THE BETRAYAL OF
THE HUMANITIES

STUDIES IN ANTISEMITISM
Alvin H. Rosenfeld, editor

THE BETRAYAL OF THE HUMANITIES

The University during the Third Reich

EDITED BY
BERNARD M. LEVINSON
AND
ROBERT P. ERICKSEN

INDIANA UNIVERSITY PRESS

This book is a publication of

Indiana University Press
Office of Scholarly Publishing
Herman B Wells Library 350
1320 East 10th Street
Bloomington, Indiana 47405 USA

iupress.org

© 2022 by Indiana University Press

All rights reserved
No part of this book may be reproduced or utilized in any form or by any means, electronic or mechanical, including photocopying and recording, or by any information storage and retrieval system, without permission in writing from the publisher. The paper used in this publication meets the minimum requirements of the American National Standard for Information Sciences—Permanence of Paper for Printed Library Materials, ANSI Z39.48-1992.

Manufactured in the United States of America

First printing 2022

Cataloging information is available from the Library of Congress.
ISBN 978-0-253-06078-5 (hardback)
ISBN 978-0-253-06079-2 (paperback)
ISBN 978-0-253-06081-5 (ebook)

CONTENTS

Contributors   vii

Illustrations   xiii

Abbreviations   xv

Preface   xvii

Introduction: The Betrayal of the Humanities under National Socialism / *Bernard M. Levinson and Robert P. Ericksen*   1

PART I. *Nazi Germany and the Historical Humanities*

1. The History of the Humanities in the Third Reich / *Alan E. Steinweis*   41
2. The "Orient" and "Us": Making Ancient Oriental Studies Relevant during the Nazi Regime / *Suzanne L. Marchand*   64
3. Luther Scholars, Jews, and Judaism during the Third Reich: From the Hallowed Halls of Academia to the Sacred Spaces of German Protestantism / *Christopher J. Probst*   114
4. Gerhard von Rad's Struggle against the Nazification of the Old Testament / *Bernard M. Levinson*   154
5. Jewish Studies in the Service of Nazi Ideology: Tübingen's Faculty of Theology as a Center for Antisemitic Research / *Anders Gerdmar*   205
6. Hermann Grapow, Egyptology, and National Socialist Initiatives for the Humanities / *Thomas Schneider*   263
7. German Assyriology: A Discipline in Troubled Waters / *Johannes Renger*   306

8. National Socialist Archaeology as a Faustian Bargain: The Contrasting Careers of Hans Reinerth and Herbert Jankuhn / *Bettina Arnold*   332

PART II. *Law, Music, and Philosophy in the Third Reich*

9. Hitler's Willing Law Professors / *Oren Gross*   361

10. The Music of Arnold Schoenberg: Catastrophe and Creation / *Michael Cherlin*   402

11. Political Philosophy: Hannah Arendt and Aurel Kolnai as Interpreters of the Nazi Totalitarian State / *Emmanuel Faye*   423

PART III. *Nazi Germany and Beyond*

12. The Nazification and Denazification of the University of Göttingen / *Robert P. Ericksen*   449

13. The University of Göttingen and Its Postwar Response to Persecuted Colleagues: A Broken Relationship / *Anikó Szabó*   491

14. Italian Fascism: Decentering Standard Assumptions about Antisemitism and Totalitarianism / *Franklin Hugh Adler*   522

15. Is There an Anti-Jewish Bias in Today's University? / *Alvin H. Rosenfeld*   545

Index of Scholars and Related Academic Figures Examined   571

Index of Paramilitary and Military Roles Held   575

Index of Universities and Academic Institutions Examined   581

Index of Authors   583

Subject Index   593

CONTRIBUTORS

FRANKLIN HUGH ADLER is the G. Theodore Mitau Professor of Political Science Emeritus at Macalester College, Saint Paul. He specializes in political theory, comparative politics, movements of the Far Right, and Holocaust studies. He is the author of *Italian Industrialists from Liberalism to Fascism: The Political Development of the Industrial Bourgeoisie, 1906–1934* (Cambridge, 1995) and has published articles in numerous academic journals. He has also contributed to the anthologies *Antonio Gramsci: Critical Assessments of Leading Political Philosophers* (Routledge, 2001) and *Dizionario del Fascismo* (Einaudi, 2002) and serves as an editor of the journal *Telos*.

BETTINA ARNOLD is Professor of Anthropology at the University of Wisconsin–Milwaukee and serves as Adjunct Curator of European Archaeology at the Milwaukee Public Museum. Her research interests include the archaeological interpretation and analysis of complex societies as reflected in mortuary contexts and in the production and consumption of alcoholic beverages and the archaeological interpretation of gender. She has also studied the sociopolitical history of archaeology and museum collecting, especially their involvement in identity construction in nineteenth- and twentieth-century nationalist and ethnic movements in Europe and the United States. She published a groundbreaking article on the use and abuse of archaeology for political purposes in Nazi Germany in *Antiquity* in 1990.

MICHAEL CHERLIN is author of *Schoenberg's Musical Imagination* (Cambridge, 2007) and *Varieties of Musical Irony: From Mozart to Mahler* (Cambridge, 2017). His essay "Ritual and Eros in James Dillon's *Come Live with Me*," a study of a contemporary setting of verses from "Song of Songs," appears in *Transformations of Musical Modernism* (Cambridge, 2015). In 2019, he was awarded a lifetime membership in the Society for Music Theory. He is Professor Emeritus, University of Minnesota.

ROBERT P. ERICKSEN is the Kurt Mayer Chair of Holocaust Studies Emeritus at Pacific Lutheran University in Tacoma, Washington. He has written or edited six books, including *Theologians under Hitler* (Yale, 1985), *Complicity in the Holocaust: Churches and Universities in Nazi Germany* (Cambridge, 2012), and *Betrayal: German Churches and the Holocaust* (edited with Susannah Heschel, Fortress, 1999). He is Fellow of the Alexander von Humboldt Foundation; serves as Chair of the Committee on Ethics, Religion, and the Holocaust at the United States Holocaust Memorial Museum; and sits on the board of editors of *Kirchliche Zeitgeschichte* and an online journal, the *Contemporary Church History Quarterly*.

EMMANUEL FAYE is Professor of Modern and Contemporary Philosophy at the University of Rouen and has written or edited ten books, including *Heidegger, l'introduction du nazisme dans la philosophie: autour des séminaires inédits de 1933–1935* (Albin Michel, 2005), which has been translated into six languages and published in English as *Heidegger: The Introduction of Nazism into Philosophy in Light of the Unpublished Seminars of 1933–1935* (Yale, 2009). He has recently published *Arendt et Heidegger: Extermination nazie et destruction de la pensée* (Albin Michel, 2016). He received an honorary doctorate from the Brazilian Academy of Philosophy and serves on the editorial board of the German open-access journal *theologie.geschichte*.

GERALD FETZ is Dean Emeritus of Humanities and Sciences and Professor Emeritus of German Studies at the University of Montana. He received his PhD at the University of Oregon. He has received major fellowships (DAAD, NEH, American Philosophical Society) and was appointed Fulbright Visiting Professor at the University of Heidelberg. He served as Secretary-Treasurer of the German Studies Association for twenty years. He was also the refounding director and chief editor of the University of Montana Press and is on the editorial board for Ariadne Press. His publications include a book on Martin Walser (Metzler, 1997), as well as articles and essays on Thomas Bernhard, Franz Kafka, Friedrich Wolf, Franz Innerhofer, Lilian Faschinger, Walser, W. Georg Sebald, and German Theater at the Wende. He is editor of a new book on Christa Wolf (Spektrum, 2021). He is currently writing a book on Vienna novels since 1945.

ANDERS GERDMAR is President of the Scandinavian School of Theology in Uppsala, Sweden. He is also Associate Professor in New Testament Exegesis at Uppsala University and Full Professor (at large) at Southeastern University, Lakeland, Florida. His research focuses on the Jewish matrix of the New Testament, the construction of Judaism and Hellenism in New Testament research, and the impact of Nazi ideology on Christian exegesis. He is the author of *Roots of Theological Antisemitism: German Biblical Interpretation and the Jews, from Herder and Semler to Kittel and Bultmann* (Brill, 2009).

OREN GROSS is the Irving Younger Professor of Law at the University of Minnesota Law School. He holds an LLB degree magna cum laude from Tel Aviv University, and LLM and SJD degrees from Harvard Law School. He has taught and held visiting positions in prominent institutions, such as Harvard Law School and Princeton University. His work has been published extensively in leading academic journals, such as the *Yale Law Journal* and *Yale Journal of International Law*. His book *Law in Times of Crisis: Emergency Powers in Theory and Practice* (Cambridge, 2006) was awarded the prestigious Certificate of Merit for Preeminent Contribution to Creative Scholarship by the American Society of International Law in 2007. His most recent book, *Guantanamo and Beyond: Exceptional Courts and Military Commissions in Comparative Perspective* (edited with Fionnuala Ni Aoláin), was published by Cambridge in 2013. In 2017, he received the Stanley V. Kinyon Tenured Faculty of the Year Award, University of Minnesota Law School.

BERNARD M. LEVINSON serves as Professor of Classical and Near Eastern Studies and of Law at the University of Minnesota, where he holds the Berman Family Chair in Jewish Studies and Hebrew Bible. His research focuses on biblical and cuneiform law, textual reinterpretation in the Second Temple period, and the relation of the Bible to Western intellectual history. The interdisciplinary significance of his work has been recognized with appointments to the Institute for Advanced Study in Princeton, the Wissenschaftskolleg zu Berlin, the National Humanities Center in North Carolina, and the Israel Institute for Advanced Studies in Jerusalem, where he codirected a research team of eight international scholars working on Pentateuchal theory. He is the author of four books, including *Deuteronomy and the Hermeneutics of Legal Innovation* (Oxford, 1997) and *Legal Revision and Religious Renewal in Ancient Israel* (Cambridge, 2008), and six edited volumes.

SUZANNE L. MARCHAND serves as the Boyd Professor of European Intellectual History at Louisiana State University, Baton Rouge. She received her BA from the University of California, Berkeley, and her PhD from the University of Chicago and spent several years at Princeton University as assistant and associate professor before being appointed to Louisiana State University in 1999. She is the author of *Down from Olympus: Archaeology and Philhellenism in Germany, 1750–1970* (Princeton, 1996); *German Orientalism in the Age of Empire: Religion, Race, and Scholarship* (Cambridge, 2009); and, most recently, *Porcelain: A History from the Heart of Europe* (Princeton, 2020); as well as many essays on the history of the humanities.

CHRISTOPHER J. PROBST is Visiting Assistant Professor of modern European history at Saint Louis University. He is author of *Demonizing the Jews: Luther and the Protestant Church in Nazi Germany* (Indiana University, 2012). He received his PhD in modern European history from Royal Holloway, University of London, in 2008 and continued his research as Charles H. Revson Foundation Fellow at the Center for Advanced Holocaust Studies of the United States Holocaust Memorial Museum.

JOHANNES RENGER is Professor Emeritus of Ancient Near Eastern Philology and History at the Freie Universität Berlin. He has published widely on the economic and social history of the ancient Near East, with a theoretical perspective based on the work of Karl Polanyi, Moses Finley, and Fernand Braudel. He has written several previous studies concerned with the history of the discipline of Assyriology. Since 1993, he has directed the Assur-Project, which is devoted to publishing the results of the excavations of the Deutsche Orient-Gesellschaft between 1903 and 1914.

ALVIN H. ROSENFELD holds the Irving M. Glazer Chair in Jewish Studies at Indiana University, where he has taught since 1968, and is Director of the university's Institute for the Study of Contemporary Antisemitism. He is the author of numerous books and articles on Holocaust literature and contemporary antisemitism and has lectured widely on these subjects in the United States, Europe, and Israel. He held a five-year presidential appointment on the United States Holocaust Memorial Council and also served on the US Holocaust Memorial Museum's Executive Committee. For ten years, he was Chair of the Academic Committee of the Museum's Center for Advanced Holocaust Studies. He has been honored with Indiana University's Distinguished Service Award, the Provost's Medal, and, most recently, the President's Medal in recognition of "sustained excellence in service, scholarly achievement, and leadership."

THOMAS SCHNEIDER is Professor of Egyptology and Near Eastern Studies at the University of British Columbia, Vancouver. After studying at Zurich, Basel, and Paris, he held a Junior Research Professorship of the Swiss National Science Foundation at the University of Basel and was Professor and Chair in Egyptology at the University of Wales, Swansea. He was also Visiting Professor at the Universities of Vienna and Heidelberg as well as the Hebrew University of Jerusalem and Associate Vice President (International) at the Southern University of Science and Technology in Shenzhen, China. He has published widely on Egyptian interconnections with the Near East, Egyptian history and chronology, language contact in ancient Egypt, and the history of Egyptology in Nazi Germany.

ALAN E. STEINWEIS is Professor of History and Raul Hilberg Distinguished Professor of Holocaust Studies at the University of Vermont. He is the author of *Art, Ideology, and Economics in Nazi Germany* (University of North Carolina, 1993), *Studying the Jew* (Harvard, 2006), and *Kristallnacht 1938* (Harvard, 2009), and is now completing a general history of Nazi Germany. He has edited eight additional volumes. In addition to numerous fellowships, he has held visiting professorships at the Universities of Hannover, Heidelberg, Frankfurt, and Munich.

ANIKÓ SZABÓ is a German historian and archivist who directs the Archive of the University of Paderborn, Germany. She has previously published a major study of the impact of National Socialist racist and political persecution on the German university system: *Vertreibung, Rückkehr, Wiedergutmachung: Göttinger Hochschullehrer im Schatten des Nationalsozialismus* (Wallstein, 2000). Her work, appearing here for the first time in English, examines the postwar experience of professors who had been persecuted and expelled from their academic positions during the Nazi period.

ILLUSTRATIONS

FIGURE 6.1: Prince August Wilhelm of Prussia, Lieutenant General Wilhelm Philipps, and Hermann Grapow at the meeting of the Prussian Academy on January 27, 1944.
FIGURE 6.2: Group photo with Egyptologists in Giza, to honor the achievements of Selim Hassan.
FIGURE 6.3: Hermann Grapow at the meeting of the Prussian Academy on January 27, 1944.

ABBREVIATIONS

AstA	Allgemeiner Studenten-Auschuss [General Association of Student Representatives]: the national student government organization in Germany
DC	Deutsche Christen [German Christians]: an enthusiastically pro-Nazi faction within the German Protestant Church
DMG	Deutsche Morgenländische Gesellschaft [German Oriental Society]: a professional organization for German Assyriologists
DSt	Deutsche Studentenschaft: the German Student Union
DVP	Deutsche Volkspartei [German People's Party]: a moderate, right-of-center political party
DVU	Deutsche Volksunion [German People's Union]: a radical right-wing political party
GUF	Gruppi universitari fascisti [Fascist University Youth]: an Italian youth organization created by the Fascist Party. GUF members automatically became Fascist Party members.
KDC	Kirchenbewegung Deutsche Christen [German Christian Church Movement]: a radical wing of the pro-Nazi German Christian (DC) church organization and political movement that was active in the German state of Thuringia
KfdK	Kampfbund für deutsche Kultur [Militant League for German Culture]: Alfred Rosenberg's semiofficial organization for winning intellectual and cultural elites to the National Socialist cause

NS	National Socialism *or* National Socialist
NSDAP	Nationalsozialistische Deutsche Arbeiterpartei [National Socialist German Workers' Party]: the Nazi Party
NSDDozB	Nationalsozialistischer Deutscher Dozentenbund [National Socialist German University Instructors' League]: a mandatory professional association that oversaw all academic personnel. Together with the head of each institution's Nazi student union, association leaders made recommendations for all academic appointments.
NSDStB	Nationalsozialistischer Deutscher Studentenbund [National Socialist German Students' League]: managed student government and other campus activities and events
OKW	Oberkommando der Wehrmacht: the High Command of the German Armed Forces
PCI	Partito Comunista Italiano [Italian Communist Party]
RMWKV	Reichsministerium für Wissenschaft, Kunst, und Volksbildung [Reich Ministry of Science, Art, and Education]
RSHA	Reichssicherheitshauptamt [Main Office for Reich Security]: responsible for surveillance of academic faculty and institutions. The SD was integrated into the RSHA in 1939.
SA	Sturmabteilung [Storm Troopers]: the *brown-shirts*, the original paramilitary wing of the National Socialist party. The SA was used to terrorize political opponents.
SD	Sicherheitsdienst: the Security Service of the SS, a unit responsible for investigating and preventing disloyalty to the Nazi regime. They were also charged with surveillance of academic faculty and institutions.
SPD	Social Democratic Party of Germany: a progressive political party
SS	Schutzstaffel: a Nazi paramilitary organization, originally part of the Sturmabteilung (SA), that was charged with surveilling and policing Germany and Nazi-occupied territories. Subunits within the SS also served in combat and ran the Nazi concentration and extermination camps.
ZDMG	*Zeitschrift der Deutschen Morgenländischen Gesellschaft*: the prestigious journal published by the German Oriental Society (DMG)

PREFACE

THE FOCUS OF THIS VOLUME is how the humanities, as the standard-bearers of the values and history of Western civilization, eagerly accommodated themselves to the political, social, and racist ideology of the governing political party in Germany under National Socialism during the period from 1933 through 1945. Science, history, and scholarship became tools of the state and aligned themselves with the agenda of the state. The contributors to this volume examine the impact of Nazi ideology on academic disciplines, university autonomy, and faculty appointment procedures and contrast the situations of German and Italian fascism. The historical span extends to the process of denazification after the war, as Germany sought to rebuild its universities, and includes the impact of antisemitism on contemporary American universities.

If only we could look back now, from this vantage point of the third decade of the twenty-first century, at those transformations of the German university to map them all as comfortably distant, as safely "then" rather than "now." And yet as this book goes to press in contemporary America, ideological forces question the integrity of democratic institutions and the electoral process, the evidence of science regarding climate change and environmental protection is dismissed, essential public health measures to protect against COVID-19 are politicized, and, on the afternoon this preface was being finalized, an armed mob (a number of whom carried Confederate or white supremacist symbols) stormed the halls of Congress. Here, too, the values that we associate with the humanities are once again under attack. With this resurgence of right-wing populism, truth risks being replaced by ideological assertion.

This volume, which closely examines a racist and antisemitic regime in which ideology *did* successfully replace truth and achieve political power, is therefore not merely of historical interest. The focus on the ideological transformation of knowledge and the threats to the autonomy of the university at times of national crisis make it deeply relevant to the present. Its chapters provide many powerful case studies of the impact of national events on the lives of individual scholars across many disciplines; it also demonstrates how disciplinary history is embedded in political and social history.

We, the two editors of this volume, are deeply committed to the ideal of the German university and the Humboldtian ideal of the Enlightenment. There is no sense of a betrayal without a prior love for the ideal that was lost: that is the logic for and the point of departure for this investigation. The German university served as the model for the American graduate school and played a key role in establishing the American system of higher education. We are equally committed to the academic and moral values of the humanities: the notion that teaching and learning are not simply about mastery of technical content but also play an essential role in the transmission of human values, in shaping us as persons, and in preserving what matters in civilization. We equally recognize that precisely those values mean that universities around the world, including American ones, must do a much better job to address matters of racial injustice, gender inequality, and class privilege in their curricula and in their appointment procedures.

In April 2012, the University of Minnesota held an international symposium, "Betrayal of the Humanities: The University during the Third Reich," hosted by Bernard M. Levinson, Berman Family Chair of Jewish Studies and Hebrew Bible, and Bruno Chaouat, then director of the Center for Holocaust and Genocide Studies. The symposium included twelve speakers, not all of whom were able to participate in the volume. Bernard M. Levinson initiated the original conference, recruited most of the contributors to this volume, and invited Robert P. Ericksen, as Kurt Mayer Chair Emeritus in Holocaust Studies at Pacific Lutheran University, to serve as coeditor with him. This volume thereby represents the collaboration of an ancient historian and a modern historian, both of whom take languages, sources, and the significance of the past seriously.

The intent has been to create a volume that brings together the study of antiquity and modernity, disciplinary history and intellectual history. The volume seeks a transdisciplinary readership and covers a distinctive range of topics. The chapters have been shaped throughout with that broader audience in mind. They do not speak merely to an in-group set of specialist readers. The editors and contributors have taken care to explain disciplinary-specific technical terminology and to avoid academic jargon. Foreign language quotations are always accompanied by a translation for the convenience of the nonspecialist reader. Cross-references have been added when contributors address shared topics across the chapters. To facilitate further research by the interested reader, each chapter includes its own bibliography, to allow a deeper dive into any of the topics discussed. The contributors include scholars from Germany, Israel, France, Sweden, Canada, and the United States, some of whose work appears here in English for the first time. The contributions gathered here have developed significantly beyond the earlier conference. We have expanded the number of contributions to fifteen. All of the original papers have gone through several stages of editorial and peer review.

Without the support of the many individuals and institutions who have given generously in many ways over many years, this volume would not exist. We must first sincerely thank the contributors of this volume for their patience, fortitude, and goodwill. It has been a long ride and they have maintained their commitment, as the volume has grown exponentially in scope far beyond the original conference. They shared our larger vision of trying to write in such a way as to reach beyond our own specific disciplinary boundaries to address a larger, transdisciplinary readership.

Several units at the University of Minnesota have generously supported this volume. The Provost's Office has a visionary initiative, the Imagine Fund grants program, which supports faculty projects in the arts, humanities, and design, as well as special projects such as conferences and interdisciplinary symposia. The Imagine Fund contributed to the original conference as well as for research toward Bernard M. Levinson's own chapter. The Center for Holocaust and Genocide Studies, directed by Professor Alejandro Baer, provided two grants in support of editing and translation. The Law School, where Bernard is an affiliated faculty member, actively encourages interdisciplinary research; Dean Garry W. Jenkins kindly extended a grant.

The Salo W. and Jeannette M. Baron Foundation, with its dedication to the connection between Jewish Studies and the humanities, provided a much appreciated grant in support of this project. In intellectual terms, we turned to colleagues for expertise at key points, given the broad range of topics covered by this volume. We therefore thank Eva von Dassow (professor of Classical and Near Eastern Studies, University of Minnesota), Saul Olyan (Samuel Ungerleider Jr. Professor of Judaic Studies and Professor of Religious Studies, Brown University), Anthony Cardozo (emeritus professor of History, Loyola University Chicago), and Anselm C. Hagedorn (professor of Old Testament, University of Osnabrück). The two anonymous readers for Indiana University Press deserve special credit. Their rigorous, detailed, and deeply engaged reader reports have left an indelible positive impact on the volume.

Ashante Thomas and Gary Dunham at Indiana University Press provided valuable editorial guidance; and Stephen Williams offered enthusiastic support for the cover design. It is an honor to have this volume accepted into the Studies in Antisemitism series under the editorship of Alvin Rosenfeld, Irving M. Glazer Chair in Jewish Studies.

Considerable effort has gone into the editing of each of the contributions to ensure consistency across chapters, especially since the authors had five different mother tongues and many more disciplinary style sheets. The labor at times seemed Herculean. For assistance with this work, thanks are extended to Sarah Shectman, PhD, a professional editor, who helped significantly with two chapters; and Justin Buol, PhD. Particular thanks go to Tina Sherman, PhD, for her careful work and research assistance on each of the chapters of this volume.

The humanities have meaning through the human relationships that sustain them. Robert would like to extend his thanks to his special partner in all of this, Dr. Judith M. Meyers. Bernard counts it as a blessing to have Dr. Hanne Løland Levinson in his life as wife and Joseph as son.

Bernard M. Levinson and Robert P. Ericksen
Minneapolis and Gig Harbor, January 6, 2021

THE BETRAYAL OF
THE HUMANITIES

THE BETRAYAL OF
THE HUMANITIES

INTRODUCTION

The Betrayal of the Humanities under National Socialism

BERNARD M. LEVINSON AND
ROBERT P. ERICKSEN

WHAT ARE THE LIES WE tell ourselves to help us sleep at night? Does each culture have its own? Must we live in fear that these lies will be exposed as lies, either to ourselves or to others? This book is predicated on the notion that a particular strand of Western education, based on and inspired by the humanities, will make us better and more humane human beings. We believe that inquiry into the human experience in subjects such as art, literature, music, philosophy, theology, and history will inspire us with the accomplishments of human societies over centuries and millennia. We will learn how others have lived. We will learn to ask questions of the past and to identify the best paths to a better life in the future. We also believe that the study of the human experience represents an important path toward greater self-knowledge, empathy, and compassion.

Yet how inherent are such aspirations to the study of the humanities? At the heart of this volume is a critical assessment of humanities scholars under the Nazi regime. As they practiced their craft, did their scholarship lead them toward greater empathy and compassion, or did they embrace Nazi values, whether out of personal conviction or to advance their careers? We know that Germany took a wrong turn in that era. Germans committed one of the worst national crimes in modern history, murdering six million Jews and five million other innocents, those whom they pointedly labeled *Lebensunwertes Leben* [life unworthy of life].[1] Since the collapse of the Nazi regime in 1945, it has been very

---

The historical portion of this chapter was prepared by Robert P. Ericksen; the chapter was then expanded by Bernard M. Levinson.

1. This concept was first developed by Karl Binding and Alfred Hoche, *Die Freigabe der Vernichtung lebensunwerten Lebens: Ihr Maß und ihre Form* (Leipzig, Germany: F. Meiner, 1920). For further study, see Hans-Walter Schmuhl, *Rassenhygiene, Nationalsozialismus,*

hard to find anyone who defends the Holocaust, or the German idea of building death camps to maximize and industrialize their efficiency at murdering Jews. Neo-Nazis and others who deny the Holocaust, or even defend it, are generally regarded as kooks who stand outside any respectable discussion. Many other brutalities are also part of the terrible reputation of Germany under Adolf Hitler, including, of course, the launching of World War II, which added at least fifty million war dead to the eleven million Holocaust victims.

Did German professors committed to the humanities tradition have to tell themselves lies about their regime's activities or about the regime's victims to sleep at night? Did they know about the Nazi atrocities and support the regime anyway, whether out of a sincere belief that it would improve society or to improve their own status within that society? Or did they look the other way, whether out of deliberate denial or out of fear for their own personal safety? Scholarship for the past two or three decades has increasingly looked at the various professions in Germany and found that the highly educated took their prominent place within the Nazi machinery of death. For example, 7 of the 15 men who met at the Wannsee Conference in January 1942, organized to plan the murder of European Jews, had earned doctorates.[2] Michael Wildt has researched 221 men who held leading positions in the SS Reich Security Main Office. They were the type of officers who organized and coordinated the *Einsatzgruppen* and *Einsatzkommando* special operations killing squads. Two-thirds of these 221 men had earned a university degree; overall, fully a third of them held doctorates. The statistics are strikingly worse for the commanders of these killing squads who had an academic background specifically within the humanities. Among the 33 Reich Security Main Office leaders who had completed a humanities degree, fully two-thirds (22) had earned doctorates.[3] Within the past three decades, many German professional groups have been studied to determine the behavior of their members during the Third Reich. In virtually all cases, the level of approval and participation was higher than expected. Most lawyers, judges, and journalists supported the Nazi state. Most doctors supported and were willing to

---

Euthanasie: Von der Verhütung zur Vernichtung "lebensunwerten Lebens," 1890–1945, Kritische Studien zur Geschichtswissenschaft 75 (Göttingen, Germany: Vandenhoeck & Ruprecht, 1987).

2. Michael Wildt, *An Uncompromising Generation: The Nazi Leadership of the Reich Security Main Office*, trans. Tom Lampert, George L. Mosse Series in Modern European Cultural and Intellectual History (Madison: University of Wisconsin Press, 2009), 18.

3. Wildt, *Uncompromising Generation*, 38, including notes 6, 7, and 8.

serve the interests of the Nazi state. Most pastors and professors of theology found a comfortable place within Hitler's Germany, often with considerable enthusiasm.[4]

At a meeting of the *Deutscher Historikertag* (the major annual meeting of the German Association of Historians) in 1998, German historians somewhat belatedly took up the subject of historians working during the Third Reich. When the volume of papers came out in 2000, that volume acknowledged what had become clear to all:

> Today we know the actual evidence, which shows that a greater number of historians served National Socialism than we previously thought. It is these stories which prove that the circle was far from being made up only of "secondary school teachers gone wild or outsiders" (Hans Rothfels) or young Party members. The circle stretches much further, even to those now considered the "founding fathers" of historical study in the Federal Republic, and this is the central finding. It was these individuals who helped in various ways, now completely undeniable, to build the "scientific foundation for discrimination against Jews and legitimizing of the *Führer*-state, with its National Socialist demands for a politics of expansion and increase in the soil of the *Volk*."[5]

During the next several years, other groups of academics, mostly in Germany, questioned the role of scholars in the humanities under Hitler. By 2007, five substantial volumes had appeared, all echoing in various ways the very uncomfortable realization of German historians at their 1998 national conference. Many or most professors working within the humanities at German universities responded to the rise of Adolf Hitler with collaboration rather than opposition. They gave their support to Nazi policies, including hostility

---

4. See, for example, Robert J. Lifton, *The Nazi Doctors: Medical Killing and the Psychology of Genocide* (New York: Basic Books, 1986); Ingo Müller, *Hitler's Justice: The Courts of the Third Reich*, trans. Deborah Lucas Schneider (Cambridge, MA: Harvard University Press, 1991); Alan E. Steinweis, *Art, Ideology, and Economics in Nazi Germany: The Reich Chambers of Music, Theater, and the Visual Arts* (Chapel Hill: North Carolina University Press, 1993); and Robert P. Ericksen, *Theologians under Hitler: Gerhard Kittel, Paul Althaus, and Emanuel Hirsch* (New Haven, CT: Yale University Press, 1985).

5. Winfried Schulze, Gerd Heim, and Thomas Ott, "Deutsche Historiker im Nationalsozialismus: Beobachtungen und Überlegungen zu einer Debatte," in *Deutsche Historiker im Nationalsozialismus*, 2nd ed., ed. Winfried Schulze and Otto Gerhard Oexle, Zeit des Nationalsozialismus (Frankfurt, Germany: Fischer, 2000), 11–50 (at 16–17). This quotation is discussed by Robert P. Ericksen, *Complicity in the Holocaust: Churches and Universities in Nazi Germany* (Cambridge: Cambridge University Press, 2012), 182.

toward Jews and other forms of brutality, which led ultimately to the horrors of the Holocaust itself.[6] In April 2012, the University of Minnesota held an international symposium, "Betrayal of the Humanities: The University during the Third Reich." Hosted by Bernard M. Levinson, Berman Family Chair of Jewish Studies and Hebrew Bible, and Bruno Chaouat, director of the Center for Holocaust and Genocide Studies, this symposium arose from the commonly held view that universities safeguard the values of Western civilization, standing as a beacon for such fundamental values as critical thought, free inquiry, and ethical research. This volume of essays, mostly drawn from that conference, acknowledges the bad news that academics and intellectuals in Nazi Germany betrayed the humanities and also betrayed the humanistic ideals of the modern university. The question is not whether there was apostasy against the values that had undergirded humanities scholarship and the academic world before the Nazi era and that have grown in strength since the collapse of the Nazi state. Rather, the essays within this volume seek to increase our understanding of the subtle *hows* and *whys* of this apostasy. These chapters look at specific disciplines and specific individuals. They examine variations in response, from full-throated enthusiasm for Nazi ideas to small examples of courageous holding back.

One additional predicament is at play here. German universities are widely considered to have been the very best in the world during the nineteenth and early twentieth century. Americans with high aspirations went to German universities during that period. They then returned to teach at Harvard and other leading universities, developing the curriculum that is the foundation for what we continue to teach at colleges and universities to this day. To give but one example: it was the nineteenth-century German, Leopold von Ranke, who

---

6. See Frank-Rutger Hausmann, ed., *Die Rolle der Geisteswissenschaften im Dritten Reich, 1933–1945*, Schriften des Historischen Kollegs, Kolloquien 53 (Munich: Oldenbourg, 2002); Hartmut Lehmann and Otto Gerhard Oexle, eds., *Nationalsozialismus in den Kulturwissenschaften*, vol. 1, *Fächer, Milieus, Karrieren*, Veröffentlichungen des Max-Planck-Instituts für Geschichte 200 and 211 (Göttingen, Germany: Vandenhoeck & Ruprecht, 2004); Hartmut Lehmann and Otto Gerhard Oexle, eds., *Nationalsozialismus in den Kulturwissenschaften*, vol. 2, *Leitbegriffe, Deutungsmuster, Paradigmenkämpfe, Erfahrungen, und Transformationen im Exil*, Veröffentlichungen des Max-Planck-Instituts für Geschichte 200 and 211 (Göttingen, Germany: Vandenhoeck & Ruprecht, 2004); and Jürgen Elvert and Jürgen Nielsen-Sikora, eds., *Kulturwissenschaften und Nationalsozialismus*, Historische Mitteilungen 72 (Stuttgart, Germany: Franz Steiner, 2008). For a similar study in English, see Anson Rabinbach and Wolfgang Bialas, eds., *Nazi Germany and the Humanities: How German Academics Embraced Nazism* (Oxford: Oneworld, 2007).

taught us how to write and document serious history.⁷ We also know that German contributions to Western culture have been enormous; consider only Bach and Beethoven, Goethe and Schiller, Kant and Schopenhauer, Nietzsche and Heidegger. Yet these contributions are not unsullied by history. In particular, Nietzsche and Heidegger, giants in the world of modern philosophy, each have their connection to Nazi Germany: Nietzsche's work (especially as redacted by his sister) was used to provide a foundation for Adolf Hitler's much cruder will to power; and Heidegger welcomed the rise of Hitler in his inaugural lecture as rector of Freiburg University in November 1933. These last two names, jarring to some readers, perhaps, thus forcefully point toward the most important question that underlies our attempt to understand German contributions to the humanities: how is it possible to reconcile Germany's prodigious cultural achievements with the equally prodigious atrocities perpetrated by Germans during the Nazi period?

This volume both acknowledges and questions the perhaps simple-minded belief that the humanities are humane and that the study of what we label "humanities" will make people better human beings. Leading universities stress the ethical significance of the humanities and highlight the centrality of the humanities to the academic curriculum. The Humanities Center at Harvard claims that "the humanities make a unique contribution in establishing—through interpretation and conversation—communities of interest and climates of opinion."⁸ This claim posits a "unique" role for the humanities and speaks to "community," though one could argue that Nazi crimes were also committed by specific "communities of interest" and in obedience to a particularly harsh "climate of opinion." The Whitney Humanities Center at Yale claims to reflect "Yale's longstanding commitment to the humanities" and emphasizes its "Tanner Lectures on Human Values" as well as its humanities major, one of Yale's "most prestigious interdepartmental undergraduate programs."⁹ This gives a stronger nod toward values, probably even "humane" values, though there is no verbal or logical guarantee that human values must always be humane.

---

7. It is commonly held that Ranke invented the footnote. For an assessment of Ranke's actual role, and the more complicated history of the footnote, see Anthony Grafton, *The Footnote: A Curious History* (Cambridge, MA: Harvard University Press, 1999).

8. Mahindra Humanities Center at Harvard, "About the Center," Harvard University, accessed September 25, 2020, http://mahindrahumanities.fas.harvard.edu/about.

9. Whitney Humanities Center, "About Us," Yale University, accessed September 25, 2020, https://whc.yale.edu/about-us.

The Great Books Program offered at the University of Chicago and elsewhere and the Directed Studies Program at Yale are each built on the assumption that certain authors, certain books, and certain ideas within our Western canon provide students with especially useful access to the humanities. Many of those authors, books, and ideas come to us from the European Renaissance that developed more than half a millennium ago. That Renaissance led to a remarkable set of accomplishments, with subsequent revolutions in science, the arts, government, and religion. Medievalists push this reverence for important influencers in the development of the humanities further back, as Norman F. Cantor indicates in his claim that "the high Middle Ages of the twelfth, thirteenth, and early fourteenth centuries ... exhibited unprecedented creativity in literature and the visual arts and remarkable advances in theology, philosophy, popular piety, government, and law."[10] Medievalists point out that it was medieval theologians and linguists who first retrieved the works of Aristotle (via Muslim scholars in North Africa) and other founding documents in the humanities canon. Medievalists thus join those who celebrate Renaissance humanism in their eagerness to raise up the great works of classical Greece and Rome, to recapture and build on Greek and Roman culture as they pursue their overarching aim: to nurture the best of human culture, the essence of humanism.

But can we really assume that humanism advocates, or even requires, a specific set of values? Latin gives us several value-laden nouns meant to describe an ideal quality, such as *gravitas* [earnestness] or *severitas* [self-control], among others. *Humanitas* is the Latin word that describes an ideal version of what a human being can be. This word gives "the implication of humane learning or culture, or a humanistic approach to the problems of the human condition."[11] It is certainly possible to find in religious traditions a foundation for humane behavior. The Golden Rule, for example, "do unto others what you would have them do unto you," is found in Judaism, Christianity, and Islam, the three Abrahamic faiths. But we also can find in the developing humanist tradition over the past millennium specific values that now seem fundamental to humanitas.

If we look at the twelfth-century Renaissance and its fruits, we find one of the founding documents of the democratic tradition, the Magna Carta (1215), or the Great Charter. As the medieval English learned to govern themselves, from the Anglo-Saxon era of Alfred the Great in the ninth century through William

---

10. Norman F. Cantor, *Inventing the Middle Ages: The Lives, Works, and Ideas of the Great Medievalists of the Twentieth Century* (New York: William Morrow, 1991), 27.

11. *Oxford English Dictionary*, 3rd ed. (2000), s.v. "humanitas."

the Conqueror in the eleventh century to King John in the early thirteenth century, royal aspirations toward arbitrary rule brushed up against the rights of citizens. In the Magna Carta, English barons coerced King John into giving up his unlimited right to rule. This document, rooted in ideas developing in England for a century or more, protected the barons from arbitrary imprisonment, protected the rights of churches, and required an assembly of barons to approve royal requests for funds, a system that gradually led to the English Parliament as it exists today. The Magna Carta did not introduce democracy, which required centuries to develop its full form. However, it did restrict royal autocracy and laid the foundations for representative government and democratic principles, human values that have only grown in our scale of values.

The fifteenth-century Renaissance illustrates another value nurtured by the humanities: an honest search for truth based on evidence. In the famous case of the Donation of Constantine, this quest for the evaluation of truth claims becomes clear. The popes and the Church of Rome had long relied on a document, ostensibly written in the early fourth century, according to which the Emperor Constantine formally ceded extensive authority, both religious and temporal, to the bishop of Rome, Pope Sylvester I. Certain inconsistencies in the document were gradually noticed, which made it unlikely to have been written in the fourth century. Lorenzo Valla, a humanist scholar in the mid-fifteenth century, made a careful study of the language of the alleged Donation of Constantine and showed conclusively that it included language and commentary that could not have been possible until much later.[12] Although Valla was himself a priest, here he used a secular form of argument and secular evidence to fully dismantle the legal and spiritual claims that had been made for several centuries by the church.

Many threads of the twelfth- and fifteenth-century Renaissances, coupled with the scientific revolution of the sixteenth and seventeenth centuries, merged into the eighteenth-century Enlightenment. Although written at a time when the masculine pronoun still functioned as a universal, Immanuel Kant's description of that crucial development remains powerful: "Enlightenment is man's emergence from his self-imposed immaturity."[13] This is the moment at which major portions of modern democratic theory and practice were given

---

12. See Lorenzo Valla, *On the Donation of Constantine*, trans. Glen W. Bowersock, I Tatti Renaissance Library 24 (Cambridge, MA: Harvard University Press, 2007).

13. Immanuel Kant, "An Answer to the Question: 'What Is Enlightenment?'" [1784], in *Perpetual Peace and Other Essays on Politics, History, and Moral Practice*, trans. Ted Humphrey (Indianapolis: Hackett, 1983), 41–48 (at 41).

their form, from the writings of John Locke to the American Declaration of Independence and the Constitution. Since that time, representative government and democratic principles have been ascendant until the spread of democracy reached its historic peak in the late twentieth century. Also since that time, science and reason have been essential to intellectual life and to the major developments of culture, from widespread education to the extraordinary impact of science and technology in our world.

What was Kant's "self-imposed immaturity" from which humans had suffered? It was the willingness of humans to accept dogmatic authority—whether exercised by kings, popes, or priests—without claiming also their own human autonomy and their right to engage human reason. These three key moments in the rise of humanism—the twelfth- and fifteenth-century Renaissances plus the Enlightenment—challenged political autocrats, eventually with all of the elements we now assume within democracy: elected governments, equality before the law, freedom of speech, freedom of opinion, and freedom of the press. These three moments also challenged religious authority, with claims for freedom of religious belief and the right to search for evidence and employ reason. Martin Luther claimed the right to read the Bible himself. Galileo claimed the right to read the heavens. Baruch Spinoza claimed the right to read the Bible with a historical-critical inquiry into its origins.[14] Each of these values has been ascendant in the last two centuries, as promoted within the modern university and by advocates and teachers of the humanities.

It is worth noting that our widespread societal support for the Enlightenment, with its heritage of science, reason, and democratic values, remains controversial to some. Spinoza's advocacy of a historical-critical reading of the Bible, as it developed from the seventeenth through the nineteenth centuries, produced many variations on how best to understand religious truth. By the twentieth century, some Christians responded with a fundamentalist insistence that every word of the Bible is inerrant and literally true. The 1925 Scopes Trial in Tennessee famously highlighted this controversy between science and a particular view of religion, between the scientific evidence for evolutionary

---

14. Baruch Spinoza, *Theological-Political Treatise*, trans. Samuel Shirley, with an introduction and annotation by Seymour Feldman, 2nd ed. (Indianapolis: Hackett, 2001). In this book, published anonymously in 1670, Spinoza advocated the rigorous application of human reason, both in understanding the Bible, religion, and theology and in developing the sort of political systems by which humans elevate themselves from the Hobbesian definition of life as "nasty, brutish, and short." See Bernard M. Levinson, *"The Right Chorale": Studies in Biblical Law and Interpretation* (Winona Lake, IN: Eisenbrauns, 2011), 11–13.

development over millions of years on Earth and religious insistence on a six-day creation and an Earth dating back only six thousand years.

Questioning of the Enlightenment heritage took a different, more political turn in 1920s Germany, when the Weimar Republic became Germany's first experiment with democracy. Professors at German universities at that time—viewing France, Great Britain, and the United States, their hated enemies in a lost war and a harsh peace—saw in those enemy nations the heirs to the Enlightenment and its advocacy for democracy. By the 1920s, the German academic community had benefited significantly from the humanities and from the fruits of the Enlightenment. They looked back with pride on academic heroes, such as the "Göttingen Seven." These seven professors, including the brothers Grimm, earned their shared fame when Ernest Augustus became king of Hannover in 1837. He rescinded a constitution granted in 1833 by his predecessor, his more liberal brother, King William IV of England.[15] The Göttingen Seven protested, were fired, and were then celebrated throughout Germany and Europe as advocates for academic freedom. By the twentieth century, German universities had secured academic freedom and near autonomy in the running of their universities, based on values within the humanities tradition.

In the Weimar era, however, many professors were ready to deplore the new Germany and its democratic values. One explicit example may be seen in the prominent German theologian, Gerhard Kittel. He gave a lecture in Sweden in 1921 describing current problems in Germany. Yes, Germany had been hurt by its loss in World War I, he said. However, the greater problem was that Germany had sold out to the Enlightenment. This meant a democratic Weimar Republic, with its protections for free speech, a free press, and an open culture. Rational secularists and Jews took advantage of that culture, according to Kittel, leading to the decadence seen in movie and stage performances, plus increases in divorce, prostitution, and venereal disease.[16]

A decade later Kittel had been appointed to the chair in New Testament theology at Tübingen University. He joined the Nazi Party in 1933 and delivered a public lecture on the "Jewish Question," endorsing the harsh stance of the Nazi state toward Jews. He blamed the decadence he deplored in Weimar Germany

---

15. Ernest Augustus, brother to King William IV, ascended the throne of Hannover when the rightful heir to William IV, Queen Victoria, was barred. Hannover, a British possession, adhered to the ancient Salic law, which disallowed female inheritance of a throne or other royal possession. Victoria could become queen of England and later empress of India, but not queen of Hannover.

16. Gerhard Kittel, *Die religiöse und die kirchliche Lage in Deutschland* (Leipzig, Germany: Dörffling & Franke, 1921), 4–7.

primarily on Jews, especially assimilated Jews, with what he considered their "self-tormenting and lacerating relativism" and their "spiritual homelessness."[17] Throughout the Hitler era, Kittel endorsed the *Weltanschauungskampf* [battle over worldviews] undertaken by the Nazi regime. The Enlightenment had softened society through its liberal, democratic ideals, he believed. The Enlightenment advocated cultural and political freedom for Jews and others who did not accept the Christian community in which they lived. Even by 1943 and 1944, after Jews had long disappeared from the streets of Germany and after Kittel himself was aware of the murder of Jews in the East, he still described Christianity and Adolf Hitler as twin bulwarks against the Jewish menace. Christianity had stigmatized Jews and placed them in ghettoes, and although the Enlightenment weakened those policies by advocating human rights, now Hitler had overthrown the Enlightenment and renewed the necessary battle against the perceived Jewish enemy.[18]

Gerhard Kittel was hardly alone in his stance. As we look at other German professors in the Nazi era, we are likely to find a similar betrayal of the humanities in their animosity toward the Enlightenment, in their unwillingness to oppose autocracy, in their unwillingness to insist on free inquiry and freedom of expression, and in their hesitancy to privilege evidence-based science if it confronted the lies Germans were telling themselves by the 1930s. These lies included delusional claims that Germany had only lost World War I because it was "stabbed in the back" by Jews and socialists. They also included the delusional claim that Jews, though less than 1 percent of the population, were a serious threat and that Jewish blood and Jewish culture endangered German survival. Did German humanists also tell themselves these lies to help them sleep at night while their nation punished Jews—who were, after all, their fellow German citizens—for their noncrimes?

I. HOLOCAUST AWARENESS

One final issue underlying this volume of essays involves the arc of Holocaust awareness, an acknowledgement of the brutal reality that helps make the

---

17. Gerhard Kittel, *Die Judenfrage* (Stuttgart, Germany: Kohlhammer, 1933), 25. See also Ericksen, *Theologians under Hitler*, 54–61.
18. See the two unpublished lectures presented by Kittel at the University of Vienna; "Die Entstehung des Judentums" (March 22, 1943) and "Das Rassenproblem der Spätantike und das Frühchristentum" (June 15, 1944). Manuscripts of both are available at the Library of Protestant Theology at Tübingen University, under the shared call number Rg III a 119 (Magazin/RARA). See also Ericksen, *Theologians under Hitler*, 28–78, for a more complete treatment of Kittel.

betrayal of humanistic values in Germany especially significant. Much was known about the early stages of the Holocaust, both to Germans and to outsiders, as it gradually developed. Hitler's antagonism toward Jews was a major foundation for his political message, and his repression of Jews was evident from the time he took power in 1933. The boycott of Jewish shops on April 1, 1933, appeared in the international press, leading to some efforts toward a counterboycott. Hitler's Berlin Olympics in 1936 led to calls for an American boycott due to Nazi antisemitism, though that did not occur. The pogrom of November 1938, *Kristallnacht*, was known to anyone reading a serious newspaper in North America or Europe. As the actual Holocaust began to unfold, with the German attack on Poland that launched World War II on September 1, 1939, American newspapers described very harsh treatment of Jews.[19] By the end of 1942, when Auschwitz was in full operation and mass killings had been occurring for more than a year, this reality was widely rumored in Germany, with many of the crucial details also accessible in the international press.[20] By the spring of 1945, as the Nazi regime collapsed, Allied troops discovered the camps, and journalists published reports with gruesome photographs that appeared even in publications such as *Life* magazine. Then the first Nuremberg trials showed video evidence and provided remarkable testimony so that extensive knowledge of the horrors spread round the world. Since that summer of 1945, Germans have lived with a stigma: the worldwide awareness that they did horrible things during World War II. Despite the enormity of this story, however, awareness of the Holocaust receded and what we now call Holocaust studies simply did not exist.

Raul Hilberg, one of the first and most important Holocaust historians, tells an ironic story about his entry into the field. In 1948, at the age of twenty-two, he began a graduate program at Columbia University. Approaching Franz Neumann, an important historian of Nazi Germany, he said he wanted to focus his doctoral research on the German murder of European Jews. Neumann

---

19. The Berlin correspondent Otto D. Tolischus already described the organized killing of Jews by Einsatzgruppen in the *New York Times* on September 9, 1939, p. 11. See Alex Grobman, "What Did They Know? The American Jewish Press and the Holocaust, 1 September 1939–17 December 1942," *American Jewish History* 68, no. 3 (1979): 327–52. http://www.jstor.org/stable/23882020.

20. See Michael Fleming, *Auschwitz, the Allies, and Censorship of the Holocaust* (Cambridge: Cambridge University Press, 2014). See also earlier studies by Deborah Lipstadt, *Beyond Belief: The American Press and the Coming of the Holocaust, 1933–1945* (New York: Free Press, 1986), and Walter Laqueur, *The Terrible Secret: Suppression of the Truth about Hitler's "Final Solution"* (New York: Little, Brown, 1980).

accepted the idea but added, "It's your funeral."[21] Fortunately, Hilberg persisted and produced a book, *The Destruction of the European Jews*, that appeared in 1961 and is still among the most thorough and significant histories of the Holocaust.[22] Christopher Browning, another important Holocaust scholar, had a similar experience. In his case, he began working in French diplomatic history at the University of Wisconsin at the end of the 1960s. A bout of mononucleosis put him in bed for a month, which gave him a chance to read Hilberg's massive study cover to cover. He then decided to write his doctoral thesis on the Nazi persecution of the Jews. His advisor agreed but said the topic had "no professional future."[23] Browning went on to publish the pathbreaking book *Ordinary Men: Reserve Police Battalion 101 and the Holocaust in Poland* as well as a number of other important works.[24]

One striking thing about the early entry by Hilberg and Browning into the field of what we would now call Holocaust studies is that neither used the word. Not only did their academic mentors not think the study of Germans murdering European Jews would lead to an academic career, but the word *Holocaust*, so ubiquitous today, was also not yet in general use. Despite the widespread knowledge of German crimes against Jews even while they were occurring, and despite the worldwide awareness of those crimes by 1945 and 1946, this story largely disappeared for at least thirty years. Early historical treatment of Nazi Germany focused on Hitler, other leaders in the Nazi hierarchy, the ways in which the Nazis came to power, and the origins and nature of World War II. Such histories barely mentioned the persecution and murder of Jews.

---

21. This story is recounted by Raul Hilberg in his memoir, *The Politics of Memory: The Journey of a Holocaust Historian* (Chicago: Ivan R. Dee, 1996), 65.

22. Raul Hilberg, *The Destruction of the European Jews* (Chicago: Quadrangle Books, 1961). This work was later significantly revised and expanded under the same title (Raul Hilberg, *The Destruction of the European Jews*, 3rd ed., 3 vols. [New Haven, CT: Yale University Press, 2003]).

23. Christopher R. Browning, "The Personal Contexts of a Holocaust Historian: War, Politics, Trials, and Professional Rivalries," in *Holocaust Scholarship: Personal Trajectories and Professional Interpretations*, ed. Christopher R. Browning et al. (London: Palgrave Macmillan, 2015), 48–66 (at 50–51).

24. Christopher R. Browning, *Ordinary Men: Reserve Police Battalion 101 and the Final Solution in Poland* (New York: HarperCollins, 1992). Browning first published his dissertation, *The Final Solution and the German Foreign Office: A Study of Referat D III of Abteilung Deutschand 1940–43* (New York: Holmes and Meier, 1978), followed by a number of books, including *The Origins of the Final Solution: The Evolution of Nazi Jewish Policy, September 1939–March 1942* (Jerusalem: Yad Vashem; Lincoln: University of Nebraska Press, 2004).

Many reasons for this thirty- or forty-year lapse can be found. Germans themselves ran for cover in 1945, as the camps were exposed and the horrors became public knowledge. Germans claimed that they did not know. If faced with evidence of their participation, they argued that they had to follow orders. American GIs began to comment that opponents of Hitler "blossomed like flowers in the spring." The Allied postwar policy of denazification, removing ex-Nazis from positions of authority in order to cleanse Germany of Nazi ideology, resulted in large amounts of dissimulation. Even Germans with deep roots in the Nazi Party and its most brutal subsets, such as the SS, claimed that they had never really been Nazis.[25] A more accurate history of German support for Nazism simply did not develop among Germans until at least the 1980s, when the children and then the grandchildren of the perpetrator generation began to write the story.

British and North American historians also tended for several decades to accept this airbrushing of the Holocaust out of the history of Nazi Germany. On the one hand, the early outbreak of the Cold War in the postwar period meant that West Germans needed to be courted to secure their reliable place on the NATO side of the conflict. That led to lots of friendly personal contact rather than harsh charges or a careful looking into the background of these new German friends. Practical reasons, such as the usefulness of Werner von Braun in American missile development, also played a role, as American officials carefully purged his actual connections to brutal Nazi policies. Nor was it only historians and bureaucrats who were slow to take up Nazi crimes committed during the Holocaust. In the first decades after 1945, Jewish survivors rarely talked about their experience, at least to the outside world. This was partially self-protective, as they tried to stifle recurring nightmares or other symptoms of posttraumatic stress. Additionally, however, survivors often discovered that others did not want to hear their horrific stories or, worse yet, did not fully believe them.[26]

---

25. See Ericksen, *Complicity in the Holocaust*, 167–91 ("Repressing and Reprocessing the Past: Denazification and Its Legacy of Dissimulation") and 192–228 ("A Closer Look: Denazification at Göttingen University").

26. See, for example, Dorothy Rabinowitz, *New Lives: Survivors of the Holocaust Living in America* (New York: Knopf, 1976); Aaron Hass, *The Aftermath: Living with the Holocaust* (Cambridge: Cambridge University Press, 1995); and a short story by Philip Roth, "Eli, the Fanatic," in *Goodbye Columbus and Five Short Stories* (New York: Penguin, 1999) 247–98. See also, however, Hasia R. Diner, *We Remember with Reverence and Love: American Jews and the Myth of Silence after the Holocaust, 1945–1962* (New York: NYU Press, 2009).

There are important exceptions to this story of reticence—or even denial—in telling the postwar story of the Holocaust. One of the most remarkable and most significant examples, especially for our purposes in this volume, involves Max Weinreich. His book, *Hitler's Professors: The Part of Scholarship in Germany's Crimes against the Jewish People*, appeared as early as March 1946.[27] Weinreich, born in a Latvian village in 1893, had quickly shown the linguistic and intellectual skills that resulted in his prodigious scholarly career, pursued both before and after *Hitler's Professors*. He spoke German in his family home and learned Russian for his early schooling, given the czar's control over Latvia at the time. By the age of thirteen, he had learned Yiddish so thoroughly that he could start writing for a Yiddish newspaper, *Die Hofnung*, published in Vilna. He attended the Classical Gymnasium in St. Petersburg and graduated at the top of his class in 1912. In 1917, due to the Russian Revolution, he fled his studies at St. Petersburg University and arrived in Vilna, then in Lithuania, which eventually became his home for the better part of two decades. First, however, he began studies at Berlin in 1919 and finished a doctorate on the history of Yiddish linguistic studies at Marburg in 1923. Back in Vilna, he taught at the Yiddish Teachers' Seminary, edited the local daily Yiddish newspaper, and joined with others who created the Jewish research institute YIVO. At its first meeting in 1925, he was selected to be president, a role he played until 1939. During those years, he wrote books, edited volumes, and started a bimonthly scholarly journal. August 1939 found Weinreich at a linguistics conference in Brussels, safely if accidentally removed from the opening weeks of World War II on the eastern front. Rather than return to Vilna (first occupied by Russians and later by Germans), he managed to reach New York, a city possessed of a significant Jewish population and a city where Yiddish was still widely spoken. He re-created his Vilna Institute in New York as the YIVO Center for Advanced Jewish Studies. One of his first of many tasks involved gathering and studying the trove of books, pamphlets, and articles that allowed him to write *Hitler's Professors*. After two additional decades of writing, editing, and nurturing projects on Yiddish studies, along with teaching stints at the City University of New York, the University of California, Los Angeles, and Columbia, he added a four-volume history of the Yiddish language to his corpus of publications before his death in 1969. The linguistics conference in Brussels in August 1939,

---

27. Max Weinreich, *Hitler's Professors: The Part of Scholarship in Germany's Crimes against the Jewish People* (New York: Yiddish Scientific Institute [YIVO], 1946; repr., foreword by Martin Gilbert, New Haven, CT: Yale University Press, 1999). Page references are to the 1999 edition.

the accident that allowed Weinreich to flee safely to New York, was fortuitous for scholarship. As for the eighty thousand Jewish residents not able to flee Vilna, only six thousand survived.[28]

Martin Gilbert's foreword to the 1999 reprint of Weinreich's work includes this description: "*Hitler's Professors* is written with great passion. Drawing on published (and often widely publicized) writings, Weinreich conveys through the quotations that he has selected the anger he felt on reading these materials for the first time."[29] Weinreich shows his passion and his intent immediately in the first two pages of this book. He notes the six million dead Jews, almost two-thirds of the nine and one-half million Jews then living in Europe. He quotes Justice Robert H. Jackson at the Nuremberg tribunal, who stated that history "does not record a crime ever perpetrated against so many victims or one ever carried out with such calculated cruelty. . . . Determination to destroy the Jews was a binding force which at all times cemented the elements of this conspiracy." Weinreich was not willing to place blame alone on "Nazi gangsters" or those indicted at Nuremberg. He added "the whole ruling class of Germany" to his list of those responsible and then this: "But the actual murderers and those who sent them out and applauded them had accomplices. German scholarship provided the ideas and techniques which led to and justified this unparalleled slaughter."[30]

Weinreich's prodigious effort by March 1946 included 240 pages of text under three themes, "Planning and Preparation," "Large Scale Experimenting," and "Execution of the Program." He begins with an early chapter on anti-Jewish scholarship in Germany before 1933, and near the end of the book he has a chapter on "An International Anti-Jewish Congress in 1944." He also adds twenty pages of reproductions of documents he has cited in the book. Early in his work, he cites two Nobel Prize–winning German scientists, Philipp Lenard and Johannes Stark, who praised Adolf Hitler as early as 1924 for his "spirit of clarity" and "inner unity," comparing Hitler's spirit to the spirit they admire in Galileo, Kepler, Newton, and Faraday. It was only three decades later, in 1977, that Alan Beyerchen took up this story and published his *Scientists under Hitler: Politics and the Physics Community in the Third Reich*.[31] Weinreich devoted five

---

28. This biographical material is found in Martin Gilbert's "Foreword to the Second Edition," in Weinreich, *Hitler's Professors* (1999), v–xi.

29. Ibid., v.

30. Weinreich, *Hitler's Professors*, 6.

31. Ibid., 11–12; Alan D. Beyerchen, *Scientists under Hitler: Politics and the Physics Community in the Third Reich* (New Haven, CT: Yale University Press, 1977).

early pages to a chapter on "The Beginning of the New Anti-Jewish Science: Gerhard Kittel." It also was first in 1977, three decades later, that Kittel's role was given a second scholarly treatment.[32]

Prior to the international development of Holocaust awareness in the late 1970s and 1980s, it was only Israel that was quick to memorialize both victims and heroes of the Holocaust. In 1953, Yad Vashem, the World Holocaust Remembrance Center, opened in Jerusalem. The center served as memorial site, museum, and archive. It was also within the families of Jewish survivors that the murder of Jews retained a strong presence, sometimes spoken and expressed, especially among fellow survivors, and sometimes only sensed as a ghostly presence, somehow known if not discussed. Recent work, especially as typified by Hasia Diner's book, *We Remember with Reverence and Love*, identifies the many important ways that the memory of the murder of six million Jews was both remembered and processed, if primarily within the Jewish community and if widely ignored for several decades in the broader scholarship and the public consciousness.[33]

It was only in 1993 that the United States Holocaust Memorial Museum, now one of the most visited sites in Washington, DC, was created. Berlin, the city where Germans planned and instigated the horrors of the Holocaust, opened an impressive Jewish Museum in 2001 and the Memorial to the Murdered Jews of Europe in 2005. Except for Yad Vashem, these institutions all represent a burgeoning interest in the Holocaust dated to the 1990s. During this same period, Holocaust museums, Holocaust centers, and Holocaust memorials spread across North America. They are now present in Canada from Vancouver to Montreal and in most major cities throughout the United States, from Seattle to Miami and Los Angeles to Boston.

Recent Holocaust awareness can also be noted in educational curricula across North America and Europe. Courses that focus on the Holocaust, in whole or in part, are taught in middle schools and high schools as well as in colleges and universities. Those Holocaust survivors reluctant to talk about their experiences in the decades after 1945, sometimes even to their own children, now speak to their grandchildren. As long as their advancing age allows, they continue to serve on Holocaust speaker bureaus and tell their stories to

---

32. Weinreich, *Hitler's Professors*, 40–45; and Robert P. Ericksen, "Theologians in the Third Reich: The Case of Gerhard Kittel," *Journal of Contemporary History* 12, no. 3 (1977), 595–622. See also Ericksen, *Theologians under Hitler*, 28–78, as well as Anders Gerdmar's treatment of Kittel in his chapter in this volume, "Jewish Studies in the Service of Nazi Ideology: Tübingen's Faculty of Theology as a Center for Antisemitic Research."

33. Diner, *We Remember with Reverence and Love*.

schoolchildren, college students, and adults in churches, synagogues, and other public settings. In the United States, it is now possible to earn a doctorate in Holocaust studies, and many graduate programs, whether in history, literature, religion, or other fields, now encourage research on the Holocaust as an appropriate option.[34]

Holocaust awareness has also spread within our popular culture. In fact, it was a television miniseries in 1978, *Holocaust*, that firmly established this word on our mental map. Broadcast on NBC over four consecutive nights, it starred Meryl Streep, among others. Re-broadcast around the world, it is even credited with awakening Holocaust awareness in Germany. Claude Lanzmann, another pioneer in this medium, persevered for nearly a decade, interviewing victims, bystanders, and perpetrators and finally releasing his monumental documentary, *Shoah*, in 1985. Steven Spielberg directed a major Holocaust film in 1993, *Schindler's List*. Though it was not the first feature film attempting to evoke the Holocaust experience, it received international critical and popular attention and led to dozens of Holocaust films since. A combination of Holocaust films and documentary programs on television has brought the story to millions.

The arc of Holocaust awareness began as a largely Jewish story, as noted previously, with Jews worldwide traumatized by the unbelievable hatred directed against them, with Jews grieving their dead, and with the new state of Israel memorializing Holocaust victims and celebrating Holocaust heroes through the creation of Yad Vashem. Holocaust awareness also began as a Nazi story, with Nazi leaders, ideas, and behavior often represented in postwar culture as the embodiment of evil. This double focus on Jews and Nazis is appropriate. Six million Jewish deaths represent more than half of the eleven million innocent victims murdered in the Holocaust. Jews were the primary target of Nazi hostility and the only group intended to be eradicated to the last man, woman, and child. Adolf Hitler and the Nazi Party are also central to this story. With their hypernationalism and brutal antisemitism, they instigated the Holocaust and coordinated its implementation.

II. THE EXPANDING SCOPE OF CONTEMPORARY HOLOCAUST STUDIES

As study of the Holocaust developed into the very large and successful enterprise that it represents today, Jewish victims and Nazi perpetrators remain

---

34. Within the United States, doctorates specifically in Holocaust studies can be earned at three institutions: Clark University in Worcester, Massachusetts; Gratz College in Philadelphia, Pennsylvania; and the University of Texas at Dallas.

central to the story. However, the scope of Holocaust studies has also grown considerably, adding complexity and breadth to the narrative. One example can be seen in Christopher Browning's breakthrough book from 1992, *Ordinary Men*.[35] He discovered five hundred middle-aged, ordinary German men drafted to serve in a reserve police battalion in Poland. They were not young enough to have been brainwashed by Nazi education or membership in the Hitler Youth. Most had reached their thirties or forties without evidence of any particular enthusiasm for the Nazi cause. And yet, when assigned the task of murdering small groups of Jews, face-to-face, and burying them in mass graves, they did so. Furthermore, they were told that they did not have to do the killing; they could be assigned other tasks, if they chose. Yet 85 to 90 percent of these ordinary men accepted their assignment, with this one reserve police battalion accounting for the deaths of eighty-five thousand Jews.

Browning's study, pointing toward the readiness of seemingly everyday people to do terrible things under the right conditions, was among the first to suggest the active participation of a larger and more diverse group of German perpetrators than previously imagined.[36] Virtually all studies in the past thirty years have pointed in the same direction. The German Wehrmacht, for example, which once tried to blame all Nazi crimes on the SS, has now conclusively been shown to have been an active participant in the killing of Jews. More important for the present volume, we now know that historians became good Nazis. Sociologists became good Nazis. Doctors became good Nazis. Lawyers and judges became good Nazis. Pastors and theologians became good Nazis. Professors in all the disciplines of the humanities became good Nazis and used their skills to support and legitimate the regime. They lent its most toxic doctrines the aura of academic respectability. An early interpretation of the Holocaust, the one most common in the first decades after 1945, essentially accepted the claims of innocence voiced by most postwar Germans. They lived in a police state, they claimed, with no realistic chance to oppose the crimes of those rabid Nazi perpetrators. Furthermore, they did not really know about the crimes, since the Nazis were so good at keeping their secrets. The picture now is less attractive. As Peter Fritzsche has written: "It should be stated clearly that Germans became Nazis because they wanted to become Nazis and because the Nazis spoke so well to their interests and inclinations."[37]

---

35. See note 24 of this introduction.
36. Max Weinreich, of course, had pointed in this general direction already in 1946, as noted previously.
37. Peter Fritzsche, *Germans into Nazis* (Cambridge, MA: Harvard University Press, 1998), 8.

These recent trends focus on explanations of how something as dreadful as the wholesale murder of Jews could have happened. The circle of guilt has spread very widely and not only to very large segments of the German people. We also know more about those many non-Germans in occupied Europe who helped make the Holocaust possible, in some cases by doing the killing themselves, in some cases by identifying Jews and their hiding places, and in some cases by national police and political leaders collaborating with Nazi occupation authorities. We also know that the United States and many other nations made it difficult for Jews to flee and find places of refuge. The trend has been clear: we now recognize a much larger measure of guilt to go around and a more complicated explanation of how this horror could have happened.

A final expansion in the arc of Holocaust awareness has involved the term *genocide*, a term first established in international law when Raphael Lemkin convinced the United Nations to make mass murder illegal by ratifying the Genocide Convention in 1948. In the past thirty years, as we enlarged our awareness of *how* the Holocaust could have happened, we also enlarged our awareness of *how often* nations have been willing to kill large groups of people. The Herrero massacre and the Armenian genocide, both prior to the Holocaust, now seem to fit under this broader umbrella, as do the Cambodian genocide, the Rwandan genocide, and the Bosnian genocide. Holocaust studies is now often referred to as Holocaust and genocide studies. Major institutions, such as the United States Holocaust Memorial Museum, have now added genocide to the scope of their concerns.

We have very good reason to maintain a strong focus on Jews and Nazis as we study the broader rubric of genocide. Hostility toward Jews has a very long pedigree in Western Christian civilization, so that the murder of Jews by a Christian nation in the twentieth century did not come from nowhere. Christian churches and Christian theologians have had to confront this reality since 1945, with major changes in practice and doctrine now widely in place.[38] However, these changes in Christian doctrine have hardly removed

---

38. Contempt for Jews, once standard Christian theology, has now largely disappeared. See, for example, *Nostra Aetate*, produced by the Catholic Church at the Second Vatican Council in 1965 and the many national and international Lutheran bodies that have condemned Luther's scurrilous diatribe, *On the Jews and Their Lies*. For a discussion of this and other writings by Luther, see chapter 3 by Christopher J. Probst in this volume, "Luther Scholars, Jews, and Judaism during the Third Reich." Note also that the United States Holocaust Memorial Museum maintains a standing Committee on Ethics, Religion, and the Holocaust, with membership from the three Abrahamic faiths: Judaism, Christianity, and Islam.

antisemitism from our world. Antisemitism now plays a very large role in the hostility of Arabs toward Jews in the Middle East. Antisemitism also remains an issue in Europe and in North America, with a troubling resurgence that has accompanied the rise of right-wing, ethnonationalistic politics in recent years.

The centrality of Germany is also important in our assessment of Holocaust and genocide, because Germany represents such a complicated problem. Few peoples contributed more to the development of Western culture than the Germans, with such luminaries as the Holy Roman emperors, Martin Luther, Bach, Beethoven, and Mozart. Germany is the most advanced, most educated country ever to perpetrate genocide. In terms of cultural significance, in terms of its place in modern science, economics, politics, and study of the humanities, Germany by the 1920s was a nation that might seem closest to what we value in ourselves and a nation least likely to turn to the murder of innocents. If we admire the accomplishments of Western culture and advocate those cultural values today, we should be very alarmed by the fact that it was highly educated, highly accomplished Germans who were ready to ostracize large groups of people and build death camps for their eradication.

Thus, while this volume maintains a focus on Jewish victims and Nazi perpetrators, it does so without losing sight of the breadth and complexity of Holocaust scholarship in recent decades. As discussed, it was Germans, and not just rabid Nazis, who made the Holocaust possible. Also, Germans had a great deal of assistance from others, both active and passive. In addition, Jews were the primary victims, yet many other groups also were targeted, from Sinti and Roma to political opponents, Russian prisoners of war, Polish intellectuals, the disabled, and homosexuals. This broader understanding of the Holocaust, with Germans plus others responsible for the killing and Jews plus others among the victims, is both more accurate and more frightening. Much or most of Holocaust studies today sees the Holocaust as a human problem, not just a German problem and not just a Jewish issue. Finally, though it goes beyond the scope of this volume, many humanities scholars at American universities conveniently looked the other way during this period or even supported ideas within the new German paradigm.[39] Advocates of Holocaust and genocide studies, advocates of teaching this story, hope to make a better world by increasing our awareness of the past and heightening our sensitivity to massive injustice in the future while trying to recognize the full complexity and the full horror of the injustice.

---

39. See Stephen H. Norwood, *The Third Reich in the Ivory Tower: Complicity and Conflict on American Campuses* (New York: Cambridge University Press, 2009).

With few exceptions, the chapters in this volume focus on one narrow segment within the arc of Holocaust awareness: the role of the humanities in German universities. This topic lagged behind as Holocaust awareness grew. It took half a century after the liberation of Auschwitz before humanities scholars today began to look at humanities scholars then, with new research on individual scholars, specific universities, specific disciplines, and the entire apparatus of academic life. It is only within the last two decades or so that the collision between what we might take to be humanities values within the university and Nazi behavior in perpetrating the Holocaust has received a steady gaze. The results are uncomfortable, both for German academics and for some academics outside Germany who at that time cast an accepting or even approving eye on German events. We must try to understand those German humanities scholars and university professors who betrayed the higher ideals of their discipline and supported the Nazi state and Nazi ideas. We should try to understand what lies they might have told themselves to justify their apparent apostasy. We also must consider to what extent our non-German forebears were complicit and whether or not we too tell ourselves lies to avoid sleepless nights. Can we really identify values within the humanities that deserve our support and merit our advocacy? Studying professors at German universities who learned to welcome and support the Nazi state should be a good place to focus our gaze as we pursue that question.

III. STRUCTURE AND CONTENTS OF THIS VOLUME

The chapters that follow examine some of the most prestigious academic disciplines of the humanities. These include disciplines to which Germany has a proper claim for having not only founded but also first introduced into the academic curriculum of the university: disciplines concerned with religious and ethical values, with creativity and thought about the best way for humans to organize themselves in society under the rule of law, disciplines concerned with reflection on the past and humanity's greatest cultural accomplishments. This volume also takes a close and hard look at some of Germany's most prestigious universities: the Humboldt University of Berlin, Georg August University of Göttingen, and Eberhard Karls University of Tübingen. These institutions, which have a distinguished history that goes back in many cases to the Reformation and the Enlightenment, had long played a major role in providing a humanities education to German citizens. They offered a home for introducing those citizens to the humanities. Laws were established in the various German *Länder* [states] to safeguard due process in the appointment of university faculty and enshrine academic freedom in order to permit universities to flourish. What went wrong? What happened at the universities and what happened to the major disciplines of the humanities under National Socialism?

In order to examine those questions, this volume is arranged in three parts: part I, "Nazi Germany and the Historical Humanities"; part II, "Law, Music, and Philosophy in the Third Reich"; and part III, "Nazi Germany and Beyond." Part I helps situate the reader within the realm of modern scholarship on the humanities under the Third Reich. These essays present their perspectives in very different ways, providing an overview of the development of post–World War II scholarship, an analysis of how Martin Luther's antisemitism influenced Nazi-era Christian theologians, and analyses of some of Germany's prestigious academic disciplines, such as Archaeology, Assyriology, Egyptology, the study of the ancient Near East (conventionally called Oriental studies), Old Testament/Hebrew Bible scholarship, New Testament scholarship, and *Judaistik* (in contrast to "Jewish Studies," *Judaistik* refers to the study of ancient Judaism within German Protestant and Catholic theological faculties, often with an aim toward missionary activity). Part II moves from the more historically and philologically oriented disciplines to law, music, and philosophy, and the way that National Socialism had a lasting impact on them. The essays in part III, "Nazi Germany and Beyond," look beyond academic disciplines and universities under the Third Reich and cast their gaze in other directions. How did Göttingen, one of Germany's most important universities, seek to rid itself of its Nazi past through the process of *Entnazifierung* [denazification], and how successful were these efforts? How did Italian fascism contrast with German National Socialism as regards antisemitism and the construction of a totalitarian state? Finally, we turn our attention to examples of antisemitism at universities of our own day to ask whether any of these contemporary struggles recall those of the past.

Part I. Nazi Germany and the Historical Humanities

We begin this volume on the betrayal of humanistic values under the Nazi regime with "The History of the Humanities in the Third Reich." Alan E. Steinweis argues that even prior to 1933, the humanities in Germany were not characterized by the tolerant, open-minded, and democratic values that the academy embraces today. Instead, professors with a conservative nationalist orientation played a dominant role in the academic study of the humanities: this was true of virtually all the disciplines. Hence, the issue of the *betrayal* of the humanities needs to be carefully phrased. It is essential to recognize that vast differences exist between the dominant orientation of the humanities in the contemporary United States and the situation in Germany prior to 1933 Germany, let alone the humanities under the Third Reich. Furthermore, critical study of Nazi-era humanities scholars remained almost entirely unexplored until the 1990s. This was due to a German academic establishment that, perhaps understandably, not only wished to avoid implicating itself but also deemed such study relatively trivial in comparison to other priorities, such as investigating the collapse of the Weimar Republic, the rise of Hitler, and the mass crimes committed by the Nazi regime. The few studies that did emerge prior to the 1990s tended to set the tone for subsequent scholarship, and Steinweis provides a clear analysis of how the academic study of Nazi-era humanities developed over the ensuing decades. Steinweis surveys disciplines like folklore and history, studies of individual universities, Nazi *Judenforschung* (the antisemitic pseudo-academic study of Judaism), and the controversial legacies of Carl Schmitt and Martin Heidegger. The ongoing contemporary interest in the ideas of Schmitt and Heidegger demonstrates that some people continue to recognize transcendent truths in the work of politically repulsive individuals. These explorations equally sound a warning that we in the academy today—no less than the prestigious professors of Nazi-era German universities—remain susceptible to moral failings in our intellectual pursuits.

Germany has long been known for its outstanding work in the linguistic, historical, and archaeological study of classical and ancient Near Eastern antiquity. With Hitler's rise to power, the prestigious German discipline of *Orientalistik* [Oriental studies] faced enormous challenges. Would a field heavily populated by scholars of Jewish ancestry, and focused heavily on the languages of the ancient Near East and South Asia, survive in the Nazis' antisemitic, xenophobic, and anti-intellectual world? During the Great War, at least, Orientalists could claim their relevance on the basis of Germany's alliance with the Ottoman Empire; but now the question of relevance became urgent. In the chapter "The 'Orient' and 'Us': Making Ancient Oriental Studies Relevant during the Nazi Regime," Suzanne L. Marchand describes the immense toll that Nazi purges took on the field. She demonstrates how scholars employed in the diverse subfields of Oriental studies (Islamic studies, Egyptology, Assyriology, Iranology, and more) undertook a variety of strategies to save both themselves and their discipline from further decimation. The chapter poses the important question: What were the intellectual and moral costs of these attempts to establish an enduring relationship between "the Orient" and "us"?

Antisemitism within the German Protestant Church has a history that goes back to the Reformation. In "Luther Scholars, Jews, and Judaism during the Third Reich," Christopher J. Probst examines the appropriation of Martin

Luther's works by German Protestant Luther scholars during the Third Reich. Luther wrote at least five treatises on the subject of "the Jews." One work in particular, *Von den Juden und ihren Lügen* [*On the Jews and Their Lies*], has fueled the greatest discussion of the reformer's attitude toward Jews. In the final section of the lengthy treatise, Luther makes seven severe recommendations to the authorities regarding Germany's Jews. Among these are calls to burn their synagogues and schools to the ground, confiscate their "prayer books and Talmudic writings," and subject them to harsh labor. These antisemitic recommendations closely correspond to the fatal measures enacted against Jews in Nazi Germany some four hundred years later. The chapter begins with a brief overview of the German Protestant Church during the Third Reich, the academic context in which Protestant theologians operated, and the roles they played in the church, academia, and broader society. The chapter's focus is the work of two Luther scholars, the respected Leipzig philologist Georg Buchwald and Moringen pastor Walter Holsten. Both scholars appropriated Luther's writings about Jews and Judaism in support of their own anti-Judaic and antisemitic views. Rather than utilizing the tools of the well-developed discipline of modern German theological studies to reflect thoughtfully on the relationship between Christianity and Judaism, they instead betrayed their commitment to the humanities by dehumanizing Jews in their theological writings.

The focus on Christian theology continues with the next two chapters. From 1933 through 1945, the Old Testament (Hebrew Bible) was under attack in Nazi Germany. Indeed, the entire notion that Christianity had any connection to Judaism was systematically denied, and the prestigious German tradition of "Old Testament" studies was compromised, as both the universities and the Protestant Church sought to align themselves with Nazi ideology. Bernard M. Levinson, in his contribution to the volume, "Gerhard von Rad's Struggle against the Nazification of the Old Testament," presents a case study of one scholar's experience, that of Gerhard von Rad (1901–1971). Later renowned as a major theologian of the Old Testament, von Rad began his academic career at the University of Jena during the Nazi rise to power. Von Rad's preoccupation with the biblical book of Deuteronomy in his writings, and the way his arguments read Christian doctrine into the text in perplexing ways, raises a series of important issues about the social location of scholarship under the National Socialist dictatorship. His experience serves as a microcosm of the larger changes taking place in the German university. Von Rad's resistance to those changes stands in contrast to the betrayal of traditional academic values by many of his colleagues. Unlike his peers, Von Rad never incorporated National Socialist ideology into his research or course work, nor did he participate in efforts by his peers to remove all traces of Judaism from the biblical text. Yet he was not unmoved by events around him. His drive to resist the nazification of his field shaped his writings in ways even he himself does not seem to have recognized. In his own way, he too ensured that Deuteronomy bore no connection to Judaism.

The focus on biblical and religious studies being turned against its ostensible object of study continues in the next chapter. In the context of the German university, Judaistik as an academic discipline engaged in the study of ancient Judaism represents a branch of Christian theology and is housed within either a Faculty of Protestant Theology or a Faculty of Catholic Theology. Although ancient Judaism was the object of study (often for the sake of background to the New Testament or for the sake of "mission" or conversion), Jews themselves almost without exception could not play an academic role either as faculty or as students.[40] In "Jewish Studies in the Service of Nazi Ideology: Tübingen's Faculty of Theology as a Center for Antisemitic Research," Anders Gerdmar investigates how the Faculty of Protestant Theology at Eberhard Karls University in Tübingen became a seedbed for the theological and political legitimation of antisemitism during the Third Reich. Several scholars from Tübingen stood at the forefront of National Socialist theology. The two most famous of them are Gerhard Kittel (1888–1948) and Walter Grundmann (1906–1976), but also noteworthy are Adolf Schlatter (1852–1938), Paul Althaus (1888–1966), and Karl Georg Kuhn (1906–1976). These scholars shared several defining characteristics, chief of which was their philological expertise in Judaistik—ironically used to show the dangers of Judaism. In addition, they held a theologically conservative perspective, advanced antisemitic and racial claims, espoused antimodernism and national chauvinism, and, to varying degrees, all embraced the idea of a National Socialist state. Gerdmar's chapter demonstrates that through their research and in their roles as educators of future ministers and teachers in Germany's churches and schools, this network of scholars became instrumental for German theological antisemitism. Toward the end of his essay, Gerdmar develops a methodological insight, drawing on network theory

---

40. For that reason, one should carefully distinguish between "Jewish Studies" as it has developed at many North American and European universities, especially after the war, and the specific theological discipline of *Judaistik* in the German context. The situation began to change with the pioneering work by Peter Schäfer to build a program in *Jüdische Studien* at the Free University of Berlin, intentionally *not* housed within a Faculty of Theology in order to free the discipline from the strictures of Protestant or Catholic theology and to permit Jews to participate.

to identify an "emotional regime" that tied these scholars and their students together. Such connections helped propagate their invidious ideas, both nationally and internationally, in the guise of reputable scholarship.

The next two chapters turn to the remarkable role that German scholarship has played in making the cultural legacy of ancient Egypt and ancient Mesopotamia accessible to the humanities. In each case there is a complicated legacy. German Egyptology properly enjoys a prestigious legacy, both within the university and in the mind of the broader public. Yet only recently has there been an attempt within the discipline to conduct research on the discipline's own history under National Socialism in a meaningful way and to bring Egyptology into dialogue with wider contemporary debates in culture and politics.[41] In his contribution to this volume, Thomas Schneider, who is one of the pioneer researchers in this field, provides a powerful analysis examining how Egyptology came to play a significant role in advancing Nazi ideology. His essay is entitled "Hermann Grapow, Egyptology, and National Socialist Initiatives for the Humanities." He provides a carefully documented, rich case study about Hermann Grapow, Professor of Egyptology at Berlin and a senior administrator at both the Prussian Academy of Sciences and the University of Berlin during the years 1938–45. Schneider demonstrates the important role played by leading academics in shaping the humanities in the Third Reich in ways that advanced Nazi racial theory. Schneider also stresses the interplay between the politics of Nazi higher education and various individual disciplines of the humanities. Through his determined ambition, Grapow rose to the positions of Vice President and Acting President of the Academy, and also became Dean, Vice President, and Acting President of the University. With his political rise, Grapow secured a position of undisputed leadership within the discipline of Egyptology. In his multiple academic and administrative roles, Grapow demonstrated a clear commitment to the National Socialist state. He regarded its doctrines as fate-given; this conviction included support for removing Jewish and politically disloyal faculty from their positions. Grapow continued to find ways to adapt and secure power even after the war. In the German Democratic Republic (East Germany), he once again assumed leading academic and administrative positions. In Schneider's fascinating study, Hermann Grapow, the leader of German Egyptology, emerges as an opportunist who (ab)used the

---

41. Stressing the interdependence of Egyptology with other cultural disciplines, see William E. Carruthers: "Introduction: Thinking about Histories of Egyptology," in *Histories of Egyptology: Interdisciplinary Measures*, ed. William E. Carruthers (New York: Routledge, 2015), 1–15.

field to further his own career and who intended to determine the discipline's course and discourse in a postwar Nazi Germany.

One of Germany's proudest contributions to the humanities is Assyriology, the study of the languages and civilizations of ancient Mesopotamia. Despite its small numbers as a discipline, Assyriology provides a crucial window into the beginnings of Western civilization—a window that had been quite literally buried in the sand for more than two millennia until the recovery and decipherment of cuneiform literature in the nineteenth century. Germans, including German Jews, played a crucial role in the development and consolidation of this discipline. In "German Assyriology: A Discipline in Troubled Waters," Johannes Renger details how Assyriology in Germany was severely affected after 1933 by the Nazi civil service laws and the widespread academic drive to read the Aryan myth back into the reconstruction of ancient history. On the one hand, the number of German Assyriologists was devastated by emigration due to Nazi policy against Jewish scholars and political opponents of the regime. On the other hand, the remaining scholars' compliance with Nazi policy undermined the integrity of the discipline. Notwithstanding the ideals of the humanities, they accepted Nazi ideology far more than they resisted it: Renger goes through each of the major scholars within the discipline to assess the extent of their indoctrination under National Socialism and to examine how the actions of Nazi-aligned Assyriologists during the Third Reich continued to impact the prestige of Germany Assyriology long after the war had ended.

Renger draws extensively on personal conversations and correspondence with German Assyriologists from that era. Thus, in addition to his scholarly arguments and his consideration of their scholarship, Renger's contribution also provides a distinctive perspective as a personal memoir from someone who, in the immediate postwar period, worked directly and built relationships with many of the protagonists being discussed. Among the scholars examined are the foundational, if controversial, Assyriologist Wolfram von Soden as well as von Soden's brilliant Jewish *Doktorvater* (doctoral dissertation director), Benno Landsberger, who was one of the most important scholars of Assyriology during this era.[42]

---

42. For alternative and more critical evaluations of Wolfram von Soden and the discipline of Assyriology during this period, see Gary Beckman, "Ancient Near Eastern 'Aryans' and the Third Reich," in *Dealing with Antiquity: Past, Present & Future—RAI Marburg*, ed. Walter Sommerfeld, Alter Orient und Altes Testament 460 (Münster, Germany: Ugarit-Verlag, 2020), 9–20, and Jakob Flygare, "Assyriology in Nazi Germany: The Case of Wolfram von Soden," in *Perspectives on the History of Ancient Near Eastern Studies*, ed. Agnès Garcia-Ventura and Lorenzo Verderame (University Park, PA: Eisenbrauns, 2020), 44–60.

Some background information on Landsberger and his relationship with von Soden provides additional context for Renger's essay. It also highlights the complexity of rehabilitating German Assyriology after World War II. Born in Austria, Landsberger fought with distinction on the eastern front during World War I, where he received three medals: a Wound Medal, the Golden Merit Cross, and the Silver Medal for Bravery, Second Class.[43] Nonetheless, in 1935, he was summarily dismissed from his position as ordinarius at Leipzig because of Germany's new racial laws. Landsberger lived in exile in Turkey until 1948, when he was appointed to the Oriental Institute of the University of Chicago.

The place of Landsberger and von Soden in Renger's essay, as well as Renger's personal relationship with each, illustrates some of the important complexities in how this volume attempts to untangle the mingling of Nazi era remnants in postwar scholarship. Von Soden was Landsberger's *Assistent*, and he had joined the Sturmabteilung (SA) already in 1933 and later spoke out against his Doktorvater while serving in the German military. Yet ironically, following the war, von Soden was only able to return to his academic career because of Landsberger's efforts on his behalf. It is remarkable that during denazification, Landsberger wrote to Göttingen University in support of von Soden's reinstatement, even as the faculty at Göttingen considered and rejected von Soden's postwar return. Landsberger's support came despite von Soden's Nazi enthusiasms and at least three nazified publications in the 1930s. While his attempt to aid von Soden in resuming his position at Göttingen was unsuccessful—von Soden ultimately failed to pass the review process of denazification—Landsberger continued to back von Soden, helping him achieve his first postwar appointment at the University of Vienna in 1955.[44] Landsberger then published with von Soden in 1965, each of them contributing prior work to produce a joint volume on Assyriology. Landsberger accepted this academic collaboration, even though he failed to persuade von Soden to alter certain of his Nazi-era interpretations of Mesopotamian cultural history.

Renger himself gained access to these matters in the 1960s while doing research in Chicago, where he also developed a close relationship with Landsberger in the last two years of Landsberger's life. This connection even included

---

43. Luděk Vacín, in collaboration with Jitka Sýkorová, *The Unknown Benno Landsberger: A Biographical Sketch of an Assyriological Altmeister's Development, Exile, and Personal Life*, Leipziger Altorientalische Studien 10 (Wiesbaden, Germany: Harrassowitz, 2018), 50.

44. Ursula Wokoeck, *German Orientalism: The Study of the Middle East and Islam from 1800 to 1945* (London: Routledge, 2009), 195.

Renger attending a private dinner organized by Landsberger in honor of von Soden in Chicago in 1967 (see chapter 7, note 38). All of this speaks to complex issues: Landsberger's loyalty to his field; his complicated relationship to Germany, despite having been forced as a Jew to give up his professorship and flee the country; and Renger's own development as a young Assyriologist establishing himself in postwar Germany.

The last chapter in this section examines the impact of Nazi investment in the field of prehistoric archaeology. In "National Socialist Archaeology as a Faustian Bargain: The Contrasting Careers of Hans Reinerth and Herbert Jankuhn," Bettina Arnold notes that although biographies of several key figures in prehistoric German archaeology under National Socialism have appeared in the last two decades, they have largely been confined to descriptive chronological narratives with little or no consideration of post-1945 life histories. Her case study utilizes a comparison of the career trajectories of prehistorians Hans Reinerth and Herbert Jankuhn—as top-ranking officials in the Rosenberg Office and the Ahnenerbe, respectively—to reveal the complexity and diversity of the motivations that led archaeologists to embrace the *Nationalsozialistische Deutsche Arbeiterpartei* [National Socialist German Workers' Party (NSDAP)] and that affected their actions between 1933 and 1945. The very different pre-, peri-, and postwar experiences of these two archaeologists reveal the extent to which the German university system first fostered and then turned a largely blind eye to the activities of archaeologists engaged in supporting the ideological program of German National Socialism.

Classified as a humanities discipline rather than a social science in Europe, prehistoric archaeology was especially well-suited to underwriting the creation of national identities in early to mid-twentieth century west-central Europe. The deep temporal reach of the archaeological record provided support for Nazi territorial claims while the ambiguity inherent in interpretations of the material record produced by largely preliterate societies facilitated tendentious manipulation of the data for political purposes. Prehistoric archaeology in Germany had largely been neglected in favor of the more prestigious fields of Classical and Near Eastern archaeology, where impressive monuments could point to the grandeur of an imperial past. Consequently, the unprecedented support provided by the NSDAP for the study of prehistory proved to be a potent lure for many professional archaeologists. The varied motivations behind their participation in the National Socialist program have received little attention to date, however, and reveal both the strengths and weaknesses of totalitarian systems that attempt to coopt research and teaching within institutions of higher learning.

Part II: Law, Music, and Philosophy in the Third Reich

While German legal scholars did not, by and large, participate directly in the crimes perpetrated by the Nazis, they facilitated those crimes by conferring a veneer of legality and legitimacy to the actions of the regime. Their legal scholarship made it possible for the Nazi leadership to proclaim, and for ordinary Germans to accept the claim, that theirs was, when all was said and done, a *Rechtsstaat* [state based on the liberal rule of law]. In his powerfully written contribution, "Hitler's Willing Law Professors," Oren Gross examines the significant role played by German law professors in creating and establishing the National Socialist legal system. Far from the claims made after the war that the number of "genuine Nazis" on faculties was very small, the majority of German legal scholars supported National Socialism. His essay focuses on the support given to the Nazis by several leading scholars while arguing that the story of the moral decline of German universities and professors in general, and of German law professors in particular, was one in which professional myopia, personal opportunism, moral weakness, antisemitism, and legal jurisprudential claims had been inexorably intermingled. That Gross weaves into his account some of his own remarkable family history makes his contribution that much more gripping.

In his poetically elegant essay "The Music of Arnold Schoenberg: Catastrophe and Creation," Michael Cherlin explores two aspects of creation in relation to catastrophe: creation as a response to catastrophe, so that newly emerging forms of creativity are part of a coping or healing process, and creation itself as entailing catastrophe, a shattering of former meaning so that new meaning might emerge. Using a dialectical paradigm derived from Harold Bloom's 1975 book *Kabbalah and Criticism*, Cherlin posits three transformative "moments" of catastrophe and creation in Schoenberg's life and works. The first moment is coincident with the upheaval in the arts in the years just prior to World War I. The second moment occurs during the interwar years, the tumultuous period that saw the virulent rise of anti-Semitism and a second sea change in Schoenberg's musical language. The first two moments of creative and personal catastrophe become the precursors to the final moment, Schoenberg's forced resignation from the Prussian Academy of Arts, his emigration to the United States, and the final stage of the composer's life.

The academic disciplines of philosophy and political science were deeply impacted by National Socialism. The Nazi connections of two luminaries of these fields, Martin Heidegger and Carl Schmitt, have long been known. But to what degree were Heidegger and Schmitt responsible for fostering and legitimizing

National Socialism? The question is all the more apposite today, since these authors continued to exert a very strong influence in the field of philosophy and political theory after 1945. Yet Hannah Arendt's well-known interpretation of Nazi totalitarianism in *The Origins of Totalitarianism* (published in 1951) lets the German intellectual elite entirely off the hook. Indeed, Arendt maintains that authors like Carl Schmitt had "no responsibility" in the Nazi phenomenon, even though Schmitt invented the concept of the totalitarian state, which Hitler notably took over in a positive sense. Emmanuel Faye, our contributor for this chapter, has done pioneering work in exposing the Nazi sympathies of Martin Heidegger. In his current study, entitled "Political Philosophy: Hannah Arendt and Aurel Kolnai as Interpreters of the Nazi Totalitarian State," Faye demonstrates that from 1950 onward, Arendt contributed more than anyone else to the promotion and defense of Heidegger. In 1969, she went so far as to acclaim him "the hidden king [who] reigned in the realm of thinking." This contrasts sharply with Aurel Kolnai, the Hungarian-born Jewish philosopher who, as early as 1938, composed *The War against the West*, a remarkable seven-hundred-page critical study on the National Socialist *Weltanschauung* [worldview]. In that study, recently translated into German, Kolnai analyzes the writings of over 120 authors who contributed to the constitution and diffusion of the National Socialist worldview in all fields, from law to theology—including philosophy, politics, and history. Thus, where Arendt excuses elite Nazi intellectuals to give them a free pass, Kolnai exposes them and holds them to account. Faye's essay helps us rediscover the value of Kolnai's work for developing an in-depth understanding of how the Nazi vision was shaped and, thereby, how to resist it.

Part III: Nazi Germany and Beyond

In his chapter, "The Nazification and Denazification of the University of Göttingen," Robert P. Ericksen begins with the widespread view that German universities in the late-nineteenth and early twentieth centuries were the best in the world. He then adds the assumption that this might have made them a natural place to question and criticize the antihumanistic Nazi ideology and the poorly educated Adolf Hitler. However, even before Hitler's rise to power in 1933, universities were subject to antisemitic prejudice and angry nationalism. Furthermore, among the student population, enthusiastic Nazis had managed to take over student government. Already by 1931, they had weaponized their antisemitism and hypernationalism with boycotts and demonstrations. Hitler's actual rise to power led to a dramatic purge of Jewish and left-wing professors beginning in April and a day for celebratory book-burning in May. Professors accepted and even supported these events, sacrificing their supposed academic ideals for a "political university" in support of the Nazi cause. Following a brief description of these trends, Ericksen employs his research into postwar denazification at Göttingen University to describe the betrayal of that university's academic values during the Nazi era and also to reflect on the difficulties of transition after 1945.

The second chapter in this section examines the process of rebuilding Göttingen University under the circumstances of postwar denazification. In the postwar period, Göttingen resided in the British Zone of Occupation. The British hoped for a practice of "indirect rule," theoretically accepting the idea of university autonomy. Their goal was for the German academic leadership at Göttingen to reform and democratize the university under a light British influence. In real terms, however, especially given the nazification of German universities that had taken place between 1933 and 1945, as described for Göttingen by Ericksen's chapter in this volume, the first stage of the process was not "light." As in other zones of occupation, the British first closed universities and developed their own vetting process, removing those faculty members they considered most egregious in their Nazi politics through a process of denazification. Then, however, the British hoped for a cooperative process in which German academics would reopen the university under their own leadership, with the British holding only a right to veto individual decisions.

In "The University of Göttingen and Its Postwar Response to Persecuted Colleagues: A Broken Relationship," Anikó Szabó offers a penetrating analysis of how this optimistic vision for rebuilding the university failed to achieve its goals. The Senate of the University of Göttingen, its highest decision-making body, established a policy of *Ergänzung der Besten* [appointing only the best] in selecting new faculty members for the regeneration of the university after the war. However, the university's use of this criterion would be implemented by academics who, even if they had passed muster during the British purge, still had lived within and often accepted many of the attitudes and practices of the Nazi regime. Furthermore, the rebuilding of the university took place during those years when German control over denazification gradually softened that process. In real terms, as a result, the implementation of *appointing only the best* primarily benefited colleagues who had been removed from their positions during the first phase of denazification as well as those who had fled positions in the Soviet zone of occupation during the postwar period. Through a series of case studies, Szabó demonstrates the many barriers to a postwar reconciliation and reconstruction of the Germany university system. She describes a fraught process whereby the very professors who prospered during the Nazi era regained their positions and continued to flourish after the war, while victims of academic persecution who had been forced to flee abroad rarely achieved a successful return to the university.

If much of the volume is rightly focused on how humanities professors under the Third Reich so eagerly acquiesced to Nazi ideology, Franklin Hugh Adler provides an important complicating perspective in his contribution, "Italian Fascism: Decentering Standard Assumptions about Antisemitism and Totalitarianism." Italian fascism lasted nearly twice as long as German fascism and, in contrast, neither racism nor antisemitism played a major role in its formation or ideology. Jews were well-integrated into Italian life, and Italy even viewed Nazis with suspicion as late as the mid-1930s. In 1938, however, the situation for Italian Jews changed drastically, when Mussolini launched a campaign against them. Adler argues that this sudden shift in attitude toward the Jews can be traced to a legitimation crisis that followed failed economic and social reforms. His analysis explores the cultural contradictions within Italian fascism. By equating Jews with a decadent bourgeois class at odds with the cultural revolution, Italy simultaneously strengthened a new alliance with Germany and gave Italians a convenient "other" to set in opposition to the fascist "New Man." Although the anti-Jewish campaign of 1938 caused many Italian Jews to flee the country, it was not accompanied by pogroms or concentration camps; it was couched in terms of "discrimination not persecution." Sadly, many Italians—including university professors—silently accepted the discrimination against their former friends and colleagues as they reaped the benefits of newly available jobs and decreased competition for academic positions and promotions. Adler's important essay reminds us that betrayals of the humanities do not always resemble the case of Nazi Germany. Such betrayals can emerge swiftly and for a variety of reasons and take a number of forms. We would do well to keep this in mind as we critically evaluate the state and moral compass of our academic disciplines in the twenty-first century.

In its final chapter, this volume extends its focus to the contemporary world. Many of those who served as faculty members and administrators of German universities during the Third Reich colluded with the Nazi regime or chose to remain passive in the face of the compromises exacted by the regime's racial principles and political program. The result radically stripped the country's institutions of higher learning of Jews on their faculties and in their student bodies. Nothing akin to the situation that prevailed in German universities during the Hitler period is observable within North American and European institutions of higher learning today. However, in his provocative contribution, "Is There an Anti-Jewish Bias in Today's University?," Alvin H. Rosenfeld maintains that contemporary American universities, like the surrounding cultures in which they exist, are not altogether free of new adaptations of the

Jewish Question. While clearly recognizing that no one is calling for a final solution, he argues that certain recent campus developments are troubling all the same. Some of the troubles relate to changing attitudes toward how the victims and perpetrators of the Nazi Final Solution of the Jewish Question should be remembered, including how they should be presented in university-level teaching and research. In some quarters, one observes feelings of impatience with Holocaust memory and resentment toward Jews for keeping such memory alive. In addition, some universities have seen the emergence of an intensely negative, aggressively hostile attitude toward Israel and its supporters, which expresses itself in well-organized Boycott, Divestment, and Sanctions (BDS) movement programs, annual Israel Apartheid weeks, and other campus manifestations of anti-Israel activity. Taken together, these developments have made a number of American university campuses no longer seem as hospitable to Jewish students and others as they once were. In the context of current debates both within Europe and North America about immigration and the status of refugees, such developments—with their inevitable echoes of a dark past—emerge as all the more troubling.

BIBLIOGRAPHY

Beckman, Gary. "Ancient Near Eastern 'Aryans' and the Third Reich." In Sommerfeld, *Dealing with Antiquity: Past, Present & Future—RAI Marburg*, 9–20.

Beyerchen, Alan D. *Scientists under Hitler: Politics and the Physics Community in the Third Reich*. New Haven, CT: Yale University Press, 1977.

Binding, Karl, and Alfred Hoche. *Die Freigabe der Vernichtung lebensunwerten Lebens: Ihr Maß und ihre Form*. Leipzig, Germany: F. Meiner, 1920.

Browning, Christopher R. *The Final Solution and the German Foreign Office: A Study of Referat D III of Abteilung Deutschand 1940–43*. New York: Holmes and Meier, 1978.

———. *Ordinary Men: Reserve Police Battalion 101 and the Final Solution in Poland*. New York: HarperCollins, 1992.

———. *The Origins of the Final Solution: The Evolution of Nazi Jewish Policy, September 1939–March 1942*. Jerusalem: Yad Vashem; Lincoln: University of Nebraska Press, 2004.

———. "The Personal Contexts of a Holocaust Historian: War, Politics, Trials, and Professional Rivalries." In Browning et al., *Holocaust Scholarship: Personal Trajectories and Professional Interpretations*, 48–66.

Browning, Christopher R., Susannah Heschel, Michael R. Marrus, and Milton Shain, eds. *Holocaust Scholarship: Personal Trajectories and Professional Interpretations*. London: Palgrave Macmillan, 2015.

Cantor, Norman F. *Inventing the Middle Ages: The Lives, Works, and Ideas of the Great Medievalists of the Twentieth Century*. New York: William Morrow, 1991.

Carruthers, William E., ed. *Histories of Egyptology: Interdisciplinary Measures*. New York: Routledge, 2015.

Carruthers, William E. "Introduction: Thinking about Histories of Egyptology." In Carruthers, *Histories of Egyptology: Interdisciplinary Measures*, 1–15.

Diner, Hasia R. *We Remember with Reverence and Love: American Jews and the Myth of Silence after the Holocaust, 1945–1962*. New York: NYU Press, 2009.

Ericksen, Robert P. *Complicity in the Holocaust: Churches and Universities in Nazi Germany*. Cambridge: Cambridge University Press, 2012.

——. "Theologians in the Third Reich: The Case of Gerhard Kittel." *Journal of Contemporary History* 12, no. 3 (1977): 595–622.

——. *Theologians under Hitler: Gerhard Kittel, Paul Althaus, and Emanuel Hirsch*. New Haven, CT: Yale University Press, 1985.

Elvert, Jürgen, and Jürgen Nielsen-Sikora, eds. *Kulturwissenschaften und Nationalsozialismus*. Historische Mitteilungen 72. Stuttgart, Germany: Franz Steiner, 2008.

Fleming, Michael. *Auschwitz, the Allies, and Censorship of the Holocaust*. Cambridge: Cambridge University Press, 2014.

Flygare, Jakob. "Assyriology in Nazi Germany: The Case of Wolfram von Soden." In Garcia-Ventura and Verderame, *Perspectives on the History of Ancient Near Eastern Studies*, 44–60.

Fritzsche, Peter. *Germans into Nazis*. Cambridge, MA: Harvard University Press, 1998.

Garcia-Ventura, Agnès, and Lorenzo Verderame, eds. *Perspectives on the History of Ancient Near Eastern Studies*. University Park, PA: Eisenbrauns, 2020.

Grafton, Anthony. *The Footnote: A Curious History*. Cambridge, MA: Harvard University Press, 1999.

Grobman, Alex. "What Did They Know? The American Jewish Press and the Holocaust, 1 September 1939–17 December 1942." *American Jewish History* 68, no. 3 (1979): 327–52.

Hass, Aaron. *The Aftermath: Living with the Holocaust*. Cambridge: Cambridge University Press, 1995.

Hausmann, Frank-Rutger, ed. *Die Rolle der Geisteswissenschaften im Dritten Reich, 1933–1945*. Schriften des Historischen Kollegs, Kolloquien 53. Munich: Oldenbourg, 2002.

Hilberg, Raul. *The Destruction of the European Jews*. 3rd ed. 3 vols. New Haven, CT: Yale University Press, 2003. First edition published 1961 by Quadrangle Books (Chicago); second edition published 1985 by Holmes and Meier (New York).

——. *The Politics of Memory: The Journey of a Holocaust Historian*. Chicago: Ivan R. Dee, 1996.

Kant, Immanuel. "An Answer to the Question: 'What Is Enlightenment?'" [1784]. In idem, *Perpetual Peace and Other Essays on Politics, History, and Moral Practice*, 41–48. Translated by Ted Humphrey. Indianapolis, IN: Hackett, 1983.

Kittel, Gerhard. "Das Rassenproblem der Spätantike und das Frühchristentum." Lecture, University of Vienna, June 15, 1944. Rg III a 119 (Magazin/RARA). Library of the Faculty of Protestant Theology. Tübingen University, Tübingen, Germany.

———. "Die Entstehung des Judentums." Lecture, University of Vienna, March 22, 1943. Rg III a 119 (Magazin/RARA). Library of the Faculty of Protestant Theology. Tübingen University, Tübingen, Germany.

———. *Die Judenfrage*. Stuttgart, Germany: Kohlhammer, 1933.

———. *Die religiöse und die kirchliche Lage in Deutschland*. Leipzig, Germany: Dörffling & Franke, 1921.

Laqueur, Walter. *The Terrible Secret: Suppression of the Truth about Hitler's "Final Solution."* New York: Little, Brown, 1980.

Lehmann, Hartmut, and Otto Gerhard Oexle, eds. *Nationalsozialismus in den Kulturwissenschaften*. Vol. 1, *Fächer, Milieus, Karrieren*. Veröffentlichungen des Max-Planck-Instituts für Geschichte 200. Göttingen, Germany: Vandenhoeck & Ruprecht, 2004.

———. *Nationalsozialismus in den Kulturwissenschaften*. Vol. 2, *Leitbegriffe, Deutungsmuster, Paradigmenkämpfe, Erfahrungen, und Transformationen im Exil*. Veröffentlichungen des Max-Planck-Instituts für Geschichte 211. Göttingen, Germany: Vandenhoeck & Ruprecht, 2004.

Levinson, Bernard M. *"The Right Chorale": Studies in Biblical Law and Interpretation*. Winona Lake, IN: Eisenbrauns, 2011.

Lifton, Robert J. *The Nazi Doctors: Medical Killing and the Psychology of Genocide*. New York: Basic Books, 1986.

Lipstadt, Deborah. *Beyond Belief: The American Press and the Coming of the Holocaust, 1933–1945*. New York: Free Press, 1986.

Mahindra Humanities Center at Harvard. "About the Center." Harvard University. Accessed September 25, 2020. http://mahindrahumanities.fas.harvard.edu/about.

Müller, Ingo. *Hitler's Justice: The Courts of the Third Reich*. Translated by Deborah Lucas Schneider. Cambridge, MA: Harvard University Press, 1991.

Norwood, Stephen H. *The Third Reich in the Ivory Tower: Complicity and Conflict on American Campuses*. New York: Cambridge University Press, 2009.

Oxford English Dictionary. 3rd ed. (2000). Oxford: Oxford University Press. http://www.oed.com/.

Rabinbach, Anson, and Wolfgang Bialas, eds. *Nazi Germany and the Humanities: How German Academics Embraced Nazism*. Oxford: Oneworld, 2007.

Rabinowitz, Dorothy. *New Lives: Survivors of the Holocaust Living in America*. New York: Knopf, 1976.

Roth, Philip. "Eli, the Fanatic." In idem, *Goodbye Columbus and Five Short Stories*, 247–98. New York: Penguin, 1999.
Schmuhl, Hans-Walter. *Rassenhygiene, Nationalsozialismus, Euthanasie: Von der Verhütung zur Vernichtung "lebensunwerten Lebens," 1890–1945*. Kritische Studien zur Geschichtswissenschaft 75. Göttingen, Germany: Vandenhoeck & Ruprecht, 1987.
Schulze, Winfried, Gerd Heim, and Thomas Ott. "Deutsche Historiker im Nationalsozialismus: Beobachtungen und Überlegungen zu einer Debatte." In Schulze and Oexle, *Deutsche Historiker im Nationalsozialismus*, 11–50.
Schulze, Winfried, and Otto Gerhard Oexle, eds. *Deutsche Historiker im Nationalsozialismus*. 2nd ed. Zeit des Nationalsozialismus. Frankfurt, Germany: Fischer, 2000.
Sommerfeld, Walter, ed. *Dealing with Antiquity: Past, Present & Future—RAI Marburg*. Alter Orient und Altes Testament 460. Münster, Germany: Ugarit-Verlag, 2020.
Spinoza, Baruch. *Theological-Political Treatise*. Translated by Samuel Shirley, with an introduction and annotation by Seymour Feldman. 2nd ed. Indianapolis: Hackett, 2001.
Steinweis, Alan E. *Art, Ideology, and Economics in Nazi Germany: The Reich Chambers of Music, Theater, and the Visual Arts*. Chapel Hill: North Carolina University Press, 1993.
Vacín, Luděk, in collaboration with Jitka Sýkorová. *The Unknown Benno Landsberger: A Biographical Sketch of an Assyriological* Altmeister's *Development, Exile, and Personal Life*. Leipziger Altorientalische Studien 10. Wiesbaden, Germany: Harrassowitz, 2018.
Valla, Lorenzo. *On the Donation of Constantine*. Translated by Glen W. Bowersock. I Tatti Renaissance Library 24. Cambridge, MA: Harvard University Press, 2007.
Vatican Council II. *Nostra Aetate*. October 28, 1965. Accessed November 5, 2021. https://www.vatican.va/archive/hist_councils/ii_vatican_council/documents/vat-ii_decl_19651028_nostra-aetate_en.html.
Weinreich, Max. *Hitler's Professors: The Part of Scholarship in Germany's Crimes against the Jewish People*. New York: Yiddish Scientific Institute (YIVO), 1946. Reprinted with foreword by Martin Gilbert. New Haven, CT: Yale University Press, 1999.
Whitney Humanities Center. "About Us." Yale University. Accessed September 25, 2020. https://whc.yale.edu/about-us.
Wildt, Michael. *An Uncompromising Generation: The Nazi Leadership of the Reich Security Main Office*. Translated by Tom Lampert. George L. Mosse Series in Modern European Cultural and Intellectual History. Madison: University of Wisconsin Press, 2009.
Wokoeck, Ursula. *German Orientalism: The Study of the Middle East and Islam from 1800 to 1945*. London: Routledge, 2009.

BERNARD M. LEVINSON is Professor of Classical and Near Eastern Studies and of Law at the University of Minnesota, where he holds the Berman Family Chair in Jewish Studies and Hebrew Bible. His research focuses on biblical and cuneiform law, textual reinterpretation in the Second Temple period, and the relation of the Bible to Western intellectual history. The interdisciplinary significance of his work has been recognized with appointments to the Institute for Advanced Study in Princeton, the Wissenschaftskolleg zu Berlin, the National Humanities Center in North Carolina, and the Israel Institute for Advanced Studies in Jerusalem, where he codirected a research team of eight international scholars working on pentateuchal theory. He is the author of four books, including *Deuteronomy and the Hermeneutics of Legal Innovation* (Oxford, 1997) and *Legal Revision and Religious Renewal in Ancient Israel* (Cambridge, 2008), and six edited volumes.

ROBERT P. ERICKSEN is the Kurt Mayer Chair of Holocaust Studies Emeritus at Pacific Lutheran University in Tacoma, Washington. He has written or edited six books, including *Theologians under Hitler* (Yale, 1985), *Complicity in the Holocaust: Churches and Universities in Nazi Germany* (Cambridge, 2012), and *Betrayal: German Churches and the Holocaust* (with Susannah Heschel, Fortress, 1999). He is a Fellow of the Alexander von Humboldt Foundation; serves as Chair of the Committee on Ethics, Religion, and the Holocaust at the United States Holocaust Memorial Museum; and sits on the board of editors of *Kirchliche Zeitgeschichte* and an online journal, the *Contemporary Church History Quarterly*.

PART I

**NAZI GERMANY AND
THE HISTORICAL HUMANITIES**

ONE

THE HISTORY OF THE HUMANITIES IN THE THIRD REICH

ALAN E. STEINWEIS

WHEN DISCUSSING THE IMPACT OF Nazi rule on the humanities in Germany, it is important to avoid retrojecting onto the past our own sense of what the humanities are or ought to be. As Suzanne L. Marchand has emphasized, the humanistic disciplines in Germany before 1933 were characterized, by and large, by a devotion to a particular set of methodologies, not by the kinds of "non-elitist, inclusionary" values that typify the humanities in today's academy.[1] This is not a moral judgment about old-fashioned scholarship but simply a fact that must be kept in mind when assessing the degree to which the history of the humanities during the Nazi period should be regarded as a "betrayal." While there is no question that the Nazi regime brought unprecedented political and ideological pressures to bear on German academic life, German universities had *not* served as beacons of tolerance, democracy, and antiestablishment thinking before 1933. The acquiescence of German scholarship in Nazi rule resulted from a variety of factors, but certainly among the most important of these was the fundamental compatibility between Nazism and the intellectual and political values of a significant segment of the conservative-nationalistic German professoriate—or, at the very least, the absence of a fundamental incompatibility. The humanistic values that were betrayed between 1933 and 1945

---

1. Suzanne L. Marchand, "Nazism, 'Orientalism,' and Humanism," in *Nazi Germany and the Humanities: How German Academics Embraced Nazism*, ed. Wolfgang Bialas and Anson Rabinbach (Oxford: Oneworld, 2006; repr., 2014), 267–305 (at 267–68). See further her contribution to this volume, "The 'Orient' and 'Us': Making Ancient Oriental Studies Relevant during the Nazi Regime."

were not so much those of the German professoriate of the time as those of today's scholars working in liberal-democratic intellectual environments.

With this caveat in mind, we can trace the post-1945 development of scholarship about the conduct of Nazi-era German humanists. The historiography has unfolded against the background of generational change and the process of "coming to terms with the past" in postwar German-speaking Europe. Consideration of the subject began very slowly and haltingly, with only a tiny number of studies appearing between 1945 and 1990. These were produced mainly in West Germany. For its part, East Germany produced no significant research on this subject,[2] although it did publish information about West German scholars with Nazi pasts as an element in its strategy to discredit the Federal Republic.[3] In Austria, where work on the Nazi period was generally neglected until the late 1980s, systematic research about Nazi-era academics has been slow to develop, although a recent excellent volume about the University of Vienna, to be discussed in this chapter, provides a solid foundation for further consideration of the subject.

Research in this area picked up in pace considerably in the 1990s, after German unification, and has undergone a dramatic efflorescence since around 2000. This development has paralleled that of the historiography of the Third Reich more generally and for many of the same reasons. In postwar West Germany, the academic establishment long remained reluctant to address the pre-1945 unpleasantness. This mirrored a broader West German tendency to strive for normalcy by repressing certain aspects of the Nazi past but also served the

---

2. On the treatment of the Nazi period in the historical writing of the German Democratic Republic, see Martin Sabrow, "Die NS-Vergangenheit in der geteilten deutschen Geschichtskultur," in *Teilung und Integration: Die doppelte deutsche Nachkriegsgeschichte als wissenschaftliches und didaktisches Problem*, ed. Christoph Klessmann and Peter Lautzas, Schriftenreihe der Bundeszentrale für politische Bildung 482 (Bonn, Germany: Bundeszentrale für politische Bildung, 2005), 132–51; and Katrin Hammerstein et al., eds., *Aufarbeitung der Diktatur—Diktat der Aufarbeitung? Normierungsprozesse beim Umgang mit diktatorischer Vergangenheit*, Diktaturen und ihre Überwindung im 20. und 21. Jahrhundert 2 (Göttingen, Germany: Wallstein, 2009).

3. See, for example, the East German disclosure of details about the Nazi career of Peter-Heinz Seraphim, a specialist on Eastern European and Jewish matters, who after 1945 secured a job at a training academy for civil servants in West Germany. See Ilse Girard, "Prof. P. H. Seraphim: 'Wissenschaftlicher' Wegbereiter faschistischer Ideologie unter Hitler und unter Adenauer," *Dokumentation der Zeit* 126 (September 1956): 355–74. On Seraphim, see Hans-Christian Petersen, *Bevölkerungsökonomie – Ostforschung –Politik: Eine biographische Studie zu Peter-Heinz Seraphim (1902–1979)*, Einzelveröffentlichungen des Deutschen Historischen Instituts Warschau 17 (Osnabrück, Germany: Fibre, 2007).

personal and professional self-interests of a professoriate that had itself been implicated in Nazism. For many years after 1945, West German academic life was dominated by scholars who had started their careers or received their degrees in the Nazi period. Moreover, as members of that generation retired, they were replaced by their students, whose personal loyalty to their mentors often took precedence over an honest confrontation with the past. This is not to suggest that West German scholars with unacknowledged Nazi-era records necessarily espoused ideas that were sympathetic to, or apologetic for, right-wing causes. Many were solidly on the left, the most notable case perhaps being that of the historian Fritz Fischer, who had trained at a Nazi-sponsored institute in the 1930s but whose work during the 1960s, which posited a continuity between the expansionistic aims of the German Empire and those of the Third Reich, was embraced by the German New Left.[4] Although a generation of historians and other scholars who came of age in the late 1960s and 1970s did much to stimulate public and scholarly discussion of the Third Reich, they rarely addressed the involvement of their own disciplines and doctoral supervisors in Nazism.[5]

We should not let the tacit conspiracy of silence in the German academic world obscure other factors accounting for the slow development of scholarship on the humanities during the Nazi period. Postwar German scholars who *did* address the Nazi era regarded other issues as more urgent: the dissolution of the Weimar Republic and Hitler's accession to power, the diplomacy of the 1930s and the origins of the Second World War, and resistance to Hitler.[6] These were also the themes that tended to dominate American and British scholarship about Nazi Germany. One can argue that German scholars failed in their unique obligation to confront the Nazi-era records of their own disciplines, but they were hardly the only ones who neglected such subjects.

---

4. Angelika Ebbinghaus and Karl Heinz Roth, "Ein abtrünniger Konservativer: Fritz Fischer," in *1999: Zeitschrift für Sozialgeschichte des 20. und 21. Jahrhunderts* 15, 1 (2000): 7–11.

5. See Rüdiger Hohls and Konrad H. Jarausch, *Versäumte Fragen: Deutsche Historiker im Schatten des Nationalsozialismus* (Stuttgart, Germany: Deutsche Verlags-Anstalt, 2000).

6. Important examples include Hans Rothfels, *Die deutsche Opposition gegen Hitler: Eine Würdigung* (Krefeld, Germany: Scherpe, 1949); Karl Dietrich Bracher, *Die Auflösung der Weimarer Republik: Eine Studie zum Problem des Machtverfalls in der Demokratie*, Schriften des Instituts für politische Wissenschaft 4 (Stuttgart, Germany: Ring, 1955); Karl Dietrich Bracher, Wolfgang Sauer, and Gerhard Schulz, *Die nationalsozialistische Machtergreifung: Studien zur Errichtung des totalitären Herrschaftssystems in Deutschland 1933/34*, Schriften des Instituts für politische Wissenschaft 14 (Cologne, Germany: Westdeutscher, 1960); and Andreas Hillgruber, *Hitlers Strategie: Politik und Kriegführung 1940–1941* (Frankfurt, Germany: Bernard & Graefe, 1965).

The intellectual life of Nazi Germany, like its cultural and artistic life, was widely and erroneously regarded—both within Germany and without—as having been characterized by a fundamental bifurcation. On one side stood the majority of German scholars, artists, and intellectuals, who kept the Nazis at arm's length, preserved their integrity, and provided a basis for the perpetuation of non-Nazi values into the post-Nazi period. On the other side stood the mediocre opportunists, the party hacks, and the ideological zealots, who attempted to infuse Nazism into the mainstream of cultural and intellectual life but were easy enough to identify and purge in 1945. The first group seemed too mundane a subject for historical inquiry; the second group seemed unworthy of the attention of serious scholars. There appeared to be no compelling reason to place the German humanities on the agenda of postwar scholarship.

This context helps explain why the first book on the subject made little impact and quickly fell into oblivion. This was *Hitler's Professors: The Part of Scholarship in Hitler's Crimes against the Jewish People*, published in 1946 by Max Weinreich.[7] One of the twentieth century's most distinguished Yiddishists, Weinreich was long associated with the Yiddish Scientific Institute (YIVO), first in Vilna and later in New York. Weinreich's indictment of German scholars for their role in legitimizing and facilitating the persecution and murder of the Jews was marked by an angry and uncompromising tone—understandable in view of how close the events in question had been and in view of the German-trained Weinreich's personal sense of betrayal by people he believed should have known better. Given the speed with which Weinreich prepared his book, and the fact that organized research on this subject was extremely difficult so soon after the war, *Hitler's Professors* was an impressive achievement. In an otherwise critical review of the book in the Jewish journal *Commentary*, Hannah Arendt praised Weinreich for having laid a foundation for future research on the subject. But Weinreich's book found no resonance in a postwar German academic establishment that was itself implicated in Nazism. Moreover, the German scholars described by Weinreich tended to fit into the category of insurgent ideological zealots and could be easily dismissed as irrelevant for understanding the mainstream of German academic life under the Nazis. Only decades later, upon its republication, did Weinreich's work receive widespread recognition for its pioneering contribution. The rediscovery of Weinreich[8] was the result of new interest in the subject

---

7. Max Weinreich, *Hitler's Professors: The Part of Scholarship in Germany's Crimes against the Jewish People* (New York: Yiddish Scientific Institute [YIVO], 1946).

8. Note the reprint of Weinreich's book by Yale University Press in 1999, with a foreword by Martin Gilbert.

of Nazi *Judenforschung* [Jewish research], which has been addressed in several recent books that are further discussed here.

Between the publication of Weinreich's book in 1946 and the 1990s, only a handful of book-length works addressed the subject of Nazi-era scholarship in the humanities. But despite the relatively small volume of material, these early works, like Weinreich's, set much of the agenda for research on the subject. Questions that were central to the early scholarship remain crucial today. What was the degree of continuity or discontinuity within university faculties from the Weimar period into the Nazi years? To what extent did German scholars "self-coordinate," that is, accommodate themselves to the ideological and political priorities of the Nazi regime? How much intellectual and professional room for maneuver did they have? What strategies did the regime use to steer scholarship in the desired ideological and political direction? What was the relationship between the established universities and the many external institutes set up by the regime? What role did scholars play, as consultants or as experts in the employ of the government and the party, in the formulation and implementation of policy?

Several of these questions were addressed in Helmut Heiber's study of the Reich Institute for the History of the New Germany. Published in 1966, the book contained a wealth of new, archive-based disclosures about the historical profession during the Nazi era.[9] Led by the right-wing historian Walter Frank, the Reich Institute was established by the Nazi regime to promote historical scholarship sympathetic to a Nazi perspective. The history of the Institute conveys the complexity of the relationship between established German academics and the Nazi regime. The Institute was founded with the support of the regime because history departments at German universities were perceived as too traditional in their orientation, resistant to an overt politicization of scholarship. But the Institute did have one major ally who had already been established on the history faculty: Karl Alexander von Müller, a conservative nationalist who had supervised Walter Frank and other doctoral students who found work with the Institute. In 1935, Müller was appointed editor of the *Historische Zeitschrift*, the premier historical journal in Germany.

---

9. Helmut Heiber, *Walter Frank und sein Reichsinstitut für Geschichte des neuen Deutschlands*, Quellen und Darstellungen zur Zeitgeschichte 13 (Stuttgart, Germany: Deutsche Verlags-Anstalt, 1966). Also worth noting is Karl Ferdinand Werner, *Das NS-Geschichtsbild und die deutsche Geschichtswissenschaft*, Lebendiges Wissen (Stuttgart, Germany: Kohlhammer, 1967), a provocative but slender book that, unlike Heiber's massive tome, has not been foundational for later research.

He commissioned Wilhelm Grau, one of his former students, and the head of the Institute's Jewish Research section, to edit a special section on the so-called "Jewish Question" in each issue of the journal.

Like the founding of the Institute itself, the new section of the journal typified the strategy for a gradual Nazification of the historical profession. Established professors remained in place, provided that they were not Jewish or socialist, and were able to carry on their teaching and scholarship largely as before. Meanwhile, institutions and personnel more in sync with the ideological priorities of the Nazi movement were grafted onto the existing system. Eventually, senior scholars would retire and be replaced by party members and others who were regarded as ideologically dependable, while the Reich Institute would provide research fellowships for doctoral students pursuing politically relevant projects. Over time, the graft would insinuate itself into the system and fundamentally transform it. This process was not aborted because of resistance from the German academic world but rather by the externally imposed destruction of the Third Reich.

Following in Heiber's footsteps, two historians produced further important studies on Nazi-era scholarship as practiced outside of university settings. In 1970, Reinhard Bollmus published *Das Amt Rosenberg und seine Gegner*, which is seen a classic example of the functionalist school of interpretation and characterized Nazi policies as the product of interagency and interpersonal rivalries.[10] The organizational empire of Alfred Rosenberg provided a space for radically politicized scholarship on cultural, artistic, historical, and racial questions and served as a base from which Rosenberg and his allies constantly denounced others for their alleged lack of loyalty to National Socialist ideology. While many regarded Rosenberg as a fringe figure, his rhetoric did contribute to the cumulative radicalization of the national discourse around Jews, race, religion, and other subjects. A similar radicalizing function was performed by the Ahnenerbe [Ancestral Heritage Research Institute] of the SS, which was the subject of a 1974 study by Michael Kater.[11] The Ahnenerbe sponsored archaeological, anthropological, linguistic, and historical research on a variety of subjects ostensibly linked to the racial origins of the Germans. It served as a source of research positions for young

---

10. Reinhard Bollmus, *Das Amt Rosenberg und seine Gegner: Studien zum Machtkampf im nationalsozialistischen Herrschaftssystem*, Studien zur Zeitgeschichte 1 (Stuttgart, Germany: Deutsche Verlags-Anstalt, 1970).

11. Michael H. Kater, *Das "Ahnenerbe" der SS 1935–1945: Ein Beitrag zur Kulturpolitik des Dritten Reiches*, Studien zur Zeitgeschichte 6 (Munich: Oldenbourg, 1974).

scholars, cosponsored projects with German universities, and placed some of its scholars in university faculties. It is worth emphasizing that both Bollmus's and Kater's books, both dating from the early 1970s, were rediscovered and published in new editions decades after their initial publication, when the question of scholarly collaboration with Nazism finally took center stage in the German academic world.[12]

In contrast to Bollmus and Kater, Volker Losemann's 1977 book on classical studies in the Third Reich focused on a university-based academic discipline.[13] Written not by a specialist in the Nazi period but rather by a historian of the ancient world, the book possessed enhanced credibility as a critique from within the discipline. As Losemann described the situation, most academic classicists were political conservatives and German nationalists. They possessed little sympathy for Nazism but did recognize certain points of overlap or convergence. These included a predilection for aristocracy and strong central leadership and a corresponding aversion to democracy in its modern form; admiration for the architecture of ancient Greece and Rome; and, more generally, an appreciation of the classical ideal of physical beauty. Several of these scholars responded to Nazi rule by authoring works pointing out these points of convergence and emphasizing the relevance of the ancient world to a proper appreciation of National Socialism. Such statements sometimes reflected the genuine sentiments of the scholars, but in other instances they represented a defensive rhetorical strategy designed to appease the regime and fend off political interference. The overall picture is one in which a few people embraced Nazism, while a much larger number accommodated themselves to it, and one must look carefully at specific cases. Losemann's book stood alone for many years but provided a foundation for subsequent research. Among the most impressive of the later studies was that by the American historian Suzanne L. Marchand. In contrast to Losemann, whose book is focused on the Nazi era, Marchand's 1996 book on archaeology and Pan-Hellenism in Germany

---

12. For new editions, see Reinhard Bollmus, *Das Amt Rosenberg und seine Gegner: Studien zum Machtkampf im nationalsozialistischen Herrschaftssystem*, Studien zur Zeitgeschichte 1, 2nd ed. (Munich: Oldenbourg, 2006); and Michael Kater, *Das "Ahnenerbe" der SS 1935–1945: Ein Beitrag zur Kulturpolitik des Dritten Reiches*, 4th ed., Studien zur Zeitgeschichte 6 (Munich: Oldenbourg, 2006). The fourth edition of Kater's study replaced the second edition (published 1997) and third edition (published 2001).

13. Volker Losemann, *Nationalsozialismus und Antike: Studien zur Entwicklung des Faches Alte Geschichte 1933–1945*, Historische Perspektiven 7 (Hamburg, Germany: Hoffmann und Campe, 1977).

examined the era from 1750 to 1970.[14] Marchand confirmed Losemann's claim that only a minority of German classicists actually welcomed Nazi rule, and she showed how most of them devoted themselves to their research while trying to avoid political involvement. It was as a result of their low political profile during the Nazi period that most were able to continue their careers in the postwar period in both West and East Germany.

In 1988, Michael Burleigh published *Germany Turns Eastwards*, the first major work on the field known as *Ostforschung* [research on the East], an umbrella term used to describe research about Eastern Europe in a variety of disciplines during the Third Reich.[15] The study of that region was well established at German universities, so there was no shortage of expertise to plan and carry out Germany's designs for colonization of the east. Because Eastern Europe was the home of the majority of Europe's Jews, scholars who had been rooted in Ostforschung were drawn into Jewish policy as well. Burleigh showed how academic research on the East was deeply racist and antisemitic and that many German scholars associated themselves with research institutes funded by the Nazi SS. The timing of Burleigh's book was a major reason for its wide impact. It appeared in 1988, just before the collapse of communism facilitated archival research in Eastern Europe, and thus served as a touchstone for many scholars who would later produce dissertations on Germany's attempted colonization of Eastern Europe. Most notable among these was the study by Götz Aly and Susanne Heim about German experts who helped plan the conquest of Eastern Europe and the accompanying genocide.[16]

More broadly, the 1990s saw an explosion of scholarship on Nazism, both in Germany and elsewhere. In Germany, this was driven by the coming of age of a young generation of scholars, whose members were less inhibited about confronting the past than either their parents or their mentors had been. In Germany and elsewhere, it was also driven by the dramatic expansion in attention given to the Holocaust. Academic life during the Nazi era became a major field of research and remains the subject of intensive, detailed investigation until the present day.

---

14. Suzanne L. Marchand, *Down from Olympus: Archaeology and Philhellenism in Germany, 1750–1970* (Princeton, NJ: Princeton University Press, 1996).

15. Michael Burleigh, *Germany Turns Eastwards: A Study of Ostforschung in the Third Reich* (Cambridge: Cambridge University Press, 1988).

16. Götz Aly and Susanne Heim, *Vordenker der Vernichtung: Auschwitz und die deutschen Pläne für eine neue europäische Ordnung* (Hamburg, Germany: Hoffmann und Campe, 1991), trans. A. G. Blunden as *Architects of Annihilation: Auschwitz and the Logic of Destruction* (Princeton, NJ: Princeton University Press, 2003).

The year 1994 saw the publication of two works in which German folklorists attempted to come to terms with the conduct of their field—known as *Volkskunde*—before 1945. The central figure in this effort was Hannjost Lixfeld, who authored one of these books—a study of the Reich Institute for German Volkskunde[17]—and edited the other: a collection of critical articles by young German folklorists who were determined to expose the unpleasant Nazi truth about their field.[18] Taken together, these two books did much to explode what they characterized as the myth of "two German folklores." This was the notion, still disturbingly widespread in German academia in the early 1990s, that during the National Socialist era, the field of Volkskunde was split into two distinct groups, the first consisting of serious scholars whose work remained largely untainted by Nazism and the second consisting of hacks, publicists, and weak scholars who championed the Nazi ideology and program. In his monograph, Lixfeld argued that folklorists played a key role in the construction of a "Germanic Ideology" in the decades before 1933, identifying and cataloging myriad peculiarly Germanic customs, habits, and values. After 1933, the Nazi regime found obvious uses for such research, to which it devoted expanded financial resources. Academic folklorists who, before 1933, had operated in what Lixfeld called the "bourgeois-national" tradition readily cooperated with regime-sponsored programs, not only out of sheer academic opportunism, but also because the tendencies of their previous work had been so proximate to the central assumptions of National Socialism. Lixfeld's conclusions were supported by those of the contributors to his anthology, who documented the Nazi attack on Jewish folklore studies, folklore research on the swastika and other symbols, and the role of folklorists in the wartime plundering of artifacts. They also underscore the racist, as opposed to merely culturally ethnocentric, underpinnings of a great deal of folklore scholarship produced during the Nazi period.

The first of a series of critical studies of the historical profession under Nazism was published in 1992 by Karen Schönwälder.[19] In this forceful indictment of her academic forbears, Schönwälder portrayed German historians as willing

---

17. Hannjost Lixfeld, *Folklore and Fascism: The Reich Institute for German Volkskunde*, ed. and trans. James R. Dow, Folklore Studies in Translation (Bloomington: Indiana University Press, 1994).

18. James R. Dow and Hannjost Lixfeld, eds., *The Nazification of an Academic Discipline: Folklore in the Third Reich*, Folklore Studies in Translation (Bloomington: Indiana University Press, 1994).

19. Karen Schönwälder, *Historiker und Politik: Geschichtswissenschaft im Nationalsozialismus*, Historische Studien 9 (Frankfurt, Germany: Campus, 1992).

collaborators of the regime. They welcomed the restoration of German power on the European continent and approved of the replacement of the messy democracy of Weimar by an authoritarian regime capable of maintaining order. Even though most of the older historians were not Nazis, they sympathized with Nazism's hostility to the labor movement and the Treaty of Versailles. Schönwälder depicts the Nazi-era historians mainly as proactive, enthusiastic supporters of the regime, a very harsh judgment that would be softened by the more nuanced analyses of later studies but one that served to stimulate a long-overdue conversation within the German historical profession.

Willi Oberkrome's book on the discipline of history during the Weimar and Nazi periods, published in 1993, was both more focused and more differentiated than Schönwälder's.[20] Oberkrome's main focus was on the practice of *Volksgeschichte* [people's history], a methodology that focused on ordinary people rather than on elites but that was rooted in a nationalist and racist (i.e., *völkisch*) sensibility, not an emancipatory or Marxist one. While it possessed the potential for promoting an innovative perspective on history from the bottom up, it tended to operate in the service of conservative and right-wing agendas and easily converged with the populist rhetoric of National Socialism. Among the most influential university chair holders in social history in postwar West Germany were Werner Conze and Theodor Schieder, historians who had been trained and professionally socialized in the Volksgeschichte movement during the Nazi period. Oberkrome did not posit an unbroken, linear development from pre-1945 Volksgeschichte to the social history of the 1970s—his analysis was too nuanced for that—but neither did he deny that Volksgeschichte constituted one strand in the very complex methodological genealogy of postwar West German social history.

Among the most impressive of the works published in the 1990s was Frank-Rutger Hausmann's richly detailed study of the operation known as *Aktion Ritterbusch*, which appeared in 1998.[21] In 1940, Paul Ritterbusch, the rector of the University of Kiel, initiated a massive networking project in the humanities, ultimately encompassing about five hundred scholars. Supported by the Reich minister of education, Bernhard Rust, the purpose of the *Aktion* was

---

20. Willi Oberkrome, *Volksgeschichte: Methodische Innovation und völkische Ideologisierung in der deutschen Geschichtswissenschaft 1918–1945*, Kritische Studien zur Geschichtswissenschaft 101 (Göttingen, Germany: Vandenhoeck & Ruprecht, 1993).

21. Frank-Rutger Hausmann, *"Deutsche Geisteswissenschaft" im Zweiten Weltkrieg: Die "Aktion Ritterbusch" (1940–1945)* (Dresden, Germany: Dresden University Press, 1998; expanded 3rd ed., Heidelberg, Germany: Synchron, 2007).

to mobilize the humanities in support of Germany's expansionistic war aims. Through a series of conferences and publication projects, the scholars would produce studies intended to legitimize German hegemony over other regions of Europe. Given the massive size of the *Aktion*, few humanities scholars in Germany remained uninvolved. Hausmann's exhaustive survey of their output confirmed the overt ideological nature of many of their publications as well as demonstrated that quite a few of the scholars maintained their intellectual integrity, producing work that they felt comfortable defending after 1945. While the overall conclusion of Hausmann's work was damning for the German humanities, it also underscored the importance of looking closely at individual cases and of avoiding attributions of guilt through association.

In 1998, the American scholar Pamela M. Potter published her important study of German musicology under Nazism, a pioneering book that remains the standard work on the subject.[22] The musical chauvinism exhibited by many German musicologists, Potter showed, played into Nazi propaganda about the cultural superiority of the Germans. The scholars employed essentialist arguments to explain differences among national musical traditions, often slipping into overt racism. They contrived theories about musical authenticity that provided an intellectual foundation for the purging of Jews from German musical life, and for the blacklisting of compositions that were regarded as inappropriate for the German musical canon. Potter demonstrated that some of the underlying assumptions about the superiority of German music remained in place after 1945, both in Germany and in other countries where the field of musicology had been heavily influenced by German scholarship.

As more was learned about the extensive involvement of the German academic world with Nazism, younger German scholars began to wonder why it had taken so long for this information to come out. A general rift opened up between scholars who came of age in the 1990s and their mentors, who had received their professional training in the 1960s and 1970s under the supervision of professors who had themselves been active during the Nazi period. This generational dispute became most heated among historians. Postwar German historical scholarship had been established and for a time dominated by scholars who had been trained during the Nazi era. Some of them had authored work that was antisemitic, anti-Slavic, and in favor of German expansionism.

---

22. Pamela M. Potter, *Most German of the Arts: Musicology and Society from the Weimar Republic to the End of Hitler's Reich* (New Haven, CT: Yale University Press, 1998), trans. Wolfram Ette as *Die deutscheste der Künste: Musikwissenschaft und Gesellschaft von der Weimarer Republik bis zum Ende des Dritten Reichs* (Stuttgart, Germany: Klett-Cotta, 2000).

The academic grandchildren of these historians would no longer tolerate the silence about this aspect of the past. The generational conflict broke out into the open dramatically in September 1998, at Germany's biannual Historikertag, the major professional meeting of the historical profession, held that year in Frankfurt, where hundreds of historians and graduate students packed the auditorium where the issue was being addressed. Resolved more than ever to set the record straight about the Nazi-era records of prominent members of their professions, a number of younger scholars embarked on ambitious biographical and prosopographical projects. Motivated by a strong sense of mission, some went about their tasks with a zeal that provoked accusations of excessive moralism and reductionist logic.[23]

There followed an impressive and controversial series of books by Ingo Haar, Michael Fahlbusch, Nikolas Berg, and Jan Eckel, just to name some of the most notable.[24] While Fahlbusch and Haar maintained their focus on the Nazi years, Berg and Eckel turned their attention to the postwar influence of German scholars who had begun their careers before 1945. Berg's study of how West German historians had approached the subject of the Holocaust touched a raw nerve and provoked much debate.[25] Berg portrayed the established scholars, institutions, and journals of the field of *Zeitgeschichte* [contemporary history] as insensitive to the experiences of Nazism's Jewish victims and dismissive of attempts by Jewish scholars to document the Holocaust. He subjected the highly influential Munich-based Insitut für Zeitgeschichte [Institute for Contemporary History] to especially withering criticism, even though many specialists in the history of Nazism and the Holocaust had tended to hold that institution in high esteem. The Institute, Berg argued, rebuffed Jewish scholars, considering them and their work to have been lacking in objectivity even while refusing to

---

23. See especially Hohls and Jarausch, *Versäumte Fragen*.

24. Ingo Haar, *Historiker im Nationalsozialismus: Deutsche Geschichtswissenschaft und der "Volkstumskampf" im Osten*, Kritische Studien zur Geschichtswissenschaft 143 (Göttingen, Germany: Vandenhoeck & Ruprecht, 2000); Michael Fahlbusch, *Wissenschaft im Dienst der nationalsozialistischen Politik? Die "Volksdeutschen Forschungsgemeinschaften" von 1931–1945* (Baden-Baden, Germany: Nomos, 1999); Nicolas Berg, *Der Holocaust und die westdeutschen Historiker: Erforschung und Erinnerung*, Moderne Zeit 3 (Göttingen, Germany: Wallstein, 2003); and Jan Eckel, *Hans Rothfels: Eine intellektuelle Biographie im 20. Jahrhundert*, Moderne Zeit 10 (Göttingen, Germany: Wallstein, 2005).

25. See the online anthology dedicated to Berg's book, Astrid M. Eckert und Vera Ziegeldorf, eds., *Der Holocaust und die westdeutschen Historiker: Eine Debatte*, Historische Forum 2, Veröffentlichungen von Clio Online 2 (Clio Online, 2004), accessed September 20, 2016, doi: 10.18452/17807.

acknowledge that German scholars who had come of age during the Nazi era may have also suffered from a certain subjectivity.

Jan Eckel's 2007 book focused on Hans Rothfels, a key figure in the founding of Zeitgeschichte and the first editor of the Institute's influential journal, the *Vierteljahrshefte für Zeitgeschichte* [Quarterly for contemporary history]. Rothfels had been a conservative-nationalist historian during the Weimar Republic but was purged from his professorial chair in Königsberg by the Nazis because of his Jewish ancestry. He tried to remain in Germany but was forced to depart, ultimately landing at the University of Chicago. He returned to Germany and a professorship at Tübingen in 1951. Eckel and others have described Rothfel's return to Germany as an essential maneuver in the restoration of the conservative-nationalist dominance in the West German historical profession, despite that tradition's record of intellectual collaboration with Nazism. This maneuver was made possible by the fact that Rothfels, despite his right-wing politics, qualified as a victim of Nazism.

A good indicator of the progress achieved in the study of the humanities during the Nazi period was the appearance of several significant anthologies between 2007 and 2010. One of these, *Nazi Germany and the Humanities*, a volume edited by Wolfgang Bialas and Anson Rabinbach, was the result of an international project involving senior scholars from both Germany and the United States.[26] The collection *Wissenschaft im Einsatz*, edited by Käte Meyer-Drawe and Kristin Platt, featured work by young German scholars, mostly theoretically inclined, and was distinguished by its attempt to contextualize the Nazi case historically through the inclusion of articles about the politicization and mobilization of scholarship in the Napoleonic Wars and in the Soviet Union.[27] Comparative approaches of this sort remain surprisingly rare in the field. The most encyclopedic treatment of the Nazi Germany case appeared in the anthology *Kulturwissenschaften und Nationalsozialismus*, edited by Jürgen Elvert and Jürgen Nielsen-Sikora. This almost thousand-page volume contains synthetic articles about twenty-eight different humanistic disciplines, including several that had received little attention previously, such as sports science, theater science, Baltic philology, and Celtic studies.[28] A similar breadth of

---

26. Wolfgang Bialas and Anson Rabinbach, eds., *Nazi Germany and the Humanities: How German Academics Embraced Nazism* (Oxford: Oneworld, 2006; repr., 2014).

27. Käte Meyer-Drawe and Kristin Platt, eds., *Wissenschaft im Einsatz*, Schriftenreihe "Genozid und Gedächtnis" (Munich: Wilhelm Fink, 2007).

28. Jürgen Elvert and Jürgen Nielsen-Sikora, eds., *Kulturwissenschaften und Nationalsozialismus*, Historische Mitteilungen 72 (Stuttgart, Germany: Franz Steiner, 2008).

coverage is on display in Frank-Rutger Hausmann's gigantic edited collection of primary sources, *Die Geisteswissenschaften im "Dritten Reich,"* which was published in 2011.[29] Meanwhile, Michael Fahlbusch and Ingo Haar published a collection of essays focusing on the role of German scholars as experts in the planning and implementation of the German "New Order" in Europe.[30] The implications of this research are significant, as it depicts German scholars not simply as having provided intellectual legitimation for Nazi expansionism but for having gone a good deal further by participating directly in the colonization of Eastern Europe.

It would not be an exaggeration to observe that the volume of work produced on these questions just in the past twenty years exceeds the totality of that which appeared between 1945 and 1990 (an observation that would hold true for the scholarship on numerous other aspects of Nazi Germany). Among the more impressive achievements in this genre of scholarship is a volume, published in 2010, about the humanities at the University of Vienna, edited by Mitchell Ash, Wolfram Niess, and Ramon Pils.[31] The book exemplifies the advantages of applying a microhistorical approach to the history of a single university. Such an approach allows for comparisons of academic units that operated in the same institutional setting, brings into focus the important role of the university's administration, and contextualizes the activities of scholars in their highly specific local cultural and political settings. The Vienna case is especially interesting for several reasons. As Austria became part of the Third Reich only in 1938, the university was subjected to Nazi rule for five years fewer than those in the "Old Reich." Nonetheless, the purge of the faculty that took place after the Anschluss was more thoroughgoing than at German universities. More than one-third of the Faculty of Philosophy was dismissed on either racial or political grounds. In some of the humanistic disciplines, however, such as German literature (*Germanistik*), in which the faculty had already been

---

29. Frank-Rutger Hausmann, *Die Geisteswissenschaften im "Dritten Reich"* (Frankfurt, Germany: Klostermann, 2011).

30. Michael Fahlbusch and Ingo Haar, eds., *Völkische Wissenschaften und Politikberatung im 20. Jahrhundert: Expertise und "Neuordnung" Europas* (Paderborn, Germany: Schöningh, 2010).

31. Mitchell G. Ash, Wolfram Niess, and Ramon Pils, eds., *Geisteswissenschaften im Nationalsozialismus: Das Beispiel der Universität Wien* (Vienna: Vienna University Press; Göttingen, Germany: V&R Unipress, 2010). Also notable is a chronologically broader volume focusing on antisemitism at the University of Vienna: Oliver Rathkolb, ed., *Der lange Schatten des Antisemitismus: Kritische Auseinandersetzungen mit der Geschichte der Universität Wien im 19. und 20. Jahrhundert*, Zeitgeschichte im Kontext 8 (Vienna: Vienna University Press; Göttingen, Germany: V&R Unipress, 2013).

dominated by German nationalists and had contained no Jews before 1938, there was significant continuity of personnel despite the Nazi takeover. But even among these nationalists there were those who proved to be less than enthusiastic about adopting Nazi racism into their teaching and research. An appreciation of this kind of nuance is a strength of the volume and a product of the microhistorical focus on one university.

The recent explosion of interest in the history of Nazi Jewish policy and the Holocaust, both in Germany and elsewhere, has focused new attention on so-called Nazi *Judenforschung* [Jewish research]. After the appearance of Max Weinreich's *Hitler's Professors* in 1946, six decades would elapse until the publication of the next book-length work on the subject, my own *Studying the Jew*.[32] Additional studies of Judenforschung have appeared since 2006, authored by, among others, Susannah Heschel, Dirk Rupnow, and Horst Junginger.[33] Notwithstanding differences of emphasis, these recent works all tend to highlight some common themes. First, there was the desire of the Nazi regime to elevate consideration of the Jewish Question to a supposedly rational, scientific level, the intention being to separate Nazi antisemitism from the emotional, irrational, and superstitious Jew hatred of earlier generations. Second, Judenforschung was perceived by its creators as a genuinely interdisciplinary field, drawing on the expertise of scholars in history, religion, theology, sociology, and "racial science." Third, Judenforschung serves as a good example of how the regime promoted change in the German academic world through the creation of a new institutional infrastructure alongside the existing university system. This included the creation of institutes and journals that were outside the governance structure of universities, the sponsorship of conferences, and the allocation of funds for graduate fellowships for the purpose of luring younger scholars into the field. Fourth, Judenforschung

---

32. Alan E. Steinweis, *Studying the Jew: Scholarly Antisemitism in Nazi Germany* (Cambridge, MA: Harvard University Press, 2006).

33. Susannah Heschel, *The Aryan Jesus: Christian Theologians and the Bible in Nazi Germany* (Princeton, NJ: Princeton University Press, 2008); Dirk Rupnow, *Judenforschung im Dritten Reich: Wissenschaft zwischen Politik, Propaganda, und Ideologie*, Historische Grundlagen der Moderne 4 (Baden-Baden, Germany: Nomos, 2011); and Horst Junginger, *Die Verwissenschaftlichung der "Judenfrage" im Nationalsozialismus*, Veröffentlichungen der Forschungsstelle Ludwigsburg der Universität Stuttgart 19 (Darmstadt, Germany: Wissenschaftliche Buchgesellschaft, 2011). Also worth noting is an earlier anthology, Andreas Hofmann und Irmtrud Wojak, eds., *"Beseitigung des jüdischen Einflusses...": Antisemitische Forschung, Eliten, und Karrieren im Nationalsozialismus*, Jahrbuch des Fritz Bauer Instituts 3 (Frankfurt, Germany: Campus, 1999).

tended to be predicated on the notion that the Jews themselves had exercised hegemonic control over Jewish studies in a way that had served their own religious, ethnic, or racial interests at the expense of the German *Volk*. Knowledge about Jews was seen as a weapon that needed to be placed in the proper hands. Non-Jewish scholars, therefore, needed to acquire the requisite language skills and command of Jewish sources, including works of scholarship produced by Jews, which could be mined for information even as their pro-Jewish arguments could be inverted for antisemitic purposes. Fifth, and finally, while most of the German scholars who had been active in Judenforschung disappeared from German academic life after 1945, there were several disturbing examples of scholars who did in fact enjoy academic careers in postwar Germany. Among them was Karl Georg Kuhn, an expert on Jewish Midrash and Talmud, who had authored vicious antisemitic works during the Nazi period but, nevertheless, after the collapse of Nazism, rose to occupy a prestigious chair at the University of Heidelberg.[34]

The Nazi-era records and intellectual legacies of two figures in particular have generated intense controversy and have transcended the national context of Germany as well as consideration of specific disciplines and institutions. These were Carl Schmitt and Martin Heidegger.[35] Both cases have implications that extend well beyond the history of central Europe in the twentieth century. There can be no doubt that both men were guilty of abominable conduct during the Nazi years. Both joined the Nazi Party (on the same day—May 1, 1933), turned their backs on their Jewish colleagues, and publicly praised Nazism and Hitler. The fact that both eventually ran into some trouble with Nazi authorities does not negate these monumental personal failings. The debates go not to their biographies but to the question of whether the legitimacy of their still influential ideas is undermined through their association with Nazism.

After 1933, Carl Schmitt crafted his writings to fit in with Nazi ideology. An especially striking example was an article he wrote following the Night of Long Knives, entitled "Der Führer schützt das Recht" ["The Führer Protects the Law"]. Schmitt's atrocious record of antisemitism has been ably documented

---

34. On Kuhn, see Junginger, *Verwissenschaftlichung der "Judenfrage,"* and Anders Gerdmar, *Roots of Theological Anti-Semitism: German Biblical Interpretation and the Jews, from Herder and Semler to Kittel and Bultmann*, Studies in Jewish History and Culture 20 (Leiden, Netherlands: Brill, 2009). See further Gerdmar's contribution to this volume, which provides an extensive discussion of Kuhn, "Jewish Studies in the Service of Nazi Ideology: Tübingen's Faculty of Theology as a Center for Antisemitic Research."

35. On Schmitt, see Oren Gross's powerful essay in this volume, "Hitler's Willing Law Professors."

by Raphael Gross.[36] Nevertheless, certain of his key ideas have survived both the Nazi years and Schmitt's own death in 1985.

Several key ideas of Schmitt continue to have resonance in contemporary political thinking. Perhaps the most characteristic is the friend-enemy distinction set out in his work *Der Begriff des Politischen*.[37] For Schmitt, the political basis of any state is the enmity of its people toward some other people or peoples. It is this enmity that defines a people and furnishes the foundation of a nation. Schmitt also expounded what he called the *Ausnahmezustand*, or "state of exception." This is a condition in which the sovereign suspends the constitution and the rule of law for the purpose of meeting an emergency and with a view to preserving the constitution and the rule of law once the emergency has passed. The importance of this idea can be grasped when we recall that, for example, President Lincoln suspended the writ of habeas corpus in 1861—clearly exceeding his executive authority. The debate about whether constitutional protections are applicable or not to suspected terrorists is a contemporary instance of a rather inexplicit use of this concept. Is the constitution being suspended in order to preserve it? Still another Schmittian idea that is certainly not politically fashionable but underlies current debate about the virtues and flaws of multiculturalism is the notion that effective democracy requires a homogeneous population. In other words, democracy is impossible except in a state populated by people who generally share the same values. This idea can be traced to Baruch Spinoza, who argued that while people should have religious freedom, it is appropriate for the government to impose uniformity in the outward manifestations of a particular religion. The viability of a profoundly multicultural country like the United States is something that Schmitt would have, by no means, taken for granted.[38]

In the case of Heidegger, the intellectual stakes are arguably even higher, as his philosophy constitutes an essential part of the foundation for the

---

36. Raphael Gross, *Carl Schmitt und die Juden: Eine deutsche Rechtslehre* (Frankfurt, Germany: Suhrkamp, 2000). Other notable books on Schmitt include Joseph W. Bendersky, *Carl Schmitt: Theorist for the Reich* (Princeton, NJ: Princeton University Press, 1983), and Bernd Rüthers, *Carl Schmitt im Dritten Reich: Wissenschaft als Zeitgeist-Verstärkung?* (Munich: Beck, 1989).

37. Originating as an article in 1927, the text was republished numerous times in modified forms. See e.g., Carl Schmitt, *Der Begriff des Politischen: Mit einer Rede über das Zeitalter der Neutralisierungen und Entpolitisierungen* (Munich: Duncker & Humblot, 1932), trans. George Schwab as *The Concept of the Political: Expanded Edition* (Chicago: University of Chicago Press, 2007).

38. For examples of recent discussions about the applicability of Schmittian ideas, see many issues of the American journal *Telos*. I am grateful to my colleague Robert D. Rachlin for sharing his insights into debates over the possible contemporary relevance of Schmitt.

postmodern movement. Heidegger's membership in the Nazi Party, his rectorship of the University of Freiburg, and his many pro-Nazi statements have all long been part of the public record. In his 1987 book, the Chilean scholar Victor Farías claimed these biographical details could not be separated from Heidegger's ideas, which Farías characterized as inherently fascist on account of their illiberalism, subordination of reason to instinct, and denial of universal truths—not coincidentally the same characteristics ascribed to postmodernism by the defenders of the positivist tradition.[39] After Hugo Ott and Rüdiger Safranski added new, unflattering details to Heidegger's biography,[40] Emmanuel Faye used records of Heidegger's seminars from the 1930s to posit an inextricable connection between the master's philosophy and his Nazism.[41] A number of scholars, most notably Richard Wolin, have focused more on the Heideggerian basis of both fascism and postmodern relativism.[42] The recent publication of Heidegger's Black Notebooks have also rekindled the debate over alleged connections between the philosopher's antisemitism and other aspects of his critique of modernism.[43]

Those who support the use of Schmittian and Heideggerian concepts have responded with a variety of arguments: the connection to fascism was biographical but not necessarily philosophical; bad men can produce good ideas; Heidegger also served as a philosophical inspiration to Zionism; an opinion is not automatically, as Leo Strauss explained, "refuted by the fact that it happens to have been shared by Hitler." (This is Strauss's famous dictum of the "reductio ad Hitlerum."[44]) Whatever one's position, there is no denying that

---

39. Victor Farías, *Heidegger and Nazism*, ed. and with foreword by Joseph Margolis and Tom Rockmore, French materials translated by Paul Burrell with the advice of Dominic Di Bernardi, German materials translated by Gabriel R. Ricci (Philadelphia: Temple University Press, 1989).

40. Hugo Ott, *Martin Heidegger: A Political Life*, trans. Allan Blunden (New York: Basic Books, 1993); Rüdiger Safranski, *Martin Heidegger: Between Good and Evil*, trans. Ewald Osers (Cambridge, MA: Harvard University Press, 1998).

41. Emmanuel Faye, *Heidegger: The Introduction of Nazism into Philosophy in Light of the Unpublished Seminars of 1933–1935*, trans. Michael B. Smith (New Haven, CT: Yale University Press, 2009). See further Faye's contribution to the present volume, "Political Philosophy."

42. Richard Wolin, *The Seduction of Unreason: The Intellectual Romance with Fascism from Nietzsche to Postmodernism* (Princeton, NJ: Princeton University Press, 2004).

43. Richard Wolin, "Heideggers 'Schwarze Hefte': Nationalsozialismus, Weltjudentum, und Seinsgeschichte," *Vierteljahrshefte für Zeitgeschichte* 63, no. 3 (2015): 379–410.

44. Leo Strauss, *Natural Right and History*, Charles R. Walgreen Foundation Lectures (Chicago: University of Chicago Press, 1953), 42–43.

decades after their deaths, the writings of Schmitt and Heidegger figure into lively debates about politics, culture, knowledge, and identity.[45] Their enduring relevance can be interpreted as evidence of their intellectual achievements. It can also be seen as evidence of our own potential for exercising poor judgment, as Germans did in the 1930s, in the defense of reason, democracy, and intellectual freedom.

BIBLIOGRAPHY

Aly, Götz, and Susanne Heim. *Vordenker der Vernichtung: Auschwitz und die deutschen Pläne für eine neue europäische Ordnung.* Hamburg, Germany: Hoffmann und Campe, 1991. Translated by A. G. Blunden as *Architects of Annihilation: Auschwitz and the Logic of Destruction.* Princeton, NJ: Princeton University Press, 2003.

Ash, Mitchell G., Wolfram Niess, and Ramon Pils, eds. *Geisteswissenschaften im Nationalsozialismus: Das Beispiel der Universität Wien.* Vienna: Vienna University Press; Göttingen, Germany: V&R Unipress, 2010.

Bendersky, Joseph W. *Carl Schmitt: Theorist for the Reich.* Princeton, NJ: Princeton University Press, 1983.

Berg, Nicolas. *Der Holocaust und die westdeutschen Historiker: Erforschung und Erinnerung.* Moderne Zeit 3. Göttingen, Germany: Wallstein, 2003.

Bialas, Wolfgang, and Anson Rabinbach, eds. *Nazi Germany and the Humanities: How German Academics Embraced Nazism.* Oxford: Oneworld, 2014. First published 2006.

Blasius, Dirk. *Carl Schmitt und der 30. Januar 1933: Studien zu Carl Schmitt.* Frankfurt, Germany: Peter Lang, 2009.

Bollmus, Reinhard. *Das Amt Rosenberg und seine Gegner: Studien zum Machtkampf im nationalsozialistischen Herrschaftssystem.* 2nd ed. Studien zur Zeitgeschichte 1. Munich: Oldenbourg, 2006. First edition published 1970 by Deutsche Verlags-Anstalt (Stuttgart, Germany).

---

45. Works on Schmitt have been especially numerous in recent years. See, for example, Claus Heimes, *Politik und Transzendenz: Ordnungsdenken bei Carl Schmitt und Eric Voegelin,* Beiträge zur politischen Wissenschaft 154 (Berlin: Duncker & Humblot, 2009); Dirk Blasius, *Carl Schmitt und der 30. Januar 1933: Studien zu Carl Schmitt* (Frankfurt, Germany: Peter Lang, 2009); Reinhard Mehring, *Carl Schmitt: Aufstieg und Fall* (Munich: Beck, 2009); Daniel Hitschler, *Zwischen Liberalismus und Existentialismus: Carl Schmitt im englischsprachigen Schrifttum,* Würzburger Universitätsschriften zu Geschichte und Politik 14 (Baden-Baden, Germany: Nomos, 2011); Stefan Breuer, *Carl Schmitt im Kontext: Intellektuellenpolitik in der Weimarer Republik* (Berlin: Akademie, 2012); and Volker Neumann, *Carl Schmitt als Jurist* (Tübingen, Germany: Mohr Siebeck, 2015).

Bracher, Karl Dietrich. *Die Auflösung der Weimarer Republik: Eine Studie zum Problem des Machtverfalls in der Demokratie*. Schriften des Instituts für politische Wissenschaft 4. Stuttgart, Germany: Ring, 1955.

Bracher, Karl Dietrich, Wolfgang Sauer, and Gerhard Schulz. *Die nationalsozialistische Machtergreifung: Studien zur Errichtung des totalitären Herrschaftssystems in Deutschland 1933/34*. Schriften des Instituts für politische Wissenschaft 14. Cologne, Germany: Westdeutscher, 1960.

Breuer, Stefan. *Carl Schmitt im Kontext: Intellektuellenpolitik in der Weimarer Republik*. Berlin: Akademie, 2012.

Burleigh, Michael. *Germany Turns Eastwards: A Study of Ostforschung in the Third Reich*. Cambridge: Cambridge University Press, 1988.

Dow, James R., and Hannjost Lixfeld, eds. *The Nazification of an Academic Discipline: Folklore in the Third Reich*. Folklore Studies in Translation. Bloomington: Indiana University Press, 1994.

Ebbinghaus, Angelika, and Karl Heinz Roth. "Ein abtrünniger Konservativer: Fritz Fischer." *1999: Zeitschrift für Sozialgeschichte des 20. und 21. Jahrhunderts* 15, 1 (2000): 7–11.

Eckel, Jan. *Hans Rothfels: Eine intellektuelle Biographie im 20. Jahrhundert*. Moderne Zeit 10. Göttingen, Germany: Wallstein, 2005.

Eckert, Astrid M., and Vera Ziegeldorf, eds. *Der Holocaust und die westdeutschen Historiker: Eine Debatte*. Historische Forum 2. Veröffentlichungen von Clio Online 2. Clio Online, 2004. Accessed September 20, 2016. DOI: 10.18452/17807.

Elvert, Jürgen, and Jürgen Nielsen-Sikora, eds. *Kulturwissenschaften und Nationalsozialismus*. Historische Mitteilungen 72. Stuttgart, Germany: Franz Steiner, 2008.

Fahlbusch, Michael. *Wissenschaft im Dienst der nationalsozialistischen Politik? Die "Volksdeutschen Forschungsgemeinschaften" von 1931–1945*. Baden-Baden, Germany: Nomos, 1999.

Fahlbusch, Michael, and Ingo Haar, eds. *Völkische Wissenschaften und Politikberatung im 20. Jahrhundert: Expertise und "Neuordnung" Europas*. Paderborn, Germany: Schöningh, 2010.

Farías, Victor. *Heidegger and Nazism*. Edited and with foreword by Joseph Margolis and Tom Rockmore. French materials translated by Paul Burrell with the advice of Dominic Di Bernardi. German materials translated by Gabriel R. Ricci. Philadelphia: Temple University Press, 1989.

Faye, Emmanuel. *Heidegger: The Introduction of Nazism into Philosophy in Light of the Unpublished Seminars of 1933–1935*. Translated by Michael B. Smith. New Haven, CT: Yale University Press, 2009.

Gerdmar, Anders. *Roots of Theological Anti-Semitism: German Biblical Interpretation and the Jews, from Herder and Semler to Kittel and Bultmann*. Studies in Jewish History and Culture 20. Leiden, Netherlands: Brill, 2009.

Girard, Ilse. "Prof. P. H. Seraphim: 'Wissenschaftlicher' Wegbereiter faschistischer Ideologie unter Hitler und unter Adenauer." *Dokumentation der Zeit* 126 (September 1956): 355–74.

Gross, Raphael. *Carl Schmitt und die Juden: Eine deutsche Rechtslehre*. Frankfurt, Germany: Suhrkamp, 2000.

Haar, Ingo. *Historiker im Nationalsozialismus: Deutsche Geschichtswissenschaft und der "Volkstumskampf" im Osten*. Kritische Studien zur Geschichtswissenschaft 143. Göttingen, Germany: Vandenhoeck & Ruprecht, 2000.

Hammerstein, Katrin, Ulrich Mählert, Julie Trappe, and Edgar Wolfrum, eds. *Aufarbeitung der Diktatur—Diktat der Aufarbeitung? Normierungsprozesse beim Umgang mit diktatorischer Vergangenheit*. Diktaturen und ihre Überwindung im 20. und 21. Jahrhundert 2. Göttingen, Germany: Wallstein, 2009.

Hausmann, Frank-Rutger. *"Deutsche Geisteswissenschaft" im Zweiten Weltkrieg: Die "Aktion Ritterbusch" (1940–1945)*. Dresden, Germany: Dresden University Press, 1998. Expanded 3rd edition published 2007 by Synchron (Heidelberg, Germany).

———. *Die Geisteswissenschaften im "Dritten Reich."* Frankfurt, Germany: Klostermann, 2011.

Heiber, Helmut. *Walter Frank und sein Reichsinstitut für Geschichte des neuen Deutschlands*. Quellen und Darstellungen zur Zeitgeschichte 13. Stuttgart, Germany: Deutsche Verlags-Anstalt, 1966.

Heimes, Claus. *Politik und Transzendenz: Ordnungsdenken bei Carl Schmitt und Eric Voegelin*. Beiträge zur politischen Wissenschaft 154. Berlin: Duncker & Humblot, 2009.

Heschel, Susannah. *The Aryan Jesus: Christian Theologians and the Bible in Nazi Germany*. Princeton, NJ: Princeton University Press, 2008.

Hillgruber, Andreas. *Hitlers Strategie: Politik und Kriegführung 1940–1941*. Frankfurt, Germany: Bernard & Graefe, 1965.

Hitschler, Daniel. *Zwischen Liberalismus und Existentialismus: Carl Schmitt im englischsprachigen Schrifttum*. Würzburger Universitätsschriften zu Geschichte und Politik 14. Baden-Baden, Germany: Nomos, 2011.

Hofmann, Andreas, and Irmtrud Wojak, eds. *"Beseitigung des jüdischen Einflusses...": Antisemitische Forschung, Eliten, und Karrieren im Nationalsozialismus*. Jahrbuch des Fritz Bauer Instituts 3. Frankfurt, Germany: Campus, 1999.

Hohls, Rüdiger, and Konrad H. Jarausch. *Versäumte Fragen: Deutsche Historiker im Schatten des Nationalsozialismus*. Stuttgart, Germany: Deutsche Verlags-Anstalt, 2000.

Junginger, Horst. *Die Verwissenschaftlichung der "Judenfrage" im Nationalsozialismus*. Veröffentlichungen der Forschungsstelle Ludwigsburg der Universität Stuttgart 19. Darmstadt, Germany: Wissenschaftliche Buchgesellschaft, 2011.

Kater, Michael H. *Das "Ahnenerbe" der SS 1935–1945: Ein Beitrag zur Kulturpolitik des Dritten Reiches*. 4th ed. Studien zur Zeitgeschichte 6. Munich: Oldenbourg, 2006. First edition published 1974 by Oldenbourg, revised in 1997 (2nd ed.) and 2001 (3rd ed.).

Lixfeld, Hannjost. *Folklore and Fascism: The Reich Institute for German Volkskunde*. Edited and translated by James R. Dow. Folklore Studies in Translation. Bloomington: Indiana University Press, 1994.

Losemann, Volker. *Nationalsozialismus und Antike: Studien zur Entwicklung des Faches Alte Geschichte 1933–1945*. Historische Perspektiven 7. Hamburg: Hoffmann und Campe, 1977.

Marchand, Suzanne L. *Down from Olympus: Archaeology and Philhellenism in Germany, 1750–1970*. Princeton, NJ: Princeton University Press, 1996.

———. "Nazism, 'Orientalism,' and Humanism." In Bialas and Rabinbach, *Nazi Germany and the Humanities*, 267–305.

Mehring, Reinhard. *Carl Schmitt: Aufstieg und Fall*. Munich: Beck, 2009.

Meyer-Drawe, Käte, and Kristin Platt, eds. *Wissenschaft im Einsatz*. Schriftenreihe "Genozid und Gedächtnis." Munich: Wilhelm Fink, 2007.

Neumann, Volker. *Carl Schmitt als Jurist*. Tübingen, Germany: Mohr Siebeck, 2015.

Oberkrome, Willi. *Volksgeschichte: Methodische Innovation und völkische Ideologisierung in der deutschen Geschichtswissenschaft 1918–1945*. Kritische Studien zur Geschichtswissenschaft 101. Göttingen, Germany: Vandenhoeck & Ruprecht, 1993.

Ott, Hugo. *Martin Heidegger: A Political Life*. Translated by Allan Blunden. New York: Basic Books, 1993.

Petersen, Hans-Christian. *Bevölkerungsökonomie – Ostforschung – Politik: Eine biographische Studie zu Peter-Heinz Seraphim (1902–1979)*. Einzelveröffentlichungen des Deutschen Historischen Instituts Warschau 17. Osnabrück, Germany: Fibre, 2007.

Potter, Pamela M. *Most German of the Arts: Musicology and Society from the Weimar Republic to the End of Hitler's Reich*. New Haven, CT: Yale University Press, 1998.

Rathkolb, Oliver, ed. *Der lange Schatten des Antisemitismus: Kritische Auseinandersetzungen mit der Geschichte der Universität Wien im 19. und 20. Jahrhundert*. Zeitgeschichte im Kontext 8. Vienna: Vienna University Press; Göttingen, Germany: V&R Unipress, 2013.

Rothfels, Hans. *Die deutsche Opposition gegen Hitler: Eine Würdigung*. Krefeld, Germany: Scherpe, 1949.

Rupnow, Dirk. *Judenforschung im Dritten Reich: Wissenschaft zwischen Politik, Propaganda, und Ideologie*. Historische Grundlagen der Moderne 4. Baden-Baden, Germany: Nomos, 2011.

Rüthers, Bernd. *Carl Schmitt im Dritten Reich: Wissenschaft als Zeitgeist-Verstärkung?* Munich: Beck, 1989.

Sabrow, Martin. "Die NS-Vergangenheit in der geteilten deutschen Geschichtskultur." In *Teilung und Integration: Die doppelte deutsche Nachkriegsgeschichte als wissenschaftliches und didaktisches Problem*, edited by Christoph Klessmann and Peter Lautzas, 132–51. Schriftenreihe der Bundeszentrale für politische Bildung 482. Bonn, Germany: Bundeszentrale für politische Bildung, 2005.

Safranski, Rüdiger. *Martin Heidegger: Between Good and Evil*. Translated by Ewald Osers. Cambridge, MA: Harvard University Press, 1998.

Schmitt, Carl. *Der Begriff des Politischen: Mit einer Rede über das Zeitalter der Neutralisierungen und Entpolitisierungen*. Munich: Duncker & Humblot, 1932. Translated by George Schwab as *The Concept of the Political: Expanded Edition*. Chicago: University of Chicago Press, 2007.

Schönwälder, Karen. *Historiker und Politik: Geschichtswissenschaft im Nationalsozialismus*. Historische Studien 9. Frankfurt, Germany: Campus, 1992.

Steinweis, Alan E. *Studying the Jew: Scholarly Antisemitism in Nazi Germany*. Cambridge, MA: Harvard University Press, 2006.

Strauss, Leo. *Natural Right and History*. Charles R. Walgreen Foundation Lectures. Chicago: University of Chicago Press, 1953.

Weinreich, Max. *Hitler's Professors: The Part of Scholarship in Germany's Crimes against the Jewish People*. New York: Yiddish Scientific Institute (YIVO), 1946. Reprinted with foreword by Martin Gilbert. New Haven, CT: Yale University Press, 1999.

Werner, Karl Ferdinand. *Das NS-Geschichtsbild und die deutsche Geschichtswissenschaft*. Lebendiges Wissen. Stuttgart, Germany: Kohlhammer, 1967.

Wolin, Richard. "Heideggers 'Schwarze Hefte': Nationalsozialismus, Weltjudentum, und Seinsgeschichte." *Vierteljahrshefte für Zeitgeschichte* 63, no. 3 (2015): 379–410.

———. *The Seduction of Unreason: The Intellectual Romance with Fascism from Nietzsche to Postmodernism*. Princeton, NJ: Princeton University Press, 2004.

ALAN E. STEINWEIS is Professor of History and Raul Hilberg Distinguished Professor of Holocaust Studies at the University of Vermont. He is the author of *Art, Ideology, and Economics in Nazi Germany* (University of North Carolina, 1993), *Studying the Jew* (Harvard, 2006), and *Kristallnacht 1938* (Harvard, 2009) and is now completing a general history of Nazi Germany. He has edited eight additional volumes. In addition to numerous fellowships, he has held visiting professorships at the Universities of Hannover, Heidelberg, Frankfurt, and Munich.

TWO

THE "ORIENT" AND "US"

Making Ancient Oriental Studies Relevant
during the Nazi Regime

SUZANNE L. MARCHAND

HOW DO HUMANISTS REACT WHEN a wave of anti-intellectualism and/or utilitarianism sweeps the nation? What strategies work and at what cost? Although the humanists profiled in this chapter operated in a political landscape far different, fortunately, from our current predicament, the answers to these questions may have something to tell us about how the humanities in Germany, and America, took on their contemporary contours. In focusing on the study of the fields that were once collectively known as *'Orientalistik'* (or *'Orientalische Philologie'*) in Germany in the years 1933–1945, this chapter uses an extreme example to open up the more general question of the problem of establishing relevance for humanists, especially for those who specialize in the study of cultures and peoples distant in time (as most German Orientalists in this era focused on the ancient world) and in space.[1]

---

1. I am well aware that in the wake of the publication of Edward Said's *Orientalism* (New York: Viking, 1978), we have recognized the prejudices and blind spots that underlay the lumping together of so many cultures of the Near East, South Asia, North Africa, and East Asia in a single discipline termed "Oriental" studies. Universities today (generally!) do not do this model, and those scholars who once were described, and called themselves, "Orientalists" no longer do so. But in an historical essay examining this once united field in the 1930s, it would be awkward to refer to it as "Near Eastern studies" or "Eastern studies." Neither of those alternative terms captures the logic that once held the discipline together: namely that it treated the history of civilizations, ancient and modern, that did not belong to Europe's classical (and secular) heritage. Similarly, when I discuss "Orientalists" here, I am also referring to scholars who devoted themselves to the study of non-western languages and cultures, not to persons outside of the scholarly world who wrote about, or depicted, the "Oriental" world.

The aim of the piece is not to condemn all attempts at relevance making or popularization; academics do need to explain to the wider public what significance our findings have, and those who invest funds in our studies deserve to have an accounting of what we do and why we do it. It should also be noted that the intent of this chapter is not to separate collaborators from victims of the Nazi regime or even to judge various shades of collaboration, of which there were many.[2] In the space of one chapter, it would be impossible to describe the fate of all those institutions that dabbled, to one extent or another, in things Eastern, much less to trace the fate of particular individuals. Rather, my aim here is first of all to recognize that there *were* a considerable number of attempts made by specialists in Oriental Studies, and notably even in the subfield discussed here, *Altorientalistik* [the discipline of ancient Near Eastern studies], to establish relevance, some born out of fear and others out of ideological dedication to the Nazi regime. Although a considerable number of scholars emigrated or were expelled from their posts (and a still uncertain number were murdered in the camps), specialists in the study of the ancient Orient did not simply retreat into positivistic "inner emigration." On the contrary, though some scholars continued to produce apparently high-quality positivistic scholarship, some of these very same people were outspoken champions of the regime and party members.[3] Many had also

---

2. The groundbreaking work remains, of course, Max Weinreich, *Hitler's Professors: The Part of Scholarship in Germany's Crimes against the Jewish People* (New York: Yiddish Scientific Institute [YIVO], 1946; repr., foreword by Martin Gilbert, New Haven, CT: Yale University Press, 1999) (page references to the 1999 edition). There have been some significant new initiatives, especially Ludmila Hanisch's pioneering works, "Akzentverschiebung—Zur Geschichte der Semitistik und Islamwissenschaft während des 'Dritten Reichs,'" *Berichte zur Wissenschaftsgeschichte* 18, no. 4 (1995): 217–26; *Die Nachfolger der Exegeten: Deutschsprachige Erforschung des Vorderen Orients in der ersten Hälfte des 20. Jahrhunderts* (Wiesbaden, Germany: Harrassowitz, 2003); and "Arabistik, Semitistik, und Islamwissenschaft," in *Kulturwissenschaften und Nationalsozialismus*, ed. Jürgen Elvert and Jürgen Niels-Sikora, Historische Mitteilungen 72 (Stuttgart, Germany: Franz Steiner, 2008), 503–25. On the discipline of Assyriology, see the contribution to the present volume by Johannes Renger, "German Assyriology: A Discipline in Troubled Waters." A number of scholars have explored the extent of collaboration within the discipline of Egyptology. The list of pro- and anti-Nazi scholars sent by the German-Jewish Egyptologist Georg Steindorff to his American colleague, John Wilson, in June 1945 provides the major point of departure for these studies. For an extensive discussion, see the contribution by Thomas Schneider to this volume, "Hermann Grapow, Egyptology, and National Socialist Initiatives for the Humanities."

3. A good example here is Carl Brockelmann, whose pathbreaking *Syrische Grammatik* appeared in 1938. His magnum opus, *Geschichte der arabischen Litteratur*, appeared in a five-volume second edition between 1937 and 1949. For a recent appraisal, see Rudolph Sellheim,

been vocal patriots during the Great War—but the context and ideological parameters of relevance-making had changed. Most importantly, after 1933, as compared with 1914, Germany did not have the Ottoman Empire on its side (and the alliance with Japan came too late and was too difficult to make use of for people whose specialties lay mostly in the Near East). This made the question of race—and how to link "the Orient" and "us"—all the more challenging for the Semitists, in particular, to deal with. Furthermore, the whole question of humankind's religious history—so central to *Altorientalistik*'s identity in the past—was of virtually no interest to the Nazis. Indeed, the Nazis put (or were seen to put) contributions to the *Volk* ahead of contributions to *Wissenschaft* (scholarship). This meant that those Orientalists (individuals who were professionally trained in *Orientalistik* and thus had learned at least one Near Eastern or Asian language) who wanted to demonstrate their relevance had to do some fancy footwork to establish a relationship between "the Orient" and "us." It is this fancy footwork—and its consequences—that lie at the heart of this chapter.

The sources for this inquiry are overwhelmingly printed ones. I am interested in the public effusions of the Orientalists, not in their private correspondence, and I draw freely on material brought to light by others who have done pioneering work in this field, including Ludmila Hanisch, Sheldon Pollock, and Frank-Rutger Hausmann.[4] All of these scholars discuss the collaborators' quests to establish relevance, but because they do not take a longer and wider view of the history of Oriental philology, they have a tendency to presume that the field's importance and relevance in Europe had never previously been disputed. This essay corrects that presumption by showing how the field had made itself useful and interesting in the eighteenth and nineteenth centuries—and why conforming to Nazi ideas required novel, and deeply consequential, rhetorical and evidentiary gymnastics. This essay is perhaps also better able to discuss the *scholarly* consequences of relevance making by excluding crucial considerations that have been explored elsewhere, such as tragic fate of exiled or murdered scholars or Orientalists'

"Brockelmann, Carl," *Encyclopaedia Iranica*, online edition, accessed November 5, 2021, https://iranicaonline.org/articles/brockelmann-carl.

4. See Hanisch, *Nachfolger*; Sheldon Pollock, "Deep Orientalism? Notes on Sanskrit and Power beyond the Raj," in *Orientalism and the Postcolonial Predicament: Perspectives on South Asia*, ed. Carol A. Breckenridge and Peter van der Veer (Philadelphia: University of Pennsylvania Press, 1993), 77–133; and Frank-Rutger Hausmann, *"Deutsche Geisteswissenschaft" im Zweiten Weltkrieg: Die "Aktion Ritterbusch" (1940–1945)* (Dresden: Dresden University Press, 1998).

contributions to propaganda efforts in the Eastern Mediterranean.[5] Here, by contrast, we will focus on the Orientalists' own effusions, and the ways in which their relevance-seeking embroiled them in the racist politics of a murderous regime.

I. ORIENTAL PHILOLOGY AND ITS PATRONS BEFORE 1933

Historians committed to denouncing the collaborationist compromises made by Nazi-era intellectuals sometimes fail to remind their readers that scholars who are not wealthy enough to support their own studies have *always* had to justify their existence to patrons in one way or another. What is interesting is not so much *that* scholars do this but rather *how* they do this and whether patrons allow those they support to seek honest results (and whether scholars in fact seek, and find, them). To understand *Orientalistik*'s development over the *longue durée*, it is important to remember that the foundations of the field lie in the period in which the Catholic Church was the great patron and that in the sixteenth century, these studies received a new lease on life in response to two major developments: the Protestant Reformation and the acceleration of European travel around the world. To be extremely schematic, one could say that these developments shaped two rather different forms of European Orientalism, one more historical, religious, and textually based and the other more practical, antiquarian, and based on present-day encounters. In reality, both had nonscholarly as well as scholarly aims and undertones: the first to enhance conversions or be of use in religious debates; the second to map, collect, and make use of other people's lands and things. In any event, it is surely the case that most of what counted as 'Oriental' *scholarship* in the early modern period was of the former variety and had as its first priority the proper translation and interpretation of the most important book of the Ancient Near East as far as Christian Europeans were concerned: the Old Testament. Just as Renaissance classicists had embraced the reading of ancient Greek and Latin texts, Christian humanists like Martin Luther and Johannes Reuchlin learned (from Jews or Jewish converts) to read Biblical Hebrew (as well as New Testament Greek). From this time onward, Oriental studies began to diversify but did so as an auxiliary science (*Hilfswissenschaft*) intended to be useful in the explication of

---

5. See Jeffrey Herf, *Nazi Propaganda for the Arab World* (New Haven, CT: Yale University Press, 2010), and David Motadel, *Islam and Nazi Germany's War* (Cambridge, MA: Belknap Press of Harvard University Press, 2014).

the Hebrew Bible.⁶ As European travel to Asia increased, moreover, the study of Eastern languages expanded as well. In this case, however, travelers, entrepreneurs, soldiers, and missionaries often learned and taught their modern language skills, suited more to conversing than to reading ancient texts, outside of university frameworks, and many leaned heavily on intermediaries. Support came from princes or, in the case of soldiers and missionaries, from the states and churches that sent scholars into the field. Royal libraries and societies competed in the buying of rare books and manuscripts, which began to pile up in the Bibilothèque du Roi in Paris, the University Library in Leiden, and the Pietist Francke Foundation Library in Halle.

By the early eighteenth century, Oriental philology was a well-developed field in many respects, but insofar as it was an academic (rather than a practical) field, it was skewed in some crucial directions. First of all, it was oriented to the study of ancient texts and, especially, ancient religious texts. Secondly, it remained in the theological faculty and was chiefly used in the interpretation of the Old Testament (meaning it was founded on Hebrew studies). Thirdly, Orientalists also had to be classicists, as much of what was considered reliable information about the ancient Orient came from Greek and Roman sources, since many Near Eastern languages had not yet been learned or deciphered in the West. Fourthly, although there was some aestheticization of its products—the *1,001 Nights* and the chinoiserie craze of the mid-century are fine examples—on the whole, Oriental studies were not seen as so intimately related to the cultural renaissance in Europe as were classical styles. As for offering models for political and religious reform, some seventeenth-century English and Dutch radicals made the case for founding new Jerusalems, and Voltaire, a few decades later, attempted to defend the rationality of the Chinese bureaucracy. Ultimately, such attempts paled in comparison to the uses made of classical antiquity for reform purposes and petered out, too, after the mid-eighteenth century. Finally, the academic field had a rather distant but important series of relationships to "practical" Orientalism. Missionaries, travelers, and dragomans collected the books, manuscripts, and ethnographic information the field depended on, as well as dictionaries and travel accounts that were vital to stay-at-home scholars, among whom those

---

6. It was useful, for example, to study languages related to Hebrew (such as Aramaic and Arabic) as well as the languages in which scriptural fragments had been preserved (such as Armenian and Ethiopic); understanding the geography, botany, and zoology of Palestine and nearby regions was also useful in explicating the biblical text, as were the histories and practices of neighboring peoples, many of them mentioned in the scriptures themselves.

in the German states figured large, having many increasingly well-respected universities but no colonies to rule. In fact, relationships between academic and practical Orientalism in the early eighteenth century were closer than they would be in centuries to come, as we explore in this chapter. But we can already see some important patterns and issues emerging with respect to German Orientalism's relevance: Orientalistik was useful chiefly for theological and historical purposes, it was dependent on Greek and Roman classics and seen as providing inferior models for reform, and it was heavily oriented to the study of the ancient Near Eastern world.

Not surprisingly, those who took most seriously the development of "modern" Oriental studies were the nations with Asian colonial interests: the Dutch, the French, and the British. Leiden University took an early lead in Arabic studies; Paris's École speciale des langues orientales, founded in the later eighteenth century, and Bengal's Fort William College, established in 1800, also mixed the historical and the practical. In German-speaking Europe, the Austrians—with their long, "hot" Ottoman border—had the most use for these modern Oriental studies, and not surprisingly, it was in Vienna that the most utilitarian school was founded in 1754, under Maria Theresa. Emphasizing modern language learning rather than biblical exegesis, that school produced Josef von Hammer-Purgstall and many other translators.[7] Farther north, the German states did not found practical schools of this nature; with no colonies, they had no need. German missionaries who needed training in modern Asian languages would for decades need to travel abroad to learn them or attend special church-supported courses. Only in the very late nineteenth century (or early twentieth) would modern non-western languages begin to be added to German university curricula.

In the Germanies, too, the study of the Orient was undergoing transformation. The Enlightenment and the institutionalization of the research imperative as the goal of the universities prompted some secularization in Orientalistik, as scholars sought to expand their understandings of historical contexts. But just as importantly, the boom in interest in the classical, and especially in the Greek world, made for monumental changes in the pursuit of humanistic knowledge. In the course of a few decades between about 1780 and 1820, theology lost its position as the "queen of the sciences," although it was kept within the university. Both pastors and textual scholars (including many Orientalists)

---

7. On this school and its most famous graduate see Paula Sutter Fichtner, *Terror and Toleration: The Habsburg Empire Confronts Islam, 1526–1850* (London: Reaktion, 2008).

would hereafter be trained at the university, with the input of clerical bodies but overseen by the states. In the wake of Wilhelm von Humboldt's widely imitated reforms at the University of Berlin, classical philology became not only a favored discipline but also a model one. Because students now needed classical language training to pass the university entrance exam (and needed a university education to move up into the state bureaucracy, clergy, or *Bildungsbürgertum* [educated elite]), classical philology became more relevant and useful than the other humanistic disciplines and certainly more so than Orientalistik. The work of earlier polymaths who lectured and wrote about both classical and biblical cultures and texts began to be seen as amateurish. After being rather interested in the Orient, and even lecturing on world history in the 1820s, in the 1830s, Leopold von Ranke, to take one example, began pronouncing the Orient unimportant and its documents untrustworthy. Although some Orientalists had managed to escape the theological for the philosophical faculty, many still were considered (or considered themselves) basically exegetes, or "language machines" whose purpose it was to teach basic Hebrew, Arabic, and perhaps Sanskrit grammar.[8]

Importantly, it was in the first decades of the nineteenth century that British and German scholars really worked out what would subsequently be known as the "Indo-European" (or, for most Germans, Indo-German) family tree. This linguistic theory linked together the "Aryan" Indians, Greeks and Romans, and modern Europeans and juxtaposed this linguistic family to that of the Semites (including ancient Hebrews and modern Arabs) as well as that of other groups about which scholars cared less, in large part because they were not mentioned in the Bible (e.g., East Asians, sub-Saharan Africans, Australian aborigines, and peoples of the New World). Those interested in the Vedas or in other Indian texts could not sensibly explain their relevance to their contemporaries by way of linking their work to biblical exegesis (though some tried), nor could they argue that they were burnishing, preserving, and passing on the great cultural legacy of the Greeks and Romans. The family tree did, however, allow them to make a case for deep linkages between the Aryans and "us" (British Orientalists could also make the practical argument from empire), and thus was born a whole series of protoracial arguments that would give Indology new cultural clout but also compromise the whole field

---

8. See Suzanne L. Marchand, *German Orientalism in the Age of Empire: Religion, Race, and Scholarship*, Publications of the German Historical Institute (New York: Cambridge University Press, 2009), 53–102.

of Indo-European linguistics in the eyes of much later generations.[9] While in the middle of the nineteenth century, Indology could also be defended on the grounds of India's place in the history of religions or its contributions to the history of poetry, science, and philosophy, by the early twentieth century it was being enrolled in a racialized quest for Aryan identity, pursued by—among others—Houston Stewart Chamberlain.

It was also in the mid-nineteenth century that German universities took the leading role in "scientific" Orientalism and began to define what it meant to be a professional Orientalist (as opposed to a dragoman or what in East Asia became known as a "China hand"). As the scholars of the period shaped their norms and research projects, they did so based on the model provided by classical philology or on much older humanistic and exegetical models. The focus continued to be on the most ancient texts and on the question of religion and its origins. Historicism convinced them that the earliest texts would reveal the most about the "essence" of each people and each faith and that the best scholars were the ones who best understood original languages and ancient histories.

It is worth making another point or two about the mid-nineteenth century before we move on. First of all, we should note that German scholarly life in this era was funded by the individual states rather than private patrons, with the important exception (especially for our field) of Jewish schools and seminaries, which was where *all* of the study of postbiblical Judaism had to take place, as it was excluded from the universities. The German aristocracy was—after the Thirty Years' War—relatively poor and uninterested in patronizing scholarship. The German middle classes too were small and relatively poor—at least until after the 1860s. A large number of scholars were the sons of clergymen, bureaucrats, or schoolteachers and, as such, did not have diverse cultural backgrounds, nor did they have private incomes. In many German states, Jews could study philosophy, law, medicine, and even theology at German universities after 1809, but very few were allowed to teach there (without converting) until after 1869. Even first- and second-generation converts were heavily discriminated against in hiring—though a high number of those who did manage to get jobs received them in Oriental studies, a field that began to flourish right about this time. The flourishing of Orientalistik, however, was less the result of student interest (which remained limited) than of competition

---

9. There is no space to investigate this more closely, but see Stefan Arvidsson, *Aryan Idols: Indo-European Mythology as Ideology and Science*, trans. Sonia Wichmann (Chicago: University of Chicago Press, 2006); and Marchand, *German Orientalism*, 123–31, 190–94, 292–321.

between universities and the discipline's ability to convince the state that scientific progress demanded the founding of a new chair. Many Orientalists continued to be wide-ranging linguists, who began (and often ended) their careers as exegetes. There were continual battles in the field over decipherments and interpretations, with none so vituperative as those involving things biblical.[10] Although many of these debates were extremely specialized and the relevance of the issues obscured by the positivistic quest to get the facts right, orientalist scholars still usually defended the importance of their work in allowing Europeans to obtain a scientific understanding of what were *their own* religious traditions (and errors).

At least until the 1890s, German Orientalists considered themselves poor sisters with respect to classical philology, whose more abundant and appealing texts and more focused and secure methodologies they envied and whose superior cultural prestige many resented. On the whole, however, the Orientalists shared the classicists' dim view of those who studied modern languages (including German) and the modern Orient, subjects that were in their eyes too culturally trivial and too much like journalism or politics to be worthy of the attention of humanistic scholarship. I will not detail here their multiple and varied relationships with German or British imperial projects, or recount the development of the various institutions that grew up after 1885 to promote the more "practical" study of the Orient. Suffice it to say that these organizations were not of much interest to university scholars, many of whom disdained them. In the words of the Sinologist Otto Franke, the reaction of the University of Berlin's faculty to the founding of the modern-oriented Seminar für Orientalische Sprachen [Seminar for Oriental Languages] in 1887 was that of "an honest woman, who had had a bastard put in her crib."[11] If, in an era in which new decipherments, finds, and publications grew exponentially, some scholars

---

10. For example, there were fierce polemics about the cuneiform "Flood" tablets deciphered by British scholar George Smith, and about the "higher criticism" of Julius Wellhausen (in Old Testament scholarship) in the 1870s. See Marchand, *German Orientalism*, 196–202, and Rudolf Smend, "Julius Wellhausen," in *From Astruc to Zimmerli: Old Testament Scholarship in Three Centuries*, trans. Margaret Kohl (Tübingen, Germany: Mohr Siebeck, 2007), 91–102. For a different set of polemics, see Suzanne L. Marchand, "Dating Zarathustra: Oriental Texts and the Problem of Persian Prehistory, 1700–1900," *Erudition and the Republic of Letters* 1 (2016): 203–45.

11. Otto Franke, *Erinnerungen aus Zwei Welten: Randglossen zur eigenen Lebensgeschichte* (Berlin: Walter de Gruyter, 1954), 37. Franke's original reads: "Ihr Verhalten war das einer ehrbaren Frau, der man einen Bastard in die Wiege gelegt hat." All translations in this essay are the author's own, unless otherwise indicated.

used imperialist metaphors to trumpet their conquests in the Ancient Near East, the real argument for relevance—especially outside of Indology—was not that their scholarly achievements helped extend Germany's power abroad but that they gave it worldwide prestige. Within *Semitistik* [Semitic studies], there were still many who argued for their importance in understanding the Bible—not least Friedrich Delitzsch, who made such a stir in the Babylon and the Bible Affair of 1901–2.[12] Among Indologists, the utility of the field was based either on a quasi-religious identity politics or the importance of the *Rig Veda* or the Buddha as models for new forms of post-Christian religious belief.[13]

During the First World War, classical, Orientalist, and Germanic philologists and archaeologists in great numbers volunteered their services and did their bit for German victory. This was made significantly easier for the Islamicists as a result of the entry of the Ottoman Empire on the side of the Central powers in November 1914, and a large proportion of these scholars lent their skills and services to the state during the war. To describe this as a "large proportion" rather than a "large number" is important, as there were relatively few German scholars trained in modern Islamic matters in 1914—most German Orientalists at the time were still at work on the ancient Orient. Among those scholars, however, a large proportion, again, volunteered their services. Perhaps the most distinguished among them, Eduard Meyer, wrote bitter diatribes attacking the English; the now aged Assyriologist Friedrich Delitzsch even wrote a bizarre little book praising the "peace-loving" but victimized Turks.[14] One of the major ways these scholars hoped to contribute was by convincing the German public that they could trust their Islamic, "oriental" partners (and vice versa), by emphasizing the long endurance of the Hellenistic world and the debts both the Christian and Islamic worlds owed to it. This was a line of thought that had been pioneered by historian of Islam Carl Becker before the war, and it was not difficult to deploy it in public lectures and the like—nor did doing so do tremendous violence to the scholarship of the day. In part because the Germans were also trying to reach out—publicly and covertly—to

---

12. For an excellent study of Delitzsch's controversial lectures and the ensuing uproar, with particular attention to their "unmitigated nationalism and anti-Christian sentiment," as well as their antisemitism, see Bill T. Arnold and David B. Weisberg, "A Centennial Review of Friedrich Delitzsch's 'Babel und Bibel' Lectures," *Journal of Biblical Literature* 121, no. 3 (2002): 441–57 (at 443). See also Marchand, *German Orientalism*, 244–49.

13. For examples, see Marchand, *German Orientalism*, 162–216.

14. See Eduard Meyer, *England: Seine staatliche und politische Entwicklung und der Krieg gegen Deutschland* (Berlin: J. G. Cotta, 1915), and Friedrich Delitzsch, *Die Welt des Islam*, Männer und Völker 2 (Berlin: Ullstein, 1915).

Muslims in the Russian, French, and British Empires, too, this was not a case in which the rhetoric of "for us" was a racist rhetoric: on the contrary. Strikingly, in this war, it was the Semitists, for the most part, who got jobs in the cultural ministry and in covert operations.[15]

The war and its loss had a powerful impact on German cultural politics. Most obviously, the war killed a disproportionate number of young scholars, and war expenditures and debts deeply impoverished the individual states and, consequently, the universities. Those who survived were less likely than the previous generations to be interested exclusively in the ancient world and less keen on becoming pure linguists.[16] Many more had begun to study the post-Christian Near East, or East Asia, once a region little touched by German scholarship. Studies of *Realien* [material culture] and of modern history grew, and the number of Asian exchange students (and anticolonial activists) in Germany had increased. More (nonconverted) Jews and women received jobs. But until his death in 1930, Eduard Meyer continued to be an extremely powerful player, as did a number of other members of the linguistic old guard, including Egyptologist Adolf Erman, Semitists Enno Littmann and Carl Brockelmann, and Indologist Heinrich Lüders. Carl Becker served twice as German cultural minister and led the liberal campaign for university reform and the modernization of *Bildung* [liberal education]—without, however, a great deal of success.

On the eve of Hitler's coming to power, German Oriental studies still could boast that its scholars were great precisely because they were the products of a largely "irrelevant" tradition, one that favored studies of the ancient world, preferred philological expertise to grand theorizing, required its practitioners to know classical as well as oriental languages, and had much to say about the history of religions (and very little to say about modern politics). Grumblings could be heard that old men—like Meyer—remained too powerful and controlled too much of the dwindling state patronage for research. In fact, however, the Weimar era witnessed a great deal of innovation in the field, perhaps in

---

15. See Marchand, *German Orientalism*, 429–63; Gottfried Hagen, "German Heralds of Holy War," *Comparative Studies of South Asia, Africa, and the Middle East* 24, no. 2 (2004): 145–62; and the essays in Charlotte Trümpler, ed., *Das grosse Spiel: Archäologie und Politik zur Zeit des Kolonialismus* (Cologne, Germany: DuMont, 2008). On the classicists, see Suzanne L. Marchand, *Down from Olympus: Archaeology and Philhellenism in Germany, 1750–1970* (Princeton, NJ: Princeton University Press, 1996), 228–62.

16. For more on Weimar Orientalism, see Suzanne L. Marchand, "Eastern Wisdom in an Era of Western Despair: Orientalism in 1920s Central Europe," in *Weimar Thought: A Contested Legacy*, ed. Peter E. Gordon and John P. McCormick (Princeton, NJ: Princeton University Press, 2013), 341–60.

part because materials collected before the war were now being sifted and in part because researchers in classics and Orientalistik devoted new attention to previously understudied areas, periods, and sites (such as Dura Europos) where cross-cultural fertilizations had taken place.[17] There were a considerable number of liberals in the field, though many older Orientalists, like their classicist brethren—formerly fans of the monarchy—now adopted what they called an apolitical stance. What this really meant was that they despised all of Weimar's parties and the democracy that they represented. Most leaned to the right—many to the far right. Apparently, quite a number were already excited about Nazism on the eve of Hitler's installation as chancellor, including a few men with Jewish ancestry, such as Anton Baumstark, who deceived himself into thinking that he would be exempted from the Nazis' circle of victims.[18]

II. THE NAZI SEIZURE OF POWER AND THE FATE OF ORIENTAL STUDIES AFTER 1933

We are now in position to see what changes the Nazi regime and its rhetoric of national emergency administered to this essentially humanistic discipline. Despite some analyses that suggest that 1933 represented a blip rather than a major break in the lives of the universities, the radical nature of the regime with respect to academia must have been apparent from the first. Well before 1933, most academics would have had encounters with Nazi students or with the Nationalsozialistischer Deutscher Dozentenbund [National Socialist German

---

17. See Suzanne L. Marchand, "From Liberalism to Neoromanticism: Albrecht Dieterich, Richard Reitzenstein, and the Religious Turn in Fin de Siècle German Classical Studies," in *Out of Arcadia: Classics and Politics in the Age of Burckhardt, Nietzsche, and Wilamowitz*, ed. Martin Ruehl and Ingo Gildenhard, Bulletin of the Institute of Classical Studies Supplement 79 (London: Institute of Classical Studies, School of Advanced Study, University of London, 2003), 129–60.

18. Markus Mode quotes the reminiscences of James Henry Breasted, who visited his Egyptological friends in Germany shortly before the Nazis' seizure of power and reported that all of them were for Hitler. See Mode, "Altertumswissenschaft und Altertumswissenschaftler unter dem NS-Regime," in *Wissenschaft unter dem NS-Regime*, ed. Burchard Brentjes and Günter Albrecht (Berlin: Peter Lang, 1992), 156–69 (at 159). On Baumstark, see Hanisch, *Nachfolger*, 120. The Egyptologist Friedrich Freiherr von Bissing had been a backer of Hitler even before the 1923 Beer Hall Putsch and joined the party in 1933. On Bissing's hypernationalist propaganda campaign during World War I and his involvement with the Nazis, see Peter Raulwing and Thomas L. Gertzen, "Friedrich Freiherr von Bissing im Blickpunkt ägyptologischer und zeithistorischer Forschungen: Die Jahre 1914 bis 1926," *Journal of Egyptian History* 5, no. 1–2 (2010): 34–119.

University Instructors' League (NSDDozB)] and could anticipate that the advent of a Nazi regime was likely to be accompanied by a vehement attack on scholarship they deemed overly positivistic and/or irrelevant to their political goals. As we know, many of those who initially welcomed this assault on traditional academic values ended up getting more transvaluation than they had bargained for.[19]

We should remember that the Nazi movement was disproportionally a youth movement, one saturated with Nietzschean and vitalistic as well as hypernationalistic and racist ideas. Remarkably, older scholars almost instinctively moved to accommodate these sentiments. In a graduation address in May 1933, Heidelberg rector Willy Andreas claimed, "The time of high-flown homeless intellectualism is definitely over and none of us who want to remain in contact with reality can allow ourselves to fall victim to an unworldly piling up of knowledge."[20] There were calls for more Germanic teaching and learning, and less attention to "alien" and "irrelevant" subjects. There were also attacks on the study of language alone, without the crucial addition of racial science. States moved quickly to create new professorships for Germanic folklore (Heidelberg, Berlin, Leipzig, Tübingen) and Germanic prehistory, two fields that had been largely scorned by the erudite classical and biblical philologists. There was an upsurge in the hypernational study of Eastern Europe known as *Ostforschung* and a less successful attempt to create a parallel, politically oriented field dubbed *Westforschung*. Both "Eastern studies" and "Western studies" looked eagerly forward to a time when they might help change Germany's borders.[21]

---

19. Heidegger is a familiar example, here; for a further analysis of his attempts to ingratiate himself with the Third Reich, and Hannah Arendt's attempts to whitewash them, see Emmanuel Faye's contribution to the present volume, "Political Philosophy: Hannah Arendt and Aurel Kolnai as Interpreters of the Nazi Totalitarian State."

20. Quoted in Steven P. Remy, "'We Are No Longer the University of the Liberal Age': The Humanities and National Socialism at Heidelberg," in *Nazi Germany and the Humanities: How German Academics Embraced Nazism*, ed. Wolfgang Bialas and Anson Rabinbach (Oxford: Oneworld, 2014), 21–49 (at 24).

21. For the classic treatment of the Amt Rosenberg (the Nazi office created and headed by the ideologue Alfred Rosenberg and dedicated to bringing existing cultural institutions into line), and particularly its role in Nazifying the study of Germanic prehistory, see Reinhard Bollmus, *Das Amt Rosenberg und seine Gegner: Studien zum Machtkampf im nationalsozialistischen Herrschaftssystem*, 2nd ed., Studien zur Zeitgeschichte 1 (Munich: R. Oldenbourg, 2006). On *Ost*- and *Westforschung*, see Michael Burleigh, *Germany Turns Eastwards: A Study of Ostforschung in the Third Reich* (New York: Cambridge University Press, 1988), and Burkhard Dietz, "Die interdisziplinäre 'Westforschung' der Weimar Republik

The onset of the Nazi regime was especially threatening to those branches of Orientalistik that were not devoted to the Indo-European Orient: Islamic studies, Jewish studies, Assyriology, and Egyptology were especially hard hit, in part because so many of these scholars had come from either Jewish backgrounds (where their training in Hebrew gave them a leg up) or from traditions of religious dissent. East Asian studies—only in its infancy—was also decimated.[22] Already in the first half of 1933, scores of junior scholars and a number of senior ones were fired, either because of their Jewish ethnicity or their political opposition to the regime, and others were forced to fight the regime to maintain their positions. Those who succeeded were forced out by 1936 at the very latest. Age, rank, scholarly prestige, and service to the nation were only grudgingly taken into account and often were not enough to prevent termination. The longserving director of Berlin's Seminar for Oriental Languages, Eugen Mittwoch, was forced to step down, despite his distinguished service in World War I (which included, incidentally, assisting in the campaign to foment jihad in the Middle East).[23] The work of the older generation came under fire; already in April 1933, a highly critical review of Eduard Meyer's final publication strongly suggested that the work of the now-deceased grand old Orientalist was both in terms of research and approach out of date.[24] In the next few years, positions were slashed, independent sources of financing were cut off, and chairs, seminars, and organizations were renamed, especially in Semitistik. By 1938, more than one-half of the chair holders in this field had changed. Some of those who left managed to find positions in England, France, Turkey, Palestine, or the United States, greatly enhancing the scholarly standing of local academic traditions and institutions and correspondingly reducing that of Germany's universities.[25] Observers could not help but notice the change; in his 1936 presidential address to

---

und der NS-Zeit als Gegenstand der Wissenschafts- und Zeitgeschichte: Überlegungen zu Forschungsstand und Forschungsperspektiven," *Geschichte im Westen* 14, no. 2 (1999): 189–209.

22. Here see Martin Kern, "The Emigration of German Sinologists, 1933–1945: Notes on the History and Historiography of Chinese Studies," *Journal of the American Oriental Society* 118, no. 4 (1998): 68–100.

23. On Mittwoch, see Marchand, *German Orientalism*, 452, 457, 479–80, and Hanisch, *Nachfolger*, 158, 198.

24. Max Pieper, "Eduard Meyers letztes Werk," *Orientalistische Literaturzeitung* 36, no. 4 (1933): 201–9.

25. Hanisch, *Nachfolger*, 134. Among those who went to Turkey were the great Assyriologist Benno Landsberger, his student Fritz Rudolf Kraus, and the Hittite specialist Hans-Gustav Güterbock. Several of these figures—as well as many others—ended up

the American Oriental Society, William Foxwell Albright described "the rapid decline of attention to our studies" in Germany since 1933.[26]

The decimation of German Indology by the 1930s, on the other hand, had little to do with the coming of the Nazis. Although the number of positions had expanded greatly at the fin de siècle, the numbers withered in the 1920s, perhaps because the Weimar regime had little money or interest in supporting what had long been a right-leaning field. It is also the case that after the Great War, Sanskrit students like Heinrich Zimmer and Betty Heimann wearied of philological positivism—and their senior colleagues resented their attempts to enliven the field with cross-disciplinary ventures. At the time of Hitler's ascent to power, some six chairs remained unfilled.[27] Indeed, some younger scholars in the field regarded the coming of the Nazis as a great opportunity to root out the positivism of the older generation and to seize some of the glory still possessed by the classicists, or by the Semitists who remained prominent in their roles as—in Hanisch's formulation—"Successors of the Exegetes." A few (mostly younger people) were driven out by the Nazis, such as Heimann, Zimmer (in 1936), and Isidore Scheftelowitz, and some Indologists committed suicide or died at the hands of the National Socialist (NS) regime, including Otto Stein, Otto Strauss, and Walter Neisser. But others—Sheldon Pollock estimates about a third of the professoriate—were not just positively inclined toward the regime but also active in the party or the Schutzstaffel (SS).[28] The Indologists, too, saw 1933 as a watershed—but in their case, it was one that might send more glory and state funding down their side of the Orientalist mountain range.

III. REINVENTING ORIENTALISTIK'S RELEVANCE: CHALLENGES AND RESPONSES

That scholars at the time quickly recognized that something very radical had happened is borne out by the immediate emigration of several scholars and the

---

later in the United States, helping to revolutionize (as Albright had predicted) the study of the ancient Near East in America. See Johannes Renger, "Altorientalistik und jüdische Gelehrte in Deutschland: Deutsche und österreichische Altorientalisten im Exil," in *Jüdische Intellektuelle und die Philologien in Deutschland, 1871–1933*, ed. Wilfried Barner and Christoph König, Marbacher Wissenschaftsgeschichte 3 (Göttingen, Germany: Wallstein, 2001), 252–61.

26. William F. Albright, "How Well Can We Know the Ancient Near East?," *Journal of the American Oriental Society* 56, no. 2 (1936): 121–44 (at 121).

27. Marchand, *German Orientalism*, 476–77; Hanisch, *Nachfolger*, 147n523.

28. Pollock, "Deep Orientalism," 94.

massive amounts of correspondence exchanged in efforts to prevent firings. Perhaps even more telling, however, are the large numbers of lectures and essays generated immediately after the Nazi seizure of power which sought to link scholarly production in some way with the sensationalist "national emergency" language Hitler himself deployed to legitimize his brutal and authoritarian new regime. Infamous books and essays were written by prominent scholars including Gerhard Kittel, Martin Heidegger, and Werner Jaeger, but many others, including many Orientalists, also felt the need, or desire, to articulate their own solutions to their nation's "emergencies."[29] As we have seen, something similar had happened at the outbreak of war in 1914—but now, Germany was not (yet) at war, and its alliance with an "Asian" power (the Axis Treaty with Japan in 1936) was still several years away. Orientalists had previously argued their importance on the grounds of their contributions to science and to religion, or to the building of Germany's prestige in the international world of scholarship, but the Nazis seemed not to care about any of these things. What could they do or say that would be useful to this new order?

This question was further complicated by some aspects of the Nazi regime that made it less likely than previous German governments to listen to, or patronize, the Orientalists. Most obviously, it was deeply antisemitic, which was naturally problematic for specialists in Semitic languages. Second, although it did not want to offend the churches, the regime was indifferent to appeals based on Christian history. Third, the regime was committed to a racial worldview, which complicated attempts to make other people's histories and cultures relevant to those at home. Fourth, the regime showed no interest in colonizing in Asia. Finally, though some of its major figures were keenly interested in either Germanic or Aryan antiquity, others were devoted to modern history and resented the relative underfunding of that field as compared to studies of the ancient world. Thus did Walter Frank in 1935 make a point of comparing the last Weimar budget for the German Archaeological Institute (931,000 Reichsmark [RM]) with that of the Imperial Historical Commission (35,000 RM), which

---

29. On Gerhard Kittel's *Die Judenfrage*, 2nd ed. (Stuttgart, Germany: Kohlhammer, 1933), see Robert P. Ericksen, *Theologians under Hitler: Gerhard Kittel, Paul Althaus, and Emanuel Hirsch* (New Haven, CT: Yale University Press, 1985), 52–78. See also Anders Gerdmar's contribution to this volume, "Jewish Studies in the Service of Nazi Ideology: Tübingen's Faculty of Theology as a Center for Antisemitic Research." On Heidegger, see (among many other treatments) Charles Bambach, *Heidegger's Roots: Nietzsche, National Socialism, and the Greeks* (Ithaca, NY: Cornell University Press, 2005), 69–111. On Jaeger, see Marchand, *Down from Olympus*, 325–27.

had overseen work on German history since 1871.[30] As we shall see, the first of these problems was almost insuperable, though some Semitists managed to figure out how to collaborate anyway, either as specialists in *Judenforschung* [literally, Jewish research, but this racialized term was used only by enemies of the Jews, who combined within it Old Testament and Talmudic studies as well as the study of modern Jewish history and culture] or as diplomats, translators, or spies in the Middle East—and might have been even more heavily implicated had the Reich won the war in North Africa.[31] Religious argumentation essentially had to be, and was, given up. As concerns racial thought, this was a card the specialists in Indo-European languages sought to play to their own benefit, while for Semitists it was something like the third rail. The demand for more modernization was, in the end, one the field could handle, at least to a certain extent.

In what follows, I want to give a sampling of some of the collaborationist language—minor and major—and show how it reflects the desperate desire of some scholars to demonstrate their loyalty and relevance. I agree with Georg Bollenbeck that we cannot deduce too much about the degree to which the writers of these pieces signed on to Nazi doctrine, compromised their scholarship, or behaved toward their colleagues from these public speeches beyond a general willingness to collaborate. As far as we know, no one was coerced into giving these talks and could have declined to participate in these events. Beyond this, Bollenbeck claims, public effusions such as these "do not permit conclusions about the various strategies of the agents within the scientific field. A public 'vow of allegiance to the regime' might form a sort of protective space within which one could pursue professional and thematically oriented

---

30. Helmut Heiber, *Walter Frank und sein Reichsinstitut für Geschichte des neuen Deutschlands* (Stuttgart, Germany: Deutsche Verlags-Anstalt, 1966), 165.

31. On Judenforschung, see Weinreich, *Hitler's Professors*; Bollmus, *Amt Rosenberg*, 119–23; and Alan E. Steinweis, "Nazi Historical Scholarship on the 'Jewish Question,'" in Bialas and Rabinbach, *Nazi Germany and the Humanities*, 399–412. On collaborationists, see Suzanne L. Marchand, "Nazism, 'Orientalism,' and Humanism," in Bialas and Rabinbach, *Nazi Germany and the Humanities*, 267–305; Renger, "Altorientalistik"; Hanisch, "Arabistik, Semitistik, und Islamwissenschaft." Herf offers some examples of Semitist collaborators such as Hans Alexander Winckler (*Nazi Propaganda*, 79–82, 118–20, 156–57). The collaboration of Egyptologists—technically Semitists—is extensively documented in Thomas Schneider, "Ägyptologen im Dritten Reich: Biographische Notizen anhand der sogennten 'Steindorff-Liste,'" *Journal of Egyptian History* 5 (2012): 120–247 (reprinted in *Egyptology from the First World War to the Third Reich: Ideology, Scholarship, and Individual Biographies*, ed. Thomas Schneider and Peter Raulwing, 120–247 [Leiden, Netherlands: Brill, 2013]) and "Hermann Grapow, Egyptology, and National Socialist Initiatives for the Humanities" (in this volume).

research."[32] What is interesting to us, however, are the ways in which the relevance and utility of the field of Oriental studies were now depicted, and the departures this represented from the public profiles the field had presented before Hitler's seizure of power.

As Hanisch has described, one of the first major flurries of relevance literature was provoked by the May 1933 memorandum produced by the right-wing Islamicists Franz Babinger and Walter Hinz entitled "The Study of the Orient in the New Germany: Current Situation and Future Tasks."[33] Babinger, who had served in Turkey during the Great War and afterward taken a position at the Seminar for Oriental Languages in Berlin, was some fifteen years older than Hinz, a party member who had gone to work for the War Ministry and only completed his habilitation in 1934. But both were clearly keen on making practical use of their studies. They stirred the pot by arguing that Germany's outdated preservation of more than twenty chairs for Semitic languages demonstrated that "the study of the Orient [*Morgenlandkunde*] remains in many ways ancillary to the study of religion and to rabbinic studies and is still pursued as such." They also claimed that the field had become "distant from this world [*weltfremd*] and had petrified into narrowly philological studies" and advocated the funding of only three centers for Oriental studies: a general one in Berlin, a linguistic center in Leipzig, and a center focused on modern Near Eastern and Balkan studies at the University of Munich.[34]

Evidently the memorandum was circulated, or leaked out, for several responses followed it, including a defense of linguistic studies written by three Leipzig chair holders, two of them fans of the regime and the other a Jewish scholar. The writers also insisted that it was religious studies that was the dependent field and that students could learn about the present by travels or reading travel literature.[35] Babinger was also (secretly) punished for his outburst by the much more discrete and old-fashioned Hans Heinrich Schaeder, Professor at the University of Berlin and the new director of the Seminar for Oriental Languages (following the firing of Mittwoch). Later in 1933, Schaeder

---

32. Georg Bollenbeck, "The Humanities in Germany after 1933: Semantic Transformations and the Nazification of the Disciplines," in Bialas and Rabinbach, *Nazi Germany and the Humanities*, 1–20 (at 12–13).

33. For a discussion of this unpublished memorandum, see Hanisch, *Nachfolger*, 144; Ursula Wokoeck, *German Orientalism: The Study of the Middle East and Islam from 1800 to 1945*, Culture and Civilization in the Middle East (London: Routledge, 2009), 189–91.

34. Hanisch, *Nachfolger*, 144; Renger, "Altorientalistik," 492–93.

35. Hanisch, *Nachfolger*, 144–45.

recommended against Babinger's appointment to fill a vacant Munich chair on the grounds that he had reservations about Babinger's personality, his scholarship, and his Aryan origins. In 1934, Babinger's career in Germany was ruined when the violently antisemitic Nazi journal *Der Stürmer* denounced him for being a *Mischlinge* [person of mixed race]; he survived by taking posts in Bulgaria, Romania, and Hungary, returning to Germany in 1948.[36] Hinz, on the other hand, who had actually studied with Schaeder, kept in good graces with the regime *and* with his colleagues. He moved on to a position in the Cultural Ministry in 1934 and then to a chair at the University of Göttingen in 1937. It is possible that during his time at the Cultural Ministry Hinz protected his field from further damage, but the degree to which he collaborated with the regime was sufficient to earn him a brief suspension after the war. Soon, however, he returned to the University of Göttingen, where he wrote both scholarly and popular books, and managed to enlarge his institute from one professorship to six.[37] Hinz's career exemplifies many others (including Schaeder's own), in which moderate collaboration did little to damage the individual's academic credentials, before or after 1945.

Though willing to work for the Nazis, Schaeder found the Babinger-Hinz plan not to his taste, and, again privately, argued against the consolidation plan by noting that condensing positions to three would harm students who wanted to study near home (a defense used then, and now, by smaller state-funded universities to combat the consolidation of programs). The most vigorous defense was mounted by Paul Kahle, the Bonn Semitist and executive director of the prestigious Deutsche Morgenländische Gesellschaft [German Oriental Society (DMG)]. Kahle took the initiative to pitch his own plan for a more relevant Orient-Institut, under his own direction, that would reach out to the present-day Middle East. The ministry came close to adopting Kahle's plan but finally decided he was politically untrustworthy and shelved it.[38]

---

36. Gerhard Grimm, "Franz Babinger (1891–1967): Ein Lebensgeschichtlicher Essay," *Die Welt des Islams* 38, no. 3 (1998): 286–333 (at 317–20). For more on Babinger's life and legacy, see Ali Anoonshahr, "Franz Babinger and the Legacy of the 'German Counter-Revolution' in Early Modern Iranian Historiography," in *Rethinking Iranian Nationalism and Modernity*, ed. Kamran Scot Aghaie and Afshin Marashi (Austin: University of Texas Press, 2014), 25–48.

37. Renger, "Altorientalistik," 492n130; Ludwig Paul, "Göttingen, University of, History of Iranian Studies," *Encyclopaedia Iranica*, online edition, 2006, accessed July 25, 2012, http://www.iranicaonline.org/articles/gttingen-university-of-history-of-iranian-studies. Hinz's work on the Safavid empire, long positively received, has recently been found to be suffused with German fascist concepts. See Anoonshahr, "Franz Babinger," 37–40.

38. Hanisch, *Nachfolger*, 144–48.

Kahle was indeed untrustworthy from the Nazi perspective. He tried to protect his Jewish assistant, Kurt Levy; in his capacity as executive director of the DMG, Kahle dragged his feet when it came to implementing Nazi racial laws. As a specialist in Hebrew literature, Kahle despaired of the loss of so many of his Jewish colleagues and tried to help them get jobs elsewhere. He had some success in this regard, but was tormented by his failure place Levy, who committed suicide in 1935.[39] As the editor of the *Zeitschrift der Deutschen Morgenländischen Gesellschaft* (*ZDMG*), Kahle refused to publish an overtly racist essay by the retired Orientalist Arthur Ungnad.[40] But he also tried to play the relevance game, at least for a time, seeking to make the *ZDMG* more popularly accessible and publishing a number of pieces there by Nazi scholars. Though most of these avoided using explicitly racialized or antisemitic language, by 1938, this barrier too was falling. The journal's report on the 1938 Orientalists' Conference, which Kahle had overseen in his hometown of Bonn, discussed several papers that were clearly racist in conception, including "The Aryan Contribution to Indian Philosophy," presented by Austrian Nazi Party member Erich Frauwallner.[41] Already known to be friendly to Jews, Kahle could no longer hold his position after his wife and son came to the aid of Jews terrorized by the Night of the Broken Glass and was forced to give up his positions and to emigrate in early 1939.[42] By this

---

39. To a directive issued by the Reichsministerium für Wissenschaft, Kunst, und Volksbildung [Reich Ministry of Science, Art, and Education (RMWKV)] in August 1933, instructing the organization to adhere to the Law for the Restoration of the Professional Civil Service (because it received more than 50 percent of its funding from the state), Kahle responded—taking his time—in October that first of all, the DMG had no real employees, and secondly, that in 1932 it had received 14,728 RM from publications and income, and only 13,200 RM from public sources, and therefore was under the 50 percent mark. Moreover, Prof. Dr. (and Geheimrat) L. Schermann had already resigned from the executive committee and the question of other members would have to be decided at the year-end meeting. See Kahle to RMWKV 6 October 1933, responding to Breuer (RMWKV to Deutsche Morgenländische Gesellschaft, 26 August 1933), both in BGStPK I HA, Rep. 76 Vc, Sekt. 1, Tit. XI, Teil I, Nr. 10, Bd. 3. See also Hanisch, *Nachfolger*, 125–26.
40. Renger, "Altorientalistik," 487.
41. "Der IX. Deutsche Orientalistentag: Bonn 1938," *Zeitschrift der Deutschen Morgenländischen Gesellschaft* 92 (1938): 3–38 (at *9–10* and *22–24* [the italic page numbers mark a supplement at the end of the journal]). Renger discusses the ambivalent career of Adam Falkenstein (see ibid., *22–24*) and his mistrust of racism and concludes that the essay might have been a subtle attempt to refute the racist ideas of Ungnad. See Renger, "Altorientalistik," 495–98.
42. Paul Kahle, *Die Universität Bonn vor und während der Nazi Zeit (1923–1939)*, bound as a single volume with Marie Kahle, *Was hätten Sie getan? Die Flucht der Familie Kahle aus Nazi Deutschland*, ed. John H. Kahle and Wilhelm Bleek (Bonn, Germany: Bouvier, 1998), 142–43.

time, the number of members in the DMG had fallen from one thousand in 1933 to about three hundred.[43]

In this context, Helmut Berve's assault on the usefulness of Orientalism to the Nazi regime, published in 1934, proved explosive. Berve, professor of ancient history and dean of the philosophical faculty at the University of Leipzig and a Nazi Party member (since 1933), made his programmatic remarks at the end of a long review of a typical product of positivistic Orientalism: a multiauthored history of the Ancient Near East, published as part of a general *Handbuch der Altertumswissenschaft* [Handbook for the Study of the Ancient World]. Berve began by summarizing the contributions—including a few written by persons who were already persona non grata in the Nazi world—but the sting was in the tail. Finishing his summary with several paragraphs on the work of Hermann Kees (a supporter of the regime) on Egyptian religion, Berve noted Kees's attempts to comprehend a religion "so foreign to our being" and his attempts to avoid modernizing it or measuring it by Greek standards. But did not this very attempt, Berve concluded, throw the whole of Egyptological science into question?

> The general situation of the human sciences is ... that today, without a specific, all-uniting system of value they can no longer be productively pursued. That is not only an inescapable consequence of our cultural or political situation in the present, which denies the right to life of value-free scholarship, but an inner necessity of scholarship itself, that must find its way back to the natural insight that Treitschke expressed so beautifully, that man can only know what he loves. But one can only love what is related to himself, and the question now unavoidably poses itself to a whole range of disciplines, that, previously, were pursued on the basis of another kind of "objective" orientation: is knowledge here in its deepest sense possible? So long as it was about the positivistic fixing of facts of a chronological or philological nature, this problem did not arise, nor could it arise. But who today satisfies himself with aspiring to the goals set by positivism? Who is willing and able to renounce the recognition of the historical materials in his own individual identity [*Eigenart*], even where the individual identity is the reason he pursues this and not that branch of science?[44]

Berve proceeded to claim that it was very difficult, and for the most part impossible, to understand the essence of another race or people; this was true of

---

43. Mode, "Altertumswissenschaft," 154.
44. Helmut Berve, "Zur Kulturgeschichte des alten Orients," *Archiv für Kulturgeschichte* 25 (1934): 216–30 (at 227–28).

the Carthaginians and of the Semitic people of the Near East, including the Jews, "even though parts of the Old Testament today form part of the indispensable repertoire of our Christian imaginary." Nor can we love Egypt, since the landscape leaves us bored and cold—"The foreignness is too great." The upshot of this was, Berve concluded, that the science of the ancient Orient, insofar as it was racially foreign "cannot satisfy the demand to establish value and loses thereby its right to life. For the need to establish value has become an inescapable reality for the historical sciences, at least in the realm of German *Geist*; it was already so before the political break came, which in some ways only brought the legitimation of a change that was irresistibly unfolding." The classicists, Berve claimed—championing his own field—had already left behind the period of pure positivism, while the era would almost surely last a bit longer in Orientalistik. But sometime in the near future, Oriental studies would discover "that it will have no specialized students who are willing to do nothing but trivial fact collecting [*nackte Sacharbeit*]." Assyriology and Egyptology would move into the background as studies of racially and culturally related peoples rose. Berve tried to conclude the essay on a positive note: the book under review was fine as a summary of the accomplishments of the positivistic age, but now it was time to move on.[45]

It is hard to know if it was the Babinger-Hinz memo, Berve's review, or a more general panic about relevance that unleashed a number of lectures in 1934 whose aim was explaining Oriental philology's utility for the present day. That Berve hit a nerve, however, is clear from a number of pieces written slightly later, as we review here. Among the 1934 essays were two that did not refer directly to Berve's assault but made rather mild attempts at linking modern Germans with the medieval Persians and ancient Assyrians—Hans Heinrich Schaeder's "Firdosi and the Germans" and Walter Andrae's *The German Excavations in Warka (Uruk)*. The first lines of Andrae's essay reveal the urgency of demonstrating the relevance of finds—even though they had long since been held in high esteem by the scholarly world and many had just been put on display in the new Pergamon Museum. "What does Uruk mean to us?" he asks. "To us, whom necessity and inner drive compel to reflect on our nation, our people, our history, in order to understand ourselves? What to us is the distant past of a foreign, dead people?" The best that Andrae could do was to argue that the Assyrians were also a people of "inner purity" who had left little in the way of

---

45. Ibid., 229–30 (the page range provided here covers all quotations in this paragraph). For more on Berve's career as a classicist and collaborator, see Volker Losemann, "Classics in the Second World War," in Bialas and Rabinbach, *Nazi Germany and the Humanities*, 313–35.

their own literary records and thus had to be described through the reports of others.⁴⁶ In earlier times, Andrae could have dispensed with these rhetorical gymnastics or might have boasted about Germany's contribution to science or to the understanding of the world of the Old Testament. Now he felt obliged to say something about why "his" Volk should care about a "foreign," long expired one. We can recognize this for what it was: a transparent attempt to demonstrate relevance, but one that shifted the ground from history, religion, and prestige to the making of racial identities.⁴⁷

Schaeder's "Firdosi and the Germans" offers another example of relevance seeking without major politicization. Here Schaeder—who leaned in conservative and neoromantic directions and collaborated to some extent but who seems not to have covered himself with ideological infamy—first defended the study of things Persian as part of Germany's "romantic tendency to seek a mirror for one's own essence in the distant and the foreign." But he finished with the rhetoric of familial if not racial relevance, declaring that in Firdosi today's German reader found more than a piece of exotic poetry. "He hears in the thousand-year-old, eternal verses the sound of a trusted, brotherly, voice—a voice that epitomizes the genius of a people of noble origin and intense determination, which has endured through periods of greatness and decline."⁴⁸

IV. INDOLOGY'S APPEAL FOR SPECIAL RELEVANCE

As one might have expected, the Indologists—who had long used the Indo-European family tree as a means to argue for their "relevance"—were not slow to deploy the rhetoric of racial relatedness. In 1934, Walther Wüst, Professor of Indology at the University of Munich, published an essay entitled "Early

---

46. Walter Andrae, *Die deutschen Ausgrabungen in Warka (Uruk)*, Deutsche Forschung aus der Arbeit der Deutschen Forschungsgesmeinschaft 25 (Berlin: Karl Siegismund, 1935), 5–6.

47. Andrae was not a Nazi. He had become enamored of the anthroposophy of Rudolf Steiner in the 1920s, and while his lectures on Assyrian art, given at the Technische Universität Berlin in winter 1933–34 do attempt to assert relevance (they were titled "What Does Ancient Oriental Art Mean for Our Age?"), they are full of esoteric ideas about humans, gods, and modern art, not antisemitic and racist commentaries. Andrae's lectures can be found among his papers at BSB, Nachlass Andrae, Mappe 142.

48. Hans Heinrich Schaeder, "Firdosi und die Deutschen," *Zeitschrift der Deutschen Morgenländischen Gesellschaft* 88 (1934): 118–29 (at 129). Schaeder did not mention the immense work that Jewish Iranist Fritz Wolff put into creating a glossary for Firdosi's *Shahnameh*. This glossary would be presented to the Iranian government as an official gift in recognition of the thousand-year anniversary of the poet in 1935, but in 1943, Wolff himself would die, along with his wife, in a concentration camp. See Hanisch, *Nachfolger*, 124.

Germanic History and Aryan Cultural History," in the Nazi journal *Süddeutsche Monatshefte*. Wüst's invocation of Indological scholarship demonstrates, as Sheldon Pollock has argued, "The propriety and need Wüst felt of legitimating the NS worldview by anchoring it in an ancient Indian *darśana* [holy perspective]."[49] But we can also examine the speech from the opposite perspective. Wüst—who joined the Nazi Party in May 1933 but had not yet joined the SS—was also defending the relevance of Sanskrit philology, something that might well have seemed "knowledge not worth knowing" to Nazi officials, despite Himmler's occasional interest in the subject.

Surprisingly, although racial linkages form the substructure of the essay, Wüst spoke little about racial profiles or migrations. Yet perhaps we should not be so surprised, since Wüst was trained as a Vedic philologist, not as a biologist. Indeed, one can read the whole piece as a defense of the usefulness of humanistic studies of the ancient world, and of the study of Indo-European languages. Even more specifically, Wüst takes pains to defend his particular subspecialty (Sanskrit linguistics) against the possible intrusion of Persian or Hittite studies. No one can challenge the right of the *Rig Veda*, he insists, to be "the oldest document of the Aryan race and the purist example of the ancient Indo-German writing."[50] In an essay full of absurd leaps from deep antiquity to the present, Wüst nonetheless warns particularly against trusting speculations about Persian history and linguistics—the implication is that in tracking the ancient Aryans, the Sanskritists, and not the Iranists, are the experts to be trusted.[51] Fittingly for a defense of one's field of research, the essay ends less with a confirmation that the linkages between ancient Aryans and modern Germans are already proven than with a call to those he terms the *Berufene* [those called to the field] (it is noteworthy that his vitalist language carefully avoids the all too positivistic or elitist terms *Gelehrten* [scholar] or *Wissenschaftler* [scientist]) to investigate these connections more extensively (which would, presumably, need state patronage to accomplish). As endorsement for this quest, he invokes the work of Houston Stewart Chamberlain, whose 1905 *Arische Weltanschauung* had called for the abandoning of classical models in favor of Aryan Indian ones.[52] Wüst ends the essay by quoting Chamberlain:

---

49. Pollock, "Deep Orientalism," 91.
50. Walther Wüst, "Deutsche Frühzeit und arische Geistesgeschichte," *Süddeutsche Monatshefte* 31, no. 12 (1934): 731–39 (at 735).
51. Ibid., 732.
52. On this book and on Chamberlain's friendship with the Indologist Leopold von Schroeder, see Marchand, *German Orientalism*, 311–21.

"Indology must help us to fix our eyes clearly on the goals of our culture—we have yet to bring a great humanistic task to fruition: for this, Aryan India is the chosen [model]."[53] For close readers, this was a carefully plotted attack on the German neoclassical tradition as well as a defense of Indology, over against the other branches of Orientalistik. Because, for Wüst, it deals with "us," racially conceived Indology can and should be the field that drives forward the German-Aryan Renaissance.

Wüst's self-mobilization caught the eye of Wolfram Sievers, managing director of the SS Ahnenerbe [Ancestral Heritage Research Institute], and by mid-1936, Wüst was reading the *Rig Veda* aloud to Heinrich Himmler. In February 1937, the Indologist was appointed Sievers's right-hand man, in part to give the organization some much-needed gravitas—for Wüst was also allowed and encouraged to keep his Munich chair.[54] The study of ancient India, it seems, was safe from further attacks on its relevance—but at the cost of linking it to the murderous SS and its higher officials' obsessions with Germanic prehistory and Aryan sun worship.[55] But if Wüst made a successful, hypercollaborationist case for Sanskrit philology, for the other fields, fears about the relevance of Oriental studies (now termed *Orientforschung*, rather than Orientalistik, suggesting a parallel to the fields of Ostforschung and Westforschung) were still around by the summer of 1934. The few attempts at full collaboration and the half-hearted self-criticisms of the field clearly were not enough to deter the regime from meddling further—or, to look at it from the more avidly collaborationist perspective, the field remained insufficiently mobilized. At about the same time as the Night of the Long Knives was unfolding, Theodor Wiegand, one of the Reich's most esteemed archaeologists and the head of the scholarly committee of the high-profile Deutsche Orient-Verein [German-Orient Association], called on all of Berlin's Orientalist organizations to participate

---

53. Wüst, "Deutsche Frühzeit," 739.

54. Heather Pringle, *The Master Plan: Himmler's Scholars and the Holocaust* (New York: Hyperion, 2006), 94–97. On Himmler's Teutonic worldview (which was intended to replace the Judeo-Christian one he despised) and his need for gravitas to justify his esoteric pursuits, see also Peter Longerich, *Heinrich Himmler*, trans. Jeremy Noakes and Lesley Sharpe (Oxford: Oxford University Press, 2012), 255–98.

55. For more on these esoteric pursuits as linked to the Orient, see Eric Kurlander, "The Orientalist Roots of National Socialism? Nazism, Occultism, and South Asian Spirituality, 1919–1945," in *Transcultural Encounters between Germany and India: Kindred Spirits in the Nineteenth and Twentieth Centuries*, ed. Joanne Miyang Cho, Eric Kurlander, and Douglas T. McGetchin, Routledge Studies in the Modern History of Asia 90 (London: Routledge, 2014), 155–69.

in a series of lectures on the subject of "German Oriental Studies [Orientforschung]: Its Significance for the Present and Its Tasks for Today." It is likely that Wiegand, who had spent his career excavating in the Near East and many years plumping for the creation of the Pergamon Museum, believed that such a collective defense of the field was vital at this point. The Ishtar Gate had just been installed in the museum, yet many more finds were awaiting study and exhibition, while excavation sites in the Near East had been handed over to the Americans, British, and French or required new infusions of cash and personnel. Wiegand invited several individual associations—including the excavation-supporting Deutsche Orient-Gesellschaft [German-Orient Society], the Gesellschaft für Islamkunde [Society for Islamic Studies], and die Gesellschaft für Ostasiatischen Kunst [Society for East Asian Art]—to participate, to which they responded positively. Many also hosted their own lectures during the next winter in order to participate fully in this series. The idea was to attract a popular audience as well as a scholarly one. Thus, those asked to give the lectures were some of the most prominent academics in the field, and also those known to be at least mildly sympathetic toward the NS regime. In 1935, its prominence enhanced by the collaboration of these other organizations, Wiegand's Orient-Verein contracted with the highly respected academic publisher Walter de Gruyter to publish six of these lectures under the title *Der Orient und Wir: Sechs Vorträge des Deutsche Orient-Vereins Berlin* [The Orient and Us: Six Lectures by the German Orient Association].

V. *THE ORIENT AND US:* VARIATIONS ON THE THEME OF RELEVANCE

A brief examination of the strategies of relevance making in these lectures shows us a range of different approaches to establishing the connection between "Orient" and "us." The first lecture was given by Wilhelm Weber, Professor of ancient history at the University of Berlin, whose title was simply "Der Alte Orient." Weber was followed by: Hans Heinrich Schaeder, whose talk was titled "Der neuere Orient"; Ernst Kühnel, Director of the Islamic Department of the Berlin State Museums ("Islamische Kunst"); Heinrich Lüders, Professor of Indology at the University of Berlin ("Indien"); and Otto Franke, Professor emeritus of Sinology at the University of Berlin ("China"). The final lecture ("Ostasiatische Kunst") was delivered by Germany's most notable expert in East Asian art history, Otto Kümmel. All of these men were very senior scholars who—with the exception of Schaeder—had made their careers before World War I and had been movers and shakers in the nation's cultural scene in various ways. Weber, for example, was a leading ancient historian. Franke had been instrumental in the signing of the treaty with Germany's Chinese protectorate, Qingdao, and was Germany's most renowned Sinologist. Kühnel was a highly accomplished archaeologist and art historian who had helped curate the monumental 1910 Exhibition, "Masterpieces of Mohammedan Art," in Munich. Kümmel was *the* proponent of East Asian and especially Japanese art and the founder in 1912 of the *Ostasiatische Zeitschrift*. He had served as director of the East Asian Collections and of the Ethnographic Museum before 1933 and in 1934 was appointed general director of the State Museums.[56] These were all heavy hitters, though they would develop different attitudes and forms of engagement with the Nazi regime.

Weber's lecture, the first, praised the regime most directly, and one can guess that Wiegand—or someone else—chose Weber more for his ideological commitment than for his scholarly credentials, as Weber's true field was not Orientalistik but the history of the Roman Empire. Eager to engage the audience and addressing a subject in which he was not an expert, Weber padded his lecture with some seventy-seven slides, which were not included in the publication but echo the increasing production of grand-scale art books in the 1910s and '20s. If philology and history did not engage contemporaries, this visual approach suggested, perhaps images would do the trick. But even before showing the slides, Weber called on his audience to recall their collective experience of "the sudden awakening and self-discovery of the German folk. With new political unity, stability, and leadership our folk embarks on its path. It has become young, newly formed from the primeval power of its life, in order to raise itself to consciousness. The dim future as a goal, the deep past as its moving power: both determine its present and give it meaning. Thus our folk strides, moved from its depths, into a century of faith."[57] What exactly Weber meant by "faith" [*Glauben*] is a bit obscure, but as the next paragraphs in the lecture make clear, he was trying in some way to link ancient and modern, Nordic and "Oriental," the achievements of (aging) scholars and the political deeds of mobilized young men. One of the next paragraphs is almost comical in its attempts at making his lecture fit the current circumstances:

> Adolf Hitler has called the young people to write the world history of Aryan humanity, a job suited to a youth movement that, carried forward by its

---

56. See Marchand, *German Orientalism*, for more on these figures.
57. Weber, "Der Alte Orient," in *Der Orient und Wir: Sechs Vorträge des Deutschen Orient-Vereins, Berlin: Oktober 1934 bis Februar 1935*, ed. Deutscher Orient-Verein (Berlin: Walter de Gruyter, 1935), 1–30 (at 3).

power, aspires to the highest achievements, the actualization of faith. If they do not refuse the Führer's call, nor lose heart in the face of the vastness [of the enterprise] and its problematical and obscure aspects, then I cannot be afraid for the sciences that throw light on the life of the oriental peoples. For new forces will take part, and new life will bloom. New laurels will be bestowed on the genius of our people.[58]

The remainder of the lecture was vague and diffuse, jumping from one culture and historical era to the next, and full of the sort of popular stereotypes Weber's pre-1933 colleagues would have found embarrassing ("oriental life" described as sensual, timeless, and irrational, as opposed to the "rational, abstracting, and organizing thought patterns of the Europeans").[59] Weber cheerfully employed racist invocations of the Nordic peoples' long history as culture creators. But more generally what Weber wanted to convey was his conviction that "the history of the millennia is [our] history. Is there any sort of development that is only rooted in the uppermost layer? . . . Everything eternally determines all life. Primeval myths and primeval forces are present in the most recent ones." We can guess the conclusion: "He who wants to write Aryan world history must know ancient Asia, the *ancient Orient*."[60] That is to say, Orientalistik is relevant! Moreover, the Third Reich's history should be *ancient* history—the modern "layer" championed by Walter Frank and his friends was derivative and trivial.

Schaeder's essay took two rather more traditional approaches to establishing relevance: the claim that Europe and Asia Minor shared Hellenistic roots (a familiar argument used during World War I) and the claim that German scholarship laid the foundations for a peaceful and disinterested policy with respect to the emerging nations of Asia. Like his liberal predecessor, C. H. Becker, Schaeder argued that Islam and Christianity shared common roots. Like Becker and other cultural propagandists, he also celebrated the arrival of a postcolonial age in which the Islamic peoples would finally be emancipated from the British, Russian, and French yokes (while treating Armenian and Zionist nationalisms as merely Allied cultural propaganda aimed at breaking up the Ottoman Empire). But the problem for the new Orient was that the more or less unified European ideal had come apart as a result of the Great War.

---

58. Ibid., 4.
59. Ibid., 13.
60. Ibid., 30 (italics original). Weber would later write an even more explicitly pro-Nazi essay for an instructor's manual for the Hitler Youth. See Losemann, "Classics in the Second World War," 326–27.

England no longer championed it, if it ever really had; its aims were only oil and cotton. The Soviet Union was spreading communist propaganda in the Orient for its own, dictatorial ends. The only people who could credibly still represent old European ideals, he strongly implied, were the Germans, who had never, as far as Schaeder intimated, wanted anything but to bring peaceful forms of modernity to the East. To his credit, Schaeder did not advocate direct meddling in politics but rather argued that German scholars continue the tradition they had been taught: "The unrestricted, careful devotion in research and teaching the essence of things oriental and their embeddedness in the course of history, in which we ourselves stand."[61] The scholar was "to remain open to oriental Being, in its alterity as in its deep relationship to us, and to understand in this process of comprehending ourselves as Germans, and to keep ever before our eyes, together with our Germanness, the undying European idea."[62] Characteristically, in these early days of the regime, Schaeder relied on his neoromantic vocabulary and did without heavy-handed political rhetoric.

If Schaeder could invoke reasonably well-known arguments, both Ernst Kühnel and Otto Kümmel felt obliged to open by admitting that the general public knew very little about their subject matter (Islamic and East Asian art, respectively). Comparing the two lectures, it is striking that Kühnel's attempt to establish relevance was far more compromising in terms of the vocabulary and reasoning he deployed—for in the end, Kümmel proved the more active and consequential collaborator. Kühnel invoked racialized histories to frame his discussion of the different forms of Islamic art and saved for last his big defense of Islamic art—that it was *not* Semitic art and indeed exhibited "striking" parallels to Nordic art. According to Kühnel, both Islamic and Nordic art sought to express their artistic imagination in stylized and schematic forms, something that in the era between the eighth and the twelfth centuries led to their joint resistance to the art of the Christian West.[63] The idea was to make Islamic art relevant by claiming it, like Nordic art, had kept itself free from the taint of what fellow pro-Nazi Orientalist art historian Josef Strzygowski called the aristocratic-papist "power art" of the Mediterranean.[64] Kümmel, on the other hand, limited himself to denouncing European ignorance of East Asian art and arguing that it had its own powerful kind of beauty, "as foreign as it may

---

61. Hans Heinrich Schaeder, "Der Neuere Orient," in *Der Orient und Wir*, 31–55 (at 53).
62. Ibid.
63. Ernst Kühnel, "Islamische Kunst," in *Der Orient und Wir*, 56–67 (at 67).
64. Strzygowski, quoted in Marchand, *German Orientalism*, 408. Kühnel cites one of Strzygowski's more racist books in his (very short) bibliography.

seem."⁶⁵ This is a case in which Bollenbeck's caution about reading politics from public pronouncements is well warranted, for Kümmel did not discredit his field by the rhetoric he used to protect it but rather disgraced himself by his actions. As museum director, Kümmel dismissed those unfriendly to the regime and prepared a lengthy list of "German" artwork held in occupied territories that might be "repatriated" by the Wehrmacht or SS. He also saw to the hiding of many of the museums' goods at the war's end.⁶⁶

Like several others, Otto Franke reflected on the unknowability of things—not something his positivist predecessors would have done: "Nothing could teach better than Chinese history that stronger than all human intelligence and will are secret powers, which remain forever hidden from our knowledge, because they are the actualization of the eternal, in which realm no human cleverness can penetrate. Only peoples who have a will to the future can become tools of providence."⁶⁷ But if that was one of Chinese history's Delphic lessons for the Germans, Franke felt he could make a stronger case for German Sinology's utility for the Chinese. One of the major tasks of modern Sinology, Franke averred, was to help China understand and reorient itself among the ruins of its Confucian culture and to place itself into a larger history of nations rather than continue to think of itself as exceptional. Perhaps the Germans more than anyone could understand China's predicament: "Were we not trodden down by despondency, caused by misfortune and shame? Were we not threatened, for a time, with being overcome by dejection and despair? Have we not also pulled ourselves up and put our faith in an 'afterwards'? Precisely from German Sinologists it must be expected that they bring to the mightily struggling people in the East an empathetic understanding."⁶⁸

Heinrich Lüders's major claim for the significance of Indology was that it had won Germany friends in the East. He told the story of having had a mill owner (naturally a Brahman) rush out to shake the hand of a German professor, on the grounds that German scholars had done so much for India.⁶⁹ Thanks especially to the Germans, the Indians could now be proud of their ancient history. Lüders also dragged in some "racial unity" talk, arguing that the writers of the *Rig Veda* were certainly emigrants from the North. He invoked

---

65. Otto Kümmel, "Ostasiatische Kunst," in *Der Orient und Wir*, 114–36 (at 136).
66. *Dictionary of Art Historians*, s.v. "Kümmel, Otto," accessed November 4, 2021, http://www.dictionaryofarthistorians.org/kummelo.html.
67. Otto Franke, "China," in *Der Orient und Wir*, 93–113 (at 112–13).
68. Ibid., 113.
69. Heinrich Lüders, "Indien," in *Der Orient und Wir*, 68–92 (at 71).

relationships between the Aryans and the *Germanen* and separated the higher-thinking Aryans from the recently discovered Indus culture of Harappa and Mohenjodaro. He confirmed that the study of religious thought still lay at the heart of Indology—but emphasized that that was not all there was of the field; political history was important, too. Opening an old Orientalist wound, he admitted that the Mahabharata was no *Iliad*, especially in its current form, in which the core epic was caked over with hundreds of years of non-epic material. Perhaps the original core could be extracted—though he thought this was more likely to be possible for the *Ramayana*. This would be the kind of work to which a nineteenth-century philologist could warm—though Lüders did not say so directly. He did, however, claim that as national consciousness rose in India, Indian scholars were taking over the study of India's cultural history, something of which the Europeans, and especially the anti-imperial Germans, could be proud.[70]

VI. WADING INTO DEEPER WATERS: RELEVANCE-TALK AFTER THE NUREMBERG RACE LAWS

We can see patterns emerging here in the Orientalists' relevance talk: in an age in which neither religion nor history worked to establish relevance, race could be made to work (for some) to cement links between "the Orient" and "us," while others (especially Semitists) might fall back on their usefulness to Nazi propagandists at work in the Near East.[71] We can never really know how well such arguments (as opposed to all sorts of other factors) worked to prevent further decimation of the Orientalists' ranks. They cannot have worked very well, for although some—like Wüst and Kümmel—succeeded in pleasing the state, the period between 1934 and 1937 saw a steady stream of Orientalists leaving the Reich. These included those "racial enemies" who had been spared the application of the Law for the Restoration of the Professional Civil Service because of their war service but who after the passage of the Nuremberg Race Laws in 1935 were compelled to retire, resign, or flee by some other means. By 1936, a new wave of fear—and opportunity seeking—was coursing through the Reich. Interdisciplinary struggles for position resumed and, with them, attacks on old-fashioned positivism and on the irrelevancies of ancient history. As Wolf

---

70. Ibid., 91–92.
71. Naturally, we should not forget that at the same time the classicists were working hard to demonstrate links between *die Antike* and *wir*, Germanists were taking full advantage of the rhetorical turn that favored the study of a racially defined "us."

Meyer-Erlach, rector of the University of Jena, put it in 1936: "The struggle is not yet over. Enough cobwebs are still hanging in the corners and nooks of the universities. There are still instructors and students whose eyes are turned backward, toward eternal yesterday's life. But we know that . . . the future is more potent than the past."[72] Not long afterward, Schaeder, in a eulogy for the Hittitologist Hans Ehelolf confessed that unlike Germanists and classicists, "the Orientalist only exceptionally has to deal with cultural manifestations that touch him as a man of his age and his people, which not only increase his knowledge, but also enrich him as a human being. His work is suited—and the more so, the more seriously he pursues it—to his isolation in the educated community [Bildungsgemeinschaft] in which he lives, to leave him to waste away as an esoteric defender of a form of knowledge not worth knowing. This danger affects more than any other the scholar of the great ancient oriental cultures."[73]

This is the context in which Egyptologist Walter Wolf, Associate Professor at the University of Leipzig and a convinced supporter of the regime, published his response to Berve's 1934 review.[74] It was imperative, Wolf wrote, to defend Egyptology's *Lebensrecht* [right to life] against Berve's frontal attack. Yet the Egyptologist opened his pamphlet with an attack not on Berve but on the just-deceased disciplinary doyen Adolf Erman, from whom the Nazis had been mean-spirited enough to take away a teaching certificate in 1936, thanks to his status as a mixed-race person. Wolf called the great Erman a "late son of the Enlightenment" and accused him of having ruined Egyptology's chances to embrace a deeper understanding of the organic unity of Egyptian culture by concentrating on details and refusing to acknowledge the irrational side of Egyptian culture. Erman's huge academic and popular impact had prevented the creation of a more vital, Nietzschean relationship between past and present. It was surely possible, Wolf argued, to develop a deeper and less life-killing approach to Egyptian culture, a culture that possessed a racially pure *Volkstum* [community] for a time—though this was lost by the time of the New Kingdom. The Leipzig professor denied Berve's claim that Egyptology could

---

72. Quoted in Weinreich, *Hitler's Professors*, 19. For more on Meyer-Erlach, see Susannah Heschel, "For 'Volk, Blood, and God': The Theological Faculty at the University of Jena during the Third Reich," in Bialas and Rabinbach, *Nazi Germany and the Humanities*, 365–98 (at 368–69). See also Levinson's contribution to this volume, "Gerhard von Rad's Struggle against the Nazification of the Old Testament."

73. Hans Heinrich Schaeder, "Hans Ehelolf," *Zeitschrift der Deutschen Morgenländischen Gesellschaft* 94 (1940): 1–11 (at 3).

74. Georg Steindorff would characterize him as a "terrible Nazi." See Raulwing and Gertzen, "Freiherr von Bissing," 92.

only belong to the age of value-free science. One could use new methods and intuition to fill in gaps in knowledge and thus understand the soul of this foreign culture. He also objected to Berve's statement that studying foreign races was pointless because Germans could not understand them; this would mean closing off too many fields of study. Finally, Wolf resorted to the relativist claim (citing here Jacob Burckhardt and Ernst Troeltsch) that there was no correct, objective method of history writing. All methods were shaped by the author's *Weltanschauung* [worldview]. But, Wolf said, it behooved contemporary Egyptologists to give up positivism: the way of the future was to abandon *Kleinarbeit* [trivial academic inquiries] and instead seek to establish relationships between the ancient past and the present world.[75]

Interestingly, Wolf's answer to Berve provoked its own response: a long essay in the *ZDMG* by the Halle Egyptologist Rudolf Anthes, who agreed that the "essence and worth of Egyptology" had now become a burning question: "Our era in particular, which ... now calls every previously valid norm into question, demands a clear answer even in this small area before it is negated, reordered, or recognized. Thus, we Germans today pose this question from a common platform: can Egyptology provide even a modest contribution to building our national, cultural life, and if so, what is its significance?"[76] To the same question, however, Anthes gave different answers. He defended his departures from Wolf on the grounds that he represented an older generation (in fact he was only four years older). Once upon a time this might have been a trump card; on the other hand, it was now something of an act of modesty. Indeed, Anthes's tone was quite friendly, and the ways in which he defended the methods of the older generation showed that he was already making compromises. Anthes, for example, defended Erman—but did so by denying that he was a "positivist" and confirming that he appreciated the irrational side of Egyptian culture. He took Wolf to task for failing to appreciate the foundational work of the tradition from which he came and insisted that Kleinarbeit needed to continue. But he insisted that specialist work could not be defended if it only created more "bloodless images" of the past.[77]

---

75. Walter Wolf, *Wesen und Wert der Ägyptologie*, Leipziger ägyptologische Studien 8 (Glückstadt: J. J. Augustin, 1937).

76. Rudolf Anthes, "Zu Walther Wolf's 'Wesen und Wert der Ägyptologie,'" *Zeitschrift der Deutschen Morgenländischen Gesellschaft* 92 (1938): 421–40 (at 422). These works are also discussed by Sergei Stadnikow in "Bedeutung des Alten Orients für deutsches Denken: Skizzen aus dem Zeitraum 1871–1945," *Propylaeum: Fachinformationsdienst Altertumswissenschaften* (2007), 23 pp., doi: 10.11588/propylaeumdok.00000040, 11–14.

77. Anthes, "Walther Wolf," 438–39.

Anthes accepted some aspects of Wolf's Spenglerian approach to cultures as closed circles—and confirmed that Egyptologists should engage in "mutual exchange" with *Rassenforschung* [racial science] to answer "fundamental racial questions."[78] He objected, mildly, to Wolf's throwing into one pot (and attempting to throw away) Augustine's worldview, German idealism, positivism, and evolutionary theory and argued that Egypt had not been an isolated entity but an organism that, like German culture, possessed a racial profile, cultivated an *Heimatskultur* [organic identity], and belonged to a greater *Kulturgemeinschaft* [cultural community]. In a final paragraph, he insisted that research should not be driven by the desire either to bury oneself with the Egyptians or to have a broad impact on our folk, but should be generated by simple curiosity and should foreground "the accuracy [*Sauberkeit*] of work." But Anthes did not claim—as had so many of the pre-Nazi generation—that Egyptian culture had influenced Greek and European culture or that it actually had some sort of relationship to German "being"; he was just trying to lay down some principles for what he called "the responsibility-conscious struggle for the meaning of the task."[79] In 1939, Anthes was prevented from returning to the classroom—though he did survive the war to become Professor at the University of Berlin, from which he moved to the University of Pennsylvania in 1950.

VII. ORIENTALISTIK AND THE SECOND WORLD WAR

Once the war began, a new round of utility questioning began. Now the sciences needed to show not only their relevance to the folk but also their *Kriegswichtigkeit,* or importance for the war effort. This applied in particular to the scholars employed by the Ahnenerbe and the other Nazi organizations, who were dependent on what we would today describe as "soft" money from the Reich itself, as opposed to university budgets, though of course those too had been slashed and would be further reduced as student numbers plummeted during the war. In the course of a total war, scholars had to fight hard for funding, and for the right to be excused from duty at the front—or the right to use precious cash for cultural purposes. Even more clearly, now, the natural sciences could defend their relevance, but the humanities? Of course one could do this, if one were a very energetic collaborator, by offering to "secure" treasures or archives abroad, volunteering to help write or broadcast propaganda in Asian

---

78. Ibid., 434.
79. Ibid., 440.

languages, or, worst of all, working for one of the many outfits pursuing the Jewish Question.[80]

But most humanists were either too old, or too deeply invested in irrelevant subjects, to take such steps. Some, surely, were happy when in early 1940 law professor and University of Kiel rector Paul Ritterbusch began agitating for the humanities to mount a campaign demonstrating that they were "crucial to the war effort." Ritterbusch's campaign became a Reich-wide crusade by 1941, when he was taken on as the department head for scholarship in the Ministry for Scholarship, Pedagogy, and Public Education.[81] Ritterbusch's point of departure was his fear that in wartime, it would be generally assumed that only the natural sciences were relevant and necessary. On the contrary, he argued, every discipline could find a way to contribute to winning the war, even if simply by offering "intellectual [*geistig*] opposition to the ideas and values of the enemy."[82] As Michael Kater notes laconically: "One would not be wrong to think that these sorts of phrases were warmly greeted by the universities and academies, for they offered a welcome pretext for all humanistic organizations in the Reich to endure, at least to a certain extent."[83] Using Ritterbusch's rhetorical device of *der Kriegseinsatz der Geisteswissenschaften* [the War Deployment of the Humanities], one could justify continuing to study almost anything—though of course it was much easier to get funding to study Germanic archaeology or folklore or racial medicine. Frank-Rutger Hausmann estimates that at least five hundred scholars collaborated with the operation that became known as Aktion Ritterbusch, about half of them academics who had received their professorships since 1933.[84] Oriental philology joined the list of disciplines participating in 1942, when Wüst—surely with the approval of his SS boss, Himmler—agreed to lend a hand.[85] A conference was scheduled and came off in early October 1942. Several important Orientalists offered lectures, which we examine more closely in the paragraphs that follow. Eleven subdepartments of Orientalist Aktion were organized and heads appointed who were, for the most part, active friends of the regime (such as Hermann Grapow for Egyptology, Erich Frauwallner for Indology, and Hans Heinrich

---

80. See Michael Kater, *Das "Ahnenerbe" der SS, 1935–1945: Ein Beitrag zur Kulturpolitik des Dritten Reiches*, 4th ed., Studien zur Zeitgeschichte 6 (Munich: Oldenbourg, 2009), 191–211.

81. For further study of Ritterbusch's campaign, see Thomas Schneider's contribution to this volume.

82. Quoted in Kater, *Ahnenerbe*, 193.

83. Ibid.

84. Hausmann, *Deutsche Geisteswissenschaft*, 20, 22.

85. Ibid., 212.

Schaeder for Indo-German-Iranian matters).[86] Quite suddenly Japan—by this time fighting on the German side—was prominently mentioned.

Both Haussmann and Hanisch have noted that the essays in the conference proceedings, some published under the title *The Orient in German Scholarship* (1944) and others under the title *Essays on Arabic, Semitic, and Islamic Studies* (also 1944), were not all suffused with Nazi terminology or reflective of the Third Reich's worldview. Hanisch argues that the conference showed that neither the division of the discipline into culture-historical and philologically oriented branches nor the continuing specialization of the field was halted by the coming of National Socialism.[87] Haussmann calls attention to the fact that most of the participants in the conference were members of the generation born about 1880 and thus almost a generation older than representatives of other disciplines. Perhaps, he suggests, this accounts for the fact that the discipline's members were less outwardly enthusiastic about the Nazi Zeitgeist than those who owed their careers to National Socialism.[88] This might be right, but there are also a number of other interesting things to observe in these essays.

Ritterbusch's opening address tackled the problem head-on: was not this whole conference, he asked, another example "of the overvaluing of [classical and Eastern] antiquity over against our own prehistory, which has had to fight so long for recognition"? Does not investment in Orientalistik conflict with the need for our own history to be taught in schools and represented by academic chairs? These and other questions can be asked, Ritterbusch noted, and it was up to the participants in the conference to "represent and defend" their tradition and to prove its "nearness to the present and its immediate relatedness to reality." Like *Anglistik* [the study of English language, literature, and culture] and *Romanistik* [the study of Romance languages, literatures, and cultures], Orientalistik was more and more leaving behind its antiquarian focus on linguistics and moving toward the study of "political-historical" realities—such as current developments in Egypt, Arabia, Turkey, and India. Orientalistik actually had a great portion of the political world to cover, and nowadays "only the superficial observer could view it as knowledge not worth knowing, whose practical worth was virtually nothing." Japan was an ally, for example, in Germany's fight with the British Empire in India and elsewhere in the East. Ritterbusch repeatedly returned to the problem that most German Orientalists dealt with the past, usually the deep past. He emphasized the

---

86. Ibid., 214n301.
87. Hanisch, *Nachfolger*, 223.
88. Hausmann, *Deutsche Geisteswissenschaft*, 217.

need for enhancing modern studies and argued that past and present simply had to be more clearly linked. In a much more aggressive way, he made the point Lüders had made in 1934: "In the Orient itself today, the study of long-past cultures is often enough an important bridge to the understanding of the present. The study of things historical has often enough demonstrated a strong link to the present and has delivered to us, in particular, a form of solidarity with the men of the Orient that is based on the image of their own historical grandeur rather than on political interests. Understanding of the past and present culture of the Orient has become the most powerful kind of intellectual propaganda in the Orient." Ritterbusch called on the Orientalists to use this propaganda, for the sake of the folk, the Führer, and "the historical mission of the Reich."[89]

Schaeder's essay, which directly followed Ritterbusch's call for more mobilization, indeed volunteered more engagement for Orientalists than before. Schaeder's title was "Asia and the Eastern Borders of European History," and its main thrust was to include the Near and Middle East into European history while expelling the ever-barbaric and "Asiatic" Russians. Schaeder complimented nineteenth-century Indo-European studies for dissolving, from one direction, a narrowly conceived "Mediterranean-Western" view of history; cuneiform studies, he argued, had destroyed this "self-narrowing" from another direction and shown us that bridges between the West and the Near East were primeval ones, which had only superficially been closed by the coming of Islam. The Greek battle for freedom from the Persians described in Herodotus, he claimed, must not obscure our understanding that in reality, this was a fight between *Brüdervölker* [brothers], not between strangers. Schaeder denounced directly the British Empire's colonial and postcolonial "rape" [*Vergewaltigung*] of the Orient and the "everlasting threat" Russia had posed for the last 1,600 years "to Europe, to Western culture, and to the men it has created. Who was and is called," Schaeder asked, "to protect European culture against the East?" Naturally, his answer was the Indo-Europeans of the past and the Germans of the present. Their greatest achievement in the past was "the task of settling and colonizing the German East. [The field's] whole significance is only clear in light of the deep background of the Asiatic threat to Europe, which in our days, greater and more terrifying than ever, has raised itself again and must be

---

89. Paul Ritterbusch, "Eröffnungsansprache," in *Der Orient in deutscher Forschung: Vorträge der Berliner Orientalistentagung, Herbst 1942*, ed. Hans Heinrich Schaeder, Deutsche Orientforschung (Leipzig, Germany: Otto Harrassowitz, 1944), 1–5 (the page range provided here covers all quotations in this paragraph).

vanquished, if Germany and Europe are to endure."[90] Now fully "mobilized," Schaeder apparently published versions of this essay in a Swedish journal and in the Hitler Youth journal *Wille und Macht*.[91]

The essay collection devoted to Semitistik was rather more muted in its attempts to demonstrate its "war significance." Carl Brockelmann's "Status and Tasks of Semitic Studies" was a rather old-fashioned defense of the field, though we can note some departures. Brockelmann left out the field's deep debts to theology, substituting instead debts to classical and Indo-European linguistics. This discipline, he argued, had experienced a great upswing when it moved on from the study of dead languages and "incorporated the fresh life-pulse of their successors thriving everywhere in Europe into its realm of research, and developed the laws of discursive life from them."[92] The Semitists too had acquired rich material from the still-living Arabic, Aramaic, and Abyssinian dialect-speakers in the latter half of the nineteenth century, Brockelmann said, but should have taken modern languages and cultures more seriously. This comment may seem unexceptional to us, but in the history of the discipline, it was quite unusual for scholars of ancient languages to suggest they had learned things from living speakers. But Brockelmann also invoked some themes calculated to please racist audiences. He reiterated the old saws that Semitic languages are inflexible and unpoetic, that the Semites created few aesthetically valuable or long-lasting monuments (explaining why scholars had to study their languages almost exclusively), and that Indo-European influence had been decisive in creating cultural flowering in the ancient world. He suggested—along lines pioneered long ago by Ernest Renan and elaborated by other racist theologians—that a Galilean/Hellenistic culture had shaped Jesus and the early Christians more than Jewish Near Eastern traditions.[93] Departing radically from his usual positivistic focus on linguistic matters, Brockelmann instead offered here a brief discussion of how the Egyptians, like the Jews and Phoenicians, differed from other members of the Oriental race, such as the Arabs, "especially in the form of the back of the head and the nose."[94] Perhaps

---

90. Hans Heinrich Schaeder, "Asien und die Ostgrenze der europäische Kultur," in *Der Orient in deutscher Forschung*, 6–17; for quotations, see pp. 8, 9, 16, 17.

91. Ibid., 17.

92. Carl Brockelmann, "Stand und Aufgaben der Semitistik," in *Beiträge zur Arabistik, Semitistik, und Islamwissenschaft*, ed. Richard Hartmann and Helmuth Scheel, Deutsche Orientforschung (Leipzig: Otto Harrassowitz, 1944), 3–41 (at 7).

93. On this tradition, see Susannah Heschel, *The Aryan Jesus: Christian Theologians and the Bible in Nazi Germany* (Princeton, NJ: Princeton University Press, 2008).

94. Brockelmann, "Stand und Aufgaben der Semitistik," 15.

the most revolting aspect of the essay was that it did not breathe a word about Jewish persecution or suffering while ending with a plea for the saving of the Nestorian Syrians (who spoke a unique form of Aramaic dialect) from "dying out" at the same time as the murder of the Jews was in full swing.[95] Brockelmann may well not have known this, but he could not have been ignorant of the large number of ethnic Jews trained in his subspecialty who had been driven out or persecuted grievously by the regime.

Following Brockelmann's essay were several more on the history of German Orientforschung, which largely stuck to the history of the discipline as a means to show its contributions to Germany's scholarly prestige. There followed, unsurprisingly, a section devoted to essays on ancient history, on the Islamic middle ages, and one entitled "Toward a History of the Present." What is striking is that of these three sections, the one on the ancient Orient was the shortest—only two essays—and that on the "history of the present" was the longest—five essays. All five of those were written by somewhat younger scholars than Brockelmann, who was seventy-four in 1942 (Walther Braune, b. 1900; Richard Hartmann, b. 1881; Franz Taeschner, b. 1888; and Gotthard Jäschke, b. 1894, who contributed two essays). All of the essays made the case for the relevance of the discipline in a particular way: by emphasizing the contribution of German scholarship to nationalist consciousness raising in the Orient. The essays demonstrated a detailed knowledge of the East's modern "players," and a series of astute, if self-serving, assessments of the demise of European colonial power and the mixed legacy of Islam. The emergence of new forms of nationalism in the Islamic world, as Walther Braune claimed, was not just a political development but represented:

> the coming into being of a new way of life, a new form of thought, a new will to create. No one can say what the already noteworthy Egyptian literature of today will mean for Asia Minor in twenty years' time, what the religious activism of the Azhar University will mean for the people of Africa, or what economic cooperation of the Arab peoples will mean for the economic order of the Old World. But it is certain that in this pivotal point between Europe, Asia, and Africa a new field of power is rising, a field of power that perhaps does not interest or cannot interest us, but which will profoundly confront us as a new factor of life.[96]

---

95. Ibid., 41.
96. Walther Braune, "Die Entwicklung des Nationalismus bei den Arabern," in Hartmann and Scheel, *Beiträge zur Arabistik*, 425–38 (at 438).

We do not know, at the moment, how many of these writers compromised themselves in other ways; as Herf has shown, there were numerous Arabic-speaking announcers and writers who helped broadcast violently antisemitic and anti-British propaganda to the Arab world during the Second World War, and we know also of several Orientalists who intrigued in Iran, Turkey, India, and elsewhere in the hopes of securing the support of these regimes for the Axis powers.[97] We can certainly conclude, however, that the regime was willing to employ directly those who really could show their relevance and utility—and in the case of many of them, it was better that they *not* advertise what they were doing for the war effort.

VIII. RETREAT FROM RELEVANCE: ORIENTALISTIK AFTER 1945

In retrospect, *not* speaking too much about one's utility during the Nazi era was the way to ensure a safe landing in the postwar era. As is well known, many heavily compromised scholars in a variety of subjects did return to the universities, sometimes after a brief suspension from their posts. In Orientalistik, the situation was no different. Very few people—all party members—were actually fired. Wüst and the very committed Egyptologist Hermann Grapow are exceptional in this regard; even Erich Frauwallner got his job at the University of Vienna back in 1951. In the immediate postwar era, the discipline seems to have reverted to high positivism, in part to return to its strengths and in part to mask its contributions to the regime. Most fields returned to the study of the deep past and of languages rather than of cultural history. Even Wüst tried this tactic. After about three years of internment, during which he repeatedly insisted that the Ahnenerbe had been a purely scholarly organization, Wüst escaped prosecution for war crimes and went back to work on his never-finished dictionary of Old Indo-Aryan.[98]

When discussion about the need to fully denazify the disciplines began in the later 1960s, the focus was on the "us" disciplines—Germanic prehistory, Germanic folklore, Indo-European philology—and of course on the discourse of race. It is only recently that spotlights have been turned on the work of the Semitists as well. Moreover, only recently have German scholars really begun to study the modern Near and Middle East and modern South and East Asia

---

97. E.g., Fritz Grobba, Max Freiherr von Oppenheim, Otto Hentig, Curt Prüfer. See Herf, *Nazi Propaganda*, and Marchand, *German Orientalism*, 487–95.

98. Pringle, *Master Plan*, 314.

in a culture-historical way. From our perspective, it appears that the Nazi era, which forbade social scientific forms of universalism and insisted on turning history into a neoromantic quest for racial origins, perverted and delayed the modernization of its once pace-setting tradition of Orientforschung. In the attempt to defend their subspecialties, scholars turned away from the more interdisciplinary and innovative methods pioneered in the Weimar era and failed to save the careers and sometimes the lives of their former colleagues in favor of claiming special and spurious links between "the Orient" and "us." Those who sought publicly and privately to make the discipline into something relevant or useful for Nazi purposes can be held responsible for that consequence as well as for the other crimes, of varying significance, to which their efforts contributed.

Of course, demands for relevance in the 1930s were not limited to Germany, nor are we without them today. Indeed, there was another major response to Helmut Berve's challenge, this one delivered by the great American Semitist William Foxwell Albright, in the form of his presidential address to the American Oriental Society in 1936. Provoked by Berve, and by the forced emigration of so many of his German Jewish colleagues, Albright entitled his lecture: "How Well Can We Know the Ancient Near East?" Albright's lecture was also a response to the shrinking of funds for research during the Depression and the forking over of so much of the money to the natural sciences rather than the humanities. I want to close by showing how Albright's efforts at relevance differed so greatly from those being made by his collaborationist colleagues in Germany—and perhaps have rather more "utility" for those of us humanists (and especially champions of the study of the ancient world) who find ourselves in similarly worrying conditions today.

IX. AN ALTERNATIVE RESPONSE TO THE PROBLEM OF ORIENTAL STUDIES' RELEVANCE: WILLIAM FOXWELL ALBRIGHT

Albright's lecture opened by posing the problem directly:

> The study of the ancient Near East stands on the frontier of humanistic research, since it is perhaps the most difficult branch of learning to justify on obvious utilitarian grounds. Not only does it belong to a remote and now relatively unimportant part of the earth, but it appertains to a time which has been called 'the past past' in the jargon of a certain group of thinkers.[99]

---

99. Albright, "How Well Can We Know," 121.

Albright noted that the field had been so prominent in Germany before 1933 that it had become a target for other disciplines—by which Albright surely meant Berve's classicists. Referring explicitly to interdisciplinary and/or inter-organizational struggles for funding, Albright noted that the United States had profited from Germany's losses, and the field had begun to flourish. But in America too, "We are always surrounded by real or potential foes who think that they can use our modest income to balance some tiny deficit in their budgets."[100] Albright then introduced Berve's attack, arguing that it was "a symptom of a widespread attitude in Germany."[101] He dismissed Berve's racial theory as unappealing to "Anglo-Saxons" (!), especially Americans. Still, Berve's comments "made it necessary for the Orientalist who would be an impartial thinker to take stock and to justify his labor to himself, as well as to others."[102]

This "taking stock" proceeded first by surveying progress made in the field, secondly by comparing ancient Oriental studies with others, thirdly by defending the utility of the field, and finally by contrasting "the nihilism of a Berve with the buoyant optimism of a [James Henry] Breasted."[103] For our purposes, it is Albright's attempt to deal with the problem of the utility of the field that is of most interest—though it is rather amusing to note that he defends the Orientalists' failure to adopt the "interpretive" methods of the classicists on the ground that adopting subjective interpretive methods would simply lead to cluttering the field with "unfounded hypotheses."[104] Albright objected strenuously to Treitschke's dictum (quoted, as we saw above, by Berve) that one can only know what he loves, and denounced as illogical Berve's "romantic" attempt to make the Egyptian landscape "foreign": to Albright—having spent twelve years in Chile and the better part of the last sixteen years in Palestine—the non-West was far more like "home" than was eastern Germany. Albright then questioned how well any biographer could know the "essence" of his subject, or any person could really understand himself; historians could not fully understand any culture. "The more we love it, in fact, the more prejudiced we become and the less able to see it in

---

100. Ibid.
101. Ibid., 122.
102. Ibid., 123.
103. Ibid. James Henry Breasted was America's first great Egyptologist and founder of Chicago's Oriental Institute. See now Jeffrey Abt, *American Egyptologist: The Life of James Henry Breasted and the Creation of His Oriental Institute* (Chicago: University of Chicago Press, 2011).
104. Albright, "How Well Can We Know," 134.

proper perspective.... Treitschke's dictum ... is thus in part directly opposed to the facts."[105]

Albright then tackled Berve's discussion of the utility of ancient Near Eastern knowledge:

> Knowledge is not only useless, we can not even obtain full possession of it unless it can somehow be made serviceable, unless it proves fruitful. This certainly does not mean that knowledge must be exposed for sale in the marketplace at the earliest opportunity; it does not mean that Egyptian medicine may supplant modern practices, nor that a knowledge of Assyrian may mysteriously bring its possessor nearer to the fountain-head of theosophic wisdom. In other words, it does not mean that knowledge should be utilitarian in the short-sighted meaning which this term generally has. But racist romanticism and instrumental pragmatism agree that knowledge must somehow be made useful if it is worth cultivation, and even if it merits the designation "knowledge." Our final task will thus be to point out some ways in which our knowledge of the Ancient Orient can be useful.[106]

Albright then proceeded to make *his* case for utility, based chiefly on the field's utility for understanding human and Western history, the history of material culture and of religious institutions "which preceded and partly inspired our own."[107] The study of the ancient Near East had benefited sociology, anthropology, and the study of law; it had also inspired and contributed to geography, geology, zoology, and paleontology. It provided a sobering lesson for modern scientific culture that rational thinking could indeed be swamped by irrational ideas and science snuffed out for generations—something Albright suggested might be happening in an astrology-mad West.

Albright ended on a note that sounds remarkably modern. The United States, he argued, had been pouring money recently into the natural and social sciences, and the humanities had not fared so well:

> In part this latent hostility to the humanities is the outcome of a feeling that research in fields relating to the past history and achievements of man is useless, especially in a new land with its history before it. It arises partly also from the short-sighted conviction that only research which yields immediate results in the form of mechanical inventions and technical processes is worth while.[108]

---

105. Ibid., 136.
106. Ibid., 137–38.
107. Ibid., 138.
108. Ibid., 143.

But it also arose, Albright explained, from the century-long bitter campaign for school reform fought by the natural scientists against the dominance of Greek and Latin languages in higher education. "This battle has long since been won, but the natural scientists have inherited from their predecessors a hostility to the very word 'humanities' which by 1920 had brought humanistic research to a singularly low level in American intellectual life."[109] That things had improved was due to the efforts especially of Breasted, who fifteen years earlier had prophesied that studies of the ancient Orient were likely to revolutionize historical thinking in a way that could only be compared to the revival of the classics in the Renaissance.[110] Albright's subtle, but evident, conclusion was that individual scholars *could* make a difference by believing in their field's prospects to work on the culture at a distance. The best one could do was to work not toward a Führer or seek immediately "useful" results but seek a Renaissance that (and here I am interpolating) would not be forced down from above—like the racist one Wüst championed—but would spread surely more slowly. If this Renaissance caught hold, it would come about gradually, without compromising the demands of scholarship, those of democracy, or those of human dignity, from scholar to scholar and student to student. Perhaps that is a model from which we too can learn some lessons about the right way to seek relevance for the humanities.

BIBLIOGRAPHY

Archival Sources

BGStPK 1. HA 76 Vc Berlin (Dahlem), Geheimes Staatsarchiv, Preußischer Kulturbesitz, Hauptarchiv. Papers of the Reichsministerium für Wissenschaft, Erziehung, und Volksbildung.

BSB, Nachlass Andrae, Berlin Staatsbibliothek, Handschriftsabteilung, Papers of Walter Andrae.

Secondary Sources

Abt, Jeffrey. *American Egyptologist: The Life of James Henry Breasted and the Creation of His Oriental Institute.* Chicago: University of Chicago Press, 2011.

Albright, William F. "How Well Can We Know the Ancient Near East?" *Journal of the American Oriental Society* 56, no. 2 (1936): 121–44.

---

109. Ibid.
110. Ibid., 144.

Andrae, Walter. *Die deutschen Ausgrabungen in Warka (Uruk)*. Deutsche Forschung aus der Arbeit der Deutschen Forschungsgesmeinschaft 25. Berlin: Karl Siegismund, 1935.

Anoonshahr, Ali. "Franz Babinger and the Legacy of the 'German Counter-Revolution' in Early Modern Iranian Historiography." In *Rethinking Iranian Nationalism and Modernity*, edited by Kamran Scot Aghaie and Afshin Marashi, 25–48. Austin: University of Texas Press, 2014.

Anthes, Rudolf. "Zu Walther Wolf's 'Wesen und Wert der Ägyptologie.'" *Zeitschrift der Deutschen Morgenländischen Gesellschaft* 92 (1938): 421–40.

Arnold, Bill T., and David B. Weisberg. "A Centennial Review of Friedrich Delitzsch's 'Babel und Bibel' Lectures." *Journal of Biblical Literature* 121, no. 3 (2002): 441–57.

Arvidsson, Stefan. *Aryan Idols: Indo-European Mythology as Ideology and Science*. Translated by Sonia Wichman. Chicago: University of Chicago Press, 2006.

Bambach, Charles. *Heidegger's Roots: Nietzsche, National Socialism, and the Greeks*. Ithaca, NY: Cornell University Press, 2005.

Berve, Helmut. "Zur Kulturgeschichte des alten Orients." *Archiv für Kulturgeschichte* 25 (1934): 216–30.

Bialas, Wolfgang, and Anson Rabinbach, eds. *Nazi Germany and the Humanities: How German Academics Embraced Nazism*. Oxford: Oneworld, 2014. Originally published 2006.

Bollenbeck, Georg. "The Humanities in Germany after 1933: Semantic Transformations and the Nazification of the Disciplines." In Bialas and Rabinbach, *Nazi Germany and the Humanities*, 1–20.

Bollmus, Reinhard. *Das Amt Rosenberg und seine Gegner: Studien zum Machtkampf im nationalsozialistischen Herrschaftssystem*. 2nd ed. Studien zur Zeitgeschichte 1. Munich: R. Oldenbourg, 2006.

Braune, Walther. "Die Entwicklung des Nationalismus bei den Arabern." In Hartmann and Scheel, *Beiträge zur Arabistik, Semitistik, und Islamwissenschaft*, 425–38.

Brockelmann, Carl. "Stand und Aufgaben der Semitistik." In Hartmann and Scheel, *Beiträge zur Arabistik, Semitistik, und Islamwissenschaft*, 3–41.

Burleigh, Michael. *Germany Turns Eastwards: A Study of Ostforschung in the Third Reich*. Cambridge: Cambridge University Press, 1988.

Delitzsch, Friedrich. *Die Welt des Islam. Männer und Völker*, vol. 2. Berlin: Ullstein, 1915.

"Der IX. Deutsche Orientalistentag: Bonn 1938." *Zeitschrift der Deutschen Morgenländischen Gesellschaft* 92 (1938): 3–38.

Deutscher Orient-Verein, ed. *Der Orient und Wir: Sechs Vorträge des Deutschen Orient-Vereins, Berlin: Oktober 1934 bis Februar 1935*. Berlin: Walter de Gruyter, 1935.

Dictionary of Art Historians. Edited by Lee Sorensen. https://arthistorians.info/.

Dietz, Burkhard. "Die interdisziplinäre 'Westforschung' der Weimar Republik und der NS-Zeit als Gegenstand der Wissenschafts- und Zeitgeschichte: Überlegungen zu Forschungsstand und Forschungsperspektiven." *Geschichte im Westen* 14, no. 2 (1999): 189–209.

Elvert, Jürgen, and Jürgen Niels-Sikora, eds. *Kulturwissenschaften und Nationalsozialismus*. Historische Mitteilungen 72. Stuttgart, Germany: Franz Steiner, 2008.

Ericksen, Robert P. *Theologians under Hitler: Gerhard Kittel, Paul Althaus, and Emanuel Hirsch*. New Haven, CT: Yale University Press, 1985.

Fichtner, Paula Sutter. *Terror and Toleration: The Habsburg Empire Confronts Islam, 1526–1850*. London: Reaktion, 2008.

Franke, Otto. "China." In Deutscher Orient-Verein, *Der Orient und Wir*, 93–113.

———. *Erinnerungen aus Zwei Welten: Randglossen zur eigenen Lebensgeschichte*. Berlin: Walter de Gruyter, 1954.

Grimm, Gerhard. "Franz Babinger (1891–1967): Ein Lebensgeschichtlicher Essay." *Die Welt des Islams* 38, no. 3 (1998): 286–333.

Hagen, Gottfried. "German Heralds of Holy War." *Comparative Studies of South Asia, Africa, and the Middle East* 24, no. 2 (2004): 145–62.

Hanisch, Ludmila. "Akzentverschiebung—Zur Geschichte der Semitistik und Islamwissenschaft während des 'Dritten Reichs.'" *Berichte zur Wissenschaftsgeschichte* 18, no. 4 (1995): 217–26.

———. "Arabistik, Semitistik, und Islamwissenschaft." In Elvert and Niels-Sikora, *Kulturwissenschaften und Nationalsozialismus*, 503–25.

———. *Die Nachfolger der Exegeten: Deutschsprachige Erforschung des Vorderen Orients in der ersten Hälfte des 20. Jahrhunderts*. Wiesbaden, Germany: Harrassowitz, 2003.

Hartmann, Richard, and Helmuth Scheel, eds. *Beiträge zur Arabistik, Semitistik, und Islamwissenschaft*. Deutsche Orientforschung. Leipzig, Germany: Otto Harrassowitz, 1944.

Hausmann, Frank-Rutger. *"Deutsche Geisteswissenschaft" im Zweiten Weltkrieg: Die "Aktion Ritterbusch" (1940–1945)*. Dresden, Germany: Dresden University Press, 1998.

Heiber, Helmut. *Walter Frank und sein Reichsinstitut für Geschichte des neuen Deutschlands*. Stuttgart, Germany: Deutsche Verlags-Anstalt, 1966.

Herf, Jeffrey. *Nazi Propaganda for the Arab World*. New Haven, CT: Yale University Press, 2010.

Heschel, Susannah. *The Aryan Jesus: Christian Theologians and the Bible in Nazi Germany*. Princeton, NJ: Princeton University Press, 2008.

———. "For 'Volk, Blood, and God': The Theological Faculty at the University of Jena during the Third Reich." In Bialas and Rabinbach, *Nazi Germany and the Humanities*, 365–98.

Kahle, Marie and Paul Kahle. *Was hätten Sie getan? / Die Universität Bonn vor und während der Nazi-Zeit (1923–1939): Die Flucht der Familie Kahle aus Nazi-Deutschland*. Edited by John H. Kahle and Wilhelm Bleek. Bonn, Germany: Bouvier, 1998.

Kater, Michael. *Das "Ahnenerbe" der SS, 1935–1945: Ein Beitrag zur Kulturpolitik des Dritten Reiches*. 4th ed. Studien zur Zeitgeschichte 6. Munich: Oldenbourg, 2006.

Kern, Martin. "The Emigration of German Sinologists, 1933–1945: Notes on the History and Historiography of Chinese Studies." *Journal of the American Oriental Society* 118, no. 4 (1998): 507–29.

Kittel, Gerhard. *Die Judenfrage*. 2nd ed. Stuttgart, Germany: Kohlhammer, 1933.

Kühnel, Ernst. "Islamische Kunst." In Deutscher Orient-Verein, *Der Orient und Wir*, 56–67.

Kümmel, Otto. "Ostasiatische Kunst." In Deutscher Orient-Verein, *Der Orient und Wir*, 114–36.

Kurlander, Eric. "The Orientalist Roots of National Socialism? Nazism, Occultism, and South Asian Spirituality, 1919–1945." In *Transcultural Encounters between Germany and India: Kindred Spirits in the Nineteenth and Twentieth Centuries*, edited by Joanne Miyang Cho, Eric Kurlander, and Douglas T. McGetchin, 155–69. Routledge Studies in the Modern History of Asia 90. London: Routledge 2014.

Longerich, Peter. *Heinrich Himmler*. Translated by Jeremy Noakes and Lesley Sharpe. Oxford: Oxford University Press, 2012.

Losemann, Volker. "Classics in the Second World War." In Bialas and Rabinbach, *Nazi Germany and the Humanities*, 313–35.

Lüders, Heinrich. "Indien." In Deutscher Orient-Verein, *Der Orient und Wir*, 68–92.

Marchand, Suzanne L. "Dating Zarathustra: Oriental Texts and the Problem of Persian Prehistory, 1700–1900." *Erudition and the Republic of Letters* 1 (2016): 203–45.

———. *Down from Olympus: Archaeology and Philhellenism in Germany, 1750–1970*. Princeton, NJ: Princeton University Press, 1996.

———. "Eastern Wisdom in an Era of Western Despair: Orientalism in 1920s Central Europe." In *Weimar Thought: A Contested Legacy*, edited by Peter E. Gordon and John P. McCormick, 341–60. Princeton, NJ: Princeton University Press, 2013.

———. "From Liberalism to Neoromanticism: Albrecht Dieterich, Richard Reitzenstein, and the Religious Turn in Fin de Siècle German Classical Studies." In *Out of Arcadia: Classics and Politics in Germany in the Age of Burckhardt, Nietzsche, and Wilamowitz*, edited by Martin Ruehl and Ingo Gildenhard, 129–60. Bulletin of the Institute of Classical Studies Supplement 79. London:

Institute of Classical Studies, School of Advanced Study, University of London, 2003.

———. *German Orientalism in the Age of Empire: Religion, Race, and Scholarship.* Publications of the German Historical Institute. New York: Cambridge University Press, 2009.

———. "Nazism, 'Orientalism,' and Humanism." In Bialas and Rabinbach, *Nazi Germany and the Humanities,* 267–305.

Meyer, Eduard. *England: Seine staatliche und politische Entwicklung und der Krieg gegen Deutschland.* Berlin: J. G. Cotta, 1915.

Mode, Markus. "Altertumswissenschaft und Altertumswissenschaftler unter dem NS-Regime." In *Wissenschaft unter dem NS-Regime,* edited by Burchard Brentjes and Günter Albrecht, 156–69. Berlin: Peter Lang, 1992.

Motadel, David. *Islam and Nazi Germany's War.* Cambridge, MA: Belknap Press of Harvard University Press, 2014.

Paul, Ludwig. "Göttingen, University of, History of Iranian Studies." *Encyclopaedia Iranica,* online edition, 2006. Accessed July 25, 2012. http://www.iranicaonline.org/articles/gttingen-university-of-history-of-iranian-studies.

Pieper, Max. "Eduard Meyers letztes Werk." *Orientalistische Literaturzeitung* 36, no. 4 (1933): 201–9.

Pollock, Sheldon. "Deep Orientalism? Notes on Sanskrit and Power beyond the Raj." In *Orientalism and the Postcolonial Predicament: Perspectives on South Asia,* edited by Carol A. Breckenridge and Peter van der Veer, 77–133. Philadelphia: University of Pennsylvania Press, 1993.

Pringle, Heather. *The Master Plan: Himmler's Scholars and the Holocaust.* New York: Hyperion, 2006.

Raulwing, Peter, and Thomas L. Gertzen. "Friedrich Wilhelm Freiherr von Bissing im Blickpunkt ägyptologischer und zeithistorischer Forschungen: die Jahre 1914 bis 1926." *Journal of Egyptian History* 5, no. 1–2 (2012): 34–119.

Remy, Steven P. "'We Are No Longer the University of the Liberal Age': The Humanities and National Socialism at Heidelberg." In Bialas and Rabinbach, *Nazi Germany and the Humanities,* 21–49.

Renger, Johannes. "Altorientalistik." In Elvert and Niels-Sikora, *Kulturwissenschaften und Nationalsozialismus,* 469–502.

———. "Altorientalistik und jüdische Gelehrte in Deutschland: Deutsche und österreichische Altorientalisten im Exil." In *Jüdische Intellektuelle und die Philologien in Deutschland, 1871–1933,* edited by Wilfried Barner and Christoph König, 247–61. Marbacher Wissenschaftsgeschichte 3. Göttingen, Germany: Wallstein, 2001.

Ritterbusch, Paul. "Eröffnungsansprache." In Schaeder, *Orient in deutscher Forschung,* 1–5.

Said, Edward. *Orientalism.* New York: Viking, 1978.

Schaeder, Hans Heinrich. "Asien und die Ostgrenze der europäische Kultur." In *Orient in deutscher Forschung*, 6–17.

———. "Der Neuere Orient." In Deutscher Orient-Verein, *Der Orient und Wir*, 31–55.

———, ed. *Der Orient in deutscher Forschung: Vorträge der Berliner Orientalistentagung, Herbst 1942*. Leipzig, Germany: Otto Harrassowitz, 1944.

———. "Firdosi und die Deutschen." *Zeitschrift der Deutschen Morgenländischen Gesellschaft* 88 (1934): 118–29.

———. "Hans Ehelolf." *Zeitschrift der Deutschen Morgenländischen Gesellschaft* 94 (1940): 1–11.

Schneider, Thomas. "Ägyptologen im Dritten Reich: Biographische Notizen anhand der sogennten 'Steindorff-Liste.'" *Journal of Egyptian History* 5, no. 1-2 (2012): 120–247. Reprinted in *Egyptology from the First World War to the Third Reich: Ideology, Scholarship, and Individual Biographies*, edited by Thomas Schneider and Peter Raulwing, 120–247. Leiden, Netherlands: Brill, 2013.

Sellheim, Rudolph. "Brockelmann, Carl." In *Encyclopaedia Iranica*, online edition. Accessed November 5, 2021. https://iranicaonline.org/articles/brockelmann-carl

Smend, Rudolf. "Julius Wellhausen." In *From Astruc to Zimmerli: Old Testament Scholarship in Three Centuries*, 91–102. Translated by Margaret Kohl. Tübingen, Germany: Mohr Siebeck, 2007.

Stadnikow, Sergei. "Die Bedeutung des Alten Orients für deutsches Denken: Skizzen aus dem Zeitraum 1871–1945." *Propylaeum: Fachinformationsdienst Altertumswissenschaften* (2007). 23 pages. doi: 10.11588/propylaeumdok.00000040.

Steinweis, Alan E. "Nazi Historical Scholarship on the 'Jewish Question.'" In Bialas and Rabinbach, *Nazi Germany and the Humanities*, 399–412.

Trümpler, Charlotte, ed. *Das grosse Spiel: Archäologie und Politik zur Zeit des Kolonialismus (1860–1940)*. Cologne, Germany: DuMont, 2008.

Walravens, Hartmut. "Sinologie." In Elvert and Niels-Sikora, *Kulturwissenschaften und Nationalsozialismus*, 526–85.

Weber, Wilhelm. "Der Alte Orient." In Deutscher Orient-Verein, *Der Orient und Wir*, 1–30.

Weinreich, Max. *Hitler's Professors: The Part of Scholarship in Germany's Crimes against the Jewish People*. New York: Yiddish Scientific Institute (YIVO), 1946. Reprinted with a foreword by Martin Gilbert. New Haven, CT: Yale University Press, 1999.

Wokoeck, Ursula. *German Orientalism: The Study of the Middle East and Islam from 1800 to 1945*. Culture and Civilization in the Middle East. London: Routledge, 2009.

Wolf, Walter. *Wesen und Wert der Ägyptologie*. Leipziger ägyptologische Studien 8. Glückstadt, Germany: J. J. Augustin, 1937.

Wüst, Walther. "Deutsche Frühzeit und arische Geistesgeschichte." *Süddeutsche Monatshefte* 31, no. 12 (1934): 731–39.

SUZANNE L. MARCHAND serves as the Boyd Professor of European Intellectual History at Louisiana State University, Baton Rouge. She received her BA from the University of California, Berkeley, and her PhD from the University of Chicago and spent several years at Princeton University as assistant and associate professor before being appointed to Louisiana State University in 1999. She is the author of *Down from Olympus: Archaeology and Philhellenism in Germany, 1750–1970* (Princeton, 1996); *German Orientalism in the Age of Empire: Religion, Race, and Scholarship* (Cambridge, 2009); and, most recently, *Porcelain: A History from the Heart of Europe* (Princeton, 2020), as well as many essays on the history of the humanities.

THREE

LUTHER SCHOLARS, JEWS, AND JUDAISM DURING THE THIRD REICH

From the Hallowed Halls of Academia to the Sacred Spaces of German Protestantism

CHRISTOPHER J. PROBST

THE ROLE OF PROTESTANTISM IN Nazi Germany has been explored very thoroughly by scholars, demonstrating that Protestants exhibited widespread apathy toward the Nazi oppression and murder of Jews. This problem is exemplified by the attitude of the great German Luther scholar George Buchwald, who wrote in 1881, "A Jew cannot be a German, because only a Christian can be a genuine German!"[1] The literature has also shown that no major faction in German Protestantism consistently spoke out in unified fashion on behalf of Jews during the Third Reich.[2] The name of Dietrich Bonhoeffer is perhaps so widely known today only because of a deeply ironic fact: very few of his fellow German Protestants, even within the generally Nazi-wary Confessing Church,

---

1. [Georg Buchwald], *Luther und die Juden: Den deutschen Studenten gewidmet von einem Kommilitonen* (Leipzig, Germany: Paul Frobberg, 1881), 3, quoting Christoph Ernst Luthardt: "'Das Deutschthum ist völlig mit dem Christenthum verschmolzen; niemand kann ein wahrer Deutscher sein, der nicht Christ ist', sprach D. Luthardt in seiner Predigt am ersten Advent.... und so stimme ich den Worten D. Luthardts völlig bei: *Ein Jude kann kein Deutscher sein, weil ein echter Deutscher nur der sein kann, der ein Christ ist!*" (my translation; emphasis added in the fuller German original). See also note 59 in this chapter. It has been impossible to find the original quote by Luthardt (1823–1902), a German Lutheran theologian who published extensive collections of his sermons.

2. See Robert P. Ericksen and Susannah Heschel, eds., *Betrayal: German Churches and the Holocaust* (Minneapolis: Fortress, 1999); Susannah Heschel, *The Aryan Jesus: Christian Theologians and the Bible in Nazi Germany* (Princeton, NJ: Princeton University Press, 2008); and Wolfgang Gerlach, *And the Witnesses Were Silent: The Confessing Church and the Persecution of the Jews*, trans. Victoria J. Barnett (Lincoln: University of Nebraska Press, 2000).

assisted the Jews of Europe in any meaningful way. Even Bonhoeffer himself did not begin to act decisively in support of German Jews until the fall of 1941, when he took part in an elaborate but successful plot called "Operation Seven" to rescue fourteen Jews.[3]

After the Second World War, German Protestant pastors and theologians bent on painting their actions and that of their churches in the most sympathetic light propagated the myth of the German Church Struggle (*Kirchenkampf*), as it came to be called by its participants, as a valiant fight against Nazism. Clashes between the Confessing Church and the German Christians actually revolved around theology and church politics. Scholars have since demythologized this legend. Many of the churches in fact cooperated with Hitler, in effect (and in many cases in actuality) promulgating Nazi ideology, including antisemitism.[4] Pro-Nazi and anti-Jewish sentiment within the German Protestant church during the Third Reich was abetted by an antidemocratic outlook and theological reappraisal spurred on by a decade-old Luther Renaissance as well as by the now ready availability of a variety of editions of Martin Luther's works.[5] The Luther Renaissance was a scholarly renewal of interest in Luther that encompassed attempts by theologians to rediscover the reformer—the German who introduced the Protestant Reformation to Europe—in the postwar era. Politically, proponents of the Luther Renaissance—who during the Third Reich included Göttingen theologian Emanuel Hirsch and his protégé, Königsberg church historian Erich Vogelsang—exhibited a pronounced tendency toward conservative views. Though the writings of the movement were

---

3. On Bonhoeffer's evolving stance toward Jews and Judaism, see Kenneth C. Barnes, "Dietrich Bonhoeffer and Hitler's Persecution of the Jews," in Ericksen and Heschel, *Betrayal*, 110–28; Eberhard Bethge, "Dietrich Bonhoeffer und die Juden," in *Die Juden und Martin Luther—Martin Luther und die Juden: Geschichte, Wirkungsgeschichte, Herausforderung*, ed. Heinz Kremers (Dusseldorf, Germany: Neukirchener, 1985), 211–49; and Christopher J. Probst, *Demonizing the Jews: Luther and the Protestant Church in Nazi Germany* (Bloomington: Indiana University Press, 2012), 6–7. On the Confessing Church, see Victoria Barnett, *For the Soul of the People: Protestant Protest against Hitler* (New York: Oxford University Press, 1992).

4. Robert P. Ericksen and Susannah Heschel, "The German Churches and the Holocaust," in *The Historiography of the Holocaust*, ed. Dan Stone (New York: Palgrave Macmillan, 2004), 296–318.

5. On both the Luther Renaissance and the publication of Luther's works after the First World War, see Probst, *Demonizing the Jews*, 25–27. Karl Kupisch discusses the political proclivities of the Luther Renaissance in Karl Kupisch, "The 'Luther Renaissance,'" *Journal of Contemporary History* 2, no. 4 (1967): 39–49 (at 41–46). See further Roland H. Bainton, "Interpretations of the Reformation," *American Historical Review* 66, no. 1 (1960): 74–84 (at 76).

primarily theological in nature, antidemocratic sentiments resonated with many of its adherents. This resurgence of interest in Luther carried over into the Nazi era. A sizable, vocal minority of German Protestants avidly and openly supported the Nazis in their nefarious goals concerning the Jewish Question.

Even so, it must also be recognized that overt resistance to Nazism and covert assistance for Jews living under Nazi oppression and threat of murder did exist in small corners of the German Protestant scene. The "Grüber Office," based in Berlin, provided Jews, who were under grave threat from the Reich, with advice about emigration, finding employment abroad, social assistance, legal matters, and educational support. Among those assisted by the Grüber Office were Jews who converted to Christianity.[6] Further, a group of pastors and parishioners sheltered at least seventeen Jewish refugees in sixty church parsonages in a so-called Rectory Chain in the state of Württemberg in southwest Germany.[7]

Though Martin Luther certainly did not invent antisemitism, one cannot discuss the question of Christian antisemitism without reference to this most prominent figure of the German Protestant Reformation. Luther wrote at least five treatises on the subject of "the Jews."[8] One work in particular, *Von den Juden und ihren Lügen*, has fueled the greatest discussion of the reformer's attitude toward Jews. *On the Jews and Their Lies* (for convenience, subsequent references employ its translated title) is rather lengthy (approximately 135 pages in the standard critical edition of Luther's works, the Weimar edition). The final section, in which Luther presents his social program concerning Jews, is the most often quoted. It is crucial to recognize, however, that these five pages are surrounded by a significant body of coherent—if often contentious—theological argumentation.[9] In this last section, Luther makes seven severe recommendations concerning Jews. Their synagogues and schools should be burned to

---

6. Gerlach, *And the Witnesses Were Silent*, 154–60.

7. Eberhard Röhm and Jörg Thierfelder, *Vernichtet, 1941–1945*, vol. 4, bk. 1 of *Juden-Christen-Deutsche, 1933–1945* (Stuttgart, Germany: Calwer, 2006), 182, 198–99; Monika Richarz, ed., *Jewish Life in Germany: Memoirs from Three Centuries*, trans. Stella P. Rosenfeld and Sidney Rosenfeld (Bloomington: Indiana University Press, 1991), 448–60.

8. See note 5 in this chapter.

9. Martin Luther, *Von den Juden und ihren Lügen*, in Martin Luther, *D. Martin Luthers Werke: Kritische Gesamtausgabe*, vol. 53 (Weimar, Germany: Böhlau, 1920), 417–552 (at 522–26); Probst, *Demonizing the Jews*, 39–58. Unless otherwise stated, all translations are mine. The standard translation is Martin Luther, "On the Jews and Their Lies, 1543," trans. Martin H. Bertram, in *Luther's Works*, vol. 47, *The Christian in Society IV*, ed. Franklin Sherman (Philadelphia: Fortress, 1971), 121–306.

the ground; their houses should be "razed and destroyed"; their "prayer books and Talmudic writings" should be confiscated; their rabbis should be "forbidden to teach henceforth on pain of loss of life and limb"; they should be denied safe conduct on the highways; usury should be prohibited to them and their gold, silver, and cash should be taken from them; and, finally, they should be subjected to harsh labor (as retribution for their supposed laziness). The anti-Jewish recommendations, of course, bear resemblance to measures carried out against Jews in Nazi Germany some four hundred years later.

The majority of German Protestant academic theologians did not appeal in the first place to Luther's writings about Jews and Judaism to support their anti-Judaic and antisemitic views but instead looked elsewhere.[10] Rather, there is a diverse, significant, and yet overlooked minority of theologians who published writings that dealt explicitly with Luther's view of the Jewish people.[11] Such works were a means of both buttressing their own often antisemitic and anti-Judaic views and encouraging the church at large to view Jews in the same light as they and Luther did.[12] The work of two such Luther scholars, the respected

---

10. Some simply stressed Luther's stature as a Germanic hero. Siegfried Leffler, who cofounded the Church Movement of German Christians (Kirchenbewegung Deutsche Christen) with Julius Leutheuser in 1927, effuses over Luther as the great German. It is Luther—this "son of the German *Volk*"—who would go "into the Most Holy as priest and theologian and speak there with God..." on behalf of the German people. This remarkable language echoes the New Testament book of Hebrews, which describes the saving work of Christ, who enters the Most Holy place alone as high priest on behalf of his people (Hebrews 9:11–12). See Susannah Heschel, "Nazifying Christian Theology: Walter Grundmann and the Institute for the Study and Eradication of Jewish Influence on German Church Life," *Church History* 63, no. 4 (1994): 587–605 (at 588). Heschel discusses Siegfried Leffler, *Christus im Dritten Reich der Deutschen: Wesen, Weg, und Ziel der Kirchenbewegung "Deutsche Christen"* (Weimar, Germany: Deutsche Christen, 1935), 69–73.

11. I deal with this question extensively in *Demonizing the Jews*. Here I will use the carefully situated case studies of Georg Buchwald and Walter Holsten, who also grappled with Luther's writings about Jews and Judaism, to demonstrate how some Protestant scholars betrayed the humanities by painting a defamatory portrait of Jews and Judaism during the Third Reich.

12. With Gavin Langmuir, I define antisemitism as "the hostility aroused by irrational thinking about 'Jews.'" It is *irrational* thought, he argues, that characterizes antisemitism; *nonrational* thought characterizes anti-Judaism. Whereas irrational thinking is the kind of thought that is in conflict with rational empirical observation, nonrational thinking does not conflict with rational thought and can utilize it in a "subordinate capacity." In its essence, nonrational language is the language of *symbol*, the kind of language found in art and affirmations of belief. See Gavin I. Langmuir, *History, Religion, and Antisemitism* (Berkeley: University of California Press, 1990), 105–7, 130, 152–53, 252–55, 275, 276; Gavin I. Langmuir, *Toward a Definition of Antisemitism* (Berkeley: University of California Press, 1990), 101; and Probst, *Demonizing the Jews*, 3–5.

Leipzig philologist Georg Buchwald and Moringen pastor and Luther scholar Walter Holsten, demonstrates both the appropriation of Luther's writings about Jews and Judaism in support of their own anti-Judaic and antisemitic views and the betrayal of the humanities that this represented. Rather than utilizing the tools of the well-developed discipline of modern German theological studies to affirm his Christian faith while thoughtfully reflecting on the relationship between Christianity and Judaism, Buchwald chose over the course of his career to analyze Luther's writings about Jews and Judaism in polemical fashion and to reflect on their implications in strident ways. Because he also served as a pastor and sought to make Luther's thought known via short selections of his works, Buchwald's influence reached beyond the hallowed halls of academia into the sacred spaces of German Protestantism, the churches. Holsten was also a pastor, his influence springing from his scholarly writings about Luther, including his commentary on Luther's writings about Jews and Turks. Before analyzing Buchwald's decades-long engagement with these writings and Holsten's influential Nazi-era Luther commentary, however, it would be helpful to establish, first, the academic context in which Protestant theologians operated; second, the roles they played in the church, the academy, and broader society; and, third, the ways that these dynamics played out at the University of Tübingen, home of Germany's most prestigious Protestant theological faculty.

I. THE POLITICAL UNIVERSITY

On April 7, 1933, the Nazi regime commenced its first wave of far-reaching repressive legislation, beginning with the Law for the Restoration of the Professional Civil Service. In the same month, the Law against the Overcrowding of German Schools and Universities was introduced. The latter law at first affected only Jewish students, as it effectively restricted the number of Jews to a maximum of 1.5 percent of the total number of students attending German schools and universities. Later amendments, however, would limit the total number of places made available in universities and drastically reduce the number of young women who could receive a university education. The enforcement of subsequently introduced legislation meant that by December 1934, Jews could no longer work as teaching assistants or lecturers in German universities.[13]

---

13. Michael Burleigh and Wolfgang Wippermann, *The Racial State: Germany, 1933–1945*, 14th printing (Cambridge: Cambridge University Press, 2007), 78–80, 214; Richard J. Evans, *The Third Reich in Power: How the Nazis Won Over the Hearts and Minds of a Nation* (London: Penguin, 2006), 297.

Despite all of this, neither Hitler nor the Nazi leadership acted with the same enthusiasm in imposing Nazi views and values in the universities as they did in the schools. Perhaps predictably then, important decisions affecting institutions of higher education—including academic appointments and funding for research—became flashpoints for typical internecine competition between government agencies, including the Education and Interior ministries. Also involved in these sorts of disputes were powerful student organizations, such as the Nationalsozialistischer Deutscher Studentenbund [National Socialist German Students' League (NSDStB)], as well as the Sturmabteilung [Storm Troopers (SA)] and university professors and rectors. In April 1935, rectors were entrusted with new and sweeping authority by the Education Ministry. In reality, that ministry's political weakness and the interference of the previously mentioned parties and organizations made this directive difficult to enforce.[14] Even so, in the case of one of the more nazified universities like Jena, a forceful persona like Wolf Meyer-Erlach, who was rector at Jena from 1935 to 1937, could, by the power of his office, attempt rather successfully to push the institution's scholarship in the direction of the Führer.[15] The regime's attempts at controlling the academy and forcing the universities to conform to the verities of a racial state shaped a context in which many German Protestant theologians would betray their commitment to the Christian tradition of viewing all human beings as having been created in the image of God by dehumanizing the Jew in their theological writings.

II. THE ROLE OF ACADEMIC THEOLOGIANS

One Nazi opponent, reporting in April 1937 to the Sozialdemokratische Partei Deutschlands [Social Democratic Party of Germany (Sopade)], compared Nazism to a religion, arguing that a "Church-State" had emerged that demanded absolute loyalty, including the submission of the soul. Yet this phenomenon emerged neither overnight nor entirely in plain sight. Instead, the observer likened it to the refurbishment of a railway bridge. Such bridges could not be

---

14. Michael Grüttner, *Studenten im Dritten Reich* (Paderborn, Germany: Ferdinand Schöningh, 1995), 87–100; Evans, *Third Reich in Power*, 291–92.

15. Probst, *Demonizing the Jews*, 68–75; Heschel, *Aryan Jesus*, 201–41. For a helpful discussion of Meyer-Erlach and the theology faculty at Jena, see Bernard M. Levinson, "Reading the Bible in Nazi Germany: Gerhard von Rad's Attempt to Reclaim the Old Testament for the Church," *Interpretation: A Journal of Bible and Theology* 62, no. 3 (2008): 238–54; and Bernard M. Levinson, "Gerhard von Rad's Struggle against the Nazification of the Old Testament," in this volume.

destroyed altogether; this would make rail travel impossible. Instead, each day individual girders and rails were replaced "until the passengers, who had either not paid much attention, or imagined bits and pieces were being refurbished, realised that they were crossing an entirely new structure."[16] In a sense, Protestant academic theologians who were supportive of the regime filled the role of ideological railway bridge worker.

Yet what general role did Protestant academic theologians play in their professional lives? First, we must recognize that, so to speak, they "served two masters." As professors in German universities, they were civil servants. As professors of Protestant theology, they also worked in conjunction with their confession and with their regional churches.[17] Yet during the Nazi regime, as a civil servant the university professor was not expected to serve typical higher education ideals such as unfettered intellectual inquiry and political objectivity. Instead, as Harvard sociologist Edward Yarnell Hartshorne observed at the time, a professor was "politically bound": "He is committed to its [i.e., the state's] philosophy and must not only refrain from criticizing the government but must openly fend for it in word, deed, and attitude."[18]

Those who were supportive of the anti-Jewish policies of Hitler and the Nazis played a very clear role, providing a sort of respectable, "scholarly" tool for the regime. The scholars that the Nazis employed to advance their antisemitic program often were very highly regarded. Among them were university professors and members of the academy, some of whom were world-famous

---

16. Michael Burleigh's summary of the conclusions of the *Deutschland-Berichte der SOPADE* (1937) entry dated April 4, 1937, 497–99, in Michael Burleigh, *The Third Reich: A New History* (London: Pan, 2001), 252.

17. To follow the example of the Hessian regional church's cooperation with the Theology Faculty of Gießen University, see Probst, *Demonizing the Jews*, 150–51. See also Eike Wolgast, "Nationalsozialistische Hochschulpolitik und die evangelisch-theologischen Fakultäten," in *Theologische Fakultäten im Nationalsozialismus*, ed. Leonore Siegele-Wenschkewitz and Carsten Nicolaisen (Göttingen, Germany: Vandenhoeck & Ruprecht, 1993), 45–79 (at 59).

18. Edward Yarnell Hartshorne Jr., "The German Universities and the Government," *Annals of the American Academy of Political and Social Science*, 200, no. 1 (1938): 210–34 (at 232). See further Edward Yarnell Hartshorne Jr., *The German Universities and National Socialism* (Cambridge, MA: Harvard University Press, 1937). Hartshorne became a key part of early efforts by the Office of Military Government, United States (OMGUS), to denazify German universities after the war. See Steven P. Remy, *The Heidelberg Myth: The Nazification and Denazification of a German University* (Cambridge, MA: Harvard University Press, 2002), 128. See further the discussion of Hartshorne in Robert Ericksen, *Complicity in the Holocaust: Churches and Universities in Nazi Germany* (Cambridge: Cambridge University Press, 2012), 140–43.

authors: "the kind of people Allied scholars used to meet and fraternize with at international congresses."[19]

How, then, may the thought of such antisemitic scholars be characterized? Alan Steinweis surmises that there were three tiers of antisemitic discourse in Nazi Germany. The bottom tier included the more tactless forms of propaganda against Jews, intended to influence those in the German populace who were less astute intellectually. The second tier encompassed "middlebrow" speech, intended to ensure the social acceptability of antisemitism among more-educated Germans.[20] The third and highest tier comprised what he calls "the product of Nazi Jewish studies," which would have included Wilhelm Grau's *Forschungen zur Judenfrage* [Research on the Jewish Question], the scholarly journal of the Reichsinstitut für Geschichte des neuen Deutschlands [Reich Institute for the History of the New Germany].[21] The ideas from this tier in fact funneled down to the other two. Steinweis's schema provides a helpful means for discussing varying kinds of antisemitic discourse in the Third Reich.

The biographies of theologian Gerhard Kittel, philosopher Martin Heidegger, and political theorist Carl Schmitt demonstrate the wellspring of esteem for Hitler among highly educated Germans who had not supported the Nazi Party prior to 1933. Heidegger (1889–1976) was rector of Freiburg University from 1933 to 1934, an early and ardent supporter of Nazism, and one of the most significant philosophers of the twentieth century. Schmitt (1888–1985) was a prominent jurist and legal theorist. Kittel (1888–1948), Professor of New Testament at Tübingen and an important figure in German Protestantism during the Nazi era, was both a member of the Nazi Party and an early member of the German Christians, the wing of the German Protestant church that

---

19. Max Weinreich, *Hitler's Professors: The Part of Scholarship in Germany's Crimes against the Jewish People* (New York: Yiddish Scientific Institute [YIVO], 1946; repr., foreword by Martin Gilbert, New Haven, CT: Yale University Press, 1999), 7.

20. Alan E. Steinweis, *Studying the Jew: Scholarly Antisemitism in Nazi Germany* (Cambridge, MA: Harvard University Press, 2006), 14–15. The first tier included films such as *Der ewige Jude*, as well as publications such as the *Völkischer Beobachter* and *Der Stürmer*. The SS newspaper *Das Schwarze Korps* falls into the second category in Steinweis's schema.

21. Steinweis, *Studying the Jew*, 15. Wilhelm Grau, a Catholic, was acting director of the Institute's Department for Research into the Jewish Question [Forschungsabteilung Judenfrage] in Munich from 1935 to 1938. See Patricia von Papen, "Vom engagierten Katholiken zum Rassenantisemiten: Die Karriere des Historikers 'der Judenfrage' Wilhelm Grau," in *Theologische Wissenschaft im "Dritten Reich": Ein ökumenisches Projekt*, ed. Georg Denzler and Leonore Siegele-Wenschkewitz (Frankfurt, Germany: Haag and Herchen, 2000), 68–113.

was most fervently pro-Nazi and antisemitic.[22] These three men offered a "restrained alternative to the old [Nazi] fighters' rage against Jews ... that neither Hitler nor his deputies could have provided."[23] The academics who supported the Nazis by dint of their advocacy for the regime's antisemitic designs for Germany, including Walter Holsten and Georg Buchwald, thus betrayed their roles as purveyors of free inquiry, providing the regime with respectability among academia both inside and outside Germany.[24]

III. PROTESTANT THEOLOGY AT TÜBINGEN DURING THE THIRD REICH: HANNS RÜCKERT

The University of Tübingen became a "political university" during the Third Reich. Tübingen already had a long and tortuous history as a place of exclusion for and condemnation of Jews and Judaism.[25] Its institutional bias against Jews and Judaism did not reverse during the era of the Weimar Republic, which Horst Junginger calls "the zenith ... of Jewish emancipation."[26] Quite the contrary, and despite the fact that the Weimar constitution guaranteed full civil rights and access to civil service employment for all, regardless of religious affiliation, the university consciously undermined such a policy so thoroughly that when the Law for the Restoration of the Professional Civil Service came into effect, the university had the lowest quota of dismissals of any German university. While other reasons for this include the national malaise in the wake of the First World War, Tübingen's centuries-long "all-encompassing nationalist Protestant consensus," which included antisemitism, contributed significantly as well.[27]

This sweeping nationalist Protestant consensus is exemplified in the work of Hanns Rückert, who was appointed to the prestigious chair of church

---

22. On the German Christians, see especially Doris L. Bergen, *Twisted Cross: The German Christian Movement in the Third Reich* (Chapel Hill: University of North Carolina Press, 1996).

23. Claudia Koonz, *The Nazi Conscience* (London: Belknap Press, 2003), 68. On Heidegger, see also Ericksen, *Complicity in the Holocaust*, 89, 92–93.

24. Due to the growing influence of German Christian theologians under the Nazi regime, Confessing Church theologians were increasingly marginalized. The theological responses of this wing of German Protestantism thus appeared, for the most part, outside of the theological faculties of the universities, in journals and circulated church newsletters.

25. Horst Junginger, *The Scientification of the "Jewish Question" in Germany* (Leiden, Netherlands: Brill, 2017), 36–68.

26. Ibid., 69–112 (at 69).

27. Ibid. (at 111).

history at Tübingen in 1931. A few months after Hitler became chancellor, the Protestant theology faculty at Tübingen affirmed its fealty to the new state, noting that "a positive attitude toward the new *Volk* movement is just as necessary as the preservation of the Church as a Church of the Word."[28] Soon after, Rückert joined the German Christian movement, as did several of his Tübingen colleagues, including Gerhard Kittel.[29] Rückert served as dean of the Faculty of Theology during the 1933–34 academic year.[30] In November 1933, he left the German Christians in the wake of Reinhold Krause's scandalous speech at the Berlin Sportpalast.[31]

In his lecture, "Luther als Deutscher" [Luther as a German], which was published in the wake of both Krause's speech and the 450th anniversary of Luther's birth, Rückert does not cite the reformer's works on Jews and Judaism or articulate overtly antisemitic views. Yet he supports romantic notions of *Heimat*,[32] *völkisch* [nationalistic] Christianity, and National Socialism.

---

28. Tübingen Faculty of Protestant Theology, April 25, 1933, Faculty Meeting Minutes, in Siegfried Bräuer, "Hanns Rückert (1901–1974)," in Rainer Lächele and Jörg Thierfelder, eds., *Wir konnten uns nicht entziehen: 30 Porträts zu Kirche und Nationalsozialismus in Württemberg* (Stuttgart, Germany: Quell, 1998), 379–97 (at 384).

29. Bräuer, "Hanns Rückert (1901–1974)," 384. Anders Gerdmar's contribution to this volume, "Jewish Studies in the Service of Nazi Ideology: Tübingen's Faculty of Theology as a Center for Antisemitic Research," demonstrates that Kittel, together with other Tübingen theologians, became instrumental for German theological antisemitism during the Third Reich.

30. Michael Wischnath, ed., *Universitätsarchiv Tübingen: Bestandsrepertorium 207. Nachlaß Hanns Rückert (1901–1974): (1917–1970)* (Universitätsarchiv Tübingen: Tübingen, 2000), 7.

31. During the infamous speech, Krause assailed the Old Testament, the Apostle Paul, and the symbol of the cross as ludicrous and weakening leftovers from Judaism (Bergen, *Twisted Cross*, 17–18, 174). See also the discussion of and quote from Krause's speech in Levinson's contribution to this volume, "Gerhard von Rad's Struggle."

32. The malleable and untranslatable German term *Heimat* conveys the sense of how, collectively, Germans living in provinces across the nation felt about their home, their land, their people. The concept developed after the unification of Germany in 1871 (and especially from the 1880s to the early 1900s). Though Heimat was promulgated primarily by members of the middle and upper classes through books, school curricula, and museums, it was an idea that cut across social, economic, political, and religious lines. As its symbols and expressions could change from one epoch to the next, the concept was supple. Yet its characteristic elements—history, nature, and folklore—remained constant. See Alon Confino, *Germany as a Culture of Remembrance: Promises and Limits of Writing History* (Chapel Hill: University of North Carolina Press, 2006), 34–35, 61–64, 64–65, 81–82, and Celia Applegate, *A Nation of Provincials: The German Idea of Heimat* (Berkeley: University of California Press, 1990), 3, 8–9.

He begins the lecture by tying together the commemoration of the founding of the German Protestant church with the ascent to power of Hitler and the Nazi regime. Rückert opines: "The Protestant church cannot and does not want to think it accidental that it can commemorate its own emergence, which coincides with the dawn of a new epoch in German history, in an instant that in turn signifies a turning point in German destiny."[33] Rückert thus implies a divine convergence between this significant anniversary in the history of German Protestantism and the coming of the Third Reich. The final section of the lecture focuses on Luther's contributions to German religious and cultural life. Noteworthy here are passages in which Rückert affirms Luther's ties to race and Heimat. Rückert stresses Luther's humanity and earthiness, contending that these characteristics are tied to "his rootedness in race, *Volkstum*, and Heimat."[34]

During the Second World War, Rückert reaffirmed the muscular views of Volk and state that he had expressed during late Weimar and the early years of the Third Reich, even if he did so with, at times, a bit more nuance and less enthusiasm. In "Die Bedeutung der Reformation für die deutsche Geschichte" [The significance of the Reformation for German history (1941)], Rückert stresses the state's duties before God while presenting Luther as not only a German but also a Western hero of the Reformation.[35] Originally given as a lecture to Wehrmacht soldiers at Tübingen, Rückert characterizes the ongoing German war effort—which was driven in no small measure by genocidal impulses and would several years later be judged an aggressive war—as a virtuous struggle.

Rückert places Luther in the service of the Christian church; the reformer's work also has resonance among the *Völker* [peoples] of the Christian West: "In spite of [Luther's] much quoted and only rarely correctly understood word: 'I was born to my Germans, I will serve them,' the community in which and from which Luther had received his commission is not his German *Volk*, but the Christian Church; just as his work also had a common Christian, Western meaning beyond the range of the German *Volk*."[36] Rückert thus carves out a space for a more universal (or, at least more European) Luther.

---

33. Hanns Rückert, "Luther als Deutscher," Luthersonderheft, *Deutsche Theologie* 1 (November 1933): 10–23 (at 10).

34. Ibid., 20–23 (at 20).

35. Hanns Rückert, "Die Bedeutung der Reformation für die deutsche Geschichte," *Deutsche Theologie* 8 (1941): 89–101.

36. Ibid., 90.

Having later established Bismarck as a benchmark for how a German leader, following Luther, should regard the problem of church and state, Rückert abruptly applies this Lutheran approach to the German present. "Even today we feel an echo of this Lutheran state thinking in what characterizes our German conception of this war as opposed to the English one: we wage this war in order to preserve and secure our *Volk*'s historical life and disdain the camouflage of the war aims with medieval crusade ideas."[37] Such a comment is not completely unsurprising given the lecture's audience. Yet it is not entirely clear which aspects of Luther's (and Bismarck's) view of the German state Hitler and the regime are echoing in their execution of aggressive war and genocide. Rückert provides only a broad rationale: "we wage this war in order to preserve and secure our Volk's historical life." Just how England "camouflage(s)" its war aims with "medieval crusade ideas" is left unexplored.[38] But the effect of such a broadside on Rückert's original audience must have been powerful. These God-fearing soldiers were receiving from a well-known church historian the imprimatur for their part in the German war effort—along with some grandiloquent propaganda against one of Germany's strongest enemies.[39]

Rückert's scholarship and speeches connecting Luther's writings to the German *Volk* and state exemplify a broader strain of nationalist Protestantism in scholarship during the Third Reich. At Tübingen, Rückert helped make the theology faculty a "respectable" scholarly tool for the regime. He was not alone in his pursuits. The remainder of this chapter examines the work of two other German scholars who leveraged Luther's writings to promote an ostensibly Christian argument in favor of antisemitism that, during the Third Reich, would have encouraged Germany's Protestant population to support the antisemitic policies and practices of the state.

---

37. Ibid., 99–100.
38. It is also deeply ironic that though Rückert could not have known it, Hitler had signed a directive on December 18, 1940—just a month before the lecture was originally given—changing the code name of the planned attack on the Soviet Union (which would begin on June 22, 1941) to Barbarossa, the nickname of Frederick I, the Holy Roman emperor who led (and died during) the Third Crusade. See Saul Friedländer, *Nazi Germany and the Jews, 1933–1945*, abridged ed. (New York: HarperPerennial, 2009), 202, and Jonathan Phillips, *The Crusades, 1095–1197* (London: Routledge, 2013), 138–52.
39. Rückert extends his takedown of England to the Enlightenment, adding France into the mix as well. In his view, while Germany "experienced and absorbed the religious depth of the Enlightenment," the English and French Enlightenments were characterized by "shallow materialism and utilitarianism" (Rückert, "Bedeutung der Reformation," 100).

IV. WALTER HOLSTEN, MORINGEN PASTOR

Born in 1908 in Osnabrück, Walter Holsten began his ministerial and academic career on the cusp of the Nazi ascent to power, receiving his doctorate in Göttingen in 1932. He became curate at Elverhausen the following year and then pastor in Moringen, near Göttingen, in September 1934. Four years later, he began serving as pastor in Hasbergen. After completing his habilitation in 1946, he became professor of religion and missions at the University of Mainz the next year. Holsten achieved Professor emeritus status in 1973 and died in Mainz in 1982.[40]

Holsten's impact on greater German Protestantism from 1933 to 1945 seems on the surface to be far less significant than that of more well-known theologians such as Protestant League president Heinrich Bornkamm and Erlangen systematic theologian and Luther Society president Paul Althaus. He was merely one pastor among thousands and held no important positions in the German Protestant Church. Yet his influence regarding Luther's views of Volk, Jews, and Judaism is highly significant. His betrayal of the humanities is exemplified by his embrace of Luther's one-sided portrayal of Jews and Judaism. Holsten's writings furthered anti-Judaic notions of Jews as a people separate from the Christian Volk as well as antisemitic images of Jews as purveyors of anti-Christian Bolshevism.

Paul Althaus, in an article titled "Der Wahrheitsgehalt der Religionen und das Evangelium" [The Validity of the Religions and the Gospel (1934)], twice referenced Holsten's *Christentum und nichtchristliche Religion nach derAuffassung Luthers* [Christianity and Non-Christian Religion According to Luther (1932)].[41] Both this work and Martin Luther's *Schriften wider Juden und Türken*

---

40. Dr. Hans Otte, Landeskirchliches Archiv Hannover, e-mail message to author, February 15, 2006. The personnel records pertaining to Holsten were destroyed in an Allied bombing raid (Henning Wrogemann, "Holsten, Walter," in *Religion in Geschichte und Gegenwart: Handwörterbuch für Theologie und Religionswissenschaft*, vol. 3, ed. Hans D. Betz et al., 4th ed. [Tübingen, Germany: Mohr Siebeck, 2000], 1872). In the German academic system, the *Habilitation* refers to the second dissertation, following the doctorate, that is necessary to write in order to seek employment as a full Professor.

41. Paul Althaus, "Der Wahrheitsgehalt der Religionen und das Evangelium: Grundsätze der theologischen Kritik aller Religion," *Neue Allgemeine Missionszeitschrift* 11, no. 10 (1934): 277–92 (at 282, 284), reprinted in *Theologische Aufsätze*, vol. 2, by Paul Althaus (Gütersloh: Bertelsmann, 1935), 65–82. Here as elsewhere in the chapter, dates included after the English translation of a German book or article title brackets refer solely to the publication date of the work in German. Most of the titles included in the chapter were never published in English translation.

[Writings against Jews and Turks (1936 and 1938)]—which included extensive commentary by Holsten—also appeared on a short list of texts and monographs recommended by Dr. Friedrich Werner, director of the main office of the German Protestant Church in Berlin, in an April 1939 memo to the leaders of all the regional Protestant churches.[42]

Holsten's comments on Luther's *Writings against Jews and Turks* were of considerable importance as an interpretive tool for German pastors and theologians serving during the Nazi regime. The collection first appeared in 1936; the second (unmodified) edition was published in 1938. His comments are especially instructive insofar as they reveal his attitude toward the Jewish Question in the midst of increasing oppression and marginalization of Jews in the Third Reich.

Holsten's detailed textual comments appear at the end of a work that includes the texts of Luther's most well-known writings about Jews and Judaism. There is a short introduction to each work as well. Some of the more relevant notations and introductory comments are worth considering. Though some of the most revealing comments are lengthy, other shorter comments illuminate a great deal as well. Holsten twice consults a dubious source without censure, in the first instance directing the reader to consult Wilhelm Grau's *Antisemitismus im späten Mittelalter* [Antisemitism in the Late Middle Ages (1934)] on the matter of Christian mission to Jews in medieval times. Grau, a Catholic, was acting director of the Department for Research into the Jewish Question within the Reich Institute for the History of the New Germany, in Munich, from 1935 to 1938. In 1940, chief Nazi Party ideologue Alfred Rosenberg appointed him director of both the Frankfurt Judaica Library and the Frankfurt branch of Rosenberg's planned

---

42. H. H. Borcherdt and Georg Merz, eds., *Schriften wider Juden und Türken*, vol. 3 of *Martin Luther: Ausgewählte Werke*, 2nd ed. (Munich: Christian Kaiser, 1938). At the suggestion of the Reich minister for church affairs, Hanns Kerrl, Werner asked these church authorities to "motivate the ministers" in their area of supervision "in an appropriate way to an engagement with the position of Luther on the Jews . . ." See *Evangelisches Zentralarchiv Berlin* 7/3688, Werner memo to regional Protestant church authorities, April 22, 1939, 243 (my translation). After the war and the Holocaust, Christian Kaiser published a third edition of *Martin Luther: Ausgewählte Werke*. Notably, none of the volumes retained the original title of *Schriften wider Juden und Türken*. They were instead republished as H. H. Borcherdt, Georg Merz, and Wilhelm Heinsius, eds., *Martin Luther: Ausgewählte Werke*, 3rd ed. (Munich: Christian Kaiser, 1948–1953). Hereafter in the chapter, I am using the English translation, *Writings Against Jews and Turks* in place of the German title of the work.

Nazi University.[43] All of these institutions were ostensibly scholarly venues for promoting antisemitic Nazi propaganda. Exhibiting a tone that reveals a general suspicion of Jewish actions and beliefs, Grau's work nevertheless manages to maintain a thin veneer of even-handedness. Yet this apparent impartiality is betrayed at times by conclusions that are not based on credible evidence.[44]

In a concluding comment on *Wider die Sabbater* [Against the Sabbatarians (1538)], Holsten avers: "Obviously the Jewish Question had not been a scholarly question for Luther, but rather [his heart] was full of it, and out of its fullness broke a river of thoughts. Will this not anyway be the case everywhere one really lives from the Scriptures?" This is probably an allusion to the words of Jesus in the Gospel of Matthew and is no doubt intended as an encouragement to personal piety.[45] Yet it is tied to an evaluation of the Jewish Question that was—for both Luther and Holsten—decidedly negative.

Holsten begins his introduction to *On the Jews and Their Lies* by noting that the work "is that writing to which Luther owes his fame as a prominent antisemite." It might be called the "arsenal" from which antisemitism got its weapons. Yet the Jewish Question is no mere academic inquiry but rather one that "had its place in his heart." Luther's heart "beat for the Word of God alone." Holsten seeks both to cloak Luther's antisemitism in pious attire and to distance himself from the "modern" antisemites.

Holsten encourages Christians to practice a "sharp mercy" toward Jews. "*Hard measures against the Jews are thus justified and required*, if a genuine mercy is behind them." Christians might be surprised, he avers, that these measures are rooted for Luther in "Christian" rather than "national or other"

---

43. Holsten, "Erläuterungen," in Borcherdt and Merz, *Schriften wider Juden und Türken*, 523–79 (at 527 [text 2, line 12]; and 535 [text 39, line 27]). The text and line numbers provided in brackets here and in what follows refer to the text by Luther on which Holsten comments. See further Patricia Kennedy Grimsted, "Roads to Ratibor: Library and Archival Plunder by the Einsatzstab Reichsleiter Rosenberg," *Holocaust and Genocide Studies* 19, no. 3 (2005): 390–458 (at 406), and von Papen, "Vom engagierten Katholiken," 68–69.

44. In one such instance, Grau leaves open the question of medieval Jewish ritual murder. It is wrong, he complains, "to accept the fact of ritual murder without reservation," which "the Christian historians above all have done." Yet, he maintains, it is "equally incorrect" to assert, as the Jewish researchers have done, that ritual murders could not possibly have occurred. See Wilhelm Grau, *Antisemitismus im späten Mittelalter: Das Ende der Regensburger Judengemeinde, 1450–1519* (Munich: Duncker and Humblot, 1934), 145.

45. Holsten, "Erläuterungen," 537 (text 60, line 33). The allusion is to "For out of the overflow of the heart the mouth speaks" (Matthew 12:34).

considerations. Yet here is where the "Christian" and the "political" meet for Luther.[46] Holsten's support for at least the principles of Nazi anti-Jewish policy is perhaps nowhere clearer than when he states that it is "the obligation of the authorities and of Christianity not to tolerate or through tolerance to encourage" a religion whose essence contradicts the truth. "Anti-Christianity" is an attack on the existence of the Volk *and therefore demands a national approach.*"[47]

As would be expected, Holsten cites the work of other prominent Luther scholars to support his interpretations of Luther. For example, in commenting at length on Luther's proposed measures against Jews, he encourages his readers to consult Althaus regarding the purportedly disparate attitudes toward work and usury held by Luther and the Jewish people.[48] Discussing a passage from *On the Jews and Their Lies*, Holsten accentuates Luther's distinction between people as they are "before the world" and as they are "before God," quoting church historian and Luther specialist Erich Vogelsang at length: "Human beings and peoples and races are thus not—[as with] the rationalism of the philosemites—all equally valuable, equal in nobility, in intelligence, in talent, in strength." The differences between peoples and races nevertheless do not matter "in the light of eternity, in the court of God," a fact that "the Jews and many antisemites do not understand."[49] Here, via Vogelsang, Holsten makes a further distinction between Christian condemnation of Jews and that of "many antisemites."

While Luther argues that the Jewish people "could not know what God's commandment is," Holsten complains that Stuttgart Protestant pastor Eduard Lamparter sees a "providential task" for Judaism in that it both stresses and protects the "ethical element in the spiritual belief in God." Following Vogelsang once again, he argues that Lamparter in his "Enlightenment liberalism" does

---

46. Ibid., 537–39 (emphasis added).
47. If no "energetic measures" are taken against Jews, he argues, Christians make themselves "jointly guilty for Jewish enmity against Christ" (Holsten, "Erläuterungen," 553–54 [emphasis added; text 189, lines 13ff.]).
48. Holsten, "Erläuterungen," 530 (text 28, lines 10ff.) and 553–54 (text 189, lines 13ff.). See also Paul Althaus, "Die Frage des Evangeliums an das moderne Judentum," *Zeitschrift für Systematische Theologie* 7 (1930): 195–215, reprinted in Althaus, *Theologische Aufsätze*, 83–103.
49. Erich Vogelsang, *Luthers Kampf Gegen die Juden* (Tübingen, Germany: J. C. B. Mohr, 1933), 12, as quoted in Holsten, "Erläuterungen," 541 (text 66, line 33). Holsten appeals to Vogelsang's work in several other places. See 544 (text 95, lines 27ff.), 545–46 (text 101, line 30), and 553–54 (text 189, lines 13–19).

not understand Luther's "fight against the Jews" or "the true relationship, the antagonism between Judaism and Christianity."[50]

Holsten also links Judaism to Bolshevism, complete with an appeal to Emanuel Hirsch, who, in addition to being a leading light of the Luther Renaissance, was also a committed member of the German Christians and the Nazi Party and a supporting member of the SS: "One can well say that the messianic expectation of post-biblical Judaism comes to maturity in Bolshevism" and (in Hirsch's words) may represent an "irreligious variety of Jewish religion." "Jewish-led Bolshevism," Holsten continues, "has no affinity with the messianic expectation of the O.T."[51]

Holsten, seemingly the coolly authoritative scholar, here takes the irrational position that Bolshevism is "Jewish-led." Somehow, the messianic expectation of postbiblical Judaism "comes to maturity in Bolshevism." He does not expand on what Bolshevism has to do with this caricatured "Jewish" variety of messianic expectation. The answer lies in the text on which Holsten is commenting. In this context, Luther says of the Jewish people, "On no more bloodthirsty and vengeful Volk has the sun ever shone." They wait on their Messiah, who would "murder and kill the whole world by his sword."[52] Holsten is indicating that this murderous Jewish messianic expectation comes to fruition in Bolshevism.

Though he held no important church-political positions within the German Protestant church, Holsten's ideas about Luther, Christianity, and Judaism traveled far and wide through Protestant circles in Nazi Germany. He apparently never joined the German Christians, the Nazi Party, or any affiliated Nazi organizations. His influence stemmed more from his writings than from his biography.

---

50. Holsten, "Erläuterungen," 544 (text 95, line 27). Holsten expresses incredulity in his reading of Lamparter, referring to him as "Protestant (!) pastor Ed. Lamparter." The Lamparter quotation is from Eduard Lamparter, *Das Judentum in seiner Kultur und religionsgeschichtlichen Erscheinung* (Gotha, Germany: Leopold Klotz, 1928), 295. Lamparter fought energetically against antisemitism in Weimar Germany. See Donald L. Niewyk, *The Jews in Weimar Germany*, 2nd ed. (New Brunswick, NJ: Transaction, 2001), 59.

51. Robert P. Ericksen, "Assessing the Heritage: German Protestant Theologians, Nazis, and the 'Jewish Question,'" in Ericksen and Heschel, *Betrayal*, 22–39 (at 26); Holsten, "Erläuterungen," 543 (text 81, 25); Emanuel Hirsch, *Die gegenwärtige geistige Lage im Spiegel philosophischer und theologischer Besinnung* (Göttingen, Germany: Vandenhoeck & Ruprecht, 1934), 24.

52. Martin Luther, *Von den Juden und ihren Lügen*, in Borcherdt and Merz, *Schriften wider Juden und Türken*, 61–228 (at 81).

In his commentary on Luther's *Writings against Jews and Turks,* Holsten quotes as serious scholarship the committed Nazi Wilhelm Grau's work on antisemitism in the Middle Ages and believes Bolshevism to be led by Jews and tied somehow to postbiblical Judaism and its purportedly murderous, false messianic expectation. Further, he appeals to Erich Vogelsang's works and those of Vogelsang's fellow Nazi and German Christian Emanuel Hirsch, in which such antisemitic views are espoused.

In both his commentary on Luther's writings about Jews and Turks, and his earlier work about Luther and non-Christian religions, Holsten consistently supports the reformer's anti-Jewish sociopolitical proposals. This is historically significant, of course, in light of the anti-Jewish legal measures that were being implemented in Nazi Germany between the appearance of the earlier work (1932) and the second edition of the latter work (1938). Yet Holsten consistently tries to portray these measures as solely inspired by religion. In contrast to many German Christians, Holsten's approach to Luther's writings about Jews and Judaism upholds traditional conservative Lutheran orthodoxy. He cannot help, however, espousing anti-Enlightenment sentiment and irrational theories about "Jewish-led" Bolshevism. Such sentiments offer one example of a betrayal of the humanities on the part of Protestant scholars whose work concerned the relationship between Christianity, Jews, and Judaism. We now turn our attention to the work of another such Luther scholar.

V. GEORG BUCHWALD, LUTHER PHILOLOGIST

It is difficult to overestimate the importance of the career of Luther philologist Georg Buchwald (1859–1947) to the discipline of Luther studies. The well-known Luther scholar Heinrich Bornkamm (1901–77) regarded Buchwald as the "'greatest Luther philologist of the deserving generation which gave us the critical Weimar edition of Luther's works and with it the foundation of the entirety of modern Luther research.'"[53] The publication of the Weimar edition of Luther's works, which became and remains the standard critical edition of Luther's writings, began in 1883, the four hundredth anniversary of Luther's birth. By 1886, the commission for their publication had already appointed the twenty-seven-year-old Buchwald as a contributor. He would edit or contribute

---

53. Heinrich Bornkamm, as quoted in Reinhold Jauernig, "Georg Buchwald in Memoriam," *Theologische Literaturzeitung* 78, no. 4 (1953): 239–52 (at 240). On Bornkamm, see also Probst, *Demonizing the Jews,* 146–55.

to at least forty-two of the volumes in the series, more than any other contributor. He also found and published many previously undiscovered Luther works, including lectures, sermons, and letters and was coeditor of the 1925 Munich edition of selected Luther works, which was utilized by scholars and laypersons alike.[54] Despite all of this, he did not edit any of the volumes containing Luther's most direct and extensive writings about Jews and Judaism, which are often referred to by German scholars as his *Judenschriften* [writings about Jews and Judaism].[55] Even so, more than any other single scholar of his era, Buchwald supplied grist for the mill of the Lutheran theologians. Even one of Buchwald's popular works about Luther (some of which will be addressed below) drew praise from Heinrich Hermelink, in the Marburg University church historian's 1935 theological journal article about recent Luther research.[56]

Buchwald was born in 1859 in Großenhain (Saxony), the son of a cloth manufacturer. He received training in ancient languages at secondary school in Dresden-Neustadt.[57] After his university studies at Leipzig, he took up teaching, first at Mittweida (1882) and then in Zwickau (1883). He received his doctorate from Leipzig in the same year that he came to Zwickau and then his licentiate in theology the next year. From 1885 to 1895, he served as sexton in churches in Zwickau and then in Leipzig. In 1896, he became the pastor of the Michaeliskirche in Leipzig. He was appointed superintendent of the Rochlitz

---

54. Jauernig, "Georg Buchwald," 240, 250; Harold J. Grimm, "Luther Research since 1920," *Journal of Modern History* 32, no. 2 (1960): 105–18 (at 107).

55. Martin Luther, *D. Martin Luthers Werke: Kritische Gesamtausgabe*, 120 vols. (Weimar, Germany: Böhlau, 1883–2009), hereafter, *Luthers Werke*. Luther's Judenschriften include *Daß Jesus Christus ein geborener Jude sei* (*That Jesus Christ Was Born a Jew* [1523] (*Luthers Werke* 11); *Wider die Sabbather: An einen guten Freund* (*Against the Sabbatarians: Letter to a Good Friend*) [1538] (*Luthers Werke* 50); *Von den Juden und ihren Lügen* (*On the Jews and Their Lies*) and *Vom Schem Hamphoras und vom Geschlecht Christi* (*On the Ineffable Name and on the Lineage of Christ*) [both titles 1543] (*Luthers Werke* 53); and *Von den letzten Worten Davids* (*On the Last Words of David*) [1543] (*Luthers Werke* 54). There are also references to Jews and Judaism in Martin Luther, *Ungedruckte Predigten D. Martin Luthers aus den Jahren 1537–1540*, ed. Georg Buchwald (Leipzig, Germany: G. Strübig, 1905), and Martin Luther, *D. Martin Luthers Letzte Streitschrift*, ed. Georg Buchwald (Leipzig, Germany: Wigand, 1893).

56. Heinrich Hermelink, "Die neuere Lutherforschung," *Theologische Rundschau* 7, no. 2 (1935): 63–85, 131–56 (at 81). Hermelink was also a contributor to the Weimar edition of Luther's works (*Luthers Werke* 39). On Hermelink, see Probst, *Demonizing the Jews*, 163–67.

57. Friedrich-Wilhelm Bautz, "Buchwald, Georg," in *Biographisch-Bibliographisches Kirchenlexikon*, 37 vols. (Herzberg: Traugott Bautz, 1990–2016), 1:794; Jauernig, "Georg Buchwald," 239.

church district in 1914, a position he held until 1923, when he received the rank of emeritus in order to dedicate himself more singularly to Luther research. He died in Rochlitz in February 1947.[58]

Buchwald's engagement with Luther's life and works was lifelong, spanning the *Kaiserreich* [Imperial Germany], the Weimar Republic, and the Third Reich. In addition to his crucial contributions to Luther scholarship, he also published selected works and excerpts from Luther's Judenschriften many times during his career. In 1881, as a university student at Leipzig, he wrote and published anonymously *Luther und die Juden* [Luther and the Jews].[59] In 1931, as part of the series "Luther's Pamphlets for Our Time," Buchwald published edited excerpts of *Daß Jesus Christus ein geborener Jude sei* [That Jesus Christ Was Born a Jew (1523)], *Against the Sabbatarians, Von den Juden und ihren Lügen* [On the Jews and Their Lies (1543)] and *Vom Schem Hamphoras und vom Geschlecht Christi* [On the Ineffable Name and on the Lineage of Christ (1543)], and material about Jews and Judaism from his "table talk" [informal conversations about various issues] and sermons.[60] Six years later, he included a section about Luther and Judaism in *Luthers ewiges Wort* [Luther's Eternal Word (1937)]. Each of these was a conscious attempt to popularize the reformer's works, something Buchwald did throughout his career. Buchwald's impact on scholarly and popular reception of Luther's views of Jews and Judaism is extremely significant. Like Holsten, Buchwald's betrayal of the humanities is exemplified by his embrace of Luther's biased portrayal of Jews and Judaism. His popularizing of Luther's Judenschriften via his many publications gave

---

58. Bautz, "Buchwald, Georg," 794; Jauernig, "Georg Buchwald," 239.

59. Anonymous [Georg Buchwald], *Luther und die Juden*; Jauernig, "Georg Buchwald," 239, 241. Jauernig asserts that Buchwald had published this work, saying "Freilich hatte er [Buchwald] schon in seiner Studienzeit Luthers Schrift 'Die Juden und ihre Lügen'— anonym. —erscheinen lassen." The bibliographic entry for the work gives the correct title: "1881 Luther und die Juden. Den deutschen Studenten gewidmet von einem Kommilitonen. Leipzig (32 S.). [Anonym. erschienen]."

60. See Georg Buchwald, ed., *Von Kaufshandlung und Wucher: Martin Luther, Luthers Flugschriften für unsere Zeit* (abbreviated here as MLLF) Booklet 1 (Dresden, Germany: Landesverein für Innere Mission, 1931); Georg Buchwald, ed., *Daß Jesus Christus ein geborener Jude sei: Ein Brief D. Martin Luthers wider die Sabbather an einen guten Freund*, MLLF Booklet 2 (Dresden, Germany: Landesverein für Innere Mission, 1931); Georg Buchwald, ed., *Von den Juden und ihren Lügen*, MLLF Booklet 3 (Dresden, Germany: Landesverein für Innere Mission, 1931); and Georg Buchwald, ed., *Vom Schem Hamphoras und vom Geschlecht Christi: Aus Predigten und Tischreden über die Juden*, MLLF Booklet 4 (Dresden, Germany: Landesverein für Innere Mission, 1931).

such one-sided views a wide audience.[61] His writings promoted antisemitic ideas of Jews as a people separate from the German Volk.

Luther and the Jews (1881)

In November 1879, not long after reading Jewish historian Heinrich Graetz's multivolume *History of the Jews*, Berlin historian Heinrich von Treitschke published an article titled "Our Prospects," which touched off a great controversy that would become known as the *Berliner Antisemitismusstreit* [Berlin Antisemitism Dispute].[62] Treitschke was angered by Graetz's historical narrative, which he thought demonstrated the traits that nearly justified the growing and vituperative antisemitism then present in Berlin. For example, both Treitschke and Graetz praise the eighteenth-century German Jewish philosopher Moses Mendelssohn. Yet Graetz attributes to Mendelssohn the revival of a German Jewish identity stripped of its supposedly less attractive medieval qualities, while Treitschke credits Mendelssohn with what he regards as an exemplary emancipation *from Jewishness* coupled with an embrace *of Germanness*. Treitschke's anger thus was based in part merely on Graetz's espousal of a positive German Jewish identity, an idea that Treitschke rejected in favor of a form of assimilation in which German Jews repressed their Jewish identity. The infamous phrase found near the end of the article, "the Jews are our misfortune"—which Treitschke may have borrowed from Luther—became forever associated with Treitschke and later served as a Nazi slogan. The Berlin historian had his "good Jews," of course. But he warned that while Jews who had immigrated to Germany arrived in poverty, their children would one day rule Germany's stock markets and newspapers.[63]

---

61. See Georg Buchwald, *Doktor Martin Luther: Ein Lebensbild für das Deutsche Haus* (Leipzig, Germany: B. G. Teubner, 1902). Buchwald treats the theme of "Luther and the Jews" here as well, 489–93. This work appeared in at least two more editions, in 1914 and 1924.

62. Heinrich von Treitschke, "Unsere Aussichten," *Preußischer Jahrbücher* 44 (1879): 559–76; Karsten Krieger, *Der "Berliner Antisemitismusstreit," 1879–1881: Eine Kontroverse um die Zugehörigkeit der deutschen Juden zur Nation—Kommentierte Quellenedition* (Munich: K. G. Saur, 2004), 1:14.

63. See especially Krieger, introduction to *Der "Berliner Antisemitismusstreit,"* x–xxxi (at x, xvi); Michael A. Meyer, "Heinrich Graetz and Heinrich von Treitschke: A Comparison of Their Historical Images of the Modern Jew," *Modern Judaism* 6, no. 1 (1986): 1–11; and Heinrich von Treitschke, *Luther und die deutsche Nation*, 2nd ed. (Berlin: G. Reimer, 1883). In *On the Jews and Their Lies*, Luther says "the Jews" are "a heavy burden to us, like a plague, pestilence, and vain misfortune in our land." See Luther, *Von den Juden und ihren Lügen*, 53:417–552 (at 520). For a brief discussion of the Berlin controversy in connection with

Initially, it was Jewish intellectuals who responded to Treitschke's attacks with articles of their own. Eventually, however, non-Jews lent their voices in opposition to Treitschke. "Manifesto of the Berlin Notables," which was signed by a number of Berlin academics—most notably Treitschke's renowned colleague Theodor Mommsen, along with seventy-five others—appeared in November 1880. The article bemoaned the fact that the "race-hate and fanaticism of the Middle Ages" had been reintroduced into modern German life. Mommsen was motivated in part by an antisemitic petition that had been circulated among students beginning in the autumn of the year that the manifesto appeared. The petition called for immigration restrictions and for limiting the number of Jewish civil servants and professionals. The controversy continued into the next year, but its reverberations lingered at least through the Third Reich.[64]

Buchwald's anonymously published *Luther and the Jews* appeared in 1881, while the controversy was still churning. He wrote the short work while a student at Leipzig, which, along with Berlin, was a center of the nascent antisemitic student movement in Germany.[65] In the introduction to the work, he addresses his "fellow students," relating the dilemma facing especially Protestant theologians in German universities in light of the circulation of "an antisemitic petition to the Reich Chancellor." Should they lend the petition their name, or would this be an un-Christian thing to do? He offers his "little book" to help solve the conundrum.[66]

Buchwald had been reflecting on an Advent sermon in which the preacher, Dr. Luthardt,[67] said that "*Deutschtum* [German-ness] has completely merged with Christianity; nobody can be a true German who is not a Christian."[68] Around the same time, Buchwald "skimmed through" Martin Luther's works. If anyone truly was a German "through and through, with heart and soul,"

"nationalistic Luther interpretation," see Jan Herman Brinks, "Luther and the German State," *Heythrop Journal* 39, no. 1 (1998): 1–17 (at 2–4).

64. Among those who had signed the petition were four thousand university students (19 percent of all students at German universities at the time). Krieger, *Der "Berliner Antisemitismusstreit*," xxvii; Norbert Kampe, "Jews and Antisemites at Universities in Imperial Germany (II): The Friedrich Wilhelms Universität of Berlin. A Case Study on the Students' 'Jewish Question,'" *Leo Baeck Institute Yearbook* 32, no. 1 (1987): 43–101.

65. Kampe, "Jews and Antisemites," 45.

66. Buchwald, *Luther und die Juden*, 3.

67. Christoph Ernst Luthardt (1823–1902), Professor of Systematic Theology at Leipzig. See Johannes Neukirch, "Luthardt, Christoph Ernst," in Biographisch-Bibliographisches Kirchenlexikon 5:440–42, and Thomas Kaufmann, *Luther's Jews: A Journey into Anti-Semitism* (Oxford: Oxford University Press, 2017), 141.

68. Buchwald, *Luther und die Juden*, 3 (quoting Luthardt).

opined the young scholar, it was Luther. Buchwald was "pleased to find confirmation" in Luther's works that Judaism and "a Deutschtum permeated by Christianity" could not exist side by side. Conceiving of the Jewish Question as either a religious or a racial question is "one-sided," he argues. Since the correct way to view it is as an "amalgamation of both," he heartily lends his agreement to Dr. Luthardt's dictum, concluding that "a Jew cannot be a German, because only a Christian can be a genuine German!"[69]

Despite this stark pronouncement, Buchwald quickly distances himself from Luther's "coarse" language and argues that not all of his proposals against "the Jews" are worthy of approval. Yet if one engages the subject, he should do so, Buchwald contends, in "the spirit in which our reformer speaks against the Jews." In combative fashion, Buchwald argues that "no one can say" that Luther's is not a true "Christian spirit"—"or do we want to take offense at the coarseness of Luther's expressions?"[70]

Buchwald will deal with Luther's opinions about "the Jews," he says, without invoking his "quite piquant and coarse" language. "On the contrary, I refuse with good right and conscience the reproach of a tendentious representation. So far as possible, I have skipped over all such remarks." But even if he had included them, Buchwald avers, this would have not been a matter serious enough for condemnation. For whoever knows Luther's "parlance" would not take offense. He speculates that if Luther could talk to nineteenth-century men, he would speak with different images than he used in the sixteenth century.

He frames *On the Jews and Their Lies* in light of Luther's Christocentrism: "With Luther Christ is beginning and end. At first the question: Can we lead the Jews to Christ? At the end the prayer: 'Christ our dear Lord, convert them mercifully!' and in the middle the question to us: How can we allow it, that a Volk live with us, who mock and ridicule our Lord and Redeemer daily?" Since, for Luther, Christ is at the center of Christianity, Buchwald argues that the reformer can "speak in truthful holy anger against the Jews."[71]

He frames the broader discussion of Luther's Judenschriften in the light of the important question, "Did Luther consider mission to the Jews possible?" He proposes first to answer this question and then to depict the picture that Luther draws of the "character of the Jews on the basis of the answer to that question." When it comes to the Jewish Question, the Christian has "above all" to answer, "Is it not the task of Christianity to call on the Jews in love rather

---

69. Ibid.
70. Ibid., 3–4.
71. Ibid., 4.

than to persecute them?" What is Luther's response to this question? The reply of Luther's earlier writings is "completely different," he contends, from the reformer's later response.[72]

Buchwald discusses next the long-term development of Luther's thinking regarding the Jewish Question. In 1537, Strasbourg-based Christian Hebraist Wolfgang Capito asked Luther to hear the plea of Josel of Rosheim, who was protector of German Jewry in the Holy Roman Empire during Luther's day, on behalf of the Jews of Saxony, who were being threatened with expulsion by John Frederick.[73] Predictably, Buchwald sides with Luther when recording the reformer's response to Josel's plea regarding the impending expulsion. In his reply to Josel, Luther emphasizes his purportedly magnanimous behavior toward German Jewry, which included both "words and writings" (Luther likely had in mind *That Jesus Christ Was Born a Jew*). Because the Jews so "shamefully abused" his service to them and did things that are intolerable to Christians, they subverted any influence Luther might have had with the princes and lords. Luther refuses to assist Josel on the grounds that he does not want to "'strengthen them in their error.'"[74] Buchwald agrees with Luther that his "friendly attitude toward the Jews certainly seems to have been recompensed badly." Further, he speculates that Luther's confrontation with three "'learned Jews'" between 1537 and 1538 (and also between his reply to Josel and the publication of *Against the Sabbatarians*) "probably" induced him to "judge the Jews more sharply."[75]

In Buchwald's analysis of Luther and "the Jews," the "bases for the impossibility of Jewish mission" lie in "Jewish character." He highlights Luther's disparaging of this "character" in the areas of their "tendentious" interpretation of scripture, their greed, and stinginess, progressing from *Against the Sabbatarians* to *On the Jews and Their Lies*. From the latter, Buchwald investigates at length the four "glories" of "the Jews"—the glories of "their descent from Abraham," circumcision, possession of the law, and possession of the land of Canaan—which prevent them from seeing the crucified Christ as Messiah.[76]

---

72. Ibid., 5.

73. Selma Stern, *Josel of Rosheim: Commander of Jewry in the Holy Roman Empire of the German Nation*, trans. Gertrude Hirschler (Philadelphia: Jewish Publication Society of America, 1965), 156–57, 175.

74. Luther, as quoted in Buchwald, *Luther und die Juden*, 6–7.

75. Buchwald, *Luther und die Juden*, 6–7. See also Mark U. Edwards Jr., *Luther's Last Battles: Politics and Polemics, 1531–46* (Ithaca, NY: Cornell University Press, 1983), 123–25.

76. Buchwald, *Luther und die Juden*, 8–12.

In two instances, Buchwald emphasizes the continuity in Luther's thinking about the Jewish people but demonstrates in both cases the greater severity of the later writings. For instance, he quotes a passage from a 1531 sermon in which Luther derides the coming Jewish Messiah as a "worldly king" who would build an "earthly *Reich*." In *On the Jews and Their Lies*, he attacks the "arrogance of nobility of blood and race" of the hoped-for Messiah of the Jews. Luther, he says, speaks "much sharper" in this later writing.[77]

In a second instance, Buchwald compares a 1521 pericope to another passage from *On the Jews and Their Lies*. In the earlier work, Luther calls "the Jews" "the greatest enemies of Christ of all time." Buchwald describes this language as "fairly mild." From *On the Jews and Their Lies*, he lists five "lies" that they have purportedly "invented." One of these "lies" is the purported Jewish designation of Jesus as the "child of a whore" and his mother, Mary, as a "whore."[78]

He pauses here to demur once again at Luther's harsh language. "The author would like also to apologize because of the quotation of these and the following passages. He fears however by omission of the same to perpetrate a dishonesty against Luther." It is these "lies of the Jews about our Lord," however, that have directly caused Luther "to propose the severe disciplinary measures against the Jews."[79] Despite his clear sympathy with the reformer—or perhaps because of it—he attempts to portray the proposed sociopolitical restrictions of *On the Jews and Their Lies* in a comprehensive theological context. Just prior to quoting excerpts from the proposals, Buchwald declares (with rather peculiar and unexplained zest, given the dire nature of the recommendations): "Let us now hear Luther's proposals concerning the Jewish Question!" After relating the recommendations in full, Buchwald closes with Luther's prayer, with which he concurs: "Christ, our dear Lord, convert them mercifully."[80]

"Luther's Pamphlets for Our Time" (1931)

In the introduction to this series, written fifty years after *Luther and the Jews*, Adolf Wendelin, at that time director of the publisher of the series, explains that the inexpensive booklets will make it possible for many "to become clear about Luther's position on questions" that deeply move the readers. They "will

---

77. Ibid., 15–16.

78. Ibid., 19. Buchwald censors Luther's formulation here, using an ellipsis to avoid the coarser language of the original: The Jews call Jesus "ein H . . . -kind [*Hurenkind*] und seine Mutter Maria eine H . . . [*Hure*]." See Luther, *Von den Juden und ihren Lügen*, 53:514.

79. Buchwald, *Luther und die Juden*, 19.

80. Ibid., 24–32.

be newly amazed thereby again and again, how clearly Luther comprehends the problems, how he foresees with a prophetic view a development which took root in the centuries after him." This "development" clearly includes the Jewish Question mentioned in the previous paragraph. "To our joy, the well-known Luther researcher Dr. Buchwald has undertaken this work."[81]

The second booklet covers *That Jesus Christ Was Born a Jew* and *Against the Sabbatarians*. In the preface, titled "Luthers Wandlungen in seiner Stellung zu den Juden" [Luther's transformations in his position on the Jews], Buchwald begins by citing a letter in which Luther sides with Johannes Reuchlin in his controversy with Johannes Pfefferkorn. Pfefferkorn (1469–1522) was a Jew who converted to Christianity but subsequently tried to have all Jewish books in the Holy Roman Empire except for the Old Testament destroyed. Reuchlin (1455–1522) was a trailblazing Christian Hebraist who opposed Pfefferkorn in this effort and was condemned by the pope for giving Christian interpretations to both the Hebrew Bible and the Kabbalah.[82] Despite his siding with Reuchlin in the controversy—a position that might on the surface appear philosemitic—Luther complains that Jews are "incorrigible" and can only become worse, not better, when rebuked.[83]

A few years later, in his 1521 *Magnificat* (translated into German and interpreted), Luther takes a "friendlier" position toward "the Jews." Here, the reformer argues that while most Jews are "obdurate," some may still convert to Christianity. Thus, Christians should not act in an "unfriendly" manner toward them. Later, however, according to Buchwald, Luther "heavily altered" this position "due to personal experiences and various tidings of the anti-Christian activities and the teachings of the Jews that were hostile to Christ." Buchwald recounts in similar fashion to his 1881 treatment (but with a bit more depth) of Luther's 1537 correspondence with Josel of Rosheim. In a page-long footnote, citing Wilhelm Walther's *Luther und die Juden und die Antisemiten* [Luther and the Jews and the Antisemites (1921)], he relates Luther's

---

81. Adolf Wendelin, introduction to *Von Kaufshandlung und Wucher: Martin Luther, Luthers Flugschriften für unsere Zeit*, Booklet 1 (Dresden, Germany: Landesverein für Innere Mission, 1931), inside cover.
82. See David H. Price, *Johannes Reuchlin and the Campaign to Destroy Jewish Books* (New York: Oxford University Press, 2011), and Heiko A. Oberman, *The Roots of Anti-Semitism in the Age of Renaissance and Reformation*, trans. James I. Porter (Philadelphia: Fortress, 1984), 11–12.
83. Buchwald, "Luthers Wandlungen in seiner Stellung zu den Juden," in *Daß Jesus Christus*, 5–6.

(once again quite negative) experiences with two Jewish Christian professors of Hebrew.[84] Buchwald's heavy emphasis on Luther's experiences as a reason for his hardening stance toward Jews and Judaism is congruent with some, though certainly not all, of his German Protestant contemporaries.[85]

Despite Luther's ever-sharpening rhetoric concerning the Jewish people, which Buchwald illustrates by reference to some brief but effective quotes, the reformer never fully abandons the hope of their conversion. Yet by the time he delivers his last sermon from the pulpit, his "admonition" against them (February 1546), his words carry not only "hope and love" but also "deeply serious" reflection. If "the Jews" want to convert and cease their blasphemy and other offenses, Christians will forgive them. If not, then Christians should not tolerate or endure them.[86] Following this general preface is an introduction to *That Jesus Christ Was Born a Jew*. There is nothing remarkable here, except for one comment that illuminates the highly regarded philologist's popularizing approach to this series of booklets. "The detailed biblical argumentation in Luther's writing hardly offers interest to today's reader. Only that which illuminates Luther's position on the Jews is communicated from it."[87] While the condensation of the reformer's thought for the German Protestant laity is understandable, this introductory comment might have led some readers to filter their perceptions of Luther's views on Jews and Judaism more through a contemporary cultural lens than through the perceived minutiae of biblical theology.

Buchwald delivers the introduction to the booklet about *On the Jews and Their Lies* in workmanlike fashion. He employs no strident rhetoric but is once again clearly sympathetic to Luther's version of events. According to Buchwald, God's wrath against the Jews is based on a litany of offenses that they have purportedly committed against Christians, including their "diatribes and lies" and "prayers against the Christians." The weight of this reality leads to a "pain" that, he argues, "overwhelms Luther and compels him to prayer for the Jews."[88] Like the final volume of Nazi philologist Theodor Pauls's 1939 three-volume work,

---

84. Buchwald, "Luthers Wandlungen," 5–7; Wilhelm Walther, *Luther und die Juden und die Antisemiten* (Leipzig, Germany: Dörffling & Franke, 1921), 9–10.

85. For example, both Ansbach pastor Hermann Steinlein and Heimsheim pastor Heinrich Fausel factored Luther's unpleasant experiences with Jews into their view of his attitude toward Jews and Judaism, but neither places as much stress on this factor as does Buchwald. See Probst, *Demonizing the Jews*, 75–79, 94–99.

86. Buchwald, "Luthers Wandlungen," 7–8.

87. Buchwald, *Daß Jesus Christus*, 9.

88. Buchwald, *Von den Juden und ihren Lügen*, 3.

Luther und die Juden [Luther and the Jews], Buchwald intersperses selected quotes from Luther's works with explanatory headings.

Pauls earned his doctorate in philology and until 1938 served as director of a secondary school for boys and girls in Senftenberg. In 1938, he became Professor at the University for Teacher Education in Hirschberg-Riesengebirge.[89] While Pauls did not sit on a Protestant theological faculty, he had a running engagement with Protestant theology via the German Christians, most notably by publishing *Luther und die Juden*, which was part of a long series of ostensibly scholarly works about "positive Christianity."[90] He also coauthored a volume on the "de-Judaizing" of Luther research with Dr. Werner Petersmann, a Breslau pastor and regional chairman of the German Christians in Silesia.[91] Pauls offered his *Luther und die Juden* as a "gift" to the antisemitic and purportedly academic Institute for the Study and Eradication of Jewish Influence on German Church Life, which was dominated by members of the German Christians and commonly called the "Eisenach Institute."[92]

Pauls's approach in this volume is really quite simple. It is a topical compendium of quotes about the Jewish Question, all taken from Luther's Judenschriften from 1538 to 1543. Pauls assigns a heading to each long quote or series of quotes. In one case, Pauls emphasizes blood by decrying a Jewish "false blood-boast"[93] in a heading concerning a passage where Luther describes the supposed error of the Jews as a fault "regarding nobility of blood and lineage."[94] In another instance, when Luther is speaking of the priority of being circumcised over and above the nobility of birth, Pauls gives the section the title "God

---

89. Peter von der Osten-Sacken, "Der Nationalsozialistische Lutherforscher Theodor Pauls: Vervollständigung eines Fragmentarischen Bildes," in *Das Mißbrauchte Evangelium: Studien zu Theologie und Praxis der Thüringer Deutsche Christen*, ed. Peter von der Osten-Sacken (Berlin: Institut Kirche und Judentum, 2002), 136–66.

90. Point twenty-four of the Nazi Party program called for a nebulous "positive Christianity" that crossed confessional boundaries, as long as it did not "endanger" the state or "conflict with the customs and moral sentiments of the Germanic race" (Alfred Rosenberg, *Das Parteiprogramm: Wesen, Grundsätze und Ziele der NSDAP*, 25th ed. [Munich: Zentralverlag der NSDAP, 1943], 13, 37–38).

91. Werner Petersmann and Theodor Pauls, *"Entjudung" selbst der Luther-Forschung in der Frage der Stellung Luthers zu den Juden!*, 3rd ed. (Bonn, Germany: Scheur, 1940).

92. Von der Osten-Sacken, "Der Nationalsozialistische Lutherforscher Theodor Pauls," 136–37. On the Institute for the Investigation and Eradication of Jewish Influence on German Church Life, see especially Heschel, *Aryan Jesus*, 67–165.

93. Theodor Pauls, *Aus Luthers Kampfschriften gegen die Juden*, vol. 3 of *Luther und die Juden* (Bonn, Germany: Scheur, 1939), 27.

94. Luther, *Von den Juden und ihren Lügen*, 421.

Commands More Than Mere Blood."[95] Luther does speak on occasion of the notion of blood when discussing the nobility of the Israelites, against which he rails.[96] Yet Pauls injects the specter of blood into his topical subheadings, even when the main idea of Luther's text is more about purported Jewish boasting or pride of ancestry. The term *blood* has racial overtones for Pauls that for Luther it clearly did not carry. The typical Nazi conception of blood bore the clear implication that Aryan blood was superior to non-Aryan and especially Jewish blood.[97]

The headings in Buchwald's work, however, generally adhere more closely to Luther's intentions. Given Luther's disdain for Jews and Judaism, this does not signify, of course, that the content of the headings is necessarily innocuous. In one section, for example, Buchwald deals with Luther's citation of examples of what he describes as "Jewish abuses against the person of Christ, against Mary, and thus against the Christians."[98] Yet the Leipzig philologist is generally more judicious in his quote selection than is Pauls, and the nazified racial rhetoric is absent. He captures the general sense of this and Luther's other *Judenschriften*. Buchwald's excerpted selections from Luther works, presented in the form of short books, made the reformer's anti-Judaic and antisemitic attitudes available to many German Protestants.[99] His approach to the Luther material, which was less tendentious than was Pauls's, might have made such attitudes more palatable, or even more attractive, to university-educated Protestants.

Luther's Eternal Word (1937)

In 1937, Buchwald edited a book-length compilation that is likely his most glowing tribute to the reformer. Despite the clear affinity for Luther's character and thought exhibited in the 1931 pamphlet series, Buchwald nevertheless demonstrated there a measure of scholarly restraint. Here, however, some of that moderation is stripped away. Crucially, in the intervening years his German readers had experienced the ascent to power of Hitler and the Nazis.

The preface sets the tone and framework for the manner in which Buchwald wants his readers to understand the excerpts from Luther's works that are to

---

95. Pauls, *Aus Luthers Kampfschriften*, 28.
96. See, e.g., Luther, *Von den Juden und ihren Lügen*, 420, 422.
97. See, e.g., Christopher M. Hutton, *Race and the Third Reich: Linguistics, Racial Anthropology and Genetics in the Dialectic of* Volk (Cambridge: Polity, 2005), 91–92, and Burleigh and Wippermann, *Racial State*, 66, 116.
98. Buchwald, *Von den Juden und ihren Lügen*, 16.
99. Ibid.

follow. Luther—here, a very *German* Luther—is presented as the translator and purifier of doctrine who had set things right for Christians in Germany. German sermons ring out from the pulpits. "The congregation prays in their mother tongue and praises God in German song. The young learn the German Catechism." Church and state are united in the fact that they serve the Volk.[100]

Following this long litany of praise for the reformer, Buchwald issues a brief, vague word of caution. "Even Luther was a child of his time. Therefore much of what he said is temporally conditioned." His last word, however, refocuses the reader on his central message. "But the fundamentals, which he drew from God's Word, retain their value and their power for all time. May our Volk draw blessing from them for time and eternity!"[101]

Buchwald divides his book into twelve "principal parts." These include "Man and God," "The Church," "The State," "The Home," and "Death and Eternal Life." The first section, "Luther the German Man," demonstrates most directly Buchwald's betrayal of the humanities.

In light of the times in which he was living, it is significant—but not surprising—that Buchwald would begin his literary tribute to Luther's "eternal word" with a section on Luther as a *German* man. The titles for many of the subsections are even more revealing: *"Alles für Deutschland,"* "The Reformation a German Affair," "German Language." One of the most striking is a brief selection of quotes under the subheading "The German Volk Need a Führer."

Without comment, Buchwald presents quotes from Luther taken from a lecture on Genesis, from his table talks, and from a sermon on Genesis. In one of these, Luther compares Germany to a beautiful stallion that has everything it needs—except a rider. Germany is "strong enough in might and men." A Führer, however, is missing.[102] Given added weight by the strong praise that the respected philologist has lavished on the reformer, this powerful imagery would have taken on fresh and menacing meaning in the wake of all that had transpired in Nazi Germany over the previous four years.

Not many pages later, and under the same principal part, "Luther the German Man," Buchwald deals with "Luther's position on the Jews" and "Luther's Judenschriften" under the subheading "Judaism." In this last subsection, he includes quotes from *That Jesus Christ Was Born a Jew*, *On the Jews and Their Lies*, and *On the Ineffable Name*. There is an implicit separation of Jewish-ness from

---

100. Georg Buchwald, preface to *Luthers ewiges Wort* (Cologne, Germany: Wartburg, 1937), no page number.
101. Ibid.
102. Buchwald, *Luthers ewiges Wort*, 21.

German-ness at work here that is similar to the explicit division he espoused in *Luther and the Jews* more than fifty years earlier. The difference, of course, is that it was now far more dangerous to be a Jew in Germany. Further, the inclusion under the outline heading "Luther the German Man" of both Germany's need for a Führer and the thoroughgoing degradation of Judaism, including the full reprint of the seven severe recommendations, hardly seems accidental.

Much of the language of the section "Luther's Position on the Jews" is nearly identical to that of the 1931 pamphlet series, suggesting that he reused and edited some of that material. In terms of text selection, however, it is noteworthy that he devotes by far the greatest space of the twelve pages to excerpts from the aggressively anti-Judaic and antisemitic *On the Jews and Their Lies* (seven pages).[103] The work in its totality is a literary hymn to the reformer's purported social and theological prescience and prowess, but it is pregnant with ominous implications for Germany's Jews.

VI. CONCLUSION

Over the course of more than half a century, first as a student of theology, then as a pastor-scholar, and finally as a seasoned and respected Luther scholar, Georg Buchwald occupied himself with the works of the seminal figure of the German Protestant Reformation. Significantly, he popularized Luther's writings about Jews and Judaism during the waning years of the Weimar Republic and included an extensive section on Luther's most infamous antisemitic work, *On the Jews and Their Lies*, in a hagiographical work about the reformer written four years after the Nazis came to power in Germany. In all of this, he remained remarkably consistent in his appraisal of Jews and Judaism and in his portrayal of the reformer's outlook on the same. Buchwald's overwhelmingly negative assessment of the Jewish people and their faith—which he made available to thousands via his publications—represents a betrayal of the humanities, including the crucial scholarly value of objectivity.

As a young theology student at Leipzig, Georg Buchwald anonymously dipped his toe in the Berlin Antisemitism Dispute. He plainly wished to make a clear statement on the issue from a Protestant Christian perspective and invoked the influential German reformer in doing so. Despite the harshness of the conclusions reached in the resulting book, *Luther and the Jews*, Buchwald evidences there, at least in small measure, the nuance of a burgeoning academic theologian. With respect to the Jewish Question, he believed that the racial

---

103. Ibid., 33–44.

and the religious should be fused. Ironically, this cool rejection of a one-sided answer leads him to the stark conclusion that a Jew cannot be a good German.

Buchwald centers Luther's answer to the Jewish Question in his Christology (doctrine of Christ). What Buchwald and Luther both apparently view as a mass Jewish rejection of Christ leads to God's wrath against them. This anti-Judaic interpretation is married to a view of Luther's personal disappointments with Jews—which he sees as a key factor in the reformer's ever-sharpening anti-Jewish tone.

The fact that Luther had some difficult personal experiences with Jews is valid enough, except that Buchwald presumes Luther's innocence in these encounters, which in fact were few and far between.[104] Further, to imply that a few such experiences should justifiably lead to a poor opinion about an entire people group is license for xenophobia at least. The weight that Buchwald places on this factor is unwarranted. The reformer's apocalyptic worldview, equally dim view of Catholicism and Islam, and worsening health are not even considered.[105] This lack of contextualization represents another aspect of Buchwald's betrayal of the academic ideals of the study of the humanities during the Third Reich.

The young scholar is so embarrassed by the reformer's crude language that he censors one of the milder pejoratives. Yet he makes clear that this difference between sixteenth- and nineteenth-century German parlances is merely a curiosity of cultural evolution. If Luther would have lived in the nineteenth century, he would not have been so vulgar in his antisemitism; perhaps he would have been, like Buchwald and many other like-minded middle-class Germans, a "respectable" antisemite. In the end, Buchwald is more than happy to make Luther's severe anti-Jewish proposals available to his fellow students in an environment that had become increasingly acrid for its Jewish minority.

Fifty years later, in the deeply troubled atmosphere of late Weimar Germany, Buchwald, now a highly regarded Luther philologist, prepared the topical booklet series "Luther's Pamphlets for Our Time." Here he places even more emphasis on Luther's series of disappointments and confrontations with Jews. The idea of Jewish mission is still present even in the later Luther, despite his souring mood and sharpening tone.

---

104. Thomas Kaufmann, "Luther and the Jews," in *Jews, Judaism, and the Reformation in Sixteenth-Century Germany*, ed. Dean Phillip Bell and Stephen G. Burnett (Leiden, Netherlands: Brill, 2006), 69–104 (at 73–76).
105. See Probst, *Demonizing the Jews*, 39–58.

A crucial comment appears in the introduction to the booklet on *That Jesus Christ Was Born a Jew*. Keenly aware of his audience, he notes that readers may not be very interested in Luther's "detailed biblical argumentation," and so only what "illuminates Luther's position on the Jews" appears. While the idea of condensing Luther's works for popular consumption is certainly reasonable, the sacrifice of the reformer's theological reasoning (much of which was anti-Judaic in nature) might have left some readers to lean more on their visceral tendencies when deciding how to view their Jewish contemporaries.

Four years into the Nazi regime, Buchwald was now in his late seventies. His 1937 work, *Luther's Eternal Word*, may be described most aptly as glowing hagiography. The reformer's influence on German life—which was indeed substantial—is nonetheless portrayed here as impeccably beneficial. The separation of Jewish-ness from German-ness so evident in the earlier anonymous work is present here in a more subtle yet unmistakable manner. While the ascent to power and rule of Hitler may have seemed to Buchwald an answer to Luther's prescient sixteenth-century observations, the Führer's antisemitic policies were in 1937 a deepening menace to Germany's beleaguered Jews (and would later become so for the Jews of Europe).

Buchwald's treatment of the issue "Luther and the Jews" was marked by a modicum of scholarship and erudition. He applied his significant intellectual prowess throughout his long career to making the thought and works of Luther available to both popular and scholarly audiences. His work, then, encompassed both the second and third tiers in Steinweis's schema, suggesting that Buchwald's views would have gained a fairly wide influence. Yet despite his scholarly bona fides, the tendentious manner in which he portrayed Jews and Judaism is palpable.

That Buchwald engaged the theme of "Luther and the Jews" for more than five decades suggests that the topic was important to him. He treated the topic in a rather consistent fashion throughout his career. Despite the many changes in the political structures, national fortunes, and religious outlook at work in Germany, this strongly suggests that, where it concerned their views about Jews and Judaism—for some Protestants at least—a modicum of continuity existed from the Kaiserreich to the Third Reich.[106]

---

106. The sharp turn toward antisemitism in Gerhard Kittel's approach to New Testament studies after the Nazis came to power, however, provides a counterpoint to this (tentative) argument. See, for example, Robert P. Ericksen, "The Case of Gerhard Kittel," in *Theologians under Hitler: Gerhard Kittel, Paul Althaus, and Emanuel Hirsch* (New Haven, CT: Yale University Press, 1985), 28–78. Yet further research is needed to determine the calculus between continuity and discontinuity in Protestant views of Jews and Judaism from the birth

Moringen pastor and Luther scholar Walter Holsten was only twenty-four years old when his first scholarly work was published. One year later, Hitler and the Nazis came to power in Germany. In 1936, in the wake of the implementation of the Nuremberg Race Laws, the first edition of the young scholar's commentary on Luther's writings about Jews and Turks appeared in print. The second edition was published in 1938, the year of the Kristallnacht [night of broken glass], with its destruction of hundreds of Jewish synagogues and thousands of Jewish businesses, public violence against Jews, and, in the week that followed, the arrest and internment of some thirty thousand Jewish men in Dachau, Buchenwald, and Sachsenhausen. In this context, Holsten betrayed the humanities (and his fellow man) by reiterating Luther's sixteenth-century justification of seven severe sociopolitical measures against German Jews and by tying the contemporary threat of Bolshevism to Jews.

The scholarly endeavors of both Buchwald and Holsten provided, especially for their fellow Protestants, theological arguments against besieged German (and indeed European) Jews. Their writings furthered the notions of Jews as a people inferior to the German Volk, as purveyors of Bolshevism, and as enemies of Christ and Christianity. Bound up as Christianity and German-ness were for Buchwald, and given Holsten's support for at least the principles of Nazi anti-Jewish policy, this signified that Jews were enemies of the German Volk at a time when they had already been thrust outside the boundaries of German society; they would soon, of course, experience the bitter realities of the Shoah. Such abuses of scholarship fly in the face of the sorts of principles to which both the academy and the church have often aspired. They represent both a betrayal and a perversion of these ideals.

BIBLIOGRAPHY

Althaus, Paul. "Der Wahrheitsgehalt der Religionen und das Evangelium: Grundsätze der theologischen Kritik aller Religion." *Neue Allgemeine Missionszeitschrift* 11, no. 10 (1934): 277–92. Reprinted in *Theologische Aufsätze*, vol. 2, by Paul Althaus, 65–82. Gütersloh, Germany: Bertelsmann, 1935.

———. "Die Frage des Evangeliums an das moderne Judentum." *Zeitschrift für Systematische Theologie* 7 (1930): 195–215. Reprinted in *Theologische Aufsätze*, vol. 2, by Paul Althaus, 83–103. Gütersloh, Germany: Bertelsmann, 1935.

---

of the modern German nation-state to the end of the Third Reich (and beyond). I am grateful to Indiana University Press for granting me permission to draw on material from *Demonizing the Jews: Luther and the Protestant Church in Nazi Germany* (Bloomington: Indiana University Press, 2012), especially in the first half of this essay.

Applegate, Celia. *A Nation of Provincials: The German Idea of Heimat*. Berkeley: University of California Press, 1990.

Bainton, Roland H. "Interpretations of the Reformation." *American Historical Review* 66, no. 1 (1960): 74–84.

Barnes, Kenneth C. "Dietrich Bonhoeffer and Hitler's Persecution of the Jews." In Ericksen and Heschel, *Betrayal*, 110–28.

Barnett, Victoria. *For the Soul of the People: Protestant Protest against Hitler*. New York: Oxford University Press, 1992.

Bautz, Friedrich-Wilhelm. "Buchwald, Georg." In *Biographisch-Bibliographisches Kirchenlexikon*, 1:794.

Bergen, Doris L. *Twisted Cross: The German Christian Movement in the Third Reich*. Chapel Hill: University of North Carolina Press, 1996.

Bethge, Eberhard. "Dietrich Bonhoeffer und die Juden." In *Die Juden und Martin Luther—Martin Luther und die Juden: Geschichte, Wirkungsgeschichte, Herausforderung*, edited by Heinz Kremers, 211–49. Dusseldorf, Germany: Neukirchener, 1985.

Biographisch-Bibliographisches Kirchenlexikon. Edited by Friedrich-Wilhelm Bautz and Traugott Bautt. 37 vols. Hamm, Germany: Traugott Bautz, 1990–2016.

Borcherdt, H. H., and Georg Merz, eds. *Schriften wider Juden und Türken*. Vol. 3 of *Martin Luther: Ausgewählte Werke*. 2nd ed. Munich: Christian Kaiser, 1938.

Borcherdt, H. H., Georg Merz, and Wilhelm Heinsius, eds. *Martin Luther: Ausgewählte Werke*. 3rd ed. Munich: Christian Kaiser, 1948–1953.

Brinks, Jan Herman. "Luther and the German State." *Heythrop Journal* 39, no. 1 (1998): 1–17.

Buchwald, Georg, ed. *Daß Jesus Christus ein geborener Jude sei: Ein Brief D. Martin Luthers wider die Sabbather an einen guten Freund*. Booklet 2 of *Martin Luther, Luthers Flugschriften für unsere Zeit* (hereafter, *MLLF*) Dresden, Germany: Landesverein für Innere Mission, 1931.

———. *Doktor Martin Luther: Ein Lebensbild für das Deutsche Haus*. Leipzig, Germany: B. G. Teubner, 1902.

———. *Luthers ewiges Wort*. Cologne, Germany: Wartburg, 1937.

[Buchwald, Georg.] *Luther und die Juden: Den deutschen Studenten gewidmet von einem Kommilitonen*. Leipzig, Germany: Paul Frobberg, 1881.

Buchwald, Georg. *Vom Schem Hamphoras und vom Geschlecht Christi: Aus Predigten und Tischreden über die Juden*. MLLF Booklet 4. Dresden, Germany: Landesverein für Innere Mission, 1931.

———. *Von den Juden und ihren Lügen*. MLLF Booklet 3. Dresden, Germany: Landesverein für Innere Mission, 1931.

———. *Von Kaufshandlung und Wucher*. MLLF Booklet 1. Dresden, Germany: Landesverein für Innere Mission, 1931.

Burleigh, Michael. *The Third Reich: A New History*. London: Pan, 2001.

Burleigh, Michael, and Wolfgang Wippermann. *The Racial State: Germany, 1933–1945*. 14th printing. Cambridge: Cambridge University Press, 2007.
Confino, Alon. *Germany as a Culture of Remembrance: Promises and Limits of Writing History*. Chapel Hill: University of North Carolina Press, 2006.
Edwards, Mark U., Jr. *Luther's Last Battles: Politics and Polemics, 1531–46*. Ithaca, NY: Cornell University Press, 1983.
Ericksen, Robert P. "Assessing the Heritage: German Protestant Theologians, Nazis, and the 'Jewish Question.'" In Ericksen and Heschel, *Betrayal*, 22–39.
———. *Complicity in the Holocaust: Churches and Universities in Nazi Germany*. Cambridge: Cambridge University Press, 2012.
———. *Theologians under Hitler: Gerhard Kittel, Paul Althaus, and Emanuel Hirsch*. New Haven, CT: Yale University Press, 1985.
Ericksen, Robert P., and Susannah Heschel, eds. *Betrayal: German Churches and the Holocaust*. Minneapolis: Fortress, 1999.
———. "The German Churches and the Holocaust." In *The Historiography of the Holocaust*, edited by Dan Stone, 296–318. New York: Palgrave Macmillan, 2004.
Evans, Richard J. *The Third Reich in Power: How the Nazis Won Over the Hearts and Minds of a Nation*. London: Penguin, 2006.
Friedländer, Saul. *Nazi Germany and the Jews, 1933–1945*. Abridged ed. New York: HarperPerennial, 2009.
Gerlach, Wolfgang. *And the Witnesses Were Silent: The Confessing Church and the Persecution of the Jews*. Translated by Victoria J. Barnett. Lincoln: University of Nebraska Press, 2000.
Grau, Wilhelm. *Antisemitismus im späten Mittelalter: Das Ende der Regensburger Judengemeinde, 1450–1519*. Munich: Duncker and Humblot, 1934.
Grimm, Harold J. "Luther Research since 1920." *Journal of Modern History* 32, no. 2 (1960): 105–18.
Grimsted, Patricia Kennedy. "Roads to Ratibor: Library and Archival Plunder by the Einsatzstab Reichsleiter Rosenberg." *Holocaust and Genocide Studies* 19, no. 3 (2005): 390–458.
Gritsch, Eric W. *Martin Luther's Anti-Semitism: Against His Better Judgment*. Grand Rapids, MI: Eerdmans, 2012.
Grüttner, Michael. *Studenten im Dritten Reich*. Paderborn, Germany: Ferdinand Schöningh, 1995.
Hartshorne, Edward Yarnell, Jr. *The German Universities and National Socialism*. Cambridge, MA: Harvard University Press, 1937.
———. "The German Universities and the Government." *Annals of the American Academy of Political and Social Science* 200, no. 1 (1938): 210–34.
Hermelink, Heinrich. "Die neuere Lutherforschung." *Theologische Rundschau* 7, no. 2 (1935): 63–85, 131–56.

Heschel, Susannah. *The Aryan Jesus: Christian Theologians and the Bible in Nazi Germany*. Princeton, NJ: Princeton University Press, 2008.

———. "Nazifying Christian Theology: Walter Grundmann and the Institute for the Study and Eradication of Jewish Influence on German Church Life." *Church History* 63, no. 4 (1994): 587–605.

Hirsch, Emanuel. *Die gegenwärtige geistige Lage im Spiegel philosophischer und theologischer Besinnung*. Göttingen, Germany: Vandenhoeck & Ruprecht, 1934.

Holsten, Walter. "Erläuterungen." In Borcherdt and Merz, *Schriften wider Juden und Türken*, 523–79.

Hutton, Christopher M. *Race and the Third Reich: Linguistics, Racial Anthropology and Genetics in the Dialectic of Volk*. Cambridge: Polity, 2005.

Jauernig, Reinhold. "Georg Buchwald in Memoriam." *Theologische Literaturzeitung* 78, no. 4 (1953): 239–52.

Junginger, Horst. *The Scientification of the "Jewish Question" in Germany*. Leiden, Netherlands: Brill, 2017.

Kampe, Norbert. "Jews and Antisemites at Universities in Imperial Germany (II): The Friedrich Wilhelms Universität of Berlin. A Case Study on the Students' 'Jewish Question.'" *Leo Baeck Institute Yearbook* 32, no. 1 (1987): 43–101.

Kaufmann, Thomas. "Luther and the Jews." In *Jews, Judaism, and the Reformation in Sixteenth-Century Germany*, edited by Dean Phillip Bell and Stephen G. Burnett, 69–104. Leiden, Netherlands: Brill, 2006.

———. *Luther's Jews: A Journey into Anti-Semitism*. Oxford: Oxford University Press, 2017.

Koonz, Claudia. *The Nazi Conscience*. London: Belknap Press, 2003.

Krieger, Karsten. *Der "Berliner Antisemitismusstreit," 1879–1881: Eine Kontroverse um die Zugehörigkeit der deutschen Juden zur Nation*. Kommentierte Quellenedition. 2 vols. Munich: K. G. Saur, 2004.

Kupisch, Karl. "The 'Luther Renaissance.'" *Journal of Contemporary History* 2, no. 4 (1967): 39–49.

Lächele, Rainer, and Jörg Thierfelder, eds. *Wir konnten uns nicht entziehen: 30 Porträts zu Kirche und Nationalsozialismus in Württemberg*. Stuttgart, Germany: Quell, 1998.

Lamparter, Eduard. *Das Judentum in seiner Kultur und religionsgeschichtlichen Erscheinung*. Gotha, Germany: Leopold Klotz, 1928.

Langmuir, Gavin I. *History, Religion, and Antisemitism*. Berkeley: University of California Press, 1990.

———. *Toward a Definition of Antisemitism*. Berkeley: University of California Press, 1990.

Leffler, Siegfried. *Christus im Dritten Reich der Deutschen: Wesen, Weg, und Ziel der Kirchenbewegung "Deutsche Christen."* Weimar, Germany: Deutsche Christen, 1935.

Levinson, Bernard M. "Reading the Bible in Nazi Germany: Gerhard von Rad's Attempt to Reclaim the Old Testament for the Church." *Interpretation: A Journal of Bible and Theology* 62, no. 3 (2008): 238–54.

Luther, Martin. *D. Martin Luthers Letzte Streitschrift*. Edited by Georg Buchwald. Leipzig, Germany: Wigand, 1893.

———. *D. Martin Luthers Werke: Kritische Gesamtausgabe*. 120 vols. Weimar, Germany: Böhlau, 1883–2009.

———. "On the Jews and Their Lies, 1543." Translated by Martin H. Bertram. In *The Christian in Society IV*, edited by Franklin Sherman, 121–306. Vol. 47 of *Luther's Works*. Philadelphia: Fortress, 1971.

———. *Ungedruckte Predigten D. Martin Luthers aus den Jahren 1537–1540*. Edited by Georg Buchwald. Leipzig, Germany: G. Strübig, 1905.

———. *Von den Juden und ihren Lügen*. In Borcherdt and Merz, *Schriften wider Juden und Türken*, 61–228.

———. *Von den Juden und ihren Lügen*. In *Schriften 1542/43*, 417–552. D. Martin Luthers Werke: Kritische Gesamtausgabe 53. Weimar, Germany: Böhlau, 1920 (Weimar edition).

Meyer, Michael A. "Heinrich Graetz and Heinrich von Treitschke: A Comparison of Their Historical Images of the Modern Jew." *Modern Judaism* 6, no. 1 (1986): 1–11.

Neukirch, Johannes. "Luthardt, Christoph Ernst." In *Biographisch-Bibliographisches Kirchenlexikon* 5:440–42.

Niewyk, Donald L. *The Jews in Weimar Germany*. 2nd ed. New Brunswick, NJ: Transaction, 2001.

Oberman, Heiko A. *The Roots of Anti-Semitism in the Age of Renaissance and Reformation*. Translated by James I. Porter. Philadelphia: Fortress, 1984.

Osten-Sacken, Peter von der, ed. *Das Mißbrauchte Evangelium: Studien zu Theologie und Praxis der Thüringer Deutsche Christen*. Berlin: Institut Kirche und Judentum, 2002.

Papen, Patricia von. "Vom engagierten Katholiken zum Rassenantisemiten: Die Karriere des Historikers 'der Judenfrage' Wilhelm Grau." In *Theologische Wissenschaft im "Dritten Reich": Ein ökumenisches Projekt*, edited by Georg Denzler and Leonore Siegele-Wenschkewitz, 68–113. Frankfurt, Germany: Haag and Herchen, 2000.

Pauls, Theodor. *Aus Luthers Kampfschriften gegen die Juden*. Vol. 3 of *Luther und die Juden*. Bonn, Germany: Scheur, 1939.

Petersmann, Werner, and Theodor Pauls. *"Entjudung" selbst der Luther-Forschung in der Frage der Stellung Luthers zu den Juden!* 3rd ed. Bonn: Scheur, 1940.

Phillips, Jonathan. *The Crusades, 1095–1197*. London: Routledge, 2013.

Price, David H. *Johannes Reuchlin and the Campaign to Destroy Jewish Books*. New York: Oxford University Press, 2011.

Probst, Christopher J. *Demonizing the Jews: Luther and the Protestant Church in Nazi Germany.* Bloomington: Indiana University Press, 2012.

———. "Protestantism in Nazi Germany: A View from the Margins." In *Life and Times in Nazi Germany*, edited by Lisa Pine, 213–38. London: Bloomsbury Academic, 2016.

Remy, Steven P. *The Heidelberg Myth: The Nazification and Denazification of a German University.* Cambridge, MA: Harvard University Press, 2002.

Richarz, Monika, ed. *Jewish Life in Germany: Memoirs from Three Centuries.* Translated by Stella P. Rosenfeld and Sidney Rosenfeld. Bloomington: Indiana University Press, 1991.

Röhm, Eberhard, and Jörg Thierfelder. *Juden-Christen-Deutsche, 1933–1945.* 4 vols. Stuttgart: Calwer, 1990–2007.

Rosenberg, Alfred. *Das Parteiprogramm: Wesen, Grundsätze und Ziele der NSDAP.* 25th ed. Munich: Zentralverlag der NSDAP, 1943.

Rückert, Hanns. "Die Bedeutung der Reformation für die deutsche Geschichte." *Deutsche Theologie* 8 (1941): 89–101.

———. "Luther als Deutscher." Luthersonderheft, *Deutsche Theologie* 1 (November 1933): 10–23.

Siegele-Wenschkewitz, Leonore, and Carsten Nicolaisen, eds. *Theologische Fakultäten im Nationalsozialismus.* Göttingen: Vandenhoeck & Ruprecht, 1993.

Steinweis, Alan E. *Studying the Jew: Scholarly Antisemitism in Nazi Germany.* Cambridge, MA: Harvard University Press, 2006.

Stern, Selma. *Josel of Rosheim: Commander of Jewry in the Holy Roman Empire of the German Nation.* Translated by Gertrude Hirschler. Philadelphia: Jewish Publication Society of America, 1965.

Treitschke, Heinrich von. *Luther und die deutsche Nation.* 2nd ed. Berlin: G. Reimer, 1883.

———. "Unsere Aussichten." *Preußischer Jahrbücher* 44 (1879): 559–76.

Vogelsang, Erich. *Luthers Kampf Gegen die Juden.* Tübingen, Germany: J. C. B. Mohr, 1933.

Walther, Wilhelm. *Luther und die Juden und die Antisemiten.* Leipzig, Germany: Dörffling & Franke, 1921.

Weinreich, Max. *Hitler's Professors: The Part of Scholarship in Germany's Crimes against the Jewish People.* New York: Yiddish Scientific Institute (YIVO), 1946. Reprinted with a foreword by Martin Gilbert. New Haven, CT: Yale University Press, 1999.

Wendelin, Adolf. Introduction to *Von Kaufshandlung und Wucher und Wucher.* In Landesverein für Innere Mission, MLLF Booklet 2, inside cover.

Wischnath, Michael, ed. *Universitätsarchiv Tübingen: Bestandsrepertorium 207. Nachlaß Hanns Rückert (1901–1974): (1917–1970).* Universitätsarchiv Tübingen: Tübingen, 2000.

Wolgast, Eike. "Nationalsozialistische Hochschulpolitik und die evangelisch-theologischen Fakultäten." In Siegele-Wenschkewitz and Nicolaisen, *Theologische Fakultäten im Nationalsozialismus*, 45–79.

Wrogemann, Henning. "Holsten, Walter." In *Religion in Geschichte und Gegenwart: Handwörterbuch für Theologie und Religionswissenschaft*. Vol. 3. Edited by Hans D. Betz et al., 1872. 4th ed. Tübingen, Germany: Mohr Siebeck, 2000.

CHRISTOPHER J. PROBST teaches courses in modern European history and Holocaust and Genocide Studies at Washington University in St. Louis and Maryville University. His publications include *Demonizing the Jews: Luther and the Protestant Church in Nazi Germany* (Indiana University Press, 2012) and "Protestantism in Nazi Germany: A View from the Margins," in *Life and Times in Nazi Germany*, edited by Lisa Pine (2016). In 2008, he was a Charles H. Revson Foundation Fellow at the Center for Advanced Holocaust Studies of the United States Holocaust Memorial Museum.

FOUR

GERHARD VON RAD'S STRUGGLE AGAINST THE NAZIFICATION OF THE OLD TESTAMENT

BERNARD M. LEVINSON

IN 1933, HITLER AND HIS Nationalsozialistische Deutsche Arbeiterpartei [National Socialist German Workers' Party], better known as the NSDAP or the "Nazi Party," gained control of the German government. During its first months in power, the government initiated a series of legal measures to eliminate all forms of influence other than the National Socialist party. Non-Nazi organizations such as trade unions, political parties, and the Protestant Church were to be brought under centralized control. The Nazis termed the pseudolegal measures taken to forcibly subordinate competing institutions and organizations, rather euphemistically, *Gleichschaltung* [alignment].

Despite its name and intent, the degree of coordination varied across different institutions, as did the approach the government took to achieve the Gleichschaltung. Within the Protestant Church, the Nazi government began supporting efforts to place the historically autonomous, individual state churches under a centralized, national structure, a *Reichskirche* [Reich Church]. The Deutsche Christen [German Christians], a rising faction within the Church seeking to align church doctrine with National Socialist ideology, gained Hitler's support to lead the new Reich Church. With NSDAP assistance, the German Christians undertook the task of managing the Church's transformation. However, the policies that they attempted to implement in the Church were polarizing, and the manner in which they forced the changes on the Church was badly managed. As a result, their biggest achievement was galvanizing widespread resistance, to both their methods and their theology. That resistance effectively thwarted the sort of Gleichschaltung within the church that both Hitler and the German

Christians desired.[1] Despite a lack of meaningful progress toward a unified Reichskirche, however, the German Christians held on to leadership positions within most of the state churches throughout the Third Reich, which allowed them to continue to pursue their efforts to nazify the Church at the local level.[2]

Relative to the Protestant Church, the push to align the German universities was less coordinated and far less controversial. While the universities were encouraged by the Education Ministry, the state police, and Nazi-aligned student and faculty organizations to devote their efforts to the priorities of the state, there was no single central authority or even a single clearly defined government plan to coordinate the alignment of these schools.[3] Rather, the government implemented two new policies to ensure that key leadership roles in the universities would be held by party loyalists and then allowed movement toward alignment with National Socialist priorities to proceed largely at its own pace. The first policy was enforcement of the 1933 Law for the Restoration of the Professional Civil Service, which in part required that Jews and those with anti-Nazi political views be purged from their positions in civil service. Since the schools were government funded, faculty and staff were civil servants, and thus were subject to the new employment restrictions. The second new policy to be implemented was overturning the historical practice

---

All English translations are by the author unless a translated volume is cited. Works translated into English are introduced by "ET:" as the notation. For ease of reference to the original documents, archival sources retain the original German terminology with the shelf and file numbers. Thanks to Robert Ericksen for his careful reading and valuable suggestions, as well as to Tina Sherman, my research assistant, for her careful work.

1. Richard Steigmann-Gall, *The Holy Reich: Nazi Conceptions of Christianity, 1919–1945* (Cambridge: Cambridge University Press, 2003), 155–66.

2. For the situation within the Roman Catholic Church, see Robert A. Krieg, *Catholic Theologians in Nazi Germany* (New York: Continuum, 2004); and Kevin P. Spicer, *Hitler's Priests: Clergy and National Socialism* (De Kalb: Northern Illinois University Press, 2008).

3. Wolfgang Bialas and Anson Rabinbach, "Introduction: The Humanities in Nazi Germany," in *Nazi Germany and the Humanities: How German Academics Embraced Nazism*, ed. Wolfgang Bialas and Anson Rabinbach (Oxford: Oneworld, 2014; originally published 2006), ix–liii. Nazification of the universities was also assisted by the efforts of two national organizations: The National Socialist German Students' League (NSDStB), which managed student government and other campus activities and events, and the National Socialist German University Instructors' League (NSDDozB), which all junior faculty members were required to join (Robert P. Ericksen, *Complicity in the Holocaust: Churches and Universities in Nazi Germany* [Cambridge: Cambridge University Press, 2012], 144).

of selecting rectors and deans by faculty election and instead making these positions political appointments.[4] The general enthusiasm among faculty and students toward politicization of the universities, coupled with the placement of party loyalists in key university leadership positions, ensured the success of the alignment of those institutions with Nazi priorities and ideology, even without the presence of a strong central authority to guide the changes.[5]

The Gleichschaltung of the Church and the universities becomes particularly instructive at their point of intersection: the study of Christian theology. A review of these two interrelated institutions reveals the impact on scholars of the Church controversy over, and the university enthusiasm for, the Gleichschaltung. It would be a much larger project to examine all of the theological crosscurrents between the Church and the universities during this era. Yet a case study of one scholar's experience, that of Gerhard von Rad (1901–1971), is a useful place to start. Von Rad, later renowned as a major theologian of the Old Testament,[6] began his academic career during the period when the Nazis rose to power. A perplexing problem in von Rad's writings raises a series of important issues about the social location of scholarship under the National Socialist dictatorship. His experience under Gleichschaltung serves as a microcosm of the larger changes taking place in the German university. Von Rad's resistance to those changes stands in contrast to the betrayal of traditional academic values, such as independence of scholarly inquiry from political interference and meritocracy in hiring decisions, by many of his colleagues. Unlike his peers, Von Rad never incorporated National Socialist ideology into his research or course work. Yet he was not unmoved by events around him. His drive to resist the nazification of his field shaped his work in ways even he himself does not seem to have recognized.

I. A PUZZLE IN VON RAD'S SCHOLARSHIP

"Was will das Deuteronomium?" ["What is the Purpose of Deuteronomy"?][7] The question of the significance of Deuteronomy preoccupied von Rad over

---

4. *Rektor* [derived from the Latin *rector* or "ruler"] is the standard German term for the chief executive of a university. The equivalent term in England would often be *chancellor* and in the North American context usually *president*.

5. Ericksen, *Complicity in the Holocaust*, 84–89 and 139–45.

6. The term "Old Testament," rather than "Hebrew Bible," is used throughout this chapter because at this point in the history of the discipline of biblical studies there was no notion of the Hebrew Bible as also a Jewish text.

7. Gerhard von Rad, *Deuteronomium-Studien*, Forschungen zur Religion und Literatur des Alten und Neuen Testaments (FRLANT) 58 (Göttingen, Germany: Vandenhoeck &

the length of his career, in both his scholarly works and those aimed at a broader readership. From his doctoral dissertation in 1929, *Das Gottesvolk im Deuteronomium* [The People of God in Deuteronomy], through his commentary on Deuteronomy in 1964 for the prestigious series Das Alte Testament Deutsch, von Rad kept returning to Deuteronomy.[8] Even where Deuteronomy was not the sole focus, it often provided the point of departure for other explorations. Just as striking as this continuing preoccupation with Deuteronomy was how von Rad described Deuteronomy: both what he affirmed and what he denied about its textual content, its priorities, and its theology.

As is well known to biblical scholars, von Rad argued that Deuteronomy is not law but rather sermons by countryside Levites who preached a renewed message of redemption. He argued that Deuteronomy's law code is not dead text but live instruction, not incomprehensible demands for works but spiritual exhortations to remember God's grace.[9] In his view, the redactors of Deuteronomy return Israel, hundreds of years after Moses, to the foot of Mount Horeb to renew Yahweh's election and salvation. From this retrospective vantage point, Deuteronomy delivers its message of Israel's election. Von Rad concluded that in its purest form, Deuteronomy declares Yahweh's constant, unconditional election of Israel to salvation. So complete and pervasive is Israel's election that the concepts of commandments and obedience are subordinated: "Die Erfüllung der Gebote ist also keineswegs

---

Ruprecht, 1947), chapter title, 48. In the second edition, the chapter title was changed to emphasize still further von Rad's focus: "Die Absicht des Deuteronomiums" (Gerhard von Rad, *Deuteronomium-Studien*, 2nd ed., FRLANT 58 [Göttingen, Germany: Vandenhoeck & Ruprecht, 1948], 49). ET: "The Purpose of Deuteronomy" (Gerhard von Rad, *Studies in Deuteronomy*, trans. David Stalker [London: SCM, 1956], 70). All references to this work henceforth are to the first edition, unless otherwise specified. That first edition was posthumously reprinted in Gerhard von Rad, *Gesammelte Studien zum Alten Testament II*, ed. Rudolf Smend, Theologische Bücherei 48 (Munich: Kaiser, 1973), 109–53 (150).

8. On von Rad's preoccupation with Deuteronomy throughout his career, see Eckart Otto's foreword to *Recht und Ethik im Alten Testament*, ed. Bernard M. Levinson and Eckart Otto, with assistance from Walter Dietrich (Münster, Germany: LIT, 2004), v. For the works in question, see Gerhard von Rad, *Das Gottesvolk im Deuteronomium*, Beiträge zur Wissenschaft vom Alten (und Neuen) Testament (BWA[N]T) 47 (Stuttgart, Germany: W. Kohlhammer, 1929); posthumously published in von Rad, *Gesammelte Studien zum Alten Testament II*, 9–108. See also Gerhard von Rad, *Das fünfte Buch Mose*, 4th ed., Das Alte Testament Deutsch 8 (Göttingen, Germany: Vandenhoeck & Ruprecht, 1983). ET: *Deuteronomy: A Commentary*, trans. Dorothea Barton, Old Testament Library 5 (Philadelphia: Westminster, 1966).

9. Jean-Louis Ska connects von Rad's distinction between law and grace to the dialectical theology of Karl Barth. See Jean-Louis Ska, *Introduction to Reading the Pentateuch*, trans. Sr. Pascale Dominique (Winona Lake, IN: Eisenbrauns, 2006), 116–23.

die Voraussetzung des Heiles" ["Fulfilling of the commandments is thus in no wise the pre-supposition of salvation"].[10] In fact, any attempts within Deuteronomy to narrow or make Yahweh's salvation conditional on obedience are seen to reflect later, secondary expansions. Only in these later additions does one find "eine gewisse Präponderanz des Gesetzes gegenüber dem Evangelium" ["a certain preponderance of Law over Gospel"].[11]

In order to present the text as sermonic exposition by countryside Levites, von Rad found it necessary to explain away some of Deuteronomy's most characteristic concepts. In his analysis, Deuteronomy became not a law book demanding obedience but rather a collection of sermons pervaded with a spiritual, even "'protestantische' Atmosphäre" ["'Protestant' atmosphere"].[12] Written laws became homiletic sermons—spiritual lessons taught by the traveling Levites—meant to encourage and inspire. Israel's obligation under Yahweh's covenant treaty for obedience to his statutes and ordinances became Israel's unconditional election to salvation. In von Rad's reading of Deuteronomy, salvation was not conditional on works. On that basis, any sections of Deuteronomy that do seem to condition salvation on legal obedience were deftly and systematically explained away: either their significance was deemphasized or they were relegated to later exilic or postexilic expansions of the text.[13]

Von Rad's writings on the Old Testament are considered classics, both in the history of the discipline of biblical studies and as examples of the form-critical approach to the biblical text, but in key areas his conclusions do not hold up under scrutiny. The difficulties with von Rad's analysis of the history of ancient Israel and the formation of the Hexateuch have been extensively discussed.[14] In general, it is difficult to find proper rationale or support for

---

10. Von Rad, *Deuteronomium-Studien*, 50 [ET: *Studies in Deuteronomy*, 72].
11. Ibid., 50 [ET: *Studies in Deuteronomy*, 72].
12. Ibid., 47 [ET: *Studies in Deuteronomy*, 68].
13. Ibid., 50 [ET: *Studies in Deuteronomy*, 72].
14. Von Rad's argument regarding the alleged emergence of the Pentateuch from a small credal statement preserved in Deuteronomy 26 (with law viewed as a late, secondary development) generated sharp and cogent challenges almost from the very beginning. His arguments have not found acceptance. For a good summary of the extensive literature, see J. Philip Hyatt, "Were There an Ancient Historical Credo in Israel and an Independent Sinai Tradition?," in *Translating and Understanding the Old Testament: Essays in Honor of Herbert Gordon May*, ed. Harry Thomas Frank and William L. Reed (Nashville: Abingdon, 1970), 152–70, and Jan Christian Gertz, "Die Stellung des kleinen geschichtlichen Credos in der Redaktionsgeschichte von Deuteronomium und Pentateuch," in *Liebe und Gebot: Studien zum Deuteronomium—Festschrift zum 70. Geburtstag von Lothar Perlitt*, ed. Reinhard Gregor

von Rad's arguments within the text of Deuteronomy. Indeed, his analysis of Deuteronomy—particularly the legal corpus of Deuteronomy 12–26—comes closer to eisegesis than to exegesis. This is a disturbing conclusion to reach regarding the work of a scholar who spent most of his career emphasizing the paramount importance of listening to the text without preconceptions about what it would say.[15] Such incongruity demands investigation. How did von Rad's own voice begin to drown out the voice of the text? Careful reflection suggests that von Rad's analysis says less about Deuteronomy than it says about the situation in which he wrote. Those points where von Rad's claims seem not to fit the text of Deuteronomy reflect the historical context of the formative part of his career: Germany, under the National Socialist dictatorship from 1933 to 1945, a time of crisis within the history of the German nation.

Two aspects of this historical context are crucial. First, the Protestant Church, within which von Rad had once served as a pastor, suffered a near fatal rupture as a result of the drive to centralize the Church and align it with Nazi ideology. This internal dispute is known by the name *Kirchenkampf* [Church Struggle]. While the German Christians' centralization effort ultimately failed, the group's supporters continued their efforts to nazify Church doctrine and liturgy throughout the Third Reich. They engaged in concerted attacks against the "Jewish" vestiges of the Church. They urged what amounted to a neo-Marcionite[16] assault on the Lutheran canon, a "cleansing" of the canon to remove anything Jewish from it. They labeled the Old Testament, the primary object of von Rad's scholarship, illegitimate and superfluous. In addition, they argued that all citations of the Old Testament within the New Testament—the liturgy, the hymnal, and the catechism—should be excised, because they were tainted by Judaism and therefore in conflict with Christianity. They believed many of the Pauline letters were similarly tainted and, therefore, should also be rejected.

Kratz and Hermann Spieckermann, FRLANT 190 (Göttingen, Germany: Vandenhoeck & Ruprecht, 2000), 30–45.

15. Rudolf Smend, *From Astruc to Zimmerli: Old Testament Scholarship in Three Centuries*, trans. M. Kohl (Tübingen, Germany: Mohr Siebeck, 2007), 170–97 (193–94).

16. Marcion was a second-century CE Christian who argued that the Jewish God of the Old Testament was a different deity than the God of the New Testament, who was the father of Jesus. He rejected both the Old Testament and the God of ancient Israel. Marcion created a new canon consisting of only eleven books, including only certain sections of the Gospel of Luke and ten of Paul's epistles, with the other scriptures of the New Testament excluded. Widely popular at the time, his teachings were condemned as heretical by Tertullian ca. 208, and rejected by the church.

Second, the University of Jena in the German state of Thuringia, where von Rad joined the Faculty of Theology in 1934, became during this period one of the leading German universities to promote National Socialist ideology. This transformation affected nearly all of its faculties, research institutes, and disciplines (including law, medicine, and the natural and social sciences). The Faculty of Theology at the University of Jena moved eagerly in the same direction. It took a leadership role in transforming the prestigious German discipline of theology into an organ for National Socialist and German Christian ideology. Faculty appointments, the curriculum, student research, and language requirements were all affected. In this context, von Rad worked to maintain his own integrity and that of the discipline.

What von Rad wrote about Deuteronomy must be understood in that specific historical location. There has been an immense amount of scholarship on German history under National Socialism. Archival work made possible since 1989, in particular, has opened a new perspective on the institutional history of Jena University during the critical period from 1933 to 1945. Yet while a number of scholars have commented on the relationship between elements of von Rad's work and National Socialist ideology, his scholarship and its specific historical and institutional context have not systematically been brought together.[17]

---

17. Though no other scholars have attempted to connect von Rad's work to his social situation in a comprehensive way, there is a great deal of information available about von Rad's life, about the Thuringian church, and about the University of Jena during the Nazi era. The two most helpful resources are Susannah Heschel, *The Aryan Jesus: Christian Theologians and the Bible in Nazi Germany* (Princeton, NJ: Princeton University Press, 2008), and Rudolf Smend, *Deutsche Alttestamentler in drei Jahrhunderten: Mit 18 Abbildungen* (Göttingen, Germany: Vandenhoeck & Ruprecht, 1989), 226–54. An abridged version of Smend's work has been published in English as *From Astruc to Zimmerli*, 170–97.

Additional helpful resources include Susanne Böhm, "Gerhard von Rad und der Streit um das Alte Testament—Unter besonderer Berücksichtigung seiner Zeit in Jena" (unpublished diploma thesis, Faculty of Theology, Fredrick Schiller University of Jena, Germany, 1996); Susanne Böhm, "Gerhard von Rad in Jena," in *Das Alte Testament—ein Geschichtsbuch?!: Geschichtsschreibung oder Geschichtsüberlieferung im antiken Israel. Festschrift für Joachim Conrad*, ed. Uwe Becker and Jürgen von Oorschot, Arbeiten zur Bibel und ihrer Geschichte 17 (Leipzig, Germany: Evangelische Verlagsanstalt, 2005), 203–40; Volker Leppin, "Vom Auseinanderbrechen zum Neuaufbau: Die Theologische Fakultät Jena um 1945," in *Hochschule im Sozialismus: Studien zur Geschichte der Friedrich-Schiller-Universität Jena (1945–1990), Band 2*, ed. Uwe Hoßfeld, Tobias Kaiser, and Heinz Mestrup, with assistance from Horst Neuper (Cologne, Germany: Böhlau, 2007), 1848–70; Eberhard H. Pältz, "Jena," *Theologische Realenzyklopädie* (*TRE*) 16 (1987): 559–63; Tobias Schüfer, "Die Theologische Fakultät Jena und die Landeskirche im Nationalsozialismus," in *Thüringer*

In his biography on Gerhard von Rad, James Crenshaw outlines the progression of von Rad's career and the development of his theology. However, Crenshaw does not develop a relationship between von Rad's political, social, and professional environment and his academic writing.[18] Conversely, Jean-Louis Ska and Walter Brueggemann have correctly noted that von Rad's concept of salvation history represents a polemic against National Socialist ideology.[19] Martin Buss also recognizes von Rad's efforts to defend the Old Testament, though he argues that von Rad was primarily motivated by Christian convictions rather than political objections to Nazi ideology.[20] However, while

---

Gratwanderungen: Beiträge zur fünfundsiebzigjährigen Geschichte der evangelischen Landeskirche Thüringens, ed. Thomas A. Seidel et al., Herbergen der Christenheit 3 (Leipzig, Germany: Evangelische Verlagsanstalt, 1998), 94–110; and Rudolf Smend, "Rad, Gerhard von," *TRE* 28 (1997): 889–91. Finally, for a study of the World War II–era publications of German Old Testament scholars (including von Rad) and their response to National Socialism, see Klaus Koenen, *Unter dem Dröhnen der Kanonen: Arbeiten zum Alten Testament aus der Zeit des Zweiten Weltkriegs* (Neukirchen-Vluyn, Germany: Neukirchener, 1998).

18. Crenshaw discusses von Rad's professional relationships, briefly references the social and historical context during his career, and analyzes the development of his theology. He also occasionally delves into motives for von Rad's activities. For example, Crenshaw attributes von Rad's resignation from his first pastoral post and his return to academic studies as von Rad's response to his concern over the problem posed by the Old Testament in a context of growing antisemitism. However, Crenshaw's discussion of the relationship between von Rad's environment and his writing is largely limited to making a connection to von Rad's moving sermons and popular writings defending the Old Testament. See James Crenshaw, *Gerhard von Rad*, Makers of the Modern Theological Mind (Waco, TX: Word Books, 1978), 18–19, 21, 34–35. In contrast, Rudolf Smend frames von Rad's early academic decisions differently. He agrees that von Rad's choice of the Old Testament as his primary research focus was made out of concern for defending the Old Testament against "antisemitic agitation," but Smend does not connect that decision to von Rad's resignation from the pastorate (Smend, *From Astruc to Zimmerli*, 174).

19. Ska hints that von Rad's reconstruction of Israelite religion was an implicit rejection of "natural religion," as favored by National Socialism (Ska, *Introduction to Reading the Pentateuch*, 116–23). Brueggemann sees in von Rad's work a rejection of the "Blood and Soil" claim of National Socialism. He also argues that scholars who later took up von Rad's theories did not sufficiently consider the extent to which those theories were "a response to the German Church crisis of the 30s" (Walter Brueggemann, "The ABC's of Old Testament Theology in the US," *Zeitschrift für die alttestamentliche Wissenschaft* 114 [2002]: 412–32 [at 413–14]).

20. Personal correspondence, April 27, 2010. Buss interprets the lack of explicit criticism of National Socialism in von Rad's writings, both before and after the war, as evidence of his "relative neutrality in state politics." He notes as evidence of von Rad's lack of political motivation that in 1934 von Rad praised a "pro-Nazi defense of the Old Testament" in one publication, but in that same year, he criticized Germanic ideology in a speech. On the

Ska, Brueggemann, and Buss see connections between von Rad's work and his historical circumstances, they all overlook the combined significance of von Rad's Lutheran background and his specific situation in Jena as factors in his passion—I use the word deliberately—to retain the Old Testament as part of the church's canon. Finally, Susannah Heschel's rich histories of the Jena faculty discuss von Rad but generally focus elsewhere than on Old Testament theology and exegesis.[21] Thus, by these and other scholars, the extent to which von Rad's exegesis arises from and reflects the historical context in which he wrote has not been fully explored.

II. KIRCHENKAMPF: THE STRUGGLE FOR CONTROL OF THE CHURCH

The struggle for control of the Church began in the state church elections in 1933. Each of the twenty-eight German Länder [states] had its own constitution, government, and church organization. This governing structure meant the states had traditionally operated with a fair degree of autonomy, particularly in matters of religion and Church governance. Yet with the backing of the NSDAP, the German Christians sought to use the state church elections to gain administrative control of the various *Landeskirchen* [state churches]. The party provided the German Christians with organizational support leading up to the elections, and government officials made participation in church elections mandatory for Protestant members of the party, instructing those members to vote for the German Christians. In addition, Hitler himself endorsed the German Christians in his national radio address just before the church elections, an action that resulted in the opposition in many states dropping out of the race altogether.[22] This strategy yielded overwhelming

---

other hand, while not specifically referring to von Rad, Buss later acknowledges that the consequences for openly opposing the state may have played a role in silencing even those who opposed Nazi policies (Martin Buss, *Biblical Form Criticism in Its Context*, Journal for the Study of the Old Testament: Supplement Series 274 [Sheffield, UK: Sheffield Academic, 1999], 331–32).

21. Susannah Heschel has produced an important series of publications on the University of Jena and its Faculty of Theology, including "The Theological Faculty at the University of Jena as 'a Stronghold of National Socialism,'" in *"Kämpferische Wissenschaft": Studien zur Universität Jena im Nationalsozialismus*, ed. Uwe Hoßfeld et al. (Cologne, Germany: Böhlau, 2003), 452–71. Citations of Heschel's work in this article will primarily reference the most comprehensive of her studies, *The Aryan Jesus: Christian Theologians and the Bible in Nazi Germany* (Princeton, NJ: Princeton University Press, 2008).

22. Steigmann-Gall, *Holy Reich*, 160–63.

victories that year in twenty-five of the twenty-eight state church elections. It elevated the German Christian supporters to leadership roles over these state churches.

Unfortunately for the German Christians, these electoral wins did not translate into widespread support for the German Christian agenda of aligning Church doctrine with National Socialist ideology. Many in the Church did initially welcome the rise to power of the NSDAP.[23] Hitler promised a revitalization of Germany's Lutheran heritage after the moral corruption and secularization of the postwar era.[24] Problems arose, however, over the issue of what the relationship would be between the Protestant Church and the new government. Traditionally, the Church had supported the state without becoming politically involved in its decisions. At the same time, the state generally did not interfere in confessional matters within the Church. The German Christians' attempt to bring the individual state churches into conformity with National Socialist ideology enflamed tensions within the church, in part because the German Christians were subverting traditional Christian theology, but also because their efforts represented a change in the traditional role of the Protestant Church within Germany—instead of an independent, nationalistic Church, the German Christians were creating a Church that would serve as a tool for the state.[25]

A striking example is the adoption of the Aryan Paragraph of the Law for the Restoration of the Professional Civil Service by the Reichskirche. The Aryan Paragraph restricted non-Aryans from holding civil service positions. While clergy and other church employees, all of whom were paid by the state, were technically bound by the requirements of the Civil Service Law, the Nazi government did not press for its implementation in the churches. The German Christians did not adopt a similar posture of restraint. Instead, they saw implementation of the Aryan Paragraph as a political opportunity. In a bid to prove their commitment to Nazi ideology, the German Christian leadership

---

23. Victoria Barnett, *For the Soul of the People: Protestant Protest against Hitler* (New York: Oxford University Press, 1992), 28.

24. Shelley Baranowski, "The Confessing Church and Antisemitism: Protestant Identity, German Nationhood, and the Exclusion of Jews," in *Betrayal: German Churches and the Holocaust*, ed. Robert P. Ericksen and Susannah Heschel (Minneapolis: Fortress, 1999), 90–109 (at 94–95). On the use of Luther's writings by German Christian and Confessing Church theologians and pastors during this period, see Christopher J. Probst, *Demonizing the Jews: Luther and the Protestant Church in Nazi Germany* (Bloomington: Indiana University Press, 2012), and his contribution to this volume.

25. Barnett, *For the Soul of the People*, 21–29, 33–35.

attempted to make this requirement binding upon the Church.[26] In practical terms, this action would prohibit baptized Jews, Protestants of Jewish ancestry, and Protestants married to non-Aryans from holding such church offices or serving as pastors. The Reichskirche imposed this qualification by the end of 1934,[27] thereby subordinating the Church to political ideology. Race transcended faith as a qualification for service in the Church.

The drive to free the Church from any taint of Jewish influence also included the call to eradicate anything related to Jewish belief or practice. The German Christians launched virulent attacks against the Old Testament. At a rally in front of twenty thousand people in November 1933, Dr. Reinhold Krause, a German Christian leader in Berlin, demanded that the Church make itself more appealing to all National Socialists by pursuing "die Befreiung vom allen Undeutschen im Gottesdienst und im Bekenntnismäßigen; Befreiung vom Alten Testament mit seiner jüdischen Lohnmoral, von diesen Viehhändler- und Zuhältergeschichten" [liberation from everything non-German in worship and confession; liberation from the Old Testament with its Jewish morality of profit and its stories of cattle traders and pimps].[28] Krause's pejorative reference to the biblical patriarchal narratives in this speech was met with applause by his audience, but the extreme nature of his attack caused significant outrage and disaffection toward the German

---

26. Ericksen, *Complicity in the Holocaust*, 26–27.
27. Baranowski, "Confessing Church," 100–101.
28. Reinhold Krause, *Rede des Gauobmannes der Glaubensbewegung "Deutsche Christen" im Groß-Berlin: Dr. Krause. Gehalten im Sportpalast am 13. November 1933* Schriftenreihe der Glaubensbewegung Deutsche Volkskirche [12 page pamphlet], [Berlin:] Glaubensbewegung Deutsche Volkskirche, 1933, 2 (translation mine). ET: Mary M. Solberg, ed. and trans., *A Church Undone: Documents from the German Christian Faith Movement, 1932–1940* (Minneapolis: Fortress, 2015), 249–62 (257–58). Krause's speech has been discussed extensively in secondary literature. See Hans Buchheim, *Glaubenskrise im Dritten Reich: Drei Kapitel nationalsozialistischer Religionspolitik* (Stuttgart, Germany: Deutsche Verlags-Anstalt, 1953), 129; Doris Bergen, "Storm Troopers of Christ: The German Christian Movement and the Ecclesiastical Final Solution," in Ericksen and Heschel, *Betrayal*, 40–67 (53); and Doris Bergen, "Old Testament, New Hatreds: The Hebrew Bible and Antisemitism in Nazi Germany," in *Sacred Text, Secular Times: The Hebrew Bible in the Modern World*, ed. Leonard J. Greenspoon and Brian F. Lebeau, Studies in Jewish Civilization 10 (Omaha, NE: Creighton University Press, 2000), 35–46. Bergen points out that the phrase "cattle traders and pimps" originated with Alfred Rosenberg as part of a Nazi construction to mask attacks against Jews as biblical truths (Bergen, "Old Testament, New Hatreds," 38). For further discussion of Krause's speech, see Christopher Probst, "Luther Scholars, Jews, and Judaism during the Third Reich: From the Hallowed Halls of Academia to the Sacred Spaces of German Protestantism," in this volume.

Christians.[29] Most Christians in Germany were not ready for drastic attacks on the biblical canon, even though Krause's antipathy toward the Old Testament accurately reflected a common Protestant critique of the supposedly "Jewish" notion that works and obedience to the law earn God's reward. According to this viewpoint, Jewish law, as encapsulated in the Old Testament, distorted and opposed the Christian notion of Christ's unconditional grace. However, actual removal of the Old Testament proved too extreme for most, as did Krause's attacks on the Apostle Paul[30] and later German Christian efforts to disprove the Jewish ancestry of Jesus and to erase Hebrew words like *hosanna* and *hallelujah* from church creeds and hymns.[31]

Opposition to the German Christian power grab initially organized itself in 1933 under the banner of the Pastors' Emergency League. Those who opposed the German Christians rejected their promotion of the National Socialist agenda within the Church and, thus, any Gleichschaltung with the Nazi government. Leaders of this movement gathered together with other German Christian opponents at Barmen in May 1934 and ratified a document known as the Barmen Declaration, which became the foundation on which members of the newly formed Bekennende Kirche [Confessing Church] defined their resistance to the German Christians. The Barmen Declaration set clear boundaries between church and state so as not to subject church government to National Socialist ideology. It rejected any attempt to turn the Church into an organ of the state. Instead the Declaration defined the Church as a community of brethren united by word and sacrament, led exclusively by the Lord Jesus Christ.[32] Karl Barth, a major drafter of the Barmen Declaration, later emphasized its message as declaring the ultimate sovereignty of Christ: "Grace *alone*! Holy Writ *alone*! Honour to God *alone* in the highest!"[33]

Yet despite their resistance on some matters of confessional autonomy, on a number of key points the Confessing Church remained silent or even held the same theological position as the German Christians. For example, the Barmen Declaration does not even mention the word *Jew* or take any stance on Nazi persecution of Jews. The Pastors' Emergency League had initially seemed

---

29. Ernst Christian Helmreich, *The German Churches under Hitler: Background, Struggle, and Epilogue* (Detroit: Wayne State University Press, 1979), 150.
30. Ericksen, *Complicity in the Holocaust*, 27.
31. Bergen, "Storm Troopers," 41.
32. Baranowski, "Confessing Church," 90–91, 96–97.
33. Karl Barth, *Trouble and Promise in the Struggle of the Church in Germany: Translation of the Substance of the Philip Maurice Deneke Lecture Delivered at Lady Margaret Hall, Oxford, on 4 March 1938*, trans. P. V. M. Benecke (Oxford: Clarendon, 1938), 21 (emphasis in the original).

sensitive to "non-Aryans," focusing its opposition to the German Christians on their effort to enforce the Aryan Paragraph within the Church. However, by the time the Barmen synod met, internal disagreements over how best to handle the plight of non-Aryans made it impossible for the synod to come to a unanimous position on the Aryan Paragraph itself.[34] The conference actually voted down a motion to take an explicit stand against it.[35]

When the Barmen Declaration omitted mention of the Aryan Paragraph, the Confessing Church showed its ambivalence to the situation of baptized German Jews, whom it should have viewed simply as fellow Christians. As for German Jews who were not baptized, the Confessing Church failed to take a stand affirming their rights as fellow German citizens.[36] As Baranowski notes, "The muted protests of the Evangelical opposition to the persecution of the Jews and other 'undesirables' contrasts markedly to its spirited defense of ecclesiastical autonomy."[37] In this respect, the Declaration reflected the claims of many leaders of the Confessing Church that their interests were purely focused on retaining confessional autonomy, and not at all intended to interfere in or criticize affairs of state. They argued that opposition to Nazi church policy was not equivalent to opposition to the Nazi government.[38]

The Barmen Declaration, with its strongly Christocentric focus, also did not speak to the contested role of the Old Testament in the Church. At the theological level, both the German Christians and the Confessing Church took for granted that a dichotomy existed between law and gospel, and both attributed to Judaism a legalism that was inimical to the Christian gospel. Given this persistent viewpoint, even within the Confessing Church, regarding the nature of the Old Testament, it is perhaps unsurprising that the biblical passages

---

34. Wolfgang Gerlach, *And the Witnesses Were Silent: The Confessing Church and the Persecution of the Jews*, ed. and trans. Victoria J. Barnett (Lincoln: University of Nebraska Press, 2000), 69–76. This work is a slightly revised translation of Gerlach's original book, *Als die Zeugen Schweigen: Bekennende Kirche und die Juden* (Berlin: Institut Kirche und Judentum, 1987).

35. Günther van Norden, "Die Barmer Theologische Erklärung und die 'Judenfrage,'" in *Das Unrechtsregime: Internationale Forschung über den Nationalsozialismus Band I: Ideologie—Herrschaftssystem—Wirkung in Europa. Festschrift für Werner Jochmann zum 65. Geburtstag*, ed. Ursula Büttner, Hamburger Beiträge zur Sozial- und Zeitgeschichte 21 (Hamburg, Germany: Christians, 1986), 315–30.

36. Dietrich Bonhoeffer seems to have been one of the few who, at an early stage, was publicly critical of the Barmen Declaration for not recognizing the larger issue. He urged that the Church should take a proper stand against the Nazi policy toward German Jews.

37. Baranowski, "Confessing Church," 99.

38. Steigmann-Gall, *Holy Reich*, 166–68.

referenced in the Barmen Declaration are taken exclusively from the New Testament. In fact, the only mention of scripture in the Declaration merely confirms that sacred scripture is the absolute source for God's will.[39]

While the differences between the German Christians and the Confessing Church regarding non-Aryans and the Old Testament were not always clearly distinguishable, the German Christians' heavy-handed attempts to seize power and change church doctrine nevertheless served as an effective catalyst for the Confessing Church to channel popular dissent. A series of events in 1934 galvanized the opposition: first, Reich Bishop Ludwig Müller unilaterally decided to merge all state church youth groups into the Hitler Youth; second, the Reichskirche issued a church decree forbidding attacks from the pulpits against the German Christian administration; and third, the Reichskirche attempted to depose the bishops of Bavaria and Württemberg.[40] As a result of public demonstrations marshaled by the Confessing Church, support for the Reichskirche among the National Socialist leadership evaporated. In 1935, the National Socialist regime withdrew its endorsement of a German Christian–led centralized Reichskirche.[41] Without this national platform, the struggle between the German Christians and the Confessing Church splintered into a decade-long clash for control of the state churches.[42] Throughout this period of conflict, the German Christians retained concentrated power in various state church organizations. The state of Thuringia, as home to the University of Jena, warrants particular attention. There an especially radical wing of the German Christians, the Kirchenbewegung Deutsche Christen [German Christian Church Movement] or KDC, was able to control the state church and extend its influence into the political, academic, and theological spheres.[43]

---

39. Van Norden, "Barmer Theologische Erklärung," 327.

40. Steigmann-Gall, *Holy Reich*, 171–75; Baranowski, "Confessing Church," 97. See also Helmreich, *German Churches under Hitler*, 153.

41. The Nazis had not yet completely given up on a unified Church, however. In 1935, after ending his support for the German Christian Reich Bishop, Ludwig Müller, Hitler created a Reich Ministry for Church Affairs, whose task was to broker a settlement among the warring factions within the Protestant Church. This effort was no more successful at unifying the Church than the German Christians' attempts had been, and in 1938 it, too, was abandoned (Steigmann-Gall, *Holy Reich*, 177–87).

42. On the history and legacy of the *Kirchenkampf*, see Matthew D. Hockenos, *A Church Divided: German Protestants Confront the Nazi Past* (Bloomington: Indiana University Press, 2004).

43. Helmreich, *German Churches under Hitler*, 151. See also Rudolf Smend, *Deutsche Alttestamentler*, 235 [ET: *From Astruc to Zimmerli*, 179], and Heschel, *Aryan Jesus*, 211, 282–83.

III. THE BETRAYAL OF TRADITIONAL ACADEMIC VALUES AT THE UNIVERSITY OF JENA

As noted in the introduction to this chapter, the experience of the Gleichschaltung in the universities was less controversial than that of the Church. Since many of the changes were self-managed in a manner and at a pace set by the university leaders, faculty members, and students, there was no strong outside authority against which to galvanize popular resistance. Nor is there much evidence that large numbers of university members were inclined to protest the changes.[44]

In the state of Thuringia, the University of Jena, where Gerhard von Rad took his first position as *Ordinarius* [tenured full Professor], moved aggressively to mold the school into the ideal National Socialist University whose primary function would be to serve the goals of the state.[45] This project had a far-reaching impact on faculty appointments, curriculum, research, and the administrative structure of the university. The transformation of the university compromised even its most prestigious faculties, like law, medicine, and theology, which increasingly promoted Aryan racial theory and eugenics. In 1941, the Faculty of Law and Economics established a new institute for *Rasse und Recht* [race and law]. The university's program in psychiatry became recognized for its specialization in heredity and race hygiene. The Faculty of Medicine established a close working relationship with Buchenwald, the concentration camp less than twenty miles distant, where some medical students trained in pathology.[46] Two university medical clinics were involved in the forced medical sterilization of approximately fourteen thousand people in the state of Thuringia between July 14, 1933, and the end of 1943. Karl Astel, an SS Colonel who would later serve as rector of the university from 1939 to

---

44. Steven P. Remy, *The Heidelberg Myth: The Nazification and Denazification of a German University* (Cambridge, MA: Harvard University Press, 2002), 11–13, 31–35.

45. Much of the difficult history of Friedrich Schiller University of Jena (the name it acquired in 1934) during the Third Reich has become available only since 1989, once the reunification of Germany permitted access to important archival sources that were previously unavailable under East German rule. The university administration should be commended for the way it has encouraged and supported critical evaluation and public exposition of its past. This support is particularly evident in two significant edited volumes. See Herbert Gottwald and Matthias Steinbach, eds., *Zwischen Wissenschaft und Politik: Studien zur Jenaer Universität im 20. Jahrhundert* (Jena, Germany: Bussert & Stadeler, 2000), and especially Hoßfeld et al., *Kämpferische Wissenschaft*.

46. See Mike Bruhn and Heike Böttner, "Studieren in Jena 1933 bis 1945: Eine Fallstudie," in Gottwald and Steinbach, *Zwischen Wissenschaft und Politik*, 107–22 (116).

1945, helped conceive and direct this program in his capacity as president of the Thuringian State Office for Matters of Race.[47] Already in that latter capacity, in a speech at the opening ceremonies for the winter semester of 1936–37, Astel stressed that the primary task of the university was to promote the values of the Third Reich.[48] As a result of the extensive alignment of academic research and curriculum with National Socialist ideology, "die Universität Jena wurde... eine der wichtigsten Hochschulen Deutschlands in der Verbreitung der Rassenfrage" [the University of Jena became... one of the most important universities in Germany in promulgating the question of race].[49]

Beyond the broader nazification movement occurring within the University of Jena, a second factor also impinged on von Rad's work environment: the Church Struggle. As previously noted, the extremist German Christian Church Movement (KDC), was active in Thuringia. By 1933, they were able to install one of their own members in the State Ministry of Education: Siegfried Leffler.[50] Using this state office, Leffler initiated a series of steps that would eventually bring Jena University's Faculty of Theology into conformity with KDC ideology, staffed and administered by KDC supporters.[51] His actions broke down the barriers of Weimar-era German civil society that maintained the independence between church, state, and university. Like the rest of the university, the Faculty of Theology would also develop into an organ of National Socialism.

Leffler's appointment of Wolf Meyer to the Chair of Practical Theology in November 1933 marked the beginning of this transformation. Meyer, a radio preacher in Bavaria and acting leader of the KDC, possessed none of the normal qualifications for a German academic appointment.[52] He had

---

47. Rüdiger Stutz, "Wissenschaft als 'Dienst an Volk und Vaterland': Die Rektoren der Universität Jena und das 'Dritte Reich,'" in Gottwald and Steinbach, *Zwischen Wissenschaft und Politik*, 123–54 (142).

48. Karl Astel, *Die Aufgabe: Rede zur Eröffnung des Winter-Semesters 1936/37 an der Thüringischen Landesuniversität Jena in Gegenwart des Reichsstatthalters und Gauleiters Fritz Sauckel, gehalten am 6. November 1936*, Jenaer Akademische Reden 24 (Jena, Germany: Gustav Fischer, 1937), 6.

49. Bruhn and Böttner, "Studieren in Jena," 117.

50. Anja Rinnen, *Kirchenmann und Nationalsozialist: Siegfried Lefflers ideelle Verschmelzung von Kirche und Drittem Reich*, Forum zur Pädagogik und Didaktik der Religion 9 (Weinheim, Germany: Deutscher Studien, 1995), 67. Originally cited by Heschel, "Theological Faculty," 453.

51. Smend, *Deutsche Alttestamentler*, 235; Heschel, *Aryan Jesus*, 211.

52. Christopher Probst, "'An Incessant Army of Demons': Wolf Meyer-Erlach, Luther, and 'the Jews' in Nazi Germany," *Holocaust and Genocide Studies* 23, no. 3 (2009): 441–60 (448); and Stutz, "Wissenschaft," 138.

not completed his *Promotion* [doctorate], let alone written his *Habilitation* [a second dissertation, which is the normal requirement in Germany for appointment as ordinarius, or full Professor, holding an academic chair]. Nor had he published anything other than political pamphlets. Nonetheless, his appointment was not disputed; other candidates were not considered.[53] In order to create an opening for Meyer, Leffler abruptly removed another professor, Waldemar Macholz, from his chair in Practical Theology.[54] After his neat removal and replacement, Macholz was shunted into the newly created Konfessionskundliche Abteilung [Ecumenical Studies Department], a position he held until his retirement in 1938.[55]

As for Wolf Meyer, he advanced rapidly to positions of academic leadership. In less than a year, he became dean of the Faculty of Theology. On April 1, 1935, Meyer was appointed rector of the university. This appointment was made on the strength of his having gained only 8 of 129 faculty votes. As rector, a position he held from 1935 to 1937, he was an ardent proponent of the German Christians and publicly declared himself a "soldier of the *Führer*."[56] He also advanced the cause of aligning the university with Nazi priorities. In his 1935 address to the school, he praised the idea of a "political" university and called on students and faculty to become "workers, fighters, and warriors" for the state.[57] Meyer seems to have been concerned with countering allegations that he might be a Jew, allegations based on his name and the fact that he had once attended, several years before, a synagogue inauguration ceremony. Lest such a damaging idea, which stigmatized him as *Synagogenmeyer*, impugn his Aryan heritage

---

53. Heschel, "Theological Faculty," 466n15 (referencing Klaus Raschzok, "Wolf Meyer-Erlach und Hans Asmussen," in *Zwischen Volk und Bekenntnis: Praktische Theologie im Dritten Reich*, ed. Klaus Raschzok [Leipzig, Germany: Evangelische Verlagsanstalt, 2000], 167–202 [at 174]).

54. Apart from the manipulation of academic procedures to accomplish an ideological goal, there seems also to have been a rather petty personal grudge involved: Macholz had given Leffler a failing grade in his second theological exam (Heschel, *Aryan Jesus*, 211). On Leffler's examination failure, see Schüfer, "Theologische Fakultät Jena," 95.

55. For the administrative history and academic staffing of the various faculties and institutes of the Fredrick Schiller University of Jena, with a particular emphasis on the Nazi period from 1932–33 to 1945–46, see Jürgen John and Oliver Lemuth, "Statistiken, Übersichten und Tabellen," in Hoßfeld et al., *Kämpferische Wissenschaft*, 1101–29. Particularly valuable is the chart showing the history of appointments to the Faculty of Theology (ibid., 1110).

56. Heschel, *Aryan Jesus*, 211–14.

57. Probst, "Incessant Army of Demons," 450.

or diminish his reputation with state officials, Wolf Meyer legally changed his surname to Meyer-Erlach in 1935.[58]

As both dean and rector, Meyer-Erlach made a concerted effort to ensure that German Christian and National Socialist supporters were appointed to the faculty, regardless of academic qualification.[59] The appointment of von Rad to the faculty in 1934 ironically supports the emphasis placed on ideology over scholarship. Of the candidates for the position, Leffler wrote:

> Herr Professor Wolf Meyer-Erlach hat mir 2 Herren genannt, einen alten Partei genossen aus Tübingen, einen jungen 29jährigen Partei genossen und ausserordentlich begabten Menschen aus Leipzig. Ich habe ihm aber gesagt, ich möchte unbedingt den Herrn aus Leipzig erst einmal sehen. Ein alterer kommt kaum in Frage, da her für die theologische Entwicklung in Sachen des Alten Testaments zu wenig elastisch ist.
>
> [Professor Wolf Meyer-Erlach has mentioned two men to me, one an old party member from Tübingen, and one a young, twenty-nine-year-old party member and extraordinarily talented man from Leipzig. I have told him I really prefer to see the gentleman from Leipzig as a start. With an elder, there is little question that he will be too inflexible in terms of theological development with respect to the Old Testament.][60]

As this letter suggests, von Rad may have gained his position because he was mistakenly assumed to hold membership in the NSDAP and to sympathize with German Christian ideology.[61] Several factors would have contributed to this mistaken impression. One was almost certainly von Rad's early academic work with Gerhard Kittel, a prominent supporter of National Socialism.[62] Von

---

58. Heschel, "Theological Faculty," 454 (citing Universitätsarchiv der Jena [hereafter, UAJ] J 92, "Promotionsakten der Theologischen Fakultät 1941–1947").

59. A number of sources analyze Meyer-Erlach's lack of academic qualifications, his tenure as rector, and his role in infusing National Socialist ideology into the university. See Hans-Joachim Sonne, *Die politische Theologie der Deutschen Christen*, Göttinger Theologische Arbeiten 21 (Göttingen, Germany: Vandenhoeck & Ruprecht, 1982), 232–49; Pältz, "Jena," 561–62; Schüfer, "Theologische Fakultät Jena," 94–110; Ralf Meister-Karanikas, "Die Thüringer evangelische Kirche und 'die Judenfrage': Notizen zur Epoche 1933–1945," in Seidel and Wiegand, *Thüringer Gratwanderungen*, 111–23; Stutz, "Wissenschaft," 123–54 (138); Probst, "Incessant Army of Demons," 441–60; and Heschel, *Aryan Jesus*, 211–40.

60. Schüfer, "Theologische Fakultät Jena," 97.

61. Ibid.

62. Heschel, *Aryan Jesus*, 214–16. Gerhard Kittel was one of the first university scholars who openly embraced the National Socialist vision of the Jews. That he was a full Professor of Theology at the prestigious University of Tübingen made his role even more significant.

Rad played a role as Old Testament editor and contributed a number of articles to Kittel's very influential project, *Theologisches Wörterbuch zum Neuen Testament*.[63]

Perhaps the most important factor was von Rad's membership in the Sturmabteilung (SA), the so-called brown shirts, which had a quite high middle-class membership, including theology professors. Von Rad's reasons for joining the SA in November 1933 are unclear, though a memoir from one of his students during this era indicates that von Rad may have been motivated more by professional necessity than by personal allegiance.[64] Von Rad resigned his membership in 1937, most likely as a result of "anti-theological" actions taken by the government during this period.[65] In 1938, von Rad indicated on a questionnaire regarding political memberships that he had resigned from the SA on June 15, 1937 "auf Grund eines Befehles der Gruppe Thüringen betreffs Theologen" [due to a command of the Thüringian group

---

While Kittel opposed the *Ausrottung* [extirpation] of the Jews by violence, the reasons were primarily practical. Kittel only belatedly condemned such a project as "absurd" and "unchristian" in the second and third editions of his *Die Judenfrage*, after he was criticized for his first edition treatment of that issue (Robert P. Ericksen, *Theologians under Hitler: Gerhard Kittel, Paul Althaus and Emanuel Hirsch* [New Haven, CT: Yale University Press, 1985], 55 [see esp. n146]). See also the pioneering work of Max Weinreich, *Hitler's Professors: The Part of Scholarship in Germany's Crimes against the Jewish People* (New York: Yiddish Scientific Institute [YIVO], 1946; repr., foreword by Martin Gilbert, New Haven, CT: Yale University Press, 1999), 40–45 (page references to the 1999 edition).

63. Gerhard Kittel and Gerhard Friedrich, eds., *Theologisches Wörterbuch zum Neuen Testament*, 10 vols. (Stuttgart, Germany: W. Kohlhammer, 1932–79). On this work's bias, see Maurice Casey, "Some Anti-Semitic Assumptions in the 'Theological Dictionary of the New Testament,'" *Novum Testamentum* 41, no. 3 (1999): 280–91.

64. As a member of the Confessing Church who answered the call to come to the University of Jena to study with von Rad, Konrad von Rabenau refers to von Rad's membership in the SA as having helped establish his credentials for appointment to the faculty. See his fascinating brief memoir: Konrad von Rabenau, "Als Student bei Gerhard von Rad in Jena 1943–1945," in *Das Alte Testament und die Kultur der Moderne*, ed. Manfred Oeming, Konrad Schmid, and Michael Welker, Altes Testament und Moderne 8 (Münster, Germany: LIT, 2004), 7–12 (10).

65. Leppin, "Vom Auseinanderbrechen," 1849 and 1865n22. There is a discrepancy in the reporting of the exact year of von Rad's resignation from the SA, because von Rad gave two different answers on two different questionnaires, one from 1938 and the other from 1945. Rüdiger Stutz posits that von Rad simply misremembered the year these events occurred when he completed the 1945 questionnaire (Thüringisches Hauptstaatsarchiv Weimar [hereafter ThHStAW], Personalakten aus dem Bereich Volksbildung 23957, "Personalakte Gerhard von Rad," Bll, 1r–2v), in which he dated his departure from the SA to 1936 (personal correspondence, May 31, 2013).

concerning theologians].⁶⁶ Rüdiger Stutz reports that in 1937, Nazi leaders in Thüringia began to enforce a strict separation of church and state. This included pressuring individuals to either resign their civil service positions and Nazi Party membership or leave the church. Stutz suggests that theologians such as von Rad may have faced a similar choice and that von Rad's response to the 1938 questionnaire indicates his decision to resign from the SA rather than leave the Church.⁶⁷ In any case, even before he went to Jena, von Rad was giving public lectures stressing that there is no access to Christ except through the Old Testament. Had his pointed declarations against German Christian theological assumptions been read, it is hard to imagine that he would have been appointed to the faculty at Jena.

The preference for ideology over scholarship at Jena became explicit in subsequent academic appointments. In 1937, Meyer-Erlach wrote in support of Heinz Eisenhuth's appointment as Professor of Systematic Theology:

> Vor allem aber bestimmt mich für Eisenhuth einzutreten die Tatsache, dass er unbedingt zuverlässiger Parteigenosse ist, der aus innerster Überzeugung treu zum Führer und zur Bewegung steht.... Gerade weil die Universität Jena bewusst eine Hochburg des Nationalsozialismus werden will, lege ich allergrössten Wert darauf, dass bei Neuberufung neben der wissenschaftlichen Tüchtigkeit die nationalsozialistische Zuverlässigkeit in 1. Linie berücksichtig wird. Bei dem traurigen Zustand der meisten theologischen Fakultäten in Deutschland, die zum grossen Teil noch nicht den Weg zu einer inneren Beziehung zum Nationalsozialismus gefunden haben, muss in Jena eine Theologische Fakultät aufgebaut werden, die im Gegensatz zu den meisten Fakultäten ganz bewusst den Nationalsozialismus bejaht.

> [First of all I am determined to speak on behalf of Eisenhuth because he is an absolutely reliable party-comrade who in his innermost conviction stands loyal to the *Führer* and his movement.... Especially because the University of Jena deliberately wants to become a stronghold of National Socialism, besides academic competence, I attach great importance to taking predominantly into account national-socialist credibility for a new appointment. Considering the sad state of most theological faculties in Germany which overall have not yet found their true connection to National

---

66. UAJ D 2312, "Fragebogen über politische Zugehörigkeit vom 22.5.1938."

67. Personal correspondence, May 24, 2013. Supporting this theory is a similar order issued by Martin Bormann, a senior Nazi Party functionary, in June 1937 that required pastors to resign from the SA (Steigmann-Gall, *Holy Reich*, 223).

Socialism, Jena needs to build a theological department which, in contrast to the majority of departments, consciously affirms National Socialism.][68]

With his credentials for the position thereby confirmed, Eisenhuth received his appointment in 1938.

A similar case is that of Walter Grundmann. In 1937, he was invited for a *Probevorlesung* [job talk] to fill the New Testament chair beginning in the 1938 school year. Grundmann was appointed despite having not written a habilitation; he had only published his doctoral dissertation along with several minor articles in Kittel's *Theologisches Wörterbuch zum Neuen Testament*. His primary academic "qualifications" were his early party membership in the NSDAP, his active involvement in the German Christians, and his authorship of myriad political pamphlets.[69] Two candidates with far better academic credentials, Günther Bornkamm and Carl Schneider, were rejected: the first, as a sympathizer with the Confessing Church; the second, for having spent time at an American seminary.[70]

By 1938, with the appointments of Meyer-Erlach, Eisenhuth, and Grundmann, the KDC controlled three of the six academic chairs in Jena's Faculty of Theology. They were often joined in their voting by Karl Heussi, who held the chair of Church history.[71] They thereby effectively controlled the direction of the Faculty of Theology, leaving von Rad and Macholz as minority dissenters. Once Macholz retired that year, the KDC supporters gained a clear majority, and Gerhard von Rad was left essentially alone within the Faculty of Theology.

---

68. Heschel, *Aryan Jesus*, 219 (citing, in a slightly different English translation, UAJ D 603, Bll, 15).

69. See Weinreich, *Hitler's Professors*, 62–67; and Heschel, *Aryan Jesus*, 219–24. Heschel notes that von Rad listed Grundmann as a second choice for the University of Jena's vacant position behind a candidate who was sympathetic to the Confessing Church.

70. Heschel, *Aryan Jesus*, 221–24.

71. Smend seems too generous in presenting Karl Heussi as a kind, apolitical figure who kept himself out of the war (*Deutsche Alttestamentler*, 235). In contrast, Heschel notes numerous instances of Heussi's siding with Meyer-Erlach, Eisenhuth, and Grundmann to support the changes at the University of Jena ("Theological Faculty," 454). This perspective is confirmed by von Rabenau, who notes that Heussi rarely voted in support of von Rad ("Als Student bei Gerhard von Rad," 11). Heschel argues that Heussi's "neutrality" facilitated the transformation of the University of Jena into a National Socialist stronghold. In addition, after the war, Heussi played an active role in rebuilding the department in such a way as to weaken the *Entnazifierung* (the denazification process), eagerly reappointing Nazi colleagues to their former positions ("Theological Faculty," 461–64). His poswar actions should not be taken as unambiguous evidence of Nazi sympathies, however, since Heussi also attempted to reinstate von Rad after the war ("Theological Faculty," 463).

Using this control, the majority within the Faculty of Theology began systematically to reshape—and subvert—the historically rich German theology curriculum. Majority members initially developed a plan to align its professorships with National Socialist interests. They intended to redefine the chair in New Testament studies into one concerned instead with the study of the Gospels and early Christianity. This limitation would in effect remove the "Jewish" Pauline letters from the curriculum and from the canon. Similarly, Old Testament studies would focus on the religious history of the ancient Near East, not the "Jewish" religion of ancient Israel. Since the courses taught in this redefined subject would no longer take account of the Old Testament, this change would allow the faculty to eliminate instruction in Hebrew. Church history, systematic theology, and practical theology would all be focused on *völkische* [Germanic][72] topics.[73] While the full plan was never implemented, the faculty did take steps in this direction.

Inevitably, one of the first targets for change was Hebrew language study. On December 12, 1938, the Jena Faculty of Theology, in its capacity as the examination committee for the state church, approved a resolution that made instruction in Hebrew optional for theology students training for the pastorate or to teach religion. In announcing this resolution, the faculty reasoned that in the study of Jesus Christ, the study of the Old Testament could be set aside. They argued that any notion of a connection between the Old Testament and the New Testament was a myth whereby Jewish Christians had falsified scripture.[74] This elimination was formally announced and implemented by the dean of the Faculty of Theology in April 1939. In alignment with the faculty's plan to change the focus of Old Testament study to the

---

72. The adjective *völkisch* is difficult to translate, especially because of the racist connotations that it acquired under National Socialism. While derived literally from the noun, *Volk* [folk, people], the simple adjective *ethnic* does not do justice to the ideological force of the term, which is therefore here rendered *Germanic*. The range of meaning is described well by Mark Allinson: "For the early German nationalists who influenced Hitler's political development, the *Volk* became an almost mystical community, linked by racial characteristics. The adjective *völkisch* represented a particular racial nationalism, based on a misguided pseudoscientific belief in notions of racial superiority and largely borrowed from Charles Darwin's work on the evolution of species and the survival of the fittest. Applied to the human race, *völkisch* agitators claimed that the Jews were an inferior, parasitic race who sought to undermine and dominate their host communities throughout the world." See Mark Allinson, *Germany and Austria 1814–2000* (London: Routledge, 2002), 86.
73. Schüfer, "Theologische Fakultät Jena," 99.
74. Böhm, "Gerhard von Rad," 32 (citing UAJ C 358).

history of religions, from that point on, history of religions replaced Hebrew as a required subject in the students' oral examinations.[75]

In addition to the elimination of the Hebrew requirement, the Faculty of Theology introduced new courses to make the curriculum more compatible with National Socialism. In particular, there was an attempt to address the question of "racial science," as was being done systematically throughout the university in many other disciplines. Of course, the Jewish Question was also immanent to the discipline of theology. The two became increasingly interlocked. Accordingly, in 1940, Meyer-Erlach, Eisenhuth, and Grundmann taught courses that included "Jesus und das Judentum," "Luther und die Juden," "Grundfragen der völkischen und religiösen Anthropologie," and "Die Idee des Reiches als Grundfrage deutscher Theologie" [Jesus and Judaism, Luther and the Jews, Fundamental Questions of Germanic and Religious Anthropology, and the Idea of the *Reich* as the Fundamental Question of German Theology].[76]

The KDC majority in the Faculty of Theology also directed student research so as to promote National Socialism. Graduate student research was held to a National Socialist litmus test and forced to comply with anti-Jewish racial theory and German Christian ideology. The controlling members of the Faculty of Theology rejected dissertations inconsistent with these perspectives while accepting and granting prizes to those that, despite slipshod scholarship, promoted National Socialist ideals. Between 1933 and 1945, forty-five doctoral dissertations were submitted to the Faculty of Theology. Ten of these were "rejected by the faculty or withdrawn by the student. . . . While some dissertations were rejected for poor quality of scholarship, the majority of dissertations were rejected because they did not champion Nazi racial theory."[77] For example, one student's dissertation argued that the ideas of Jesus must be understood in an Old Testament context. Even after a revision, the dissertation was rejected because, as Meyer-Erlach explained, "Es fehlt dem Theologen die Erkenntnis des Nationalsozialismus, daß die Rassenfrage die Grundfrage für alles ist" ["The theologian lacks the recognition by National Socialism that the question of race is the fundamental question for everything"].[78]

The attempt to transform the theology curriculum in light of National Socialist ideology is also evident elsewhere. In 1939, Grundmann, who held

---

75. Heschel, *Aryan Jesus*, 229–30.
76. Heschel, "Theological Faculty," 458.
77. Ibid., 459.
78. Heschel, *Aryan Jesus*, 237 (citing, with a different English translation, UAJ J 90, "Promotionsakten der Theologischen Fakultät, 1939–1941").

the New Testament Chair, created an Institut zur Erforschung und Beseitigung des jüdischen Einflusses auf das deutsche kirchliche Leben [Institute for the Investigation and Eradication of Jewish Influence on German Church Life] under the direction and extensive financial support of the Thuringian state church. It was housed in the church's training seminary in Eisenach.[79] Although the Institute was constructed away from the University of Jena, its ties with the university remained prominent. Members of Jena's Faculty of Theology, including Meyer-Erlach, Eisenhuth, and Grundmann, actively published under the Institute's name.

At the opening ceremonies of the Institute, Grundmann delivered a keynote address that included a powerful antisemitic slogan: "Die Entjudung des religiösen Lebens als Aufgabe deutscher Theologie und Kirche" [The "de-Jewing" of religious life as the task of German Theology and Church].[80] He argued that German Christianity was completely independent of any Jewish origins. There was no continuity between the Old Testament and Christ. In fact, the Jewish Old Testament was a roadblock to German Christianity. To eliminate this obstruction, von Rad's colleagues scoured church materials in search of any conceivable "Jewish" vestige. They rewrote the New Testament, the hymnal and the catechism so as to eliminate Hebrew words, Old Testament references, and all links between Jesus and Judaism. They also sought to connect famous past Christian theologians to their cause. According to an administrative document from the Institute, Meyer-Erlach's role was to clarify "the attitude of great religious figures towards Judaism (Luther, Herder, Stöcker, etc.)."[81] Widely sold throughout Germany, the various publications by "academic" authors added a patina of scholarship to the Institute's positions.[82] They transformed "their antisemitic ideas into respectable teachings of Christian theology."[83]

---

79. For a brief, early (1946) assessment of Grundmann and the Institute, see Weinreich, *Hitler's Professors*, 62–67.

80. The speech was later published as Walter Grundmann, *Die Entjudung des religiösen Lebens als Aufgabe deutscher Theologie und Kirche* (Weimar, Germany: Deutsche Christen, 1939). For the most extensive study of Grundmann's career, see Roland Deines, Volker Leppin, and Karl-Wilhelm Niebuhr, eds., *Walter Grundmann: Ein Neutestamentler im Dritten Reich*, Arbeiten zur Kirchen- und Theologiegeschichte 21 (Leipzig, Germany: Evangelische Verlagsanstalt, 2007).

81. Probst, "Incessant Army of Demons," 451.

82. Susannah Heschel, "When Jesus Was an Aryan: The Protestant Church and Antisemitic Propaganda," in Ericksen and Heschel, *Betrayal*, 68–89. See also Heschel, *Aryan Jesus*, 107–65.

83. Heschel, "When Jesus Was an Aryan," 80.

This, then, was the environment within which von Rad developed his arguments about the Old Testament. The Protestant church and the Faculty of Theology at Jena were deeply divided over issues of Germanic theology and the place of the Old Testament in the Christian faith, and Nazi ideology was spreading within the university with little to hinder its progress. At the same time, the field of theology as a whole was falling out of favor with the state. What was von Rad's response to this environment?

IV. VON RAD'S EXPERIENCE AT JENA

Von Rad arrived in Jena near the beginning of the process of the university's transformation into a National Socialist stronghold. He was appointed to its Faculty of Theology in the winter semester of 1934–35, and he remained there, under very difficult circumstances, until his conscription into the Reichsluftschutzbund [the Reich Air Defense League] in August 1944.[84] Von Rad's activities during his tenure at Jena make clear where his sympathies lay in the Church Struggle. He attended and spoke at Confessing Church meetings and lectures, both in Jena and throughout Germany, and he formally joined the organization in 1939.[85] The titles of some of the lectures that were published make clear von Rad's ongoing commitment during this period to the importance of the Old Testament for Christianity: *Das Alte Testament: Gottes Wort für die Deutschen!* [The Old *Testament: God's Word for the* Germans!]; *Die bleibende Bedeutung des Alten Testaments* [The Enduring Significance of the Old Testament]; and "Warum unterrichtet die Kirche im Alten Testament?" [Why Does the Church Teach the Old Testament?].[86] In addition, in 1939 von Rad published a eulogy recognizing the significance of Friedrich Rittelmeyer, one of his confirmation teachers.[87] There, he tried to strike a balance between valuing preaching that

---

84. See Gerhard von Rad, *Erinnerungen aus der Kriegsgefangenschaft Frühjahr 1945* (Neukirchen-Vluyn, Germany: Neukirchener Verlag, 1976).

85. Smend describes von Rad's work with the Confessing Church as follows: "He preached in the illegal church hall of the Lutheran Confessing community in Jena, and spoke year out, year in, up and down the country, holding innumerable lectures to students, to clergy meetings, to illegal courses for further education, and to individual congregations, lectures which were often followed by discussion.... For the lecturer himself, it often seemed as if the time-consuming journeys (which were even more difficult in wartime) annoyingly kept him from the scholarly work he was really supposed to be doing" (*From Astruc to Zimmerli*, 180).

86. Smend, *From Astruc to Zimmerli*, 180. See note 106 in this chapter for a more complete list of von Rad's publications from this era, including full citation details.

87. Gerhard von Rad, "Friedrich Rittelmeyer," *Theologische Blätter* 18 (1939): 129.

speaks to contemporary issues and cautioning against allowing contemporary ideology to distort the word of God.[88] Finally, von Rad's stress, in his academic work, on ancient Israel's opposition to Canaanite fertility religion, and his corresponding deemphasis on the role of creation theology, has been seen as a thinly veiled polemic against Nationalist Socialist Volk ideology.[89]

That von Rad threw in his lot with the Confessing Church should not be surprising. He was a former pastor in the Bavarian church, the conservative culture of which would have made von Rad sensitive to issues of encroachment on traditional ecclesiastical autonomy. He was also an unabashed "member of 'the *Epistle to the Romans* generation,'"[90] a reference to Karl Barth's 1919 work and his philosophy of letting the biblical text speak for itself. The German Christian manipulations of the Bible violated that guiding principle. More practically, as an Old Testament scholar, von Rad's work on the Bible was more likely to find an audience within the Confessing Church than anywhere else.

Ironically, the Church Struggle is primarily relevant to von Rad's social situation in Jena because of von Rad's own involvement with the Confessing Church. The German Christian control of the Thuringian church was strong, and the Confessing Church was almost nonexistent in the region.[91] Had von Rad not aligned himself with the Confessing Church, he probably could have passed most of his tenure at Jena without being much affected by the Church Struggle. Instead, he likely witnessed firsthand the struggles of the small number of Confessing Church pastors to retain their church positions and find places for their congregations to meet. He was also certainly aware of the challenges Confessing Church-aligned theology students had in completing their education once Confessing Church seminaries and theological exams were declared illegal in 1937.[92] Indeed, von Rad directly assisted some

---

88. Martin Hauger, "'But We Were in the Wilderness, and There God Speaks Quite Differently': On the Significance of Preaching in the Theology and Work of Gerhard von Rad," *Interpretation* 62, no. 3 (2008): 278–92. Hauger's study has now been expanded into a valuable investigation of von Rad's early sermons: Martin Hauger, *Gerhard von Rads frühe Predigten: Eine historisch-homiletische Untersuchung*, Arbeiten zur Praktischen Theologie 51 (Leipzig, Germany: Evangelische Verlagsanstalt, 2013), with extended discussion of what von Rad learned from Rittelmeyer at 120–214.

89. For a fuller exposition of these aspects of von Rad's scholarship, see Bernard M. Levinson, *Defending the Old Testament in Nazi Germany: Gerhard von Rad's Struggle to Transform Law into Gospel* (Atlanta, GA: Society of Biblical Literature, 2022).

90. Smend, *From Astruc to Zimmerli*, 173.

91. Barnett, *For the Soul of the People*, 82.

92. Ibid., 82, 86–87.

of these theology students as one of the few university theology professors to offer them additional practical instruction during their holiday breaks.[93] Perhaps surprisingly, von Rad's connection to the Confessing Church also may have helped save his own job in his last years at the University of Jena. By 1941, the Confessing Church had begun to send between two and four students to the University of Jena "in order to make certain that von Rad had an audience at his lectures."[94]

In the Church Struggle, von Rad sided with those fighting for confessional autonomy from Nazi ideology and with those advocating for letting the Bible speak for itself. This was also the case at the university, where von Rad's actions consistently demonstrated his desire for intellectual independence and his respect for the authoritative voice of scripture. He voted in the minority against the ideologically based appointments of Grundmann and Eisenhuth.[95] On the subject of the study of Hebrew by students of theology, von Rad argued powerfully that the elimination of the Hebrew requirement was an attack on Christianity. Macholz and Heussi joined him in this dissent, and the three of them were thereby able to temporarily delay the implementation of this change.[96] However, after the retirement of Macholz, the resolution passed. Thus, unfortunately, von Rad ultimately fought a losing battle in resisting the nazification of the Faculty of Theology.

The one point on which von Rad's rejection of the push to nazify the university was most successful was in von Rad's own course offerings. While the Faculty of Theology taught courses in "racial science" and the Jewish Question, von Rad made his own statement, resisting the ideological subversion of the curriculum. He held lectures and seminars on Exodus, Psalms, Jeremiah, and Old Testament Theology.[97] Such courses were "sein wirksamstes Kampfmittel" [his most effective weapon].[98]

---

93. Jörg Thierfelder, "Ersatzveranstaltungen der Bekennenden Kirche," in *Theologische Fakultäten im Nationalsozialismus*, ed. Leonore Siegele-Wenschkewitz and Carsten Nicolaisen, Arbeiten zur kirchlichen Zeitgeschichte, series B, vol. 18 (Göttingen, Germany: Vandenhoeck & Ruprecht, 1993), 291–301 (at 296). Thanks to Robert Ericksen for the reference.

94. Heschel, *Aryan Jesus*, 240. Heschel indicates two students for 1941–42, while an eyewitness speaks of being one of four students sent to Jena in the fall of 1943 (Von Rabenau, "Als Student bei Gerhard von Rad," 7).

95. Heschel, *Aryan Jesus*, 217, 223.

96. Ibid., 229.

97. Böhm, "Gerhard von Rad," appendix 2.

98. Von Rabenau, "Als Student bei Gerhard von Rad," 11.

In this environment, from the very beginning, von Rad failed to gain any significant student support or following. In the winter semester of 1935–36, the first academic year after von Rad's appointment for which full data is available, there were 155 students registered in the Faculty of Theology at the University of Jena.[99] During that same semester, von Rad's Psalms course enrolled just 4 students, while his Jeremiah course and Deutero-Isaiah seminar enrolled 2 each.[100] By the winter semester of 1941–42, enrollment for the Faculty of Theology as a whole had declined to just 10 students.[101] Von Rad's enrollments for his three classes remained identical to those previously given (4/2/2); indeed, his enrollments are almost static every semester from his appointment right through the summer of 1944.[102] Perhaps the most telling measure of von Rad's academic isolation is the fact that only one of the aforementioned 45 doctoral dissertations submitted to the Faculty of Theology during his tenure at the University of Jena was directed by von Rad.[103]

The evidence thus indicates that von Rad's position as an Old Testament scholar, with sympathies for the Confessing Church, often placed him outside the mainstream in the Faculty of Theology at Jena. Throughout most of his tenure there, von Rad resisted the attempts by his colleagues to subordinate new faculty appointments, the curriculum, language requirements, and student research to National Socialist ideology.[104] He was an isolated scholar working in an academic environment that was hostile to his religious affiliation with

---

99. Böhm, "Gerhard von Rad," appendix 1. It is worth noting that at a number of points, the enrollment data provided by Böhm and Heschel differ somewhat. Hopefully, future investigations of the archival sources will include an attempt to reconcile differences in the data from this historically fraught period.

100. Böhm, "Gerhard von Rad," appendix 2.

101. Ibid., appendix 1.

102. Böhm, "Gerhard von Rad," appendix 2. For the semester after von Rad was drafted, the winter of 1944–45, enrollment in the Jena Theology Program was just one student (Heschel, *Aryan Jesus*, 240).

103. Böhm, "Gerhard von Rad," 31. Note that the calculation of the total number of dissertations actually begins a year prior to von Rad's appointment. Heschel provides a breakdown of the dissertation supervisors and a fascinating report of the debates to enforce or circumvent academic standards (*Aryan Jesus*, 232–40).

104. It is therefore astonishing that the editors of the most comprehensive volume on the University of Jena (Hoßfeld et al., *"Kämpferische Wissenschaft"*) make absolutely no mention of Gerhard von Rad while responding to the important question of whether there are examples of resistance or civil disobedience by any members of the university community. This omission occurs in the volume's introduction (Axel Burchardt, "Das Bild von der 'braunen Universität' greift zu kurz: Interview mit den Herausgebern des Studienbandes," 9–22 [at 16]).

the Confessing Church and his scholarly interests in the Old Testament. He witnessed indictments of Jewish legalism against the Old Testament by his colleagues at Jena, by the German Christians, and even by some in the Confessing Church.

This historical situation, however, illuminates the distinctive aspects of von Rad's exegesis: in particular, of course, the need to deny that Deuteronomy is law. For von Rad, the National Socialist and German Christian attacks against the Old Testament as Jewish challenged his belief in the Old Testament as both a testament of Christ and a history of God's saving grace.[105] He fought back by defending the relevance of the Old Testament within the Church and by positioning the Bible in such a way as to resist the discipline of theology from being co-opted by National Socialism.

V. VON RAD'S RESPONSE IN HIS WRITINGS

In the midst of the assaults against the Old Testament, Gerhard von Rad took a public stand during the 1930s and early 1940s to defend the Old Testament.[106]

---

105. As Gary Knoppers observed, "For von Rad, Christianity was inherently a historical religion. Von Rad's understanding of the very identity of Christianity as one of *Heilsgeschichte* must have made him recoil against any approach that would flatten out the long story of scripture or reduce his religion to one of simple morality" (personal correspondence, September 30, 2004).

106. The monographs in question include the principled public lectures given by Albrecht Alt, Joachim Begrich, and Gerhard von Rad at Leipzig and then published under their names with the pointed title: *Führung zum Christentum durch das Alte Testament: Drei Vorträge* (Leipzig, Germany: Dörffling & Franke, 1934). In addition are von Rad's independent monographs and essays: "Das Christuszeugnis des Alten Testaments: Eine Auseinandersetzung mit Wilhelm Vischers gleichnamigem Buch," *Theologische Blätter* 14 (1935): 249–54; *Das Alte Testament: Gottes Wort für die Deutschen*, Klares Ziel 1 (Berlin: Ostwerk, 1937); "Gesetz und Evangelium im Alten Testament. Gedanken zu dem Buch von E. Hirsch: Das Alte Testament und die Predigt des Evangeliums," *Theologische Blätter* 16 (1937): 41–47; "Die bleibende Bedeutung des Alten Testaments," *Der Kindergottesdienst* 47 (1937): 9–10; "Alttestamentliche Glaubensaussagen vom Leben und vom Tod," *Allgemeinen Evangelischen-Lutherischen Kirchenzeitung* 71 (1938): 826–34; *Fragen der Schriftauslegung im Alten Testament*, Theologia militans 20 (Leipzig, Germany: A. Deichert, 1938); "Warum unterrichtet die Kirche im Alten Testament?," *An der Lebensquelle, Ev. Gemeindebote für den Kirchenbezirk Baden-Baden* 20 (1939): 6–7; *Moses*, Wege in die Bibel 3 (Göttingen, Germany: Vandenhoeck & Ruprecht, 1940); "Vom Menschenbild des Alten Testaments," in *Der alte und der neue Mensch: Aufsätze zur theologischen Anthropologie*, by Gerhard von Rad et al., Beiträge zur evangelischen Theologie 8 (Munich: A. Lempp, 1942), 5–23; and "Das Alte Testament in der katholischen Kirche: Gedanken zum dem 'Werkbuch der Bibel' von E. Kalt," *Theologische Blätter* 21 (1942): 177–81.

The sheer number of his essays published during this period with *Alte Testament* in the title testifies to its centrality for von Rad.[107] Von Rad's theological position is already articulated in his lecture, entitled "Das Ergebnis" [The conclusion] delivered on February 15, 1934, in Leipzig.[108] In the face of German Christian efforts to position the Old Testament as a treacherous Jewish text, von Rad developed theological arguments to claim the Old Testament as a vital witness of Christ for the Church. Moreover, von Rad argued against any conclusions that would excise the Old Testament from Christianity or fundamentally alter its meaning for Christianity. For example, Theodor Fritsch, the virulent anti-Semite, contended that Christianity must be severed from the "Jewish" Old Testament. Alternatively, Martin Buber, the Jewish theologian, contended that the Old Testament was essential to Judaism and that early Christianity was a development from within Judaism rather than a separate religion.[109] Von Rad rejected both of these positions and concluded instead: "Es ist offensichtlich unmöglich, Jesus vom Alten Testament zu trennen!" [It is obviously impossible to separate Jesus from the Old Testament!][110] In a pointed allusion to Matthew 11:6, von Rad concluded his argument: "In dem Maß, in dem wir uns am Alten Testament ärgern, ärgern wir uns auch an Christus" [To the extent that we are offended by the Old Testament, we are also offended by Christ].[111] Regardless of whether a Christian or Jewish

---

107. Regarding these essays, Smend notes: "Die Titel sprechen für sich. Was man ihnen nicht immer ansieht, ist das Bemühen, das Alte Testament selber zu Wort kommen zu lassen" (*Deutsche Alttestamentler*, 237) [ET: The titles speak for themselves. What is not always recognized is the endeavor to allow the Old Testament to speak for itself (*From Astruc to Zimmerli*, 180 [modifying the published translation])].

108. The lecture was published as Gerhard von Rad, "Das Ergebnis," in Alt, Begrich, and von Rad, *Führung zum Christentum durch das Alte Testament*, 54–70.

109. It is disturbing that von Rad would even equate, as two contrasting understandings of the Old Testament, the vitriol of Fritsch with the scholarship of Martin Buber. Von Rad was tendentiously responding to two essays included in Martin Buber, *Vom Geist des Judentums: Reden und Geleitwörte* (Leipzig: Kurt Wolff, 1916). The two essays in question are available in translation as Martin Buber, "The Spirit of the Orient and Judaism," and "Jewish Religiosity," in *On Judaism*, ed. Nahum M. Glatzer (New York: Schocken, 1967), 56–78 and 79–94, respectively.

110. Von Rad, "Ergebnis," 69. In taking this stand, von Rad attempted to counter a common instinct for supersession that united the German Christians and the Confessing Church. Both sides of the theological debate assumed "a New Testament that does not so much fulfill the Hebrew Bible as supersede it and, perhaps, contradict it," as well as "a radical discontinuity between the Old and New Testaments." See Micha Brumlik, "Post-Holocaust Theology," in Ericksen and Heschel, *Betrayal*, 169–88 (171–72).

111. Von Rad, "Ergebnis," 70.

theologian advocated it, every argument against the inherent Christianity of the Old Testament was in essence an argument against Christ. The Old Testament could not be separated from Christ, nor as a result could it be separated from the Church.

Building the Academic Defense: Introducing the Levitical Sermon Form

Von Rad duplicated his defense of the Old Testament as a Christian document in his academic writings. However, his argument shifted from theological to exegetical. He attempted to demonstrate that the Old Testament was Christian in the very *Gattung* [form] of the material.[112] In "Das Ergebnis," von Rad had argued for Christianity as the theological heir to the Old Testament. In his essay, "The Levitical Sermon in I and II Chronicles," von Rad directed his exegesis to the parenesis in Deuteronomy and Chronicles.[113] He claimed these texts for the Church by positioning them as material created within a familiar Christian form, the sermon.

Von Rad reasoned that the parenetic material was no longer written text, but rather it was sermons created by traveling Levites. He rescued the Old Testament from the realm of dead Jewish letter by placing it into the familiar and superior oral sermon tradition. Von Rad quoted Ludwig Köhler's verdict that "die Predigt, die größte und beste Form der Menschenbelehrung, sie setzt damals ein" ["the sermon, the greatest and best form of human instruction, begins at this time"].[114] For von Rad, Köhler's definition was "unmittelbar überzeugend" ["wholly convincing"].[115] Köhler was commenting on the introductory chapters in Deuteronomy, but von Rad applied this approach to identify the sermon form in Chronicles. He argued that Chronicles, once properly

---

112. In German biblical scholarship of this period, the term *Gattung* [form] had a technical meaning going back to Norse sagas. It designated the underlying structure of a narrative, which was presumed to have an originally oral setting in life.

113. Gerhard von Rad, "Die levitische Predigt in den Büchern der Chronik," in *Festschrift Otto Procksch zum sechzigsten Geburtstag am 9. August 1934 überreicht: Sonderdruck, Die Bezeichnungen für Land und Volk im Alten Testament*, ed. Leonhard Rost (Leipzig, Germany: A. Deichert'sche, 1934), 113–24, repr. in Gerhard von Rad, *Gesammelte Studien zum Alten Testament I*, 4th ed., TB 8 (Munich: C. Kaiser, 1971), 248–61. [ET: "The Levitical Sermon in I and II Chronicles," in *The Problem of the Hexateuch and Other Essays*, trans. E. W. Trueman Dicken (London: SCM, 1966), 267–80.]

114. Von Rad, "Levitische Predigt," 113 [ET: "Levitical Sermon," 267]. Von Rad quotes Ludwig Köhler, "Die hebräische Rechtsgemeinde: Festrede des Rektors Prof. Dr. Ludwig Köhler gehalten an der 98. Stiftungsfeier der Universität am 29. April 1931" (Zürich: Art. Institut Orell Füssli, 1931), 17.

115. Von Rad, "Levitische Predigt," 113 [ET: "Levitical Sermon," 267].

understood, challenges the common assumption of a postexilic decline into *Nomismus* [narrow legalism].[116] Sermonic exhortation, the instruction to the community provided by the Levitical preacher, redeems the text from being read as mere law.[117] Moreover, by making the sermon form rather than law central to Chronicles, the Old Testament text was made much more accessible to the Christian reader, since it was now presented as kerygma.

Unfortunately, von Rad's argument was based on a faulty premise. With its assumption of the text's origin in oral preaching, Köhler's entire line of thought failed to do justice to the literary and exegetical sophistication of Deuteronomy.[118] There is extensive evidence for Deuteronomy as a literary work composed by authors working with prior texts, both Israelite and ancient Near Eastern, and embracing concepts of law, treaty, and covenant.[119] If Köhler was wrong about the form of the introductory chapters of Deuteronomy, then von Rad compounded the error by basing his analysis of Chronicles on Köhler's study of Deuteronomy.

Deploying the Academic Defense: Applying the Levitical Sermon Form to Law

During von Rad's tenure at Jena, pressure increased to dismiss the Old Testament as irrelevant, Jewish, and anti-Christian. His introduction of the familiar Christian sermon form in Chronicles and Deuteronomy in 1934 allowed von Rad to reinsert portions of the Old Testament into the Christian tradition. However, his analysis left Deuteronomy's law code unredeemed. His exegesis had yet to reclaim Deuteronomy's core legal text as relevant for the Church. As noted previously, both German Christian and Confessing Church supporters attacked the Old Testament as merely "Jewish" legalism. Contending with their argument was critical to von Rad's defense of the Old Testament.

Von Rad's 1938 work, *Das formgeschichtliche Problem des Hexateuchs* ["The Form-Critical Problem of the Hexateuch"], had little to say about law. While it discusses Deuteronomy 5–11 as a hortatory allocution or sermon, the legal

---

116. Ibid., 124 [ET: "Levitical Sermon," 277].
117. Ibid.
118. See Marc Z. Brettler, "A 'Literary Sermon' in Deuteronomy 4," in *"A Wise and Discerning Mind": Essays in Honor of Burke O. Long*, ed. Saul M. Olyan and Robert C. Culley, Brown Judaic Studies 325 (Providence, RI: Brown Judaic Studies, 2000), 33–50.
119. See Bernard M. Levinson, *Legal Revision and Religious Renewal in Ancient Israel* (Cambridge: Cambridge University Press, 2008), and Bernard M. Levinson and Jeffrey Stackert, "Between the Covenant Code and Esarhaddon's Succession Treaty: Deuteronomy 13 and the Composition of Deuteronomy," *Journal of Ancient Judaism* 3 (2012): 123–40.

section of Deuteronomy (Deuteronomy 12–26) is not analyzed in this way.[120] It suggests that Deuteronomy's law code arises from a covenant ceremony whereby the law is read publicly. Only with *Deuteronomium-Studien* [*Studies in Deuteronomy*] does von Rad turn his attention meaningfully to the legal corpus of Deuteronomy. This work was written shortly after the war ended, in the winter of 1945/1946, when he was appointed to Göttingen. Von Rad extends the approach that he had developed for his analysis of Chronicles and applies it to the laws of Deuteronomy: he isolates the now familiar Gattung of the Levitical sermon.

Von Rad thus extends his theory of the oral sermon Gattung from the literary frame of Deuteronomy to the law code. What he had earlier considered as public reading of the law (Deuteronomy 12–26) he transforms into the Levitical sermon form or public preaching. In contrast to his early analysis of the Levitical sermon, von Rad spends little time discussing the detailed structure of the sermon form in Deuteronomy's laws.[121] He simply presents Deuteronomy 12–26 as the kernels of older original legal material that Levitical preachers have transformed into hortatory sermons. The law code is thus explained in homiletic terms: "Das ist gepredigtes Gesetz!" ["It is the Law preached!"][122]

Deuteronomy thus represents the transformation of law into homily. In order to drive this point home, von Rad shunts Deuteronomy's legal revision—the legal component—to a stage prior to the work of the Levitical preachers. Only their sermons constitute Deuteronomy proper. The legal scaffold on which von Rad hangs these sermons was built some time earlier. Von Rad solves the problem of law in Deuteronomy by means of diachronic analysis. What one considers law in Deuteronomy is either prior to or subsequent to Deuteronomy. But Deuteronomy proper is not law. The problem with this solution is that von Rad's attempt to maintain the dichotomy between preaching and law forced him to create a literary layer and a social location

---

120. Gerhard von Rad, *Das formgeschichtliche Problem des Hexateuchs*, BWA(N)T 78 (Stuttgart, Germany: W. Kohlhammer, 1938), 24–30, repr. von Rad, *Gesammelte Studien zum Alten Testament I*, 9–86 (at 34–40). ET: *The Problem of the Hexateuch and Other Essays*, trans. E. W. Trueman Dicken (London: Oliver & Boyd, 1966), 1–78 (at 26–33). Dicken's translation has also recently been reprinted in a new collection of von Rad's writings: Gerhard von Rad, *From Genesis to Chronicles: Explorations in Old Testament Theology*, ed. K. C. Hanson, Fortress Classics in Biblical Studies (Minneapolis: Fortress, 2005), 1–58 (at 20–25).

121. Von Rad noted that the Chronicler should not be credited with creating the sermon form. Instead, he merely reuses a common and well-known form, that of Levitical tradition ("Levitische Predigt," 122).

122. Von Rad, *Deuteronomium-Studien*, 10 [ET: idem., *Studies in Deuteronomy*, 16].

that was driven by his hypothesis. Von Rad posited that a keen eye could penetrate "hinter der homiletischen Verkleidung noch mannigfaches Material" ["behind the homiletic dress and sort out materials of many different kinds"].[123] However, this pre-Deuteronomic stage had no clear literary level or social location.[124]

Von Rad does concede potential difficulties in his analysis. A number of Deuteronomy's casuistic laws are completely devoid of parenetic dressing. As such, they read like pure law, unaccompanied by homily. Von Rad explains the contradictory evidence away. That which is law in Deuteronomy—that which cannot be incorporated into the model of the Levitical sermon—is presented as "trivial," "rare," or as a secondary overlay that derives from the redactional history of the legal corpus.[125] Only by such arbitrary means could von Rad preserve the purity of Deuteronomy as Levitical sermonizing.

The form-critical method permits recovery of the original kerygma of Deuteronomy, which must never be confused with "Jewish" legalism. Israel's election and salvation are not conditional on obedience to the law. Rather, the Israelites receive salvation through their faith in Yahweh. "Ja, man kann es geradezu als das Programm des Dt. bezeichnen, eine Gemeinde mit reinem Jahwe-Glauben im Kulturland herauszustellen" ["Thus we have in Deuteronomy the most comprehensive example of a theological restatement of old traditions in which the later Israel could become at the same time the message of Yahweh"].[126] This reconstruction of a pristine Yahwistic faith, which is to serve as the foundation for community life, is not weighted down by law. For von Rad, Gospel subsumes Law. Only through secondary additions does Deuteronomy later begin to show "eine gewisse Präponderanz

---

123. Ibid., 12 [ET: idem, *Studies in Deuteronomy*, 17].

124. Moshe Weinfeld points out that von Rad holds two mutually exclusive positions regarding the *Sitz im Leben* of the Levitical sermons. In "Levitische Predigt" (1934), von Rad argues that it is a matter of postexilic sermonizing. Only *as a result of centralization* were the Levites required, by default, to engage in a new sphere of activity: religious instruction. *Deuteronomium-Studien* (1947), by contrast, regards this sermonic activity as the original role of the countryside Levites and as responsible for the composition of Deuteronomy. As such, this key Levitical activity is here understood to precede, not follow, centralization. The main issue, of course, is that the two inconsistent positions are never reconciled or integrated by von Rad. See Weinfeld, "Deuteronomy: The Present State of Inquiry," *Journal of Biblical Literature* 86 (1987): 249–62 (at 252–53), repr. in *A Song of Power and the Power of Song: Essays on the Book of Deuteronomy*, ed. Duane L. Christensen, Sources for Biblical and Theological Study 3 (Winona Lake, IN: Eisenbrauns, 1993), 21–35.

125. Von Rad, *Deuteronomium-Studien*, 14–15 [ET: idem, *Studies in Deuteronomy*, 22].

126. Ibid., 49 [ET: idem, *Studies in Deuteronomy*, 71].

des Gesetzes gegenüber dem Evangelium" ["a certain preponderance of Law over Gospel"].[127]

This discussion of von Rad's exegesis over the course of his career would not be complete without a brief note about his methodology. In both his 1929 doctoral dissertation and his 1930 habilitation,[128] von Rad indicated that his goal was to let the text speak for itself. In fact, for his habilitation, he specifically rejected a suggestion that he focus on "the discovery of liturgies in the Chronicler,"[129] because he did not want to assume the presence of particular forms or genres in the text. Yet just a few years later, in 1934, his approach to studying the sermon form in Chronicles appears to have been completely different. This time, instead of letting the text drive the direction of the form analysis, he approached the text with the intention of looking for the sermon form. Thus, in his study of the Levitical sermon in Chronicles, he was, perhaps for the first time, taking a theory and applying it to the text rather than studying the text and waiting for a pattern to emerge. It is not clear whether von Rad even noticed this shift in his approach, since he never ceased to speak of the importance of letting the text speak for itself. Yet this change may be the key to explaining his later exegesis and the fact that there is no discernable shift in his thinking in the postwar period. Unbeknownst to the scholar, the need to defend the Old Testament had deafened him to the voice of the text.

VI. METHODOLOGICAL CHALLENGES IN RELATING VON RAD'S ACTIONS TO HIS SOCIAL LOCATION

It is possible to object that von Rad may not have been influenced by his social location, and that his presentation of Deuteronomy in terms of grace rather than law simply represents an extension of conventional Lutheran theology.[130]

---

127. Ibid., 50 [ET: idem, *Studies in Deuteronomy*, 72].

128. Von Rad's habilitation was entitled *Das Geschichtsbild des chronistischen Werkes* [The conception of history in the Chronicler's work] (BWA[N]T 54 [Stuttgart, Germany: W. Kohlhammer, 1930]).

129. Smend, *From Astruc to Zimmerli*, 176.

130. The focus here will be primarily on Lutheranism, because von Rad was Lutheran. Note, however, that there were three mainstream Protestant denominations in Germany during this era: Lutheran, Reformed (or Calvinist), and United, which combined elements of both Lutheran and Reformed theology (Barnett, *For the Soul of the People*, 5). Since von Rad was a theology student, he likely would have been familiar with Reformed and United theology in addition to his own Lutheranism. Even if he did not gain such an understanding of the doctrinal differences between the denominations through his studies, von Rad almost

In that way, one might claim that he was completely untouched by the events taking place all around him. Here it may be helpful to frame the discussion with two specific questions. First, if von Rad's work was affected by his social location, is there evidence of an otherwise unexplained shift in his thinking after he moved to Jena? And second, is National Socialism necessarily a factor in his exegesis, or could von Rad's conclusions be explained simply as a result of his Lutheran background? In reality, neither question can be empirically tested, because there was never a time in von Rad's scholarly career when antisemitism and questions about the place of the Old Testament in the church were *not* a part of his social location. Even during the early years of his education, in the 1920s, the situation in Germany was one of gradually escalating völkisch-ness and antisemitism, not one in which such voices suddenly burst onto the scene with the rise of the Third Reich.

In addition, the hypothesis that von Rad's approach simply represents an extension of traditional Lutheran theology seems unlikely. There does not seem to be a clear path from Lutheran theology to von Rad's argument about Deuteronomy, because the law was not a problem for Lutheran theology. While Lutherans depended on grace for salvation, they acknowledged the usefulness of the law to restrain sin and to encourage penitence in the sinner. Reformed (or Calvinist) theology had a distinctive "third use" of the law, with which von Rad would also have been familiar: as a guide for right living.[131] The important point, though, is that in both Lutheranism and Reformed theology, it is clear that the law remained law. Neither denomination argued, as von Rad did with Deuteronomy, that the legal material in the Old Testament was not actually law but represented a form of theological grace that enabled Israel's salvation.[132]

---

certainly would have been exposed to them during the period of the Church Struggle. One of the original goals for the Reich Church was that it would have a unified confessional stance, but doctrinal differences between the denominations hindered that effort. Indeed, those differences had been an impediment to any serious discussion of forming a national Protestant Church in Germany even before the Nazis came to power (Steigmann-Gall, *Holy Reich*, 156).

131. John E. Witte Jr. and Thomas C. Arthur, "The Three Uses of the Law: A Protestant Source of the Purposes of Criminal Punishment?," *Journal of Law and Religion* 10, no. 2 (1993–94): 433–65. Witte and Arthur argue that Lutheran theology also included this third use of the law, and that Lutheran and Reformed theology simply emphasized the three uses differently (ibid., 436n8).

132. Some Lutheran critics of the Barmen Declaration, and Karl Barth's follow-up essay, "Gospel and Law," argued that Barth obscured the distinction between law and gospel through his claim that the two were unified in Jesus Christ, that the law came from the gospel and could only be understood through the gospel. Even in this formulation, though, the law

Moreover, prior to the advent of National Socialism, the question of the place of the Old Testament in the Bible was not a mainstream issue. Scholars had raised the subject,[133] but there was no large-scale movement to remove the law from the Old Testament or to remove the Old Testament from the Bible. Thus, in the absence of National Socialism, it seems that von Rad's interpretation of Deuteronomy as grace, and not law, would have been a solution in search of a problem. With no real threat to the Old Testament or the law as part of the Lutheran canon, there would be no need to revalidate the usefulness of the law. Under such conditions, what impulse would have led von Rad to redefine law as grace?

There is one additional thought to keep in mind about the question of imposing Lutheran theology on the Old Testament: Even if the idea did not arise directly from that theology, the question remains as to why von Rad would have followed the impulse to apply a Protestant concept, the sermon form, to Deuteronomy. Was it subconscious: his mind seeing something familiar and making an unexpected intuitive leap? Or was it deliberate: von Rad seeking something familiar in order to prove a point about the relevance of the Old Testament for Christianity? Given the constraints discussed here, perhaps the best approach is the one used in this chapter: lay out the evidence of the events occurring during the formative part of von Rad's career and assess the extent to which his distinctive defense of Deuteronomy as neither law nor Jewish might, in part, have been an indirect response to the escalating National Socialist rhetoric of his social location.

VII. THE AMBIGUITY OF VON RAD'S POSITION REGARDING THE OLD TESTAMENT

There is a point when the history of scholarship must become instead cultural and intellectual history and where the discipline of biblical studies can only explain its development by turning to the broader social and political world. The available evidence suggests that von Rad's moving affirmations about Deuteronomy—and especially his ardent striving to deny even the faintest hint of law to Deuteronomy—speak to the historical context in which von Rad

---

remained law. Barth's goal was not to redefine the nature of the law as law but rather to draw a distinction between God's laws and earthly laws. He did this in order to undermine German Christian claims that the laws of the Nazi government were divinely ordained (Hockenos, *Church Divided*, 26).

133. Steigmann-Gall, *Holy Reich*, 40–41.

wrote during the formative part of his career: Germany, under the National Socialist dictatorship from 1933 to 1945. At every key point, the language that von Rad employs to defend Deuteronomy resonates with issues that engaged him personally, academically, and theologically. Von Rad's professional life and scholarly accomplishments provide poignant testimony to that period. Through his scholarship, von Rad took a stand.

To be clear, however, the argument here is not that von Rad was a progressive thinker. His defense of the Old Testament never rose to a defense of Judaism. Indeed, from a modern perspective, von Rad's transformation of law into sermons in Deuteronomy could be seen as being as much a "de-Jewing" of the text as any of the actions taken by his German Christian peers.[134] However, such a position would anachronistically assume that von Rad saw the texts as Jewish in the first place. It is hard now, eight decades later, to imagine how different the discipline of biblical studies looked during the 1930s. In today's world, the term "Hebrew Bible," as opposed to "Old Testament," has become nearly de rigueur in biblical scholarship. Colleagues take for granted the connection of "the Old Testament" to Judaism, both ancient and modern. Participation by both Jewish and Israeli scholars in the discipline has become the norm, not the exception. But Old Testament scholarship, in its origins, was a Christian theological discipline in which Jews rarely played a significant role.[135]

Von Rad's perspective was shaped by this disciplinary context. In 1934, in a debate with Martin Buber, von Rad maintained: "The entire difficult question about whether the Old Testament belongs to the Jews or to the Church can only be decided by Christ alone."[136] With such a mindset, it is doubtful that von Rad ever imagined his work might be relevant to a Jewish reader. Ironically, Nazi-sympathizing parties like the German Christians were actually the innovators in making the strong—and for them, pejorative— identification between the Old Testament and Jewish religion and identity—in

---

134. Susannah Heschel has helpfully encouraged me to consider this alternative analysis of the evidence (private communication, December 3, 2010), as has my colleague, Oren Gross.

135. For a broader discussion of these issues, see Jon D. Levenson, "The Hebrew Bible, the Old Testament, and Historical Criticism," in *The Hebrew Bible, the Old Testament, and Historical Criticism: Jews and Christians in Biblical Studies* (Louisville, KY: Westminster/ John Knox, 1993), 1–32. See further Anders Gerdmar, *Roots of Theological Anti-Semitism: German Biblical Interpretation and the Jews, from Herder and Semler to Kittel and Bultmann*, Studies in Jewish History and Culture 20 (Leiden, Netherlands: Brill, 2009), 45–46, 69–70, and his contribution to the present volume, "Jewish Studies in the Service of Nazi Ideology: Tübingen's Faculty of Theology as a Center for Antisemitic Research."

136. Von Rad, "Ergebnis," 70.

viewing the Old Testament as Jewish. They "Judaized" the Old Testament in order to remove it from the canon. Von Rad's efforts were aimed at resisting both of these transformations. In the face of the neo-Marcionite heresy of the German Christians, von Rad sought to preserve traditional Christianity and Old Testament scholarship, in effect perpetuating the exclusion of Jews and Judaism from what was, in his view, an intra-Christian debate.

The analytical model of *Deuteronomium-Studien* constrained von Rad in his later work. He could not break through or move beyond the antithetical categories that he had constructed. Deuteronomy always stood over against the dissolution of the saving ordinance (gospel) into community dictates (law): "Damit wurde es [Heilsordnung] endlich zum 'Gesetz' im landläufigen Sinn des Wortes, das wörtlich, ja buchstäblich befolgt sein wollte" ["In this way it finally became a 'law' in the normal sense of the term, a law which had to be adhered to word by word, indeed letter by letter"].[137] From this vantage point, Deuteronomy represented: "eine letzte Gegenwehr gegen eine beginnende Vergesetzlichung" [a last stand against an incipient degeneration into legalism].[138] In this way, von Rad became a victim of the historical context in which he found himself. The continuing need to defend the Old Testament as kerygmatic proclamation—as properly "Christian" rather than "Jewish"—meant that he could not allow the text to speak for itself. Deuteronomy could never be law, let alone incarnate both law and grace. Subsequent biblical scholarship (Protestant, Catholic, and Jewish), perhaps freed from some of the historical constraints imposed on von Rad, has moved away from many of his intellectual and theological assumptions that law and grace must stand in opposition to each other. These more recent approaches emphasize the carefully crafted textuality of Deuteronomy, the extensive literary traditions on which it draws, and the inseparability of religion and law.[139]

---

137. Gerhard von Rad, *Theologie des Alten Testaments I*, 10th ed. (Munich: C. Kaiser, 1992), 201 [ET: idem, *Old Testament Theology*, trans. David Stalker, 2 vols. (New York: Harper & Brothers, 1962), 1:201].

138. Von Rad, *Theologie des Alten Testaments I*, 201 [ET: "a last stand against the beginning of a legalization" (idem, *Old Testament Theology*, 1:201 [correcting the published translation])].

139. The key intellectual and methodological breakthrough was provided by Moshe Weinfeld, *Deuteronomy and the Deuteronomic School* (Oxford: Clarendon, 1972; Winona Lake, IN: Eisenbrauns, 1992). See further Bernard M. Levinson, *Deuteronomy and the Hermeneutics of Legal Innovation* (Oxford: Oxford University Press, 1998); Norbert Lohfink, *Das Hauptgebot: Eine Untersuchung literarischer Einleitungsfragen zu Dtn 5–11* (Rome: Pontifical Biblical Institute, 1963); and Timo Veijola, "The Deuteronomistic Roots of Judaism," in *Sefer*

VIII. DENAZIFICATION AND ITS LEGACY IN THE POSTWAR PERIOD

After the war, the Allied powers began a program of denazifying German institutions [*Entnazifierung*].[140] In principle, the goal was to remove Nazi sympathizers from leadership roles and replace them with Germans who had not actively supported the Nazi government. In practice, Germans at many institutions often defended their friends and colleagues against charges of Nazi collaboration, thereby rendering the denazification process somewhat toothless. Thuringia provides a good example of this type of dysfunction, both in the state church and in the Faculty of Theology at Jena. As occurred elsewhere, members of the Confessing Church in Thuringia assumed power after the war, but rather than expel those church pastors and leaders who had aligned themselves with the German Christian movement, it appears that the Church instead chose to attempt to "reeducate" them. In addition, the Thuringian church also proved a haven for theologians who lost their academic positions at the university.[141]

Such was the case for Grundmann and Eisenhuth. After several years of defending himself in the denazification process, Grundmann received a rural pastorate in the Thuringian church in 1952. Just two years later, he assumed the role of rector of the Thuringian seminary at Eisenach, from which position he published extensively on the New Testament during the 1950s and 1960s. It is clear that any attempt at "reeducation" in the case of Grundmann was futile. Even after the war, Grundmann maintained his consistent view that the Church ought to serve the interests of the state and tailor its theology for such purposes. It was out of these convictions that he enthusiastically

---

Moshe: The Moshe Weinfeld Jubilee Volume, Studies in the Bible and the Ancient Near East, Qumran, and Post-Biblical Judaism, ed. Chaim Cohen, Avi Hurvitz, and Shalom M. Paul (Winona Lake, IN: Eisenbrauns, 2004), 459–78.

140. On the process of denazification, see Robert P. Ericksen, "The Nazification and Denazification of the University of Göttingen" (in this volume).

141. Heschel, *Aryan Jesus*, 245–49. Thuringia may be an extreme example of this type of weak denazification, but a similar tendency to avoid imposing consequences on German Christians and to provide a new home for displaced university professors also existed in other states. See, for example, Gerhard Besier, *"Selbstreinigung" unter britischer Besatzungsherrschaft: Die Evangelisch-Lutherische Landeskirche Hannovers und ihr Landesbischof Marahrens, 1945–1947*, Studien zur Kirchengeschichte Niedersachsens 27, (Göttingen, Germany: Vandenhoeck & Ruprecht, 1986). Thanks to Robert Ericksen for the reference.

collaborated with the Stasi (Ministerium für Staatssicherheit) in the GDR after the war, reporting on his colleagues in the Church.[142] Eisenhuth was much more quickly superficially "rehabilitated" by the Church. In 1946, he was assigned to a pastoral position in Jena, and in 1952, he was promoted to superintendent of the church in Eisenach. Meyer-Erlach was the only core member of the Faculty of Theology who was not welcomed by the Thuringian church, despite a vigorous self-defense in which he disavowed any antisemitic views and instead claimed that he was always a Jewish sympathizer and a target of the Nazi state. He eventually left the GDR altogether in 1950 and took up a pastorate near Frankfurt.[143]

Although there had been some preliminary interest in having Gerhard von Rad return to help rebuild the Faculty of Theology at Jena, those plans never materialized into any formal offer. This must have created a situation of immense disappointment for von Rad, who had been drafted into the German army in the summer of 1944 and captured by the Americans in April 1945. He spent the last months of the war as a prisoner of war. Upon his release in June, von Rad traveled to his family's summer home on Lake Chiemsee in Bavaria, where he awaited an invitation to resume his faculty appointment. The invitation never came. After waiting until nearly the end of the year, von Rad reluctantly accepted a position at Göttingen instead.[144] He taught there from 1946–49 before moving to the University of Heidelberg where he taught until his death in 1971.

A cursory look at the evidence of denazification efforts in the Thuringian church and at the University of Jena might suggest that the university was more effective and the church more lenient. This is not entirely accurate, however, since two of the faculty positions left empty by the departures of Grundmann, Eisenhuth, Meyer-Erlach, and von Rad were eventually filled by individuals with their own Nazi and German Christian histories.[145] In general, the letters and other documents describing denazification efforts in Thuringia leave the

---

142. See Lukas Bormann, "Walter Grundmann und das Ministerium für Statssicherheit—Chronik einer Zusammenheit aus Überzeugung (1956–1969)," *Kirchliche Zeitgeschichte* 22 (2009): 595–632.

143. Heschel, *Aryan Jesus*, 249–72.

144. Smend, *From Astruc to Zimmerli*, 184–85; Böhm, "Gerhard von Rad in Jena," 225–26; and Leppin, "Vom Auseinanderbrechen," 1851.

145. Heschel, "For 'Volk, Blood, and God': The Theological Faculty at the University of Jena during the Third Reich," in *Nazi Germany and the Humanities*, ed. Wolfgang Bialas and Anson Rabinbach (Oxford: Oneworld, 2007), 365–98 (at 387–88); and Leppin, "Vom Auseinanderbrechen," 1851.

impression of individuals denying their own histories, rather than confronting and learning from them, and of peers and colleagues exculpating one another for their past errors, rather than holding each other accountable. In this respect, Thuringia is merely an example, though a particularly clear one, of behavior that was rather common in Germany under denazification. Within this dynamic, the Church in effect provided cover and a career path for theology professors who could not survive even the limited denazification in the university theology faculties.

Too often, "history of scholarship" as a category is restricted to who has said what about specific problem X or Y—as if the discipline were not part of a broader social, cultural, and intellectual history, both shaping that history and being shaped by it. The effect of the weak denazification of the Thuringian Church and the University of Jena was that a group of German Christian educators and church leaders continued to work and publish in their fields, and thereby influence the development of Old and New Testament scholarship, long after the Nazi era came to a close.[146] Some of this theological and biblical scholarship was never fully divorced of its antisemitic roots. In the broader scope of the history of the Third Reich, it seems the intersection of the two institutions—the Church and the university—in the field of theology presents two betrayals: one during nazification and one during denazification. In between these two betrayals stood von Rad, a scholar who actively resisted the nazification of his field but whose scholarship was nonetheless significantly compromised in the process.

BIBLIOGRAPHY

Archival Sources

ThHStAW   Thüringisches Hauptstaatsarchiv Weimar
UAJ   Universitätsarchiv der Friedrich-Schiller-Universität Jena

---

146. For example, Grundmann's New Testament commentaries were popular at universities in Germany after the war, meaning a generation of biblical scholars used his work on a regular basis in their studies. The most recent edition of his commentary on the Gospel of Mark is still available for purchase on the publisher's website (*Das Evangelium nach Markus*, 10th ed., Theologischer Handkommentar zum Neuen Testament 2 [Leipzig, Germany: Evangelische Verlagsanstalt, 1989], accessed November 28, 2013, http://www.eva-leipzig.de/product_info.php?info=p2260_Das-Evangelium-nach-Markus.html).

Secondary Sources

Allinson, Mark. *Germany and Austria 1814–2000*. London: Routledge, 2002.

Alt, Albrecht, Joachim Begrich, and Gerhard von Rad. *Führung zum Christentum durch das Alte Testament: Drei Vorträge*. Leipzig, Germany: Dörffling & Franke, 1934.

Astel, Karl. *Die Aufgabe: Rede zur Eröffnung des Winter-Semesters 1936/37 an der Thüringischen Landesuniversität Jena in Gegenwart des Reichsstatthalters und Gauleiters Fritz Sauckel, gehalten am 6. November 1936*. Jenaer Akademische Reden 24. Jena, Germany: Gustav Fischer, 1937.

Baranowski, Shelley. "The Confessing Church and Antisemitism: Protestant Identity, German Nationhood, and the Exclusion of Jews." In Ericksen and Heschel, *Betrayal*, 90–109.

Barnett, Victoria. *For the Soul of the People: Protestant Protest against Hitler*. New York: Oxford University Press, 1992.

Barth, Karl. *Trouble and Promise in the Struggle of the Church in Germany: Translation of the Substance of the Philip Maurice Deneke Lecture Delivered at Lady Margaret Hall, Oxford, on 4 March 1938*. Translated by P. V. M. Benecke. Oxford: Clarendon, 1938.

Bergen, Doris L. "Old Testament, New Hatreds: The Hebrew Bible and Antisemitism in Nazi Germany." In *Sacred Text, Secular Times: The Hebrew Bible in the Modern World*, edited by Leonard J. Greenspoon and Brian F. Lebeau, 35–46. Studies in Jewish Civilization 10. Omaha, NE: Creighton University Press, 2000."

———. "Storm Troopers of Christ: The German Christian Movement and the Ecclesiastical Final Solution." In Ericksen and Heschel, *Betrayal*, 40–67.

Besier, Gerhard. *"Selbstreinigung" unter britischer Besatzungsherrschaft: Die Evangelisch-Lutherische Landeskirche Hannovers und ihr Landesbischof Marahrens, 1945–1947*. Studien zur Kirchengeschichte Niedersachsens 27. Göttingen, Germany: Vandenhoeck & Ruprecht, 1986.

Bialas, Wolfgang, and Anson Rabinbach, eds. *Nazi Germany and the Humanities: How German Academics Embraced Nazism*. Oxford: Oneworld, 2014. Originally published 2006.

Böhm, Susanne. "Gerhard von Rad in Jena." In *Das Alte Testament—ein Geschichtsbuch?!: Geschichtsschreibung oder Geschichtsüberlieferung im antiken Israel. Festschrift für Joachim Conrad*, edited by Uwe Becker and Jürgen von Oorschot, 203–40. Arbeiten zur Bibel und ihrer Geschichte 17. Leipzig, Germany: Evangelische Verlagsanstalt, 2005.

———. "Gerhard von Rad und der Streit um das Alte Testament—Unter besonderer Berücksichtigung seiner Zeit in Jena." Unpublished diploma thesis, Faculty of Theology, Fredrick Schiller University of Jena, Germany, 1996.

Bormann, Lukas. "Walter Grundmann und das Ministerium für Statssicherheit—Chronik einer Zusammenheit aus Überzeugung (1956–1969)." *Kirchliche Zeitgeschichte* 22 (2009): 595–632.
Brettler, Marc Z. "A 'Literary Sermon' in Deuteronomy 4." In *"A Wise and Discerning Mind": Essays in Honor of Burke O. Long*, edited by Saul M. Olyan and Robert C. Culley, 33–50. Brown Judaic Studies 325. Providence, RI: Brown Judaic Studies, 2000.
Brueggemann, Walter. "The ABC's of Old Testament Theology in the US." *Zeitschrift für die alttestamentliche Wissenschaft* 114 (2002): 412–32.
Bruhn, Mike, and Heike Böttner. "Studieren in Jena 1933 bis 1945: Eine Fallstudie." In Gottwald and Steinbach, *Zwischen Wissenschaft und Politik*, 107–22.
Brumlik, Micha. "Post-Holocaust Theology." In Ericksen and Heschel, *Betrayal*, 169–88.
Buber, Martin. "Jewish Religiosity" [German original, 1910]. In *On Judaism*, edited by Nahum M. Glatzer, 79–94. New York: Schocken, 1967.
———. "The Spirit of the Orient and Judaism" In *On Judaism*, edited by Nahum M. Glatzer, 56–78. New York: Schocken, 1967. Originally published in German in 1916.
———. *Vom Geist des Judentums: Reden und Geleitwörte*. Leipzig, Germany: Kurt Wolff, 1916.
Buchheim, Hans. *Glaubenskrise im Dritten Reich: Drei Kapitel nationalsozialistischer Religionspolitik*. Stuttgart, Germany: Deutsche Verlags-Anstalt, 1953.
Burchardt, Axel. "Das Bild von der 'braunen Universität' greift zu kurz: Interview mit den Herausgebern des Studienbandes." In Hoßfeld et al., *Kämpferische Wissenschaft*, 9–22.
Buss, Martin. *Biblical Form Criticism in Its Context*. Journal for the Study of the Old Testament: Supplement Series 274. Sheffield, UK: Sheffield Academic, 1999.
Casey, Maurice. "Some Anti-Semitic Assumptions in the 'Theological Dictionary of the New Testament.'" *Novum Testamentum* 41, no. 3 (1999): 280–91.
Crenshaw, James L. *Gerhard von Rad*. Makers of the Modern Theological Mind. Waco, TX: Word Books, 1978.
Deines, Roland, Volker Leppin, and Karl-Wilhelm Niebuhr, eds. *Walter Grundmann: Ein Neutestamentler im Dritten Reich*. Arbeiten zur Kirchen- und Theologiegeschichte 21. Leipzig, Germany: Evangelische Verlagsanstalt, 2007.
Ericksen, Robert P. *Complicity in the Holocaust: Churches and Universities in Nazi Germany*. Cambridge: Cambridge University Press, 2012.
———. *Theologians under Hitler: Gerhard Kittel, Paul Althaus and Emanuel Hirsch*. New Haven, CT: Yale University Press, 1985.
Ericksen, Robert P., and Susannah Heschel, eds. *Betrayal: German Churches and the Holocaust*. Minneapolis: Fortress, 1999.

Gerdmar, Anders. *Roots of Theological Anti-Semitism: German Biblical Interpretation and the Jews, from Herder and Semler to Kittel and Bultmann*. Studies in Jewish History and Culture 20. Leiden, Netherlands: Brill, 2009.

Gerlach, Wolfgang. *And the Witnesses Were Silent: The Confessing Church and the Persecution of the Jews*. Edited and translated by Victoria J. Barnett. Lincoln: University of Nebraska Press, 2000. Originally published in German as *Als die Zeugen Schweigen: Bekennende Kirche und die Juden*. Berlin: Institut Kirche und Judentum, 1987.

Gertz, Jan Christian. "Die Stellung des kleinen geschichtlichen Credos in der Redaktionsgeschichte von Deuteronomium und Pentateuch." In *Liebe und Gebot: Studien zum Deuteronomium—Festschrift zum 70. Geburtstag von Lothar Perlitt*, edited by Reinhard Gregor Kratz and Hermann Spieckermann, 30–45. Forschungen zur Religion und Literatur des Alten und Neuen Testaments 190. Göttingen, Germany: Vandenhoeck & Ruprecht, 2000.

Gottwald, Herbert, and Matthias Steinbach, eds. *Zwischen Wissenschaft und Politik: Studien zur Jenaer Universität im 20. Jahrhundert*. Jena, Germany: Bussert & Stadeler, 2000.

Grundmann, Walter. *Das Evangelium nach Markus*. 10th ed. Theologischer Handkommentar zum Neuen Testament 2. Leipzig, Germany: Evangelische Verlagsanstalt, 1989.

———. *Die Entjudung des religiösen Lebens als Aufgabe deutscher Theologie und Kirche*. Weimar, Germany: Deutsche Christen, 1939.

Hauger, Martin. "'But We Were in the Wilderness, and There God Speaks Quite Differently': On the Significance of Preaching in the Theology and Work of Gerhard von Rad." *Interpretation* 62, no. 3 (2008): 287–92.

———. *Gerhard von Rads frühe Predigten: Eine historisch-homiletische Untersuchung*. Arbeiten zur Praktischen Theologie 51. Leipzig, Germany: Evangelische Verlagsanstalt, 2013.

Helmreich, Ernst Christian. *The German Churches under Hitler: Background, Struggle, and Epilogue*. Detroit: Wayne State University Press, 1979.

Heschel, Susannah. *The Aryan Jesus: Christian Theologians and the Bible in Nazi Germany*. Princeton, NJ: Princeton University Press, 2008.

———. "For 'Volk, Blood, and God': The Theological Faculty at the University of Jena during the Third Reich." In *Nazi Germany and the Humanities*, edited by Wolfgang Bialas and Anson Rabinbach, 365–98. Oxford: Oneworld, 2007.

———. "The Theological Faculty at the University of Jena as 'a Stronghold of National Socialism.'" In Hoßfeld et al., *Kämpferische Wissenschaft*, 452–70.

———. "When Jesus Was an Aryan: The Protestant Church and Antisemitic Propaganda." In Ericksen and Heschel, *Betrayal*, 68–89.

Hockenos, Matthew D. *A Church Divided: German Protestants Confront the Nazi Past*. Bloomington: Indiana University Press, 2004.

Hoßfeld, Uwe, Jürgen John, Oliver Lemuth, and Rüdiger Stutz, eds. *"Kämpferische Wissenschaft": Studien zur Universität Jena im Nationalsozialismus.* Cologne, Germany: Böhlau, 2003.

Hyatt, J. Philip. "Were There an Ancient Historical Credo in Israel and an Independent Sinai Tradition?" In *Translating and Understanding the Old Testament: Essays in Honor of Herbert Gordon May*, edited by Harry Thomas Frank and William L. Reed, 152–70. Nashville, TN: Abingdon, 1970.

John, Jürgen, and Oliver Lemuth. "Statistiken, Übersichten und Tabellen." In Hoßfeld et al., *Kämpferische Wissenschaft*, 1101–29.

Kittel, Gerhard, and Gerhard Friedrich, eds. *Theologisches Wörterbuch zum Neuen Testament.* 10 vols. Stuttgart: W. Kohlhammer, 1932–79.

Koenen, Klaus. *Unter dem Dröhnen der Kanonen: Arbeiten zum Alten Testament aus der Zeit des Zweiten Weltkriegs.* Neukirchen-Vluyn: Neukirchener, 1998.

Köhler, Ludwig. "Die hebräische Rechtsgemeinde: Festrede des Rektors Prof. Dr. Ludwig Köhler gehalten an der 98. Stiftungsfeier der Universität am 29. April 1931." Zürich: Art. Institut Orell Füssli, 1931.

Krause, Reinhold. *Rede des Gauobmannes der Glaubensbewegung "Deutsche Christen" im Groß-Berlin: Dr. Krause. Gehalten im Sportpalast am 13. November 1933.* Schriftenreihe der Glaubensbewegung Deutsche Volkskirche [12 page pamphlet]. [Berlin:] Glaubensbewegung Deutsche Volkskirche, 1933. Translated with annotations in Solberg, *Church Undone*, 249–62.

Krieg, Robert A. *Catholic Theologians in Nazi Germany.* New York: Continuum, 2004.

Leppin, Volker. "Vom Auseinanderbrechen zum Neuaufbau: Die Theologische Fakultät Jena um 1945." In *Hochschule im Sozialismus: Studien zur Geschichte der Friedrich-Schiller-Universität Jena (1945–1990), Band 2*, edited by Uwe Hoßfeld, Tobias Kaiser, and Heinz Mestrup, with assistance from Horst Neuper, 1848–70. Cologne, Germany: Böhlau, 2007.

Levenson, Jon D. *The Hebrew Bible, the Old Testament, and Historical Criticism: Jews and Christians in Biblical Studies.* Louisville, KY: Westminster/John Knox, 1993.

Levinson, Bernard M. *Defending the Old Testament in Nazi Germany: Gerhard von Rad's Struggle to Transform Law into Gospel.* Atlanta, GA: Society of Biblical Literature, 2022.

———. *Deuteronomy and the Hermeneutics of Legal Innovation.* Oxford: Oxford University Press, 1998.

———. *Legal Revision and Religious Renewal in Ancient Israel.* Cambridge: Cambridge University Press, 2008.

———. "Reading the Bible in Nazi Germany: Gerhard von Rad's Attempt to Reclaim the Old Testament for the Church." *Interpretation* 62, no. 3 (2008): 238–54.

Levinson, Bernard M., and Eckart Otto, eds., with assistance from Walter Dietrich. *Recht und Ethik im Alten Testament*. Münster, Germany: LIT, 2004.

Levinson, Bernard M., and Jeffrey Stackert. "Between the Covenant Code and Esarhaddon's Succession Treaty: Deuteronomy 13 and the Composition of Deuteronomy." *Journal of Ancient Judaism* 3 (2012): 123–40.

Lohfink, Norbert. *Das Hauptgebot: Eine Untersuchung literarischer Einleitungsfragen zu Dtn 5–11*. Rome: Pontifical Biblical Institute, 1963.

Meister-Karanikas, Ralf. "Die Thüringer evangelische Kirche und 'die Judenfrage': Notizen zur Epoche 1933–1945." In Seidel and Wiegand, *Thüringer Gratwanderungen*, 111–23.

Norden, Günther van. "Die Barmer Theologische Erklärung und die 'Judenfrage.'" In *Das Unrechtsregime: Internationale Forschung über den Nationalsozialismus Band I: Ideologie—Herrschaftssystem—Wirkung in Europa. Festschrift für Werner Jochmann zum 65. Geburtstag*, edited by Ursula Büttner, 315–30. Hamburger Beiträge zur Sozial- und Zeitgeschichte 21. Hamburg, Germany: Christians, 1986.

Pältz, Eberhard H. "Jena." *Theologische Realenzyklopädie* 16 (1987): 559–63.

Probst, Christopher. *Demonizing the Jews: Luther and the Protestant Church in Nazi Germany*. Bloomington, Indiana University Press, 2012.

———. "'An Incessant Army of Demons': Wolf Meyer-Erlach, Luther, and 'the Jews' in Nazi Germany." *Holocaust and Genocide Studies* 23, no. 3 (2009): 441–60.

Rabenau, Konrad von. "Als Student bei Gerhard von Rad in Jena 1943–1945." In *Das Alte Testament und die Kultur der Moderne*, edited by Manfred Oeming, Konrad Schmid, and Michael Welker, 7–12. Altes Testament und Moderne 8. Münster, Germany: LIT, 2004.

Rad, Gerhard von. "Alttestamentliche Glaubensaussagen vom Leben und vom Tod." *Allgemeinen Evangelischen-Lutherischen Kirchenzeitung* 71 (1938): 826–34.

———. *Das Alte Testament: Gottes Wort für die Deutschen*. Klares Ziel 1. Berlin: Ostwerk, 1937.

———. "Das Alte Testament in der katholischen Kirche: Gedanken zum dem 'Werkbuch der Bibel' von E. Kalt." *Theologische Blätter* 21 (1942): 177–81.

———. "Das Christuszeugnis des Alten Testaments: Eine Auseinandersetzung mit Wilhelm Vischers gleichnamigem Buch." *Theologische Blätter* 14 (1935): 249–54.

———. "Das Ergebnis." In Alt, Begrich, and Rad, *Führung zum Christentum durch das Alte Testament*, 54–70. Leipzig, Germany: Dörffling & Franke, 1934.

———. *Das formgeschichtliche Problem des Hexateuchs*. Beiträge zur Wissenschaft vom Alten (und Neuen) Testament 78. Stuttgart, Germany: W. Kohlhammer, 1938. Reprinted in von Rad, *Gesammelte Studien zum Alten Testament I*, 9–86. Translated in English as "The Form-Critical Problem of the Hexateuch," in von Rad, *Problem of the Hexateuch*, 1–78. Reprinted in Gerhard von Rad, *From*

Genesis to Chronicles: Explorations in Old Testament Theology, edited by K. C. Hanson, 1–58. Fortress Classics in Biblical Studies. Minneapolis: Fortress, 2005.

———. *Das fünfte Buch Mose*. 4th ed. Das Alte Testament Deutsch 8. Göttingen, Germany: Vandenhoeck & Ruprecht, 1983. Translated by Dorothea Barton as *Deuteronomy: A Commentary*. Old Testament Library 5. Philadelphia: Westminster, 1966.

———. *Das Geschichtsbild des chronistischen Werkes*. Beiträge zur Wissenschaft vom Alten (und Neuen) Testament 54. Stuttgart, Germany: W. Kohlhammer, 1930.

———. *Das Gottesvolk im Deuteronomium*. Beiträge zur Wissenschaft vom Alten (und Neuen) Testament 47. Stuttgart, Germany: W. Kohlhammer, 1929. Reprinted in von Rad, *Gesammelte Studien zum Alten Testament II*, 9–108.

———. *Deuteronomium-Studien*. 2nd ed. Forschungen zur Religion und Literatur des Alten und Neuen Testaments 58. Göttingen, Germany: Vandenhoeck & Ruprecht, 1948. First edition reprinted in von Rad, *Gesammelte Studien zum Alten Testament II*, 109–53. Translated by David Stalker as *Studies in Deuteronomy*. 2nd ed. London: SCM, 1956.

———. "Die bleibende Bedeutung des Alten Testaments." Der *Kindergottesdienst* 47 (1937): 9–10.

———. "Die levitische Predigt in den Büchern der Chronik." In *Festschrift Otto Procksch zum sechzigsten Geburtstag am 9. August 1934 überreicht: Sonderdruck, Die Bezeichnungen für Land und Volk im Alten Testament*, edited by Leonhard Rost, 113–24. Leipzig, Germany: A. Deichert'sche, 1934. Reprinted in von Rad, *Gesammelte Studien zum Alten Testament I*, 248–61. Translated in English as "The Levitical Sermon in I and II Chronicles," in von Rad *Problem of the Hexateuch*, 267–80.

———. *Erinnerungen aus der Kriegsgefangenschaft Frühjahr 1945*. Neukirchen-Vluyn, Germany: Neukirchener Verlag, 1976.

———. *Fragen der Schriftauslegung im Alten Testament*. Theologia militans 20. Leipzig, Germany: A. Deichert, 1938.

———. "Friedrich Rittelmeyer" [obituary]. Theologische Blätter 18 (1939): 129.

———. *Gesammelte Studien zum Alten Testament I*. 4th ed. Theologische Bücherei: Neudrucke und Berichte aus dem 20. Jahrhundert 8. Munich: C. Kaiser, 1971.

———. *Gesammelte Studien zum Alten Testament II*. Edited by Rudolf Smend. Theologische Bücherei: Neudrucke und Berichte aus dem 20. Jahrhundert 48. Munich: Kaiser, 1973.

———. "Gesetz und Evangelium im Alten Testament. Gedanken zu dem Buch von E. Hirsch: Das Alte Testament und die Predigt des Evangeliums." *Theologische Blätter* 16 (1937): 41–47.

———. *Moses*. Wege in die Bibel 3. Göttingen, Germany: Vandenhoeck & Ruprecht, 1940.

———. *The Problem of the Hexateuch and Other Essays.* Translated by E. W. Trueman Dicken. London: SCM, 1966.

———. *Theologie des Alten Testaments I.* 10th ed. Munich: C. Kaiser, 1992. Translated by David Stalker as *Old Testament Theology.* 2 vols. New York: Harper and Brothers, 1962.

———. "Vom Menschenbild des Alten Testaments." In Gerhard von Rad, Heinrich Schlier, Edmund Schlink, and Ernst Wolf, *Der alte und der neue Mensch: Aufsätze zur theologischen Anthropologie,* 5–23. Beiträge zur evangelischen Theologie 8. Munich: A. Lempp, 1942.

———. "Warum unterrichtet die Kirche im Alten Testament?" *An der Lebensquelle, Ev. Gemeindebote für den Kirchenbezirk Baden-Baden* 20 (1939): 6–7.

Raschzok, Klaus. "Wolf Meyer-Erlach und Hans Asmussen." In *Zwischen Volk und Bekenntnis: Praktische Theologie im Dritten Reich,* edited by Klaus Raschzok, 167–202. Leipzig, Germany: Evangelische Verlagsanstalt, 2000.

Remy, Steven P. *The Heidelberg Myth: The Nazification and Denazification of a German University.* Cambridge, MA: Harvard University Press, 2002.

Rinnen, Anja. *Kirchenmann und Nationalsozialist: Siegfried Lefflers ideelle Verschmelzung von Kirche und Drittem Reich.* Forum zur Pädagogik und Didaktik der Religion 9. Weinheim, Germany: Deutscher Studien, 1995.

Schüfer, Tobias. "Die Theologische Fakultät Jena und die Landeskirche im Nationalsozialismus." In Seidel and Wiegand, *Thüringer Gratwanderungen,* 94–110.

Seidel, Thomas A. "Die 'Entnazifierungs-Akte Grundmann': Anmerkungen zur Karriere eines vormals führenden DC-Theologen." In Deines, Leppin, and Niebuhr, *Walter Grundmann,* 349–69.

Seidel, Thomas A., and Dietmar Wiegand, eds. *Thüringer Gratwanderungen: Beiträge zur fünfundsiebzigjährigen Geschichte der evangelischen Landeskirche Thüringens.* Herbergen der Christenheit 3. Leipzig, Germany: Evangelische Verlagsanstalt, 1998.

Ska, Jean-Louis. *Introduction to Reading the Pentateuch.* Translated by Sr. Pascale Dominique. Winona Lake, IN: Eisenbrauns, 2006.

Smend, Rudolf. *Deutsche Alttestamentler in drei Jahrhunderten: Mit 18 Abbildungen.* Göttingen, Germany: Vandenhoeck & Ruprecht, 1989. Abridged translation published as idem, *From Astruc to Zimmerli: Old Testament Scholarship in Three Centuries.* Translated by M. Kohl. Tübingen: Mohr Siebeck, 2007.

———. "Rad, Gerhard von." *Theologische Realenzyklopädie* 28 (1997): 889–91.

Solberg, Mary M., ed. and trans. *A Church Undone: Documents from the German Christian Faith Movement, 1932–1940.* Minneapolis: Fortress, 2015.

Sonne, Hans-Joachim. *Die politische Theologie der Deutschen Christen: Einheit und Vielfalt deutsch-christlichen Denkens, dargestellt anhand des Bundes für Deutsche Kirche, der Thüringer Kirchenbewegung "Deutsche Christen" und der*

Christlich-Deutschen Bewegung. Göttinger Theologische Arbeiten 21. Göttingen, Germany: Vandenhoeck & Ruprecht, 1982.

Spicer, Kevin P. *Hitler's Priests: Clergy and National Socialism.* De Kalb: Northern Illinois University Press, 2008.

Stegmann, Erich. *Der Kirchenkampf in der Thüringer Evangelischen Kirche 1933–1945.* Berlin: Evangelische Verlagsanstalt, 1984.

Steigmann-Gall, Richard. *The Holy Reich: Nazi Conceptions of Christianity, 1919–1945.* Cambridge: Cambridge University Press, 2003.

Stutz, Rüdiger. "Wissenschaft als 'Dienst an Volk und Vaterland': Die Rektoren der Universität Jena und das 'Dritte Reich.'" In Gottwald and Steinbach, *Zwischen Wissenschaft und Politik,* 123–54.

Thierfelder, Jörg. "Ersatzveranstaltungen der Bekennenden Kirche." In *Theologische Fakultäten im Nationalsozialismus,* edited by Leonore Siegele-Wenschkewitz and Carsten Nicolaisen, 291–301. Arbeiten zur kirchlichen Zeitgeschichte, Series B, Volume 18. Göttingen, Germany: Vandenhoeck & Ruprecht, 1993.

Veijola, Timo. "The Deuteronomistic Roots of Judaism." In *Sefer Moshe: The Moshe Weinfeld Jubilee Volume,* Studies in the Bible and the Ancient Near East, Qumran, and Post-Biblical Judaism, ed. Chaim Cohen, Avi Hurvitz, and Shalom M. Paul, 459–78. Winona Lake, IN: Eisenbrauns, 2004.

Weinfeld, Moshe. *Deuteronomy and the Deuteronomic School.* Oxford: Clarendon, 1972. Reprint, Winona Lake, IN: Eisenbrauns, 1992.

———. "Deuteronomy: The Present State of Inquiry." *Journal of Biblical Literature* 86 (1987): 249–62. Reprinted in *A Song of Power and the Power of Song: Essays on the Book of Deuteronomy,* edited by Duane L. Christensen, 21–35. Sources for Biblical and Theological Study 3. Winona Lake, IN: Eisenbrauns, 1993.

Weinreich, Max. *Hitler's Professors: The Part of Scholarship in Germany's Crimes against the Jewish People.* New York: Yiddish Scientific Institute (YIVO), 1946. Reprinted with a foreword by Martin Gilbert. New Haven, CT: Yale University Press, 1999.

Weyde, Karl William. "Hellig krig i Det gamle testamentet og Tysklands krig i de to verdenskrigene: Et sentralt tema hos fremtredende gammeltestamentlere på 1900-tallet" [Holy war in the Old Testament and Germany's war in the two world wars: A central theme of prominent Old Testament academics of the 20th century]. *Teologisk Tidsskrift* 2 (2013): 136–53 (Norwegian; English abstract).

Witte, John E., Jr., and Thomas C. Arthur. "The Three Uses of the Law: A Protestant Source of the Purposes of Criminal Punishment?" *Journal of Law and Religion* 10, no. 2 (1993–94): 433–65.

BERNARD M. LEVINSON serves as Professor of Classical and Near Eastern Studies and of Law at the University of Minnesota, where he holds the Berman

Family Chair in Jewish Studies and Hebrew Bible. His research focuses on biblical and cuneiform law, textual reinterpretation in the Second Temple period, and the relation of the Bible to Western intellectual history. The interdisciplinary significance of his work has been recognized with appointments to the Institute for Advanced Study in Princeton, the *Wissenschaftskolleg zu Berlin*, the National Humanities Center in North Carolina, and the Israel Institute for Advanced Studies in Jerusalem, where he codirected a research team of eight international scholars working on Pentateuchal theory. He is the author of four books, including *Deuteronomy and the Hermeneutics of Legal Innovation* (Oxford, 1997) and *Legal Revision and Religious Renewal in Ancient Israel* (Cambridge, 2008), and six edited volumes.

FIVE

JEWISH STUDIES IN THE SERVICE OF NAZI IDEOLOGY

Tübingen's Faculty of Theology as a Center for Antisemitic Research

ANDERS GERDMAR

WHEN HITLER WAS PLANNING HIS strategy to seize political power and introduce new antisemitic policies in Germany, he knew that legitimation from Protestant academic theologians would be invaluable.[1] But was finding such support too bold a wish? One of the dominant ideological forces in the German population was, of course, Lutheran Protestantism. The question, however, was whether Christian clergy, committed to the care of souls, would be willing to help legitimate the oppression of Jews, regarded as God's chosen people. The situation in the Pietist German state of Schwaben, and its academic capital, Tübingen, provides an excellent case study of how German scholars provided a theological justification for Hitler's actions. Most well-known is Gerhard Kittel (1888–1948), the entrepreneurial Tübingen New Testament professor and author of the still prominent handbook of New Testament studies, *Theologisches Wörterbuch zum Neuen Testament*, who early on formulated

---

1. Leonore Siegele-Wenschkewitz, *Nazionalsozialismus und Kirchen: Religionspolitik von Partei und Staat bis 1935*, Tübinger Schriften zur Sozial- und Zeitgeschichte 5 (Düsseldorf, Germany: Droste, 1974), 44–46. See also Kurt Dietrich Schmidt, "Der Widerstand der Kirche im Dritten Reich," *Lutherische Monatshefte* 1, no. 8 (1962): 366–70, on Hitler's strategic propaganda to win the Christians, although Hitler himself was at odds with Christianity and the church. His personal animus was kept secret during most of the Nazi period. See Eike Wolgast, "Nationalsozialistische Hochschulpolitik und die evangelischtheologischen Fakultäten," in *Theologische Fakultäten im Nationalsozialismus*, ed. Leonore Siegele-Wenschkewitz and Carsten Nicolaisen, Arbeiten zur kirchlichen Zeitgeschichte, series B: Darstellungen (Göttingen, Germany: Vandenhoeck & Ruprecht, 1993), 45–80 (at 49).

a theological foundation for antisemitism for the Third Reich.[2] But he was not the only one. What I have termed the *Tübingen network* also included three other scholars: Paul Althaus (1888–1966), the Professor of Systematic and New Testament theology at Erlangen and an architect of a political theology for the "New Germany" who demonstrated a lifelong indebtedness to his Tübingen inheritance; Karl Georg Kuhn (1906–1976), an expert in Old Testament and Judaism, who during the National Socialist period was an antisemitic specialist in the Talmud; and Walter Grundmann (1906–1976), the Jena Professor of New Testament and Völkische Theology whose membership in this group is too little appreciated. That Kittel and Althaus were closely connected with Adolf Schlatter (1852–1938) and were part of a Tübingen network is well-known.[3] Kuhn, whose National Socialist past has been increasingly recognized, was academically related to Kittel and Schlatter as well.[4] Grundmann came to the Swabian university town as a young man; his *Doktorvater* [doctoral advisor]

---

2. See Gerhard Kittel, *Die Judenfrage*, 2nd ed. (Stuttgart: Kohlhammer, 1933), and below. For an overview of the research about Kittel, see Anders Gerdmar, *Roots of Theological Anti-Semitism: German Biblical Interpretation and the Jews, from Herder and Semler to Kittel and Bultmann*, Studies in Jewish History and Culture 20 (Leiden, Netherlands: Brill, 2009), 417–530, and Horst Junginger, *Die Verwissenschaftlichung der "Judenfrage" im Nationalsozialismus*, Veröffentlichungen der Forschungsstelle Ludwigsburg der Universität Stuttgart 19 (Darmstadt, Germany: Wissenschaftliche Buchgesellschaft, 2011), 133–78. For the history of the University of Tübingen under National Socialism, see Uwe Dietrich Adam, *Hochschule und Nationalsozialismus: Die Universität Tübingen im Dritten Reich; Mit einem Anhang von Wilfried Setzler "Die Tübinger Studentenfrequenz im Dritten Reich,"* Contubernium 23 (Tübingen, Germany: Mohr, 1977), and Benigna Schönhagen, *Tübingen unterm Hakenkreuz: Eine Universitätsstadt in der Zeit des Nationalsozialismus*, Beiträge zur Tübinger Geschichte 4 (Stuttgart, Germany: Theiss, 1991).

3. Dora Schlatter, letter regarding the connection between Adolf Schlatter and Gerhard Kittel (Abschrift), 1947, file 162/31.2, Universitätsarchiv Tübingen, Germany.

4. See Horst Junginger, "Das Bild der Juden in der nationalsozialistischen Judenforschung," in *Die kulturelle Seite des Antisemitismus: Zwischen Aufklärung und Shoah*, ed. Andrea Hoffmann (Tübingen, Germany: Tübinger Vereinigung für Volkskunde, 2006), 171–220; Horst Junginger, "'Judenforschung' in Tübingen: Von der jüdischen zur antijüdischen Religionswissenschaft," *Jahrbuch des Simon-Dubnow-Instituts* 5 (2006): 375–98; Junginger, *Die Verwissenschaftlichung der "Judenfrage" im Nationalsozialismus*. See also Alan E. Steinweis, *Studying the Jew: Scholarly Antisemitism in Nazi Germany* (Cambridge, MA: Harvard University Press, 2008). The National Socialist history of Karl Georg Kuhn has been focused on recently by Gerd Theissen, *Neutestamentliche Wissenschaft vor und nach 1945: Karl Georg Kuhn und Günther Bornkamm*, Schriften der Philosophisch-historischen Klasse der Heidelberger Akademie der Wissenschaften 47 (Heidelberg, Germany: Universitätsverlag Winter, 2009), and Junginger, *Verwissenschaftlichung der "Judenfrage" im Nationalsozialismus*, 179–210.

was Gerhard Kittel, under whom he also served as *wissenschaftlicher Assistent* [research assistant] from 1930 to 1932. I suggest here that Grundmann's Tübingen background decisively contributed to both his political and his theological development, even though in some respects he went much further in both than did his Tübingen colleagues. The fifth and most important figure in the group was Schlatter, who created and guaranteed the scholarly and spiritual environment in which the aforementioned scholars could develop their ideas, including antisemitic ones.

However, my primary focus in this chapter is not on these individual professors. I seek rather to explore how and why the prestigious theological faculty at Tübingen became a seedbed and, indeed, a think tank for the theological and political legitimation of antisemitism. The prominent Eberhard Karls University of Tübingen produced a greater number of influential Bible scholars with a National Socialist and antisemitic stance than any other German Protestant theological faculty. What factors—academic, political, religious, and social—contributed to this development? The influence of the faculty becomes even more significant when one considers its impact on the students it trained to serve as ministers and teachers in churches and schools. These scholars were important not only in the theological world but as key figures in the antisemitic project of the new Germany. As Alan Steinweis notes, these Tübingen scholars were what the National Socialist authorities had been waiting for.[5] Few non-Jewish scholars elsewhere had any expertise in Jewish studies; at Tübingen there was a long tradition of studying Jews and Judaism and great erudition in the Jewish literary heritage. Thus, the University of Tübingen could play a leading role as a center for Judenforschung, research into Judaism conducted by non-Jews during the Nazi regime as a form of antisemitism. Even under National Socialism, Germany thought of itself as a *Bildungsnation* [the Enlightenment ideal of a well-educated and highly cultured citizenry], and Hitler had repeatedly called for a scientific understanding of the "Jewish Problem." And since Jews by now were excluded from academia—precisely because they were Jews—they could not be used in antisemitic Judenforschung. There is no doubt that this Tübingen played an important role in German theological scholarship during the National Socialist period. Analysis of that academic context helps account for the role that theology played in the ideological legitimation of antisemitic policies—namely, in the betrayal of Christian theology.

---

5. Steinweis, *Studying the Jew*, 11.

In this chapter, I argue that the decisive factor in the role that Tübingen would play was the theologically legitimated political ideas nurtured by the group of scholars who were part of this network, influenced especially by Adolf Schlatter but later also by Gerhard Kittel.[6] It is true that Schlatter's connection to National Socialism or German antisemitism is seldom noted, perhaps because he was not a member of the Nationalsozialistische Deutsche Arbeiterpartei [National Socialist German Workers' Party (NSDAP)] and also because he was and still is seen more as a generator of "positive" or confessional biblical theology than a key figure in the lead-up to German antisemitism. My use of the term *network* here indicates not that these scholars formed any permanent group with equally intensive contact but that at different points in their careers these men all had some relationship to a Tübingen network and, to different degrees, to the charismatic and strong personality of Adolf Schlatter.

Thus, the Tübingen network became influential not only in the important academic centers of Tübingen, Erlangen, Munich, and Jena but also on a national level, where its scholars served as theological experts.[7] Schlatter, Kittel, and Kuhn were noted for their expertise in Judaism. The study of Tübingen thus provides a case study in how academic theology can function as an *ancilla antisemitica*, a handmaiden to antisemitism, even as biblical theology in Tübingen purported to serve as an *ancilla fidei*, a handmaiden of faith. This situation demonstrates how a small academic environment could wield significant influence and shape the course of German antisemitism during the National Socialist period.

---

6. For Schlatter, see Werner Neuer, *Adolf Schlatter: Ein Leben für Theologie und Kirche* (Stuttgart, Germany: Calwer, 1996), and Gerdmar, *Roots of Theological Anti-Semitism*, 253–318. I am well aware of the difficulty with terms like *network, group*, etc., and use them here in a tentative way to focus on the fact that these scholars were not mere individuals, each developing his ideas in isolation. Rather, there were relationships between them, and they did find themselves in a common location, even a particular discipline at a particular academic institution; there was a set of relationships between the "members" of the group.

7. See below on Kittel's and Kuhn's involvement in the Forschungsabteilung Judenfrage [Department for Research into the Jewish Question] at the Reichsinstitut für Geschichte des neuen Deutschlands [Reich Institute for the History of the New Germany]; Grundmann's involvement in the Institut zur Erforschung und Beseitigung des jüdischen Einflusses auf das deutsche kirchliche Leben [Institute for the Investigation and Eradication of Jewish Influence on German Church Life] in Eisenach; and Althaus's role in supporting antisemitic policies through writings and expert opinions in the Third Reich.

I. TÜBINGEN: CENTER FOR JEWISH STUDIES AND ANTISEMITISM

In his infamous book *Die Judenfrage* (1933), which went through three editions in just two years, Gerhard Kittel said that there was no Jewish Problem at the University of Tübingen, either in the faculty or in the student body.[8] But this fact had a long prehistory. In the same year that Count Eberhard im Bart (1445–1496) founded the university (1477), he also expelled all the Jews from the city of Tübingen.[9] The university charter mentioned the risk of having Jews around. Even through the mid-1920s Jewish students were not allowed as members of the student leagues in Tübingen, and in 1926, the National Socialist German Student League was established. In 1922, the university administration officially stated that it wanted no *rassefremde Ausländer* [foreigners of other race] at the university.[10] The policy was successful: Jewish students represented only half a percent of the student body at Tübingen, compared with 3.5 percent in German academia at large.[11] In 1931, the last Jewish full Professor, a Professor of Theoretical Physics named Alfred Landé, left Tübingen; when he was appointed, it had been remarked that this (in fact nonconfessional) Jewish professor would not be a good example for the youth studying at the University of Tübingen.[12] In 1932, the entire student league went in a National Socialist direction and became a corporate member of Kampfbund für deutsche Kultur [Militant League for German Culture (KfdK)],[13] Alfred Rosenberg's semiofficial organization for winning intellectual and cultural elites to the National Socialist cause.[14] These observations indicate that academic Tübingen became National Socialist even before the *Machtübernahme*—that is, before it became politically correct or expedient to be so. In reality, there was no Jewish Problem to deal with because the university was already *Judenrein* [a Nazi term designating an area "cleansed" or freed of Jews], as was noted by its senate in February 1933.[15]

Ironically enough, theology at the University of Tübingen, especially New Testament exegesis, was known for its competency in Judaism. In 1898, the

---

8. Kittel, *Judenfrage*, 35.
9. Junginger, *Verwissenschaftlichung der "Judenfrage" im Nationalsozialismus*, 47.
10. Ibid., 115, quoting Schönhagen, *Tübingen unterm Hakenkreuz*, 84.
11. Junginger, *Verwissenschaftlichung der "Judenfrage" im Nationalsozialismus*, 115n91.
12. Ibid., 117.
13. Adam, *Hochschule und Nationalsozialismus*, 24.
14. Junginger, *Verwissenschaftlichung der "Judenfrage" im Nationalsozialismus*, 128.
15. Ibid., 128.

Swiss New Testament scholar Schlatter was appointed to Tübingen. Schlatter's background was in an ecumenically oriented Swiss Pietism, and in his circles, there was an interest in evangelizing Jews and in Jewish studies.[16] In line with this background, Schlatter in 1882 made it his program to "get to know the Jews." He said to himself: "You must go into the Jewish literature; Philo and the apocalyptics (whom I knew) are not enough; Judaism, to which the New Testament stood in fruitful fellowship and heated struggle, was the Palestinian one, Pharisaism, which you must get to know on the basis of its own testimonies."[17] He noted that he was alone in this endeavor: New Testament scholarship concentrated only on the Greek texts. Finding the rabbinical literature aesthetically unattractive and challenging to the logical capacities of the reader, Schlatter nevertheless believed that the New Testament historian needed firsthand knowledge of it, since Jesus lived in this environment. But Schlatter also expresses his reverence for the religious earnestness of the Pharisees.[18]

Although in 1882 Schlatter could feel alone in his urge to go to the roots of the Judaism of the New Testament period, there was a parallel development in Germany. In 1883, Hermann Strack started the Institutum Judaicum in Berlin, and in 1886, Franz Delitzsch started one in Leipzig.[19] These scholars were like Schlatter in some ways—espousing evangelizing missions to Jews and quality scholarship in Jewish sources in the original languages—but they also took a clear stance against antisemitism, despite harboring negative stereotypes about Jews. Both produced important Semitic scholarship, which was appreciated by Jewish scholars.[20] Even more appreciated, perhaps, were their anti-antisemitic pamphlets.[21] At the same time, Delitzsch had a deep quarrel with liberal Judaism and especially its claims on Jesus as a part of Judaism.[22]

---

16. See Gerdmar, *Roots of Theological Anti-Semitism*, 191–251.

17. Adolf Schlatter, *Adolf Schlatters Rückblick auf seine Lebensarbeit: Zu seinem hundertsten Geburtstag*, ed. Theodor Schlatter, Beiträge zur Förderung christlicher Theologie (Gütersloh, Germany: C. Bertelsmann, 1952), 120 (my translation).

18. See Gerdmar, *Roots of Theological Anti-Semitism*, 254–55.

19. Ibid., 213–37 (for Delitzsch and his institute), 239–51 (for Strack).

20. Franz Delitzsch, *Zur Geschichte der jüdischen Poësie vom Abschluss der heiligen Schriften Alten Bundes bis auf die neueste Zeit* (Leipzig, Germany: Karl Tauchnitz, 1836); Hermann L. Strack, *Einleitung in Talmud und Midras*, 5th ed. (Munich: C. H. Beck'sche, 1920).

21. See Hermann Strack, *Der Blutaberglaube in der Menschheit, Blutmorde, und Blutritus*, 4th ed., Schriften des Institutum Judaicum in Berlin 14 (Leipzig, Germany: J. C. Hinrichs'sche, 1892).

22. Franz Delitzsch, *Jesus und Hillel: Mit Rücksicht auf Renan und Geiger* (Erlangen, Germany: A. Deichert, 1867).

When Gerhard Kittel came to Tübingen, Schlatter's passion for Jewish studies and the tradition from the Leipzig Institutum Judaicum would join together, Kittel having grown up close to the latter. These two professors, seemingly close both in scholarship and in personal relations, could be called the hub of the Tübingen network. But Schlatter had already nurtured these interests for over forty years when Kittel arrived. It was Schlatter's great entrepreneurial spirit that created the Jewish studies–oriented environment in Tübingen, making the beautiful little Swabian town by the Neckar River a center for Jewish studies under Christian auspices. The result was one of those centers of excellence that funding authorities so cherish today: a center for Jewish studies. In consequence, the rector of the University of Tübingen could later brag that Tübingen played a pioneering role in the scholarly struggle against antisemitism.[23]

II. THE INDIVIDUAL SCHOLARS AND THEIR BACKGROUNDS

Before looking at specific aspects of the Tübingen network, an examination of the individual scholars who were key members of this network is in order. This section reviews the history and work of Adolf Schlatter, Gerhard Kittel, Karl George Kuhn, Paul Althaus, and Walter Grundmann. Each of these men had a different relationship to Tübingen and to each other, yet they all had enough in common to be seen as a group.

Adolf Schlatter: The Tübingen Pioneer in Theology and Judaica

Due both to the fact that he was there before the others and to his role as theologian, teacher, and inspirer to the rest, Adolf Schlatter was the foundation of this network. Born in 1852, Schlatter was appointed to Tübingen as a New Testament professor in 1898. His family was deeply rooted in both Lutheran and Reformed Pietism with an ecumenical outlook. He studied in Basel and Tübingen, and in his circles, there was a strong interest in Jewish studies as

---

23. Helmut Heiber, *Walter Frank und sein Reichsinstitut für Geschichte des neuen Deutschland*, Quellen und Darstellungen zur Zeitgeschichte 13 (Stuttgart, Germany: Deutsche Verlags-Anstalt, 1966), 454. Tübingen's front-line position as a center of National Socialist Judenforschung is also noted in Horst Junginger, "Antisemitismus in Theorie und Praxis: Tübingen als Zentrum der nationalsozialistischen 'Judenforschung,'" in *Die Universität Tübingen im Nationalsozialismus*, ed. Urban Wiesing et al., Contubernium 73 (Stuttgart, Germany: Franz Steiner, 2010), 483.

well as attempts to convert Jews.[24] Schlatter's plan to familiarize himself with Judaism and Jewish history would remain his program throughout his career.[25] Theologically, Schlatter belonged to the conservative camp, which was why he became a professor in Berlin in 1893, where he represented the so-called positive school, a group of thinkers who stood in sharp opposition to the dominant liberal theology represented by Adolf von Harnack.[26] The conflict between these theological parties was deep and would deepen further while Schlatter was in Berlin.[27] Schlatter's time in Berlin was also important politically, as he became acquainted with the Lutheran Pietist and conservative court preacher Adolf Stoecker (1835–1909). In 1878, the latter became the founder of the Christian Social Party, which purposed to be an alternative to the growing socialist movement, and Schlatter reported on his positive encounters with Stoecker.[28] During the Berlin years Schlatter's relationship with Stoecker deepened, Schlatter seeing Stoecker as a "wholesome element in our Prussia and especially in our Berlin."[29] This observation, written in 1892, before his time in Berlin, may bear on Schlatter's political stance, and there is nothing to suggest that Schlatter quarreled with Stoecker's political leanings. Stoecker's movement was conservative-monarchist, but he is most well-known as the father of political, religiously founded antisemitism,[30] and he managed to make antisemitism a viable popular movement. In Schlatter's own words, his contact with

---

24. For this, see Gerdmar, *Roots of Theological Anti-Semitism*, 191–251, and Neuer, *Adolf Schlatter*, 179–80. For Beck's influence on the young Schlatter, see Neuer, *Adolf Schlatter*, 66–77.

25. A. Schlatter, *Adolf Schlatters Rückblick auf seine Lebensarbeit*, 120.

26. Neuer, *Adolf Schlatter*, 308–9. For Harnack and Judaism, as well as his correspondence with Houston Steward Chamberlain, see Wolfram Kinzig, *Harnack, Marcion, und das Judentum: Nebst einer kommentierten Edition des Briefwechsels Adolf von Harnacks mit Houston Steward Chamberlain*, Arbeiten zur Kirchen- und Theologiegeschichte 13 (Leipzig, Germany: Evangelische Verlagsanstalt, 2004). Christian Wiese, *Wissenschaft des Judentums und protestantische Theologie im wilhelminischen Deutschland: Ein Schrei ins Leere?*, Schriftenreihe wissenschaftlicher Abhandlungen des Leo Baeck Instituts 61 (Tübingen, Germany: Mohr Siebeck, 1999), discusses the relationship between Judaism and Protestant theology of the period.

27. See A. Schlatter, *Adolf Schlatters Rückblick auf seine Lebensarbeit*, 181–87, and Neuer, *Adolf Schlatter*, 311–16, 318–23.

28. Neuer, *Adolf Schlatter*, 262.

29. Ibid.

30. Werner Bergmann, "Stoecker, Adolf," in *Handbuch des Antisemitismus: Judenfeindschaft in Geschichte und Gegenwart*, vol. 2, bk. 2, Personen, im Auftrag von Zentrum für Antisemitismusforschung der Technischen Universität Berlin, ed. Wolfgang Benz (Berlin: K. G. Saur, 2009), 798–802 (at 798–99).

Stoecker was "the greatest that Berlin brought me."[31] The context of this remark was his conflict with liberal theology,[32] but Schlatter also seems to have stood close to Stoecker more generally. They certainly had a theological position in common, as both were part of a conservative-Pietist network that included Friedrich Bodelschwingh the elder, a key leader of German Lutheran Pietism.[33]

Schlatter was often regarded as an outsider, neither Lutheran nor born a German, but in some respects he was also a free and creative thinker.[34] He was a prolific writer and thereby exerted considerable influence in Germany and beyond—as he still does—as a cherished theologian in certain evangelical and conservative Protestant circles, especially in the United States and Germany.[35] His passion to understand Jews and Judaism led him to a range of research enterprises meant to enhance knowledge of "Palestinian Judaism"—a term often used in scholarly discourse to describe the Judaism of Jesus's time within the land of Israel, in contrast to the various diaspora communities.[36] Schlatter held simultaneously a deep interest in Judaism and a strong opposition to it. He boldly defended the Jewishness of both Jesus—Jesus was "a Jew, who is God"—and of Paul.[37] In his view early Christianity was deeply rooted in Palestinian Judaism. His arguments contributed to the ongoing German debate on the Jewishness of Jesus.[38]

---

31. A. Schlatter, *Adolf Schlatters Rückblick auf seine Lebensarbeit*, 187.

32. Neuer, *Adolf Schlatter*, 322.

33. For the contacts between Stoecker and Bodelschwingh, see Walter Frank, *Hofprediger Adolf Stoecker und die christlichsoziale Bewegung* (Berlin: Reimar Hobbing, 1928), index, s.v. "Bodelschwingh."

34. On his outsider status, see Roland Deines, *Die Pharisäer: Ihr Verständnis im Spiegel der christlichen und jüdischen Forschung seit Wellhausen und Graetz*, Wissenschaftliche Untersuchungen zum Neuen Testament 101 (Tübingen, Germany: Mohr Siebeck, 1997), 405, and Gerdmar, *Roots of Theological Anti-Semitism*, 255–56.

35. For example, Schlatter's 1885 book, *Der Glaube im Neuen Testament*, is being translated and published under the title *Faith in the New Testament* as part of the widespread Logos Bible Software (Cliff Kvidahl, "Adolf Schlatter [1852–1938]," Logos [blog], May 19, 2012, accessed December 29, 2020, https://blog.logos.com/2012/05/adolf-schlatter-1852-1938/).

36. Examples are Adolf Schlatter, *Der Glaube im Neuen Testament*, 2nd ed. (Stuttgart, Germany: Calwer, 1896); Adolf Schlatter, *Jochanan ben Zakkai, der Zeitgenosse der Apostel*, Beiträge zur Förderung christlicher Theologie 3/4 (Gütersloh, Germany: C. Bertelsmann, 1899); and Adolf Schlatter, *Israels Geschichte von Alexander dem Großen bis Hadrian*, Reiche der Alten Welt 3 (Calw, Germany: Verlag der Vereinsbuchhandlung, 1901).

37. Gerdmar, *Roots of Theological Anti-Semitism*, 303.

38. As raised by Houston Steward Chamberlain, *Die Grundlagen des neunzehnten Jahrhunderts*, vol. 1, 3rd ed. (Munich: F. Bruckmann A.-G, 1901). Such thinking also shows up in the work of influential theologians like Emanuel Hirsch, *Das Wesen des Christentums*

In 1935, Schlatter revealed himself as an antisemite, though there is evidence of similar attitudes from his work from the 1920s.[39] At Christmastime that year, he composed the pamphlet *Wird der Jude über uns siegen?* [Will the Jew prevail over us?]. Fifty thousand copies of this pamphlet were distributed immediately after the passage of the Nuremberg racial legislation. Unrealistically, he believed the Jews would join the National Socialists in opposing Christianity. Although scholars evaluate the pamphlet differently, its antisemitic stance is quite evident.[40] It provoked National Socialists, because Schlatter vehemently criticized any alternative, non-Christian celebrations of Christmas.[41] He also concocted a National Socialist–Jewish conspiracy, since, allegedly, the Jews also opposed Christmas. The pamphlet included a series of classical antisemitic stereotypes of Jewish conspiracies.[42] This was not the first or the only antisemitic statement by Schlatter, whose attitude was profoundly ambivalent: belief in the salvific historical role of the Jews alongside a sharp prejudice against contemporary Judaism.[43]

Schlatter had a complex relationship to the National Socialist state. On the one hand, he welcomed the Nazi seizure of power in 1933 and signed the so-called Tübinger Sätze [Tübingen Statements], which state: "We are full of gratitude to God, that he, as the Lord of history, has given our people, in Adolf Hitler, the Führer and Savior [*Führer und Retter*], from deep trouble."[44] This statement was formulated one month after the boycott of the Jews, and the document was an attempt to bridge the relationship between the Bekennende Kirche [Confessing Church], which sought to maintain the independence of the church, and the "brown" Deutsche Christen [German Christians].[45]

(Weimar, Germany: Deutsche Christen, 1939), republished in his *Gesammelte Werke*, ed. Arnulf von Scheliha, vol. 19 (Waltrop, Germany: Hartmut Spenner, 2004). See further Alan T. Davies, "The Aryan Christ: A Motif in Christian Anti-Semitism," *Journal of Ecumenical Studies* 12 (1975): 569–79, and Susannah Heschel, *The Aryan Jesus: Christian Theologians and the Nazi Bible in Nazi Germany* (Princeton, NJ: Princeton University Press, 2008).

39. Gerdmar, Roots of Theological Anti-Semitism, 272–75.
40. Ibid., 306.
41. Adolf Schlatter, *Wird der Jude über uns siegen? Ein Wort für die Weihnachtszeit*, Freizeit-Blätter 8 (Essen an der Ruhr, Germany: Freizeiten-Verlag zu Velbert im Rheinland, 1935), 3.
42. Gerdmar, *Roots of Theological Anti-Semitism*, 306–18.
43. Ibid., 253–326.
44. Quoted in Gerhard Schäfer, *Die evangelische Landeskirche in Württemberg und der Nationalsozialismus: Eine Dokumentation zum Kirchenkampf*, vol. 3, *Der Einbruch des Reichsbischofs in die württ. Landeskirche 1934* (Stuttgart, Germany: Calwer, 1974), 335.
45. For a concise discussion of the conflict that arose within Germany between the various German Christian groups, which advocated the alignment of the church with

On the other hand, even though he saw the Führer as divinely ordained, he maintained his criticism of National Socialism for denying Christian values, for including pagan elements, and for a "Caesarism" that went too far.[46] At the same time, he seemed to flirt or at least wish to dialogue with the politically powerful or with the National Socialist Christians, as when he wrote about the total church in the total state: "If the total state creates the willing German, it brings great blessing to the church."[47] Thus, even though Schlatter kept a critical distance, he was nevertheless eager for the church to stay on speaking terms with the SA-man.[48] He raised that to a priority over protecting the church's own Jewish-Christian brethren.[49] In that context, his view on the order of creation as legitimating the present rule, including that of the Führer, played an important role and was echoed in Althaus's theology of the *Ordnungen* [orders] (see below).

Schlatter was no Nazi, but by theological principle, he was a supporter of the powers that be, in this case the National Socialist regime. He was not a fervent antisemite, as his successor Kittel was, but he held and expressed antisemitic ideas. He could have taken a clear stand against antisemitism but did not, instead signing the Tübinger Sätze. His cultural, antisemitic criticism of contemporary Judaism was deeply rooted in and reminiscent of Stoecker's

---

National Socialist policies, and the Confessing Church, which sought to preserve church autonomy, see the chapter by Bernard Levinson, "Gerhard von Rad's Struggle against the Nazification of the Old Testament," in this volume.

46. Gerdmar, *Roots of Theological Anti-Semitism*, 281.

47. Adolf Schlatter, *Die neue deutsche Art in der Kirche*, Sonderdrucke des Monatsblattes "Beth-El" 14 (Bethel bei Bielefeld, Germany: Anstalt Bethel, 1933). The notion of the Total Church connects with the judicial philosophy of Carl Schmitt, who was the first to talk about the Total State. See my discussion of this aspect of Schlatter's work in Gerdmar, *Roots of Theological Anti-Semitism*, 292–301.

48. "SA-man" stands for members of the Sturmabteilung (Storm Troopers), which was the paramilitary wing of the National Socialist Party used to terrorize political opponents. Initially, as in 1933, when Schlatter wrote this pamphlet, the membership of the SA consisted largely of demobilized German soldiers, often unemployed. In Schlatter's text, the "SA-man" seems to stand for the "man of the street," normal German citizens, whom Schlatter sought to reach. See his early commentary, *Der Römerbrief: Ein Hilfsbüchlein für Bibelleser* (Stuttgart, Germany: Calwer, 1887), 3; and Adolf Schlatter, *Adolf Schlatters Rückblick auf seine Lebensarbeit: Zu seinem hundertsten Geburtstag herausgegeben von Theodor Schlatter* (Gütersloh, Germany: C. Bertelsmann, 1952), 123. Of course, Schlatter must have known the violent character of the SA.

49. This is indicated in his dealings with the Bethel Confession; see Gerdmar, *Roots of Theological Anti-Semitism*, 281–92.

agitation in Berlin in the late nineteenth century.[50] Although Schlatter never stood on the barricades like Kuhn or Kittel, he served as the patriarch of the Tübingen group, which spearheaded antisemitic research into Judaism and mentored younger scholars. His major role as facilitator of such ideas should not be underestimated.

Gerhard Kittel: Antisemitic Expert in Judaism

Gerhard Kittel's father was the famous Old Testament scholar Rudolf Kittel. Raised in the Lutheran Pietist tradition, the younger Kittel was introduced to Jewish studies through his father's involvement in the Institutum Judaicum Delitzschianum in Leipzig. Part of Gerhard Kittel's initial work indeed made some progress in understanding the Jewish background to the New Testament, providing an alternative to liberal, idealistic research into Judaism that was less favorable to Jews and Judaism. Kittel's *Die Probleme des palästinischen Spätjudentums und das Urchristentum*, published in 1926, showed an unusual appreciation of Palestinian Judaism as the background of early Christianity. Dedicated to Kittel's Jewish teacher Israel I. Kahan, the book argued that Jesus and his disciples were Palestinian Jews, even though Kittel also established that there was a fundamental opposition between Jesus and Palestinian rabbinism and scribes.[51] However, he also found many points of contact between Palestinian Judaism and early Christianity.[52] In seeing such connections, he broke with the research tradition of Wilhelm Bousset, Hugo Gressmann, and the history of religions school.[53] However, Kittel ultimately saw no possibility of harmonizing Judaism and Christianity: "Where Judaism wants to remain Judaism, it can do nothing but declare a fight regarding the claim of Jesus."[54] Thus Kittel ended up with an ambiguous view: on the one

---

50. Adolf Stoecker, *Christlich-Sozial: Reden und Aufsätze* (Berlin: Verlag der Buchhandlung der Berliner Stadtmission, 1890), 359–494.

51. Gerhard Kittel, *Die Probleme des palästinischen Spätjudentums und das Urchristentum*, Beiträge zur Wissenschaft vom Alten und Neuen Testament 3/1 (Stuttgart, Germany: W. Kohlhammer, 1926), 3. See also Gerdmar, *Roots of Theological Anti-Semitism*, 423–24.

52. Kittel, *Probleme des palästinischen Spätjudentums und das Urchristentum*, 45–51 (my translation).

53. Ibid., 4n3. The work he criticizes is Wilhelm Bousset and Hugo Gressmann, *Die Religion des Judentums im späthellenistischen Zeitalter, verfasst von Wilhelm Bousset, herausgegeben von Hugo Gressmann*, Handbuch zum Neuen Testament 21 (Tübingen, Germany: J. C. B. Mohr [Paul Siebeck], 1926), which is Gressmann's revision of Bousset's influential work.

54. Kittel, *Probleme des palästinischen Spätjudentums und das Urchristentum*, 140 (my translation).

hand, there was a clear affinity between Judaism and early Christianity, but on the other, there was a deep conflict between them because, he contended, Judaism found its culmination in Jesus. Despite this problematic ambivalence, Kittel must be seen as a pioneer in his description of Palestinian Judaism: very few of his contemporary colleagues describing classical Judaism were competent to consult actual rabbinic sources.

Nevertheless, in 1933 Kittel wrote the pamphlet *Die Judenfrage*, which was quickly published in three editions. Here he argued for an apartheid policy toward German Jewry, but only after having discussed other models for dealing with the Jewish Problem, including elimination and emigration.[55] With this work, Kittel became simultaneously the most prominent specialist in Jews and Judaism and a leading figure of antisemitism in German academia. What may look like a conversion under the gallows was not. It is true that Kittel became a member of the National Socialist Party in 1933, but he had already been involved in the KfdK for some years.[56] The goal of this organization was to win the German elite over to the National Socialist cause, attracting "personalities in German cultural life who, at least initially, refuse a tie to any party."[57] In the KfdK, other organizations, and in fellowship with both students and other scholars, Kittel had ample opportunity to develop his antisemitic ideas. Therefore, it is not that surprising that *Die Judenfrage*, building on a speech from June 1, 1933, evidenced a fully grown antisemitic ideology; it is not a pamphlet formulated only two months after the Nazi *Machtübernahme* [seizure of power] but a thoroughly developed antisemitic product. In his unpublished postwar attempt at self-exculpation, "Meine Verteidigung" [My defense, 1946], Kittel explained that he had not changed his ideas on "the Jewish Problem" from what he espoused 1933.[58] Even after the Holocaust, he upheld his view on the sharp

---

55. Kittel, *Judenfrage*, 13–18.
56. For the KfdK, see Jürgen Gimmel, *Die politische Organisation kulturellen Ressentiments: Der "Kampfbund für deutsche Kultur" und das bildungsbürgerliche Unbehagen an der Moderne*, Schriftenreihe der Stipendiatinnen und Stipendiaten der Friedrich-Ebert-Stiftung 10 (Münster, Germany: LIT, 2001). For the evidence of his membership, see Gerdmar, *Roots of Theological Anti-Semitism*, 447–48.
57. Gimmel, *Politische Organisation kulturellen Ressentiments*, 274–75, quoted from a KfdK document. Kittel had also been a member of several other organizations with a nationalist and/or antisemitic stance, including the Kyffhäuser-Verband of the Vereine deutscher Studenten and Deutsche Vaterlandspartei (Leonore Siegele-Wenschkewitz, *Neutestamentliche Wissenschaft vor der Judenfrage: Gerhard Kittels theologische Arbeit im Wandel deutscher Geschichte*, Theologische Existenz heute 208 [Munich: Chr. Kaiser, 1980], 79).
58. Gerhard Kittel, "Meine Verteidigung, Neue erweiterte Niederschrift: November/Dezember 1946," 1946, file 162/31.1, Universitätsarchiv Tübingen, Germany.

anti-Jewish position of the New Testament and regretted that he had not earlier intervened in the political discussion of the Jewish Problem.[59] He could then have provided an alternative to the explosive antisemitism that erupted after 1933, he contended. It is evident that for Kittel, even in 1946, there was without a doubt a Jewish Problem that could not be ignored or minimized; modern Judaism was still like a red flag in front of a bull for him. To Kittel, even in custody for his antisemitic activities, the opposition between Christianity and Judaism was fierce, even metaphysical, and even in his self-exculpatory statement after the war, where he would have benefited from minimizing his antisemitism, Kittel still stood up for his book, *Die Judenfrage*.

As noted, Kittel is most famous for his editorship of *Theologisches Wörterbuch zum Neuen Testament*, which became a prestigious international propaganda asset for Germany, demonstrating that Germany was still a nation producing great scholarship. Gathering a host of Bible scholars to write articles on almost every Greek word in the New Testament, Kittel was able to set this mammoth ten-volume work in motion in 1928. The project was finished by his disciple Georg Friedrich only in 1958.[60] However, the lion's share of his own scholarly work during the National Socialist years was not in New Testament but in antisemitic research and was carried out in the Forschungsabteilung Judenfrage [Department for Research into the Jewish Question] at the Reichsinstitut für Geschichte des neuen Deutschlands [Reich Institute for the History of the New Germany]. The Institute was heavily politicized, having been founded by the antisemitic historian Walter Frank.[61] For a number of years, Kittel focused his main scholarly strengths on questions pertaining to racial mixing, a politically hot question in National Socialist Germany.[62] Building on his background in

---

59. Ibid., 7–8.

60. Gerhard Kittel and Gerhard Friedrich, eds., *Theologisches Wörterbuch zum Neuen Testament*, 10 vols. (Stuttgart, Germany: W. Kohlhammer, 1932–79), trans. G. W. Bromiley as *Theological Dictionary of the New Testament*, 10 vols. (Grand Rapids, MI: Eerdmans, 1964–76).

61. For Walter Frank, see Heiber, *Walter Frank und sein Reichsinstitut für Geschichte des neuen Deutschland*. Frank's views of Jews and Judaism were in line with those of the antisemitic court chaplain Adolf Stoecker, about whom he wrote his doctoral dissertation. See Junginger, *Verwissenschaftlichung der "Judenfrage" im Nationalsozialismus*, 229.

62. Gerhard Kittel, "Das Urteil über die Rassenmischung im Judentum und in der biblischen Religion," *Der Biologe* 6, no. 1 (1937): 342–53, and Gerhard Kittel, "Das Konnubium mit den Nicht-Juden im antiken Judentum," in *Forschungen zur Judenfrage: Sitzungsberichte der Zweiten Arbeitstagung der Forschungsabteilung Judenfrage des Reichsinstituts für Geschichte des neuen Deutschlands vom 12. bis 14. Mai 1937* (Hamburg, Germany: Hanseatische Verlagsanstalt, 1937), 30–62. See also Robert P. Ericksen, "Christians and the Holocaust: The Wartime Writings of Gerhard Kittel," in *Remembering for the Future: Working Papers and*

Jewish history in antiquity, Kittel paid particular attention to intermarriage.[63] This research had an obvious antisemitic agenda in *Das Antike Weltjudentum: Tatsachen, Texte, Bilder* [World Judaism in antiquity: Facts, texts, pictures], coauthored with Eugen Fischer in 1943.[64] His work was especially toxic in "Die Behandlung des Nichtjuden nach dem Talmud" [The treatment of non-Jews according to the Talmud], published by Joseph Goebbels's propaganda ministry in the inaugural issue of an antisemitic magazine. Here, with the Nazi persecution of Jewish citizens fully underway, Kittel alleged that the Talmud sanctions Jews to kill non-Jews.[65] The latter may be the worst example of antisemitic pseudo-scholarship by the Tübingen professor. Kittel retained his position at Tübingen until his suspension by the French military authorities on October 25, 1945. He died in July 1948, shortly after his return to Tübingen from an internment camp, an important reason for his detention having been his involvement in the Department for Research into the Jewish Question.

Karl Georg Kuhn: National Socialist Talmud Expert

Karl Georg Kuhn was born in 1906 to a Pietist Protestant family.[66] His father was a preacher and was later employed by the YMCA. As with many of the Tübingen scholars, Kuhn's interest in Semitic languages was not merely academic but grew from a desire to know the world around the New Testament.[67] Kuhn was introduced to rabbinic literature by Israel Rabin at the Breslau Rabbinical Seminary. He chose to continue his studies in Tübingen, where Adolf Schlatter and Gerhard Kittel were teaching. It was Kittel, who would become his colleague in the Department for Research into the Jewish

---

Addenda, ed. Yehuda Bauer et al. (Oxford: Pergamon, 1989), 2400–14, and Gerdmar, *Roots of Theological Anti-Semitism*, 478–92.

63. This was a key area of research at the Department for Research into the Jewish Question. See Junginger, *Verwissenschaftlichung der "Judenfrage" im Nationalsozialismus*, 229.

64. Gerhard Kittel and Eugen Fischer, *Das antike Weltjudentum: Tatsachen, Texte, Bilder*, Forschungen zur Judenfrage: Schriften des Rechtsinstituts für Geschichte des neuen Deutschlands 7 (Hamburg, Germany: Hanseatische Verlagsanstalt, 1943).

65. Gerhard Kittel, "Die Behandlung des Nichtjuden nach dem Talmud," *Archiv für Judenfragen: Schriften zur geistigen Überwindung des Judentums*, ed. Friedrich Löffler, Gruppe A 1/Heft 1 (Berlin: Mier and Glasemann, 1943), 7–17.

66. Theissen, *Neutestamentliche Wissenschaft vor und nach 1945*, 17. This was also his own description of himself (101).

67. Gert Jeremias, "Karl-Georg Kuhn (1906–1976)," in *Neutestamentliche Wissenschaft nach 1945: Hauptvertreter der deutschsprachigen Exegese in der Darstellung ihrer Schüler*, ed. Cilliers Breytenbach and Rudolf Hoppe (Göttingen, Germany: Neukirchener Verlag, 2008), 297–312 (at 299).

Question, who inspired Kuhn to take on the translation and commentary of the Midrash Sifre to Numbers[68] and who is regarded as his mentor.[69] Work on rabbinics was typical of several Tübingen scholars; Kittel himself had long been involved in editing rabbinic texts. In 1932, he became the editor of the still highly regarded monograph series Rabbinische Texte, which provided German translations and commentaries on classical rabbinic literature. In 1928, at the age of twenty-two, Kuhn began working on the translation, and in 1931 he completed his doctorate in Oriental studies under Enno Littmann (1875–1958).

It was Kittel who brought Kuhn, as young as he was, into the world of scholarship, assigning him to work on the Judaism-related parts of many articles in the *Theological Dictionary of the New Testament*.[70] Although he never formally held the position, Kuhn was regarded as Kittel's assistant, a sign of their closeness, and he taught rabbinic literature together with his mentor. Kuhn became a member of the National Socialist Party in September 1932 and of the Sturmabteilung [Storm Troopers (SA)] in April 1933, steps he later defended as a reaction to his fiancée having left him and her having become a Communist.[71] Immediately, Kuhn made a career in the National Socialist Party, becoming a spokesman and cultural officer of the Tübingen National Socialist Party and the leader of ideological training.[72] He is even reported to have taught in an academic setting in his SA uniform, including the honorary dagger.[73] For a time, his Communist former fiancée and his Jewish contacts caused him some problems with the National Socialist Party, but in defending himself, he took a clear stand for National Socialism. Gerhard Kittel aided him by assuring party officials that Kuhn espoused a spotless National Socialist ideology.[74] This also indicates that Kittel shared the same political stance and indeed enjoyed some authority in the party. Kuhn was no secondary figure in Tübingen National Socialism. On the day of the Jewish boycott,

---

68. Theissen, *Neutestamentliche Wissenschaft vor und nach 1945*, 17.
69. Junginger, Verwissenschaftlichung der "Judenfrage" im Nationalsozialismus, 182.
70. Ibid.
71. Theissen, *Neutestamentliche Wissenschaft vor und nach 1945*, 18–19n8; Junginger, *Verwissenschaftlichung der "Judenfrage" im Nationalsozialismus*, 47.
72. Junginger, "Bild der Juden in der nationalsozialistischen Judenforschung," 179–80.
73. M. A. Beek, review of *Achtzehngebet und Vater unser und der Reim*, by Karl Georg Kuhn, *Vox Theologica* 21, no. 1 (1950): 21–22; Junginger, "Bild der Juden in der nationalsozialistischen Judenforschung," 180.
74. Junginger, "Bild der Juden in der nationalsozialistischen Judenforschung," 180.

April 1, 1933, he was the one to give the official speech from the pulpit of the city hall in Tübingen urging citizens to boycott Jewish shops.[75]

After his habilitation in Tübingen in 1934, Kuhn held no regular position, but in 1936, he was appointed as a part-time teacher in the language, literature, and history of the Jews, especially the Jewish Problem, in Tübingen.[76] At the same time, he received an appointment in the Department for Research into the Jewish Question (referred to in the rest of the chapter as the Department). Kuhn had already been working there for six months when it was officially inaugurated in Munich in November 1936, and he became a leading Talmud specialist in the Nazi academic establishment.[77] Tübingen played an important role for the Department, as Kuhn, his teacher Kittel, and his Tübingen assistant Günter Schlichting devoted their main scholarly activity to the Jewish Problem. Schlichting, who had belonged to the National Socialist Party since 1930, was recruited to the Department as a result of his extraordinary skills in Hebrew, Aramaic, and Yiddish, and he was tasked with building a major library for the Department in a short time.[78] The library was meant to be a weapon for the German people in the struggle against the Jews. In gathering valuable books for the library, Kuhn also visited the Warsaw Ghetto in June 1940 with the explicit purpose of stealing—or, using the Nazi euphemism, *Sicherstellung* [securing]—books, Talmudic manuscripts, and libraries from the rich Jewish heritage of Poland.[79] Neither Schlichting nor Kuhn seems to have been inhibited by any moral doubts when stealing books from Jewish synagogues and libraries.

---

75. Ibid.
76. Junginger, "'Judenforschung' in Tübingen," 380.
77. Junginger, "Bild der Juden in der nationalsozialistischen Judenforschung," 181.
78. Ibid. See further Heiber, *Walter Frank und sein Reichsinstitut für Geschichte des neuen Deutschland*, 436, 440–41. According to Heiber, Schlichting was a passionate National Socialist but was also "Mann der Bekenntnisfront" (a man of the confessing front, presumably meaning a member of the Confessing Church)." In Amsterdam he had obtained, probably dishonestly, an old copy of the medieval Jewish libel, *Toledot Jeschu*, which he later edited and published.
79. Junginger, "Bild der Juden in der nationalsozialistischen Judenforschung," 186. Adam Czerniakow, *The Warsaw Diary of Adam Czerniakow: Prelude to Doom*, ed. Raul Hilberg, Stanislaw Staron, and Josef Kermisz, trans. Stanislaw Staron and the staff of Yad Vashem (New York: Stein and Day, 1979), 158, mentions Dr. Kuhn, the university lecturer from Tübingen, in the entry for June 6–7, 1940: "The Museum was unlocked—the collection and showcases are gone." From this, it seems clear that Kuhn was involved in extensive pillaging of books and manuscripts from the Warsaw Ghetto.

Kittel, Kuhn, and the Tübingen philosopher Max Wundt were also instrumental to the propaganda work of the Department, giving popular public lectures on the Jewish Problem that attracted sizable audiences.[80] The University of Tübingen and its theologians thereby became known as significant fighters in what was called the scholarly fight against Judaism.[81] In 1942, Kuhn was appointed extracurricular professor; however, by this time, Germany was already practically devoid of Jews, and the Final Solution had gone so far that the original project to strengthen scholarship on Judaism had grown less important. Nevertheless, Kuhn was already regarded as a Talmud expert in the National Socialist research apparatus.

After the war, the denazification court looked forgivingly on Kuhn's work in the Department, accepting his explanation that he only intended to avert antisemitism.[82] The court benevolently agreed that his work was purely scholarly: it did not find any antisemitic tendencies in his publications, nor did it see any antisemitism in his Berlin speech about the talmudic way of thinking. Kuhn claimed that the speech, urging support for the 1933 economic boycott against the Jews of Germany was a noble attempt to avert something worse.[83] The court improbably ruled that Kuhn should be regarded as having been an enemy of the Third Reich![84] In light of what he actually had said in those speeches, Kuhn's excuses ring false indeed. Originally in 1933, when he defended himself against the charge of having held pro-Jewish tendencies, he affirmed: "My conviction on this point has fundamentally changed, as was proven by my entrance into the Nazi Party and, even more clearly, by the speech I gave this spring on Boycott Day at the marketplace rally of the Tübingen NSDAP [National Socialist Party]."[85] Kuhn accordingly won the approval of the party, with Kittel's

---

80. Junginger, "Bild der Juden in der nationalsozialistischen Judenforschung," 184–85.
81. Ibid., 185.
82. Ibid., 213.
83. Theissen, *Neutestamentliche Wissenschaft vor und nach 1945*, 20n11. How people after the war explained their involvement in National Socialist politics and activities connected with it is a research area in its own right. See the chapter by Robert P. Ericksen in this volume, "The Nazification and Denazification of the University of Göttingen."
84. Junginger, "Antisemitismus in Theorie und Praxis," 544–45.
85. "So hat sich meine Überzeugung in diesem Punkte eben gründlich geändert, wie schon mein Eintritt in die NSDAP in März 1932 beweist, und noch deutlicher meine Rede, die ich bei der Kundgebung der NSDAP Tübingen anlässlich des Boykott-Tages in diesem Frühjahr auf dem Marktplatz hielt" (Karl-Georg Kuhn, Der Kreis-U.Schl.A. Tübingen attention Max Stockburger, October 16, 1933, file 126a/284, Universitätsarchiv Tübingen, Germany). The file pertains to the National Socialist tribunal Untersuchung und Schlichtungs-Ausschuss.

supporting statement that Kuhn shared his views on the Jewish Problem as described in *Die Judenfrage*.[86]

Kuhn did master the scholarly craft, but it is evident that his scholarship from this time was motivated by an anti-Jewish and antisemitic agenda. One example is his inauguration lecture as senior lecturer [*Privatdozent*] in the Faculty of Philosophy at Tübingen on December 19, 1934. The first part of the lecture was later published in the journal *Deutsche Theologie*.[87] Kuhn assumed that there was a Jewish Problem, and it is clear that the context was the political issue of how to deal with it. Kuhn argued that the "eternal Jew," earlier in the text named Ahasveros, was by necessity doomed to be a foreigner. But wherever Jews dwell, he argued, they try to gain power and become a threat to the "host peoples."[88] In a cool and scholarly manner, Kuhn had begun the lecture by drawing a history of the Jews, but soon it became clear that there was a political agenda behind his scholarly argument. As the title of the article indicates, Kuhn contends that the spread of Judaism is rooted in the inner conditions and structure of Judaism.[89] Kuhn advanced two main ideological positions. He contended, first, that the Jewish people had no original connection to the land of Israel,[90] and, second, that the essence of Judaism was to be a foreign entity.[91] He made several claims to distance Judaism from Israel. The cradle of Judaism was Babylon, not ancient Israel. The Babylonian exile meant the end of the history of Israel and the beginning of the history of Judaism. This also meant Israel's transformation from a national religion of a people, Israel, into a universal world religion.[92] The Jerusalem temple lost its vital role, argued Kuhn, and the Jews no longer needed a homeland.[93]

Kuhn grossly oversimplified Jewish history, trying to create a breach between old Israel and Judaism that would allow him to identify with old Israel and still see Judaism as something new and different. In his overall argument this became important: Jews are not connected with the old homeland of Israel but are forever foreigners. Since the Jews now centered their faith on the Torah

---

86. Gerhard Kittel to Max Stockburger, October 10, 1933, file 126a/284, Universitätsarchiv Tübingen, Germany.
87. Karl Georg Kuhn, "Die inneren Voraussetzungen der jüdischen Ausbreitung," *Deutsche Theologie* 2 (1935): 9–17 (at 17).
88. Ibid., 17 (Ahasveros is mentioned on p. 16).
89. Ibid., 10.
90. Ibid., 10.
91. Ibid., 17.
92. Ibid., 10.
93. Ibid., 11, 15.

and not the temple or the land of Israel, they were a people without any geographical center. Instead, the crucial condition for the Jews was their religion; it is of no importance to Jews where they are on earth, Kuhn argued.[94] Although the homeland was originally important to Israel, this ended with the exile.[95]

Kuhn here ignored the fact that there was a return to and rebuilding of the temple and city of Jerusalem after the exile and that the land was and had been regarded as the self-evident homeland of the Jews. To take only one postexilic example, Philo of Alexandria (20 BCE–50 CE) called Jerusalem his *mētropolis*, his mother city.[96] Kuhn went a long way to try to prove his point,[97] but he had to suppress evidence of the continuing prominent role of the land of Israel and Jerusalem for the Jewish people. Kuhn had a clear agenda to show that the Jew was and would always be Ahasveros, the "Wandering Jew." In the last line of the article, Kuhn's nationalist agenda became evident: "There is only one possible way to handle the Jewish Problem, namely . . . energetically, again and again, direct [the Jews] back into their place."[98] Before this, Kuhn had discussed different solutions to the Jewish Problem, one being the expulsion of all Jews to another country, not necessarily Palestine. However, here Kuhn argued that Jews of necessity were bound to live as foreigners among other people until an eschatological time.[99] One probable interpretation of Kuhn's proposal to send the Jews back to their place is that he intended to return them to some kind of ghetto, an idea that accords with that of Kuhn's teacher Gerhard Kittel.[100] In any case, it is clear that Kuhn's speech had an antisemitic agenda and played into the hands of the political authorities. That this was the core of the speech for the audience is confirmed by the newspaper *Tübinger Chronik*, which used Kuhn's political suggestions to summarize the speech.[101]

In his subsequent productions in the notorious Nazi journal, *Forschungen zur Judenfrage* [Research into the Jewish Question], Kuhn became more and more clearly antisemitic. For example, his pamphlet *Die Judenfrage als*

---

94. Ibid., 14–15.
95. Ibid., 15.
96. Philo, *On the Embassy to Gaius*, 36:281. Aryeh Kasher, "Diaspora I/2," in *Theologische Realenzyklopädie* (Berlin: Walter de Gruyter, 1981), 8:711–17 (at 716).
97. Kuhn, "Inneren Voraussetzungen der jüdischen Ausbreitung," 16–17.
98. Ibid., 17.
99. Ibid., 16.
100. See Kittel, *Judenfrage*, 40–69, where he envisions the ghettoization of German Jewry.
101. Karl-Georg Kuhn, "Die Ausbreitung des Judentums in der antiken Welt" (lecture reported in *Tübinger Chronik*, December 17, 1934). The first part was later republished as Kuhn, "Die inneren Voraussetzungen der jüdischen Ausbreitung," 9–17.

weltgeschichtliches Problem [The Jewish Question as world historical problem, 1939] is thoroughly antisemitic. To Kuhn, the Jewish Problem rested in Judaism itself and was independent of the culture the Jews were living in.[102] Kuhn attempted what must be regarded as a quasi-sociological discussion, stating that the Jewish Problem was based on the racial composition and biologically hereditary disposition of the Jews.[103] Following the Nuremberg Race Laws of 1935 and the pogrom of November 9, 1938 (Kristallnacht), Kuhn praised Hitler for having created a historical opportunity to solve the Jewish Problem.[104]

Kuhn contributed to the myth of Jewish evil by absurdly alleging that there is a talmudic right for a Jew to kill non-Jews.[105] The work of Kittel and Kuhn in the Propaganda Ministry's Department for Research into the Jewish Question advanced National Socialist policies and gave scholarly support to the antisemitic measures. Kittel's many articles on racial mixing, for example, undergirded the Nuremberg Race Laws, as did Kuhn's caricatures of talmudic thinking. In many ways, Kittel and Kuhn were speaking with the same voice, stressing the danger of the emancipation of the Jews.[106] Kuhn also lectured to elite military trainees at the National Socialist *Ordensburgen* [special schools developed for the upper echelon of the Nazi military].[107] He adjusted his profile to his audience: in church contexts, he was probably perceived differently than he was in the Department or in the National Socialist Party. In a church environment, he would speak positively of the Old Testament, advocate a salvation-historical theology, and present a comparatively modest view of racial antisemitism.[108] This is not to soften or redeem his antisemitism; it is only to show that he was capable of presenting completely different faces in different arenas.

---

102. Karl Georg Kuhn, *Die Judenfrage als weltgeschichtliches Problem*, Schriften des Reichsinstitutes für Geschichte des neuen Deutschlands (Hamburg, Germany: Hanseatische Verlagsanstalt, 1939), 8.

103. Ibid., 29.

104. Ibid., 47. This speech was held during a session in the Department for Research into the Jewish Question, November 30–December 3, 1938.

105. Karl Georg Kuhn, *Ursprung und Wesen des talmudischen Einstellung zum Nichtjuden*, Forschungen zur Judenfrage: Sitzungsberichte der Dritten Arbeitstagung des Reichsinstitutes für Geschichte des neuen Deutschlands 3 (Hamburg, Germany: Hanseatische Verlagsanstalt, 1938), 228–29. See further Theissen, *Neutestamentliche Wissenschaft vor und nach 1945*, 30.

106. Theissen, *Neutestamentliche Wissenschaft vor und nach 1945*, 35–36. For Kittel, see Gerdmar, *Roots of Theological Anti-Semitism*, 511–13.

107. Theissen, *Neutestamentliche Wissenschaft vor und nach 1945*, 33.

108. Ibid., 39. Kuhn could fall back on his background, since these views were the general tendency of the movement in which he was raised.

Kuhn went through the denazification process without any difficulties, a fact that is deeply disturbing given his clear antisemitic and National Socialist history. Thus he could teach in Göttingen beginning in 1949, though not without opposition due to his past.[109] He was rejected as Chair in New Testament studies at Mainz in 1952, but in 1954, he was appointed professor at Heidelberg. His luck depended on the recently found Qumran texts, for the study of which his philological skills were perfect. Kuhn became famous as a pioneer in Qumran research and mentor of many New Testament scholars. However, he refused to withdraw his works from the Department.[110] When he was elected to the Heidelberger Akademie der Wissenschaften [Heidelberg Academy of Sciences], his problematic articles from the past were not even mentioned.[111] Though the terminology is problematic, Gerd Theissen notes that Kuhn "was a philosemite before he converted to an antisemite."[112] During the case against him in the National Socialist Party in 1933, Kuhn confessed that he "may once have" uttered something pro-Jewish but that he had fundamentally changed, as demonstrated by his early membership in the National Socialist Party.[113] In this case where he was being criticized by National Socialist Party members, Kuhn naturally wished to deny his pro-Jewish past, although there is little doubt that in Breslau (present-day Wrocław) he would have had positive contacts with Jews and Judaism. The parallel to Kittel is evident, Kittel having dedicated his *Probleme des palästinischen Spätjudentums und das Urchristentum* [The problems of Palestinian late Judaism and early Christianity] to Israel Kahan.[114] However, just as Kittel could espouse strongly anti-Jewish attitudes at the same time that he was a friend of some Jewish individuals, a specialist in Judaism, and even a pioneer in creating a more historically reliable picture of Judaism than most of his contemporary exegetes, Kuhn may have gone through a similar process.[115]

---

109. Ibid., 48–49.

110. Ibid., 52–54.

111. For the background and also the professors signing the recommendation for Kuhn (among them G. Bornkamm and G. von Rad), see Theissen, *Neutestamentliche Wissenschaft vor und nach 1945*, 58–64. For von Rad, see also Levinson, "Gerhard von Rad's Struggle" (in this volume).

112. Theissen, *Neutestamentliche Wissenschaft vor und nach 1945*, 58–64, 10. As to the terminology, see Gerdmar, *Roots of Theological Anti-Semitism*, 5–8, 594.

113. Karl Georg Kuhn to the Untersuchung und Schlichtungs-Ausschuss, to the attention of Max Stockburger, Tübingen, October 10, 1933, file 126a/284, Universitätsarchiv Tübingen, Germany.

114. Kittel, *Probleme des palästinischen Spätjudentums und das Urchristentum*.

115. On the compartmentalized views of Kittel, see Gerdmar, *Roots of Theological Anti-Semitism*, 607–8.

In fact, most of the scholars discussed here share this combination of anti-Jewish views and apparent academic expertise in Judaism.[116] Nevertheless, Kuhn probably already held views similar to those of the National Socialist Party during his studies in Breslau, intimating that he began to relate to National Socialists at that time.[117] The contradiction evident in the lives of these scholars—beginning with an interest in and a certain knowledge of Judaism and ending, or even being combined, with a consistently antisemitic stance—can be observed to different degrees among many of the scholars in the confessional German tradition of Christian scholarship on Judaism: Schlatter, Delitzsch, Strack, Kittel, and Grundmann.[118] Alan Levenson calls Delitzsch and Strack "defenders and detractors."[119] I have elsewhere tried to explain these contradictions with the concept of compartmentalization (see also below).[120] This does not redeem their antisemitism, but it tries to explain the obvious contradictions. In Kittel's case, the history ends with his death, before he could begin a new, postwar career. In Kuhn's case, however, the fact that he could continue almost as if nothing had happened during the National Socialist period is startling.

---

116. Theissen, *Neutestamentliche Wissenschaft vor und nach 1945*, 105–7, may well overstate Kuhn's early positive attitude toward Judaism. Theissen's arguments are ex silentio, and one must appreciate that these scholars knew perfectly well how to adjust their writings to the expected audience. Kittel also knew how to behave in an international forum of scholars, and the *Theological Dictionary of the New Testament* is surprisingly free overall from political or anti-Jewish tendencies. This was not because the authors were not antisemitic—a great number were—but because politicized material would have served the propaganda goals of this publication badly. For analyses of the *Theological Dictionary of the New Testament*, see Maurice Casey, "Antisemitic Assumptions in the Theological Dictionary of the New Testament," *Novum Testamentum* 41, no. 3 (1999): 280–91; J. S. Vos, "Antijudaismus/Antisemitismus im Theologischen Wörterbuch zum Neuen Testament," *Nederlands Theologisch Tijdschrift* 35 (1984): 89–110; and Gerdmar, *Roots of Theological Anti-Semitism*, 474–78. Further on Kittel, see also Levinson, "Gerhard von Rad's Struggle" (in this volume).

117. Kuhn to the Untersuchung und Schlichtungs-Ausschuss, October 10, 1933.

118. For a discussion of each of these scholars and their relationship to Judaism, see the respective chapters in Gerdmar, *Roots of Theological Anti-Semitism*.

119. See Alan Levenson, "Missionary Protestants as Defenders and Detractors of Judaism: Franz Delitzsch and Hermann Strack," *Jewish Quarterly Review* 92, no. 3–4 (2002): 383–420: "How can we come to terms with the apparent contradiction that the most determined defenders of Judaism publicly and its most sympathetic interpreters theologically were the same people who actively strove for the Jews' disappearance?" (387).

120. Gerdmar, *Roots of Theological Anti-Semitism*, 606–9.

Paul Althaus: Political Theology for the "New Germany"

The Tübingen environment also impacted the political theology of the Third Reich through the work of the influential German scholar Paul Althaus (1888–1966), systematic theologian, New Testament scholar, and Luther specialist. Althaus began his studies at Tübingen in 1906 and afterward spent three semesters in Göttingen. His link to Tübingen came through the Luther specialist Karl Holl, but for the areas of theology for which he has become infamous—creation and the theology of orders—Althaus's personal and theological relationship with his teacher Adolf Schlatter was decisive.[121] Schlatter's hermeneutics, a kind of commonsense theological empiricism pivoting around the notion of *Sehakt* [act of seeing], and his position of *Vermittlung* [mediation] became decisive for Althaus.[122] Equally important were Schlatter's theological reflections on creation, nature, and revelation and his efforts to find a link between natural theology and a "Christological-narrowing doctrine of revelation."[123] Walter Wimmer calls Schlatter "one of the most important ancestors of Althaus's *Uroffenbarungslehre*" [doctrine of original revelation].[124] Schlatter's theology of the orders probably provided a background to Althaus's own fully developed theology of the Ordnungen.[125] Althaus developed such ideas in order to legitimate the National Socialist state (see below).

Althaus's father, also named Paul Althaus, a Lutheran minister and later a Professor of Systematic Theology, raised his son in "the spirit of a living Lutheran minister's home."[126] Althaus's early years were characterized by the "positive Lutheran" Erlangen theology, with a conservative and warm religiosity. Althaus was deeply influenced by the so-called Luther Renaissance

---

121. Walter Wimmer, Eschatologie der Rechtfertigung: Paul Althaus' Vermittlungsversuch zwischen uneschatologischer und nureschatologischer Theologie, Minerva-Fachserie Theologie (Munich: Minerva-Publikation, 1979), 16. Althaus called Schlatter his teacher and was also entrusted by Schlatter with the editorship of Schlatter's Beiträge zur Förderung christlicher Theologie; see Paul Althaus, "Zum Gedächtnis der abgerufenen Herausgeber der 'Beiträge,'" in Adolf Schlatter und Wilhelm Lütgert zum Gedächtnis, ed. Paul Althaus, Beiträge zur Förderung christlicher Theologie 40 (Gütersloh, Germany: C. Bertelsmann, 1938), 9–15 (at 15).
122. Eckhart Lessing, "Paul Althaus," in *Geschichte der deutschsprachigen evangelischen Theologie von Albrecht Ritschl bis zur Gegenwart*, 3 vols. (Göttingen, Germany: Vandenhoeck & Ruprecht, 2000–2009), 1:80–86.
123. Wimmer, *Eschatologie*, 16.
124. Ibid.
125. For Schlatter's view, see Gerdmar, *Roots of Theological Anti-Semitism*, 287, 296–99.
126. Wimmer, *Eschatologie*, 9.

but also by the combination of Lutheran and subjectivistic theology that was specific to Erlangen, which he later modified.[127] Politics also mattered to Althaus, who was engaged early on in a conservative political cultural criticism rooted in both the church and the idea of the German people.[128] During the 1920s, he was involved in a variety of conservative and antidemocratic movements and initiatives.[129]

As 1933 dawned, Althaus welcomed the country's new political direction, supporting the Aryanization of the church and openly supporting Hitler. In his book, *Die deutsche Stunde der Kirche* ["The German Hour of the Church," 1934], he wrote that "the Protestant churches had greeted the German turn in 1933 as a gift and miracle from God."[130] In this book, Althaus theologized the German National Socialist turn, including the theology of the Deutsche Christen and the SA man, as in line with classical Protestant theology of nature as God's *Uroffenbarung* [original revelation]. The Nazi political order was rooted in God's creation, he claimed, and in the voice of the Führer the people were hearing "more than a human voice."[131] Althaus also used the concept of salvation history to interpret the "German hour of the church" and encouraged a "political preaching" that addressed the questions of the present time, for example, how parliamentarianism led the German people to disaster.[132] Althaus upgraded the current historical development in Germany to something where "God is": "God is in the history of the people and God is acting with the individual through the salvation history in its suprahistorical presentness.... God is also working a history with the nations."[133] Though he maintained the specific role of biblical salvation history, Althaus used the concept of salvation history to make German politics part of God's actions, a stance that would have a direct bearing on concrete decisions.

---

127. Ibid., 21.
128. Roland Liebenberg, *Der Gott der feldgrauen Männer: Die theozentrische Erfahrungstheologie von Paul Althaus d. J. im Ersten Weltkrieg*, Arbeiten zur Kirchen- und Theologiegeschichte 22 (Leipzig, Germany: Evangelische Verlagsanstalt, 2008), 12n7. Liebenberg's work is a rich source for Althaus's background.
129. Ibid., 12.
130. Paul Althaus, *Die deutsche Stunde der Kirche*, 3rd ed. (Göttingen, Germany: Vandenhoeck & Ruprecht, 1934), 5. For the term's translation and discussion, see Ericksen, *Theologians under Hitler*, 86.
131. Ibid., 8–12 (quote at 12).
132. Ibid., 17–19.
133. "Gott ist in der Volksgeschichte und Gott handelt mit dem Einzelnen durch die Heilsgeschichte in ihrer übergeschichtlichen Gegenwärtigkeit.... Gott [waltet] auch mit den Völkern eine Geschichte" (Althaus, *Deutsche Stunde der Kirche*, 23).

These basic nationalistic thoughts seem to have been deeply rooted in Althaus's thinking and were no result of a sudden conversion in January 1933. Furthermore, Althaus had revealed his stance on Judaism and German Jewry as early as 1930, talking about Judaism as a *"völkisch* problem": "To listen to the theological question [raised by Judaism] does not mean to deny the völkisch one, to treat the *völkisch* problem, which is facing us through the fact that Jewish people are living among us, in a humanitarian-liberal way. And yet is it for the moment even more important to emphasize the opposite: it would be bad for German Christianity, due to mere numbness [*Benommenheit*] because of the *völkisch* question, to miss the theological one! Both should be heard and dealt with."[134]

It is evident even at this early point that Althaus saw Judaism as a problem—he believed the Jews were a separate people living among the German people—and that he resisted humanitarian-liberal policies. This harsh stance is rooted in a solid and long-standing exaltation of the German people both as an ethnic unity and as something blessed by God.[135] His view that the gospel of Jesus was the point of confrontation with Judaism was shared with Kittel and Schlatter, among others. The same is true for his discussion of *das innere Schicksal des Judentums*: "Therefore we also know the inner destiny of Judaism is even today being decided by the words of judgment and promise by Jesus over Israel: 'You will not see me until you say: Blessed is the one who comes in the name of the Lord' (Matt 23:39)."[136] Althaus interprets the words of Jesus as a prediction of the fall of the temple and the diaspora of the Jews.

In *Die Deutsche Stunde*, Althaus also welcomed the new National Socialist rule, with its harsher punishments, steps against corruption, defense against the "powers of disintegration in literature and theater," and desire to raise the people to a socialism of action [*Sozialismus der Tat*]. But he worried that the churches would not support the change, noting that the church also had to preach the law—the orders, Althaus's special area.[137]

---

134. Paul Althaus, "Die Frage des Evangeliums an das moderne Judentum," *Zeitschrift für systematische Theologie* 7, no. 2 (1930): 195–215 (at 196).

135. See Althaus's articles from 1916 and 1932, reprinted in Althaus, *Deutsche Stunde der Kirche*, 34–49, 55–60.

136. Paul Althaus, "Die Frage des Evangeliums an das moderne Judentum," *Zeitschrift für systematische Theologie* 7 (1929): 195–215.

137. Paul Althaus and Werner Elert, "Theologische Gutachten über die Zulassung von Christen jüdischer Herkunft zu den Ämtern der deutschen evangelischen Kirche," *Theologische Blätter* 12, no. 11 (1933): 321–24; Tanja Hetzer, *"Deutsche Stunde": Volksgemeinschaft und Antisemitismus in der politischen Theologie bei Althaus*, Beiträge zur Geschichtswissenschaft (Munich: Allitera, 2009), 159–60.

Two aspects of Althaus's theological political work were instrumental in legitimizing antisemitic National Socialist policies: his theology of the orders of creation and his public defense of the Aryan legislation.[138] In *Theologie der Ordnungen* (1933), Althaus's use of the language of the systematic theologian may seem obscure, but in the political context of the time, the message was clear: the present political order, the National Socialist state, is part of God's created order,[139] and our boundedness to the people [*Volksgebundenheit*] includes a conscience that wishes to sacrifice itself for the people. Here we must observe the special nationalist tone in the German word *Volk*.[140] For Althaus, the ethical binding of the Volk to the state was biblical, and he stressed that the theology of the Ordnungen had a role to play in the new Germany. The voice of "positive Christianity" must not stop, and ethical reflection must deal with such questions as race or eugenics.[141] However, according to his doctrine of the two kingdoms, Althaus saw these questions as the task not of theologians per se. In the area of eugenics, he argued, we must listen to doctors who are Christians.[142] Althaus's argument became useful in the political context of his theology of the Ordnungen, giving divine sanction to the National Socialist state and to its political measures as part of God's creation. Althaus's theology of the orders and of creation legitimated völkisch ideology and antisemitism and thereby contributed to paving the way for the Holocaust.

The same position appeared in the *Ansbacher Ratschlag* [Ansbach memorandum, June 1934], which Althaus signed, in which the law is said to "bind us to the degree [*Stand*, in the sense of social rank] to which we are called by God. It thus obliges us to the natural orders, to which we are submitted, as family, Volk, race [i.e., blood relationship, *Blutzusammenhang*]."[143] Again the Führer was greeted as a gift from God. Thus, Althaus used his considerable authority to legitimate the new social order of National Socialist Germany, including racial politics, eugenics, and political antisemitism.

---

138. Robert P. Ericksen, *Theologians under Hitler: Gerhard Kittel, Paul Althaus, and Emanuel Hirsch* (New Haven, CT: Yale University Press, 1985), 100–105. With Ericksen, I choose to use the German term, which has connotations other than mere *order*.
139. Paul Althaus, *Theologie der Ordnungen*, 2nd ed. (Gütersloh, Germany: Bertelsmann, 1935), 15–16.
140. Ibid., 17.
141. Ibid., 44.
142. Ibid., 44–46.
143. Quoted in Hetzer, *Deutsche Stunde*, 258. On the Ansbach Memorandum as an attempt by theologians sympathetic to Nationalist Socialist ideology to refute the Barmen Declaration, see Ericksen, *Theologians under Hitler*, 87–90.

The second aspect, Althaus's overtly antisemitic statements as part of the expert opinion that he and Werner Elert gave regarding the Aryan legislation on September 25, 1933, was strategic for the German discussion of the right of baptized Jewish Christian ministers to keep their ministries.[144] The two theologians stated that race was part of the God-given order, that the boundedness of the church to the *Volkstum* [national identity] made it important to appreciate ethnicity as a factor, and that the Jews could not be regarded as part of the German people.[145] Moreover, this being a biological-historical matter, they argued that the relationship between German-ness and Jewishness must be dealt with by the state and not by the church alone. They argued that keeping Jewish ministers in the German church would seriously hinder the mission of the church to the German people and should be an exception rather than the rule.[146]

Here Althaus's theology of the Ordnungen received a practical application, giving race and German antisemitic policy divine sanction. In his *Obrigkeit und Führertum* [Authority and führerism, 1936], Althaus discussed transformations in the conception of state leadership from the perspective of German Protestant theology.[147] Althaus saw a need to renew the understanding of the state and its authorities on an apostolic-Lutheran foundation in view of what he regarded as the dissolution of true statehood during the Weimar regime.[148] This caused him to reflect on revolution as a political weapon, seeing the 1919 revolution as an egotistic one but the 1933 revolution as righteous.[149] Such a revolution had as its goal an unselfish service to the nation and the people, and Althaus sought to confront a pacifist position, seeing the righteous revolution as a way to overthrow an illegitimate, "foreign" rule [*Fremdherrschaft*].[150] It is evident that in Althaus's world, this foreign rule was the Weimar Republic. The discussion shows Althaus's deep contempt for the Weimar period. The National Socialist kind of rhetoric was absent, probably because the paper was written

---

144. This caused considerable debate among German theologians and was addressed, for example, by Rudolf Bultmann; see Gerdmar, *Roots of Theological Anti-Semitism*, 396–98.

145. This dichotomy between German and Jewish is already evident in the early work of Johannes Wolfgang von Goethe. See Bernard M. Levinson, "Goethe's Analysis of Exodus 34 and Its Influence on Julius Wellhausen: The *Pfropfung* of the Documentary Hypothesis," *Zeitschrift für die alttestamentliche Wissenschaft* 114, no. 2 (2002): 212–23.

146. Quoted in Hetzer, *Deutsche Stunde*, 251–56.

147. Paul Althaus, *Obrigkeit und Führertum: Wandlungen des evangelischen Staatsethos* (Gütersloh, Germany: C. Bertelsmann, 1936).

148. Ibid., 5.

149. Ibid., 56.

150. Ibid., 58.

with a view to the 1937 World Conference for Practical Theology in Oxford.[151] However, it is evident that Althaus sought to justify the 1933 German revolution to an international audience.

Although Althaus maintained the scholarly tone of a professional systematic theologian, the positions he argued varied considerably. His theology migrated through strong nationalism, centered on the heroic ideals of the soldier and sacrifice in World War I,[152] offering vehement criticism of the democratic Weimar state, and finally being a tool in the hands of the National Socialist regime, for whose policies he provided the strongest possible support: divine legitimation. The connections to his network in Tübingen and to his teachers Karl Holl and Adolf Schlatter (with whom he had a key relationship for more than thirty years) were crucial to Althaus's development and nationalist ideology.

Walter Grundmann: The Enfant Terrible of German Protestantism

Walter Grundmann is most well-known as the German theologian who went farthest in nazifying Christian theology. No significant scholarly achievements made him famous, but he was the dominant theologian and entrepreneur behind the Institut zur Erforschung und Beseitigung des jüdischen Einflüsses auf das deutsche kirchliche Leben [Institute for the Investigation and Eradication of Jewish Influence on German Church Life, referred to below as the Institute]. Grundmann had a meteoric career in the National Socialist Party, belonging to the "old fighters" who were members of the party even before 1933, after which membership became more common. He had joined on December 1, 1930, and could therefore be entrusted with positions of leadership.[153] In 1932, he was made leader of the National Socialist Pastors' League [Pfarrerbund], and he was among the founders of the German Christian Church Movement in Saxony in 1933, the same year that he was appointed to the Oberkirchenrat [governing council] of the state church. Grundmann became a national figure through his authorship of Die 28 Thesen der sächsischen Volkskirche erläutert [The twenty-eight theses of the Saxon people's church explained], which became a form of confession first for the German Christians in Saxony and later for several other state churches.[154] When the

---

151. Ibid., 59.
152. See Liebenberg, Gott der feldgrauen Männer.
153. Grundmann was member number 382544 (archive card, BA NSDAP Gaukartei, Bundesarchiv Koblenz, Germany).
154. The text of the confession is in Kurt Dietrich Schmidt, Die Bekenntnisse und grundsätzlichen Äusserungen zur Kirchenfrage des Jahres 1933, vol. 1 (Göttingen, Germany: Vandenhoeck & Ruprecht, 1934).

national movement accepted the theses, Grundmann became a leading ideologue in the movement. On November 1, 1936, Grundmann, having just turned thirty, became acting Professor of New Testament and völkisch theology at the University of Jena, and two years later, he was promoted by the rector of the university, Wolf Meyer-Erlach, to regular full Professor with tenure.[155] As a key figure in the Institute for the Investigation and Eradication of Jewish Influence on German Church Life, founded in 1937, Grundmann was intensely active, together with a large group of noted theologians and churchmen, in developing a dejudaized Christianity. This was part of a larger strategy of the German Christians, who on July 14, 1937, issued a new platform, signed by the leader of the Saxony Deutsche Christen, Siegfried Leffler:

> The national German Christian Church Movement stands for the overcoming and eradication of all Jewish and foreign völkisch spirit in church teaching and ways of life; it confesses German Christianity to be the racially appropriate religion of the German Volk. Christ is not the scion and fulfiller of Judaism but rather its deadly enemy and conqueror.[156]

Walter Grundmann and the Institute became leading forces in implementing this platform, and Grundmann crowned this career by writing the book *Jesus der Galiläer und das Judentum* (1940),[157] depicting Jesus as a non-Jewish Galilean. Here he lived up to the title of his Jena professorship—professor of völkisch theology and New Testament—though he compromised the latter in order to prioritize the former. Grundmann and the Institute indeed tried systematically to eradicate Judaism from German church life by, for example, making a dejudaized Bible, hymnal, and catechism.[158] He also forged a syncretistic synthesis between Christianity and völkisch theology, regarding a eugenically pure nation as a sign of the kingdom of God.[159]

Grundmann's legacy is not as a great scholar but rather as one of the most politicized exegetes of the twentieth century. His fame during the Third Reich had to do with becoming one of the first theologians of the German

---

155. Briefly reviewing Grundmann's career at Jena, see Levinson, "Gerhard von Rad's Struggle" (in this volume).

156. Quoted from Heschel, *Aryan Jesus*, 71. Heschel summarizes much of the research to date and provides biographical details.

157. Walter Grundmann, *Jesus der Galiläer und das Judentum*, Veröffentlichungen des Instituts zur Erforschung des jüdischen Einflusses auf das deutsche kirchliche Leben (Leipzig, Germany: Georg Wigand, 1940).

158. See Heschel, *Aryan Jesus*, 106–65.

159. See Gerdmar, *Roots of Theological Anti-Semitism*, 552–53.

Christian Church Movement, and his work at the Institute has received even more attention.[160] But his time and relationships in Tübingen, which he regarded as "decisive for [his] thinking and his life," have not been the subject of scholarly attention.[161] Indeed, because he was an enfant terrible, the normal procedure was to try to dissociate oneself or others from him. The fact that Grundmann and Kittel took different paths in relation to the German Christians is another sign that Grundmann was disconnected from Tübingen; Gerhard Kittel left the German Christians after the so-called Sports Palace scandal on November 13, 1933, but Grundmann stayed and became a leading figure.[162] In his later defense, Kittel used this departure as a sign that he had kept a distance from National Socialist theology.[163] As will be demonstrated here, however, Kittel and Grundmann did keep in touch, despite their differing views on some things. Moreover, Grundmann held Schlatter in high regard his whole life. Thus, Werner Neuer may be right that there is no extant correspondence between Schlatter and Grundmann—although papers may have been weeded through before being presented to an archive, so this in only an argument from silence—but Grundmann certainly confessed to his dependence on his Tübingen mentor.[164]

Grundmann took his first steps on the theological path at Tübingen. Born in 1906, like Kuhn, Grundmann's career had a fast ascent. He was twenty-five years old when he defended his thesis in July 1931. Kittel was his Doktorvater and suggested the topic for his dissertation. Between 1930 and 1932, Grundmann was academic assistant to Kittel and worked with him on the first edition of the *Theological Dictionary of the New Testament*. His move to Tübingen was probably in line with his upbringing and with the theological tendencies he had developed. Grundmann confessed that he had a Pietist background, inspired

---

160. Grundmann is hardly noted for any special scholarly achievement, being fairly mediocre as a scholar.

161. Heschel, *Aryan Jesus*, 179, quoting his curriculum vitae, April 25, 1931 (file 162/92, Universitätsarchiv Tübingen, Germany). For Grundmann in general, see Heschel, *Aryan Jesus*, which summarizes her extensive research on Grundmann; Peter von der Osten-Sacken, ed., *Das mißbrauchte Evangelium: Studien zu Theologie und Praxis der Thüringer Deutschen Christen*, Studien zu Kirche und Israel 20 (Berlin: Institut Kirche und Judentum, 2002); Roland Deines, Volker Leppin, and Karl-Wilhelm Niebuhr, eds., *Walter Grundmann: Ein Neutestamentler im Dritten Reich*, Arbeiten zur Kirchen- und Theologiegeschichte (Leipzig, Germany: Evangelische Verlagsanstalt, 2007); and Gerdmar, *Roots of Theological Anti-Semitism*, 531–76.

162. Gerdmar, *Roots of Theological Anti-Semitism*, 547.
163. Kittel, "Meine Verteidigung," 16.
164. See below in this chapter.

by his father; his youthful involvement in the YMCA and Bible studies also shaped his beliefs. The predominant source for this spiritual background is his own autobiographical essay, "Erkenntnis und Wahrheit," written in 1969, during his time in East Germany.[165] There is no reason to doubt this description of his past since he had nothing to gain by it. To the contrary, as a member of the East German church establishment, he wrote with an eye to the new authorities and, probably, to the Stasi as well.[166] Nevertheless, he did confess to his Pietist beginnings even though he also later said that he, like his father, had "overcome" his Pietism.[167]

Grundmann's academic life began in Leipzig under Johannes Leipoldt, and in 1927, he came to Tübingen. Grundmann described Kittel as "my Tübingen teacher and Doktorvater"[168] and spoke of his teacher in friendly terms. It seems that Grundmann and his wife had a warm relationship with Kittel, socializing with the Kittel family in their home and their summer house.[169] Later correspondence from Grundmann shows that they had an ongoing relationship. Kittel sent his articles to Grundmann—Grundmann received several letters without having time to answer—and Grundmann asked if he could come to visit Kittel with his family during the summer holiday.[170] There would have been little for Grundmann to gain by emphasizing a warm relationship with Kittel, especially as the latter would have been regarded as a reactionary and antisemitic National Socialist in East Germany.

Grundmann described the role of Schlatter in his life in even more positive terms, vividly noting the impression he made on the young Grundmann and acknowledging Schlatter's lasting influence.[171] Thus, although Grundmann

---

165. Walter Grundmann, "Erkenntnis und Wahrheit: Aus meinem Leben," 15, unpublished typescript, Eisenach, 1969, file D 40/689, Landeskirchenarchiv Eisenach, Germany.

166. For Grundmann's history in East Germany, see Susannah Heschel, "Deutsche Theologen für Hitler: Walter Grundmann und das Eisenacher 'Institut zur Erforschung und Beseitigung des jüdischen Einflusses auf das deutsche kirchliche Leben,'" in Deines, Leppin, and Niebuhr, *Walter Grundmann*, 70–90 (at 85–88); and Wolfgang Schenk, "Der Jenaer Jesus: Zu Werk und Wirkung des völkischen Theologen Walter Grundmann und seiner Kollegen," in Osten-Sacken, *Das mißbrauchte Evangelium*, 167–279.

167. Grundmann, "Erkenntnis und Wahrheit," 15.

168. Ibid., 22.

169. Ibid.

170. Walter Grundmann to Gerhard Kittel, July 1, 1938, Bestand DC III 2 f 1938, Landeskirchenarchiv Eisenach, Germany. Grundmann's Jena colleague von Rad, who had worked with Kittel in the past, also planned to join them. For von Rad, see Levinson, "Gerhard von Rad's Struggle" (in this volume).

171. Grundmann, "Erkenntnis und Wahrheit," 19–21.

had in many ways moved to a different flank in German church life than the Tübingen one, he confessed a theological closeness to Schlatter. After Schlatter's death, Grundmann arranged a commemorative lecture at the "brown" University of Jena.[172] Grundmann regarded his Tübingen time as a decisive period in his theological life and Schlatter's theology as fundamental. Kittel's role in this development should not be minimized either. Thus, Grundmann must be regarded, at least for his beginnings, as a child of the Tübingen research environment, even though considerable forces made the young man go his own way in the turbulent years to follow.

III. THE TÜBINGEN NETWORK AS INSTRUMENTAL TO GERMAN THEOLOGICAL ANTISEMITISM

The research tradition in Tübingen and the network described here became instrumental to German theological antisemitism during the National Socialist years. The ideological formula, embryonic though it may have been for Schlatter and the Tübingen network, developed into a key ideological force in the Third Reich. Whether or not this development was intentional, Schlatter, Kittel, and their ideas influenced every member of the group. As is natural in any network, the impact on each individual varied. Some were perhaps closer to Kittel, as was the case for Kuhn, and Kittel himself was close to Schlatter.[173] Schlatter in turn was part of a longer tradition in which Adolf Stoecker played an important role, and Kittel brought his Leipzig background with him. And it is not difficult to see some of the spirit of Stoecker and the tradition of which he was a part among the Tübingen group.[174] As with any tradition, the Tübingen research tradition was fluid, but at the same time it had some thoroughgoing characteristics. These fall under five headings that more or less united the

---

172. Uwe Hoßfeld et al., eds, "Kämpferische Wissenschaft": Studien zur Universität Jena im Nationalsozialismus (Weimar, Germany: Böhlau, 2003).

173. As is stated in Neuer, *Adolf Schlatter*, 786, 792, 798, 801, Kittel constantly supported Schlatter's projects.

174. This is not to say that it is typical of the conservative theologians to be antisemitic or that the Enlightenment-oriented tradition is innocent. For example, Hermann Strack, who was at home in the same tradition as Stoecker, took a bold stand for the Jews and against Stoecker. At the same time, the liberal-front figure Adolf von Harnack received much criticism for his view of Jews and Judaism as expressed in his *Wesen des Christentums*; see Wiese, *Wissenschaft des Judentums und protestantische Theologie im wilhelminischen Deutschland*, 160–69. For an overview of the stance of different frontiers in German exegesis toward Jews and Judaism, see Gerdmar, *Roots of Theological Anti-Semitism*, 577–613.

group: expertise in Jewish studies; an environment marked by conservative theology; a common base in a theology of creation; a shared antimodernism, chauvinism, antisemitism, and allegiance to National Socialism; and a connection to the Tübingen network as an "emotional regime."[175]

Expertise in Jewish Studies

The Judaica profile of New Testament studies at Tübingen attracted several of the scholars discussed here, from the experienced Kittel to the young Kuhn. By the same token, the specialization of the Tübingen network in Judaica was a key factor in the elevation of the Swabian group to its prominent position as experts on Judaism in National Socialist Germany. The absurdity, of course, was that Jews on principle were excluded from research and writing on Judaism. Schlatter's focus on the Jewish background to the New Testament and then on Jews and Judaism stood fully in the tradition of Pietist missions to and research into Judaism, as exemplified by the Instituta Judaica in Leipzig and Berlin. Founded in an effort to win Jews to the Christian faith, the Instituta Judaica also engaged in serious research on Jewish sources and text editions of the Mishnah, Talmuds, and midrash. Kittel was deeply rooted in this tradition; his father was a member of the board of Delitzsch's institute, and he himself was a typical representative of it.[176] Well versed in Semitic and Greek Jewish sources, Schlatter and Kittel cherished the old Palestinian Judaism.[177] As much as Kittel abhorred modern Judaism, he had a certain respect for contemporary Orthodox Judaism.[178] Kittel and Kuhn both were partly trained by rabbis and probably had a good grasp of the methods used in rabbinic theology at the time. Kittel was "born" with Semitic languages, and Kuhn mastered them. In the debate over the depiction of Judaism in the works of Bousset and Gressmann, the chief representatives of the history of religion school, Kittel sided with the Jewish voices[179] against the liberal theologians.[180] True, some of the best defenders of German Jewry against antisemitic assaults like blood libels (Delitzsch,

---

175. In the subsequent sections, I do not repeat references already presented in the discussion of the individual scholars.
176. Deines, *Pharisäer*, 418n33.
177. See A. Schlatter, *Jochanan ben Zakkai, der Zeitgenosse der Apostel*; Kittel, *Probleme des palästinischen Spätjudentums und das Urchristentum*; and Gerdmar, *Roots of Theological Antisemitism*, 427–28.
178. Kittel, *Probleme des palästinischen Spätjudentums und das Urchristentum*, 94.
179. Felix Perles, *Bousset's Religion des Judentums im neutestamentlichen Zeitalter kritisch untersucht* (Berlin: Wolf Peiser, 1903).
180. Kittel, *Probleme des palästinischen Spätjudentums und das Urchristentum*, 14–17.

Strack) stood in the Pietist tradition of Judaic-studies, and as noted, traditional cultural antisemitism held that Jews were proud and arrogant, among other stereotypes.[181] There was also a negative attitude toward liberal and assimilated Judaism, which was seen as a threat to Christianity and a major reason for the degeneration of German culture.[182] This was fully in line with Stoecker's views, for example. We do not have much information about Grundmann's Jewish erudition, but he certainly had the opportunity to explore Judaica, and in his scholarly work he was adept at citing rabbinic sources.[183] Nevertheless, he was instrumental in ousting Hebrew studies from the University of Jena, though this may well have been political opportunism.[184] Althaus also engaged with Jewish theology and welcomed a new seriousness about religious and not only cultural Judaism, sharing Schlatter and Kittel's perspective.

There was a strange doubleness at the foundation of this movement, an interest in and fascination with everything Jewish, a belief that the Jews were the chosen people, but at the same time anti-Jewish and often antisemitic views. The "symbolic Jew" held an important place in the symbolic world,[185] but ironically this went together with a very negative view of the Jew next door. The Jews rejected Jesus, they killed him, and old and new stereotypes merged, as in the appearance of Ahasveros in scholarly writing. Even after the war, Kittel held firm to his anti-Judaism, which in his case was difficult to distinguish from antisemitism, as a necessary part of Christian theology. For Kittel, the opposition between Judaism and Christianity was not merely historical but metaphysical.[186] This double relationship to Jews and Judaism, reflecting a strangely compartmentalized view, was part of the setting of the Tübingen research tradition.[187] Scholars might have a personal relationship with and sometimes take the risk of standing up for Jewish friends, despite maintaining that Jews were inferior and occasionally even supporting

---

181. Gerdmar, *Roots of Theological Anti-Semitism*, 191–326.

182. Delitzsch, *Jesus und Hillel*; Kittel, *Probleme des palästinischen Spätjudentums und das Urchristentum*, 90, mentioning Walter Rathenau as an example.

183. As demonstrated in his inaugural lecture at Jena, Walter Grundmann, *Die Frage der ältesten Gestalt und des ursprünglichen Sinnes der Bergrede Jesu*, Schriften zur Nationalkirche 10 (Weimar, Germany: Verlag Deutsche Christen, 1939), 8–10.

184. Susannah Heschel, "The Theological Faculty of the University of Jena during the Third Reich" (paper presented at the Nineteenth International Congress of Historical Sciences, University of Oslo, Norway, August 6–13, 2000), accessed July 29, 2012, http://www.oslo2000.uio.no/AIO/AIO16/group%208/Heschel.pdf.

185. Gerdmar, *Roots of Theological Anti-Semitism*, 590–91.

186. Kittel, "Meine Verteidigung," 6.

187. Gerdmar, *Roots of Theological Anti-Semitism*, 607–8.

policies that discriminated against Jews. Others might have a passion for Jewish studies and evangelizing missions to Jews while still expressing antisemitic prejudices. Being personally acquainted with Jews did not exclude a person from being antisemitic. Kittel, for example, referred to a number of Jewish acquaintances yet fervently promoted antisemitic policies.

Taking a psychological-anthropological perspective, Claudia Strauss maintains that "everyone's belief system is partly compartmentalised and partly integrated."[188] There are situations in which the same individual seems to hold competing views, as was the case with New Testament scholars in the Tübingen circle. Tübingen provided an environment in which it became paradoxically possible to develop both a relatively deep understanding of Judaism and its sources and a belief in Jesus's alleged fierce opposition to his contemporary Judaism, leading to an aversion to everything Jewish.

An Environment Marked by Conservative Theology

German theology has been characterized by what Friedrich Wilhelm Graf called *die Spaltung des Protestantismus*, the "division of German Protestantism into a liberal-bourgeois cultural Protestantism, relatively open to modernity, and a conservative, neo-Pietist or Lutheran confessional church Protestantism."[189] Schlatter and the other theologians originally found themselves on the conservative side of this divide.[190] As noted, Schlatter was a key figure in

---

188. Claudia Strauss, "Research on Cultural Discontinuities," in *A Cognitive Theory of Cultural Meaning*, ed. Claudia Strauss and Naomi Quinn, Publications of the Society for Psychological Anthropology (Cambridge: Cambridge University Press, 1997), 210–51 (at 215).

189. Friedrich Wilhelm Graf, *Der Protestantismus: Geschichte und Gegenwart*, C. H. Beck Wissen (Munich: C. H. Beck, 2006), 11–12.

190. This does not imply that confessional theology was more easily merged to adjust to antisemitism than was liberal theology, as is illustrated by the discussion between Karl Barth and Rudolf Bultmann. The former expected the latter to join the National Socialist Deutsche Christen due to his theological stance. Accordingly, Barth saw a greater openness for National Socialism among liberal theologians. See Jack Forstman, *Christian Faith in Dark Times: Theological Conflicts in the Shadow of Hitler* (Louisville, KY: Westminster John Knox Press, 1992), 203–9. For the position of the Confessing Church on antisemitism, see Wolfgang Gerlach, *And the Witnesses Were Silent: The Confessing Church and the Persecution of the Jews*, trans. Victoria J. Barnett (Lincoln: University of Nebraska Press, 2000). The Confessing Church more often than not took issue with the state over the freedom of the church to have Jewish-Christian clergy or to teach Christianity to non-Aryan Christian schoolchildren. Its guilt lay in that most of its representatives took issue with the state on the Jewish-Christian question but not on the social situation of the Jews. For Bultmann's stand on the Jews, see Gerdmar, *Roots of Theological Anti-Semitism*, 373–411.

the conservative camp, amply illustrated by his Berlin experience. The choice to appoint him as a professor at Tübingen was a strategic one because he was seen as a follower of Johann Albrecht Bengel and Johann Tobias Beck.[191] His chair was new, and his appointment was motivated by the belief that the chair should be occupied by a man who stood for "biblical truth and the confession of the church."[192] Rudolf Bultmann and Schlatter represented two sharp alternatives in German church life, and Schlatter saw Bultmann's line as leading to atheism.[193] Kittel had a similar background in the conservative camp, although he was distinctly Lutheran, as was Althaus. Kuhn and Grundmann's choice to stay in Tübingen, as with Schlatter or Kittel, shows that they were at home, at least originally, with the direction in Tübingen. Schlatter was a well-known representative of the biblicist line[194] and was critical of historical-critical exegesis. In turn, Kittel was chosen because of his theological direction. Schlatter had wanted Kittel to succeed him as New Testament Chair at Tübingen, although Wilhelm Heitmüller (1869–1926), a leading figure in the history of religion school who held an entirely different view than Schlatter's, was called to the professorship.[195] Only after Heitmüller's death in 1926 did Kittel get the position, and only then did Schlatter feel that his longtime chair was in good hands, allowing him to withdraw from teaching.[196] Given that his father was the renowned Old Testament scholar Rudolf Kittel, it was natural for Kittel to take a stand for the Old Testament. This was also the reason he broke early with the Deutsche Christen, who wanted to dismiss the Old Testament.[197] Looking back, Kittel ascertained that his theological position had been "a witness to the truth, especially the biblical religion," and his conservative profile is evident throughout.[198]

Althaus, from his youth until at least 1947, took a conservative position in the German exegetical debate, in opposition to Emanuel Hirsch and Rudolf

---

191. Neuer, *Adolf Schlatter*, 359.
192. Ibid.
193. Grundmann, "Erkenntnis und Wahrheit," 23.
194. That a student studied for a semester or a year in one place was commonplace in German academic life, but being a doctoral student or even assistant normally implied a closer relationship and sharing of values.
195. Schlatter continued lecturing for fifteen semesters (!) after his formal retirement, to secure the direction of New Testament studies in Tübingen (Neuer, *Adolf Schlatter*, 592).
196. Ibid., 308–9, 621.
197. Doris L. Bergen, *Twisted Cross: The German Christian Movement in the Third Reich* (Chapel Hill: University of North Carolina Press, 1996), 174.
198. Kittel, "Meine Verteidigung," 44.

Bultmann.[199] He too was clearly influenced by his father, by Martin Kähler, and by Schlatter.[200] Kuhn, however, in his introductory lecture at the Heidelberg Academy in 1964, distanced himself from what he called Tübingen theology.[201] He described his theology as inspired by Julius Wellhausen and Bultmann, not by Schlatter or Kittel.[202] In spite of his own preferences, his parents had made him choose Tübingen and Schlatter before Marburg and Bultmann, he contended.[203] He stayed at Tübingen because of an opportunity to receive a stipend and to be involved in Kittel's rabbinical research project. Neither the theology of Schlatter and Heim nor "Tübingen theology" had attracted Kuhn, and the same was true for Kittel.[204]

Owing to the lack of sources and to Kuhn's need to navigate the politics of church and academia in the 1960s, it is difficult to evaluate his view of the past from Heidelberg. Given the strong opposition between confessional and liberal theology in German academia, it is unlikely that Kuhn would have taken the path to Tübingen had he not shared at least the basic views of Tübingen theology. The evidence also points to a very close relationship between Kittel and Kuhn.[205] Kuhn's description of his closeness to Wellhausen and Bultmann is hardly plausible. By 1964, Bultmann was in vogue, and a confession of sympathies with Kittel, by then well-known as an antisemite, and Schlatter, the advocate of conservative exegesis, was not.[206] Rather, it seems likely that by the 1960s, Kuhn was not eager to connect himself with Tübingen, Schlatter, or Kittel, not to mention his antisemitic past, and the question is how reliable this Heidelberg lecture was in this regard. This distancing seems to have been a pattern for Kuhn. Gert Jeremias holds that Kittel was Kuhn's most important teacher, even though Kuhn later said it was Littmann,

---

199. Martin Meiser, *Paul Althaus als Neutestamentler: Eine Untersuchung der Werke, Briefe, unveröffentlichten Manuskripte und Randbemerkungen*, Calwer Theologische Monographien (Stuttgart, Germany: Calwer, 1993), 391–93. On Emanuel Hirsch, the influential New Testament scholar at the University of Göttingen who embraced Nazi ideology, see Ericksen, *Theologians under Hitler*, 120–97.
200. Meiser, *Paul Althaus*, 393.
201. See also Theissen, *Neutestamentliche Wissenschaft vor und nach 1945*, 102.
202. Quoted extensively by Theissen, *Neutestamentliche Wissenschaft vor und nach 1945*, 101–2.
203. Ibid., 101.
204. Ibid., 102.
205. Jeremias, "Karl-Georg Kuhn," 299; Junginger, "Bild der Juden in der nationalsozialistischen Judenforschung," 180.
206. See the discussion in Theissen, *Neutestamentliche Wissenschaft vor und nach 1945*, 112.

seeing this as a way to dissociate himself from Kittel.[207] The fact is that Kuhn took over as Kittel's assistant after Charles Horowitz (1890–1969) could not continue because he was a Jew.[208] Kuhn cotaught rabbinical texts with Kittel for years,[209] and Kuhn and Kittel must be regarded as close partners in their work at the Department for Research into the Jewish Question. At every turn, Kuhn seems to have been Kittel's closest coworker and was regarded by the nazified university administration as the self-evident successor to Kittel at Tübingen.[210] As Theissen notes, it is true that Kuhn did not sign the Tübinger Sätze,[211] but this is an argument from silence; we do not know whether he was invited to sign the document. Given his activities in and for the party in 1933, it is unlikely that he would have declined to sign it had he been invited. A closer analysis of the writings of Kittel and Kuhn during their time in the Department would most probably show a far-reaching unity. Their respective publications clearly indicate that they shared the same perspective.[212] Thus, it seems reasonable to suggest that Kuhn's distancing himself from his Tübingen mentors and teachers was more a rationalization than a realistic description of what really happened.

As for Grundmann, there is positive evidence that he regarded Schlatter as an important figure. He confessed to having been deeply fascinated with Schlatter as a spiritual mentor, learning from him "that faith creates joy in the heart" and spending time with him every Monday, when Schlatter invited people to a weekly open house.[213] Schlatter had opened the Bible to Grundmann, he contended, saying, "my own exegetical work always goes to school with him."[214] Grundmann regarded Schlatter's joyful and confident Christianity as the way forward against the background of crisis theology. He described Schlatter's teaching at length, emphasizing his message of grace and joy and relating his theology of creation to the meaning of salvation, the role of the Holy Spirit, and the overall role of a theology of creation. Grundmann concluded:

---

207. Jeremias, "Karl-Georg Kuhn," 299.
208. Junginger, *Verwissenschaftlichung der "Judenfrage" im Nationalsozialismus*, 143–44.
209. Ibid., 193.
210. Ibid., 195.
211. Theissen, *Neutestamentliche Wissenschaft vor und nach 1945*, 115. Theissen states that it was inconceivable that Kuhn would stand on the side of the Confessing Church, but this is not a foregone conclusion. Schlatter was no Deutsche Christ, standing closer to the Confessing Church, but he did sign the Tübinger Sätze.
212. The indications are many, but such a study is beyond the scope of this chapter.
213. For this and the following, see Grundmann, "Erkenntnis und Wahrheit," 15–21.
214. Ibid., 21.

"This has become an unalienable insight for my own theological thinking." Moreover, in a 1938 letter to Kittel, Grundmann wrote: "The news about the death of Schlatter has moved me greatly. Here we have had a commemorative lecture arranged by the Department and the student association, which I held in his memory. We have done this with good conscience, since we know what we all owe Schlatter. For one cannot just immediately confiscate Schlatter from the Confessing Church, as it appears some of the contributions in the commemorative booklet have done."[215] Grundmann regarded Schlatter as an asset for his new theological project, the National Socialist affiliated Deutsche Christen, and did not accept that Schlatter should only be seen as a theologian for the Confessing Church. Schlatter had in fact showed Grundmann and the Deutsche Christen a surprising degree of openness. When others had rejected the twenty-eight theses of the Saxon church, a National Socialist church confession written by Grundmann, Schlatter had held them to be fairly moderate. Although theologically questionable, this confession was not reason enough to withhold Christian fellowship from a church.[216] Schlatter took a mediating position, which may very well be what Grundmann had in mind.

In another letter the same year, Grundmann mentioned that Schlatter's theology was "fundamental to my theological thought."[217] It seems that Grundmann's original position was more conservative and thus less likely to deviate from church doctrine. This conservatism would suggest that at one time, Grundmann's beliefs aligned with some of the nonnegotiable tenets of Tübingen theology, including holding that Jews were the people of God, that Jesus was Jewish, and that the Old Testament was an important part of Christian scripture and belief. However, the evidence suggests that, after leaving his alma mater, Grundmann began to align more with liberal approaches to scripture. In his work at the Institute for the Investigation and Eradication of Jewish Influence on German Church Life, he utilized the methodology of biblical form-criticism, which was abhorred in Tübingen.[218] More significantly, his efforts to remove Jewish influence from the Bible and the church would have required him to abandon some aspects of conservative Tübingen theology. For example, the dejudaized Bible produced by the Institute suffered from the significant

---

215. Grundmann to Kittel, July 1, 1938.
216. See Gerdmar, *Roots of Theological Anti-Semitism*, 292.
217. Walter Grundmann to Gerhard Kittel, December 11, 1938, Bestand DC III 2 f 1938, Landeskirchenarchiv Eisenach, Germany.
218. Grundmann employs the form-critical method in his *Jesus der Galiläer und das Judentum*.

omission of the Old Testament.[219] In producing this new Bible, Grundmann must have moved from his early Pietist faith in the Old Testament, through ambivalence to it in 1933, to complete rejection of the Old Testament as a Jewish book by 1939.[220] Most probably this was politically conditioned, and if he was serious in what he had once said about his dependence on Schlatter, he may have started off his career with a greater appreciation of the Old Testament. In these areas—the stance toward the Old Testament and the question of Jesus's Jewishness—no bridge was possible between the Confessing Church and the Deutsche Christen.

But Kittel and Grundmann could agree to disagree. Enclosed in a 1940 letter to Kittel, Grundmann sent his book *Jesus der Galiläer und das Judentum*, commenting that Kittel would probably not agree with some things in the book, as he had gathered through earlier talks.[221] However, this correspondence indicates that the two professors maintained an ongoing relationship and that, in spite of later developments, Grundmann saw himself as in some sense a disciple of Schlatter, even thirty years after his teacher's death. The missional aspect was also important for Grundmann, who saw his work in the Saxony Deutsche Christen as *Volksmission*, evangelism to the people. It was not only politics but *Kerygmatik, Evangelium*, and *Politische Theologie* [preaching, gospel, and political theology]. The task was to win the unchurched—people in the SA and other groups in the new Germany—for the faith, and the Volks-missions had a "prophetic office in the history of its people and the world."[222] In this synthesis of politics and evangelism, the latter was not unimportant to Grundmann, who used methods that were standard in his Christian upbringing in the YMCA.[223]

---

219. This dejudaized "Bible," which omitted the Old Testament, was called *Die Botschaft Gottes* [The Message of God]. See Birgit Jerke, "Wie wurde das Neue Testament zu einem sogenannten *Volkstestament* 'entjudet'? Aus der Arbeit des Eisenacher 'Institut zur Erforschung und Beseitigung des jüdischen Einflusses auf das deutsche kirchliche Leben,'" in *Christlicher Antijudaismus und Antisemitismus: Theologische und kirchliche Programme Deutscher Christen*, ed. Leonore Siegele-Wenschkewitz (Frankfurt, Germany: Haag und Herchen, 1994), 201–34; Anders Gerdmar, "Ett nytt evangelium" [A Novel Gospel], *Dagens Nyheter*, December 21, 2003 (in Swedish); and Heschel, *Aryan Jesus*, 106–11.

220. Klaus-Peter Adam, "Der theologische Werdegang Walter Grundmanns bis zum Erscheinen der *28 Thesen der sächsischen Volkskirche zum inneren Aufbau der Deutschen Evangelischen Kirche* Ende 1933," in Siegele-Wenschkewitz, *Christlicher Antijudaismus und Antisemitismus*, 171–99 (at 183–84).

221. Walter Grundmann to Gerhard Kittel, April 11, 1940, Bestand DC III 2 f 1940, Landeskirchenarchiv Eisenach, Germany.

222. Adam, "Theologische Werdegang Walter Grundmanns," 180.

223. Ibid.

All five of these scholars, from Schlatter to Kuhn, had much in common, theologically at least, during their Tübingen years. They came from Lutheran or Reformed Pietist backgrounds, lived in an environment regarded as a bastion of the "positive" or confessional flank of German theology, and saw historical-critical and liberal theology as a threat. This was the theological profile of Tübingen and the Tübingen network at the outset, even though Grundmann, for example, clearly departed from this tradition during the Third Reich.

A Common Base in a Theology of Creation

Part of Schlatter's theological profile was a theology of creation and history that would inspire younger theologians and contribute to the bridging of theology and ideology in the Third Reich. As noted previously, a theology of creation played a decisive role in Paul Althaus's thought in particular, but Althaus was also inspired by Schlatter. This theology in turn legitimated racist thinking, race being regarded as one of the divinely given orders. Althaus's theological language was sophisticated, and he had his own linguistic jargon that must be taken into account. But it is nevertheless clear that his theology of the Ordnungen treated race as part of the divinely ordained structure. Grundmann was more straightforward but held the same fundamental belief, evident in his formulation of the foundations of the Deutsche Christen theology. Upon their ascent to power in 1933, the Nazis instituted the infamous Aryan Paragraph, requiring that all civil servants had to be of "Aryan" descent and were barred from office if they had Jewish parents or grandparents. Grundmann legitimizes this legislation by, in effect, inscribing it into the story of creation in Genesis 1:

> From the natural gifts of blood and race the history of a people is formed.... This becoming a people means for us National Socialists the fulfillment of a divine word of creation: Let there be a *Volk*! And there was a *Volk*.... This means that we are creating a *Volkskirche* that confesses to blood and race as God's gifts of creation, from which time and again a people also comes into being.[224]

At the foundation of this thinking is a reinterpretation of Luther's theology of the two kingdoms, the political and the spiritual. Althaus and Grundmann both explicitly noted Schlatter's unique contribution to a theology of creation.

---

224. Walter Grundmann, *Die 28 Thesen der sächsischen Volkskirche erläutert*, Schriften der Deutschen Christen (Dresden, Germany: Deutsch-christlicher Verlag, 1934), 14, 15–16.

According to Althaus, Schlatter widened theology to focus not only on the work of Christ—as did Albrecht Ritschl and Karl Barth—but on creation.²²⁵ Schlatter managed the narrow road between natural theology and a Christomonism, argued Althaus, and his new understanding of the general revelation made it possible for God to be perceived in all natural and cultural manifestations of human life.²²⁶ He thus built a bridge from mere theology not only to a growing interest in a piety of nature but also to cultural and political action. This stance provided an impetus to give creation, and thus also the Ordnungen, a larger place in Nazi theology. Read in the political context of the Third Reich, these meant nothing other than a divinely legitimated new space for the new rule, although Althaus was not explicit. But as noted, in his discussion and revision of the Bethel Confession, Schlatter used the two-kingdom doctrine and creation theology to provide divine legitimacy to the current political system²²⁷ so that the new political order and the SA man became more important than the Jewish-Christian brethren. Schlatter's theology of creation thus gave divine legitimation to the existing political order in a way that did not accord with a Lutheran view of the two kingdoms.

Schlatter's theology of creation, nature, and history and his theological understanding of the people and history were also significant for Grundmann, providing a theological framework for understanding the import of the National Socialist political turn in German history. In his article celebrating Schlatter's eighty-fifth birthday, Grundmann said that both Schlatter's theology and his appearance provided strength to him and his generation during the 1920s.²²⁸ But he went even further: "Adolf Schlatter paved a way for us from theology to National Socialism."²²⁹ Schlatter taught a theology related to nature and history, "summarized in nationhood [Volkstum]."²³⁰ His stake in nationhood was evident in his actions, his son having died for Germany in World War I, a sacrifice Schlatter was also willing to make for the people.²³¹ This attitude to the German nation was also manifest in Schlatter's theology, which refused to

---

225. Paul Althaus, "Adolf Schlatters Gabe an die systematische Theologie," in Althaus, *Adolf Schlatter und Wilhelm Lütgert*, 31–40 (at 32).
226. Ibid., 33–34.
227. Gerdmar, *Roots of Theological Anti-Semitism*, 284.
228. Walter Grundmann, "Adolf Schlatter: Ein Wort des Grußes und des Gedenkens zu einem 85. Geburtstag am 16. August," *Deutsche Frömmigkeit* 8 (1937): 10–14 (at 10).
229. Ibid., 11.
230. Ibid.
231. Ibid.

disconnect the things of Christ from the things of nature, that is, the current historical and political situation.[232] Thus, Grundmann saw Schlatter's theology as legitimating political developments in Germany:[233] "Our German nationhood is his [God's] work, our Christianity is his work. There is only one love, which no longer can be divided,"[234] Schlatter said. Morever, Schlatter's reluctance to fully break with the Deutsche Christen also meant support for Grundmann, who personified Deutsche Christen theology. In regard to Schlatter, Grundmann affirmed: "Much has linked me to him, and *one of the great joys of my life* is that his son, Theodor Schlatter, told me that his father thought highly of me and had stood up for me during the time of the *Kirchenkampf* [Church Struggle], when I frequently faced hostility."[235] Grundmann mentioned this to show that Schlatter did not reject him, even though he was an outspoken National Socialist and antisemite.

These examples illustrate the extent to which Schlatter's theology of creation paved the way for a political theology of the Third Reich, merging Christianity and nation in a new and symbiotic way of thinking. Althaus provided the clearest example, with the most developed reflection on creation and Third Reich politics inspired by Schlatter's creation theology. Grundmann's political theology also benefited from his connection to Schlatter and Schlatter's theology of nature, history, and nationhood, which paved the way for National Socialism. It does not seem likely that Grundmann had much to gain from honoring Schlatter in 1937.

A Shared Antimodernism, Chauvinism, Antisemitism, and Allegiance to National Socialism

In different ways each of the members of the Tübingen group showed antimodernist, chauvinist, and antisemitic leanings, and several were full-scale National Socialists. The 1920s were characterized by modernism, the aftermath of the national catastrophe following World War I, and conservatives often blamed Jews for increasing immorality. This gloom after Germany's loss and humiliation dominated the political atmosphere, formulated not least as an antimodernist criticism of the Weimar Republic and the degeneration it was believed to have caused. Kittel, for example, though he seldom spoke up politically before 1933, fiercely attacked the memory of Walther Rathenau (1867–1922), the

---

232. Ibid., 12–13.
233. Ibid.
234. Ibid., 13.
235. Grundmann, "Erkenntnis und Wahrheit," 21 (my emphasis).

minister for foreign affairs of the Weimar Republic who was murdered in 1922. A leftist Jewish democrat and, in German right-wing circles, a symbol of the Weimar Republic, Rathenau was an example of degeneration and of moralism without religion in Kittel's view.[236] The Weimar Republic itself stood for the national failure of Germany. Whereas Rathenau combined modernism, Jewishness, and left-wing democratic politics, Kittel's own antimodernist and culturally conservative stance belonged to Alfred Rosenberg's deeply conservative, de facto National Socialist movement, the KfdK.

Moreover, in Althaus we find a chauvinist patriotism alongside a deeply conservative masculine hero-soldier ideal.[237] The military chaplain and then professor developed a völkisch and religiously founded men's patriotism during World War I.[238] By 1917, he already supported racial hygiene, saying that Germany needed strong men of good breed.[239] Both Schlatter and Grundmann admired the nationalist, antidemocratic, and antisemitic Stoecker.

This national chauvinism was evident among all of the Tübingen scholars discussed here, as was the corresponding antisemitism. The Volk, the people, was central to the rhetoric of these scholars, fully thematized by Grundmann but present in the work of Kittel, Schlatter, Althaus, and Kuhn as well. This was in no way unique, the concept of the German Volk being prominent in German cultural and political discourse beginning in Herder's time. During the first decades of the twentieth century, the Volk idea took on additional significance, and many hopes for Germany's emergence as a leading nation were attached to it. *Völkisch* became the primary buzzword of the National Socialist movement,[240] taking on not merely ethnic but metaphysical meaning during the first decades of the twentieth century. Use of the term tapped into the ongoing political discourse, in which the Volk stood for that metaphysical entity that pervaded the racist National Socialist imagination. Antisemitism was closely

---

236. Kittel, *Probleme des palästinischen Spätjudentums und das Urchristentum*, 94.
237. Liebenberg, *Gott der feldgrauen Männer*, 149–51.
238. Ibid., 477.
239. Ibid., 496.
240. For the meaning of *Volk* and *völkisch*, see Norbert Götz, "Volk, völkisch," in *World Fascism: A Historical Encyclopedia*, ed. Cyprian Balmires (Santa Barbara, CA: ABC-CLIO, 2006), 703–4. For *völkisch*, see Uwe Puschner, *Die völkische Bewegung im wilhelminischen Kaiserreich: Sprache—Rasse—Religion* (Darmstadt, Germany: Wissenschaftliche Buchgesellschaft, 2001); and Uwe Puschner, "Völkisch: Plädoyer für einen 'engen' Begriff," in *"Erziehung zum deutschen Menschen": Völkische und nationalkonservative Erwachsenenbildung in der Weimarer Republik*, ed. Paul Ciupke, Klaus Heuer, Franz-Josef Jelich, and Justus H. Ulbricht. Geschichte und Erwachsenenbildung (Essen, Germany: Klartext, 2007), 53–66.

intertwined with this national chauvinism in turn, as Jews were regarded as a foreign Volk. Some of these scholars even theologized the notions of race and Volk. Althaus included race among the divinely created orders, and Grundmann even used the Third Reich rhetoric of blood, soil, and race, something Schlatter and Kittel were reluctant to do. Nevertheless, all five—Schlatter, Althaus, Kittel, Grundmann, and Kuhn—held that Jews and Judaism in Germany constituted a Jewish Problem.[241] All were in line with the racist direction of the new Germany.

As for National Socialism, all five were either National Socialists or sympathizers. Two of the five, Kuhn and Grundmann, were *Alte Kämpfer*, that is, people who were National Socialist Party members before Hitler came to power. Kittel became a member on May 1, 1933. Schlatter and Althaus may not have been members for different reasons. Schlatter maintained a critical though ambivalent attitude toward the National Socialist Party having to do mainly with pagan elements of its ideology. As with most people on the confessional flank, Schlatter believed it was most important not to compromise the church and to keep it clean of pagan elements.

Although not all five were National Socialists, each, to different degrees and in different ways, supported the Führer and the German state. They signed declarations of loyalty, implying support for its fundamental antisemitic views on Jews and Judaism. Modern Judaism was regarded as a threat to the Christian Germany they envisioned and wanted to defend. They would accuse the Jews of practicing an unchecked capitalism that had become an economic, spiritual, and moral danger to Germany.[242] This view of Jews and Judaism was only part of the combination of ideological-political attitudes that to varying degrees characterized the Tübingen network: antimodernism, antisemitism, German chauvinism, antidemocratic ideals, and völkisch and National Socialist ideology.

A Connection to the Tübingen Network as an "Emotional Regime"

An elusive but important element of an academic institution is the social fellowship in which ideas are developed and nurtured into traditions. The salon, a home-based fellowship in a spiritual or political-ideological key, had long been part of German culture, just as home meetings were part of Pietist culture. The Tübingen fellowship and the numerous contacts between these scholars over the years were decisive for their development, for both edification and the

---

241. Althaus, "Frage des Evangeliums an das moderne Judentum," 196.
242. See Gerdmar, *Roots of Theological Anti-Semitism*, 178–79.

shaping of attitudes. Only twenty-one and twenty-two years old, respectively, Grundmann and Kuhn came to Tübingen at a time in life when the individual is being formed religiously, academically, and socially. Grundmann's report suggests that Tübingen's close and socially warm environment formed him both as a Christian and as a theologian. It was also in the strongly National Socialist Tübingen that they became early party members, and the young men may have inspired their mentor and teacher Kittel with their National Socialist commitments and ideas.

The close relationship with Tübingen was in Althaus's past by 1933, but Schlatter's ideas had been decisive, and his influence prevailed. For decades Althaus was attached to Schlatter, even though he was no longer present in Tübingen when antisemitism came into vogue.[243] Althaus was also entrusted with the series Beiträge zur Förderung christlicher Theologie just before Schlatter's death.[244] In his obituary he once more called Schlatter his teacher.[245] Grundmann attended regular events in Schlatter's home, and the joy and fervor of the old professor made an impression on him.[246] The collegial correspondence between Grundmann and Kittel witnesses to continued fellowship after the Tübingen years. And the relationship between Kittel and Schlatter seems to have been close as well. Kittel mourned Schlatter's death as the death of an Elijah who was both a father and a chariot of Israel.[247] Ten years later he pointed to his closeness to his mentor: "During the years up until the death of Schlatter in the summer of 1938, he [Kittel, who writes about himself in the third person] had not taken any step in the controversial area [of Kittel's relationship to National Socialism] without speaking to him [Schlatter]."[248] In a letter to defend Kittel in the proceedings against him after the war, Schlatter's daughter Dora also testified to Schlatter and Kittel's closeness.[249] There is no reason to doubt this report, though it may have had an apologetic function. And despite Kuhn's later attempts to distance himself from Schlatter's theology especially, he too confessed to Schlatter's influence in other areas over the course of many conversations.[250]

---

243. Neuer, *Adolf Schlatter*, 724.
244. Althaus, "Zum Gedächtnis der abgerufenen Herausgeber der 'Beiträge,'" 13.
245. Ibid., 15.
246. Grundmann, "Erkenntnis und Wahrheit," 19.
247. Gerhard Kittel, "Adolf Schlatter," in Althaus, *Adolf Schlatter und Wilhelm Lütgert*, 16–30 (at 16).
248. Kittel, "Meine Verteidigung," 45.
249. D. Schlatter, letter, 1947.
250. Quoted in Theissen, *Neutestamentliche Wissenschaft vor und nach 1945*, 102.

This last point is tentative but nevertheless important. In his book on the French Revolution, William Reddy discusses "emotional regimes," which he defines as "a set of normative emotions ... as a necessary underpinning of any stable political regime."[251] Without going into a larger methodological discussion of the history of emotions and emotional regimes, I suggest that the social and emotional environment of the Tübingen network played a decisive role in the development and institution of National Socialist attitudes and ideas. We may seldom talk of academics as emotional beings or social animals, but we all are, and these people were. The similarities in ideas and attitudes, the methodological affinities, but also the relative impact of these scholars on views of Jews and Judaism in the Third Reich would not be as great were it not for the power of the social network, or emotional regime, which is so effective in shaping attitudes in a group like the one discussed here.[252] Equally significant to this emotional regime were the strong symbols around which the scholars could unite: faith and the church, the German nation and Volk and its struggle for a new historical role, and war and the sacrifices to which heroic men were called, including a military- and uniform-loving culture. Equally emotional was the negative symbolism of the lost war and its attending humiliations, of Schlatter's lost son, and of the Weimar Republic, regarded as a failure. The Jew and world Judaism were constructed as irrational threats and symbols of anything that opposed Christianity and Germany.[253] Grundmann ended his article about the eighty-year-old Schlatter, who personified many of the ideas that formed the Tübingen network, as follows: "We see in Adolf Schlatter something, which we need more urgently today than ever: a Christianity that is obedient to God,

---

251. William M. Reddy, *The Navigation of Feeling: A Framework for the History of Emotions* (Cambridge: Cambridge University Press, 2001), 129.

252. On the growing research into emotional regimes in religion, see Ole Riis and Linda Woodhead, *A Sociology of Religious Emotion* (Oxford: Oxford University Press, 2010): "Religious emotions are simply those emotions that are integral to religious communities and their sacred symbols. As such, religious emotion can include any conceivable feeling, from tender love to violent hatred and disgust. The authorities in a religious community focus attention on a certain set of coordinated feelings, whose status is confirmed through the social and ritual life of the group and in its symbols. Thereby, the community establishes an emotional regime in terms of which its members learn to identify some emotions as legitimate and prescribed, and others as forbidden or distracting" (212).

253. Ibid., 212. On the role of such symbols, they state: "the capacity of symbolic objects to evoke powerful emotions seems to increase with the size of the group for which the symbol is moving. The most powerful of all are those that symbolize and help constitute an entire society; they can be animate (an animal, a charismatic leader), inanimate (a national flag, a crucifix), or intermediate (a relic of a saint, a memorialized leader)" (38).

connected to the people, full of joy and confidence, that lives from the God who gives and has a living unity of theology and piety and that therefore is fruitful."[254] From this center, the emotional regime of the Tübingen network received its direction and strength.

IV. CONCLUSION

Tübingen during the National Socialist period, and for decades before, supported a research tradition that became instrumental for the development of German antisemitism. This environment influenced the scholars described in this article, and Tübingen, with its rare combination of conservative theology, Judaica research, antisemitism, antimodernist chauvinism, and social-emotional relationships became a seedbed for anti-Jewish and antisemitic research and theology.

No doubt Adolf Schlatter stood as the unifying figure in this network, providing the inspiration for the tendencies discussed herein and arousing with his charisma considerable enthusiasm among his disciples and associates. It was precisely this combination of social environment and research into Judaism that led the New Testament Department at Tübingen to its role in the betrayal of Christian theology. Several factors contributed: the combination of anti-Judaism or antisemitism and expertise in Judaism; a theological tradition that could be used to divinely legitimate the new regime; a social network of scholars and colleagues and even friends with a common background and history; and a specific cultural-political milieu that fostered men with a heart for the nation who were mourning the loss of an emperor—but welcoming a Führer. In addition, the expulsion of any Jewish participation in *Wissenschaft des Judentums* [academic Jewish studies] from the German university allowed the Tübingen department to become a leader in Protestant Jewish studies and a most useful servant of the National Socialist regime.

Of course, the long tradition of a *Judenrein* University of Tübingen supported the development of this antisemitic research enterprise. Without the legitimation provided by the scholars and the anti-Jewish research tradition that developed at Tübingen, the history of theological antisemitism and German antisemitism at large would have looked quite different. Walter Grundmann would not have become a symbol of the Nazi depravation of German theology. Gerhard Kittel would not have become both one of the most famous

---

254. Grundmann, "Adolf Schlatter," 13.

exegetes and one of the most infamous antisemites. Paul Althaus might not have developed his creation theology, which legitimated his influence on Aryan legislation in the church. Karl Georg Kuhn would not have constructed an Old Testament history to fit völkisch ideals. The lesson for anyone with a Protestant background is to explore the relationship between Protestant root beliefs and antisemitism and to attempt to recover the inherent, organic connection between Christianity and Judaism. The lesson for academia and society at large is to watch for both old and new antisemitism, for mechanisms that, as history shows, tend to marginalize or stigmatize Jews and Judaism and to legitimate political measures targeting the Jewish people. If such an awareness had been present in Germany, fewer Jewish persons would have been transported on the railway tracks from Germany to Auschwitz. Instead, this betrayal of the Christian belief that every human is immensely valuable, created in God's image, paved the way not only for the spiritual elimination of Jewish influence but also for the Holocaust.

BIBLIOGRAPHY

Archival Sources

Bundesarchiv Koblenz
Landeskirchenarchiv Eisenach
Universitätsarchiv Tübingen

Secondary Sources

Adam, Klaus-Peter. "Der theologische Werdegang Walter Grundmanns bis zum Erscheinen der *28 Thesen der sächsischen Volkskirche zum inneren Aufbau der Deutschen Evangelischen Kirche* Ende 1933." In Siegele-Wenschkewitz, *Christlicher Antijudaismus und Antisemitismus*, 171–99.
Adam, Uwe Dietrich. *Hochschule und Nationalsozialismus: Die Universität Tübingen im Dritten Reich; Mit einem Anhang von Wilfried Setzler "Die Tübinger Studentenfrequenz im Dritten Reich."* Contubernium 23. Tübingen, Germany: Mohr Siebeck, 1977.
Althaus, Paul. "Adolf Schlatters Gabe an die systematische Theologie." In Althaus, *Adolf Schlatter und Wilhelm Lütgert*, 31–40.
———, ed. *Adolf Schlatter und Wilhelm Lütgert zum Gedächtnis*. Beiträge zur Förderung christlicher Theologie 40. Gütersloh, Germany: C. Bertelsmann, 1938.
———. *Die deutsche Stunde der Kirche*. 3rd ed. Göttingen, Germany: Vandenhoeck & Ruprecht, 1934.

———. "Die Frage des Evangeliums an das moderne Judentum." *Zeitschrift für systematische Theologie* 7, no. 2 (1930): 195–215.
———. *Obrigkeit und Führertum: Wandlungen des evangelischen Staatsethos.* Gütersloh, Germany: C. Bertelsmann, 1936.
———. *Theologie der Ordnungen.* 2nd ed. Gütersloh, Germany: Bertelsmann, 1935.
———. "Zum Gedächtnis der abgerufenen Herausgeber der 'Beiträge.'" In Althaus, *Adolf Schlatter und Wilhelm Lütgert*, 9–15.
Althaus, Paul, and Werner Elert. "Theologische Gutachten über die Zulassung von Christen jüdischer Herkunft zu den Ämtern der deutschen evangelischen Kirche." *Theologische Blätter* 12, no. 11 (1933): 321–24.
Beek, M. A. Review of *Achtzehngebet und Vater unser und der Reim*, by Karl Georg Kuhn. *Vox Theologica* 21, no. 1 (1950): 21–22.
Bergen, Doris L. *Twisted Cross: The German Christian Movement in the Third Reich.* Chapel Hill: University of North Carolina Press, 1996.
Bergmann, Werner. "Stoecker, Adolf." In *Handbuch des Antisemitismus: Judenfeindschaft in Geschichte und Gegenwart, im Auftrag von Zentrum für Antisemitismusforschung der Technischen Universität Berlin.* Vol. 2, bk. 2, *Personen, im Auftrag von Zentrum für Antisemitismusforschung der Technischen Universität Berlin*, edited by Wolfgang Benz, 798–802. Berlin: K. G. Saur, 2009.
Bousset, Wilhelm, and Hugo Gressmann. *Die Religion des Judentums im späthellenistischen Zeitalter, verfasst von Wilhelm Bousset, herausgegeben von Hugo Gressmann.* Handbuch zum Neuen Testament 21. Tübingen, Germany: J. C. B. Mohr (Paul Siebeck), 1926.
Casey, Maurice. "Antisemitic Assumptions in the Theological Dictionary of the New Testament." *Novum Testamentum* 41, no. 3 (1999): 280–91.
Chamberlain, Houston Steward. *Die Grundlagen des neunzehnten Jahrhunderts.* 3rd ed. Vol. 1. Munich: F. Bruckmann A.-G., 1901.
Czerniakow, Adam. *The Warsaw Diary of Adam Czerniakow: Prelude to Doom.* Edited by Raul Hilberg, Stanislaw Staron, and Josef Kermisz. Translated by Stanislaw Staron and the Staff of Yad Vashem. New York: Stein and Day, 1979.
Davies, Alan T. "The Aryan Christ: A Motif in Christian Anti-Semitism." *Journal of Ecumenical Studies* 12 (1975): 569–79.
Deines, Roland. *Die Pharisäer: Ihr Verständnis im Spiegel der christlichen und jüdischen Forschung seit Wellhausen und Graetz.* Wissenschaftliche Untersuchungen zum Neuen Testament 101. Tübingen, Germany: Mohr Siebeck, 1997.
Deines, Roland, Volker Leppin, and Karl-Wilhelm Niebuhr, eds. *Walter Grundmann: Ein Neutestamentler im Dritten Reich.* Arbeiten zur Kirchen- und Theologiegeschichte. Leipzig: Evangelische Verlagsanstalt, 2007.
Delitzsch, Franz. *Jesus und Hillel: Mit Rücksicht auf Renan und Geiger.* Erlangen, Germany: A. Deichert, 1867.

———. *Zur Geschichte der jüdischen Poësie vom Abschluss der heiligen Schriften Alten Bundes bis auf die neueste Zeit*. Leipzig: Karl Tauchnitz, 1836.

Ericksen, Robert P. "Christians and the Holocaust: The Wartime Writings of Gerhard Kittel." In *Remembering for the Future: Working Papers and Addenda*, edited by Yehuda Bauer et al., 2400–14. Oxford: Pergamon, 1989.

———. *Theologians under Hitler: Gerhard Kittel, Paul Althaus, and Emanuel Hirsch*. New Haven, CT: Yale University Press, 1985.

Forstman, Jack. *Christian Faith in Dark Times: Theological Conflicts in the Shadow of Hitler*. Louisville, KY: Westminster John Knox Press, 1992.

Frank, Walter. *Hofprediger Adolf Stoecker und die christlichsoziale Bewegung*. Berlin: Reimar Hobbing, 1928.

Gerdmar, Anders. "Ett nytt evangelium." [A New Gospel] *Dagens Nyheter*, December 21, 2003.

———. *Roots of Theological Anti-Semitism: German Biblical Interpretation and the Jews, from Herder and Semler to Kittel and Bultmann*. Studies in Jewish History and Culture 20. Leiden, Netherlands: Brill, 2009.

Gerlach, Wolfgang. *And the Witnesses Were Silent: The Confessing Church and the Persecution of the Jews*. Translated by Victoria J. Barnett. Lincoln: University of Nebraska Press, 2000.

Gimmel, Jürgen. *Die politische Organisation kulturellen Ressentiments: Der "Kampfbund für deutsche Kultur" und das bildungsbürgerliche Unbehagen an der Moderne*. Schriftenreihe der Stipendiatinnen und Stipendiaten der Friedrich-Ebert-Stiftung 10. Münster, Germany: LIT, 2001.

Götz, Norbert. "Volk, völkisch." In *World Fascism: A Historical Encyclopedia*, edited by Cyprian Balmires, 703–4. Santa Barbara, CA: ABC-CLIO, 2006.

Graf, Friedrich Wilhelm. *Der Protestantismus: Geschichte und Gegenwart*. C. H. Beck Wissen. Munich: C. H. Beck, 2006.

Grundmann, Walter. "Adolf Schlatter: Ein Wort des Grußes und des Gedenkens zu einem 85. Geburtstag am 16. August." *Deutsche Frömmigkeit* 8 (1937): 10–14.

———. *Die 28 Thesen der sächsischen Volkskirche erläutert*. Schriften der Deutschen Christen. Dresden, Germany: Deutsch-christlicher, 1934.

———. *Die Frage der ältesten Gestalt und des ursprünglichen Sinnes der Bergrede Jesu*. Schriften zur Nationalkirche 10. Weimar, Germany: Deutsche Christen, 1939.

———. "Erkenntnis und Wahrheit: Aus meinem Leben." Unpublished typescript, Eisenach, 1969. File D 40/689, Landeskirchenarchiv Eisenach, Germany.

———. *Jesus der Galiläer und das Judentum*. Veröffentlichungen des Instituts zur Erforschung des jüdischen Einflusses auf das deutsche kirchliche Leben. Leipzig, Germany: Georg Wigand, 1940.

———. Letter to Gerhard Kittel, April 11, 1940. Bestand DC III 2 f 1940, Landeskirchenarchiv Eisenach, Germany.

———. Letter to Gerhard Kittel, December 11, 1938. Bestand DC III 2 f 1938, Landeskirchenarchiv Eisenach, Germany.

———. Letter to Gerhard Kittel, July 1, 1938. Bestand DC III 2 f 1938, Landeskirchenarchiv Eisenach, Germany.

Heiber, Helmut. *Walter Frank und sein Reichsinstitut für Geschichte des neuen Deutschland*. Quellen und Darstellungen zur Zeitgeschichte 13. Stuttgart, Germany: Deutsche Verlags-Anstalt, 1966.

Heschel, Susannah. *The Aryan Jesus: Christian Theologians and the Nazi Bible in Nazi Germany*. Princeton, NJ: Princeton University Press, 2008.

———. "Deutsche Theologen für Hitler: Walter Grundmann und das Eisenacher 'Institut zur Erforschung und Beseitigung des jüdischen Einflusses auf das deutsche kirchliche Leben.'" In Deines, Leppin, and Niebuhr, *Walter Grundmann*, 70–90.

———. "The Theological Faculty of the University of Jena during the Third Reich." Paper presented at the Nineteenth International Congress of Historical Sciences, University of Oslo, Norway, August 6–13, 2000. Accessed July 29, 2012. http://www.oslo2000.uio.no/AIO/AIO16/group%208/Heschel.pdf.

Hetzer, Tanja. *"Deutsche Stunde": Volksgemeinschaft und Antisemitismus in der politischen Theologie bei Althaus*. Beiträge zur Geschichtswissenschaft. Munich: Allitera, 2009.

Hirsch, Emanuel. *Das Wesen des Christentums*. Weimar, Germany: Deutsche Christen, 1939. Republished as vol. 19 of *Gesammelte Werke*, edited by Arnulf von Scheliha. Waltrop, Germany: Hartmut Spenner, 2004.

Hoßfeld, Uwe, Jürgen John, Oliver Lemuth, and Rüdiger Stutz, eds. *"Kämpferische Wissenschaft": Studien zur Universität Jena im Nationalsozialismus*. Cologne, Germany: Böhlau, 2003.

Jeremias, Gert. "Karl-Georg Kuhn (1906–1976)." In *Neutestamentliche Wissenschaft nach 1945: Hauptvertreter der deutschsprachigen Exegese in der Darstellung ihrer Schüler*, edited by Cilliers Breytenbach and Rudolf Hoppe, 297–312. Göttingen, Germany: Neukirchener, 2008.

Jerke, Birgit. "Wie wurde das Neue Testament zu einem sogenannten *Volkstestament* 'entjudet'? Aus der Arbeit des Eisenacher 'Institut zur Erforschung und Beseitigung des jüdischen Einflusses auf das deutsche kirchliche Leben.'" In Siegele-Wenschkewitz, *Christlicher Antijudaismus und Antisemitismus*, 201–34.

Junginger, Horst. "Antisemitismus in Theorie und Praxis: Tübingen als Zentrum der nationalsozialistischen 'Judenforschung.'" In *Die Universität Tübingen im Nationalsozialismus*, edited by Urban Wiesing, Klaus-Rainer Brintzinger, Bernd Grün, Horst Junginger, and Susanne Michl, 483–558. Contubernium 73. Stuttgart, Germany: Franz Steiner, 2010.

———. "Das Bild der Juden in der nationalsozialistischen Judenforschung." In *Die kulturelle Seite des Antisemitismus: Zwischen Aufklärung und Shoah*, edited by Andrea Hoffmann, 171–220. Tübingen, Germany: Tübinger Vereinigung für Volkskunde, 2006.

———. *Die Verwissenschaftlichung der "Judenfrage" im Nationalsozialismus*. Veröffentlichungen der Forschungsstelle Ludwigsburg der Universität Stuttgart 19. Darmstadt, Germany: Wissenschaftliche Buchgesellschaft, 2011.

———. "'Judenforschung' in Tübingen: Von der jüdischen zur antijüdischen Religionswissenschaft." *Jahrbuch des Simon-Dubnow-Instituts* 5 (2006): 375–98.

Kasher, Aryeh. "Diaspora I/2." In *Theologische Realenzyklopädie*, 8:711–17. Berlin: Walter de Gruyter, 1981.

Kinzig, Wolfram. *Harnack, Marcion, und das Judentum: Nebst einer kommentierten Edition des Briefwechsels Adolf von Harnacks mit Houston Steward Chamberlain*. Arbeiten zur Kirchen- und Theologiegeschichte 13. Leipzig, Germany: Evangelische Verlagsanstalt, 2004.

Kittel, Gerhard. "Adolf Schlatter." In Althaus, *Adolf Schlatter und Wilhelm Lütgert*, 16–30.

———. "Das Konnubium mit den Nicht-Juden im antiken Judentum." In *Forschungen zur Judenfrage: Sitzungsberichte der Zweiten Arbeitstagung der Forschungsabteilung Judenfrage des Reichsinstituts für Geschichte des neuen Deutschlands vom 12. bis 14. Mai 1937*, 30–62. Hamburg, Germany: Hanseatische Verlagsanstalt, 1937.

———. "Das Urteil über die Rassenmischung im Judentum und in der biblischen Religion." *Der Biologe* 6, no. 1 (1937): 342–53.

———. "Die Behandlung des Nichtjuden nach dem Talmud." In *Archiv für Judenfragen: Schriften zur geistigen Überwindung des Judentums*, edited by Friedrich Löffler, 7–17. Gruppe A 1/Heft 1. Berlin: Mier and Glasemann, 1943.

———. *Die Judenfrage*. 2nd ed. Stuttgart, Germany: Kohlhammer, 1933.

———. *Die Probleme des palästinischen Spätjudentums und das Urchristentum*. Beiträge zur Wissenschaft vom Alten und Neuen Testament 3/1. Stuttgart, Germany: W. Kohlhammer, 1926.

———. Letter to Max Stockburger, October 10, 1933. File 126a/284, Universitätsarchiv Tübingen, Germany.

———. "Meine Verteidigung, Neue erweiterte Niederschrift: November/Dezember 1946," 1946. File 162/31.1, Universitätsarchiv Tübingen, Germany.

Kittel, Gerhard, and Eugen Fischer. *Das antike Weltjudentum: Tatsachen, Texte, Bilder*. Forschungen zur Judenfrage: Schriften des Rechtsinstituts für Geschichte des neuen Deutschlands 7. Hamburg: Hanseatische Verlagsanstalt, 1943.

Kittel, Gerhard, and Gerhard Friedrich, eds. *Theologisches Wörterbuch zum Neuen Testament*. 10 vols. Stuttgart, Germany: W. Kohlhammer, 1932–79. Translated by G. W. Bromiley as *Theological Dictionary of the New Testament*. 10 vols. Grand Rapids, MI: Eerdmans, 1964–76.

Kuhn, Karl Georg. "Die Ausbreitung des Judentums in der antiken Welt." Lecture reported in *Tübinger Chronik*, December 17, 1934.

———. "Die inneren Voraussetzungen der jüdischen Ausbreitung." *Deutsche Theologie* 2 (1935): 9–17.

———. *Die Judenfrage als weltgeschichtliches Problem*. Schriften des Reichsinstitutes für Geschichte des neuen Deutschlands. Hamburg: Hanseatische Verlagsanstalt, 1939.

———. Letter to the Untersuchung und Schlichtungs-Ausschuss [Committee for Investigation and Settlement], to the attention of Max Stockburger, Tübingen, October 10, 1933. File 126a/284, Universitätsarchiv Tübingen, Germany.

———. *Ursprung und Wesen des talmudischen Einstellung zum Nichtjuden*. Forschungen zur Judenfrage: Sitzungsberichte der Dritten Arbeitstagung des Reichsinstituts für Geschichte des neuen Deutschlands 3. Hamburg, Germany: Hanseatische Verlagsanstalt, 1938.

Kvidahl, Cliff. "Adolf Schlatter (1852–1938)." *Logos* (blog), May 19, 2012. Accessed December 29, 2020. https://blog.logos.com/2012/05/adolf-schlatter-1852-1938/.

Lessing, Eckhart. *Geschichte der deutschsprachigen evangelischen Theologie von Albrecht Ritschl bis zur Gegenwart*. 3 vols. Göttingen, Germany: Vandenhoeck & Ruprecht, 2000–2009.

Levenson, Alan. "Missionary Protestants as Defenders and Detractors of Judaism: Franz Delitzsch and Hermann Strack." *Jewish Quarterly Review* 92, no. 3–4 (2002): 383–420.

Levinson, Bernard M. "Goethe's Analysis of Exodus 34 and Its Influence on Julius Wellhausen: The *Pfropfung* of the Documentary Hypothesis," *Zeitschrift für die alttestamentliche Wissenschaft* 114, no. 2 (2002): 212–23.

Liebenberg, Roland. *Der Gott der feldgrauen Männer: Die theozentrische Erfahrungstheologie von Paul Althaus d. J. im Ersten Weltkrieg*. Arbeiten zur Kirchen- und Theologiegeschichte 22. Leipzig, Germany: Evangelische Verlagsanstalt, 2008.

Meiser, Martin. *Paul Althaus als Neutestamentler: Eine Untersuchung der Werke, Briefe, unveröffentlichten Manuskripte, und Randbemerkungen*. Calwer Theologische Monographien. Stuttgart, Germany: Calwer, 1993.

Neuer, Werner. *Adolf Schlatter: Ein Leben für Theologie und Kirche*. Stuttgart: Calwer, 1996.

Osten-Sacken, Peter von der, ed. *Das mißbrauchte Evangelium: Studien zu Theologie und Praxis der Thüringer Deutschen Christen*. Studien zu Kirche und Israel 20. Berlin: Institut Kirche und Judentum, 2002.

Perles, Felix. *Bousset's Religion des Judentums im neutestamentlichen Zeitalter kritisch untersucht*. Berlin: Wolf Peiser, 1903.

Philo. *On the Embassy to Gaius. General Indexes.* Translated by F. H. Colson. Index by J. W. Earp. Loeb Classical Library 379. Cambridge, MA: Harvard University Press, 1962.

Puschner, Uwe. *Die völkische Bewegung im wilhelminischen Kaiserreich: Sprache, Rasse, Religion.* Darmstadt, Germany: Wissenschaftliche Buchgesellschaft, 2001.

———. "Völkisch: Plädoyer für einen 'engen' Begriff." In *"Erziehung zum deutschen Menschen": Völkische und nationalkonservative Erwachsenenbildung in der Weimarer Republik,* edited by Paul Ciupke, Klaus Heuer, Franz-Josef Jelich, and Justus H. Ulbricht, 53–66. Geschichte und Erwachsenenbildung. Essen, Germany: Klartext, 2007.

Reddy, William M. *The Navigation of Feeling: A Framework for the History of Emotions.* Cambridge: Cambridge University Press, 2001.

Riis, Ole, and Linda Woodhead. *A Sociology of Religious Emotion.* Oxford: Oxford University Press, 2010.

Schäfer, Gerhard. *Die evangelische Landeskirche in Württemberg und der Nationalsozialismus: Eine Dokumentation zum Kirchenkampf.* Vol. 3, *Der Einbruch des Reichsbischofs in die württ. Landeskirche 1934.* Stuttgart, Germany: Calwer, 1974.

Schenk, Wolfgang. "Der Jenaer Jesus: Zu werk und Wirkung des völkischen Theologen Walter Grundmann und seiner Kollegen." In Osten-Sacken, *Das mißbrauchte Evangelium,* 167–279.

Schlatter, Adolf. *Adolf Schlatters Rückblick auf seine Lebensarbeit: Zu seinem hundertsten Geburtstag herausgegeben von Theodor Schlatter.* Edited by Theodor Schlatter. Beiträge zur Förderung christlicher Theologie. Gütersloh, Germany: C. Bertelsmann, 1952.

———. *Der Glaube im Neuen Testament.* 2nd ed. Stuttgart, Germany: Calwer, 1896.

———. *Der Römerbrief. Ein Hilfsbüchlein für Bibelleser.* Stuttgart, Germany: Calwer Verlag, 1887.

———. *Die neue deutsche Art in der Kirche.* Sonderdrucke des Monatsblattes "Beth-El" 14. Bethel bei Bielefeld, Germany: Anstalt Bethel, 1933.

———. *Israels Geschichte von Alexander dem Großen bis Hadrian.* Reiche der Alten Welt 3. Calw, Germany: Verlag der Vereinsbuchhandlung, 1901.

———. *Jochanan ben Zakkai, der Zeitgenosse der Apostel.* Beiträge zur Förderung christlicher Theologie 3/4. Gütersloh, Germany: C. Bertelsmann, 1899.

———. *Wird der Jude über uns siegen? Ein Wort für die Weihnachtszeit.* Freizeit-Blätter 8. Essen an der Ruhr, Germany: Freizeiten-Verlag zu Velbert im Rheinland, 1935.

Schlatter, Dora. Letter regarding the connection between Adolf Schlatter and Gerhard Kittel (Abschrift), 1947. File 162/31.2, Universitätsarchiv Tübingen, Germany.

Schmidt, Kurt Dietrich. "Der Widerstand der Kirche im Dritten Reich." *Lutherische Monatshefte* 1, no. 8 (1962): 366–70.

———. *Die Bekenntnisse und grundsätzlichen Äusserungen zur Kirchenfrage des Jahres 1933.* Vol. 1. Göttingen, Germany: Vandenhoeck & Ruprecht, 1934.

Schönhagen, Benigna. *Tübingen unterm Hakenkreuz: Eine Universitätsstadt in der Zeit des Nationalsozialismus.* Beiträge zur Tübinger Geschichte 4. Stuttgart, Germany: Theiss, 1991.

Siegele-Wenschkewitz, Leonore, ed. *Christlicher Antijudaismus und Antisemitismus: Theologische und kirchliche Programme Deutscher Christen.* Arnoldsheiner Texte. Frankfurt, Germany: Haag und Herchen, 1994.

———. *Nazionalsozialismus und Kirchen: Religionspolitik von Partei und Staat bis 1935.* Tübinger Schriften zur Sozial- und Zeitgeschichte 5. Düsseldorf, Germany: Droste, 1974.

———. *Neutestamentliche Wissenschaft vor der Judenfrage: Gerhard Kittels theologische Arbeit im Wandel deutscher Geschichte.* Theologische Existenz heute 208. Munich: Chr. Kaiser, 1980.

Steinweis, Alan E. *Studying the Jew: Scholarly Antisemitism in Nazi Germany.* Cambridge, MA: Harvard University Press, 2008.

Stoecker, Adolf. *Christlich-Sozial: Reden und Aufsätze.* Berlin: Verlag der Buchhandlung der Berliner Stadtmission, 1890.

Strack, Hermann L. *Der Blutaberglaube in der Menschheit, Blutmorde, und Blutritus.* 4th ed. Schriften des Institutum Judaicum in Berlin 14. Leipzig, Germany: J. C. Hinrichs'sche, 1892.

———. *Einleitung in Talmud und Midras.* 5th ed. Munich: C. H. Beck'sche, 1920.

Strauss, Claudia. "Research on Cultural Discontinuities." In *A Cognitive Theory of Cultural Meaning,* edited by Claudia Strauss and Naomi Quinn, 210–51. Publications of the Society for Psychological Anthropology. Cambridge: Cambridge University Press, 1997.

Theissen, Gerd. *Neutestamentliche Wissenschaft vor und nach 1945: Karl Georg Kuhn und Günther Bornkamm.* Schriften der Philosophisch-historischen Klasse der Heidelberger Akademie der Wissenschaften 47. Heidelberg, Germany: Universitätsverlag Winter, 2009.

Vos, J. S. "Antijudaismus/Antisemitismus im Theologischen Wörterbuch zum Neuen Testament." *Nederlands Theologisch Tijdschrift* 35 (1984): 89–110.

Wiese, Christian. *Wissenschaft des Judentums und protestantische Theologie im wilhelminischen Deutschland: Ein Schrei ins Leere?* Schriftenreihe wissenschaftlicher Abhandlungen des Leo Baeck Instituts 61. Tübingen, Germany: Mohr Siebeck, 1999.

Wimmer, Walter. *Eschatologie der Rechtfertigung: Paul Althaus' Vermittlungsversuch zwischen uneschatologischer und nureschatologischer Theologie.* Minerva-Fachserie Theologie. Munich: Minerva-Publikation, 1979.

Wolgast, Eike. "Nationalsozialistische Hochschulpolitik und die evangelischtheologischen Fakultäten." In *Theologische Fakultäten im Nationalsozialismus,* edited by Leonore Siegele-Wenschkewitz and Carsten

Nicolaisen, 45–80. Arbeiten zur kirchlichen Zeitgeschichte, Reihe B: Darstellungen. Göttingen, Germany: Vandenhoeck & Ruprecht, 1993.

ANDERS GERDMAR is President of the Scandinavian School of Theology in Uppsala, Sweden. He is also Associate Professor in New Testament Exegesis at Uppsala University and Full Professor (at large) at Southeastern University, Lakeland, Florida. His research focuses on the Jewish matrix of the New Testament, the construction of Judaism and Hellenism in New Testament research, and the impact of Nazi ideology on Christian exegesis. He is the author of *Roots of Theological Antisemitism: German Biblical Interpretation and the Jews, from Herder and Semler to Kittel and Bultmann* (Brill, 2009).

SIX

HERMANN GRAPOW, EGYPTOLOGY, AND NATIONAL SOCIALIST INITIATIVES FOR THE HUMANITIES

THOMAS SCHNEIDER

I. INTRODUCTION

On February 25, 1935, Hermann Grapow, who was a longtime researcher for the Berlin Egyptian Dictionary project,[1] wrote to Georg Steindorff, retired Professor of Egyptology at Leipzig, about his miserable professional position: "I am everywhere on the outside; this is true. Nowhere am I in a position to say anything decisive, I do not belong to any scholarly corporation of stature.

I would like to extend my gratitude to Bernard M. Levinson for inviting me to contribute to this volume. I am in his and Christine Johnston's debt for their help in editing this chapter. I am indebted to the Social Sciences and Humanities Research Council of Canada (SSHRC) for its financial support of the project "Egyptology in the Nazi Era: National Socialism and the Profile of a Humanistic Discipline, 1933–1945." I thank Thomas Gertzen for the archival research he conducted as a SSHRC project assistant; Silke Roth and Francis Breyer for earlier research on the project; Edmund Meltzer for advisory work; and Peter Raulwing and Christine Johnston for bibliographical help. The translations of all German primary and secondary sources are my own.

1. This major effort to produce a comprehensive *Wörterbuch der ägyptischen Sprache* [Dictionary of the Egyptian Language] originated in 1897. The work was interrupted during World War II but then continued after the war until 1961. In 1992, the effort was revived, under the name *Altägyptisches Wörterbuch*, with the goal of producing an electronic dictionary and text corpus. The current iteration of the project, initiated in 2013, carries the name "Strukturen und Transformationen des Wortschatzes der ägyptischen Sprache." For more information, see the project's website (Strukturen und Transformationen des Wortschatzes der ägyptischen Sprache: Text- und Wissenskultur im Alten Ägypten [Altägyptisches Wörterbuch], "Einführung," Berlin-Brandenburgische Akademie der Wissenschaften [BBAW], accessed August 3, 2020, http://aaew.bbaw.de/projekt) and, especially, the summary of the project's history (Stefan Gunert and Ingelore Hafemann, "Abriss der Geschichte des Wörterbuch-Unternehmens," BBAW, accessed August 3, 2020, http://aaew.bbaw.de/projekt/geschichte).

Soon a 'man of fifty years,' I am sitting in my corner 'in the shadow of titans.'"[2] He added on August 15, 1935: "It is not an alluring prospect... to remain eliminated from any actual power and influence."[3] Grapow had been deliberately prevented by the discipline's leadership from assuming an academic chair in 1927 to ensure that he would continue working on the Berlin dictionary project. Five years after his 1935 letters, Grapow had not only risen to assume the Chair in Egyptology at the University of Berlin (in 1938) but also had become the Dean of its Faculty of Philosophy. In 1943, he became deputy president and acting president of the university while serving as vice president and acting president of the Prussian Academy of Sciences. From relatively humble beginnings as the son of a Rostock grocery store owner, Grapow had quickly ascended to a leading position in Nazi Germany, and he was well-connected with ministers of the National Socialist government and the state's elite.[4] The photo shown in figure 6.1, taken at the meeting of the Prussian Academy on January 27, 1944, reflects this ascent. In this photograph, Grapow converses with Prince August Wilhelm of Prussia, the son of Emperor Wilhelm II and Sturmabteilung [Storm Troopers (SA)] *Obergruppenführer* (the highest SA rank), and Lieutenant General Wilhelm Philipps, head of the Amtsgruppe für Industrielle Rüstung—Waffen und Gerät [Group for Weapons and Equipment Manufacture].

Having risen to the top of the most important university of the Reich, and the state's most significant academy, Grapow also engaged in a number of initiatives to mobilize the humanities to implement National Socialist political goals. He was active in three major Nazi academic programs: the Aktion Ritterbusch (more formally known as the War Deployment of the Humanities), the "Committee for the Study of White Africa," and the SS publication project *Studienführer* [academic study guide]. Grapow's active engagement in these programs has not previously been taken into account in assessments either of his activities or of German Egyptology in the Nazi period more generally.

---

2. Thomas L. Gertzen, *Die Berliner Schule der Ägyptologie im Dritten Reich: Begegnung mit Hermann Grapow* (Berlin: Kadmos, 2015), 84; Thomas L. Gertzen, "'In Deutschland steht Ihnen Ihre Abstammung entgegen'—Zur Bedeutung von Judentum und Konfessionalismus für die wissenschaftliche Laufbahn Georg Steindorffs und seiner Rolle innerhalb der École de Berlin," in *Georg Steindorff und die deutsche Ägyptologie im 20 Jahrhundert: Wissenshintergründe und Forschungstransfers*, ed. Susanne Voss and Dietrich Raue, Zeitschrift für ägyptische Sprache und Altertumskunde Supplement 5 (Berlin: Walter de Gruyter, 2016), 333–400 (at 368–69).

3. Gertzen, "In Deutschland," 369.

4. Gertzen, *Berliner Schule*, 45; Alexandra Cappel, "Adolf Erman und Georg Steindorff: Zur Dynamik eines Lehrer-Schüler-Verhältnisses," in Voss and Raue, *Georg Steindorff*, 7–90 (at 63–68).

Figure 6.1. Meeting of the Prussian Academy on January 27, 1944, to celebrate the Friedrichstag (in honor of Friedrich the Great) and the foundation of the Reich. *From left to right*: Prince August Wilhelm of Prussia, son of Emperor Wilhelm II and SA Obergruppenführer; Lieutenant General Wilhelm Philipps, head of the Amtsgruppe für Industrielle Rüstung—Waffen und Gerät; Hermann Grapow. Photo courtesy of the archive of the *Süddeutsche Zeitung*, Munich.

In this chapter, I contextualize Grapow's career between 1938 and 1945. I will devote particular attention to recent scholarship on the ideological transformation and political use of the humanities under National Socialism. I will argue that Grapow endorsed the Nazi state and its agenda in a prominent position for two main reasons: (1) out of personal opportunism—he sought to advance his professional and social standing; and (2) to enhance, under his leadership, the academic position of Egyptology in a future National Socialist state—which Grapow believed to be fate-given and an inevitable historical event. Previous scholarship has tended to absolve Grapow by claiming that he was not motivated by ideological agreement with the Nazi regime and did not actively exploit the political situation for his and the discipline's advancement. I will demonstrate, however, that his actions, far from being benign, could have done lasting intellectual and institutional damage to German Egyptology. For any assessment of the impact of scholars' actions on the humanities during the

Nazi period, Grapow provides a valuable case study of how important it is to understand the motives of individuals in their choice to conform to the new doctrine of the state.

II. TENDENCIES OF RECENT SCHOLARSHIP ON EGYPTOLOGY IN NAZI GERMANY

In order to establish my position, I describe some of the current debate about this key period in the history of Egyptology. German Egyptology under National Socialism is a new topic of research.[5] Only recently has there been an attempt in Egyptology to conduct research on the discipline's history in a more reflective and contextualized way. In this respect, William Carruthers has emphasized the interdependence of Egyptology and contemporary debates in culture and politics.[6] With regard to Egyptology in Nazi Germany, extensive documentary evidence allows for a proper contextualization of the Egyptological discourse and the political roles of individuals and institutions from the Weimar Republic to the postwar period. The focus of the recent scholarly debate has been on two figureheads of German Egyptology who appeared to represent opposite positions: Georg Steindorff (1861–1951), on the one hand,[7]

---

5. Thomas Schneider, "Ägyptologen im Dritten Reich: Biographische Notizen anhand der sogenannten 'Steindorff-Liste,'" *Journal of Egyptian History* 5 (2012): 119–246; Susanne Bickel et al., eds., *Ägyptologen und Ägyptologien zwischen Kaiserreich und Gründung der beiden deutschen Staaten: Reflexionen zur Geschichte und Episteme eines altertumswissenschaftlichen Fachs im 150. Jahr der Zeitschrift für Ägyptische Sprache und Altertumskunde*, Zeitschrift für ägyptische Sprache und Altertumskunde Supplement 1 (Berlin: Akademie, 2013); Thomas Schneider, "'Eine Führernatur, wie sie der neue Staat braucht!' Hermann Kees' Tätigkeit in Göttingen 1924–1945 und die Kontroverse um Entnazifizierung und Wiedereinstellung in der Nachkriegszeit," *Studien zur altägyptischen Kultur* 45 (2015): 333–81; Susanne Voss and Dietrich Raue, eds., *Georg Steindorff und die deutsche Ägyptologie im 20 Jahrhundert: Wissenshintergründe und Forschungstransfers*, Zeitschrift für ägyptisch Sprache und Altertumskunde Supplement 5 (Berlin: Walter de Gruyter, 2016); Susanne Voss, *Die Geschichte der Abteilung Kairo des DAI im Spannungsfeld deutscher politischer Interessen*, vol. 2, *1929–1966* (Rahden, Germany: Leidorf, 2017). For an overview of the entire topic, see Thomas Schneider, "Egyptology in Nazi Germany: Ideology, Scholarship, Careers" (public lecture in memory of Hans Jakob Polotsky at the Halbert Centre for Canadian Studies, Hebrew University, December 11, 2018), accessed July 4, 2020, https://openscholar.huji.ac.il/polotskynow.

6. William E. Carruthers, "Introduction: Thinking about Histories of Egyptology," in *Histories of Egyptology: Interdisciplinary Measures*, ed. William E. Carruthers (New York: Routledge, 2015), 1–15.

7. On Steindorff, see Elke Blumenthal et al., *Georg Steindorff: Stationen eines Lebens*, Kleine Schriften des Ägyptischen Museums der Universität Leipzig 11 (Berlin: Manetho, 2017); Voss and Raue, *Georg Steindorff*; and Sandra Müller, *Georg Steindorff im Spiegel seiner*

and Hermann Grapow (1885–1967), on the other.[8] Figure 6.2 shows the two in Giza, Egypt, on March 25, 1933, next to the British Egyptologist Percy E. Newberry (1869–1949). Steindorff was chairholder in Egyptology at the University of Leipzig until 1934 and a former rector of the university (1923); he was the nestor of the discipline in Germany. Of Jewish descent, he emigrated with his wife from Germany to the United States in March 1939 and was the most distinguished German Egyptologist to do so.

Spurred by the military events of 1944 that made an end of the war imminent, Steindorff composed a letter in his American exile that named Egyptologists who had proven themselves to be "men of honor" and others whom he accused for their involvement with Nazism.[9] In June 1945, he distributed copies of the letter among leading Egyptologists outside Germany. The first on his list of incriminated individuals was Hermann Grapow, about whom Steindorff wrote:

> Dr. Hermann Grapow, professor of Egyptology and member of the Berlin Academy of Science, a man of truly base character. You know him by name as a pupil and collaborator of Erman. So long as Erman lived, he posed as a democrat. Later however, especially after Sethe passed away, he showed his true colors as an arch-Nazi, and used every means to be Erman's and Sethe's successor in the professorship at the university. He persecuted everybody who did not say "Heil Hitler!" and did not follow the Nazi flag. Finally he succeeded. In my opinion there is no one who excelled Grapow in meanness, hatefulness and denunciation of those who were not of his political opinion.[10]

These accusations were repeated a year later, on June 4, 1946, when Steindorff sent a formal letter of charges against Hermann Grapow to the American authorities who had taken Grapow into custody.[11] As argued by Susanne Voss

---

Tagebücher, Kleine Schriften des Ägyptischen Museums, Georg Steindorff, der Universität Leipzig 9 (Leipzig, Germany: Leipziger Uni-Verlag, 2012). On Steindorff's conversion to Christianity and the question of his cultural identity in Germany, see now in detail Thomas L. Gertzen, *Judentum und Konfession in der Geschichte der deutschsprachigen Ägyptologie*, Europäisch-jüdische Studien 32 (Berlin: de Gruyter Oldenbourg, 2017).

    8. On Grapow, see Gertzen, *Berliner Schule*.
    9. For the history of the letter, see Susanne Voss, "Wissenshintergründe...—Die Ägyptologie als 'völkische' Wissenschaft entlang des Nachlasses Georg Steindorffs von der Weimarer Republik über die NS- bis zur Nachkriegszeit," in Voss and Raue, *Georg Steindorff*, 105–332 (at 302–17). On the possibility of differing interpretations, see Dietrich Raue "Der 'J'accuse'—Brief an John A. Wilson: Drei Ansichten von Georg Steindorff," in Bickel et al., *Ägyptologen und Ägyptologien*, 345–76.
    10. Schneider, "Ägyptologen," 145–46, 232.
    11. Gertzen, "In Deutschland," 375–79.

Figure 6.2. Group photo with Egyptologists in Giza, to honor the achievements of Selim Hassan. *In the first row, from right to left*: Banub Habachi, Hermann Grapow, Percy Newberry, Georg Steindorff, Hermann Junker, and Selim Hassan. First published in the newspaper *Al Balagh* on March 25, 1933. Newberry Collection NEWB1/02/01. ©Griffith Institute, University of Oxford.

and Thomas Gertzen, the condemnations made by Steindorff cannot, however, be assessed without considering both the political position of those individuals during the Nazi period, and Steindorff's own personal relationship with them. These judgments were also made with strategic consideration as to their potential harm and benefit to Steindorff's own interests as a protagonist of a new postwar German Egyptology.[12] In a similar vein, Steindorff's removal as the editor of the leading German Egyptological journal, the *Zeitschrift für ägyptische Sprache und Altertumskunde*, should not be seen exclusively under a political angle—Steindorff enjoyed significant privileges in the initial years of the Nazi regime[13]—but also in the context of a generational conflict within the

---

12. Voss, "Wissenshintergründe," 310, 314–15; Gertzen, *Berliner Schule*, 82–95; Voss, "In Deutschland," 365–80.

13. Voss, "Wissenshintergründe," 269–70.

discipline as to the assumption of leadership in German Egyptology.[14] Thomas Gertzen has given a detailed analysis of the increasing discord between Steindorff and Grapow, fueled by the ousting of Steindorff from academic functions that had political, personal, and disciplinary motivations.[15]

A more accurate contextualization of Steindorff by recent scholarship demonstrates that Steindorff himself had championed völkische Wissenschaft [racial scholarship] and posited the existence of a genuine Egyptian race with Nordic features in early Egypt.[16] This helped the discipline maintain its position throughout the Weimar Republic, in a difficult academic climate. Under the influence of the political events in Nazi Germany and his exile, Steindorff's position changed, and in his 1942 book, *When Egypt Ruled the East*, he assigned Semites a larger role in Egypt's cultural development. As Susanne Voss concludes: "This meant, at least partially, a return to Petrie's view of the 'dynastic race' as a 'Semitic Messianic leader' and to the *ex oriente lux* theory of the Empire, which—given the publication year of the book, 1942, and the anti-Semitic doctrine in Steindorff's lost home country—evokes a distinctly pro-Jewish intention."[17] In this context, it is essential to see that after his conversion from Judaism to Protestantism in 1885, Steindorff saw himself no longer as Jewish but as German (he even made subsequent antisemitic statements). After 1933, he did not understand that in the new Nazi legislation, Jewishness was defined biologically and no longer culturally.[18] At the same time, he offered his resignation from the Board of the Association of Saxonian Civil Servants as an act of preemptive obedience in both 1933 and 1935. Moreover, he himself excluded a Jewish author from publishing in the journal that he edited, the *Zeitschrift für ägyptische Sprache und Altertumskunde*.[19]

In his new introduction to the history of Egyptology and its methodology, Thomas Gertzen has chosen both Georg Steindorff and Hermann Grapow as model cases for the pitfalls of modern assessment.[20] Both in that volume and in a separate monograph devoted to Grapow,[21] Gertzen advocates employing an

---

14. Ibid., 270–71, 276.
15. Gertzen, "In Deutschland," 362–64.
16. Voss, "Wissenshintergründe."
17. Ibid., 301.
18. Gertzen, "In Deutschland," 389–91.
19. Voss, "Wissenshintergründe," 274–75.
20. Thomas L. Gertzen, *Einführung in die Wissenschaftsgeschichte der Ägyptologie*, Einführungen und Quellentexte zur Ägyptologie 10 (Berlin: LIT, 2017), 91–103, 187.
21. Gertzen, *Berliner Schule*.

Indizienparadigma [evidence-based paradigm][22] for historical evaluations. He argues against convicting Grapow too easily: "Moreover, it becomes apparent that we need to abstain from an extreme dichotomy between 'good' and 'evil,' between 'politically incriminated' and 'innocent,' or even 'victim of National Socialism' and 'arch-Nazi.' Hermann Grapow's scholarly biography does not allow for a simple judgment for the time of National Socialism. Further studies will further differentiate the picture worked out in this study. However, they will not change anything about the fundamental complexity of the matter."[23]

In what follows, I add aspects of Grapow's activity during the Third Reich that have not been acknowledged by Gertzen. These issues include the "War Deployment of the Humanities" initiative, the "White Africa" committee, and the SS study guide project. I will also reevaluate the evidence that was previously known and, in conclusion, challenge Gertzen's assessment of Grapow's role in the Third Reich. In a concluding section, I will review Grapow's postwar career in East Germany, where he was once again able to rise to leadership roles in the totalitarian system of the German Democratic Republic. This will further corroborate how systematically his professional career unfolded under National Socialism and the leadership role Grapow might have wished to play in the humanities had Nazi Germany won the war.

III. HERMANN GRAPOW AND THE POLITICAL AGENDAS OF NATIONAL SOCIALISM

Hermann Grapow (b. Rostock, September 1, 1885; d. Berlin, August 24, 1967) was appointed to the vacant Chair in Egyptology at Berlin on February 1, 1938, after the two preferred candidates (Hermann Junker and Hermann Kees) declined it.[24] He had filled the chair on an acting basis since August 1934. In the spring of 1937, Grapow entered the Nationalsozialistische Deutsche Arbeiterpartei [National Socialist German Workers' Party (NSDAP)][25] (where a

---

22. Ibid., 23–25, 121; Gertzen, *Einführung*, 185.
23. Gertzen, *Berliner Schule*, 136.
24. Biographical information on Grapow in Gertzen, *Berliner Schule*, 27–33; Schneider, "Ägyptologen," 157–65; and Erika Endesfelder, "Die Ägyptologie an der Berliner Universität: Zur Geschichte eines Fachgebietes," *Berichte: Humboldt-Universität zu Berlin* 8, no. 6 (1988): 42–48.
25. Peter Walther, "'Arisierung,' Nazifizierung und Militarisierung: Die Akademie im 'Dritten Reich,'" in *Die Preußische Akademie der Wissenschaften zu Berlin 1914–1945*, ed. Wolfram Fischer, Rainer Hohlfeld, and Peter Nötzoldt, Interdisziplinäre Arbeitsgruppe der Berlin-Brandenburgischen Akademie der Wissenschaften, Forschungsberichte 8 (Berlin: Akademie, 2000), 87–118 (at 89n5). The application for membership was submitted on June

moratorium on new members had been in place from 1933 until April 1937). In a letter to the Dean dated June 18, 1937, he stated that for some years before 1937, he had been an "inactive" member of a local NSDAP group.[26] According to a survey conducted by the party in 1939, he was also a "Supporting Member" of the SS.[27] Additionally, Grapow was a member of the NS Deutscher Dozentenbund [National Socialist German University Instructors' League], the NS Volkswohlfahrt [National Socialist People's Welfare Organization], and the NS Lehrerbund [the National Socialist German Teachers' League], as well as the Reichsluftschutzbund [the Reich Air Defense League] and the Kolonialbund [the Colonial League].[28] In the aforementioned letter to the Dean, he declared that since the end of 1936, he had been active as a *Blockwart* [block warden—a low Nazi Party rank in charge of a city neighborhood] and that on April 20, 1937, he swore his allegiance to the Führer. Max Vasmer (1886–1962), professor of Slavonic philology at Berlin from 1925 to 1947, saw Grapow's career in retrospect as a textbook example of a previously unsuccessful scholar who was raised into the professoriate by National Socialism.[29] There is no evidence in support of this claim, however, as there were hardly any candidates available to fill academic positions in Egyptology in Germany during the period of Grapow's rise.[30]

It is essential to see the date of his appointment in February 1938 as a turning point in Grapow's career and to differentiate between pre-1938 and post-1938 phases. Having been fortunate to be appointed to the professorship, he appears

---

25, 1937; however, May 1, 1937, was considered the date of Grapow's admission to the party. His membership in the NSDAP is also listed in Ernst Klee, *Das Kulturlexikon zum Dritten Reich: Wer war was vor und nach 1945* (Frankfurt, Germany: S. Fischer, 2007), 196; Ludmilla Hanisch, *Die Nachfolger der Exegeten: Deutschsprachige Erforschung des Vorderen Orients in der ersten Hälfte des 20 Jahrhunderts* (Wiesbaden, Germany: Harrassowitz, 2003), 135n479; and Siegward Lönnendonker, *Freie Universität Berlin: Gründung einer politischen Universität* (Berlin: Ducker and Humblot, 1988), 52n9.

26. According to the letter (as cited in Gertzen, "In Deutschland," 375n174), the local NSDAP group was that of Schmargendorf, a neighborhood of Berlin, whereas a personal questionnaire cited by Gertzen (*Berliner Schule*, 32) identifies the local group instead as "Rüdesheimer Platz" (like Schmargendorf, part of the same Berlin district of Wilmersdorf).

27. Walther, "Arisierung," 89n6; Schneider, "Ägyptologen," 158; and Gertzen, *Berliner Schule*, 91. Regarding the "Sponsoring Membership" in the SS, see John M. Steiner, *Power Politics and Social Change in National Socialist Germany* (The Hague: Mouton and Co., 1975), 51, and 230n29.

28. Gertzen, *Berliner Schule*, 91.

29. Marie-Louise Bott, *Die Haltung der Berliner Universität im Nationalsozialismus: Die Rückschau Max Vasmers 1948*, Neues aus der Geschichte der Humboldt-Universität zu Berlin 1 (Berlin: Humboldt-Universität, 2009), 101, 111–12.

30. Schneider, "Ägyptologen," 159; Gertzen, *Berliner Schule*, 53.

to have used this position of power to ascend further. In 1938, he was elected ordinary member of the academy, and in 1939, he became acting *Sekretar* [head] of the Philosophical-Historical Class. From 1940 through 1945, he served as Dean of the Faculty of Philosophy and, starting in 1943, *Prorektor* [Deputy Rector] and acting Rector of the University of Berlin. Simultaneously, he held the positions of vice president and acting president of the Prussian Academy of Sciences (see section V for more details).[31] This also meant that he had become the most politically powerful German Egyptologist, claiming primacy in German Egyptology. At the very least, this achievement required an alignment with National Socialism.

Max Vasmer, in his 1948 retrospective, characterized Grapow as initially a "respectable" National Socialist who then "swung round" and occupied high positions.[32] In his 2011 monograph on the humanities in the Third Reich, Frank-Rutger Hausmann comments on the involvement of university professors in National Socialism as follows:

> It appears that civil courage was not among the virtues of German professors, and the professors were not willing or in a position to apply the results of their research to reality. Had they done this, they would have had to realize, e.g., the groundlessness of racial studies ... and recognize the purported identity of modern Germans [Deutsche] with the Nordic Germans [Germanen] as charlatanry. Even remaining silent would very well have been possible.... After the end of the war, only few scholars confessed to their völkisch-racial statements. The majority of them pointed to "covert speaking": such passages were said to have been pronounced with a twinkle in one's eye; therefore, they would have been marked for the then reader as not serious and as required by the times.... Scholarship [*Wissenschaft*] does not allow for ambiguity. How, otherwise, should a reader, with regard to Nationalism, have differentiated between the "opponents," the "believers," and the "indifferent," if ambiguous speaking was the order of the day? ... And it is also permissible to speculate: had National Socialism been successful in the long term, then the same statements that conformed with ideology, and were later declared not to have been meant seriously, would have been used as a sign of consent. Academic publishing is not arbitrary. The authors must have been aware of the fact that utterances of that kind harmed not only their own reputation but also that of the disciplines represented by them, and that

---

31. Wolfram Fischer, Rainer Hohlfeld, and Peter Nötzoldt, "Die Berliner Akademie in Republik und Diktatur," in Fischer, Hohlfeld, and Nötzoldt, *Preußische Akademie der Wissenschaften*, 517–66 (at 561, 564).

32. Bott, *Haltung der Berliner Universität*, 77 and 175.

they were interpreted as support for the Nazi system and helped legitimize it. This is true in particular, if a scholar celebrates Hitler as the greatest German politician, assumes a 1000-year-long rule of the "Third Reich," regards the German race as the most valuable, predicts the final victory and ties to it, and justifies with it, scholarly statements.[33]

Hermann Grapow's pertinent statements in addresses given to the Prussian Academy of Sciences and his involvement in National Socialist initiatives for the humanities will have to be judged against this asessment by Hausmann, but they need equally to be qualified by Grapow's own career ambitions and his position in German Egyptology.

The War Deployment of the Humanities (Aktion Ritterbusch)

The expansion war of the Nazi regime after September 1939, and its subsequent military successes between 1939 and 1941, created euphoria among many scholars who also emphasized the contributions of academics to the war efforts. Hermann Kees, Professor of Egyptology at Göttingen and vice president (after 1939), and later president (1942–44), of the Philosophical-Historical Class of the Göttingen Academy of Arts and Sciences,[34] praised the achievements of the *Männer der Wissenschaft* [men of academia]; in particular, he lauded the scientists behind the "amazing successes" of German weapons and inventions—most of which had to remain classified until the end of the war—and the "total war" that shed a bright light on this fact:

> But there is one thing we can say, and even more so as it gives the entire people the proud confidence that the men of academia are standing on their post und fulfill tasks that nobody else can take off their shoulders: The amazing successes of the German weapons and inventions, of our planes, submarines, communication systems, and of our chemistry speak a language of unsurpasssable intensity. Now, their inventors, whose names are known to every German child—and rightly so—grew up in the discipline of German scholarship [*Wissenschaft*] which, in the most painstaking and selfless kind of work, has laid the foundations and the theoretical prerequisites for them. It is precisely the total war that sheds a bright light on this—it is the best, even

---

33. Frank-Rutger Hausmann, *Die Geisteswissenschaften im "Dritten Reich"* (Frankfurt, Germany: Vittorio Klostermann, 2011), 26–27.
34. On Kees, see Schneider, "Eine Führernatur." See further Henning Franzmeier and Anke Weber, "'Andererseits finde ich, dass man jetzt nicht so tun soll, als wäre nichts gewesen': Die deutsche Ägyptologie in den Jahren 1945–1949 im Spiegel der Korrespondenz mit dem Verlag J. C. Hinrichs," in Bickel et al., *Ägyptologen und Ägyptologien*, 128–33.

if harshest teacher for the people, an indispensable weapon it possesses in its intellectual education.[35]

This statement by Kees singled out the direct impact of scientists and engineers. By contrast, the Kriegseinsatz der Geisteswissenschaften [War Deployment of the Humanities] initiative (also called the Aktion Ritterbusch after its initiator and director, Paul Ritterbusch) was a major National Socialist project to engage the humanities at German universities in a quasi-military fight to attain superiority within Europe, to provide the military efforts a purpose, and to define the prospective order of a New Europe after the war.[36] At the same time, the project was to prepare and propel the postwar restructuring and modernization of research in the humanities, including a new National Socialist metadiscourse.[37] Between 1941 and 1944, the Kriegseinsatz published 43 monographs and 24 edited volumes with 299 contributions ranging from ancient studies to international law, authored by scholars that both adhered to and opposed National Socialism. It was initiated and led by Paul Ritterbusch (1900–1945), Professor of Law at the University of Kiel after 1933 (and Rector of the university, 1935–41). Ritterbusch was commissioned with the execution of the project on February 3, 1940. After May 1941, he assumed this task as a *Ministerialdirigent* [section head] at the Reichsministerium für Wissenschaft, Erziehung, und Volksbildung [Reich Ministry of Science, Education, and Public Instruction] while also a Professor at the University of Berlin. In his 1941 essay, "Europe and the Reich," Ritterbusch emphasized the importance of the humanities to the German war effort:

---

35. Hermann Kees, "Die Wissenschaftlichen Arbeiten der Akademie im Jahre 1941/2," in *Jahrbuch der Akademie der Wissenschaften in Göttingen für das Geschäftsjahr 1941/2* (Göttingen, Germany: Vandenhoeck & Ruprecht, 1942), 5–14 (at 8–9); cited after Hausmann, *Geisteswissenschaften*, 85.

36. Frank-Rutger Hausmann, *"Deutsche Geisteswissenschaft" im Zweiten Weltkrieg: Die "Aktion Ritterbusch" (1940–1945)*, 3rd ed., Studien zur Wissenschafts-und Universitätsgeschichte 12 (Heidelberg, Germany: Synchron Publishers, 2007); Wolfgang Bialas and Anson Rabinbach, "Introduction: The Humanities in Nazi Germany," in *Nazi Germany and the Humanities: How German Academics Embraced Nazism*, ed. Wolfgang Bialas and Anson Rabinbach (2006; Oxford: Oneworld, 2014), ix–liii (at xxx–xxxi); Hausmann, *Geisteswissenschaften*, 84–85; Utz Maas, *Sprachforschung in der Zeit des Nationalsozialismus: Verfolgung, Vertreibung, Politisierung und die inhaltliche Neuausrichtung der Sprachwissenschaft*, Studia Linguistica Germanica 124 (Berlin: Walter de Gruyter, 2016), 429–30.

37. Hausmann, "Deutsche Geisteswissenschaft," 31, 33–34, 178; cf. Ludwig Jaeger, "Siege auf dem geistigen Schlachtfeld," review of *'Deutsche Geisteswissenschaft' im Zweiten Weltkrieg– Die 'Aktion Ritterbusch' (1940–1945)*, by F.-R. Hausmann (2001), IASL online, January 16, 2001, accessed July 4, 2020, http://www.iaslonline.lmu.de/index.php?vorgang_id=2246.

Today is it evident that the war is not just a combat of the purely technological-material weapons but moreover, an intellectual combat, a combat of scholarly capability and the research capacity of peoples. To accord to the humanities greatest care is therefore a simple law for a people's self-preservation, its military strength and combat power. Besides the soldier, there stands the academic scholar with equal necessity. Soldier and scholar are bound together in the closest possible way, as this war demonstrates. By the side of the best soldier of this world there must stand the best scholar of this world. The one cannot do without the other in the war of the present time.[38]

Hermann Grapow, in an address to the academy made in 1940, envisaged the academy similarly as "a modern army of academic soldiers," although he singled out the physical service of the young academy researchers who were drafted to the Wehrmacht. He confidently expected an upturn for the humanities when "the Führer as the man of German destiny" will have brought about the victory:

> We want to be a modern army of academic soldiers! In the decisive battle for Germany's future, the Philosophical-Historical Class, within the academy, stands on the front, through its young assistants called up into the Wehrmacht: Of them, who at one point are to carry on our and so equally their own work and to complete it, and to take on new tasks, we also think in this hour. When they return to their workplaces as fellow victors, they shall resume their academic activity with full powers, and we hope that they will have their well-deserved share in the new upturn which we can expect after the victory in the second Frederician Epoch of our history, brought about by the Führer as the man of German destiny—for scholarship in general, so also especially for the humanities in our academy.[39]

In 1941–42, Grapow spoke about the crucial support that the Academy and Egyptology lent to "the battle for Germany's greatness and future security":

---

38. Eugen Ritterbusch, "Europa und das Reich: Zur Berliner Buch- und Dokumentationsschau 'Deutsche Wissenschaft im Kampf um Reich und Lebensraum'," in *Gesetzgebung und Literatur* 22 (1941/2), 157–59; cited after Hausmann, *Geisteswissenschaften*, 84.

39. Hermann Grapow, "Über die Unternehmungen der Philosophisch-historischen Klasse," in *Vier Vorträge von Th. Vahlen, E. Heymann, L. Bieberbach und H. Grapow*, Vorträge und Schriften 1 (Berlin: Preußische Akademie der Wissenschaften, 1940), 42; quoted by Wolfram Fischer, Rainer Hohlfeld, and Peter Nötzoldt, eds., *Die Preußische Akademie der Wissenschaften zu Berlin 1914–1945*, Interdisziplinäre Arbeitsgruppe der Berlin-Brandenburgischen Akademie der Wissenschaften, Forschungsberichte 8 (Berlin: Akademie, 2000), 115; Schneider, "Ägyptologen," 160; Walther, "Arisierung," 115–16.

"The Academy in its totality stands spiritually and, through its young assistants who have been called to the Wehrmacht, even physically in the battle for Germany's greatness and future security. In this engagement Egyptology is also participating in the Academy with all available resources: Dr. Erich Lüddeckens was called to arms at the end of November 1939, Dr. Rudolf Hecker in February 1940 and Doctoral Candidate Fritz Hintze in March 1940. All three are on the front."[40]

A first working meeting of German Near Eastern scholars within the War Deployment of the Humanities was convened at the Prussian Academy of Sciences in Berlin from September 30 to October 3, 1942.[41] The proceedings were published under the title *Der Orient in Deutscher Forschung* [The Orient in German research] in 1944;[42] a second volume, *Beiträge zur Arabistik, Semitistik, und Islamwissenschaft* (edited by Richard Hartmann and Helmuth Scheel), was published the same year. It brought together all the important German Near Eastern scholars who had not been victims of persecution or forced emigration; the purpose was to showcase the capacity of German Orientalistik [Near, Middle, and Far Eastern studies] even during the war.[43] The opening and concluding remarks were by Paul Ritterbusch, as the director of the project,

---

40. Hermann Grapow, transcription of oral report during the proceedings of the Prussian Academy, in *Jahrbuch der Preußischen Akademie der Wissenschaften 1941* (Berlin: Verlag der Akademie in Kommission bei Walter de Gruyter, 1942), 64; discussion by Schneider, "Ägyptologen," 160. The drafted Egyptologists mentioned here were all research assistants in the Berlin dictionary project that Grapow continued to oversee in conjunction with Danish Egyptologist Wolja Erichsen (1890–1966, an employee of the project in Berlin until 1944). Erich Lüddeckens (b. June 15, 1913; d. July 1, 2004; Professor of Egyptology at the University of Würzburg, 1964–1981) was a member of the Waffen-SS (SS number 203768); he had been conscripted in 1938 by the SS Death's Head Regiment "Ostmark" as a *Rottenführer* [SS section leader] and by 1942 was an *Unterscharführer* [junior squad commander] of the Waffen-SS assigned to the SS *Führungshauptamt* [SS headquarters] in Berlin. Rudolf Hecker (b. December 13, 1912) fell on October 24, 1943, on the eastern front. Fritz Hintze (b. April 18, 1915; d. March 30, 1993; later a Professor of Egyptology in East Berlin, 1951–1980) had been a squad leader of the Hitler Youth (since June 1, 1933) and a member of the National Socialist German Student Union (since February 1940).

41. The German title was *Arbeitstagung deutscher Orientalisten und orientalistischer Archäologen im Kriegseinsatz der Deutschen Geisteswissenschaft.* The meeting was advertised in the 1943 issue of the prominent journal, *Zeitschrift der Deutschen Morgenländischen Gesellschaft.* See also Ursula Wokoeck, *German Orientalism: The Study of the Middle East and Islam from 1800 to 1945* (London: Routledge, 2009), 199–201.

42. Hans Heinrich Schaeder, ed., *Der Orient in deutscher Forschung: Vorträge der Berliner Orientalistentagung Herbst 1942* (Leipzig, Germany: Otto Harrassowitz, 1944).

43. Hausmann, *Geisteswissenschaften*, 415.

and Walther Wüst, respectively. Walther Wüst (1901–1993), Professor of Indo-Germanic studies at Munich, was one of the most prolific politicians of higher education of the National Socialist state, Rector of the University of Munich, and president of the SS research organization Ahnenerbe [Ancestral Heritage Research Institute].[44] It is significant that among all professors of Egyptology in Germany (of whom Hermann Kees and Walther Wolf would have been other likely candidates), Hermann Grapow assumed the chairmanship of Egyptology within the War Deployment project.[45] This selection affirms his academic leadership of the discipline. He also contributed, as did fellow Egyptologist Hermann Junker, to the published proceedings[46] and to a monograph series: Deutsche Geisteswissenschaft.[47]

THE COMMITTEE FOR THE STUDY OF WHITE AFRICA

In 1941, Hermann Grapow,[48] together with Eugen Fischer (1874–1967; director of the Kaiser Wilhelm Institute for Anthropology, Human Heredity, and Eugenics and Professor of Anthropology)[49] and Diedrich Westermann (1875–1956; Professor of African languages)[50]—both fellow-members of the Prussian Academy and faculty colleagues at the university—made a request to the academy to establish an academy-wide committee for the study of White Africa.[51] The request followed a presentation to the academy on May

---

44. Maximilian Schreiber, *Walther Wüst: Dekan und Rektor der Universität München 1935–1945* (Munich: Herbert Utz, 2008).
45. Hausmann, *Geisteswissenschaften*, 214n329.
46. Hermann Grapow, "Ägyptisch: Vom Lebenslauf einer altafrikanischen Sprache," in Schaeder, *Orient in Deutscher Forschung*, 205–16; Hermann Junker, "Deutsche Ausgrabungen in Ägypten in Vergangenheit und Zukunft," in Schaeder, *Orient in Deutscher Forschung*, 82–93.
47. Michael Grüttner and Heinz-Elmar Tenorth, *Geschichte der Universität Unter den Linden*, vol. 2, *Die Berliner Universität zwischen den Weltkriegen, 1918–1945* (Berlin: Akademie, 2012).
48. On Grapow's role as a research desideratum, see Gertzen, *Berliner Schule*, 91n50.
49. Niels C. Lösch, *Rasse als Konstrukt: Leben und Werk Eugen Fischers* (Frankfurt, Germany: Peter Lang, 1997).
50. Helma Pasch, "Westermann, Diedrich Hermann," *Biographisch-Bibliographisches Kirchenlexikon* 24 (2005): 1531–47.
51. Lösch, *Rasse als Konstrukt*, 377; Peter Rohrbacher, *Die Geschichte des Hamiten-Mythos*, Beiträge zur Afrikanistik 71 (Vienna: AFRO-PUB 2002), 202–3; Hans-Walter Schmuhl, *Grenzüberschreitungen: Das Kaiser-Wilhelm-Institut für Anthropologie, menschliche Erblehre, und Eugenik, 1927–1945* (Göttingen, Germany: Wallstein, 2005), 436–43 (published in English as *The Kaiser Wilhelm Institute for Anthropology, Human Heredity, and Eugenics,*

8, 1941, by Eugen Fischer that was titled "Problems of White Africa." Fischer has been described as "maybe the most influential anthropologist and racial scholar of the Weimar Republic and the Third Reich" and, therefore, a "trailblazer of the lethal racial ideology."[52] In his presentation, Fischer outlined the opportunities and tasks that resulted from the new political and military situation. On February 11, 1941, the first German troops had arrived in Tripoli to support the Italians, which was the start of the German campaign in North Africa. Fischer emphasized how fundamentally different the Africa north of the Sahara was from "the rest of Africa, the Africa of negroes, Black Africa," not only in terms of its natural environment but in particular its "races and human cultures." He argued that North Africa should be considered part of the European Mediterranean and included in all research questions related to Europe. Fischer's concept of a blond North African "Western race" contrasted with the more standard "Nordic" hypothesis dominant in Nazi doctrine. He expressed concern that, with the modern development of North

---

1927–1945: Crossing Boundaries. Boston Studies in the Philosophy of Science 259 [Berlin: Springer, 2008], 339–40); Petra Hoffmann, *Weibliche Arbeitswelten in der Wissenschaft: Frauen an der Preußischen Akademie der Wissenschaften zu Berlin, 1890–1945* (Bielefeldt, Germany: transcript, 2011), 71; Ekkehard Ellinger, *Deutsche Orientalistik zur Zeit des Nationalsozialismus, 1933–1945* (Edingen-Neckarhausen, Germany: Deux Mondes, 2006), 148; Karla Poewe, "Liberalism, German Missionaries and National Socialism," in *Mission und Macht im Wandel politischer Orientierungen: Europäische Missionsgesellschaften in politischen Spannungsfeldern in Afrika und Asien zwischen 1800 und 1945*, ed. Ulrich van der Heyden and Holger Stoecker, Missionsgeschichtliches Archiv 10 (Stuttgart, Germany: Franz Steiner, 2005), 633–61 (at 643); Udo Mischek, "Autorität außerhalb des Fachs—Diedrich Westermann und Eugen Fischer," in *Ethnologie und Nationalsozialismus*, ed. Bernhard Streck (Gehren, Germany: Escher, 2000), 69–82 (at 77); Hans-Walter Schmuhl, "'Neue Rehobother Bastardstudien': Eugen Fischer und die Anthropometrie zwischen Kolonialforschung und nationalsozialistischer Rassenpolitik," in *Anthropometrie: Zur Vorgeschichte des Menschen nach Maß*, ed. Gert Theile (Munich: Wilhelm Fink, 2005), 277–306; Fischer, Hohlfeld, and Nötzoldt, "Berliner Akademie," 525–26; Holger Stoecker, *Afrikawissenschaften in Berlin von 1919 bis 1945: Zur Geschichte und Topographie eines wissenschaftlichen Netzwerkes* (Stuttgart, Germany: Franz Steiner, 2008), 245; Peter Rohrbacher, "Dominik Josef Wölfel (1888–1963), Sprachwissenschafter, Afrikanist, Völkerkundler (2010)," Afrikanist, accessed July 4, 2020, http://www.afrikanistik.at.

52. Ulrich Marsch, review of *Rasse als Konstrukt: Leben und Werk Eugen Fischers*, by Niels C. Loesch, H-Soz-u-Kult (July 1998), H-Net Reviews, University of Michigan Department of History, accessed July 4, 2020, http://www.h-net.org/reviews/showrev.php?id=16100. See also Werner Brill, "Sonderpädagogik und Behinderung im Nationalsozialismus," in *Die Berliner Universität in der NS-Zeit*, vol. 2, *Fachbereiche und Fakultäten*, ed. Rüdiger vom Bruch, Christoph Jahr, and Rebecca Schaarschmidt (Stuttgart, Germany: Franz Steiner, 2005), 229–42 (at 239–40).

Africa through rail and air traffic, precious cultural and linguistic evidence was threatened. Fischer justified his request to form a committee on White Africa as follows:

> After the war, the development of the Sahara through highways, flight connections, and the only just started construction of a trans-Saharan railway will certainly be taken up anew and more intensely so. This will entail an increasing destruction of the preserved evidence of the white African past. Since we will make, in the future, extensive use of the trans-Saharan routes for our colonies, but more particularly, since the problems of White Africa are so closely tied to the problems of race, prehistory and language that are so dear to us, German scholarship can and must not flinch from this task.[53]

The subsequently formed committee consisted of the applicants (Grapow, Fischer, and Westermann); Hans Stille (1876–1966), geologist; Richard Hartmann (1881–1965), Professor of Islamic Studies; Norbert Krebs (1876–1947), Professor of Geography; and Helmuth Scheel (1895–1967), nonacademic and director of the Prussian Academy. Eugen Fischer served as its president.

Fischer propagated the significance of genetic and racial research for the "momentous expansion of the Greater Germanic Reich."[54] Like Fischer, several of the committee members had been deeply involved in the ideology and initiatives of the Third Reich. Norbert Krebs had championed the idea of *Lebensraum im Osten* [living space in the East],[55] while Richard Hartmann was a consultant to the SS and taught at the school opened in Dresden by Amin al-Husseini, grand mufti of Jerusalem, which prepared imams for service in the SS and regular Muslim units.[56] On the other hand, Hans Stille

---

53. Lösch, *Rasse als Konstrukt*, 377.
54. Brill, "Sonderpädagogik," 239.
55. Oliver Rathkolb et al., "Straßennamen Wiens seit 1860 als 'Politische Erinnerungsorte': Forschungsprojektendbericht (2013)," Vienna, July 2013, accessed July 4, 2020 (at 285–87), https://www.wien.gv.at/kultur/abteilung/pdf/strassennamenbericht.pdf; David Thomas Murphy, *The Heroic Earth: Geopolitical Thought in Weimar Germany, 1918–1933* (Kent, OH: Kent State University Press, 1997), 242.
56. David Motadel, *Islam and Nazi Germany's War* (Cambridge, MA: Harvard University Press, 2014), 32; Barry Rubin and Wolfgang G. Schwanitz, *Nazis, Islamists, and the Making of the Modern Middle East* (New Haven, CT: Yale University Press, 2014), 155. Note that Joachim Lerchenmüller (*"Keltischer Sprengstoff": Eine wissenschaftsgeschichtliche Studie über die Keltologie von 1900 bis 1945* [Tübingen, Germany: Max Niemeyer, 1997], 355n20), confuses this Richard Hartmann (b. August 6, 1881) with a different Richard Hartmann (b. September 21, 1901) who was an SS *Sturmbannführer*.

would contend with Grapow for the presidency of the Prussian Academy in 1943–44; however, he did not receive support from the Ministry of Education (see section V.). The membership on the committee also established networks that would remain valuable after the war: Westermann and Hartmann, with Grapow, would establish the Institut für Orientforschung [Institute for Near Eastern Research] in East Berlin. Scheel, in turn, defended Grapow after the war (see section VI.).

The Kommission für die Erforschung Weißafrikas [Committee for the Study of White Africa], as it was then called, met twice in 1942 (February 12 and July 9). The decision was made to publish a large opus relating to the racial and anthropological questions of white Africa, necessitating the formation of working groups on culture, anthropology, prehistory, history, religion, and languages.[57] The concept of "White Africa" itself was based on the work of the Viennese anthropologist and linguist Dominik Josef Wölfel (1888–1963), who had introduced this term first in 1939 at the instigation of Eugen Fischer. Wölfel had been a student of Westermann and later assisted the Committee on White Africa as a research collaborator.[58] At the very time when the committee was established, research on "White Africa" was also pursued in the SS Ahnenerbe by Otto Rössler.[59] Rössler was ultimately appointed director of a newly established Lehr- und Forschungsstätte für nordwestafrikanische Kulturwissenschaft [Teaching and Research Institute for North African Cultural Studies] on January 20, 1943.[60] The concept of "White Africa" integrates elements such as Georg Moeller's hypothesis of the diffusion of a Nordic race through Libyan North Africa to Egypt, which was influential in Egyptology in the 1920s and 1930s.[61] Although Lösch maintains that the committee's genesis was mainly an expression of the euphoria after the initial military successes, it subscribed to

---

57. Fischer, Hohlfeld, and Nötzoldt, "Berliner Akademie," 525–30. In contrast, Lösch (*Rasse als Konstrukt*, 377) writes that the committee did not pursue any significant further activities as a consequence of the military developments.

58. Rohrbacher, "Dominik Josef Wölfel"; Rathkolb et al., "Straßennamen Wiens," 297–99.

59. Gerd Simon, Horst Junginger, and Ulrich Schermaul, "Vom Antisemiten zum Semitistik-Professor: Chronologie Rössler, Otto," Universität Tübingen, first research 1986, provisional final version June 8, 2007, introduction and addition in November 2010, accessed July 4, 2020, https://homepages.uni-tuebingen.de/gerd.simon/ChrRoessler.pdf; Schneider, "Ägyptologen," 229n442.

60. And maybe in competition with the committee: Rössler attempted to force Wölfel to release his research materials on the Canary Islanders and their language, which Wölfel was able to prevent.

61. Voss, "Wissenshintergründe," 120–29.

a "racist and expansionist-colonialist ideology,"[62] and was intended to broker racial studies for the Prussian Academy.[63]

THE SS STUDY GUIDE PROJECT

Grapow had also consented to contribute an introductory volume on Egyptology for the series Schriftenreihe zur Einführung in das gesamte wissenschaftliche Studium: Der Studienführer [Series of introduction guides for the entire domain of academic study: The study guide]; his intended volume carried the number 34B.[64] The series had been developed in 1938 by leading SS officials in collaboration with the Reichsstudentenwerk [Reich's Association for Student Affairs] and the Heidelberg academic publishing house Carl Winter. The goal was to publish around three hundred volumes to outline the curriculum and contents for all degree programs offered within the territory of the German Reich. Each volume would provide the discipline's pertinent bibliography "with a concise but academically and ideologically reliable assessment."[65] The series was organized into eight sections (I: Cultural Studies; II: Law and Economics; III: Natural Sciences and Mathematics; IV: Medicine and Pharmacy; V: Agriculture and Forestry; VI: Engineering; VII: Military Studies; VIII: International Geography). The chairman of the project, its general editor, and the section editors were all, with one exception, high-ranking SS Officers.[66] The editor for Section I (Cultural Studies), to which Grapow's volume was assigned, was Walther Wüst, SS *Oberführer* and president of the SS Ahnenerbe. Indeed, the SS organization was almost certainly, as Jagemann suspects, the driving force behind the project. It appears to have been the intention of the editors to recruit highly respected university professors as study guide authors in order to minimize the resistance to ideological indoctrination in the individual disciplines. As of October 1944, 10 study guides had been published, 10 guides were in press, 21 manuscripts had been submitted to the publisher, and a total of 102 authors had been issued contracts to prepare the full 108 volumes.[67] Out of the several scholars who held chairs in Egyptology, it was Grapow who was enlisted for the study guide. This undertaking confirms his intent to assert

---

62. Hoffmann, *Weibliche Arbeitswelten*, 71.
63. Ellinger, *Deutsche Orientalistik*, 148.
64. Norbert Jagemann, *"Der Studienführer": Zur Wissenschaftspolitik der SS*, Studien zur Zeitgeschichte 47 (Hamburg, Germany: Dr. Kovač, 2005), 146.
65. Jagemann, *Studienführer*, 146.
66. Ibid., 64 chart 1.
67. Ibid., 119.

control over the discourse in German Egyptology and to preserve Egyptology as a discipline within the Reich's humanities.[68] His appointment likely also reflects his commitment to the goals of the Studienführer initiative.[69]

IV. THREE CASES OF HERMANN GRAPOW'S PREEMPTIVE OBEDIENCE IN THE THIRD REICH

Grapow's role in the Third Reich has been assessed in past scholarship with a focus on his personal involvement in cases where colleagues were persecuted by the Nazi regime, most comprehensively by Thomas Gertzen in his 2015 book on Grapow. Gertzen concluded that these persecutions were not an indication of Grapow's political views but, at most, a survival strategy. I present them here again to suggest that, together with Grapow's political offices and his involvement in the humanities initiatives, they contribute to a consistent picture of Grapow's complicity with the Nazi regime and his political opportunism in furthering his career.

The most famous of these cases is the removal of Georg Steindorff in 1937 from the editorship of the leading German Egyptological journal, *Zeitschrift für ägyptische Sprache und Altertumskunde*.[70] Grapow pressured Steindorff to resign from the editorial position, which, in Steindorff's own words, was a "stab in the back" that created an irretrievable rift between the once close colleagues.[71] After the war, Steindorff discredited Grapow as an "arch-Nazi" and "one of the worst academic criminals" who, as a scholar, "violated all ethical principles that are valid in scholarship."[72] As was indicated previously, recent scholarship suggests that there were two reasons for these attacks: first, Steindorff's bitterness

---

68. See here also the remark by Anne C. Nagel, *Hitlers Bildungsreformer: Das Reichsministerium für Wissenschaft, Erziehung und Volksbildung 1934–1945* (Frankfurt, Germany: Fischer, 2012), 287: "Small specialized disciplines such as Art History, Egyptology and Oriental Studies with less direct practical applicability survived because they were prestigious and because it was rightly feared that neglecting them would harm the reputation of the German Reich abroad. However, according to the new authorities, the times of *l'art pour l'art*, of scholarship for the sake of scholarship, were over."

69. In this context, it can also be mentioned that Grapow attended the opening of the German Academic Institute in Budapest, one of the institutes established by the Nazi state to promote German culture abroad (Hausmann, "Auch im Krieg," 154n18).

70. Alexandra Cappel, "Adolf Erman und Georg Steindorff," 8–13; Gertzen, "In Deutschland," 365–80; Alexandra Cappel, *Berliner Schule*, 82–85.

71. Gertzen, *Berliner Schule*, 82–83.

72. Ibid., 85–86.

about his 1937 removal and, second, his effort to prevent Grapow from assuming a leading role in postwar Egyptology.

The rift between Steindorff and Grapow was mutual: after the war, Grapow spoke about Steindorff disparagingly as "the angered old rabbi from USA."[73] Steindorff equally accused Grapow of benefiting from his resignation in 1937, which may be a truthful assessment—while the Nazi measures of persecution provided the context for Steindorff's removal, they also gave Grapow a convenient opening for a generational change in Egyptology. The same exploitation of a political circumstance for Grapow's personal benefit and the future configuration of German Egyptology can be seen in 1939, when Grapow intervened with the Nazi minister of the interior, Wilhelm Frick, to facilitate Steindorff's emigration (whereas Steindorff's sister Lucie was deported and murdered in 1942).[74]

It is noteworthy that personal motives and the interests of a national German Egyptology, rather than Grapow's political views, may also have been responsible for Grapow's denunciation of the Belgian Egyptologist Jean Capart[75] (1877–1947; in 1940, president of the Académie royale de Belgique [Royal Academy of Belgium]) to the Nazi Secret State Police, the Gestapo, in 1940.[76] In the *Chronique d'Égypte* of 1940, Jean Capart referenced Hermann Grapow's obituary of Adolf Erman and added the note: "What this scholar [Erman] has done for Egyptology and for his country has unfortunately not spared him the measures that darkened his last days." Through Theodor Vahlen, president of the academy and SS *Brigadeführer* [brigadier general], Grapow requested a clarification of who was behind these "false and unjust rumors that are injurious to the Third Reich and have for years been circulated by the Jewish, anti-National Socialist side." He also sought clarification as to whether Capart's statements were written after the German conquest of Belgium, which would suggest that they should "be evaluated as covert sabotage." Although Grapow

---

73. Schneider, "Ägyptologen," 163–64; Cappel, "Adolf Erman," 11; Gertzen, "In Deutschland," 373, 379n189.
74. Gertzen misunderstands the point I was trying to make (see references in note 73). I do not understand Grapow's assistance itself as an attempt to portray himself as a savior figure. Rather, the later portrayal of the help he provided in 1939 as given in his biography was a deliberate move to recast himself as a helper of Steindorff during the Nazi period.
75. Arpag Mekhitarian, "Capart (Jean-François-Désiré) 21.2.1877–16.6.1947," in *Biographie Nationale: Dernier supplément* 16 (1985–1986): 140–51 (without mention of this event).
76. The description of this event follows Stefan Rebenich, "Adolf Erman und die Berliner Akademie der Wissenschaften," in *Ägyptologie als Wissenschaft: Adolf Erman (1854–1937) in seiner Zeit*, ed. Bernd Schipper (Berlin: Walter de Gruyter, 2006), 340–70 (at 363–65), and Gertzen, *Berliner Schule*, 101–8.

did not consider the latter to be likely, the information was sent on to Heinrich Himmler, SS *Reichsführer* and head of the Gestapo.

Capart's statements during his interrogation in Belgium, documented by a protocol signed by the head of the Reich's Main Security Office, Reinhard Heydrich, led to a sharp reaction by Grapow. In this interrogation, Capart insinuated that Erman's Egyptological colleagues (in particular Grapow) had personally told him how dissatisfied Erman was with the political events since the Nazi takeover of power. Grapow was, however, "not convinced of the harmlessness of Mr. Capart in this matter." The director of the Berlin Academy, Helmuth Scheel, was sent to Brussels and reported Capart's "hostile attitude to Germany" to the Reich's education minister, Bernhard Rust. In the end, Capart did not face more serious consequences but had to apologize to Grapow for his statements. Thomas Gertzen plausibly suggests that the motivation for Grapow to denounce Capart was not his political position but rather the situation of competition between German and Belgian Egyptology and the wish to demonstrate his own loyalty to the Nazi state.[77]

A third example of Grapow's preemptive obedience is the case of the nationally minded Latinist Eduard Norden (1868–1941), in which Grapow showed not only his unwillingness to interfere with the persecution of a close faculty colleague but also his eagerness to dispel all doubts about his loyalty to the Führer.[78] Norden, Rector of the university in 1928 and the recipient of an honorary doctorate from Harvard University in 1936 as "the most famous Latinist in the world,"[79] had exuberantly welcomed Hitler's seizure of power. He was of Jewish descent and was thus forced to retire in 1935 and excluded from all academic institutions. Shortly before the outbreak of war in 1939, he succeeded in fleeing to Zurich. When one of Norden's former students, Horst Ducki, in a courageous petition to Adolf Hitler, demanded that Norden's termination be revoked and that he be declared a "full Aryan" with all rights and duties (on October 25, 1939), he named, among others, Hermann Grapow as a witness who would intercede on Norden's behalf. Instead Grapow immediately distanced himself from this petition in a written statement sent on October 31, 1939, to both the president and the director of the Academy of Arts and Sciences, the Rector of the university, and the local head of the NS Deutscher

---

77. Gertzen, *Berliner Schule*, 103–8.
78. Wilt Aden Schröder, *Der Altertumswissenschaftler Eduard Norden (1868–1941): Das Schicksal eines deutschen Gelehrten jüdischer Abkunft. Mit den Briefen Eduard Nordens an seinen Lehrer Hermann Usener aus den Jahren 1891 bis 1902*, Spudasmata 73 (Hildesheim, Germany: Georg Olms, 1999), 49, 174–75, 177–78; Hanisch, *Nachfolger der Exegeten*, 212.
79. Schröder, *Eduard Norden*, 43.

Dozentenbund [National Socialist German University Instructors' League]. His behavior shows, in Gertzen's view, a high degree of uncertainty and concern about his own person and position as the decisive factors, disguised by declarations of loyalty to the regime.[80] It is obvious that Grapow was anxious to quickly avert what could jeopardize his career by reaffirming his loyalty. He certainly did not want to put to the test how politically stable his position was at the University of Berlin.

V. BECOMING A TITAN: CAREER AND COMPLICITY

The necessity to assess careers during the Third Reich in a carefully contextualized way and with sufficient supporting evidence has been emphasized in recent scholarship. Therefore, the assessment made here examines Grapow's self-presentation as a National Socialist along with his ascent to a position of political power, social prestige, and intellectual authority. I demonstrate that this ascent, which also meant gaining primacy in his own field of Egyptology, was a major motivation for Grapow. Starting in 1938, Grapow stepped out of the corner, where he had been sitting in the shadow of titans, to become a titan himself, within the higher education landscape of the Third Reich and in Egyptology, more particularly.

From a letter of Danish Egyptologist Hans Osterfeld Lange (1863–1943) to Adolf Erman dated May 9, 1934, we learn that Hermann Grapow was "obsessed by the new course"[81] and, according to a letter from Georg Steindorff to Adolf Erman from May 16, 1933, that he was "unreservedly enthused with the academic events in the country."[82] As we saw previously, Grapow had been an "inactive" member of a local NSDAP group since 1933, a formal party member since 1937, a "Supporting Member" of the SS, and a member of three additional Nazi organizations (the NS Dozentenbund, the NS Lehrerbund, and the NS Volkswohlfahrt). Grapow was also active in nonparty organizations like the Reich Air Defense League and the Colonial League. While there is no evidence that he had been politically active before 1933, he stated himself that since the end of 1936, he had been active on behalf of the party as a Blockwart. Grapow may also have been awarded the golden party badge of the NSDAP,

---

80. Gertzen, *Berliner Schule*, 96–101.
81. Hans Kloft, Thomas Elsmann, and Sabine Gorsemann, eds., *Der Nachlaß Adolf Erman*, Veröffentlichungen der Abteilung Gesellschaftswissenschaften 38 (Bremen, Germany: Universität Bremen/Bibliothek, 1982), 51.
82. Ibid., 44.

which was conferred for merits on behalf of the Nazi Party.[83] Gertzen argues that Steindorff's accusation made in his 1946 letter—that Grapow "persecuted everybody who did not say 'Heil Hitler!' and did not follow the Nazi flag" in his path to success—was probably correct, since these were the responsibilities of a Blockwart.[84]

Recent scholarship on the Berlin Academy during the Third Reich has repeatedly emphasized that the resignation of its leadership on December 22, 1938 (including secretary Max Planck), cleared the way for a National Socialist leadership obligated to the Führer Principle [*Führerprinzip*] and, with it, *Gleichschaltung* [alignment].[85] The new leadership consisted of "Nazi activists," including Hermann Grapow, and was installed by the Ministry of Education without proffering the actual academy members a voice in the decision.[86] What this activism could have meant in the case of Grapow is not clear; however, it may have included pronouncements such as Grapow's defense of the newly imposed National Socialist president of the academy and SS Brigadeführer, Theodor Vahlen: "If Mr. Planck imagines that only eighty-year-old Nobel Laureates are in a position to represent the interests of German scholarship abroad in a worthy fashion, he should not forget that the interests of German

---

83. Frank Biermann and Ralf Herpolsheimer, *Zeitungswissenschaftler im Dritten Reich: Sieben biographische Studien* (Cologne, Germany: Hayit, 1984), 255. Grapow may be wearing the badge on the photograph reprinted here as figure 6.1, but due to the figure's limited resolution, a definitive confirmation is not possible.

84. Gertzen, *Berliner Schule*, 91–92.

85. Dieter Hoffmann, "Das Verhältnis der Akademie zu Republik und Diktatur: Max Planck als Sekretär," in Fischer, Hohlfeld, and Nötzoldt, *Preußische Akademie der Wissenschaften*, 53–85 (at 79–80). Within this volume, see the discussion of Gleichschaltung provided by Bernard M. Levinson, "Gerhard von Rad's Struggle against the Nazification of the Old Testament."

86. Peter Nötzoldt, "Die Akademien der Wissenschaften zwischen Kaiser-Wilhelm-Gesellschaft und Notgemeinschaft der Deutschen Wissenschaft," *Sitzungsberichte der Leibniz-Sozietät der Wissenschaften zu Berlin* 98 (2008): 83–104 (at 98–99); Fischer, Hohlfeld, and Nötzoldt, "Berliner Akademie," 525–26. See further the critical self-reflection of its own history by the Berlin Academy of Sciences in Peter Nötzoldt, ed., *Vertrieben aus rassistischen Gründen: Die Akademie der Wissenschaften 1933–45. Ausstellung im Rahmen des Berliner Themenjahres 2013 "Zerstörte Vielfalt: Berlin 1933–1945"* (Berlin: Berlin-Brandenburgische Akademie der Wissenschaften, 2014), 102. Finally, Rolf Winau notes that under Vahlen, and then Grapow, the academy was increasingly integrated into the National Socialist *Wissenschaftssystem*. See his "Die Preußische Akademie der Wissenschaften im Dritten Reich," in *Die Elite der Nation im Dritten Reich: Das Verhältnis von Akademien und ihrem wissenschaftlichen Umfeld zum Nationalsozialismus*, ed. Eduard Seidler, Christoph J. Scriba, and Wieland Berg, Acta historica Leopoldina 22 (Leipzig, Germany: Barth, 1995), 75–88 (at 83).

scholarship at home, and insofar as they affect our Academy, at this time are safeguarded precisely by you [Theodor Vahlen]."[87]

On March 25, 1943, Education Minister Bernhard Rust determined that an acting president should lead the academy until the election of a president; Grapow was proposed by Ludwig Bieberbach (1886–1982; member of the SA and the NSDAP, founder of "German mathematics," and active in the expulsion of Jewish faculty from the university) as a candidate. During April 1943, an agreement could not be reached between the academy and the ministry about a president, as the academy's preferred candidate, geologist Hans Stille (1876–1966), did not have the ministry's approval. Instead, Grapow was elected vice president on May 6, 1943. When, in the spring of 1944, it appeared as though Stille could defeat Grapow in an election for the presidency, Minister Rust declared through Grapow on July 13, 1944, that he "prohibits any activity that could relate to the election of a president." This allowed Grapow to remain acting president until the end of the war (see fig. 6.3).[88]

As noted earlier, Grapow praised "the Führer as the man of German destiny" who would bring about the "second Frederician epoch of our history" in meetings of the academy. He also used similar wording in a dedication during the presentation of the complete edition of the letters of Frederick the Great to the Minister Rust.[89] Grapow and Rust were good personal friends,[90] and according to a letter from Grapow cited later in this chapter (of September 20, 1945), he

---

87. Stefan Rebenich, "Zwischen Anpassung und Widerstand? Die Berliner Akademie der Wissenschaften von 1933 bis 1945," in *Antike und Altertumswissenschaft in der Zeit von Faschismus und Nationalsozialismus: Kolloquium Universität Zürich, 14–17 Oktober 1998*, ed. Beat Näf (Mandelbachtal, Germany: Edition Cicero, 2001), 203–44 (at 206). See further Schneider, "Ägyptologen," 162–63.

88. Fischer, Hohlfeld, and Nötzoldt, "Berliner Akademie," 563–64; Johannes Irmscher, "Johannes Stroux, der erste Präsident der Deutschen Akademie der Wissenschaften zu Berlin," *Sitzungsberichte der Leibniz-Sozietät* 15, no. 7 (1996): 37–41 (at 37). Gertzen has viewed these events as a compromise between the traditional right of the academy to elect a president and the Führerprinzip (*Berliner Schule*, 76). However, Grapow absented himself from a visit of academy members on April 7, 1943, during which they requested that the ministry not impose its candidate—he was "not keen to participate in this"—and Minister Rust was not available for the meeting. In turn, Grapow, Bieberbach, and Academy Director Helmuth Scheel had a meeting with Rust on April 12 to discuss further procedure, and on May 6, Grapow succeeded to be elected and to assume the role of acting president. De facto, Rust had been able to install his candidate Grapow in the academy's top position.

89. Gertzen, *Berliner Schule*, 78n13; Laetitia Boehm, "Langzeitvorhaben als Akademieaufgabe: Geschichtswissenschaft in Berlin und in München," in Fischer, Hohlfeld, and Nötzoldt, *Preußische Akademie der Wissenschaften*, 391–434 (at 409).

90. Winau, "Preußische Akademie," 88.

Figure 6.3. Meeting of the Prussian Academy on January 27, 1944, to celebrate the Friedrichstag and the foundation of the Reich. Grapow at the swastika-festooned lectern. Photo courtesy of the archive of the *Süddeutsche Zeitung*, Munich.

also entertained relations with other ministers and with the highest officials of the Nazi regime.[91]

Anti-Jewish resentments by Grapow are well documented. In his accusation of Capart, he spoke out against "unjust rumors that are injurious to the Third Reich and have for years been circulated by the Jewish, anti–National Socialist side." With regard to Steindorff, Grapow admonished a colleague, saying: "You are not possibly going to believe this Jew more than myself!"[92] In the statement

---

91. Rudolf Mentzel (1900–1987; president of the *Deutsche Forschungsgesellschaft* and head of the Amt Wissenschaft [Office for Research] in the Ministry of Education; brigadier general in the SS); Minister of Propaganda Joseph Goebbels (1897–1945); Hjalmar Schacht (1877–1970; president of the Reichsbank, 1933–39; minister of the economy, 1933–37, Minister without Portfolio until 1943); Nazi chief ideologue Alfred Rosenberg (1893–1946); and Minister of the Interior Wilhelm Frick (1877–1946).

Grapow also indicates that he helped Steindorff emigrate through the minister of the interior, Wilhelm Frick, and that he was also informed in strict confidence about the intention of the Ministry of Propaganda to remove Steindorff from his editorships.

92. Gertzen, "In Deutschland," 379; see also Franzmeier and Weber, "Andererseits finde ich," 138.

Grapow made in the case of Norden, his final words subordinate his own views to a strong declaration of loyalty to the Nazi regime: "As far as I myself am concerned, I probably don't need to explicitly emphasize my own view, as a member of the party and political leader sworn to the Führer."[93] Whether this was simply a "survival strategy"[94]—one that merely adopted "Nazi appearances" as a cover[95]—or a statement of "absolute loyalty"[96] that requires no further qualification remains to be seen. Suffice it to say for now that contemporary witnesses perceived Grapow to be *NS-gläubig* [a believer in Nazism].[97] Similarly, close allies of his in the academy (such as Ludwig Bieberbach) were self-declared Nazis and antisemites.

In a letter to Steindorff on February 25, 1935, Grapow presented the National Socialist regime as inevitable: "It has been determined legally to be so in general! The times have simply become different! It has to be accepted as fate!" His loyalty and need to adapt to the new situation can be seen thus as the consequence of his acceptance of this "fate." This overarching concern to maintain the impression of being a loyal National Socialist, evident also in Grapow's handling of the cases of Steindorff and Capart, shines through in his "Epistle of a man disappearing in darkness," which he wrote to publisher Leopold Klotz on January 29, 1946. Here Grapow recalls the "personal danger of being perceived as an anti-Nazi":

> Nonetheless I have cause to be thankful to God that both dear ones could die in peace [Grapow's sister and father in January 1945, TS] and I could still take care of the last things, and that they did not learn anything of all this tremendousness, also not of the following letter of the present Rector of the University of Berlin, who writes to the full Professor, the devoted Dean and Deputy Rector of many years in the following manner (NB without any personal word at all, either from him himself or from the Dean, Mr. Deubner![98]): "The Rector and Senate of the University have taken the measures that are necessary for the dismissal of all erstwhile members of the NSDAP and of the candidates for membership. In pursuance of these measures, you are therefore dismissed, effective immediately. The Rector

---

93. Gertzen, *Berliner Schule*, 100.
94. Ibid., 101.
95. Ibid., 80. For "fate" quote in next paragraph, Gertzen, *Deutschland*, 326.
96. Schneider, "Ägyptologen," 159.
97. Hans Dieter Schäfer, *Das gespaltene Bewusstsein* (Göttingen, Germany: Wallstein 2009), 236; cf. also Wolfdietrich Hartung and Werner Scheler, eds., *Die Berliner Akademie nach 1945: Zeitzeugen berichten*, Abhandlungen der Leibniz-Sozietät 6 (Berlin: Trafo, 2001), 78 (Grapow was a staunch National Socialist).
98. The philologist and historian of religion Ludwig Deubner (1877–1946).

signed Stroux."⁹⁹ Thus! So this is the gratitude for the fact that often enough I took a stand against the Party for the whole and its members [Grapow then singles out how, after having been informed that the Ministry of Propaganda wanted to remove Steindorff forcefully from the editorships of the *Zeitschrift für ägyptische Sprache und Altertumskunde* and the *Urkunden des ägyptischen Altertums*, he was able to persuade him to renounce "with composure and voluntarily what could no longer stay in his hands"].... God knows how many such commissions I had to assume in the course of the years, confidentially and often in personal danger of being perceived as an anti-Nazi.¹⁰⁰

In addition to his contacts within the inner circle of the Nazi regime and other high officials of the Nazi state through his official positions, Grapow was, through the three National Socialist initiatives discussed previously, part of a network of high SS officials who propagated racist and expansionist ideologies. In his collaboration with them, he supported those ideologies, at least in a passive manner. As part of the senior leadership of the Prussian Academy from 1938 and the University of Berlin from 1940, and then as the acting president of both institutions (1943–45), he lent support to the Nazi state in an extremely prominent way. As argued by Wolfgang Mommsen, even the academy was an effective instrument of Nazi propaganda.¹⁰¹

In her 1988 overview of the history of Egyptology at the University of Berlin during the Third Reich, Erika Endesfelder spoke in Grapow's defense: "Although Grapow had never abused his prominent position during the Third Reich in a manner that was malicious and damaging to scholarship, it was self-evident that after the defeat of fascism, at the reopening of the university, he could no longer be tolerated in active university teaching service."¹⁰²

This absolving interpretation needs to be criticized. Grapow was actively involved and (in the case of the Committee for the Study of White Africa) even initiated projects in support of National Socialist, racial, and colonial agendas. His work should indeed be assessed as "malicious and damaging to scholarship." It should also be pointed out that Endesfelder, prior to her professorship in Egyptology at East Berlin, had herself been an official of the totalitarian state of the German Democratic Republic (GDR). She served as

---

99. The Latinist Johannes Stroux (1886–1954).
100. Schneider, "Ägyptologen," 163–64.
101. Wolfgang J. Mommsen, "Wissenschaft, Krieg und die Berliner Akademie der Wissenschaften: Die Preußische Akademie der Wissenschaften in den beiden Weltkriegen," in Fischer, Hohlfeld, and Nötzoldt, *Preußische Akademie der Wissenschaften*, 3–23 (at 21).
102. Endesfelder, "Ägyptologie," 43.

an aide to Karl-Heinz Wirzberger, the Rector of the Humboldt University in Berlin, who was also a member of the Socialist Unity Party and the GDR Parliament. Endesfelder also held the political position of cultural attaché of the GDR in Cairo.[103]

Nonetheless, on the basis of Max Vasmer's 1948 retrospective, Thomas Gertzen has attempted to dismiss Grapow's intent and culpability. He argues that Grapow's rise to high positions in the academy and the university was in fact due to a lack of personnel and not Grapow's commitment to National Socialism.[104] This apologetic claim lacks validity for two reasons. First, Grapow made himself available to the positions of leadership that he assumed between 1938 and 1945. Had he wished to abstain from any involvement in the National Socialist politics of higher education, even for his personal safety, he could have restricted himself to his academic duties of teaching and research. This is what other colleagues did (e.g., Hans Bonnet, Professor of Egyptology at Bonn). Even in the event of limited personnel, there was no external compulsion for Grapow to assume the positions he took up. Second, even as late as 1943, Grapow was not the only available candidate for the presidency of the academy. When it became clear that Grapow would not receive the majority of votes, the minister of education, Bernhard Rust, stepped in and summarily prevented the academy from conducting a vote. This move effectively confirmed Grapow as acting president of the academy, an office he held until 1945. Grapow thus owed both his academy leadership appointments in 1938 and 1943 to the Reich's minister, who also approved his appointment as a Dean in 1940 and then as Deputy Rector and acting Rector of the University of Berlin in 1945. It is a moot point to consider whether he would have had the same career within the context of the Weimar Republic.[105]

It is very likely that Grapow sought out these positions deliberately.[106] Fritz Hartung (1883–1967; Professor of Modern History in Berlin) voiced suspicions in a letter to Albert Brackmann (1871–1952; Professor of History and Director of the Reichsarchiv) that Grapow "aspired to the presidency of the Academy with all available means."[107]

---

103. Petra Andrássy, "Erika Endesfelder zum Gedenken (2015)," Institut für Archäologie der Humboldt-Universität zu Berlin, accessed October 24, 2021, https://www.archaeologie.hu-berlin.de/de/aegy_anoa_old/personen/nachruf-prof.-erika-endesfelder.
104. Gertzen, *Berliner Schule*, 74.
105. Ibid., 131.
106. Ibid., 132; also considers Grapow's "career goals."
107. Joseph Lemberg, *Der Historiker ohne Eigenschaften: Eine Problemgeschichte des Mediävisten Friedrich Baethgen*, Campus Historische Studien 71 (Frankfurt, Germany:

In his recent assessments of Hermann Grapow's political views, Thomas Gertzen maintains that Grapow's political commitment to National Socialist ideology was merely limited and superficial. Gertzen insists that Grapow was not the arch-Nazi that Steindorff characterized him as being. Instead, he argues that Steindorff's condemnation represented his attempt to prevent Grapow from assuming a leading role in Egyptology in postwar Germany.[108] With the one exception of Jean Capart, Gertzen also maintains that Grapow did not take advantage of the means available through the Third Reich to harm colleagues who were being persecuted for racial or political reasons or to seek advantage from their disenfranchisement or murder.[109] This position echoes sentiments presented in a letter from Helmuth Scheel, the former director of the Prussian Academy and a close companion of Grapow, to Wolja Erichsen (1890–1966; Danish Egyptologist and, until 1944, coeditor of the Berlin dictionary with Grapow), written on April 8, 1946. In the letter, Scheel criticizes the "persecutions of the Christians"—that is, of former members of the NSDAP—and argues that, compared to other colleagues, Grapow should be exonerated: "I think that in this perspective, there vanishes the guilt of Grapow who as we know is always somewhat violent in, to say so, his actions but at the bottom of his heart, is the most good-natured human being that you can imagine. He has certainly not got anybody into a KZ [concentration camp] or harmed him otherwise."[110]

An even bolder strategy of argument employed after the war was to portray Grapow as an outright defender of academia against Nazi politics. In a letter to Grapow dated August 18, 1945, Grapow's publisher Leopold Klotz lauds him as someone who "mustered the courage and the strength to remain on his post in the interest of scholarship and in order to salvage what was left of its [the discipline's] reputation, despite the many inconsistencies." Klotz also refers to Grapow's "inner conflict of conscience" experienced during these years,

---

Campus, 2015), 347. He mentions that this included regular coffee invitations after academy meetings and that it explains Grapow's change of course in the controversial case of the appointment of the historian Theodor Mayer—as Dean in 1942, Grapow had prevented the appointment but supported it when he was made acting president of the academy in 1943.

108. Gertzen, *Berliner Schule*, 94–95, 132.

109. Ibid., 132.

110. "Ich finde demgegenüber verschwindet Grapows Schuld, der ja immer etwas gewalttätig—na sagen wir, tut—und im Grunde seines Herzens der gutmütigste Mensch ist, den man sich denken kann. Er hat bestimmt niemanden ins KZ gebracht oder ihn sonst geschädigt." The letter is part of the papers of Wolja Erichsen at the Biblioteca e Archivi di Egittologia, Università degli Studi di Milano (dossier 3/ Grapow). Alexander Scharff, in a letter to Erichsen dated February 22, 1948, in the same papers, calls Scheel and Grapow "zwei ausgesprochene Hitlerianer" [two avowed Hitlerians].

and his constant efforts to avert "wrong dispositions dictated by the party."[111] Grapow is also credited with "having done everything in order to save our discipline from Nazi demonism" in a plea for help passed on to Steindorff in 1946 (authored by Liselotte Richter).[112] Similarly, the Dean of the Faculty of Philosophy of the Humboldt University emphasized in Grapow's activity that he had "always been eager to save the academic spirit" and had "been a good comrade to his colleagues, even those who were not in the party"; however, at the same time he misrepresents his party affiliations.[113]

In postwar statements, Grapow also portrayed himself as a staunch defender of the academy and, more generally, scholarship [Wissenschaft], against Nazi politics. An example of this characterization can be found in a letter Grapow wrote to his publisher Leopold Klotz (1878–1956) on September 20, 1945: "I do not want to be just tolerated, I request recognition for many a hard battle that I fought, by using my positions and by offering to resign from them, with Messrs. Rust, Mentzel and Göbbels [sic] and Schacht and Rosenberg and the other rascals, to my own harm, but for my conscience."[114]

---

111. Gertzen, *Berliner Schule*, 87, 110.

112. The author of the plea is not identified in the letter written by Ludwig Edelstein at the request of Erich Frank, Professor of Philosophy at Marburg (Gertzen, "In Deutschland," 375). However, the letter mentions that the female author is a former student of Frank's, works at the Berlin Academy, and is the editor of a publication on Leibniz that "has just appeared." Liselotte Richter (1906–1968) did her doctorate (1934) at Marburg with Frank, worked at the academy's Leibniz project, and published in 1946 "Leibniz und sein Russlandbild." From 1947, she was professor of philosophy and philosophy of religions in Berlin. In the letter by Scheel to Erichsen cited in note 110, there is also this passage following his comments on Grapow: "By the way, Liselotte Richter is again in Berlin, district councilor. She has been KPD [Communist Party of Germany] since 1929, and is for Grapow. She thinks that you are the only one who could exonerate Grapow effectively. Maybe you could ponder whether to provide a kind of assessment about Grapow."

A similar letter dated April 24, 1946, from Scheel to Erichsen (in the correspondence of Erichsen in the Danish National Archives in Copenhagen) mentions the plea letter: "Dann liegt ein Brief von Frl. Dr. Liselotte Richter (früher Leibniz–Kommission) bei. Sie ist jetzt Leiterin der Volksbildung in Charlottenburg, seit 1929 KPD (wie Sie wohl wissen). Sie setzt sich sehr für Grapow ein. Hoffentlich können Sie ihrem Wunsch entsprechen. Grapow hat ja so wenig Freunde, nur Klotz und Spranger haben für ihn ein Zeugnis ausgestellt" [Enclosed is also a letter by Ms. Dr. Liselotte Richter (formerly Leibniz Committee). She is now the director of People's Education in Charlottenburg, German Communist Party since 1929 (as I assume you know). She supports Grapow's cause very much. I hope you can comply with her wish. As you know, Grapow has so few friends, just Klotz and Spranger have vouched for him].

113. Gertzen, *Berliner Schule*, 90–91.

114. Ibid., 137–38. On Leopold Klotz, see Franzmeier and Weber, "Andererseits finde ich," 141–48.

The incident with Rust that Grapow refers to is related in an account drafted after the war. When Rust accused members of the academy of conspiring against him, Grapow declared his solidarity with those colleagues and offered his instantaneous resignation from all functions at the academy and the university. In the end, Rust backed down and reaffirmed Grapow in his positions.[115] Rather than seeing Grapow's intervention as a battle with Rust at Grapow's peril, his action can also be understood as confirming Grapow's powerful political position and his safe standing among Nazi ministers. The other direct contacts mentioned here with the innermost circle of the National Socialist government confirm this conclusion. Especially striking in this regard is the way that Grapow downplayed the main Nazi war criminals as mere *Strolche* [rascals].

In the face of the praise of colleagues and Grapow's own proclamations, the de facto exclusion of the Jewish members of the academy in 1938 needs to be recalled.[116] In an apologetic report of activities read out by Grapow in the first session of the Prussian Academy of Sciences after the end of the war, on June 6, 1945, Grapow attempted to cleanse the academy and absolve himself of all blame.[117] In particular, he maintained that the academy had disobeyed the directives of the ministry and the State Security Office to expel its foreign members and had not even expelled its three Jewish members. As a matter of fact, however, the three members themselves resigned in order to forestall their expulsion once Max Planck, as secretary, had informed them of the state directive.[118] This is clearly tantamount to an expulsion. Grapow's emphatic denial of this fact represents an implicit acknowledgment of having done harm to colleagues who were subject to racial persecution. One month after the initial resignations, academy members who had Jewish ancestors or Jewish or half-Jewish spouses [*Mischlinge* and *jüdisch Versippte*] were asked to resign. The contracts of the remaining non-Aryan research assistants were similarly terminated. Non-Aryan members of the academy living outside of Germany were excluded by 1942.[119]

---

115. Gertzen, *Berliner Schule*, supplement.
116. Walther, "Arisierung," 87–118.
117. Ibid., 87–88.
118. Ibid., 93–94. See further Nötzoldt, *Vertrieben aus rassistischen Gründen*, 95–96. Grapow's report about these events is there labeled a "forgery."
119. Peter Nötzoldt and Peter Walther, "The Prussian Academy of Sciences during the Third Reich," *Minerva* 42, no.4 (2004): 421–44 (at 431–33), also refute Grapow's claim.

VI. CONCLUSION

In 1973, Grapow's brief autobiographical sketch, *Meine Begegnung mit einigen Ägyptologen* [My encounter with some Egyptologists], was published posthumously.[120] This work is essentially a series of anecdotes without any reference to the historical and political context of his career. It may have served to portray Grapow as an internationally respected Egyptologist who was not involved in contemporary politics.[121] In light of Grapow's view that the history of Germany is an unalterable destiny to which one has to acquiesce, it could also be seen as an attempt to dismiss such history as of little relevance as long as the individual is able to adjust.

In fact, Grapow was quite adept at "adjusting." Despite his dismissal from university service in 1945, and though he may initially have hoped that he could continue as president of the university beyond the end of the war,[122] he quickly established a new career for himself in the Soviet Occupation Zone and then the GDR.[123] In a letter to Wolja Erichsen dated May 26, 1947, the chair holder of Egyptology in Munich, Alexander Scharff (1892–1950), commented on these developments as follows:

> Berlin has lost its significant academic role; at fault for it are solely the Nazis, whose factionist Grapow was. Now it seems that he's dallying with the Russians, but in this Western Germany will not partake.... If Grapow gets once again to the top, then we will have all the Nazis again in his following such as Kees, Wolf and Schott, all of whom would be wise to stay for a bit more in the background because they bawled so much "Heil H...." The old Steindorff, with whom I have resumed a very pleasant correspondence, is said, as I am hearing from Egypt, to have mailed a list of those German Egyptologists who were Nazis and those who were not.[124]

---

120. According to a letter from Grapow from July 24, 1963, to Wolja Erichsen in the papers of Wolja Erichsen at the Biblioteca e Archivi di Egittologia, Università degli Studi di Milano (dossier 3/Grapow), the idea was due to Siegfried Morenz and Hildegard von Deines: "Morenz and Frau von Deines put the bee in my bonnet. If I'll publish it? ... Let's see."
121. Schneider, "Ägyptologen," 164.
122. Winau, "Preußische Akademie," 88.
123. Walther, "Arisierung," 116.
124. "Berlin hat seine bedeutende wissenschaftl[iche] Rolle ausgespielt; daran sind allein die Nazis, deren Parteigänger Gr[apow] war, schuld. Jetzt liebäugelt er offenbar mit den Russen, aber da tut das westliche Deutschland nicht mit.... Wenn Gr[apow] wieder obenauf kommt, dann haben wir sofort die ganzen Nazis wieder in seinem Gefolge wie Kees, Wolf und Schott, die alle ruhig noch eine Weile im Hintergrund bleiben sollten, weil sie so laut Heil H.... geschrieen haben.... Vom alten Steindorff, mit dem ich auch wieder einen

The threat of seeing Grapow and other former National Socialists resume a position of power in postwar Egyptology is here pitched clearly; it confirms that Steindorff's verdicts in his letter were also an expression of that fear. Yet Grapow ascended again. In 1947, with Diedrich Westermann and Richard Hartmann—his former coapplicant and member, respectively, on the "White Africa Committee"—he founded an Institut für Orientforschung at the Berlin Academy. In 1951, he became director of one of its divisions and in 1956 director of the Institute itself (1956–62). On the grounds of his scholarly merits, he twice received the National Prize of the GDR (in 1953 and again in 1959).[125] In 1955, Grapow was honored with a Festschrift.[126] At that time, his colleague Hermann Kees, at Göttingen, who was the same age as Grapow (b. 1886), lost his battle for reemployment at the university and reflected on a "life that had become senseless."[127] Grapow, however, who had left his corner "in the shadow of titans" in 1938, had ascended to positions much more influential than those held by Kees; he was, as he wrote to his publisher Leopold Klotz, "fourfold crowned (even the Pope has one crown less)."[128] Within German Egyptology, he had become the most prominent figure.[129] As chair holder in Egyptology at Berlin, he portrayed himself as the legitimate successor of the discipline's German titans Richard Lepsius (1810–1884), Adolf Erman (1854–1937), and Kurt Sethe (1869–1934).[130]

One might contend that Grapow, who was so adaptable to political change and obedient to state authority, merely appropriated the doctrine of the National Socialist state in a utilitarian way since that state gave him the opportunity for major professional advancement.[131] From that perspective, Nazism merely provided the means to an end, and Grapow's attitude was simply opportunistic.[132] However, Bialas and Rabinbach provide a valuable corrective to that kind of simplistic approach in their analysis of research on the humanities during the Third Reich:

---

sehr netten Briefverkehr habe, soll, wie ich aus Ägypten hörte, eine Liste der deutschen Ägyptologen versandt worden sein, welche Nazi waren und welche nicht" (letter in the papers of Wolja Erichsen at the Biblioteca e Archivi di Egittologia, Università degli Studi di Milano).
  125. Endesfelder, "Ägyptologie," 42–43.
  126. Schneider, "Ägyptologen," 164–65.
  127. Schneider, "Eine Führernatur," 367–68.
  128. Franzmeier and Weber, "Andererseits finde ich," 135 (letter to Leopold Klotz from September 1945).
  129. Gertzen, *Einführung*, 96.
  130. Gertzen, "In Deutschland," 388.
  131. Gertzen, *Berliner Schule*, 95.
  132. Gertzen, "In Deutschland," 389, 392.

The line between conviction and career could never be clearly drawn, nor was the distinction ever firmly established, between National Socialist politics and ideology on the one side and the discursive practices and mentalities of the academic community on the other.... Explanations of the behavior of the professors, framed in terms of either ideological commitment or opportunistic behavior, only beg the question of whether motivation can ever be understood in terms of such a stark polarity between personal gain and idealistic investment.... Intellectual fealty to National Socialism required not so much ideological consistency as an ethos or *Gesinnung*, a willingness to adhere to the general precepts of the worldview, which was vague and indistinct enough to embrace a variety of related perspectives. A great deal of confusion over the Nazification of the humanities derives from the difficulty in drawing a firm line between "Nazi ideology" and the wide spectrum of modes of accommodation and participation characteristic of the academic community.... What was important was not the coherence of the worldview but that it served "as a unifying principle for a large and diverse group of people. What mattered was the appeal to the worldview rather than the worldview itself."[133]

In this respect, it seems essential to point again to the three major humanities initiatives in which Grapow participated or—in the case of the White Africa Committee—that he helped launch. The War Deployment initiative was intended to provide the infrastructure for academic research in the future postwar National Socialist state. The White Africa project was intended to provide racial and colonialist justification to postwar claims of a National Socialist state to the resources of North Africa. The *Studienführer* project sought to align postwar instruction in the humanities with National Socialist ideology.

The evidence demonstrates that Hermann Grapow—as the leading Egyptologist of his discipline and as acting president of both the Prussian Academy of Sciences and the University of Berlin—embraced National Socialist agendas as a pathway for future research and teaching. He condoned the Nazi regime's "fate-given" racist and expansionist politics. He eagerly anticipated a fair share in "the new upturn which we can expect after the victory in the second Frederician epoch of our history, brought about by the Führer as the man of German destiny: for scholarship in general, so also especially for the humanities in our academy."[134] There is no doubt that Grapow envisioned himself as a titan in

---

133. Bialas and Rabinbach, "Introduction," xxxix–xl.
134. Grapow (cited previously at note 39).

German Egyptology and sought to play a leading role in the humanities more broadly within the future National Socialist state.[135]

BIBLIOGRAPHY

Archival Sources

Biblioteca e Archivi di Egittologia. Università degli Studi di Milano. Papers of Wolja Erichsen. https://archivi.unimi.it/Ente/biblioteca-e-archivi-di-egittologia/.

Danish National Archives. Copenhagen, Denmark. Correspondence of Wolja Erichsen.

Secondary Sources

Andrássy, Petra. "Erika Endesfelder zum Gedenken (2015)." Institut für Archäologie der Humboldt-Universität zu Berlin. Accessed October 24, 2021. https://www.archaeologie.hu-berlin.de/de/aegy_anoa_old/personen/nachruf-prof.-erika-endesfelder.

Bialas, Wolfgang, and Anson Rabinbach. "Introduction: The Humanities in Nazi Germany." In *Nazi Germany and the Humanities: How German Academics Embraced Nazism*, edited by Wolfgang Bialas and Anson Rabinbach, ix–liii. Oxford: Oneworld, 2014. Originally published 2006.

Bickel, Susanne, Hans-Werner Fischer-Elfert, Antonio Loprieno, and Sebastian Richter, eds. *Ägyptologen und Ägyptologien zwischen Kaiserreich und Gründung der beiden deutschen Staaten: Reflexionen zur Geschichte und Episteme eines altertumswissenschaftlichen Fachs im 150. Jahr der Zeitschrift für Ägyptische Sprache und Altertumskunde*. Zeitschrift für ägyptische Sprache und Altertumskunde Supplement 1. Berlin: Akademie, 2013.

Biermann, Frank, and Ralf Herpolsheimer. *Zeitungswissenschaftler im Dritten Reich: Sieben biographische Studien*. Cologne, Germany: Hayit, 1984.

Blumenthal, Elke, Hans-W. Fischer-Elfert, Friederike Kampp-Seyfried, Dietrich Raue, and Tonio Sebastian Richter. *Georg Steindorff: Stationen eines Lebens*. Kleine Schriften des Ägyptischen Museums der Universität Leipzig 11. Berlin: Manetho, 2017.

---

135. In a letter to Wolja Erichsen dated March 24, 1948 (papers of Wolja Erichsen at the Biblioteca e Archivi di Egittologia, Università degli Studi di Milano), Alexander Scharff alleges Grapow to have exercised an "Egyptological Nazi dictatorship" from Berlin for almost twelve years.

Boehm, Laetitia. "Langzeitvorhaben als Akademieaufgabe: Geschichtswissenschaft in Berlin und in München." In Fischer, Hohlfeld, and Nötzoldt, *Preußische Akademie der Wissenschaften*, 391–434.

Bott, Marie-Louise. *Die Haltung der Berliner Universität im Nationalsozialismus: Die Rückschau Max Vasmers 1948*. Neues aus der Geschichte der Humboldt-Universität zu Berlin 1. Berlin: Humboldt-Universität, 2009.

Brill, Werner. "Sonderpädagogik und Behinderung im Nationalsozialismus." In *Die Berliner Universität in der NS-Zeit*. Vol. 2, *Fachbereiche und Fakultäten*, edited by Rüdiger vom Bruch, Christoph Jahr, and Rebecca Schaarschmidt, 229–42. Stuttgart, Germany: Franz Steiner, 2005.

Cappel, Alexandra. "Adolf Erman und Georg Steindorff: Zur Dynamik eines Lehrer-Schüler-Verhältnisses." In Voss and Raue, *Georg Steindorff*, 7–90.

Carruthers, William E. "Introduction: Thinking about Histories of Egyptology." In *Histories of Egyptology: Interdisciplinary Measures*, edited by William E. Carruthers, 1–15. New York: Routledge, 2015.

Ellinger, Ekkehard. *Deutsche Orientalistik zur Zeit des Nationalsozialismus, 1933–1945*. Edingen-Neckarhausen, Germany: Deux Mondes, 2006.

Endesfelder, Erika. "Die Ägyptologie an der Berliner Universität: Zur Geschichte eines Fachgebietes." *Berichte: Humboldt-Universität zu Berlin* 8, no. 6 (1988): 42–48.

Fischer, Wolfram, Rainer Hohlfeld, and Peter Nötzoldt. "Die Berliner Akademie in Republik und Diktatur." In Fischer, Hohlfeld, and Nötzoldt, *Preußische Akademie der Wissenschaften*, 517–66.

———, eds. *Die Preußische Akademie der Wissenschaften zu Berlin 1914–1945*. Interdisziplinäre Arbeitsgruppe der Berlin-Brandenburgischen Akademie der Wissenschaften, Forschungsberichte 8. Berlin: Akademie, 2000.

Franzmeier, Henning, and Anke Weber. "'Andererseits finde ich, dass man jetzt nicht so tun soll, als wäre nichts gewesen': Die deutsche Ägyptologie in den Jahren 1945–1949 im Spiegel der Korrespondenz mit dem Verlag J. C. Hinrichs." In Bickel et al., *Ägyptologen und Ägyptologien*, 113–52.

Gertzen, Thomas L. *Die Berliner Schule der Ägyptologie im Dritten Reich: Begegnung mit Hermann Grapow*. Berlin: Kadmos, 2015.

———. *Einführung in die Wissenschaftsgeschichte der Ägyptologie*. Einführungen und Quellentexte zur Ägyptologie 10. Berlin: LIT, 2017.

———. "'In Deutschland steht Ihnen Ihre Abstammung entgegen'—Zur Bedeutung von Judentum und Konfessionalismus für die wissenschaftliche Laufbahn Georg Steindorffs und seiner Rolle innerhalb der École de Berlin." In Voss and Raue, *Georg Steindorff*, 333–400.

———. *Judentum und Konfession in der Geschichte der deutschsprachigen Ägyptologie*. Europäisch-jüdische Studien 32. Berlin: de Gruyter Oldenbourg, 2017.

Grapow, Hermann. "Ägyptisch: Vom Lebenslauf einer altafrikanischen Sprache." In Schaeder, *Orient in Deutscher Forschung*, 205–16.

———. *Meine Begegnung mit einigen Ägyptologen*. Berlin: Seitz, 1973.
———. "Über die Unternehmungen der Philosophisch-historischen Klasse." In *Vier Vorträge von Th. Vahlen, E. Heymann, L. Bieberbach und H. Grapow*, 30–43. Vorträge und Schriften 1. Berlin: Preußische Akademie der Wissenschaften, 1940.
———. "Wörterbuch der ägyptischen Sprache" [transcribed statement made by Grapow during the proceedings of the Prussian Academy]. In *Jahrbuch der Preußischen Akademie der Wissenschaften Jahrgang 1941*, 64. Berlin: Verlag der Akademie der Wissenschaften in Kommission bei Walter de Gruyter, 1942.
Grüttner, Michael, and Heinz-Elmar Tenorth. *Geschichte der Universität Unter den Linden*. Vol. 2, *Die Berliner Universität zwischen den Weltkriegen, 1918–1945*. Berlin: Akademie, 2012.
Gunert, Stefan, and Ingelore Hafemann. "Abriss der Geschichte des Wörterbuch-Unternehmens." Berlin-Brandenburgische Akademie der Wissenschaften. Accessed August 3, 2020. http://aaew.bbaw.de/projekt/geschichte.
Hanisch, Ludmilla. *Die Nachfolger der Exegeten: Deutschsprachige Erforschung des Vorderen Orients in der ersten Hälfte des 20 Jahrhunderts*. Wiesbaden, Germany: Harrassowitz, 2003.
Hartung, Wolfdietrich, and Werner Scheler, eds. *Die Berliner Akademie nach 1945: Zeitzeugen berichten*. Abhandlungen der Leibniz-Sozietät 6. Berlin: Trafo, 2001.
Hausmann, Frank-Rutger. *"Auch im Krieg schweigen die Musen nicht": Die Deutschen Wissenschaftlichen Institute im Zweiten Weltkrieg*. Göttingen, Germany: Vandenhoeck & Ruprecht, 2002.
———. *"Deutsche Geisteswissenschaft" im Zweiten Weltkrieg: Die "Aktion Ritterbusch" (1940–1945)*. 3rd ed. Studien zur Wissenschafts-und Universitätsgeschichte 12. Heidelberg, Germany: Synchron Publishers, 2007.
———. *Die Geisteswissenschaften im "Dritten Reich."* Frankfurt, Germany: Vittorio Klostermann, 2011.
Hoffmann, Dieter. "Das Verhältnis der Akademie zu Republik und Diktatur: Max Planck als Sekretär." In Fischer, Hohlfeld, and Nötzoldt, *Preußische Akademie der Wissenschaften*, 53–85.
Hoffmann, Petra. *Weibliche Arbeitswelten in der Wissenschaft: Frauen an der Preußischen Akademie der Wissenschaften zu Berlin, 1890–1945*. Bielefeldt, Germany: transcript, 2011.
Irmscher, Johannes. "Johannes Stroux, der erste Präsident der Deutschen Akademie der Wissenschaften zu Berlin," *Sitzungsberichte der Leibniz-Sozietät* 15, no. 7 (1996): 37–41.
Jaeger, Ludwig. "Siege auf dem geistigen Schlachtfeld." Review of *'Deutsche Geisteswissenschaft' im Zweiten Weltkrieg—Die 'Aktion Ritterbusch'(1940–1945)*, by F.-R. Hausmann. *Internationales Archiv für Sozialgeschichte der deutschen*

Literatur (IASL) Online, January 16, 2001. Accessed July 4, 2020. http://www
.iaslonline.lmu.de/index.php?vorgang_id=2246.
Jagemann, Norbert. *"Der Studienführer": Zur Wissenschaftspolitik der SS*. Studien zur Zeitgeschichte 47. Hamburg, Germany: Dr. Kovač, 2005.
Junker, Hermann. "Deutsche Ausgrabungen in Ägypten in Vergangenheit und Zukunft." In Schaeder, *Orient in Deutscher Forschung*, 82–93.
Kees, Hermann. "Die Wissenschaftlichen Arbeiten der Akademie im Jahre 1941/2." In *Jahrbuch der Akademie der Wissenschaften in Göttingen für das Geschäftsjahr 1941/2*, 5–14. Göttingen, Germany: Vandenhoeck & Ruprecht, 1942.
Klee, Ernst. *Das Kulturlexikon zum Dritten Reich: Wer war was vor und nach 1945*. Frankfurt, Germany: S. Fischer, 2007.
Kloft, Hans, Thomas Elsmann, and Sabine Gorsemann, eds. *Der Nachlaß Adolf Erman*. Veröffentlichungen der Abteilung Gesellschaftswissenschaften 38. Bremen, Germany: Universität Bremen/Bibliothek, 1982.
Lemberg, Joseph. *Der Historiker ohne Eigenschaften: Eine Problemgeschichte des Mediävisten Friedrich Baethgen*. Campus Historische Studien 71. Frankfurt, Germany: Campus, 2015.
Lerchenmüller, Joachim. *"Keltischer Sprengstoff": Eine wissenschaftsgeschichtliche Studie über die Keltologie von 1900 bis 1945*. Tübingen, Germany: Max Niemeyer, 1997.
Lönnendonker, Siegward. *Freie Universität Berlin: Gründung einer politischen Universität*. Berlin: Ducker and Humblot, 1988.
Lösch, Niels C. *Rasse als Konstrukt: Leben und Werk Eugen Fischers*. Frankfurt, Germany: Peter Lang, 1997.
Maas, Utz. *Sprachforschung in der Zeit des Nationalsozialismus: Verfolgung, Vertreibung, Politisierung und die inhaltliche Neuausrichtung der Sprachwissenschaft*. Studia Linguistica Germanica 124. Berlin: Walter de Gruyter, 2016.
Marsch, Ulrich. Review of *Rasse als Konstrukt: Leben und Werk Eugen Fischers* (1998), by Niels C. Loesch. H-Soz-u-Kult (July 1998). H-Net Reviews. University of Michigan Department of History. Accessed July 4, 2020. http://www.h-net.org/reviews/showrev.php?id=16100.
Mekhitarian, Arpag. "Capart (Jean-François-Désiré) 21.2.1877–16.6.1947." In *Biographie Nationale: Dernier supplément* 16 (1985–86): 140–51.
Mischek, Udo. "Autorität außerhalb des Fachs—Diedrich Westermann und Eugen Fischer." In *Ethnologie und Nationalsozialismus*, edited by Bernhard Streck, 69–82. Gehren, Germany: Escher, 2000.
Mommsen, Wolfgang J. "Wissenschaft, Krieg und die Berliner Akademie der Wissenschaften: Die Preußische Akademie der Wissenschaften in den beiden Weltkriegen." In Fischer, Hohlfeld, and Nötzoldt, *Preußische Akademie der Wissenschaften*, 3–23.

Motadel, David. *Islam and Nazi Germany's War.* Cambridge, MA: Harvard University Press, 2014.

Müller, Sandra. *Georg Steindorff im Spiegel seiner Tagebücher.* Kleine Schriften des Ägyptischen Museums, Georg Steindorff, der Universität Leipzig 9. Leipzig, Germany: Leipziger Uni-Verlag, 2012.

Murphy, David Thomas. *The Heroic Earth: Geopolitical Thought in Weimar Germany, 1918–1933.* Kent, OH: Kent State University Press, 1997.

Nagel, Anne C. *Hitlers Bildungsreformer: Das Reichsministerium für Wissenschaft, Erziehung und Volksbildung 1934–1945.* Frankfurt, Germany: Fischer, 2012.

Nötzoldt, Peter. "Die Akademien der Wissenschaften zwischen Kaiser-Wilhelm-Gesellschaft und Notgemeinschaft der Deutschen Wissenschaft." *Sitzungsberichte der Leibniz-Sozietät der Wissenschaften zu Berlin* 98 (2008): 83–104.

———, ed. *Vertrieben aus rassistischen Gründen: Die Akademie der Wissenschaften 1933–45. Ausstellung im Rahmen des Berliner Themenjahres 2013 "Zerstörte Vielfalt: Berlin 1933–1945."* Berlin: Berlin-Brandenburgische Akademie der Wissenschaften, 2014. Accessed October 24, 2021. https://www.bbaw.de/filesz-bbaw/user_upload/publikationen/ausstellung-vertrieben-aus.pdf.

———, and Peter Walther. "The Prussian Academy of Sciences during the Third Reich." *Minerva* 42, no. 4 (2004): 421–44.

Pasch, Helma. "Westermann, Diedrich Hermann." *Biographisch-Bibliographisches Kirchenlexikon* 24 (2005): 1531–47.

Poewe, Karla. "Liberalism, German Missionaries and National Socialism." In *Mission und Macht im Wandel politischer Orientierungen: Europäische Missionsgesellschaften in politischen Spannungsfeldern in Afrika und Asien zwischen 1800 und 1945,* edited by Ulrich van der Heyden and Holger Stoecker, 633–61. Missionsgeschichtliches Archiv 10. Stuttgart, Germany: Franz Steiner, 2005.

Rathkolb, Oliver, Peter Autengruber, Birgit Nemec, and Florian Wenninger. "Straßennamen Wiens seit 1860 als 'Politische Erinnerungsorte': Forschungsprojektendbericht." Vienna, July 2013. Accessed July 4, 2020. https://www.wien.gv.at/kultur/abteilung/pdf/strassennamenbericht.pdf.

Raue, Dietrich. "Der 'J'accuse'—Brief an John A. Wilson: Drei Ansichten von Georg Steindorff." In Bickel et al., *Ägyptologen und Ägyptologien,* 345–76.

Rebenich, Stefan. "Adolf Erman und die Berliner Akademie der Wissenschaften." In *Ägyptologie als Wissenschaft: Adolf Erman (1854–1937) in seiner Zeit,* edited by Bernd Schipper, 340–70. Berlin: Walter de Gruyter, 2006.

———. "Zwischen Anpassung und Widerstand? Die Berliner Akademie der Wissenschaften von 1933 bis 1945." In *Antike und Altertumswissenschaft in der Zeit von Faschismus und Nationalsozialismus: Kolloquium Universität Zürich, 14–17 Oktober 1998,* edited by Beat Näf, 203–44. Mandelbachtal, Germany: Edition Cicero, 2001.

Reineke, Walter F. "Das Wörterbuch der ägyptischen Sprache: Zur Geschichte eines großen wissenschaftlichen Unternehmens der Berliner Akademie der Wissenschaften zwischen 1945 und 1992." In *Textcorpus und Wörterbuch: Aspekte zur ägyptischen Lexikographie*, edited by Stefan Grunert and Ingelore Hafemann, xi–xlv. Leiden, Netherlands: Brill, 1993.

Ritterbusch, Eugen. "Europa und das Reich: Zur Berliner Buch- und Dokumentationsschau 'Deutsche Wissenschaft im Kampf um Reich und Lebensraum.'" *Gesetzgebung und Literatur* 22 (1941/2): 157–59.

Rohrbacher, Peter. *Die Geschichte des Hamiten-Mythos*. Beiträge zur Afrikanistik 71. Vienna: AFRO-PUB, 2002.

———. "Dominik Josef Wölfel (1888–1963), Sprachwissenschafter, Afrikanist, Völkerkundler (2010)." Afrikanistik. Accessed July 4, 2020. http://www.afrikanistik.at.

Rubin, Barry, and Wolfgang G. Schwanitz. *Nazis, Islamists, and the Making of the Modern Middle East*. New Haven, CT: Yale University Press, 2014.

Schaeder, Hans Heinrich, ed. *Der Orient in deutscher Forschung: Vorträge der Berliner Orientalistentagung Herbst 1942*. Leipzig, Germany: Otto Harrassowitz, 1944.

Schäfer, Hans Dieter. *Das gespaltene Bewusstsein*. Göttingen, Germany: Wallstein 2009.

Schmuhl, Hans-Walter. *Grenzüberschreitungen: Das Kaiser-Wilhelm-Institut für Anthropologie, menschliche Erblehre, und Eugenik, 1927–1945*. Göttingen, Germany: Wallstein, 2005.

———. *The Kaiser Wilhelm Institute for Anthropology, Human Heredity, and Eugenics, 1927–1945: Crossing Boundaries*. Boston Studies in the Philosophy of Science 259. Berlin: Springer, 2008.

———. "'Neue Rehobother Bastardstudien': Eugen Fischer und die Anthropometrie zwischen Kolonialforschung und nationalsozialistischer Rassenpolitik." In *Anthropometrie: Zur Vorgeschichte des Menschen nach Maß*, edited by Gert Theile, 277–306. Munich: Wilhelm Fink, 2005.

Schneider, Thomas. "Ägyptologen im Dritten Reich: Biographische Notizen anhand der sogenannten 'Steindorff-Liste'." *Journal of Egyptian History* 5 (2012): 119–246. Reprinted in Thomas Schneider and Peter Raulwing, eds., *Egyptology from the First World War to the Third Reich: Ideology, Scholarship, and Individual Biographies*. Leiden, Netherlands: Brill, 2013.

———. "Egyptology in Nazi Germany: Ideology, Scholarship, Careers." Public lecture in memory of Hans Jakob Polotsky at the Halbert Centre for Canadian Studies, Hebrew University, December 11, 2018. Accessed July 4, 2020. https://openscholar.huji.ac.il/polotskynow.

———. "'Eine Führernatur, wie sie der neue Staat braucht!' Hermann Kees' Tätigkeit in Göttingen 1924–1945 und die Kontroverse um Entnazifizierung und

Wiedereinstellung in der Nachkriegszeit." *Studien zur altägyptischen Kultur* 45 (2015): 333–81.

Schreiber, Maximilian. *Walther Wüst: Dekan und Rektor der Universität München 1935–1945*. Munich: Herbert Utz, 2008.

Schröder, Wilt Aden. *Der Altertumswissenschaftler Eduard Norden (1868–1941): Das Schicksal eines deutschen Gelehrten jüdischer Abkunft. Mit den Briefen Eduard Nordens an seinen Lehrer Hermann Usener aus den Jahren 1891 bis 1902*. Spudasmata 73. Hildesheim: Georg Olms, 1999.

Simon, Gerd, with Horst Junginger and Ulrich Schermaul. "Vom Antisemiten zum Semitistik-Professor: Chronologie Rössler, Otto." Universität Tübingen, first research 1986, provisional final version June 8, 2007, introduction and addition in November 2010. Accessed July 4, 2020. https://homepages.uni-tuebingen.de/gerd.simon/ChrRoessler.pdf.

Steiner, John M. *Power Politics and Social Change in National Socialist Germany*. The Hague: Mouton, 1975.

Stoecker, Holger. *Afrikawissenschaften in Berlin von 1919 bis 1945: Zur Geschichte und Topographie eines wissenschaftlichen Netzwerkes*. Stuttgart, Germany: Franz Steiner, 2008.

Strukturen und Transformationen des Wortschatzes der ägyptischen Sprache: Text- und Wissenskultur im Alten Ägypten (Altägyptisches Wörterbuch). "Einführung." Berlin-Brandenburgische Akademie der Wissenschaften. Accessed August 3, 2020. http://aaew.bbaw.de/projekt.

Voss, Susanne. *Die Geschichte der Abteilung Kairo des DAI im Spannungsfeld deutscher politischer Interessen*. Vol. 2, *1929–1966*. Rahden, Germany: Leidorf, 2017.

———. "Wissenshintergründe ... —Die Ägyptologie als 'völkische' Wissenschaft entlang des Nachlasses Georg Steindorffs von der Weimarer Republik über die NS- bis zur Nachkriegszeit." In Voss and Raue, *Georg Steindorff*, 105–332.

Voss, Susanne, and Dietrich Raue, eds. *Georg Steindorff und die deutsche Ägyptologie im 20 Jahrhundert: Wissenshintergründe und Forschungstransfers*. Zeitschrift für ägyptische Sprache und Altertumskunde Supplement 5. Berlin: Walter de Gruyter, 2016.

Walther, Peter. "'Arisierung,' Nazifizierung und Militarisierung: Die Akademie im 'Dritten Reich.'" In Fischer, Hohlfeld, and Nötzoldt, *Preußische Akademie der Wissenschaften*, 87–118.

Winau, Rolf. "Die Preußische Akademie der Wissenschaften im Dritten Reich." In *Die Elite der Nation im Dritten Reich: Das Verhältnis von Akademien und ihrem wissenschaftlichen Umfeld zum Nationalsozialismus*, edited by Eduard Seidler, Christoph J. Scriba, and Wieland Berg, 75–88. Acta Historica Leopoldina 22. Leipzig, Germany: Barth, 1995.

Wokoeck, Ursula. *German Orientalism: The Study of the Middle East and Islam from 1800 to 1945*. London: Routledge, 2009.

THOMAS SCHNEIDER is Professor of Egyptology and Near Eastern Studies at the University of British Columbia, Vancouver. After studying at Zurich, Basel, and Paris, he held a Junior Research Professorship of the Swiss National Science Foundation at the University of Basel and was Professor and Chair in Egyptology at the University of Wales, Swansea. He was also Visiting Professor at the Universities of Vienna and Heidelberg as well as the Hebrew University of Jerusalem and Associate Vice President (International) at the Southern University of Science and Technology in Shenzhen, China. He has published widely on Egyptian interconnections with the Near East, Egyptian history and chronology, language contact in ancient Egypt, and the history of Egyptology in Nazi Germany.

SEVEN

GERMAN ASSYRIOLOGY
A Discipline in Troubled Waters

JOHANNES RENGER

THE QUESTION OF BETRAYAL IS a question asked in hindsight, looking back at events that took place in a past that has since become a closed chapter. The idea that they were betraying something may have been barely perceptible to many of those individuals who were later perceived as having participated in or contributed to the disastrous events that we now see so clearly from our own vantage point. In addition to the question of who was responsible for the betrayal of the humanities in interwar Germany—whether academic institutions or elements of the National Socialist (Nazi) regime—we may also ask whether those who were responsible within the humanities acted consciously, deliberately, and in full knowledge of what they were doing. Many of them accepted or actively supported Nazi doctrines or convictions, together with and within their respective institutions. But doubtless some became aware of the consequences of Nazi politics only accidentally or incrementally. In the early years of the Nazi regime (1933–34), many held on to the vain hope that things would become bearable with time. Even some Jewish professors and Jews active in other areas of German life expected to be able to continue working in Germany. Some did not want to envision the consequences of Nazi policies on universities or on society in general. Even among those who would suffer terribly but a few years later, many were too credulous to see the writing on the wall. Very few foresaw the looming disaster from the very beginning.

Assyriology, or ancient Near Eastern studies, is a discipline with a long tradition, but this tradition has always been represented by a limited number of scholars, then as now. As a result, political developments in Germany during the Third Reich had an outsized influence on the field, especially as Nazi policy and the outbreak of war impacted academic institutions. The loss of prominent scholars to emigration and to military service left a notable gap in German Assyriology. The following pages represent an attempt to state the facts as I know them and to relate what I have learned through personal acquaintance with a number of Assyriologists who worked in the 1930s and thereafter.[1] I begin with a brief review of the general impact of Nazi laws and policies on the field of Assyriology, noting in particular some of the scholars who were expelled from their positions, but who continued to work in the field long after World War II ended. Among these scholars is Benno Landsberger, the brilliant German-Jewish Assyriologist, who was replaced by one of his own students, for whom he eventually helped secure a position after the war. The rest of the chapter examines the extent to which Assyriology served as an instrument of Nazi ideology through an analysis of the life and work of several scholars. The three most prominent of these scholars were full Professors of Assyriology in 1933 who held an outstanding international reputation: Wolfram von Soden (associate professor in Göttingen from 1936 to 1940 and chair in Berlin beginning in 1940); Bruno Meissner (retired in 1936 from the chair in Berlin); and Arthur Ungnad (retired in 1930 from the chair in Breslau). In addition to these three scholars, I also briefly discuss the careers of Carl Frank, Eckhard Unger, Viktor Christian, and Walter Hinz. All of these scholars embraced Nazi ideology, though to varying degrees.

I. THE IMPACT OF NAZI LAWS AND REGULATIONS

On April 14, 1933, the Nazi regime issued the Gesetz zur Wiederherstellung des Berufsbeamtentums [Law for the Restoration of the Professional Civil Service], claiming that the law was intended to "restore" the civil service and make it more "professional." In actuality, the Civil Service Law served primarily as a means of removing civil servants from their positions in the administration of

---

1. In researching this paper, I consulted the German Federal Archives, the archives of various universities, and the personal communications of some of the scholars discussed here. I also consulted the relevant scholarly publications and obituaries of the people who figure in this chapter and contacted colleagues familiar with or involved in the discipline of Assyriology in the years 1933–45. The use of unpublished personal correspondence has been crucial to this study. Many previous formal histories of the discipline have been based on scholars' obituaries that, quite conveniently, omit the crucial years from 1933 to 1945. This essay draws in part on my previous study, "Altorientalistik," in *Kulturwissenschaften und Nationalsozialismus*, ed. Jürgen Elvert and Jürgen Nielsen-Sikora, Historische Mitteilungen 72 (Stuttgart, Germany: Franz Steiner, 2008), 469–502. My gratitude goes to my colleague David Alan Warburton, who read the original draft of this article, gave valuable advice, and corrected my English.

the state, public institutions, and universities if they were Jewish, had Jewish ancestors, had a Jewish spouse, or if they were considered "unreliable" because of their political allegiance or connections. (This last category targeted members of the pre-1933 Social Democratic and Communist Parties). An additional aim was to "cleanse" universities of "un-German" persons. As a result, about one-third of university personnel (junior and professorial appointments)—that is, about three thousand persons—were expelled. Some went immediately into exile for fear of persecution. The Civil Service Law was also intended to guarantee that appointees would support the Nazi regime without any reservations. The Saxon Ministry of Public Instruction stipulated that new appointments must demonstrate not only scholarly excellence but also suitability as teachers and leaders in educating future students to be potential supporters of the Nazi regime. A university teacher was to be regarded as the "military leader" of the students. Although party membership played a role, it was not always instrumental for appointment and could be waived depending on local situations or outstanding scholarly qualifications.[2]

On September 15, 1935, the regime enacted the Reichsbürgergesetz [Reich Citizenship Law], one of the two Nuremberg Race Laws, which stripped non-Aryans of rights by creating a lower category of citizenship. In order to comply with the civil service and citizenship laws, many universities enacted regulations to create academic bodies like the Nationaler Ausschuss für die Erneuerung der Universität Leipzig. While ostensibly, as its name implies, a "National Committee for Renewing Leipzig University," in reality it served as a platform to drive out Jewish academics as well as scholars who were members of the Social Democratic Party (SPD, a progressive political party) or other non-conservative political parties.[3] Such regulations showed the extent to which the universities were aligning themselves politically with National Socialist doctrine by eliminating intellectual or political dissent by faculty. Beyond the expulsion of scholars from their positions, the new laws and regulations also led to administrative hindrance, harassment, and even persecution of academics. Participation at international scholarly meetings required permission from the dean on the basis of a recommendation by the Nazi Party.[4] The government

---

2. Ludmilla Hanisch, "Arabistik, Semitistik, und Islamwissenschaft," in Elvert and Nielsen-Sikora, *Kulturwissenschaften und Nationalsozialismus*, 503–25 (at 514).

3. See Hans Christian Petersen and Jan Kusber, "Osteuropäische Geschichte und Ostforschung," in Elvert and Nielsen-Sikora, *Kulturwissenschaften und Nationalsozialismus*, 289–311 (at 296).

4. Renger, "Altorientalistik," 470.

tried to bar nonconformist scholars from presenting their work or representing their disciplines abroad, because they could not be trusted to reflect the ideals of the "new" Germany.

The Situation in German Universities

Soon after January 1933, academic officials and bodies within German universities (rectors, deans, and faculties) began to follow the directives of the regime. They became willing partners in its ideological goals. Some professors acted readily or even enthusiastically to implement the demands and expectations of the regime. Others conformed merely to advance their academic careers. Still others avoided Nazi demands by focusing on topics with no connection to official Nazi doctrines, only occasionally nodding to Nazi expectations in their writings.[5] A survey of publications in certain disciplines of the humanities shows that many scholars took refuge from Nazi ideology by concentrating on "safe" topics of a rather antiquarian character, such as philology or the editing of texts.[6] In other words, the situation varied between distance in some cases and affinity or even active support for, complicity in, or allegiance to the regime in others.[7] Although there were occasional signs of resistance or courageous dissent, very few academics openly rejected the expectations of the regime. Even scholars with an outstanding international reputation were well aware of the risks. When Benno Landsberger—the leading Assyriologist of his time, both in Germany and internationally—was expelled from the University of Leipzig in April 1935, at the age of forty-five, five professors—among them Werner Heisenberg (the Nobel Prize winner in physics in 1932), Bernhardt Schweitzer (a classical archaeologist), and Bartel Leendert van der Waerden (a professor of mathematics at Leipzig)—unsuccessfully protested Landsberger's dismissal. Van der Waerden was subsequently himself threatened with dismissal by the very dean whom they had petitioned.[8]

---

5. Thomas Schneider, "Ägyptologen im Dritten Reich: Biographische Notizen anhand der sogenannten 'Steindorff-Liste,'" *Journal of Egyptian History* 5, no. 1 (2012): 120–247 (at 207–8).

6. Ludmilla Hanisch refers to the Swedish Orientalist H. S. Nyberg, who observed in 1937 that German Assyriologists had retreated into the solitude of their studies (*sich in die Einsamkeit der Studierstube zurückgezogen hätten*). See Ludmilla Hanisch, *Die Nachfolger der Exegeten: Deutschsprachige Erforschung des Vorderen Orients in der ersten Hälfte des 20. Jahrhunderts* (Wiesbaden, Germany: Harrassowitz, 2003), 153.

7. Horst Junginger, "Religionswissenschaft," in Elvert and Nielsen-Sikora, *Kulturwissenschaften und Nationalsozialismus*, 52–86 (at 68–70).

8. Renger, "Altorientalistik," 475.

Academic Dismissal and Exile

The position of Assyriology as a discipline became precarious in the years following 1933. Several positions became vacant because of retirement (for example, Bruno Meissner in Berlin). More importantly, though, several major professors were dismissed and exiled at the beginning of the Nazi period because they were Jews: in addition to the aforementioned Benno Landsberger in Leipzig, Ernst Herzfeld in Berlin and Julius Lewy and Hildegard Lewy in Giessen also lost their positions.[9] Albrecht Götze fled Marburg in March of 1933 under dramatic circumstances in order to avoid being sent to a concentration camp because of his active leftist political engagement against the Nazi Party.[10] Otto Neugebauer, one of the most important scholars of Babylonian mathematics and astronomy, went into exile early in 1933 when he refused to take the oath of loyalty to Hitler that was demanded of all civil servants and professors. In addition, a number of younger Assyriologists were forced to emigrate: Martin David, Hugo Figulla, Hans Gustav Güterbock, Fritz Rudolf Kraus, Paul Kraus, and Hermann Pick, followed by Leo Oppenheim and Edith Porada after the annexation of Austria in 1938.[11]

New Appointments

Vacancies in Assyriological positions were not always filled. For example, no successor was appointed for Julius Lewy in Giessen. On the other hand, the

---

9. In the Institute of Archaeology at Hebrew University, Jerusalem, documents from the estate of Benno Landberger were discovered by Nathan Wasserman. They contain private letters, manuscripts of public lectures, photos, notes, and notebooks from his time as a student in Leipzig. As far as I can tell, all of these documents are from the days before Landsberger went into exile. The material was cataloged by Michael P. Streck, Leipzig. For further information, see Michael P. Streck and Nathan Wasserman, "Landsberger Archive," accessed October 16, 2021, https://altorient.gko.uni-leipzig.de/landsberger.html.

10. See Harald Maier-Metz, *Entlassungsgrund: Pazifismus. Albrecht Götze, der Fall Gumbel, und die Marburger Universität 1930–1946*, Academia Marburgensis 13 (Münster, Germany: Waxmann, 2015).

11. David, Güterbock and F. R. Kraus were students of Landsberger. For letters exchanged between Kraus in Istanbul and Landsberger in Ankara, see Jan Schmidt, "Exil im Orient: Die Briefe von Fritz Rudolf Kraus aus Istanbul, 1937–1949," in *Der Orient in akademischer Optik: Beiträge zur Genese einer Wissenschaftsdisziplin*, ed. Ludmilla Hanisch, Orientwissenschaftliche Hefte 20 (Halle [Saale], Germany: OWZ, 2006), 145–54, and Jan Schmidt, ed., *Dreizehn Jahre Istanbul (1937–1949): Der deutsche Assyriologe Fritz Rudolf Kraus und sein Briefwechsel im türkischen Exil*, 2 vols. (Leiden, Netherlands: Brill, 2014). Nearly every day after my work on the *Chicago Assyrian Dictionary*, I would talk to Landsberger in his office, from the fall of 1966 until his death in the spring of 1968. We talked about everything from lexicography to his memories concerning his students and colleagues.

Marburg faculty gave Götze's professorship to Carl Frank, a mediocre scholar and political opportunist. When it came to replacements for Bruno Meissner in Berlin and Benno Landsberger in Leipzig—the two most prominent positions in Germany—the universities' respective faculties emphasized Indo-European studies [*Indogermanisch*, as it was called among German scholars] in their new appointments. Accordingly, the new Leipzig chair in Assyriology, Johannes Friedrich, was a Hittitologist. After his appointment, Friedrich found a way to avoid becoming a member of the Nazi Party or paying tribute to Nazi ideology. He served as the rector of the University of Leipzig during the 1948–49 academic year, before leaving in 1950 for the Freie Universität Berlin, in the western part of Berlin.

In Berlin, similar arguments were cited in favor of the appointment of Hans Ehelolf, who actually died before the faculty reached a decision. Bruno Meissner tried to influence the faculty's deliberations, but his letters show that his interventions were mainly determined by personal prejudices or irrational aversions to some of the contenders. He argued against von Soden, saying he was still too young. Von Soden's connections to (the Jewish) Benno Landsberger, his teacher, coupled with the scholarly rivalry between Meissner's school of Assyriology and Landsberger's "Leipzig school," also played a role. Meissner preferred Erich Ebeling, with whom he had been associated for many years as editor of the respected *Reallexikon der Assyriologie* (1928–).[12] But Ebeling was hardly eligible, because he had steadfastly refused to join the Nazi Party. In the end, the faculty appointed von Soden, who at thirty-two years old was one of the leading Assyriologists in Germany, with stupendous scholarly achievements to his credit. His early membership in the Sturmabteilung [Storm Troopers (SA)] may have played a role, although von Soden had only become a party member more recently.[13] Archaeologist Eckhard Unger, who succeeded the dismissed Ernst Herzfeld in ancient Near Eastern archaeology at Berlin, had been a party member since 1932, though such allegiance was probably not decisive in his appointment.

II. OFFICES AND OTHER INSTITUTIONS OF THE NAZI PARTY

In addition to the April 1933 Law for the Restoration of the Professional Civil Service and instructions to universities by local ministries (such as the Saxon

---

12. Erich Ebeling and Bruno Meissner, eds., *Reallexikon der Assyriologie* (Berlin: Walter de Gruyter, 1928–2018).

13. On the gap between von Soden joining the SA and the Nazi Party, see section 4, under "Wolfram von Soden," with the associated note explaining von Soden's biographical information. See also Renger, "Altorientalistik," 476–77, 483.

Ministry of Public Instruction, as noted previously), the Nazi Party established several bodies intended to foster ideological conformity in the academic realm. Two institutions were foremost among these: (1) the Ahnenerbe [Ancestral Heritage Research Institute], a Nazi think tank instituted in 1935 by Heinrich Himmler, chief of the Schutzstaffel (SS), which was meant to promote academic teaching and research about the superiority of the Aryan race, and (2) its rival, with similar goals, the Amt Rosenberg, with its Hohe Schule [Advanced School of the National Socialist German Workers' Party (NSDAP)], chartered on January 29, 1940, after a long period of planning, which sought to create a university for the Nazi elite.[14]

Despite their common aim of Nazi academic indoctrination, the Ahnenerbe and the Amt Rosenberg came into frequent conflict over areas of competence and jurisdiction. As is typical in autocratic states, their actions were at times disorganized. Walter Frank, a Nazi historian, and others in the circle of Reichsleiter Alfred Rosenberg, the head of the Amt Rosenberg, struggled to position themselves as leaders on the *Judenfrage* [Jewish Question]. Bernhard Rust, the Reichsminister for Science, Education, and Public Instruction, and Martin Mutschmann, the governor of the state of Saxony, came into similar conflict when Mutschmann dismissed five Jewish professors from the universities of Dresden and Leipzig in the spring of 1935, among them the Assyriologist Benno Landsberger. Rust regarded himself as the only responsible authority to act in such cases and therefore appealed directly to Hitler, who in the end let Mutschmann have his way, perhaps because Mutschmann had lent him considerable sums of money in the years before 1933.[15]

Besides the Ahnenerbe and the Hohe Schule, both of which were intended to be alternative elite universities, several party offices were established to observe, control, and direct scholarship and research at universities and other academic institutions. These were integrated into the SS or put under the direct supervision of Rosenberg, who belonged to the inner circle of the Nazi

---

14. See Michael Kater, *Das "Ahnenerbe" der SS, 1935–1945: Ein Beitrag zur Kulturpolitik des Dritten Reiches*, 4th ed., Studien zur Zeitgeschichte 6 (Munich: Oldenbourg, 2006); Junginger, "Religionswissenschaft," 77–79; Schneider, "Ägyptologen im Dritten Reich," 165; Hanisch, *Nachfolger der Exegeten*, 150–52; and Renger, "Altorientalistik," 470–71. For the Amt Rosenberg, see the bibliography in Stefan Altekamp, "Klassische Archäologie," in Elvert and Nielsen-Sikora, *Kulturwissenschaften und Nationalsozialismus*, 167–209 (at 197n130); Gerd Simon, "Zur Schulung der Elite im 3. Reich," accessed July 17, 2017, https://homepages.uni-tuebingen.de/gerd.simon/elite1.htm; and Thomas Schneider's contribution to this volume, "Hermann Grapow, Egyptology, and National Socialist Initiatives for the Humanities."

15. Renger, "Altorientalistik," 475.

hierarchy. First among these was the Hauptamt Wissenschaft [Main Office for Scholarship], headed by Rosenberg. Second was the Sicherheitsdienst [SD, the security service of the SS], a kind of political FBI, which was led by Reinhard Heydrich. The SD was eventually integrated into the Reichssicherheitshauptamt [RSHA, Main Office for Reich Security] in 1939.[16] Both the SD and the RSHA were responsible for surveillance of academic faculty and institutions.[17] The office of Rudolf Hess, Hitler's deputy in the Nazi Party, also issued recommendations in particular cases.[18] In addition, the leading functionaries of the Nationalsozialistischer Deutscher Dozentenbund [National Socialist German University Instructors' League (NSDDozB)], a kind of mandatory professional association, kept an eye on all academic personnel; together with the head of each institution's Nazi student union, the NSDDozB made recommendations for all academic appointments.[19] Working together, these institutions exerted considerable control over German universities and the academic freedom of the scholars working at them.

The primary ideological directive for research and teaching at universities under the Nazi regime was the concept of race as an overriding social and cultural issue. Scientific research, hitherto the mainstay of German academia, was to be replaced by race science, culminating in the absurd idea of an "Aryan" physics freed from the ideas of Albert Einstein.[20] Rosenberg was the driving force in this regard, seeing himself as the guardian of Nazi ideology. He was the founding personality of a state religion—the veneration of *Germanentum* [Teutonicism]—which was premised on a so-called *arische Weltanschauungslehre* [Aryan worldview].[21] Himmler, too, promoted ostensible German and

---

16. For intervention in decisions concerning academic appointments, see Hans-Joachim Dahms, "Philosophie," in Elvert and Nielsen-Sikora, *Kulturwissenschaften und Nationalsozialismus*, 19–51 (at 48n136).

17. In 1938, the RSHA stated that the discipline of Ancient History had not made sufficient efforts toward developing a Nazi concept of history. For the SD's role in the appointment of Adam Falkenstein as associate professor in Göttingen in 1940, see his personnel files in Renger, "Altorientalistik," 497. Falkenstein's precarious political position is treated extensively on pages 495–98. After Falkenstein was drafted for the army, he was eventually stationed in Turkey for military intelligence. In the spring of 1941, he took part in the unsuccessful German campaign under Fritz Grobba, a German diplomat, which was supposed to aid the Iraqi army in maintaining its régime after the coup d'état against the British.

18. Further on Paul Koschaker, see discussion of Walther Hinz in section 4 in this chapter.

19. Renger, "Altorientalistik," 470.

20. Helmut W. Schaller, "Südosteuropaforschung," in Elvert and Nielsen-Sikora, *Kulturwissenschaften und Nationalsozialismus*, 312–36 (at 329).

21. Junginger, "Religionswissenschaft," 72.

Teutonic beliefs, culture, and values as the nucleus of a new religion. The Amt Rosenberg and the Ahnenerbe issued constant "admonitions" because humanities faculties did not participate adequately in discussions concerning this most important ideological discourse "of our time,"[22] suggesting that the authorities were not always successful in their attempts to remake academia in their image.

The work of J. W. Hauer, an engaged supporter of the Nazi regime and a professor of religion at the University of Tübingen, provides one example of how this ideological drive intersected with Assyriology and other Near Eastern disciplines. Hauer made the case for promoting an Indo-Germanic worldview and the concept of race in a March 4, 1935, memorandum to the Reichsministerium für Wissenschaft, Erziehung, und Volksbildung [Reich Ministry of Science, Education, and Public Instruction]. The memorandum was, among other things, directed against one of the most reputable journals in the fields of Assyriology and Oriental studies, the *Orientalistische Literaturzeitung*, which had been founded by Felix Peiser, a Jewish Assyriologist, in 1898. Walter Wreszinski, a Jewish Egyptologist at the University of Königsberg, succeeded Peiser, serving as editor from 1921 to 1934. He was followed by Richard Hartmann, an Arabist, who served as editor until 1961. Hauer argued in his memorandum that it was necessary to restructure German universities so that race would be at the center of teaching and research. In disciplines like Egyptology, for instance, Hauer believed an orientation toward the ideological was essential. Since these disciplines were influenced by a Near Eastern–Semitic worldview that had spread into Judaism and Christianity, Hauer claimed that there was no alternative but to implement a Nazi Weltanschauung as a countermeasure. He claimed that this Indo-Germanic worldview was essential to give the Third Reich a firm ideological foundation.[23] Thus the academic discipline of *Religionswissenschaft* [the history of religions] at Tübingen and elsewhere was transformed into a discipline of antisemitism.[24]

III. ASSYRIOLOGY IN TROUBLED WATERS

Among the several disciplines focusing on the Middle East or ancient Near East, Arabic and Turkish studies grew increasingly prominent because they were relevant to Nazi foreign policy. Other disciplines, such as Assyriology

---

22. See Hanisch, *Nachfolger der Exegeten*.
23. Schneider, "Ägyptologen im Dritten Reich," 125.
24. Junginger, "Religionswissenschaft," 70–83.

and Egyptology, were less central, but their relatively obscure status did not shield them completely from ideological interference.[25] Because Assyriology was usually taught by scholars holding chairs in Semitic languages, Assyriologists had to cope with Nazi bias against anything having to do with Semitics. As a result, many chairs in Semitic philology were renamed, becoming chairs in Oriental languages or the like. The word *Semitic* was forcefully rejected. Terms such as *Morgenlandforschung* were favored instead. The word, derived from Martin Luther's translation of the Greek word *anatolé* in Matt 2:1, had been adopted for Near Eastern studies in the middle of the nineteenth century. The overriding emphasis on race in all matters meant that the declared antisemitism of the Nazi regime became the matrix through which other civilizations and cultures were henceforth seen and interpreted. This created some problems for disciplines that were supposed to be free of Semitic taint. The Roman emperor Septimius Severus, for example, was of undeniably Punic (and therefore Semitic) origin, and the Punic Carthaginians were initially victorious in their series of wars with Rome. The Oriental customs of the Aryan Persians under Islam were also seen as "Semitic degeneration."[26]

Some Assyriologists pointed to the vast and successful empires of the Babylonians and Assyrians in an effort to mitigate antisemitic bias against Assyriology. For example, in *Der Aufstieg des Assyrerreiches als geschichtliches Problem* [The rise of the Assyrian Empire as a historical problem], Wolfram von Soden claimed that the belligerent attitude and military prowess of the Assyrians were uncharacteristic of Semitic peoples and should therefore be attributed to the influence of a nonsemitic, and specifically Aryan, population.[27] The Assyrians allegedly shared their land with hypothetical mountainous people

---

25. Two recent books examine Near Eastern Studies or *Orientalistik* (i.e., studies concerning Arabic and Turkish) in Germany between 1933 and 1945: Hanisch, *Nachfolger der Exegeten*, and Ekkehard Ellinger, *Deutsche Orientalistik zur Zeit des Nationalsozialismus 1933–1945*, Thèses 4 (Edingen-Neckarhausen, Germany: Deux Mondes, 2006). See further the contribution to this volume by Suzanne L. Marchand, "The 'Orient' and 'Us': Making Ancient Oriental Studies Relevant during the Nazi Regime." For Egyptology, see Schneider, "Ägyptologen im Dritten Reich," and his contribution to this volume. On Assyriology, see the publications by Johannes Renger in the bibliography at the end of this chapter.

26. Joseph Wiesehöfer, "Alte Geschichte," in Elvert and Nielsen-Sikora, *Kulturwissenschaften und Nationalsozialismus*, 210–22 (at 216). Wilhelm Eilers, the Iranist who in 1941 served in the German Archaeological Institute in Isfahan, also lamented in a letter the degeneration of the Indo-European Iranians by the Semites (personal communication to Johannes Renger by Ignace J. Gelb, who had access to German documents in 1945 while serving for the Office of Strategic Services [OSS]).

27. Wolfram von Soden, *Der Aufstieg des Assyrerreiches als geschichtliches Problem*, Der Alte Orient 37/1 (Leipzig, Germany: J. C. Hinrichs, 1937). Eckart Frahm, "Images of Assyria

from the East who were not Semitic in background and given the name of *Bergvölker* [mountain tribes]. Arthur Ungnad in 1923 posited the influence of this Aryan population as a decisive factor in the history of the Assyrians; subsequently ancient Near Eastern archaeologist Anton Moortgat claimed to be able to identify the *Bergvölker* in Near Eastern reliefs and cylinder seals.[28] Von Soden's monograph was critically reviewed and his claims forcefully rejected by William Foxwell Albright:

> While the reviewer ... considers the racial philosophy of history as purely fictitious, he cheerfully admits that one's cultural background has very profound influence on one's intellectual orientation. The well-known polarity of German intellectual activity, which combines sober, slightly pedestrian patience in research ... with a tendency to indulge in far-reaching speculations in a transmundane metaphysical sphere, is nowhere better illustrated than in the sharply defined, relatively insignificant field of Assyriology. German Assyriology has not only given us Delitzsch and Landsberger (both accidentally non-Aryan) but also Winckler and Jeremias (both accidentally Aryan). The reviewer earnestly hopes that the author [i.e., von Soden] remains in the first group and does not shift to the second. ... Certain tendencies in the present study make one hesitate to predict what will happen.[29]

---

in Nineteenth- and Twentieth-Century Western Scholarship," in *Orientalism, Assyriology, and the Bible*, ed. Steven W. Holloway, Hebrew Bible Monographs 10 (Sheffield, UK: Sheffield Phoenix Press, 2006), 74–94 (at 86), astutely points out that "the weak foundations of his arguments must have been obvious even to von Soden himself, who in later publications never repeated his racial explanation for the spirit of the Middle-Assyrian age." But see section 4, under "Wolfram von Soden," with the associated note explaining von Soden's family background. [Editors' note: In addition, however, such a racialized Aryan explanation of the evidence would no longer have been respectable in the postwar period. The mere fact of their not surfacing again in his work may or may not, therefore, speak to whether von Soden was no longer persuaded by them.]

28. Arthur Ungnad, *Die ältesten Völkerwanderungen Vorderasiens: Ein Beitrag zur Geschichte und Kultur der Semiten, Arier, Hethiter, und Subaräer* (Breslau, Germany: Selbstverlag, 1923); Anton Moortgat, *Die Bildende Kunst des Alten Orients und die Bergvölker* (Berlin: Schoetz, 1932).

29. William Foxwell Albright, review of *Der Aufstieg des Assyrerreiches als geschichtliches Problem* by Wolfram von Soden, *Orientalia*, n.s. 8 (1939): 120–23 (at 120). It is not clear what Albright meant by describing Delitzsch as non-Aryan; the description makes no sense. The tendency to explain history as resulting from ethnic or even racial reasons was strictly denied by Thorkild Jacobsen. See Jerrold S. Cooper, "Sumerian and Aryan Racial Theory: Academic Politics and Parisian Assyriology," *Revue de l'histoire des religions* 210 (1993): 169–205.

IV. PROMINENT ASSYRIOLOGISTS WHO EMBRACED NAZI IDEOLOGY

To more fully examine the effect of Nazism on the field of Assyriology, the remainder of this chapter will focus on the histories of seven scholars. After first summarizing the most relevant details of their individual careers and publications during the Nazi era in this section, the final section of the chapter will then address the extent to which they played a role in the promotion of Nazi ideology within the field of Assyriology.

Wolfram von Soden

Wolfram von Soden (1908–1996) joined the SA in 1933 and the Nazi Party in 1937.[30] He became an associate professor in Göttingen in 1936. From 1940 to 1945, he held a chair in Berlin, but he actually never taught there because he was serving in the military as an Arabic interpreter. Von Soden wrote three works that exhibit Nazi ideology: (1) "Leistung und Grenze sumerischer und babylonischer Wissenschaft" [The accomplishment and limits of Sumerian and Babylonian science]; (2) *Der Aufstieg des Assyrerreiches als geschichtliches Problem* (mentioned previously); and (3) "Neue Untersuchungen über die Bedeutung der Indogermanen für den Alten Orient" [New studies in the significance of the Indo-Europeans for the ancient Near East].[31] I will focus here on the first

---

30. It is worth noting Wolfram von Soden's family background. His father Hans von Soden, professor of church history at the Theologische Fakultät of the University of Marburg, was a leading figure in the *Bekennende Kirche* (Confessing Church) and an engaged opponent of Nazi politics. This led to considerable, intense conflicts with his father (personal communication from the family, October 1996; see also Renger, "Altorientalistik," 481). Regarding von Soden's membership in the Nazi Party, Rykle Borger states in his obituary for von Soden, on the basis of an earlier interview with von Soden, that he joined the Nazi Party in 1944. The Document Center, however, has the personnel file dating his joining the NSDAP already in 1937. It should be noted that the NSDAP stopped the admission of new party members in the spring of 1933 and opened its ranks again in 1937. Thus, after joining the SA, he joined the Nazi Party as soon as he was able. See Renger, "Altorientalistik," 481n73.

31. "Leistung und Grenze sumerischer und babylonischer Wissenschaft" was published in *Die Welt als Geschichte* 2 (1936): 411–64 and 509–57. The article was reprinted with additions and corrections in Benno Landsberger and Wolfram von Soden, *Die Eigenbegrifflichkeit der babylonischen Welt*, Libelli 142 (Darmstadt, Germany: Wissenschaftliche Buchgesellschaft, 1965), 21–133. In the reprint, von Soden provided some later reflections on the original publication. Landsberger privately communicated to me that he had unsuccessfully tried to persuade von Soden to correct some of his unacceptable statements (Benno Landsberger, conversation with the author, 1967). For discussion of *Der Aufstieg des Assyrerreiches*

of these publications, "Leistung und Grenze," which is "the most scholarly and the most valuable [to Assyriology]" of the three works but which also exemplifies how Nazi ideology informs all three publications.[32] Although "Leistung und Grenze" includes a straightforward presentation of evidence, von Soden's conclusions in comparing the ancient Near Eastern (that is, Semitic) system of thought to the allegedly superior Indo-Germanic intellectual system are highly problematic. For example, though he discusses the Babylonians' exceptional cultural achievements, he nevertheless maintains that science in the strict sense of the word was only possible for the specific Aryan intellectual capacity of the Indo-Germanic Greeks or of the Indian subcontinent.[33] To the best of my knowledge, there exists no critical review of the work in a scholarly journal outside Germany.

In hindsight, one may surmise that the work—which stresses in great detail the enormous cultural achievements of ancient Mesopotamian scholars—was meant to defend Mesopotamian civilization and thus the discipline of Assyriology against an aggressive, antisemitic Nazi ideological bias, although the defense takes the form of supporting that very ideological bias. Such an assumption is plausible given that Helmuth Berve, a leading scholar of Greek history, denied Egyptology its very existence because its subject was an alien race that could not be understood from a Nazi point of view.[34] It is also noteworthy in this context that von Soden referred to his teacher Landsberger (by then in exile in Ankara) for decisive factual details, and he did not refrain—despite official directives—from quoting Landsberger in other publications. When

---

als geschichtliches Problem, see section 3, "Assyriology in Troubled Waters." "Neue Untersuchungen über die Bedeutung der Indogermanen für den Alten Orient" was published in *Göttingische Gelehrte Anzeigen* 200 (1938): 195–216. For a detailed study of these three works by von Soden, see Jakob Flygare, "Assyriology under Nazism: A Contextual Analysis of Three Texts by Wolfram von Soden from 1936–38," *Journal of Associated Graduates in Near Eastern Studies* 11 (2006): 3–42. See further Jakob Flygare, "Assyriologi under nazismen: En kontekstuel undersøgelse af tre tekster af Wolfram von Soden fra 1936–38," Master's thesis, University of Copenhagen, 2005.

32. Flygare, "Assyriology under Nazism," 4. Flygare describes *Aufstieg des Assyrerreiches* as "overtly politicized" and "not . . . of any value to Assyriology," and he says of von Soden's work in "Neue Untersuchungen" that "he appears as a talented scholar who is arguing on an absurd ideological basis" (ibid., 4–5). See further Flygare's recent publication, "Assyriology in Nazi Germany: The Case of Wolfram von Soden," in *Perspectives on the History of Ancient Near Eastern Studies,* ed. Agnès Garcia-Ventura and Lorenzo Verderame (University Park, PA: Eisenbrauns, 2020): 44–60.

33. Renger, "Altorientalistik," 482–83.

34. Schneider, "Ägyptologen im Dritten Reich," 183.

von Soden succeeded Landsberger as the editor of *Zeitschrift für Assyriologie*, he did not hesitate to publish an article by his teacher Landsberger, and he kept Landsberger's name, as former editor, on the title page of the journal, drawing the ire of Eckhard Unger, an ancient Near Eastern archaeologist who was a dedicated member of the Nazi Party.[35]

Landsberger and von Soden's relationship continued after World War II. In 1952, as a result of correspondence between W. F. Albright and Landsberger,[36] Landsberger accepted von Soden's dedication of his epochal Akkadian grammar (*Grundriss der akkadischen Grammatik*) to him because many of von Soden's new insights went back to Landsberger's work. When the Faculty of Göttingen refused to reinstall von Soden to his former position the same year, Landsberger wrote a letter on von Soden's behalf to the dean of the Faculty of Philosophy, arguing that it was shameful that such an eminent scholar should not find an adequate academic position merely because of his uncritical political utterances. According to Landsberger, the faculty's decision was detrimental to the discipline of Assyriology.[37] That might be accurate. However, that decision in Göttingen, coupled with von Soden's failure to secure an appointment in Germany until 1961, despite his scholarly credentials, certainly must represent the judgment of postwar German colleagues about the seriousness of the pro-Nazi stance he had maintained. While Landsberger's support assisted von Soden's return to academia, von Soden remained controversial even after his appointment at Vienna. When von Soden visited Chicago on the occasion of the annual conference of the discipline (Rencontre Assyriologique Internationale) in 1967, nonetheless, Landsberger invited a number of colleagues to a welcome dinner in "honor of Wolfram Freiherr von Soden."[38] At the same time, because of von Soden's presence at this major conference, F. R. Kraus, who had been forced to leave Germany and go into exile in Turkey because he was seen as half Jewish under Nazi law (and therefore unable to hold an academic position or other employment), refused to attend.[39]

---

35. Renger, "Altorientalistik," 483.
36. Benno Landsberger, personal communication to the author, 1967.
37. Renger, "Altorientalistik," 483.
38. The quoted phrase comes from the artfully designed invitation that Landsberger sent. The author of this chapter and his wife were invited to the restaurant dinner, along with the Oppenheims, the Gelbs, Thorkild Jacobsen, Rykle Borger, and the Rowtons.
39. Thus in a letter to Landsberger; according to an oral personal communication from Landsberger to the present author, summer 1967.

Bruno Meissner

Bruno Meissner (1868–1947) joined the Nazi Party in March 1933. Immediately after Hitler assumed power, he offered a university-wide series of lectures designed to indoctrinate students into Nazi ideology. The focus of the course was a central theme of Nazi ideology: "Introduction to the Races in the Ancient Near East." When he applied to participate in an international congress in Rome, he was commended for supporting the Nazi Party at the university. But one should also note that between 1934 and 1936, two Jewish students—Moritz Seidmann and Markus Ehrenkranz (who changed his name to Mordechai Zer-Kavod after he emigrated to Palestine)—received their doctorates under his supervision. Besides the course on race, Meissner's scholarship was devoted entirely to his Akkadian dictionary and to the *Reallexikon der Assyriologie*, neither of which shows any sign of Nazi ideology. His attempt to integrate the *Reallexikon* into the Ahnenerbe proved futile.

Arthur Ungnad

Arthur Ungnad (1879–1945), who retired from the University of Breslau in 1930 due to poor health, had a great international reputation.[40] Around the turn of the century, he began to argue that the Subarians, a nonsemitic ethnic population in the northern part of Mesopotamia, were the founders of the Assyrian state.[41] Such a thesis was, of course, a bold attempt to deny any Semitic roots for the powerful Assyrian empire, as well as for the discipline of Assyriology. In 1923, he published his ideas in his book *Die ältesten Völkerwanderungen Vorderasiens: Ein Beitrag zur Geschichte und Kultur der Semiten, Arier, Hethiter, und Subaräer* [The earliest migrations of the Middle East: A contribution to the history and culture of the Semites, Aryans, Hittites, and Subarians], maintaining that ethnic characteristics played an important role in ancient Near Eastern history. In 1935, he sought to publish an article developing these ideas in the prestigious journal, *Zeitschrift der Deutschen Morgenländischen Gesellschaft*. The journal's editor was Paul Kahle, a leading Semitist (who was subsequently dismissed from the University of Bonn in 1939 and forced to emigrate to England because his wife and son had supported Jewish victims of the November pogroms of 1938). Kahle rejected Ungnad's manuscript, writing: "Ich bin der

---

40. For details, see Renger, "Altorientalistik," 487–89.
41. As noted previously, the role of nonsemitic ethnic elements from the East was also the subject of Anton Moortgat's book, *Die bildende Kunst des Alten Orients und die Bergvölker* (1932).

Ansicht, wenn etwas über Rasse in Deutschland publiziert wird und unter der Aegide der Deutschen Morgenländischen Gesellschaft erscheint, muß es wissenschaftlich ganz einwandfrei sein" [In my view, if something concerning race is to be published in Germany and appear under the aegis of the German Oriental Society, it must be completely irreproachable scholarship].[42]

Carl Frank and Eckhard Unger

Carl Frank (in Marburg) and Eckhard Unger (in Istanbul and later Berlin) were known, dedicated members of the Nazi Party. They were regarded as marginal members in the field of Assyriology, however, never as influential scholars. They had no students, and their scholarly shortcomings were aggravated by their disreputable personal behavior. Frank (1881–1945) was an associate professor of Assyriology in Strassburg until 1918 and a full Professor in Marburg from 1936 until 1945. In the spring of 1933, he joined the Nazi Party, giving up his membership in the Deutsch-Nationale Volkspartei.[43] Unger (1884–1966) was an archaeologist and a staunch member of the Nazi Party, which he joined on January 1, 1932. In 1930, he became a nontenured associate professor of Near Eastern archaeology in Berlin; from 1932 to 1935, he was the director of the Museum for the Ancient Orient in Istanbul; and from 1938 until 1945, he was a tenured associate professor in Berlin.[44] He believed that some ancient Near Eastern phenomena (including the swastika) should be seen as precursors of important Nazi ideas. Unger's controversial scholarship and his rather absurd ideas were harshly reviewed by von Soden, leading to a vicious controversy between the two that almost ended up in civil court.[45]

Viktor Christian

The two figures of greatest interest in terms of Nazi involvement are Viktor Christian and Walther Hinz. Even before 1933, Christian (1886–1961) was actively engaged in the Nazi movement in Austria. He was dismissed from

---

42. Paul Kahle, letter to the famous Arabist, Karl Brockelmann, dated March 15, 1935; as cited in Hanisch, *Nachfolger der Exegeten*, 154n548. In 1936, Ungnad nonetheless published the text as a book: *Subartu: Beiträge zur Kulturgeschichte und Rassenforschung Vorderasiens* (Berlin: Walter de Gruyter, 1936). See Renger, "Altorientalistik," 488. On Kahle's dismissal and emigration, see Junginger, "Religionswissenschaft," 67.
43. Renger, "Altorientalistik," 485–87.
44. Ibid., 489–91.
45. For von Soden's extensive critique of Unger's ideas, see his "Neue Untersuchungen über die Bedeutung der Indogermanen für den Alten Orient," *Göttingische Gelehrte Anzeigen* 200 (1938): 195–216.

his university position in Vienna after the Dolfuss putsch in 1934 and was reinstalled after Austria's annexation by Hitler in March 1938.[46] He became a member of the SS and section head within the Ahnenerbe and thus a member of Himmler's personal staff. Nevertheless, Christian faced censure by the NSDDozB and SD for having acted too leniently, as dean, toward Catholic colleagues sympathetic to the Vatican and for having been too friendly to Jewish colleagues. These problems ended after Himmler intervened directly on February 26, 1942.[47] As section head of the Ahnenerbe, Christian brought the *Wiener Zeitschrift für die Kunde des Morgenlandes*, the illustrious journal of the Oriental Institute of the University of Vienna, under its jurisdiction. In his own writings he contributed to a new interpretation of history, arguing forcefully that Nordic, and specifically Indo-Germanic, peoples had appeared in the Near East and left their mark before Semites arrived there.[48]

Walther Hinz

Walther Hinz (1906–1992), who studied journalism, oriental languages, and East European history, on which he wrote his dissertation, served in the German counterespionage services in Turkey between 1942 and 1945. He authored a lengthy memorandum concerning Oriental studies (see below) and was an expert on ancient Iran and its languages. He had studied in Leipzig, where he was well acquainted with Benno Landsberger and Paul Koschaker, the most eminent historian of Roman and ancient Near Eastern law.[49] Until 1937—before his appointment as professor of Iranian studies in Göttingen—he worked as a civil service official first in the Ministry of Defense and then, after 1934, in the Reich Ministry of Science, Education, and Public Instruction. There are indications that Hinz aided in arranging Adam Falkenstein's appointment as an associate of Paul Koschaker in Berlin (see below).[50]

---

46. In July 1934, Nazi activists led a coup d'état in which Austria's chancellor, Engelbert Dolfuss, was killed. Despite Dolfuss's assassination, the coup attempt failed. For extensive excerpts from Christian's personnel file at the University of Vienna, see Gerd Simon, "Chronologie Viktor Christian," accessed August 23, 2018, https://homepages.uni-tuebingen.de/gerd.simon/ChrChristian.pdf, and Gerd Simon, "Tödlicher Bücherwahn: Der letzte Wiener Universitätsrektor im 3. Reich und der Tod seines Kollegen Norbert Jokl," accessed August 23, 2018, https://homepages.uni-tuebingen.de/gerd.simon/buecherwahn.pdf.

47. On Himmler's intervention, see Bundesarchiv Berlin, Berlin Document Center, Akte Ahnenerbe, Blatt 115.

48. Renger, "Altorientalistik," 484–85.

49. Georg Neumann, "Paul Koschaker in Tübingen (1941–1946)," *Zeitschrift für altorientalische und biblische Rechtsgeschichte* 18 (2012): 23–36.

50. Renger, "Altorientalistik," 496.

In his reminiscences about this period, Koschaker recalled that in connection with the negotiations for his appointment in Berlin, the ministry offered to find a position for Landsberger at the Vorderasiatisches Museum, so that he could work in relative seclusion and so that the two could continue their collaboration.[51] It is likely that Hinz was active in this regard. However, Landsberger's emigration to Turkey in 1935 rendered this superfluous. Landsberger himself remembered Hinz as having been very considerate and courteous toward him when he came to visit him in his SS uniform at the Institute in Leipzig between 1933 and 1935.[52]

V. ASSYRIOLOGY AND THE LEGITIMATION AND PROPAGATION OF NAZI POSITIONS

Assyriology did not occupy a significant place in the general Nazi concept of history, which was more focused on the (early) history of Europe. Thus, two questions arise with regard to the role of Assyriology or of individual Assyriologists in the process of legitimizing Nazi ideology and politics: (1) Was Assyriology used to legitimize and propagate Nazi positions and to what extent? (2) How did individual scholars actively contribute? There are some indications that Nazi institutions used the discipline for ideological purposes. Viktor Christian, in particular, was active as a leading figure in the Ahnenerbe, but his attempts and those of Alfred Rosenberg's Hohe Schule bore no fruit, since most Assyriologists had been drafted for service in the army.

German Academic Societies for Oriental Studies and the Propagation of Nazi Ideas

During the Nazi era, Germany had two major academic societies for scholars in Oriental studies: the Deutsche Morgenländische Gesellschaft and the Deutsche Orient-Gesellschaft. Information concerning the role of the Deutsche Morgenländische Gesellschaft in the years from 1933 to 1945 is lacking, but the Deutsche Orient-Gesellschaft encountered serious problems with the regime, which forced the society to expel its many Jewish members in 1938.[53] Unlike

---

51. Ibid., 479.
52. Benno Landsberger, personal communication to the author, 1967.
53. See Gernot Wilhelm, ed., *Zwischen Tigris und Nil: 100 Jahre Ausgrabungen der Deutschen Orient-Gesellschaft in Vorderasien und Ägypten* (Mainz, Germany: Philipp von Zabern, 1998), 10. See also Renger, "Altorientalistik," 498.

other disciplines, Assyriology in Germany had no institutionalized association, no platform to formulate common goals or voice common concerns. Assyriologists would have had an opportunity to meet at the annual meetings of the Deutsche Morgenländische Gesellschaft and the Deutsche Orient-Gesellschaft, but there are no indications that Assyriologists used these groups' meetings to discuss or formulate common goals or policy statements on any pressing matters. Nor do we know which members of the discipline attended the meetings or whether private conversations may have touched on political developments.

It appears that Assyriologists of the younger generation kept themselves away from involvement with the regime. The outbreak of the war—at which point most of them were drafted for military service—brought scholarship in the discipline to a standstill. Of the three senior scholars in the field, one—von Soden—was also in the army. Johannes Friedrich remained in Leipzig, where he lived and worked in scholarly solitude. Only Viktor Christian continued to present his ideas in public lectures and in writing. As the last rector of the University of Vienna before 1945, he worked actively for the regime.

Scholarly Positions in Conformity with Nazi Ideas

The main question here regards whether Nazi ideology penetrated into the discipline of Assyriology. To be sure, four scholars of national and international standing in the field—Arthur Ungnad, Bruno Meissner, Wolfram von Soden, and Viktor Christian—disseminated ideas that reflected Nazi doctrine. At issue are Ungnad with his last book, von Soden with the two major articles mentioned previously, and Bruno Meissner with his participation in a university-wide lecture series for the indoctrination of the student body in 1934–35. None of these three seems to have had a visible or lasting impact on the discipline of Assyriology. Their opinions never found their way into general history textbooks and therefore to a wider scholarly public (with the exception of a reprint that combined von Soden's article with another by Landsberger).[54] Viktor Christian vigorously offered his theses on the Indo-Germanic origins of Mesopotamian culture, but they have, to my knowledge, never found

---

54. As far as I remember from my days as a student, von Soden's article *Der Aufstieg des Assyrerreiches* never played even the slightest role in our understanding of ancient Near Eastern history. The republication of von Soden's article "Leistung und Grenze sumerischer und babylonischer Wissenschaft" (see section 4, under "Wolfram von Soden," with the associated note, regarding his publications that exhibit Nazi ideology) is interesting in several

recognition among Assyriologists. The main scholarly interests of Ungnad, von Soden, Meissner, and of the discipline as a whole were characterized by narrowly philological concerns: editions of texts and lexicographical, grammatical, and encyclopedic works. A number of German Assyriologists—among them Meissner and von Soden—provided manuscripts of important text corpora for the *Chicago Assyrian Dictionary* before 1939, to serve as the basis for the dictionary files.[55]

The Ahnenerbe and the Hohe Schule (Advanced School of the NSDAP)

There were, however, attempts from outside the field of Assyriology to integrate the discipline into a research and teaching agenda that would advance Nazi ideology. Himmler's Ahnenerbe and Rosenberg's Hohe Schule both tried to muster Assyriologists for their purposes. Rosenberg's office put together extensive lists of academic personnel they considered suitable for inclusion in the activities of the Hohe Schule on the basis of their scholarly reputation, regardless of party membership. Among the scholars listed was Adam Falkenstein, a Sumerologist.[56] However, the outbreak of World War II meant that nothing of substance in this regard happened. The activities of the Ahnenerbe were a limited success as far as Assyriology was concerned. The Ahnenerbe, through Viktor Christian in Vienna, did take over the *Wiener Zeitschrift für die Kunde des Morgenlandes*. A similar attempt, with the same goal, was directed against the highly regarded *Archiv für Religionswissenschaft*, which was taken over by the Ahnenerbe in 1939 and transformed into a Nazi journal.[57] The aforementioned attempt to bring the *Reallexikon der Assyriologie* under the control of the Ahnenerbe, however, was unsuccessful.

---

respects. As published, aside from an afterword, von Soden declined to make any changes to his contribution. Yet Landsberger mentioned in personal communication to me that (a) he tried unsuccessfully to persuade von Soden to correct some of his erroneous statements and (b) he had at first hesitated to have his article republished together with von Soden's in the same booklet of the Wissenschaftliche Buchgesellschaft.

55. The introduction to volume A, bk. 1 (pp. xiii–xiv) lists the following German Assyriologists as active for the *Chicago Assyrian Dictionary* in the years 1933–45: Martin David, Erich Ebeling, Wilhelm Eilers, Benno Landsberger, Julius Lewy, Bruno Meissner, Albert Schott, and Wolfram von Soden, from whom manuscripts were received. Oluf Krückmann was not able to provide a manuscript. Others were asked but could not, for one reason or another, accept the assignment: Hans Bauer, Viktor Christian, Hans Ehelolf, Arthur Ungnad, and Ernst Friedrich Weidner.

56. Renger, "Altorientalistik," 497, with n162.

57. Junginger, "Religionswissenschaft," 77.

*The Position Paper "The Study of the Ancient Near East in the
New Germany: Present Status and Future Tasks"*

Of particular interest is a memorandum dated May 15, 1933—that is, in the first few months of the Nazi regime. Written by Walther Hinz (Iranian studies) and Franz Babinger (Turkish studies), the memorandum, entitled "Die Morgenlandforschung im neuen Deutschland: Stand und künftige Aufgaben" [The study of the ancient Near East in the new Germany: Present status and future tasks] was submitted to the Ministries of Cultural Affairs in the states of Prussia, Bavaria, and Saxony.[58] Hinz and Babinger issued a broad condemnation about the way in which Oriental studies (especially general or comparative Semitics, Arabic, Turkology, Egyptology, and Assyriology) were being conducted. They criticized the orientation of these disciplines as excessively philological without taking into account contemporary relevance. Hinz and Babinger considered Oriental studies to have been overly influenced by rabbinic studies or methods—as they saw it—and to have too strong an emphasis on the history of religions.[59] They proposed a more historical orientation that would give increased consideration to cultural, social, and historical questions, as was the case at the time in France and England. As a consequence, they suggested that Oriental studies be concentrated at just three universities—Berlin, Leipzig, and Munich—with an emphasis on research and teaching that was beneficial for the new Nazi politics. Their memorandum was immediately rebutted by Landsberger and by the Arabists Erich Bräunlich and August Fischer (the latter of whom leaned positively toward the Nazi Party).[60] Others, like Hans Heinrich Schaeder (Iranian studies), Enno Littmann (Arabist), and Paul Kahle (Semitist), followed.

Hinz and Babinger's ideas concerning Oriental studies in Germany were more clearly articulated and disseminated by Alfred Rosenberg's Hohe Schule and Heinrich Himmler's Ahnenerbe. However, the general idea of including historical, sociological, and cultural aspects in the teaching curriculum and research programs was not an entirely new invention. Carl Heinrich Becker had proposed similar ideas well before 1933. Becker, a Professor of Islamic studies, was a dedicated democrat, a deputy minister [*Staatssekretär*], and minister of cultural affairs of Prussia from 1925 to 1930, in a Social Democratic cabinet. His

---

58. See Hanisch, *Nachfolger der Exegeten*, 144–45; Hanisch, "Arabistik, Semitistik, und Islamwissenschaft," 515.
59. Renger, "Altorientalistik," 492.
60. Hanisch, *Nachfolger der Exegeten*, 144–45, with n515.

main intention was to integrate religious, historical, and sociological aspects into a holistic program of Islamic studies. Similar ideas were proposed for other disciplines as well: by Wolfram Eberhardt (who emigrated in 1933) in Far Eastern studies, Hans Heinrich Schaeder in Iranian languages and religious history, and Hermann Kees in Egyptology.

VI. CONCLUSION

Assyriology in Germany was indeed a discipline in troubled waters. As a result of retirement, exile, and emigration, it lost its prominent role in the discipline to other countries in Europe and North America. The further loss—as casualties of the war—of some promising young scholars who remained in Germany made a new start in the field difficult after 1945. Yet the emigration of leading German scholars to foreign countries resulted in the astonishing progress of Assyriology in these countries. Benno Landsberger, Hans-Gustav Güterbock, and Fritz Rudolf Kraus immigrated to Turkey, successfully establishing Assyriology and Hittitology there. Julius and Hildegard Lewy, Albrecht Götze, Ernst Herzfeld, and Otto Neugebauer immigrated to the United States immediately after 1933. They were followed by Leo Oppenheim and Edith Porada in 1940, together with Landsberger and Güterbock, who left Turkey in 1948 after the Turkish authorities terminated the contracts of refugees from Germany. These scholars were instrumental in giving ancient Near Eastern studies in the United States a remarkable boost.

The attempts by the Nazi regime and its institutions to use Assyriology for legitimizing purposes, as was the case with other disciplines of the humanities, more or less failed, in no small part as a result of attrition in a field that had been dominated by Jews. Though a few publications were influenced by Nazi ideology, Assyriology as a whole did not fulfill Nazi expectations. Other disciplines are known to have been involved more substantially with the Nazis through prominent members who still held important positions for a number of years after 1945 and thus continued to influence the character and development of their fields. In contrast, German Assyriology began its course after 1945 with just two persons, Adam Falkenstein and Johannes Friedrich, neither of whom served Nazi demands. Wolfram von Soden had a chance to resume his academic career back in Germany only in 1961, in Münster (after becoming a professor in Vienna in 1954). For many years Falkenstein, who died in 1966, and von Soden, who retired in 1976, represented German Assyriology more or less exclusively. Internationally, they were among the leading scholars in the field. Falkenstein, who attracted many students from both Germany and abroad, gave Sumerology its decisive direction for years to come. Von Soden brought Assyriology to a new level of sophistication with his magisterial dictionary and his still standard grammar of the Akkadian language. These two educated a new and influential generation of Assyriologists. Ideas tainted by remnants of Nazi ideology had no possibility of influencing the discipline in the period following 1945.

BIBLIOGRAPHY

Archival Sources

Bundesarchiv Berlin, Berlin Document Center, Akte Ahnenerbe, Blatt 115
Landsberger Archives in Leipzig and Jerusalem, website hosted by Altorientalisches Institut, University of Leipzig, and by the Hebrew University of Jerusalem. Supervised by Professors Michael P. Streck (Leipzig) and Nathan Wasserman (Jerusalem). http://altorient.gko.uni-leipzig.de/landsberger.html.

Secondary Sources

Ackermann, Zeno. "Anglistik und Amerikanistik." In Elvert and Nielsen-Sikora, *Kulturwissenschaften und Nationalsozialismus*, 647–68.
Albright, William Foxwell. Review of *Der Aufstieg des Assyrerreiches als geschichtliches Problem* by Wolfram von Soden. *Orientalia*, n.s. 8 (1939): 120–23.
Almgren, Birgitta. "Germanistik." In Elvert and Nielsen-Sikora, *Kulturwissenschaften und Nationalsozialismus*, 625–46.
Altekamp, Stefan. "Klassische Archäologie." In Elvert and Nielsen-Sikora, *Kulturwissenschaften und Nationalsozialismus*, 167–209.
Barner, Wilfried, and Christoph König, eds. *Jüdische Intellektuelle und die Philologien in Deutschland 1871–1933*. Marbacher Wissenschaftsgeschichte 3. Göttingen, Germany: Wallstein, 2001.
Beckman, Gary. "Ancient Near Eastern 'Aryans' and the Third Reich." In *Dealing with Antiquity: Past, Present & Future. RAI Marburg*, edited by Walter Sommerfeld, 9–20. Alter Orient und Altes Testament 460. Münster, Germany: Ugarit-Verlag, 2020.
Cooper, Jerrold S. "Sumerian and Aryan Racial Theory: Academic Politics and Parisian Assyriology." *Revue de l'histoire des religions* 210 (1993): 169–205.
Dahms, Hans-Joachim. "Philosophie." In Elvert and Nielsen-Sikora, *Kulturwissenschaften und Nationalsozialismus*, 19–51.
Ebeling, Erich, and Bruno Meissner, eds. *Reallexikon der Assyriologie*. Berlin: Walter de Gruyter, 1928–2018.
Ellinger, Ekkehard. *Deutsche Orientalistik zur Zeit des Nationalsozialismus 1933–1945*. Thèses 4. Edingen-Neckarshausen, Germany: Deux Mondes, 2006.

Elvert, Jürgen, and Jürgen Nielsen-Sikora, eds. *Kulturwissenschaften und Nationalsozialismus*. Historische Mitteilungen 72. Stuttgart, Germany: Franz Steiner, 2008.

Flygare, Jakob. "Assyriologi under nazismen: en kontekstuel undersøgelse af tre tekster af Wolfram von Soden fra 1936–38." Master's thesis, University of Copenhagen, 2005.

———. "Assyriology in Nazi Germany: The Case of Wolfram von Soden." In *Perspectives on the History of Ancient Near Eastern Studies*, edited by Agnès Garcia-Ventura and Lorenzo Verderame, 44–60. University Park, PA: Eisenbrauns, 2020.

———. "Assyriology under Nazism: A Contextual Analysis of Three Texts by Wolfram von Soden from 1936–38." *Journal of Associated Graduates in Near Eastern Studies* 11 (2006): 3–42.

Frahm, Eckart. "Images of Assyria in Nineteenth- and Twentieth-Century Western Scholarship." In *Orientalism, Assyriology, and the Bible*, edited by Steven W. Holloway, 74–94. Hebrew Bible Monographs 10. Sheffield, UK: Sheffield Phoenix Press, 2006.

Hanisch, Ludmilla. "Arabistik, Semitistik, und Islamwissenschaft." In Elvert and Nielsen-Sikora, *Kulturwissenschaften und Nationalsozialismus*, 503–25.

———. *Die Nachfolger der Exegeten: Deutschsprachige Erforschung des Vorderen Orients in der ersten Hälfte des 20. Jahrhunderts*. Wiesbaden, Germany: Harrassowitz, 2003.

Hutter, Manfred. "Der Assyriologe Albert Schott (1901–1945)." In *Die Bonner Orient- und Asienwissenschaften: Eine Geschichte in 22 Porträts*, edited by Harald Meyer, Christine Schirrmacher, and Ulrich Vollmer, 215–31. Independent monograph published by the journal *Orientierungen*. Gossenberg, Austria: Ostasien, 2018.

Junginger, Horst. "Religionswissenschaft." In Elvert and Nielsen-Sikora, *Kulturwissenschaften und Nationalsozialismus*, 52–86.

Kater, Michael. *Das "Ahnenerbe" der SS, 1935–1945: Ein Beitrag zur Kulturpolitik des Dritten Reiches*. 4th ed. Studien zur Zeitgeschichte 6. Munich: Oldenbourg, 2006.

Maier-Metz, Harald. *Entlassungsgrund: Pazifismus. Albrecht Götze, der Fall Gumbel, und die Marburger Universität 1930–1946*. Academia Marburgensis 13. Münster, Germany: Waxmann, 2015.

Moortgat, Anton. *Die bildende Kunst des Alten Orients und die Bergvölker*. Berlin: Schoetz, 1932.

Neumann, Georg. "Paul Koschaker in Tübingen (1941–1946)." *Zeitschrift für altorientalische und biblische Rechtsgeschichte* 18 (2012): 23–36.

Petersen, Hans-Christian, and Jan Kusber. "Osteuropäische Geschichte und Ostforschung." In Elvert and Nielsen-Sikora, *Kulturwissenschaften und Nationalsozialismus*, 289–311.

Renger, Johannes. "Altorientalistik." In Elvert and Nielsen-Sikora, *Kulturwissenschaften und Nationalsozialismus*, 469–502.

———. "Altorientalistik und jüdische Gelehrte in Deutschland: Deutsche und österreichische Altorientalisten im Exil." In *Jüdische Intellektuelle und die Philologien in Deutschland 1871–1933*, edited by Wilfred Barner and Christoph König, 247–61. Marbacher Wissenschaftsgeschichte 3. Göttingen, Germany: Wallstein, 2001.

———. "Die Geschichte der Altorientalistik und der vorderasiatischen Archäologie in Berlin von 1875 bis 1945." In *Ergänzungsband zum Katalog der Ausstellung "Berlin und die Antike,"* edited by Willmuth Arenhövel and Christa Schreiber, 151–92. Berlin: Deutsches Archäologisches Institut, 1979.

Schaller, Helmut W. "Südosteuropaforschung." In Elvert and Nielsen-Sikora, *Kulturwissenschaften und Nationalsozialismus*, 312–36.

Schmidt, Jan, ed. *Dreizehn Jahre Istanbul (1937–1949): Der deutsche Assyriologe Fritz Rudolf Kraus und sein Briefwechsel im türkischen Exil*. 2 vols. Leiden, Netherlands: Brill, 2014.

———. "Exil im Orient: Die Briefe von Fritz Rudolf Kraus aus Istanbul, 1937–1949." In *Der Orient in akademischer Optik: Beiträge zur Genese einer Wissenschaftsdisziplin*, edited by Ludmilla Hanisch, 145–54. Orientwissenschaftliche Hefte 20. Halle (Saale), Germany: OWZ, 2006.

Schmidt, Wolfgang. *Neuphilologie als Auslandswissenschaft auf der Grundlage des Sprachstudiums*. Marburg: Elwert, 1934.

Schneider, Thomas. "Ägyptologen im Dritten Reich: Biographische Notizen anhand der sogenannten 'Steindorff-Liste.'" *Journal of Egyptian History* 5, no. 1 (2012): 120–247. Reprinted in *Egyptology from the First World War to the Third Reich: Ideology, Scholarship, and Individual Biographies*, edited by Thomas Schneider and Peter Raulwing, 120–247. Leiden, Netherlands: Brill, 2013.

Simon, Gerd. "Chronologie Viktor Christian." Accessed August 23, 2018. https://homepages.uni-tuebingen.de/gerd.simon/ChrChristian.pdf.

———. "Tödlicher Bücherwahn: Der letzte Wiener Universitätsrektor im 3. Reich und der Tod seines Kollegen Norbert Jokl." Accessed August 23, 2018. https://homepages.uni-tuebingen.de/gerd.simon/buecherwahn.pdf.

———. "Zur Schulung der Elite im 3. Reich." Accessed July 17, 2017. https://homepages.uni-tuebingen.de/gerd.simon/elite1.htm.

Soden, Wolfram von. *Der Aufstieg des Assyrerreichs als geschichtliches Problem*. Der Alte Orient 37/1–2. Leipzig, Germany: J. C. Hinrichs, 1937.

———. "Leistung und Grenze sumerischer und babylonischer Wissenschaft." *Die Welt als Geschichte* 2 (1936): 411–64 and 509–57. Reprinted with additions and corrections in Benno Landsberger and Wolfram von Soden, *Die Eigenbegrifflichkeit der babylonischen Welt*, 21–133. Libelli 142. Darmstadt, Germany: Wissenschaftliche Buchgesellschaft, 1965.

———. "Neue Untersuchungen über die Bedeutung der Indogermanen für den Alten Orient." *Göttingische Gelehrte Anzeigen* 200 (1938): 195–216.

Streck, Michael P., and Nathan Wasserman. "Landsberger Archive." Accessed October 16, 2021. https://altorient.gko.uni-leipzig.de/landsberger.html.

Ungnad, Arthur. *Die ältesten Völkerwanderungen Vorderasiens: Ein Beitrag zur Geschichte und Kultur der Semiten, Arier, Hethiter, und Subaräer.* Breslau, Germany: Selbstverlag, 1923.

———. *Subartu: Beiträge zur Kulturgeschichte und Völkerkunde Vorderasiens.* Berlin/Leipzig: Walter de Gruyter, 1936.

Wiesehöfer, Joseph. "Alte Geschichte." In Elvert and Nielsen-Sikora, *Kulturwissenschaften und Nationalsozialismus*, 210–22.

Wilhelm, Gernot, ed. *Zwischen Tigris und Nil: 100 Jahre Ausgrabungen der Deutschen Orient-Gesellschaft in Vorderasien und Ägypten.* Mainz, Germany: Philipp von Zabern, 1998.

JOHANNES RENGER is Professor Emeritus of Ancient Near Eastern Philology and History at the Freie Universität Berlin. He has published widely on the economic and social history of the ancient Near East, with a theoretical perspective based on the work of Karl Polanyi, Moses Finley, and Fernand Braudel. He has written several previous studies concerned with the history of the discipline of Assyriology. Since 1993, he has directed the Assur-Project, which is devoted to publishing the results of the excavations of the Deutsche Orient-Gesellschaft between 1903 and 1914.

EIGHT

NATIONAL SOCIALIST ARCHAEOLOGY AS A FAUSTIAN BARGAIN

The Contrasting Careers of Hans Reinerth and Herbert Jankuhn

BETTINA ARNOLD

HOW DO WE MAKE SENSE of the indefensible? The search for rational explanations for the Holocaust and its attendant horrors has preoccupied scholars for almost a century, and attempts to understand it have ranged from systemic, birds-eye view analyses to first-person, worms-eye view narratives, with variable success. Does it matter whether scholars at German universities embraced Nazi values out of personal conviction or opportunistically to advance their careers? Can small subversions, what Scott has called the "weapons of the weak," be identified in some of the seemingly committed Nazi Party operatives, including contradictory and even overtly risky behavior that is at odds with professional survival?[1] To what extent can the postwar period provide clues as to how willing the universities were to engage in honest self-analysis of the role played by academics in the destructive agenda of the Nationalsozialistische Deutsche Arbeiterpartei [National Socialist German Workers' Party (NSDAP)]? Biographical exegesis has the potential to reveal both the strengths and weaknesses of totalitarian systems attempting to coopt institutions of higher learning. A careful examination of the evidence makes it possible to differentiate between what Anne Applebaum, quoting Stanley Hoffmann, calls "collaborationisms and dissidences."[2] Moreover, we must try to differentiate

---

1. James C. Scott, *Weapons of the Weak: Everyday Forms of Peasant Resistance* (New Haven, CT: Yale University Press, 2008).

2. In a recent article for the *Atlantic*, Anne Applebaum quotes Stanley Hoffmann's study of collaboration in France during World War II, in which he argued that "a careful historian would have—almost—to write a huge series of case histories; for there seem to have been almost as many collaborationisms as there were practitioners of collaboration." See Anne Applebaum, "The Collaborators: What Causes People to Abandon Their Principles

these phenomena if we are to understand what makes totalitarian regimes possible. The most effective way to penetrate the apparent uniformity of the facade presented by the official documentary record is through a close reading of life histories that expose the bargains made to justify the betrayal of principles, what Hoffmann called "a series of small Munichs."³

Prior to the 1930s, prehistoric German archaeology had been an underfunded humanities discipline overshadowed by the more prestigious fields of classical and Near Eastern archaeology. During the Nazi era, the state interest in promoting German history and German identity included investing and exploiting prehistoric German archaeology. The Nazis used this "scholarship" to advance their ideological program, providing alleged historical and archaeological evidence to legitimate their claims of Aryan racial superiority. Although biographies of several key figures in the discipline have appeared in the last two decades, they have largely been confined to descriptive chronological narratives of their subjects' activities under National Socialism, with little or no consideration of post-1945 life histories. This study takes a different approach, comparing the career trajectories of prehistorians Hans Reinerth and Herbert Jankuhn, top-ranking officials in charge of archaeological research programs in the Amt Rosenberg [Rosenberg Office] and the SS Ahnenerbe [Ancestral Heritage Research Institute], respectively. It explores the motivations of Reinerth and Jankuhn for participating in and supporting the National Socialist program and asks what they sacrificed in exchange for the funding and prestige the new regime provided for their work.

The pre-, peri-, and postwar experiences of these two archaeologists also reveal the self-serving and often arbitrary ways that the German university system, and related institutions such as museums and institutes, first supported and then turned a largely blind eye to the activities of archaeologists engaged in underwriting the ideological program of German National Socialism. The

---

in Support of a Corrupt Regime? And How Do They Find Their Way Back?" *Atlantic,* July/August 2020, 48–62, citing Stanley Hoffmann, "Collaborationism in France during World War II," *Journal of Modern History* 40, no. 3 (1968): 375–95 (at 375).

3. Hoffmann, "Collaborationism," 378. The Munich Agreement was an agreement concluded at Munich on September 30, 1938, by Nazi Germany, the United Kingdom, the French Third Republic and the Kingdom of Italy ceding the Sudeten German territory of Czechoslovakia to Germany. Most of Europe celebrated the agreement, because it prevented the war threatened by Hitler, who announced it would be his last territorial claim in Europe. The choice seemed to be between war and appeasement, but as hindsight has shown, sacrificing the Sudetenland was pointless. Hoffmann uses this example to demonstrate the small steps that can imperceptibly lead to dire consequences.

reluctance of the German university system after 1945 to engage critically, or at all, with the legacy of the Faustian bargain that they had accepted in order to develop prehistoric archaeology as a discipline had, and continues to have, a corrosive effect on the field.[4]

I. ARCHAEOLOGY AS A HANDMAIDEN OF THE STATE

All archaeological research is to some extent political because of its dependence on funding that may be associated with an obligation to provide data or interpretations to suit the entity that is covering the costs of the fieldwork, analysis, and publication of those data. The fact that selective cooption of the past by the state is especially visible in totalitarian regimes such as Nazi Germany should not lead to the conclusion that it is specific to such extreme contexts.[5] However, the prevalence of ideologically compromised archaeological research in totalitarian systems suggests there may be a predictive value to exploring in greater depth what motivates scholars to participate in such political distortion of their research. Based on extensive archival documentation and recent biographical analyses, it is clear that German archaeologists decided when to join the NSDAP, the SS Ahnenerbe, and the Rosenberg Office based on expedience as well as conviction. When individual scholars chose to join the party (before or after 1933, when Hitler came to power) and whether they opted for the Rosenberg Office or the Ahnenerbe are revealing to a certain extent, but in order to be able to function professionally at all, the minimum requirement was party membership. A certain amount of subversive and obstructive activity can also be identified in the records, illuminating the schizophrenic and compartmentalized nature of life and academic research in a totalitarian regime. Focusing on individual archaeologists working within a specific set of conditions and circumstances makes it possible to contextualize and critique assumptions about the historical uniqueness of German nationalism.

Race, as defined by German National Socialism, was what qualified one to be a member of the Germanic community known as the Third Reich. It was more important than religion, language or place of birth. It was the basis for

---

4. The discussion that follows is based on previously unpublished archival material, part of a research project funded by a 1995 Wenner-Gren Foundation for Anthropological Research Post-PhD grant. Recent publications outlining the roles of Reinerth and Jankuhn in the fierce competition between the Amt Rosenberg and the SS Ahnenerbe for control of prehistoric archaeological research in National Socialist Germany are also included in the discussion.

5. Bettina Arnold, "The Contested Past," *Anthropology Today* 15, no. 4 (1999): 1–4.

the "imagined community," defined by territory that could be demonstrated archaeologically or historically as being or having been occupied by Germanic peoples, including England and most of Scandinavia.[6] Germans carried the nation-state within their bloodline and, by physically occupying territory, made that place a permanent part of their cultural identity. This persistent imbrication of blood, land, material culture, and identity conferred importance on the identification of "Germanic" material culture in the archaeological record of eastern and northern Europe, underwriting the National Socialist program of territorial expansion. It is, however, important to remember that this phenomenon had its roots in the nineteenth century, when nationalism had become a blood sport among European states, both metaphorically and literally.[7] Prehistoric archaeology was especially well-suited to underwriting the creation of national identities in early to mid-twentieth century west-central Europe.[8] The deep temporal reach of the archaeological record provided support for territorial claims while the ambiguity inherent in interpretations of the material record produced by largely preliterate societies facilitated the manipulation of the data for political purposes.

Archaeology thus provided the legitimating link with the deep past that German nationalists needed to establish their policies of territorial expansion and, ultimately, racial genocide.[9] For example, numerous scholars have discussed the role of Gustaf Kossinna in developing the concept of defining ethnic boundaries on the basis of material culture patterns in the archaeological record.[10] Kossinna's methodology was not the result of parthenogenesis, however. In fact, his "settlement archaeological method," which allowed him to identify ethnic boundaries on the basis of material culture patterns in the

---

6. On the concept of a nation as an "imagined community," see Benedict Anderson, *Imagined Communities: Reflections on the Origin and Spread of Nationalism*, rev. and ext. ed. (London: Verso, 1991). Anderson argues that nation-states were made possible only after the introduction of print media, which allowed a feeling of belonging to a clearly defined group to connect individuals who would never physically encounter one another face to face.

7. Marion Bertram, "Zur Situation der deutschen Ur- und Frühgeschichtsforschung während der Zeit der faschistischen Diktatur," *Forschungen u. Berichte* 31 (1991): 23–42 (at 23).

8. Bettina Arnold, "The Past as Propaganda: Totalitarian Archaeology in Nazi Germany," *Antiquity* 64, issue 244 (1990): 464–78.

9. Ibid.; Michael H. Kater, *Das "Ahnenerbe" der SS 1935–1945: Ein Beitrag zur Kulturpolitik des Dritten Reiches*, Studien zur Zeitgeschichte 6 (Stuttgart, Germany: Deutsche Verlags-Anstalt, 1974), 21.

10. Dirk Mahsarski and Gunter Schöbel, "Von Gustaf Kossinna zur NS-Archäologie," in *Graben für Germanien: Archäologie unterm Hakenkreuz*, ed. Sandra Geringer et al. (Stuttgart, Germany: Konrad Theiss, 2013), 31–36.

archaeological record,[11] was dependent on previous work done by Montelius, Müllenhoff and others. Kossinna's approach to the identification of ethnic groups in the archaeological record was significantly affected by his early training in philology. A close reading of his work (especially the 1911 publication *Die Herkunft der Germanen*) reveals his dependence on textual and toponymic evidence for confirmation of "culture boundaries" [*Kulturkreis*] in spite of his supposed purely "archaeological" approach to the identification of past ethnic groups.[12]

Kossinna concluded that Germanic people had their antecedents in northern Europe in the Upper Paleolithic, and although some of these groups migrated out of what later became Scandinavia and Germany, those that did not retained the racial and cultural characteristics of that original population. He argued that separation of the German language from the Indogermanic Ursprache occurred sometime in what we would now call the late Bronze Age—that is, around 1000–900 BCE. After World War I, had ended, Kossinna attempted to apply this synergistic combination of linguistic and archaeological evidence directly to the political process by sending one of his publications to Versailles in which he argued that the Weichsel area should be retained by Germany on the basis of archaeological evidence for prehistoric occupation by Germanic peoples.[13] Similar arguments of cultural, ethnic, and "racial" continuity were used to justify both the invasion of Poland and the extermination of the Jews.

II. THE OBLIGATIONS OF THE PATRON-CLIENT SYSTEM

Ulrike Sommer provides a useful overview of prehistoric archaeology in German universities from 1822, when J. G. G. Büsching became the titular chair for "Historical Auxiliary Disciplines and Germanic Antiquities" at Breslau. The first Chair in Prehistory at the University of Munich was not established until 1866, at which time the field was still linked to physical anthropology. Most prehistoric excavations were carried out by local antiquarians and curated in local museums until the early twentieth century, when prehistoric archaeology began to be linked explicitly with ethnography and folklore. By 1902, lectures on prehistory were being offered at seven universities; twenty years later, the number had increased to seventeen, but it was still not possible to earn a degree

---

11. Gustaf Kossinna, *Die deutsche Vorgeschichte: Eine hervorragend nationale Wissenschaft* (Würzburg, Germany: Curt Kabitzsch, 1912).

12. Gustaf Kossinna, *Die Herkunft der Germanen: Zur Methode der Siedlungsarchäologie* (Würzburg, Germany: Curt Kabitzsch, 1911).

13. Arnold, "Past as Propaganda," 467.

in prehistoric archaeology because no professorship in the field existed. Sommer highlights the range of fields from which the earliest professors of prehistory were drawn, including medicine, art history, physical anthropology, ethnography, and linguistics.[14] This absence of a clearly defined identity made the discipline vulnerable to manipulation and dependent on state patronage to a greater extent than was true for ancillary fields such as classical or biblical archaeology after 1933.[15]

It is also worth remembering that the 1920s were a time of great economic hardship across Germany and the rest of the globe, which is why, when the flow of funds allowed universities, museums, and institutes to begin engaging in excavations and scholarship again, they were disinclined to look too closely at the fine print. Almost all of the professorships in prehistoric archaeology that exist in Germany today were established before the outbreak of war in 1939.[16] The massive expansion of infrastructure in Germany after 1933, including the Autobahn, airports, and other projects, resulted in an unprecedented number of rescue excavations. These projects, in turn, led to the employment and training of a generation of field archaeologists.[17] Several major research excavations were beneficiaries of this new, politically tainted largesse. These excavations included the Viking trading post at Haithabu (led by Jankuhn) and the Iron Age burial mound at the Hohmichele (led by Gustav Riek), both of which were funded by the Ahnenerbe. Riek, who like Reinerth was a student of the archaeologist R. R. Schmidt, edged out Reinerth in the battle between the Ahnenerbe and the Rosenberg Office over the right to excavate at the Hohmichele.

The unprecedented support provided by the NSDAP proved to be a potent lure for many professional archaeologists. The so-called four-leaf clover of the *Weltanschauungswissenschaften* includes the four disciplines that served as the basis for the National Socialist worldview. These four disciplines, which used scholarship allegedly to confirm the superiority of the Aryan race, included race studies [*Rassenkunde*], folk studies [*Volkskunde* and *Volkskunst*], ideographic studies [*Sinnbildforschung*, the study of the specific characteristics

---

14. Ulrike Sommer, "The Teaching of Archaeology in West Germany," in *Archaeology, Ideology, and Society*, ed. Heinrich Härke, Gesellschaften und Staaten 7 (Frankfurt, Germany: Peter Lang, 2002), 205–43.

15. Henning Hassmann, "Archaeology in the 'Third Reich,'" in Härke, *Archaeology, Ideology, and Society*, 67–142 (at 77).

16. Uta Halle and Dirk Mahsarski, "Forschungsstrukturen," in Geringer et al., *Graben für Germanien*, 57–64 (at 58).

17. Uta Halle, "Wichtige Ausgrabungen der NS-Zeit," in Geringer et al., *Graben für Germanien*, 72.

that determine group identity], and prehistory.[18] The main goal for all of these disciplines was to demonstrate the racial and cultural superiority as well as the autochthonous development of the German people,[19] literally weaponizing prehistoric archaeology[20] and making it an indispensable part of the National Socialist program. Archaeologists were expected to support the party line on the innate racial purity and superiority of Nordic/Aryan peoples, their northern origins, and their migration into all parts of the Old World that eventually produced evidence of advanced cultures. This included Greek civilization, which had supposedly been colonized by Nordic peoples fleeing southward to escape a natural catastrophe in northern Europe. Party ideologues like Alfred Rosenberg borrowed heavily from earlier writers on racial doctrine, especially Houston Stewart Chamberlain, an expatriate Englishman, and Arthur le Comte de Gobineau, a French diplomat and publicist, as well as the racialist views of Hans F. K. Günther.[21]

The basic operating principle of Nazi racial doctrine was that races are not created equal and that some are inherently superior to others. For committed National Socialists there was no doubt about the natural superiority of the German people (the "Master Race," according to followers of Gobineau and Chamberlain). The role of archaeology was to excavate and identify prehistoric Germanic territory (Kossinna's culture boundaries concept came in handy here) that was now in the possession of "inferior" races like the Slavic peoples of eastern Europe. Archaeological discoveries were intended to justify the removal or extermination of these "squatters," by force if necessary, and the return of these ancient Germanic homelands to the German people. The term *Lebensraum* was used to describe this territorial expansion. Translated literally, it means "living space." For the Nazis, it meant living space for ethnic Germans, theirs by right to reclaim from "inferior" races and cultures.[22]

Well-organized propaganda is one of the most effective means of controlling large numbers of people, and high-ranking Nazi officials recognized and took advantage of this. The visual and "hands-on" appeal of prehistoric archaeology

---

18. Leonhard Franz, *Vorgeschichte und Zeitgeschehen* (Leipzig, Germany: Kabitzsch, 1938), 48, cited in Henning Hassmann and Detlef Jantzen, "'Die deutsche Vorgeschichte—Eine nationale Wissenschaft': Das Kieler Museum vorgeschichtlicher Altertümer im Dritten Reich," *Offa* 51 (1994): 9–23 (at 10).

19. Franz, *Vorgeschichte*, 30.

20. Hans Reinerth, "Die politische Waffe der Vorgeschichtsforschung," *Volk und Heimat* 4 (1937): 89–90.

21. Bertram, "Zur Situation," 23.

22. Arnold, "Past as Propaganda," 464–65.

was exploited by the Nazi regime for its own purposes, even though not all the party leaders were particularly interested in prehistory. Hitler and Goebbels were both lukewarm in their enthusiasm even though they were only too happy to exploit and manipulate archaeological evidence.[23] In order to make sure that as many people as possible were exposed to the myth-making in which prehistoric archaeology played such a major role, the party put a lot of effort into public education. The Rosenberg Office's blueprint for the politicization of prehistoric archaeology included specifically pedagogical goals, such as the introduction of German prehistory in schools, the establishment of academic chairs and institutes for prehistory at universities and other secondary schools, and funding local museums in order to make prehistory more accessible to a broader spectrum of the population.[24]

Open-air museums like Unteruhldingen on Lake Constance were established and became a required part of school and other community outings.[25] Documentary films, doctored to include footage of party rallies and other obvious propaganda symbolism, presented the German people with visual images of their links to prehistoric cultures and emphasized their "innate superiority" over other peoples. The filmmaker and archaeologist Lothar Zotz was a pioneer in the field of archaeological documentaries, and many of his films were shown at district party meetings, which were attended by whole villages. Some of his films were clearly edited and overdubbed by party ideologues before being shown.[26]

Newly established archaeological field schools catered to ordinary citizens, schoolchildren, and soldiers; participants learned field techniques as well as how to reproduce prehistoric crafts like pottery, weaving, and metalwork. Reenactments of prehistoric events became a common part of local celebrations,

---

23. Bertram, "Zur Situation," 26.

24. Hans Reinerth, "Deutsche Vorgeschichte und ihre Pflege im nationalsozialistischen Staat," *Deutsches Bildungswesen* 1 (1933): 47–50; Henning Hassmann, "Archäologie und Jugend im 'Dritten Reich': Ur- und Frühgeschichte als Mittel der politisch-ideologischen Indoktrination von Kindern und Jugendlichen," in *Prähistorie und Nationalsozialismus: Die mittel- und osteuropäische Ur- und Frühgeschichtsforschung in den Jahren 1933–1945*, ed. Achim Leube (Heidelberg, Germany: Synchron, 2002), 107–46.

25. Gunter Schöbel, *Pfahlbaumuseum Unteruhldingen: Museumsgeschichte Teil 1 (1922–1949)* (Überlingen, Germany: Pfahlbaumuseum, 2001).

26. Miriam Sénécheau, "Archäologie im Schulbuch: Themen der Ur- und Frühgeschichte im Spannungsfeld zwischen Lehrplanforderungen, Fachdiskussion, und populären Geschichtsvorstellungen Schulbücher, Unterrichtsfilme, Kinder-, und Jugendliteratur" (PhD diss., University of Freiburg, Germany, 2006); Hassmann, "Archäologie und Jugend im 'Dritten Reich,'" 127.

and a conscious effort was made to link all communities with a particular local archaeological site or tradition. Many of these activities were obviously intended to make indoctrination easier and to ensure control over the information people received regarding the German past. Exaggerated claims, outright fabrications, and significant omissions were characteristic of most of the educational materials dealing with prehistoric archaeology that were produced during this time. On the other hand, these programs provided the foundation for the exemplary public education system that still provides German citizens with information on archaeological topics today. Many amateur archaeological organizations were first founded during this time. Preservation and conservation of archaeological resources were their primary goals. In many ways the years between 1933 and 1945 witnessed an unprecedented upsurge in public interest in prehistoric archaeology, not all of it controlled by the authorities.

After 1933, there were two separate institutions within the Nazi Party battling it out for control over archaeological research and excavation in Germany and other parts of Europe: the Rosenberg Office and the SS Ahnenerbe.[27] The resulting bureaucratic Darwinism to some extent stymied efforts to ideologically streamline the discipline, a situation that appears to have been consciously exploited by some individuals within the Ahnenerbe who recognized that the rift created space for a certain amount of scholarly autonomy. The Rosenberg Office was established in 1933 by Rosenberg, the official party ideologue, a man with a gift for twisting the truth to his own ends. His 1930 publication *Der Mythus des 20. Jahrhunderts* [The myth of the twentieth century] was full of distortions and lies, judiciously mixed with quotations from and references to great scholarly and literary works.[28] He was rabidly antisemitic, and many of his writings attempted to prove the existence of an international Jewish conspiracy aimed at destroying the superior "Nordic" German civilization morally, economically, and racially. He recognized that archaeological research could be manipulated to yield maximum propaganda value. Rosenberg had plans for a national archaeological office, with his right-hand man Hans Reinerth at its head, that would centralize all archaeological research, including fieldwork. Fortunately, this plan was never realized, for reasons discussed further in this chapter. Rosenberg was tried and executed at Nuremberg in 1946.

---

27. Reinhard Bollmus, *Das Amt Rosenberg und seine Gegner: Studien zum Machtkampf im nationalsozialistischen Herrschaftssystem* (Stuttgart, Germany: Deutsche Verlags-Anstalt, 1970); and Kater, *Ahnenerbe*.

28. Alfred Rosenberg, *Der Mythus des 20. Jahrhunderts: Eine Wertung der seelisch-geistigen Gestaltenkämpfe unserer Zeit* (Munich: Hoheneichen, 1930).

The rival organization that also supported archaeological research from 1935 on was Heinrich Himmler's SS Ahnenerbe [Ancestral Heritage Research Institute].[29] Himmler gradually worked his way up in the Nazi Party hierarchy to become chief of the Secret Police (Gestapo) and the Reich commissar for the Consolidation of German Nationhood. Himmler was a complex, self-contradictory individual, and his attitude toward prehistoric archaeology was characteristically ambivalent. On the one hand, he was genuinely fascinated by the past, especially the material culture of prehistoric societies. On the other hand, his interest in the occult made him particularly susceptible to the claims of the lunatic fringe and their pseudo-scientific methodology. His Ahnenerbe archaeologists conducted excavations as widely divergent in scholarly value as Herbert Jankuhn's project at the Viking trading post of Haithabu (a model example of scientifically conducted settlement archaeology) and Julius Andree's "discovery" of the "Germanic cult site" at the Externsteine (based on fraudulent and misleading claims about the archaeological discoveries supposedly made at the site).[30]

III. HANS REINERTH AND HERBERT JANKUHN: UNEARTHING THE ARCHIVAL EVIDENCE

The National Socialist correspondents and memo writers whose missives now sit bound in file folders, ring binders, and digital repositories in Potsdam, Koblenz, Munich, and Prague reveal far more than their authors presumably had intended about individual allegiances, motivations, and political orientation. What is missing is as revealing as what is present—in the case of Herbert Jankuhn in particular, whose high-ranking position in the SS Ahnenerbe should have left a significant paper trail, noticeable gaps in the documentary record indicate that someone had done some housecleaning before the archives were no longer accessible without permission. The documentary records for other prominent archaeologists who, unlike Jankuhn, had not survived the war, are by contrast largely intact.

The correspondence files and report records of granting agencies prove especially fruitful, since they document who was obtaining funds for research and excavation projects, what kinds of selection criteria were being applied, and how those selection criteria changed over time. Identifying what the Germans call *Seilschaften*, literally generational "chains" linking graduate students

---

29. See Kater, *Ahnenerbe*.
30. Halle, "Wichtige Ausgrabungen," 65–73.

and advisors to one another, is critical to understanding individual career trajectories.[31] Personnel files and personal correspondence, as well as excavation reports, museum exhibit catalogs, and press coverage of archaeological research, prove extremely informative. Paradoxically enough, one of the things that saved German prehistoric archaeology from being completely coopted by the party was the bitterness of the ongoing feuds between rival factions within the archaeological community itself. The battle lines delineated professional specializations (classical/Near Eastern or provincial Roman archaeology versus German prehistoric archaeology) as well as geography and "ethnicity" (the northeastern portion of the German nation versus the southwest). Personal and institutional vendettas on the part of individual researchers are also well documented in the archives. These contributed to the failure of the Nazi Party to organize a single national archaeological organization, originally planned by the Rosenberg Office to be run by Rosenberg's operative Hans Reinerth.

IV. HANS REINERTH (1900–1990)

Gunter Schöbel has spent a significant portion of his career as director of the open-air museum at Unteruhldingen that Reinerth took over in 1937; in that capacity, he has published numerous biographical overviews of Reinerth's contributions to the field, especially of wetland archaeology, as well as the controversies that dogged his career.[32] Reinerth was born in Bistritz, Siebenbürgen, an area that was part of the Austro-Hungarian Empire at the time of his birth. By 1922, when he became a German citizen, ethnic Germans in the region had become first Hungarian and then Romanian. It is probably not a coincidence that early and enthusiastic supporters of the National Socialist program within the community of academic archaeologists, including Gustaf Kossinna, were often from peripheral regions that had been subjected to this kind of identity whiplash in the aftermath of World War I, including Gustaf Kossinna. Shifting geopolitical borders, especially in eastern Europe after World War I, literally disconnected German-speaking communities in Russia, Poland, and the Baltic states from their sense of belonging to the imagined community represented by the German nation-state first created at the end of the Franco-Prussian war in 1871. Reinerth focused on Swiss Neolithic lake-dwelling cultures for his

---

31. Sommer, "Teaching of Archaeology," 208–9.
32. Gunter Schöbel, "Hans Reinerth: From Archaeologist to Reichsamtsleiter," in *L'archéologie nazie en Europe de l'Ouest*, ed. Jean-Pierre Legendre, Laurent Olivier, and Bernadette Schnitzler (Gollion, Switzerland: Infolio, 2007), 45–59.

postdoctoral thesis work, which he completed at the University of Tübingen under the supervision of Schmidt.[33] The temporal and geographic scope of Reinerth's thesis and his previous experience excavating sites in the Federsee region were the reasons he was tapped to conduct systematic excavations there when continued discoveries of wetland sites in the 1920s led to a request by the local historical society for a professionally trained archaeologist.[34]

If a single theme emerges from the documentation, it is that expedience determined the political orientation of many of the archaeologists who were active in Germany between 1933 and 1945. Reinerth is a particularly good example of this phenomenon, as has been explicitly pointed out by several scholars who specifically reference the way the party intentionally promoted academic outsiders in a cynical and effective attempt to control the production and dissemination of knowledge.[35] Reinerth was a strategic choice to head the Department for Prehistory established within the Rosenberg Office in 1934 not only because of his active involvement in the ideological streamlining [Gleichschaltung] of existing organizations such as the Reichsbund für Deutsche Vorgeschichte [National Union for German Prehistory] but also because he felt he had been passed over for academic preferment and made no bones about his embittered attitude toward the establishment archaeologists who had been more successful at achieving professional success.[36]

His frustration and disappointment were to some extent justified, given the decade he had spent directing the extremely successful and innovative excavations at the late Bronze Age pile dwelling settlement of Wasserburg Buchau between 1920 and 1930.[37] The project attracted archaeological visitors from the United Kingdom, including Grahame Clark and other prominent prehistorians of the day and by rights should have provided Reinerth with the necessary entrée into the archaeological establishment he was so desperate to join.[38] His

---

33. Ibid., 47.
34. Ralf Baumeister, "Im Brennpunkt siedlungsarchäologischer Forschung: Das Federseemuseum—Einblicke in die Erforschung der Pfahlbauten seit 100 Jahren," *Denkmalpflege in Baden-Württemberg* 4 (2019): 255–61 (at 256).
35. Hassmann and Jantzen, "Die deutsche Vorgeschichte," 9.
36. Hassmann, "Archaeology," 78–79.
37. Erwin Keefer, "Hans Reinerth," in *Die Suche nach der Vergangenheit: 120 Jahre Archäologie am Federsee*, edited by Erwin Keefer (Stuttgart, Germany: Landesdenkmalamt, 1992), 41–48 (at 41–42).
38. Tim Kerig, "Grahame Clark und die mitteleuropäische Archäologie: Eine vergleichende Rezeptionsgeschichte," *Ethnographisch-Archäologische Zeitschrift* 52, no. 1 (2011): 83–103 (at 87).

publications during the ten years of excavations in the Federsee area were extremely popular, largely due to their easy and accessible tone, but no final excavation report about the "Swabian Troy," as the Wasserburg Buchau was dubbed following his use of the phrase, ever appeared.[39] In the years that followed, Reinerth applied unsuccessfully for academic positions in Prague, Heidelberg, Jena, Hamburg, Tübingen, and Berlin. He does not seem to have actively explored the possibilities for preferment in the NSDAP until after charges were brought against him that he had been intriguing against Schmidt, his Tübingen mentor. This led to his being effectively blackballed and destroyed any chance he might have had of obtaining a position in the German academic system, with its strong emphasis on the adviser-advisee relationship.[40]

Reinerth's motives for joining the NSDAP and the Rosenberg Office seem, at first glance, to be relatively straightforward, given the timing of his first official publication in 1932 in the *Nationalistische Monatsheften* [National Socialist Monthly], in which he lamented the previous neglect of German prehistory by the state and the great hope represented by the NSDAP for the field to come into its own.[41] He appears to have been less than enthusiastic when first approached by Rosenberg in 1928 on the recommendation of Kossinna, who saw in the young prehistorian a suitable successor for his Berlin chair in prehistoric archaeology. At the same time, Kossinna invited Reinerth to join the Kampfbund für deutsche Kultur [Militant League for German Culture (KfDK)] and saw to it that he was elected as secretary of the Gesellschaft für Deutsche Vorgeschichte [Society for German Prehistory] in 1929. Apparently Reinerth did not respond to Rosenberg's initial overtures, and it was not until 1931, after the Schmidt affair, that he seems to have decided his only option was to throw his lot in with the NSDAP and the Rosenberg Office. As Mahsarski and Schöbel note, the tone of his letters to colleagues became radicalized within days of his becoming a member of the NSDAP and the KfDK.[42]

Whatever his merits as an archaeologist may have been, there is no doubt that Reinerth had a long memory and made a bad enemy, engaging in personal feuds with several prominent archaeologists, some of whom later claimed to

---

39. Keefer, "Hans Reinerth," 44. See also Hans Reinerth, *Pfahlbauten am Bodensee*, 14th ed. (Überlingen, Germany: August Feyel, 1986).

40. Sommer, "Teaching of Archaeology," 208.

41. Hans Reinerth, "Deutsche Vorgeschichte," *Nationalsozialistische Monatshefte* 27 (June 1932): 241–56.

42. Mahsarski and Schöbel, "Von Gustaf Kossinna," 36. This radicalization manifested itself in his use of stock phrases employed by the NSDAP to describe racialist and nationalist goals and aims.

have joined the SS Ahnenerbe at least partly to protect themselves against Reinerth's witch-hunting campaigns.[43] He was involved in numerous high-profile conflicts and succeeded in getting at least one colleague fired, all of which contributed to his being largely frozen out of the profession in the aftermath of the war. One of these feuds involved a competition with the Tübingen prehistorian Gustav Riek—best known for his excavations of Upper Paleolithic cave sites in Swabia that have produced some of the earliest portable art in the world[44]—over the excavation of the second-largest Iron Age burial mound in Europe, the Hohmichele.[45] Reinerth was also embroiled in legal proceedings with the archaeologist Bolko von Richthofen centered on allegations by the latter that he had allegedly made cynical use of the Nazi Party in furthering his academic career.[46] The relationship between the two men had once been cordial enough for Reinerth to support von Richthofen as a replacement for Karl Hermann Jakob-Friesen, head of the Professional Union of German Prehistorians, at the annual congress for that organization in 1934.[47]

In addition to claiming that Reinerth was a careerist rather than a committed Nazi, von Richthofen accused Reinerth of fraternization with members of the Jewish community in Bad Buchau, the hometown of Albert Einstein's family. Prominent members of the Jewish community in Bad Buchau had supported Reinerth's investigations of the late Bronze Age Wasserburg Buchau, both financially and directly through their participation in the excavations. Chief among Reinerth's supporters in the Bad Buchau Jewish community was Moritz Vierfelder (1877–1961), whose family owned and operated a successful bakery and café in the Hofgartenstrasse, which was the center of Jewish life in the town, until he and his family were forced to emigrate, ultimately settling in Youngstown, Ohio.[48] Vierfelder served as secretary of the Verein für Altertumspflege und Heimatkunde Buchau [Buchau Association for the Preservation of Antiquity and Local History] during the period of Reinerth's excavations in the Federsee area, and his signature appears in the lower left on the

---

43. Keefer, "Hans Reinerth," 48.
44. Nicholas Conard, "A Female Figurine from the Basal Aurignacian of Hohle Fels Cave in Southwestern Germany," *Nature* 459 (2009): 248–52.
45. Gustav Riek and Hans-Jürgen Hundt, *Der Hohmichele: Ein Fürstengrab der späten Hallstattzeit bei der Heuneburg. Heuneburgstudien I*, Römisch-Germanische Forschungen 25 (Berlin: De Gruyer, 1962).
46. Bundesarchiv Koblenz R 21/73.
47. Bollmus, *Amt Rosenberg*, 316n166.
48. Josef Mohn, *Der Leidensweg unter dem Hakenkreuz: Aus der Geschichte von Stadt und Stift Buchau* (Bad Buchau: A. Sandmaier and Sohn, 1970).

excavations permits issued for participants in 1924. In the exhibition catalog commemorating 120 years of excavations in the Federsee area, Erwin Keefer credits Vierfelder with coining the motto for archaeological investigations of wetland sites in the region: "If Schussenried has become the anthropologists' Mecca, Buchau must certainly be considered the Medina of prehistoric archaeologists."[49]

The archival evidence suggests that Reinerth's reputation for being a tireless persecutor of colleagues who were either openly critical of the National Socialist program and/or of Jewish descent was more complicated than might initially appear.[50] He was certainly implicated in the harassment and eventual removal from office of Gerhard Bersu, who was the First Director of the Roman and Germanic Studies Commission in Frankfurt. Bersu was removed from that position in 1935 because his father (apparently unbeknownst to him until the passage of the Nuremberg Race Laws) was Jewish. On the other hand, Moritz Vierfelder, writing from Youngstown, Ohio, in 1947, during Reinerth's denazification proceedings, testified as follows:

> I was in Germany until 1939 and, as a Jew, had to suffer together with my family.... But I can prove that Dr. Reinerth never, not even in the Nazi period, changed his political disposition. He always remained what he used to be for me, during the years of scientific cooperation before 1933: a true and good friend who always stood up for me.... When, in the autumn of 1938, the synagogue in Buchau was burned and destroyed, it was again Dr. Reinerth who made it possible for the important valuable cultural items and documents from the synagogue to be saved from the Nazi plunderers and took them for safekeeping to the Federsee Museum. I can furthermore testify that, at my request, Dr. Reinerth returned the eighteen valuable Torah scrolls to the Jewish community.[51]

On the one hand, the archival record confirms that Reinerth, who came from a family without financial means, was undoubtedly an unprincipled and ruthless careerist. He single-handedly destroyed the professional and personal lives of a large number of German prehistorians during his tenure in the Rosenberg Office, as noted above. On the other hand, his famous excavations at the Bronze Age lake shore settlement of the Wasserburg Buchau in the 1920s were

---

49. Keefer, "Hans Reinerth," 36.
50. On Reinerth's reputation, see Hassmann, "Archaeology," 82.
51. See Schöbel, "Hans Reinerth," 57, based on documents in the Pfahlbau-Museum Archiv at Unteruhldingen.

supported by members of the Jewish community of the town, some of whom he continued to visit well into the late 1930s, when it had become risky to do so. He also maintained ties to a number of Jewish archaeologists outside Germany until relatively late in his career. The privileged, aristocratic Bolko von Richthofen, on the other hand, was a committed anti-Semite whose rightwing activities continued into the postwar period and who managed to entirely escape any professional fallout from his National Socialist career. Unlike Reinerth, who became a convenient whipping boy for apologists after World War II, von Richthofen continued to subscribe to some of the most reprehensible hyperdiffusionist and racist models current during the 1930s and '40s. He remains an inspirational figure for right-wing radical elements in Germany today, and there have been no attempts to produce a definitive biography revealing the extent of the ideological load he carried during his academic career both under the Nazis and afterward.[52]

V. HERBERT JANKUHN (1905–1990)

If Hans Reinerth was the quintessential academic outsider, Herbert Jankuhn represented his opposite in a number of important respects. What they shared with other enthusiastic and early converts to National Socialism among academic archaeologists is their early experiences as ethnic German minorities on the geographic fringes of Germany. Jankuhn was born in Angerburg, East Prussia; his paternal grandfather was Lithuanian, while his mother was a Masur, a German-speaking ethnic minority in Poland.[53] His academic training included close contact with Carl Schuchhardt and Wilhelm Unverzagt, which should have predisposed him to be critical of the work of Gustaf Kossinna, given the negative stance of these scholars toward an explicitly nationalist German prehistory. Like Reinerth, Jankuhn was associated early in his career with an important site with obvious political propaganda value—the UNESCO World Heritage Viking Age site of Hedeby (Haithabu), where he began conducting excavations in 1930.[54]

---

52. Tobias Weger, "Bolko Freiherr von Richthofen und Helmut Preidel," in *Politik und Wissenschaft in der prähistorischen Archäologie: Perspektiven aus Sachsen, Böhmen, und Schlesien*, ed. Judith Schachtmann, Michael Strobel, and Thomas Widera (Göttingen, Germany: V&R Unipress, 2009), 125–48 (at 140).

53. Heiko Steuer, "Herbert Jankuhn und seine Darstellungen zur Germanen- und Wikingerzeit," in *Eine hervorragend nationale Wissenschaft*, ed. Heiko Steuer (Berlin: de Gruyter, 2001), 417–73.

54. Halle, "Wichtige Ausgrabungen," 72. The site is one of the most important Viking trading centers of the eighth to eleventh centuries in Europe.

Over the course of the next eight years, the financial and administrative support of the SS Ahnenerbe allowed Jankuhn to develop the project into one of the largest and most innovative excavations in the world. Unlike Reinerth's Federsee excavations, Jankuhn's Haithabu project results were first published in 1936 and have continued since then in a dedicated publication series.[55]

By 1938, Jankuhn had achieved the rank of SS *Untersturmführer* [lit. junior storm leader, first commissioned SS officer rank], and in 1940, he became head of the Lehr- und Forschungsstelle Ausgrabungen [Excavation and Archaeology Department] for the SS Ahnenerbe. In this capacity, he was sent to Oslo, Norway, in 1940 as part of a Kommando of two hundred men, members of the Gestapo, the SD, and the Waffen-SS, in order to neutralize resistance to the German occupation. His activities at that time included the arrest and imprisonment of Anton Wilhelm Brøgger, one of the directors of the Oldsaksamling, the Norwegian Museum of Cultural History.[56] In 1941, Jankuhn became the head of "Sonderkommando Jankuhn," which was tasked with scouring the collections of various museums in the Soviet Union for material culture that could be used to support the theory that the southeastern front region had been colonized by Germanic peoples. This supposed research activity frequently took the form of the "protective seizure" of interesting objects in Scandinavia and the Crimea and their transport back to Germany. Before the war ended, Jankuhn was on the list for promotion to SS *Sturmbannführer* "Fachführer" [assault unit leader, academic specialist, roughly equivalent to a major] in the Waffen-SS.

It seems incredible, given all of this evidence for his culpability, that he nonetheless attempted to claim that he had been forced to join the SS under duress and had only loosely been associated with the Waffen-SS.[57] Presumably, it is not a coincidence that the official archives in Berlin-Dahlem and Koblenz contained suspiciously little documentation related to his military career or anything that might have potentially incriminated him in the event of additional investigations being conducted after his internment from 1945 to 1948 had ended. Unlike Reinerth, Jankuhn emerged relatively unscathed

---

55. Herbert Jankuhn, *Die Ausgrabungen in Haithabu (1937–1939): Vorläufiger Grabungsbericht* (Berlin-Dahlem: Ahnenerbe-Stiftung, 1943); Herbert Jankuhn, *Haithabu: Ein Handelsplatz der Wikingerzeit*, 3rd ed. (Neumünster, Germany: Karl Wachholtz, 1956).

56. Dirk Mahsarski, "Skandinavien und die 'Germanische Leitstelle,'" in Geringer et al., *Graben für Germanien*, 147–53.

57. Wolfgang Pape, "Zehn Prähistoriker aus Deutschland," in Steuer, *Hervorragend nationale Wissenschaft*, 55–99 (at 69n69).

from the postwar denazification proceedings, which were anything but rigorous.[58] He was able to continue teaching and supervising graduate students, many of whom went on to have distinguished careers especially in settlement archaeology. He was technically banned from teaching after his release from prison but was able to serve as a guest lecturer in Hamburg and Kiel between 1949 and 1956, when he accepted a professorship at Göttingen, from which he retired in 1973.[59] While at least in Germany his academic reputation appears to have been largely unaffected by his wartime activities, this did not extend to all European countries. In particular, Norway is conspicuously absent in the list of honors and society memberships listed in Jankuhn's obituary, and Norwegian archaeologist Anders Hagen, who published one of the earliest discussions of German archaeology under National Socialism, made it clear that Jankuhn was not welcome to come to the University of Bergen to give a lecture when he offered to do so in 1968.[60]

VI. SYNTHESIS AND CONCLUSIONS

As the career trajectories of Reinerth and Jankuhn demonstrate, it is too simple, and too simplistic, to claim that all Germans who were Nazi Party members were "Hitler's willing executioners."[61] In order to understand the Faustian bargain made by individuals and institutions in prehistoric German archaeology between 1933 and 1945, it is essential to consider the choices made by individuals within their respective contexts, rehumanizing the analytical process while gaining useful insights not only into how such regimes developed in the past but how they might develop in the future. Just as individual Jews were murdered in the Holocaust, individual Germans made decisions regarding their part in the creation and destruction of National Socialist Germany. If we are to make any sense of what happened in Germany between

---

58. Bettina Arnold and Henning Hassmann, "Archaeology in Nazi Germany: The Legacy of the Faustian Bargain," in *Nationalism, Politics and the Practice of Archaeology*, ed. Philip L. Kohl and Clare Fawcett (Cambridge: Cambridge University Press, 1995), 70–81.

59. Steuer, "Herbert Jankuhn," 424–25.

60. Heather Pringle, *The Master Plan: Himmler's Scholars and the Holocaust* (New York: Hyperion, 2006), 312. See also Anders Hagen, "Arkeologi og politik," *Viking* 49 (1985/86): 269–78.

61. Daniel Jonah Goldhagen, *Hitler's Willing Executioners: Ordinary Germans and the Holocaust* (New York: Alfred A. Knopf, 1996).

1933 and 1945, we have to focus on the individual.[62] Archaeologists, though their field was considered useful by the Nazi Party, were generally peripheral figures, with one or two notable exceptions. The available documentation makes it possible to discuss the relationship between archaeology and politics in more concrete terms while illuminating the precarious nature of life in a totalitarian regime.

The career trajectories of Reinerth and Jankuhn reflect the fates of the two competing organizations within the Nazi Party that were locked in battle over mainstreaming prehistoric archaeological research within a single umbrella organization. Several interesting patterns emerge in this comparison: (1) what individuals actually did or what was done to them during the 1930s and '40s while the Nazis were in power is more revealing of their ideological load than how they were characterized in secondary and secondhand sources in the postwar period; (2) documentary evidence is frequently scanty for individuals who survived the war and were able to engage in a post-1945 sanitization of their personal records, making this source of evidence potentially limited in its salience; (3) the postwar archaeological establishment was never fully denazified, so the treatment of certain individuals after 1945 can also provide insights into their ideological load during the twelve years of National Socialist hegemony; (4) while academic outsiders represented the bleeding edge of the turn toward racialist and nationalist ideology within the German university system in the 1930s, they found supporters within the establishment without whose assistance the political cooption of higher education would not have been possible.

It is not a coincidence that Gustaf Kossinna, Hans Reinerth, Herbert Jankuhn, and Bolko von Richthofen were all ethnic Germans whose birthplaces (in Poland, in Russia, or in the Baltic states) were lost in the aftermath of World War I. Their sense of themselves as Germans was under threat, and this existential identity crisis appears to have been one of the reasons for their embrace of a totalitarian system that held out the possibility of recovering that identity. In Reinerth's case, the additional sense of personal grievance and desire to revenge himself on his detractors were further motivations that underscore the way totalitarian systems cynically manipulate individuals vulnerable to such persuasion. In Jankuhn's case, by contrast, as Monika Steinel

---

62. Johan Callmer, "Archäologie und Nationalsozialismus als Gegenstand der modernen Forschung," in Leube, *Prähistorie und Nationalsozialismus*, 3–9 (at 8); Frederick Jagust, "Follow the Money: Bemerkungen zum Verhältnis von Geld, Prähistorie, und Nationalsozialismus," in Schachtmann, Strobel, and Widera, *Politik und Wissenschaft*, 285–99 (at 298).

has aptly put it, "it seems that active involvement in National Socialist organizations and the creation of ideologically expedient archaeologies had little to no bearing on his post-war career. In his case, as in many others, practical considerations such as the need to rebuild civil society triumphed over ethical concerns."[63]

The motivation on the part of universities, museums, and institutes to actively aid and abet the Nazi ideological program was based in large part on the sudden post-1933 windfall of previously undreamed of resources for prehistoric archaeology.[64] What cannot be as simply explained, however, is the way the German university system was willing to rehire archaeologists like Jankuhn after 1945 while freezing out those like Reinerth. In 2002, Johan Callmer wrote of the situation in German prehistoric archaeological scholarship: "The main problem in the post-war period is the silence. Very few of the active participants unburdened themselves publicly, and the number of scholars who produced anything in writing is smaller still."[65] This long silence in the academy regarding the events of the 1930s and '40s was made possible by the creation of two figurative sin-eaters or straw men: pre-1933 this role was assigned to Gustaf Kossinna, while post-1945, to a large extent, Hans Reinerth was the chosen scapegoat.[66] This was made explicit in 1949 at the annual meeting of the West- und Süddeutschen Verbandes für Altertumsforschung [West and South German Association for Research on Antiquity], at which the assembled archaeologists passed a resolution essentially blaming the abuses of archaeological research during the twelve years of National Socialist rule on Hans Reinerth.[67] Reinerth's excommunication created a cone of silence that allowed prehistoric

---

63. Monika E. Steinel, "Archaeology, National Socialism, and Rehabilitation: The Case of Herbert Jankuhn," in *Ethics and the Archaeology of Violence*, ed. Alfredo González-Ruibal and Gabriel Moshenska, Ethical Archaeologies: The Politics of Social Justice 2 (New York: Springer, 2015), 153–66.

64. Jagust, "Follow the Money," 298.

65. "Das größte Problem der Epoche nach dem Krieg ist das Schweigen. Nur wenige der Akteure haben öffentlich etwas erzählt und noch geringer ist die Zahl jener, die etwas geschrieben haben." See Callmer, "Archäologie und Nationalsozialismus," 8 (my translation). Evidence suggests that this may be changing, however—unfortunately and not coincidentally just as the last members of the generation with firsthand knowledge of events that could challenge aspects of the official documentary record are shuffling off this mortal coil.

66. Martijn Eickhoff et al., "Die Fortsetzung der archäologischen Karrieren," in Geringer et al., *Graben für Germanien*, 164–71 (at 165). See also Jagust, "Follow the Money," 296.

67. Gunter Schöbel, "Hans Reinerth: Forscher—NS-Funktionär—Museumsleiter," in Leube, *Prähistorie und Nationalsozialismus*, 321–96 (at 321).

archaeology in Germany to skip blithely over the entire question of guilt and blame, let alone critical self-assessment, until the 1990s.[68] Reinerth's punishment extended over half of his lifetime until his death in 1990.

The question remains: does it matter whether these men were both committed Nazis—that is, to what extent should a critical assessment of the discipline move beyond the simple precept that all archaeologists at the time were equally culpable?[69] Hoffmann distinguishes between what he calls servile and ideological collaborationisms in Vichy France. Servile collaborationism results from a reluctant recognition of necessity, whereas ideological collaborationism manifests itself as deliberate, voluntary, and based on conviction.[70] This classificatory scheme could also be applied to prehistoric archaeologists in Germany between 1933 and 1945. Reinerth appears to have belonged to the former category, while Jankuhn conforms more obviously to the latter. Following Jankuhn's death in 1990, an obituary appeared in the Nouvelle Droite magazine, *Nouvelle Ecole*, in which Alain de Benoist, the journal's editor and the head of far right Groupement de recherche et d'études pour la civilisation européenne [Research and Study Group for European Civilization], acknowledged Jankuhn as one of the "sponsors" of the magazine.[71]

The defamatory letters circulated by Bolko von Richthofen about Reinerth in 1938 culminated in legal proceedings documented in the Bundesarchiv Koblenz (R21/73). The letters were presumably motivated as much by personal enmity as by the desire to expose what was referred to as "Anfechtbares eines Nationalsozialisten unwürdiges Verhalten in der Judenfrage" [impugnable conduct unbecoming a National Socialist in regard to the Jewish Question]. They also reveal a less-than-consistent attitude toward the party line than would be expected of a high-ranking party official. In addition to general complaints about Reinerth's abrasive personality and accusations that he had joined the party out of personal ambition rather than conviction, Reinerth was accused by a number of well-respected and (in the postwar period) gainfully employed archaeologists of fraternization with Jews, especially the Bad Buchau baker and café owner Moritz Vierfelder, a major supporter of the Wasserburg Buchau excavations in the 1920s. When viewed through a contemporary lens, the statements outlined in the document expose the anti-Semitic leanings of these men

---

68. Jagust, "Follow the Money," 285.
69. Eickhoff et al., "Fortsetzung," 164.
70. Hoffmann, "Collaborationism," 379.
71. Maurice Olender, *Race and Erudition*, trans. Jane Marie Todd (Cambridge, MA: Harvard University Press, 2009), 63.

while casting doubt on Reinerth's commitment to this particularly heinous aspect of the Nazi ideological program.[72]

The legal document in the Bundesarchiv Koblenz, dated March 2, 1939, is thirty-five pages long and includes the testimony of fifty-five witnesses (including Herbert Jankuhn) against Reinerth. Virtually all of the accusers were either members of the Ahnenerbe or otherwise aligned against the Rosenberg Office, which makes this document not only a testament to the extent of the enmity Reinerth had engendered but goes some way to explaining why he was unable to obtain an academic position after 1945. Gunter Schöbel describes the final denouement of Reinerth's Nazi career as follows: "In March 1946, Reinerth was arrested by the French military police at Lake Constance after being denounced by his colleagues, and in 1949, he was classified as a perpetrator of the Nazi regime by the Allies. After the required period of penance he was rehabilitated in the eyes of the law but not in those of his colleagues."[73]

Jankuhn and Reinerth were born within five years of one another and died in the same year. While they shared an origin story as ethnic Germans whose homelands vanished in the aftermath of the Treaty of Versailles; fought against the perception that they were "ambitious ethnic Germans" from Poland and Romania, respectively;[74] and rose to the top archaeological positions in their respective NSDAP organizations, their postwar careers were very different. The institutional culpability in this case is represented not so much by the refusal to rehabilitate Reinerth, who was no poster child for collegiality, but rather by the willingness to give a free pass to Jankuhn, whose ideological load was certainly on a par with that of his more-maligned colleague. A recent master's thesis analyzed the publications of both Reinerth and Jankuhn in order to test the generally accepted fiction that the former had been more ideologically compromised than the latter and concluded that a double standard had been applied in their postwar treatment that was not justified based on their written output.[75]

The general pardon delivered by universities, museums, and institutes to most of the Ahnenerbe archaeologists has been recently criticized.[76] Given

---

72. Schöbel, "Hans Reinerth," 57.
73. Ibid., 55.
74. Ibid.
75. Krall, Katharina, "Prähistorie im Nationalsozialismus: Ein Vergleich der Schriften von Herbert Jankuhn und Hans Reinerth zwischen 1933 und 1939" (Master's thesis, University of Konstanz, Germany, 2005).
76. Eickhoff et al., "Fortsetzung," 171.

that virtually all of the principals have since died, however, the potential professional risks attendant on whistleblowing have been significantly reduced. Archaeologists after 1945 who knew both Reinerth's and Jankuhn's histories but chose to sacrifice the one and not the other made those institutional decisions and actions possible. It is here that we must focus our attention when attempting to understand the betrayal of the humanities and the social sciences by German universities both before and after World War II.[77] In particular the lesson for today is that we would do well to pay heed to the disenfranchised and disaffected when considering where the seeds of totalitarianism are most likely to fall on fruitful ground. We ignore these warnings from the past at our peril.

BIBLIOGRAPHY

Archival Sources

Bundesarchiv Koblenz

Secondary Sources

Anderson, Benedict. *Imagined Communities: Reflections on the Origin and Spread of Nationalism*. Rev. and ext. ed. London: Verso, 2006.

Applebaum, Anne. "The Collaborators: What Causes People to Abandon Their Principles in Support of a Corrupt Regime? And How Do They Find Their Way Back?" *Atlantic*, July/August 2020, 49–62.

Arnold, Bettina. "The Contested Past." *Anthropology Today* 15, no. 4 (1999): 1–4.

———. "The Past as Propaganda: Totalitarian Archaeology in Nazi Germany." *Antiquity* 64, no. 244 (1990): 464–78.

Arnold, Bettina, and Henning Hassmann. "Archaeology in Nazi Germany: The Legacy of the Faustian Bargain." In *Nationalism, Politics, and the Practice of Archaeology*, edited by Philip L. Kohl and Clare Fawcett, 70–81. Cambridge: Cambridge University Press, 1995.

Baumeister, Ralf. "Im Brennpunkt siedlungsarchäologischer Forschung: Das Federseemuseum—Einblicke in die Erforschung der Pfahlbauten seit 100 Jahren." *Denkmalpflege in Baden-Württemberg* 4 (2019): 255–61.

Bertram, Marion. "Zur Situation der deutschen Ur- und Frühgeschichtsforschung während der Zeit der faschistischen Diktatur." *Forschungen und Berichte* 31 (1991): 23–42.

---

77. Jagust, "Follow the Money," 298.

Bollmus, Reinhard. *Das Amt Rosenberg und seine Gegner: Studien zum Machtkampf im nationalsozialistischen Herrschaftssystem*. Stuttgart, Germany: Deutsche Verlags-Anstalt, 1970.

Callmer, Johan. "Archäologie und Nationalsozialismus als Gegenstand der modernen Forschung." In Leube, *Prähistorie und Nationalsozialismus*, 3–9.

Conard, Nicholas. "A Female Figurine from the Basal Aurignacian of Hohle Fels Cave in Southwestern Germany." *Nature* 459 (2009): 248–52.

Eickhoff, Martijn, Uta Halle, Jean-Pierre Legendre, and Otto H. Urban. "Die Fortsetzung der archäologischen Karrieren." In Geringer et al., *Graben für Germanien*, 164–71.

Franz, Leonhard. *Vorgeschichte und Zeitgeschehen*. Leipzig, Germany: Kabitzsch, 1938.

Geringer, Sandra, Frauke Von der Haar, Uta Halle, Dirk Mahsarski, and Karin Walter, eds. *Graben für Germanien: Archäologie unterm Hakenkreuz*. Stuttgart, Germany: Konrad Theiss, 2013.

Goldhagen, Daniel Jonah. *Hitler's Willing Executioners: Ordinary Germans and the Holocaust*. New York: Alfred A. Knopf, 1996.

Hagen, Anders. "Arkeologi og politik." *Viking* 49 (1985/86): 269–78.

Halle, Uta. "Wichtige Ausgrabungen der NS-Zeit." In Geringer et al., *Graben für Germanien*, 65–73.

Halle, Uta, and Dirk Mahsarski. "Forschungsstrukturen." In Geringer et al., *Graben für Germanien*, 57–64.

Härke, Heinrich, ed. *Archaeology, Ideology, and Society*. Gesellschaften und Staaten 7. Frankfurt, Germany: Peter Lang, 2002.

Hassmann, Henning. "Archaeology in the Third Reich." In Härke, *Archaeology, Ideology, and Society*, 67–142.

———. "Archäologie und Jugend im 'Dritten Reich': Ur- und Frühgeschichte als Mittel der politisch-ideologischen Indoktrination von Kindern und Jugendlichen." In Leube, *Prähistorie und Nationalsozialismus*, 107–46.

Hassmann, Henning, and Detlef Jantzen. "'Die deutsche Vorgeschichte—Eine nationale Wissenschaft': Das Kieler Museum vorgeschichtlicher Altertümer im Dritten Reich." *Offa* 51 (1994): 9–23.

Hoffmann, Stanley. "Collaborationism in France during World War II." *Journal of Modern History* 40, no. 3 (1968): 375–95.

Jagust, Frederick. "Follow the Money: Bemerkungen zum Verhältnis von Geld, Prähistorie, und Nationalsozialismus." In Schachtmann, Strobel, and Widera, *Politik und Wissenschaft*, 285–99.

Jankuhn, Herbert. *Die Ausgrabungen in Haithabu (1937–1939): Vorläufiger Grabungsbericht*. Berlin-Dahlem: Ahnenerbe-Stiftung, 1943.

———. *Haithabu: Ein Handelsplatz der Wikingerzeit*. 3rd ed. Neumünster, Germany: Karl Wachholtz, 1956.

Kater, Michael H. *Das "Ahnenerbe" der SS 1935–1945: Ein Beitrag zur Kulturpolitik des Dritten Reiches*. Studien zur Zeitgeschichte 6. Stuttgart, Germany: Deutsche Verlags-Anstalt, 1974.

Keefer, Erwin. "Hans Reinerth." In *Die Suche nach der Vergangenheit: 120 Jahre Archäologie am Federsee*, edited by Erwin Keefer, 41–48. Stuttgart, Germany: Landesdenkmalamt, 1992.

Kerig, Tim. "Grahame Clark und die mitteleuropäische Archäologie: Eine vergleichende Rezeptionsgeschichte." *Ethnographisch-Archäologische Zeitschrift* 52, no. 1 (2011): 83–103.

Kossinna, Gustaf. *Die deutsche Vorgeschichte: Eine hervorragend nationale Wissenschaft*. Würzburg, Germany: Curt Kabitzsch, 1912.

———. *Die Herkunft der Germanen: Zur Methode der Siedlungsarchäologie*. Würzburg, Germany: Curt Kabitzsch, 1911.

Krall, Katharina. "Prähistorie im Nationalsozialismus: Ein Vergleich der Schriften von Herbert Jankuhn und Hans Reinerth zwischen 1933 und 1939." Master's thesis, University of Konstanz, Germany, 2005.

Leube, Achim, ed. *Prähistorie und Nationalsozialismus: Die mittel- und osteuropäische Ur- und Frühgeschichtsforschung in den Jahren 1933–1945*. Heidelberg, Germany: Synchron, 2002.

Mahsarski, Dirk. "Skandinavien und die 'Germanische Leitstelle.'" In Geringer et al., *Graben für Germanien*, 147–53.

Mahsarski, Dirk, and Gunter Schöbel. "Von Gustaf Kossinna zur NS-Archäologie." In Geringer et al., *Graben für Germanien*, 31–36.

Mohn, Josef. *Der Leidensweg unter dem Hakenkreuz: Aus der Geschichte von Stadt und Stift Buchau*. Bad Buchau, Germany: A. Sandmaier and Sohn, 1970.

Olender, Maurice. *Race and Erudition*. Translated by Jane Marie Todd. Cambridge, MA: Harvard University Press, 2009.

Pape, Wolfgang. "Zehn Prähistoriker aus Deutschland." In Steuer, *Hervorragend nationale Wissenschaft*, 55–99.

Pringle, Heather. *The Master Plan: Himmler's Scholars and the Holocaust*. New York: Hyperion, 2006.

Reinerth, Hans. "Deutsche Vorgeschichte." *Nationalsozialistische Monatshefte* 27 (June 1932): 241–56.

———. "Deutsche Vorgeschichte und ihre Pflege im nationalsozialistischen Staat." *Deutsches Bildungswesen* 1 (1933): 47–50.

———. "Die politische Waffe der Vorgeschichtsforschung." *Volk und Heimat* 4 (1937): 89–90.

———. *Pfahlbauten am Bodensee*. 14th ed. Überlingen, Germany: August Feyel, 1986.

Riek, Gustav, and Hans-Jürgen Hundt. *Der Hohmichele: Ein Fürstengrab der späten Hallstattzeit bei der Heuneburg*. Heuneburgstudien I. Römisch-Germanische Forschungen 25. Berlin: De Gruyer, 1962.

Rosenberg, Alfred. *Der Mythus des 20. Jahrhunderts: Eine Wertung der seelisch-geistigen Gestaltenkämpfe unserer Zeit*. Munich: Hoheneichen, 1930.
Schachtmann, Judith, Michael Strobel, and Thomas Widera, eds. *Politik und Wissenschaft in der prähistorischen Archäologie: Perspektiven aus Sachsen, Böhmen, und Schlesien*. Göttingen, Germany: V&R Unipress, 2009.
Schöbel, Gunter. "Hans Reinerth: Forscher—NS-Funktionär—Museumsleiter." In Leube, *Prähistorie und Nationalsozialismus*, 321–96.
———. "Hans Reinerth: From archaeologist to Reichsamtsleiter." In *L'archéologie nazie en Europe de l'Ouest*, edited by Jean-Pierre Legendre, Laurent Olivier, and Bernadette Schnitzler, 45–59. Gollion, Switzerland: Infolio, 2007.
———. *Pfahlbaumuseum Unteruhldingen: Museumsgeschichte Teil 1 (1922–1949)*. Überlingen, Germany: Pfahlbaumuseum, 2001.
Scott, James C. *Weapons of the Weak: Everyday Forms of Peasant Resistance*. New Haven, CT: Yale University Press, 2008.
Sénécheau, Miriam. "Archäologie im Schulbuch: Themen der Ur- und Frühgeschichte im Spannungsfeld zwischen Lehrplanforderungen, Fachdiskussion, und populären Geschichtsvorstellungen Schulbücher, Unterrichtsfilme, Kinder-, und Jugendliteratur." PhD diss., University of Freiburg, Germany, 2006.
Sommer, Ulrike. "The Teaching of Archaeology in West Germany." In Härke, *Archaeology, Ideology, and Society*, 205–43.
Steinel, Monika E. "Archaeology, National Socialism, and Rehabilitation: The Case of Herbert Jankuhn." In *Ethics and the Archaeology of Violence*, edited by Alfredo González-Ruibal and Gabriel Moshenska, 153–66. Ethical Archaeologies: The Politics of Social Justice 2. New York: Springer, 2015.
Steuer, Heiko. "Herbert Jankuhn und seine Darstellungen zur Germanen- und Wikingerzeit." In Steuer, *Hervorragend nationale Wissenschaft*, 417–73.
———, ed. *Eine hervorragend nationale Wissenschaft*. Berlin: de Gruyter, 2001.
Weger, Tobias. "Bolko Freiherr von Richthofen und Helmut Preidel." In Schachtmann, Strobel, and Widera, *Politik und Wissenschaft*, 125–48.

BETTINA ARNOLD is Professor of Anthropology at the University of Wisconsin–Milwaukee and serves as Adjunct Curator of European Archaeology at the Milwaukee Public Museum. Her research interests include the archaeological interpretation and analysis of complex societies as reflected in mortuary contexts and in the production and consumption of alcoholic beverages and the archaeological interpretation of gender. She has also studied the sociopolitical history of archaeology and museum collecting, especially their involvement in identity construction in nineteenth- and twentieth-century nationalist and ethnic movements in Europe and the United States. She published a groundbreaking article on the use and abuse of archaeology for political purposes in Nazi Germany in *Antiquity* in 1990.

PART II

LAW, MUSIC, AND PHILOSOPHY IN THE THIRD REICH

NINE

HITLER'S WILLING LAW PROFESSORS

OREN GROSS

"The dagger of the assassin was concealed beneath the robe of the jurist."[1]

I. INTRODUCTION: HERR SAUL LANDE AUS WARSCHAU

On November 12, 1938, three days after Kristallnacht, the Faculty of Law of the University of Leipzig awarded a doctoral degree in law. The new doctor had studied in Leipzig between 1926 and 1933 and wrote his dissertation under the supervision of Professor Paul Koschaker, the great Roman law scholar. Yet that particular doctorate was anything but ordinary, for the university bestowed this highest degree on a Jewish student. Signed by the Dean of the Faculty of Law, Professor Hans Oppikofer, and stamped with the seal of the university, bearing the formal symbol of the Nazi party, an eagle atop a swastika, the certificate conferred on "Herrn Saul Lande aus Warschau" the degree of *Doktor der*

In memory of my great-grandparents Yossef and Ester and my great-uncles and aunt Arie-Leib, Yehuda-Tsvi, and Haya and their families from Lesko (Linsk) Poland, who were murdered in the Belzec extermination camp in 1942. May their souls be bound up in the bond of life. Earlier drafts of the work were presented at the Center for Ethics, Emory University; the Legal History Workshop, University of Minnesota Law School; the University of Minnesota Law School's Faculty Works in Progress; and the 2020 American Society of Comparative Law Annual Meeting. I have benefited greatly from the comments of all the participants in those. I have particularly benefited from comments, suggestions, and insights by David Abraham, Arnon Gutfeld, Eric Weitz, Adam Levitin, Andreas Zimmerman, Bernard Levinson, Robert Ericksen, Scott Dewey, Ryan Greenwood, Hubert Lang, Edward Queen, Achilles Skordas, and Deborah Lipstadt. Of course, all errors remain my own.

1. Trials of War Criminals before the Nuernberg Military Tribunals under Control Council Law No. 10: Nuernberg, October 1946–April 1949, vol. 3, "The Justice Case" (The United States of America v. Altstoetter et al.) (Washington, DC: United States Government Printing Office, 1951), 985.

Rechte.[2] Thus, Lande became the last Jew to be awarded a doctorate in law (and presumably the last Jew to be awarded a doctorate in any academic discipline) by a German university prior to World War II.[3] Not less amazing is the fact that the doctoral work, entitled *Teilunwirksamkeit letztwilliger Verfügungen* [Partial Inefficacy of Testamentary Dispositions], was published in 1938 in Dresden by M. Dittert and Co.[4] Indeed, the University of Leipzig awarded Lande his doctorate, and the work was published, possibly in absentia.[5] Lande had already escaped from Nazi Germany and settled in Palestine in 1935, where he became a practicing attorney in Tel Aviv shortly thereafter[6] and where I, his eldest grandson, was born thirty years later.

Personally and professionally, Saul Lande was among the lucky ones. His story as a law student and a legal professional is unique and, to this day, remains inexplicable in parts. It runs against the grain not only of Nazi targeting of Jews in general but, specifically, of their targeting of Jewish jurists—judges, lawyers, law professors and lecturers, and students. Prior to 1933, the practice of law had been a highly coveted occupation for German (and Austrian) Jews. As Ingo Müller notes, "The numerous forms of discrimination faced by Jews ... had led them to enter the unrestricted professions. . . . This was true above all in the field of law, where the lifting of all restrictions on admission to the bar made the private practice of law one of the most attractive careers for educated Jews."[7] Jews were represented at the bar in significantly higher proportion compared with their percentage of the population. For example, in Berlin, 60 percent of all private practitioners were Jewish.[8]

---

2. For a copy of the certificate, see Hubert Lang, *Zwischen allen Stühlen: Juristen jüdischer Herkunft in Leipzig (1848–1953)* (Leipzig, Germany: Biographiezentrum, 2014), 444.

3. Ibid., 445.

4. A copy of the published work is on file with the author.

5. An article published in the Israeli daily *Ha'Aretz* about Lande's story claims that he did, in fact, travel back to Leipzig to receive the doctoral degree (Ofer Aderet, "A Jew from Palestine Was Awarded Law Degree from Nazi Germany, Exhibition Reveals," *Ha'Aretz*, April 18, 2012, https://www.haaretz.com/jewish/1.5214906). Lande's daughter, Rina Gross, says that to the best of her knowledge he did not return to Germany in 1938 (in an interview with the author).

6. At least one letter sent from Germany to Dr. Lande in "Tel Aviv, Palestine" included a price quote for the publication of his dissertation by another press and ended with the salutation "Heil Hitler!" See Aderet, "Jew From Palestine."

7. Ingo Müller, *Hitler's Justice: The Courts of the Third Reich*, trans. Deborah Lucas Schneider (Cambridge, MA: Harvard University Press, 1991), 59.

8. Ibid., 60.

On April 7, 1933, just over two months after Hitler was appointed chancellor, two new laws were promulgated. The Law on the Admission to the Bar targeted lawyers, decreeing that attorneys of non-Aryan descent could be excluded from the bar. The practical result of that Law was that lawyers of Jewish descent had to reapply for admission to the bar. Only those who had been admitted before August 8, 1914 [*Altanwälte*], who had fought at the front line in the First World War [*Frontkämpfer*],[9] or who had a father or son killed in the war, were exempted and permitted to continue to practice law without seeking readmission.[10]

Within months of the passage of the new law, the number of Jewish lawyers in Germany dropped by over 30 percent, from 4,585 to 3,167.[11] However, the vast majority of Jewish lawyers affected by the law did, in fact, apply for readmission to the bar. For example, 1,761 of 1,835 Jewish lawyers in Berlin opted to do so.[12] Jewish lawyers continued practicing despite the adverse conditions in which they had found themselves. Even as late as 1938, some 10 percent of practicing lawyers in Germany—1,753 out of 17,360—were Jewish.[13] The final move to eliminate the "Jewish lawyer" came in the aftermath of the Anschluss in March 1938, bringing the city of Vienna, where 80 percent of lawyers had been Jewish,[14] into the Nazi fold. On September 27, 1938, Hitler signed a decree that disbarred all remaining Jewish lawyers as of November 30, 1938, allowing for a very small number of former lawyers to assume a newly created position of *Konsulent* [legal advisor] enabling them to handle only Jewish interests and affairs.[15] Unlike lawyers, the legal advisors were not considered "guardians of the law" or, indeed, "lawyer-like actor[s]."[16] Thus, as of the end of November, the legal profession became *entjudet* [free of Jews].

II. HITLER'S MANDARIN INTELLECTUALS

The second law issued on April 7, 1933, the Gesetz zur Wiederherstellung des Berufsbeamtentums [Law for the Restoration of the Professional Civil Service],

---

9. Douglas G. Morris, "Discrimination, Degradation, Defiance: Jewish Lawyers under Nazism," in *The Law in Nazi Germany: Ideology, Opportunism, and the Perversion of Justice*, ed. Alan E. Steinweis and Robert D. Rachlin (New York: Berghahn, 2013), 105–35 (at 114–18).
10. Müller, *Hitler's Justice*, 60–61.
11. Morris, "Discrimination," 113.
12. Ibid., 114.
13. Ibid., 129.
14. Müller, *Hitler's Justice*, 60; Morris, "Discrimination," 129.
15. Morris, "Discrimination," 130.
16. Ibid.

decreed that unreliable elements and non-Aryans were to be dismissed from public service. In accordance with that law, Jewish judges had to retire, and Jewish law professors were dismissed from their university positions. Nearly 1,700 faculty members, comprising 15 percent of the universities' teaching staff, lost their jobs.[17] Eighty percent of those fired were Jewish.[18] In the case of faculties of law in German universities, the situation was even worse.[19] Almost a third—120 of 378[20]—of those teaching were subsequently removed from their positions, the vast majority on racial grounds.[21] The vacant positions were filled in short order by "promising untenured faculty colleagues with a 'nationalistic orientation.'"[22] By 1939, 45 percent of German university professors had been appointed during the Third Reich, and by 1945, about two-thirds of university teachers belonged to the Nationalsozialistische Deutsche Arbeiterpartei [National Socialist German Workers' Party (NSDAP)].[23] In law faculties the number was, of course, higher with 60 percent of professors appointed in or since 1933.[24] The once fiercely independent, apolitical, and revered German universities now embraced their new character as political institutions[25] fully

---

17. Edward Yarnall Hartshorne Jr., *The German Universities and National Socialism* (Cambridge, MA: Harvard University Press, 1937), 99, states that 1,684 were dismissed.

18. Amy R. Sims, "Intellectuals in Crisis: Historians under Hitler," *Virginia Quarterly Review* 54, no. 2 (1978): 246–62 (at 254). Not all universities were similarly affected; some "were virtually untouched by the dismissals." However, rather than reflecting resistance to Nazi personnel policies, such differences merely reflected "the varying willingness of universities during the Weimar Republic to admit Jews, Social Democrats, or left liberals into their faculties. As a rule of thumb, the more open universities were prior to 1933, the more profoundly they were affected by the dismissals after 1933" (Michael Grüttner, "German Universities under the Swastika," in *Universities under Dictatorship*, ed. John Connelly and Michael Grüttner [University Park: Pennsylvania State University Press, 2005], 75–111 [at 91]).

19. Hartshorne notes that "the proportion of Jews in the field of Law was disproportionately large" (*German Universities and National Socialism*, 100).

20. Müller, *Hitler's Justice*, 69. Hartshorne puts the number of those dismissed from the faculties of law at 132 (*German Universities and National Socialism*, 98–99).

21. Hartshorne, *German Universities and National Socialism*, 100. Hartshorne suggests that "the 'Non-Aryans,' who constituted 17.5 per cent of the total staff of the pre-Nazi Law Faculties, make up 78.5 per cent of the dismissals."

22. Müller, *Hitler's Justice*, 69. See also Grüttner, "Universities," 85.

23. Grüttner, "Universities," 93.

24. Müller, *Hitler's Justice*, 235.

25. Gustav Adolf Rein, *Die Idee der politischen Universität* (Hamburg, Germany: Hanseatische Verlagsanstalt, 1933).

coordinated and regulated by the regime.[26] At the same time, the universities lost their position as "the crux of the educational system,"[27] with enrollment dropping down, "as a result of a deliberate policy," from a total of 97,576 students enrolled in 1932 to mere 51,527 in 1938.[28] Furthermore, as the ranks of the professoriate swelled with supporters of National Socialism, so too did the ranks of their students; by 1938, more than 90 percent of them were organized in the National Socialist German Students' League.[29]

III. THE SPIRIT OF NATIONAL SOCIALISM

Once the ranks of university professors had been filled with supporters of the Nazi Party, German academia turned with much zeal and enthusiasm to the project of justifying and legitimating the actions of the regime. Looking at the record of one of the most renowned German universities—Ruprecht Karls University in Heidelberg—Steven Remy finds that the engagement of its professoriate with National Socialism had been "extensive."[30] Professors from all faculties made "tangible contributions" to the "policies of 'racial purification' and territorial expansion ... the 'Volksgemeinschaft,' and the 'German spirit' in scholarship."[31] In turn, "the willing participation of the academic elite at Heidelberg and other universities was of vital importance to the regime's project of 'racial' purification at home, the concomitant war of expansion, and its imperialist economic and cultural offensives in occupied Europe."[32]

---

26. Sims, "Historians," 254–55, details some additional milestones in the process: "In August 1933, admission to the university became contingent upon four months of compulsory service in the Nazi labor force.... Instead of being elected, the rector had to be selected by the regime for his political reliability. And instead of being a symbolic head, he held very real power. In December 1933, professors hired after 1918 had to take a new oath of loyalty to *Volk* and Fatherland. By August 1934, civil servants had to swear loyalty to Adolf Hitler."
27. Franz L. Neumann, *Behemoth: The Structure and Practice of National Socialism, 1933–1944*, 2nd ed. (London: Oxford University Press, 1944), 399.
28. Neumann, *Behemoth*, 399.
29. Ibid. See also R. G. S. Weber, *The German Student Corps in the Third Reich* (Basingstoke, UK: Palgrave Macmillan, 1986).
30. Steven P. Remy, *The Heidelberg Myth: The Nazification and Denazification of a German University* (Cambridge, MA: Harvard University Press, 2002), 1.
31. Ibid., 239. For a detailed discussion of the contributions of jurists to the development of National Socialist law in various fields of law, see Michael Stolleis, "Law and Lawyers Preparing the Holocaust," *Annual Review of Law and Social Science* 3 (2007): 213–31.
32. Remy, *Heidelberg*, 1.

German legal academics responded with at least as much zeal and enthusiasm in support of the Nazi cause as their colleagues in other disciplines.[33] As Michael Stolleis notes, "An eager rush to publish set in as early as the spring of 1933."[34] Professors of law were "astoundingly productive" in creating and establishing a "'National Socialist legal system.' They saw it as their task to bring about a 'coordination' of the legal profession's thinking parallel to the 'coordination' of legal institutions which had already occurred."[35] Much like members of the German judiciary and bar, law professors threw themselves into the task of providing legitimacy and a cloak of legality to the regime's actions. Indeed, "it was in the writings of . . . scholars that the judges of the Third Reich found guidelines for their verdicts and lethal interpretations."[36]

German legal academia, like German higher education generally, accepted willingly and enthusiastically the notion that scholarship was impossible without a foundation of values, which were, of course, those of National Socialism. As Carl Schmitt declared: "The whole of German law today . . . must be governed solely and exclusively by the spirit of National Socialism. . . . Every interpretation must be an interpretation according to National Socialism."[37] Similarly, "All vague concepts, all so-called omnibus clauses, are to be made absolute and unconditional in accordance with National Socialism."[38] The tradition of "neutral research" was displaced by the notion of research as "the institutional reality of the spiritual realm,"[39] leading to the ominous conclusion

---

33. Arthur Kaufmann, "National Socialism and German Jurisprudence from 1933 to 1945," *Cardozo Law Review* 9 (1988): 1629–49 (at 1630). Kaufmann notes that "the majority of legal philosophers not only did not oppose National Socialism, they firmly and unequivocally supported almost all of the important goals of the new 'völkische bewegung' (popular movement), including their racial policies" (ibid.). Müller's assessment of the culpability of law professors during this era is similarly grim: "An essential role in the decline of law during the Third Reich was played by law professors at German universities. They provided a philosophical cloak for the Nazis' arbitrary acts and crimes. . . . There was virtually no outrage perpetrated by the Nazis which was not praised during the regime as 'supremely just' and defended after the war by the same scholars, with equally dubious arguments, as 'justifiable' or even 'advisable' from a legal point of view" (*Hitler's Justice*, 68).
34. Michael Stolleis, *A History of Public Law in Germany, 1914–1945*, trans. Thomas Dunlap (Oxford: Oxford University Press, 2004), 364.
35. Müller, *Hitler's Justice*, 70.
36. Ibid., 68.
37. Kaufmann, "Jurisprudence," 1644 (quoting Carl Schmitt).
38. Ibid., 1645 (quoting Carl Schmitt).
39. Max Weinreich, *Hitler's Professors: The Part of Scholarship in Germany's Crimes against the Jewish People* (London: Yiddish Scientific Institute [YIVO], 1946; repr., foreword by Martin Gilbert, New Haven, CT: Yale University Press, 1999), 37. See also Remy, *Heidelberg*, 6–7.

that "[since] the national goal is to be considered without further ceremony a motive for excluding guilt... [e]xterminating without remainder the inner enemy is doubtlessly part of restituting German honor."[40] The guiding theme of academic research became the "German spirit," which "encompassed streams of völkisch nationalism, anti-Semitism, and biological and cultural racism and entailed an antipositivist conception of scholarship that placed all research and teaching in the service of the 'people's community,' defined in racist terms."[41] Hans Schemm, the chief of the National Socialist Teachers' League—whose membership stood at 220,000 by late 1933[42]—captured the shift when he stated that, "From now on, it is not up to you to decide the truth of anything, but to determine whether it conforms to the meaning of the National Socialist Revolution."[43]

That same German spirit, and the meaning of the National Socialist revolution, expressed through and reflected in German "common law," entailed the exclusion of "non-German" elements from all legal spheres.[44] In fact, many legal scholars had been hard at work preparing Hitler's path to power by setting the stage for the dismantling of the Weimar Republic and its constitution. The "Mandarin intellectuals," as Fritz Ringer referred to university professors,[45] were mostly conservative nationalists and antirepublican long before 1932.[46] They ferociously attacked liberalism, individualism (including any notion of individual basic rights),[47] and parliamentary democracy as incorporated and reflected in the "system" of the Weimar constitution. The "demise in Germany of liberal law, the transformation of the German legal system, and the creation of a new anti-liberal Nazi legal order,"[48] had all, in turn, been entangled "like vines" with the elimination of Jewish lawyers, who, in addition to being

---

40. Weinreich, *Professors*, 37. On the use of "irrational language"—such as honor, loyalty, blood and soil, heroic—by legal scholars supporting the regime, see Kaufmann, "Jurisprudence," 1638–41.
41. Remy, *Heidelberg*, 6.
42. Claudia Koonz, *The Nazi Conscience* (Cambridge, MA: Belknap Press of Harvard University Press, 2003), 133.
43. Ibid., 136–37.
44. Remy, *Heidelberg*, 43.
45. Fritz K. Ringer, *The Decline of the German Mandarins: The German Academic Community, 1890–1933* (Hanover, NH: University Press of New England, 1969), 5–6.
46. Remy, *Heidelberg*, 7–10.
47. Kaufmann, "Jurisprudence," 1635.
48. Morris, "Discrimination," 107.

considered the ultimate *artfremde* [foreign "other"], were mostly liberals.[49] Thus, as "the ground at Heidelberg and other universities was well prepared for the Nazi seizure of power," National Socialism's "intellectual preconditions were being formed outside National Socialism itself."[50]

"All Honourable Men"[51]

Arthur Kaufmann notes that "among legal philosophers—who actually should have been the main custodians of the right to oppose—hardly any opposition was voiced."[52] In fact, "The majority of German legal philosophers . . . supported the National Socialists in very different ways."[53] Arthur Kaufmann and Mathias Reimann focus on the role played by several leading German scholars, including Theodor Maunz, Ernst Forsthoff and Karl Larenz.[54] I will briefly follow their examples before turning in the next section to focus on the greatest legal asset at the disposal of the Nazis, Carl Schmitt.

"Every German lawyer," writes Reimann, "knows [Theodor] Maunz as the coauthor of the most authoritative commentary on the West German constitution and for writing one of the leading treatises on constitutional law and the system of government."[55] Indeed, Maunz has been so highly regarded in postwar Germany that he became known as "der Kronjurist des Grundgesetzes" [the crown jurist of the Basic Law], a reference to his status as the leading expert on the West German constitution.[56] For twenty years, between 1932 and 1952, Maunz taught (and since 1937, was a full Professor) at the University of Freiburg before moving to the Ludwig Maximilian University in Munich.

---

49. In a 1936 conference on "Jewry in Jurisprudence" (see notes 162–66 and the accompanying text in this chapter), one of Germany's leading professors of constitutional and administrative law, Theodor Maunz elaborated on the "fatal predilection of Jewish theorists of administrative law for the liberal doctrine of the Rechtsstaat." See Michael Stolleis, *The Law under the Swastika: Studies on Legal History in Nazi Germany*, trans. Thomas Dunlap (Chicago: University of Chicago Press, 1998), 187.

50. Remy, *Heidelberg*, 11.

51. William Shakespeare, *The Tragedy of Julius Caesar*, 3.2.83.

52. Kaufmann, "Jurisprudence," 1634.

53. Ibid., 1635.

54. Mathias Reimann, "National Socialist Jurisprudence and Academic Continuity: A Comment on Professor Kaufmann's Article," *Cardozo Law Review* 9 (1988): 1651–62 (at 1652–55).

55. Ibid., 1653.

56. Gerhard Mauz, "'Ich bin nicht nur wütend,'" *Der Spiegel*, October 18, 1993, http://www.spiegel.de/spiegel/print/d-13680349.html.

He later served as minister of education for Bavaria. However, that "kind and reclusive" man[57] had also been "one of the most ardent supporters of National Socialism."[58] Stolleis's assessment of Maunz is a bit more benign: "Maunz was a *Vernunftrepublikaner* [republican by reason] and supporter of the *Rechtsstaat* [rule of law] when that was still part of the traditional code of conduct at the end of the Weimar Republic; he was a National Socialist as long as the others were, and a little bit more so and for a little longer; then he was once again a legal positivist with a touch of natural law. It all depended on the time and circumstances, like a chameleon that has the ability to adjust its color and temperature to the environment."[59]

Yet there is no disputing that Maunz fully immersed himself in, and supported, National Socialism. In his 1934 work on the *Neue Grundlagen des Verwaltungsrechts* [New Foundations of Administrative Law], Maunz explained: "The central legal structure, behind which all other legal structures have to follow, is the political Führer.... [A]ny judicial activity in the field of administrative law is impossible. It follows that the administration of justice can never hinder the political decisions of the Führer."[60] Following that logic, Maunz pronounced arrests by the Gestapo to constitute "sovereign acts" that fall outside any possible judicial scrutiny and review.[61] After all, he claimed, the source of legality for any police action was none other than the will of the Führer. Maunz argued that notions such as individual rights and separation of powers belonged in the liberal state and decried them as guarantors of the bourgeois concept of freedom and as such incompatible with the National Socialist state where the "powers are united in the person of the Führer."[62] Similarly to the expropriation of a person's liberty, Maunz expounded on a "National Socialist right of expropriation" of property that hinged on the national community and the proclaimed will of the Führer.[63] Maunz's legalistic contortions in the service of National Socialism can also be seen in his treatment of the principle of equality. According to Maunz, German law did contain this principle, but

---

57. Stolleis, *Swastika*, 185, describes the obituaries for Maunz upon his death.
58. Reimann, "Continuity," 1652.
59. Stolleis, *Swastika*, 189.
60. Theodor Maunz, *Neue Grundlagen des Verwaltungsrechts*, Der Deutsche Staat der Gegenwart 9 (Hamburg, Germany: Hanseatische Verlagsanstalt, 1934), 48, 55. On Maunz's contribution to the creation of a National Socialist administrative law, see Stolleis, *History*, 382–83.
61. Stolleis, *Swastika*, 187.
62. Theodor Maunz, *Verwaltung* (Hamburg, Germany: Hanseatische Verlagsanstalt), 42.
63. Kaufmann, "Jurisprudence," 1635.

it was based on race rather than relating to all human beings as such. Thus, the foreign other could be excluded from, for example, local swimming pools, without such an exclusion violating the law; indeed, such exclusion would be considered as upholding the law.[64] Last, but certainly not least, in the infamous 1936 conference on "Jewry in Jurisprudence,"[65] Maunz emphasized the "fatal predilection of Jewish theorists of administrative law for the liberal doctrine of the *Rechtsstaat*."[66]

Ernst Forsthoff is considered Carl Schmitt's "model pupil."[67] He was another member of the professoriate who had become an ardent supporter of National Socialism in the early 1930s. Like many others he benefited from the dismissal of Jews and unreliable professors from German universities. Beginning his teaching career in Frankfurt in 1933, he succeeded to the chair previously held by Herman Heller, before moving to Hamburg, Königsberg, Vienna, and Heidelberg between 1935 and 1945. In his 1933, forty-eight-page essay, "Der Totale Staat" [The Total State], Forsthoff developed the argument that a "total state" was superior to a liberal democracy. Indeed, he declared that liberalism was finished.[68] The Weimar Republic—an "unprecedented fourteen-year-long path of suffering"[69]—was to be replaced by a national state in which every individual would be placed under complete obligation to the nation.[70] Individuals were to alienate their autonomy and subordinate to race, the Volk, and the state,[71] and be prepared "to give oneself up to society."[72] It was the decision-making realm of the state that served as the ultimate source of public order.[73] This

---

64. Ibid., 1637.
65. See notes 165–69 and the accompanying text in this chapter.
66. Stolleis, *Swastika*, 187.
67. Florian Meinel, "Ernst Forsthoff and the Intellectual History of German Administrative Law," *German Law Journal* 8 (2007): 785–99 (at 787) (quoting Peer Zumbansen).
68. Ernst Forsthoff, *Der Totale Staat* (Hamburg, Germany: Hanseatische Verlagsanstalt, 1933), 7.
69. Forsthoff as quoted in Kaufmann, "Jurisprudence," 1639.
70. Forsthoff, *Totale Staat*, 42. According to Stolleis, "What Forsthoff envisaged was not totalitarian despotism, but the authoritarian state of the 'conservative revolution' that would reconcile conservatism and modernity, a commitment to values and efficiency. Neither parties nor associations, neither parliament nor public opinion should be allowed to impair the goal of an objective, task-oriented administration" (*History*, 374).
71. Peter C. Caldwell, "Ernst Forsthoff and the Legacy of Radical Conservative State Theory in the Federal Republic of Germany," *History of Political Thought* 15, no. 4 (1994): 615–41 (at 616).
72. Caldwell, "Forsthoff," 619.
73. Ibid., 618.

"kind, learned, and cultivated human being"[74]—who just happened to be a member of the Nazi Party, the SA, and the Nationalsozialistischer Deutscher Dozentenbund [National Socialist German University Instructors' League]—then embraced National Socialist authoritarianism and expressed openly his antisemitic views, including the statement that the "essentially different Jew" had become an enemy that had to be rendered harmless.[75] In similar vein, his *Deutsche Geschichte in Dokumenten seit 1918* [German history in documents since 1918] "could not have been a stronger propaganda tract had it been written by Joseph Goebbels himself."[76] In that volume, Forsthoff "justifie[d] every major public policy of the regime up to 1938."[77] Unlike Maunz's perverse insistence that the principle of equality still prevailed under National Socialism, Forsthoff openly challenged the "horrendous" notions of egalitarianism and egalitarian democracy.[78] He disagreed with Otto Koellreutter that concentration camps were incompatible with the National Socialist conception of the Rechtsstaat[79] and argued that "individualistic liberalism must no longer be allowed to enjoy the privilege of publicity in Germany."[80]

Karl Larenz is "a name every first-year German law student will know," wrote Mathias Reimann in 1988.[81] He was a professor of civil law, appointed in 1933 at the University of Kiel to the chair previously held by Gerhart Husserl, who had been dismissed from his position for being a Jew. Larenz became a leading member of what was known as the Kiel school, "an attempt to give

---

74. Kaufmann, "Jurisprudence," 1642.
75. Peter C. Caldwell, "Ernst Forsthoff in Frankfurt: Political Mobilization and the Abandonment of Scholarly Responsibility," in *"Politisierung der Wissenschaft": Jüdische Wissenschaftler und ihre Gegner an der Universität Frankfurt am Main vor und nach 1933*, ed. Moritz Epple et al., Schriftenreihe des Frankfurter Universitätsarchivs 5 (Göttingen, Germany: Wallstein, 2016), 249–84 (at 269). Unlike several of his colleagues, first and foremost Carl Schmitt, Forsthoff was willing to acknowledge, at least rhetorically, the possibility of "the Jew" ceasing to be the "enemy." This could happen, he argues, "only if the Jews give up any attempt to participate in the spiritual, intellectual and political existence of the German people, and withdraw completely into their Jewishness."
76. Remy, *Heidelberg*, 191.
77. Ibid., 88.
78. Kaufmann, "Jurisprudence," 1637, citing Forsthoff, *Totale Staat*, 24.
79. Stolleis, *History*, 355.
80. Kaufmann, "Jurisprudence," 1634, citing Forsthoff, *Totale Staat*, 33.
81. Reimann, "Continuity," 1653. Reimann ("Continuity," 1654) further notes that, "Larenz authored the leading treatises on core subjects in private law. Here, his authority equals the highest courts' [sic]. Moreover, his work on legal methodology is generally regarded as second to none."

National Socialism ... some kind of intellectual form, especially through the application of a modernized Hegelian legal philosophy."[82] Ensconced in the "shock troop university" that was Kiel,[83] Larenz proclaimed that only *Volksgenossen* [national comrades] were entitled to legal responsibility (a notion closely linked to the idea of legal entity) and, in fact, that even among them, not everybody was equally so entitled.[84] Like his other colleagues mentioned previously, Larenz based the legality and validity of any decision and law exclusively on the Führer's will. Hence, "a law based on his will is not subject to judicial review."[85]

Unlike his younger colleagues, Maunz, Forsthoff, and Larenz, who were appointed into positions vacated by the dismissal of Jewish colleagues, Otto Koellreutter became a full Professor at the University of Halle in 1920 before moving to Jena a year later and to Munich (which he described as "the capital of the [Nazi] movement") in 1933.[86] He became the Dean of the law faculty in the same year, making the university an institution "clearly dominated by National Socialists."[87] Also unlike many of his colleagues, he cast his lot with National Socialism before the fateful spring of 1933.[88] In 1932, Koellreutter was the "first state law teacher to sign an electoral proclamation in support of the NSDAP."[89] Together with his great academic rival, Carl Schmitt,[90] Koellreutter was "the most prominent among the renowned scholars who professed themselves followers of National Socialism."[91] Koellreutter, who in earlier writings extolled the eternal and timeless values of the Rechtsstaat, now was at pains to prove his allegiance to National Socialism by claiming the desirability and superiority of the "national *Rechtsstaat*."[92] In his 1933 brochure, "Vom Sinn und Wesen der Nationalen Revolution" [On the meaning and essence of the national revolution],[93] in arguments similar

---

82. Stolleis, *History*, 291–92.
83. Ibid., 291.
84. Kaufmann, "Jurisprudence," 1636.
85. Ibid., 1640.
86. Stolleis, *History*, 289.
87. Ibid., 300.
88. Caldwell, "Forsthoff," 623.
89. Stolleis, *History*, 163.
90. On the dispute between Schmitt and Koellreutter in which each charged the other party with liberal tendencies and their struggle over the fate of the Association of Teachers of State Law, see Stolleis, *History*, 327–31, 354–55.
91. Stolleis, *Swastika*, 97.
92. Stolleis, *History*, 354.
93. Otto Koellreutter, *Vom Sinn und Wesen der Nationalen Revolution*, Recht und Staat in Geschichte und Gegenwart 101 (Tübingen, Germany: J. C. B. Mohr, 1933).

to those we have already seen, Koellreutter pronounced liberalism to be a failure, rejected any notion of individual rights in favor of obligations of individuals to the community and the nation, and, somewhat ironically, followed his great foe Carl Schmitt's friend-foe dichotomy. With Koellreutter, who was awarded several honors and distinctions for his fighting in World War I, including the Iron Cross First Class, much of his support of Nazism was clearly linked to his strong opposition to the Weimar Republic and his perception of the need for a strong national power. That led him to declare in 1932 that while the Nazi Party was constitutional, the Communist Party was not, despite the fact that both sought to dismantle the Weimar Republic and constitution.[94]

IV. KRONJURIST DES DRITTEN REICHES

No single member of the Mandarin legal elite had a more pernicious impact on the collapse of Weimar and the rise of the Nazi state than Carl Schmitt. None made greater contributions to the weakening and eventual dismantling of the Weimar Republic and its constitution. None rose as fully in support of the racial policies of the Nazi regime, while also theorizing about, legalizing, and legitimizing the phenomenon of the Führer. Dubbed the "crown jurist of the Third Reich,"[95] Schmitt, the first and most prominent constitutional theorist and political thinker to join the cause of National Socialism and lend his active support to the Nazis,[96] "developed for Hitler the legal-philosophical outlines for the constitution of the Third Reich and wrote that the pivot was Hitler's status as both head of state and party leader."[97]

Attacking Weimar

According to its detractors among conservative legal theorists and political thinkers, the liberal Weimar system with its focus on individual rights and parliamentarism and its positivist underpinnings was inherently deficient. Against

---

94. Otto Koellreutter, *Parteien und Verfassung im heutigen Deutschland* (Leipzig, Germany: Hirschfeld, 1932).
95. Franz Neumann refers to Schmitt as "the most intelligent and reliable of all National Socialist constitutional lawyers" (*Behemoth*, 49). Similarly, Schmitt was recognized by the regime as "the most renowned national constitutionalist in Germany." See Yvonne Sherratt, *Hitler's Philosophers* (New Haven, CT: Yale University Press, 2013), 99.
96. Stolleis, *Swastika*, 92, 97.
97. Sherratt, *Philosophers*, 100.

Weimar's built-in culture of discussion and debate, they presented the capacity to decide.[98] Against Weimar's "effeminate passivity"[99] they posited the "masculine cult of action and will."[100] Weimar's focus on legislators and judges was cast aside in favor of the sovereign dictator. Its liberal insistence on individual rights was to be replaced by the *Volksgemeinschaft* [national community], its pluralism and "emotional pantheism"[101] substituted by coordination[102] and *Artgleichheit* [racial homogeneity]. Its "cosmic tolerance," which meant that "there [was] no longer anything that one could love and honestly hate"[103] gave way to the dichotomy between friend and foe/enemy.[104] Finally, liberalism's misguided (or even deceitful) attachment to general norms that applied at all times and in all situations was challenged by the notion of the exception.

It was this last concept— the *Ausnahmezustand* [exception]—that served as Carl Schmitt's main weapon in his attack on Weimar's constitutionalism and liberalism.[105] According to Schmitt, the existence of exceptional situations refuted the formal face of legal liberalism, which argued that preestablished general norms covered and applied to all possible situations.[106] The need to decide the exceptional, concrete situation emphasized the central role of political

---

98. Neumann, *Behemoth*, 45. Neumann discusses Carl Schmitt's decisionism, that is, "the demand for action instead of deliberation, for decision instead of evaluation."

99. Carl Schmitt, *Political Romanticism*, trans. Guy Oakes (Cambridge, MA: MIT Press, 1986), 128.

100. Jeffrey Herf, *Reactionary Modernism: Technology, Culture, and Politics in Weimar and the Third Reich* (Cambridge: Cambridge University Press, 1984), 118. As he shows: "A masculine cult of action and will permeates Schmitt's protest against the rationalization of political conflict and is meant to distinguish this cult from nineteenth century German romanticism, which is viewed as effeminate and hence passive and apolitical."

101. Schmitt, *Romanticism*, 128.

102. The Nazis "sought to control virtually every aspect of life in Germany through the 'coordination' of public and private life with the regime's ideological objectives. Universities were to be no exception." See Remy, *Heidelberg*, 4.

103. Schmitt, *Romanticism*, 128.

104. Carl Schmitt, *The Concept of the Political*, trans. George Schwab (New Brunswick, NJ: Rutgers University Press, 1976; repr. and expanded, Chicago: University of Chicago Press, 2007), 26. Schmitt argues that "the specific political distinction to which political actions and motives can be reduced is that between friend and enemy."

105. This section of the paper draws heavily from Oren Gross and Fionnuala Ní Aoláin, *Law in Times of Crisis: Emergency Powers in Theory and Practice* (Cambridge: Cambridge University Press, 2006), 162–68.

106. Schmitt's theory of the exception, as well as his general jurisprudential approach, was a rejection of the neo-Kantian, formalist, and positivist jurisprudence of Hans Kelsen. See, for example, David Dyzenhaus, "'Now the Machine Runs Itself': Carl Schmitt on Hobbes

decision-makers who had to decide how to deal with the exception on a case-by-case basis. The exception required concrete decisions that were not, and could not be, constrained or guided by any sort of a priori rules.

The first of the four chapters on the concept of sovereignty, which together comprise Schmitt's 1922 book, *Political Theology*, revolves around the concept of "the exception" and its relationship to the idea of sovereignty. Schmitt makes clear the link between the two concepts in the very first sentence of the book, where he declares that the "sovereign is he who decides on the exception."[107] He goes on to emphasize the point that "it is precisely the exception that makes relevant the subject of sovereignty, that is, the whole question of sovereignty."[108]

Schmitt considers the exception to be the purest expression and reflection of the political.[109] "The specific political distinction to which political actions and motives can be reduced," writes Schmitt, "is that between friend and enemy."[110] It is the ever-present possibility of combat that gives the friend-foe dichotomy its real meaning. "The friend, enemy, and combat concepts receive their real meaning precisely because they refer to the real possibility of physical killing. War follows from enmity. War is the existential negation of the enemy. It is the most extreme consequence of enmity."[111] Characterized as a case of "extreme peril, a danger to the existence of the state, or the like,"[112] the clearest instance of a state of exception is an armed conflict, whether of an international or internal nature. War constitutes the core of the exception and, as such, paints the exception with the colors of the political. It is thus that the inherent link

---

and Kelsen," *Cardozo Law Review* 16 (1994): 1–19 (at 10–14). See also Volker Neumann, "Carl Schmitt: Introduction," in *Weimar: A Jurisprudence of Crisis*, ed. Arthur J. Jacobson and Bernhard Schlink, trans. Belinda Cooper, Philosophy, Social Theory, and the Rule of Law 8 (Berkeley: University of California Press, 2000), 280–89 (at 283). Neumann argues that "opposition, even hostility to Hans Kelsen is a key to all of Schmitt's works." This theory also rejects Kelsen's belief that a legal norm could be devised so as to regulate all different aspects of reality and his concomitant refusal to acknowledge the existence of states of exception that could not be regulated by a priori established legal norms.

107. Carl Schmitt, *Political Theology: Four Chapters on the Concept of Sovereignty*, trans. George Schwab (Cambridge, MA: MIT Press, 1985), 5.

108. Ibid., 6.

109. William E. Scheuerman, *Between the Norm and the Exception: The Frankfurt School and the Rule of Law* (Cambridge, MA: MIT Press, 1994), 67.

110. Schmitt, *Concept of the Political*, 26. On Schmitt's definition of politics as the only clear example of a politics-as-power definition, see Judith N. Shklar, *Legalism: Law, Morals, and Political Trials* (Cambridge, MA: Harvard University Press, 1964), 125.

111. Schmitt, *Concept of the Political*, 33.

112. Schmitt, *Political Theology*, 6.

between the political and the exception is fully established, for "the exceptional case has an especially decisive meaning which exposes the core of the matter. For only in real combat is revealed the most extreme consequence of the political grouping of friend and enemy. From this most extreme possibility human life derives its specifically political tension."[113] Since every sphere of human conduct could potentially rise to the level of the political—"if it is sufficiently strong to group human beings effectively according to friend and enemy"[114]—the exception inevitably permeates all aspects of human existence, and deciding on it becomes the single most important moment in every respect of human activity.[115]

Important as it is, Schmitt does not define this central term. In fact, he argues that no such definition is at all possible. He contends that "the exception, which is not codified in the existing legal order, can at best be characterized as a case of extreme peril, a danger to the existence of the state, or the like."[116] However, the exception "cannot be circumscribed factually and made to conform to a preformed law."[117] While existential crises facing the state may be said to constitute the core of the exception, the external limits and boundaries of its penumbra are unclear, and cannot be made clear in advance. It is this fundamental characteristic of the exception which negates any belief in the possibility of constructing, in advance, a set of general, objective norms that will cover all future situations, without any need for further subjective discretion and decision-making, and which are independent of a mechanistic, technical application of the general norms to concrete scenarios. In exceptional circumstances, when the normal state of affairs is interrupted, regular legal norms are no longer applicable and cannot fulfill their ordinary regulatory function. "For a legal order to make sense, a normal situation must exist."[118] General norms are limited in their scope of application to those circumstances in which the normal state of affairs prevails. Crises undermine this factual basis and thus pull the rug out from under the feet of ordinary norms. Law is not omnipresent and omnipotent; general a priori rules cannot regulate the exception. "There

---

113. Schmitt, *Concept of the Political*, 35.
114. Ibid., 37.
115. George Schwab, *The Challenge of the Exception: An Introduction to the Political Ideas of Carl Schmitt between 1921 and 1936*, 2nd ed. (New York: Greenwood Press, 1989), 73–75.
116. Schmitt, *Political Theology*, 6.
117. Ibid.
118. Ibid.

exists no norm that is applicable to chaos."[119] The exception resides in those areas where the norm breaks down and loses its "immanent validity."[120] This, together with the idea that the exception "cannot be circumscribed factually and made to conform to a preformed law,"[121] makes it *normless*.

In *Political Theology*, Schmitt endorses a revolutionary model of sovereign dictatorship.[122] He contends that the exception is characterized by "principally unlimited authority, which means the suspension of the entire existing order."[123] Even more significant is the sovereign dictator's power to actively change the existing legal order and transform it, in whole or in part, into something else. It is not only that the exception confirms the rule and that the rule's very existence "derives only from the exception"[124] but rather that the exception gobbles up the normal case and becomes, in and of itself, the ordinary, general rule. There is no place to continue talking about rule and exception. "The rule proves nothing; the exception proves everything: It confirms not only the rule but also its existence, which derives only from the exception."[125] Inasmuch as crises represent the sphere of the political, and given the primacy of politics over all other spheres of human endeavor—it is the exception that defines the norm, not vice versa. The exception is primary to the norm and defines and informs that norm.[126] "The rule proves nothing; the exception proves everything."[127]

---

119. Ibid.
120. Ibid.
121. Ibid.
122. John P. McCormick, *Carl Schmitt's Critique of Liberalism: Against Politics as Technology* (Cambridge: Cambridge University Press, 1997), 133–41. In contrast, see Renato Cristi, *Carl Schmitt and Authoritarian Liberalism: Strong State, Free Economy* (Cardiff, UK: University of Wales Press, 1998), 63–70. Cristi argues that in *The Dictatorship*, Schmitt has already promoted the idea of the sovereign dictatorship over the alternative commissarial model as a means of reinvigorating "the monarchical principle" and countering the use by Marxism of the sovereign dictatorship model.
123. Schmitt, *Political Theology*, 12.
124. Ibid., 15.
125. Ibid.
126. Carlo Galli, "Carl Schmitt's Antiliberalism: Its Theoretical and Historical Sources and Its Philosophical and Political Meaning," *Cardozo Law Review* 21 (2000): 1597–617 (at 1616): "From a liberal standpoint exception is exception, not the rule. In other words, it is obvious that in any liberal theory contingency can't ever take the dramatic aspect it takes in Schmitt's thought.... Liberals can't agree that contingency is not simply concreteness, nor relativism, but the original and permanent tragedy of politics."
127. Schmitt, *Political Theology*, 15. Schmitt quotes Søren Kierkegaard when the latter states: "The exception explains the general and itself. And if one wants to study the general

Schmitt's ultimate goal is not merely subjecting the normal to the exception. Rather, it is the complete destruction of the normal case and its replacement by the *exceptionless* exception. In describing the exception, Schmitt states:

> The precise details of an emergency cannot be anticipated, nor can one spell out what may take place in such a case, especially when it is truly a matter of an extreme emergency and of how it is to be eliminated. The precondition as well as the content of jurisdictional competence in such a case must necessarily be unlimited.... If such action is not subject to controls, if it is not hampered in some way by checks and balances, as is the case in a liberal constitution, then it is clear who the sovereign is. He decides whether there is an extreme emergency as well as what must be done to eliminate it.[128]

The sovereign dictator enjoys unlimited powers.[129] Such unlimited powers pertain both to his unfettered discretion as to whether an exception, in fact, exists, as well as to what measures ought to be taken in order to counter the concrete threat. The only logical outcome of Schmitt's collapsing together the power to decide the existence of the exception and the breadth of counter-emergency powers to be used in order to bring the exception to a conclusion, and depositing them both in the hands of one person, is that the dictator's unlimited powers are never turned off. The dictator is the person who needs to decide that the normal state of affairs has been replaced by an extreme case and then decide what powers to use to counter the particular danger. However, the exception is a possibility that may never be discounted or disregarded.[130] It may occur at any given time, without prior warning, and create a "danger to the

---

correctly, one only needs to look around for a true exception. It reveals everything more clearly than does the general. Endless talk about the general becomes boring; there are exceptions. If they cannot be explained, then the general also cannot be explained. The difficulty is usually not noticed because the general is not thought about with passion but with a comfortable superficiality. The exception, on the other hand, thinks the general with intense passion." For a slightly different translation, see Søren Kierkegaard, *"Repetition" and "Philosophical Crumbs,"* trans. M. G. Piety, Oxford World's Classics (Oxford: Oxford University Press, 2009), 78. Schmitt has modified and adapted Kierkegaard's original formulation in several significant respects.

128. Schmitt, *Political Theology*, 6–7.

129. Ibid., 12: "Not every extraordinary measure, not every police emergency measure or emergency decree, is necessarily an exception. What characterizes an exception is principally unlimited authority, which means the suspension of the entire existing order."

130. Galli refers to Schmitt's "dramatic theory of modern politics as permanent crisis" ("Antiliberalism," 1615).

existence of the state."[131] What ought to count is not the actual occurrence of an exception but rather the *possibility* of its taking place, and in a world governed by the exception, such a possibility is all the more inevitable.[132] The existence of an exception or a possibility thereof means that the sovereign must always be vigilant and, in fact, paranoid.[133] The result is that the sovereign is not only the one who decides on the exception but also the one who definitely decides whether the normal situation actually exists.[134]

It is only the sovereign dictator who can authoritatively distinguish the exception from the normal and decide to take state action. At the same time, Schmitt considers sovereignty and the powers attached to it as indivisible.[135] Thus, one cannot say that only part of the sovereign's power is operational at any given moment. Subject to the personal decision of the sovereign dictator, the sovereign's unlimited powers may be put to use at any time. No external, objective limitations may be imposed on the exercise of these powers. Hence, should the sovereign dictator so desire, his unlimited powers—originally designed to apply to the exceptional case—may come to control the norm, indeed, *be* the norm.

Schmitt argues that the political will only disappear in "a world in which the *possibility* of war is utterly eliminated, a completely pacified globe."[136] Only such a world—in which the distinction between friend and foe is obsolete—can be a world without politics. "The phenomenon of the political can be understood only in the context of the ever present *possibility* of the friend-and-enemy grouping."[137] In a world governed by the exceptionless exception, however, there is an ongoing possibility of external conflicts among collectivities of people, as well as internal conflicts within any given collectivity, which may create the need to distinguish between friend and foe, thus invoking a political decision. With this exceptionless exception worldview, where the political is ever present and ever relevant and where ordinary day-to-day questions are very much interested in,

---

131. Schmitt, *Political Theology*, 6.
132. Of course, a world governed by a permanent exception is a fit description of Schmitt's assessment of his own environment when writing *Political Theology* in 1922.
133. Anthony Carty, "Interwar German Theories of International Law: The Psychoanalytical and Phenomenological Perspectives of Hans Kelsen and Carl Schmitt," *Cardozo Law Review* 16 (1995): 1235–92 (at 1237). As Carty points out: "For Schmitt[,] paranoia is all that stands between [the German] people and the specter of extinction."
134. Schmitt, *Political Theology*, 13.
135. Ibid., 8.
136. Schmitt, *Concept of the Political*, 35 (emphasis added).
137. Ibid. (emphasis added).

and concerned with, the concept of sovereignty,[138] Hobbes's twentieth-century self-proclaimed heir[139] throws us back into the Hobbesian state of nature.

In fact, Schmitt goes much farther than Hobbes. Hobbes's absolutist model of political and legal authority contains some external limit on the powers exercised by the sovereign—namely, those derived from the supreme principle of self-preservation, which also means individual self-preservation. Hobbes's theory leaves room for the individual in the overall framework, inter alia, by acknowledging her right to resist the dictates of the sovereign when the latter attempts to take her life.[140] This right of resistance presents an outer limit on the Leviathan's otherwise sweeping power and authority. However, even this minimal limitation is removed by Schmitt, as he considers this aspect of Hobbes's theory to undermine the effectiveness, and indeed the viability, of the Englishman's position.

Schmitt leaves no defense mechanisms against the "strong total state."[141] After all, "What characterizes an exception is principally unlimited authority, which means the suspension of the entire existing order. In such a situation it is clear that the state remains, whereas law recedes. Because the exception is different from anarchy and chaos, order in the juristic sense still prevails even if it is not of the ordinary kind."[142] However, to argue that an order that is characterized by an "unlimited authority" of the sovereign dictator is an "order in the juristic sense" means nothing. Furthermore, since the normal case and the exception collapse into one exceptionless exception, this disorderly order also becomes the "ordinary kind" of order in the Schmittian state. In that Schmittian state, nothing can withstand the sovereign dictator. There is no immovable wall that can withstand his unstoppable force. The ever-existing exception

---

138. Contrast this with Schmitt's critique of liberal jurisprudence as one "concerned with ordinary day-to-day questions [and having] practically no interest in the concept of sovereignty." See Schmitt, *Political Theology*, 12.

139. Carl Schmitt, *The Leviathan in the State Theory of Thomas Hobbes: Meaning and Failure of a Political Symbol*, trans. George Schwab and Erna Hilfstein (Westport, CT: Greenwood, 1996; repr., Chicago: University of Chicago Press, 2008). See also David Dyzenhaus, *Legality and Legitimacy: Carl Schmitt, Hans Kelsen, and Hermann Heller in Weimar* (Oxford: Oxford University Press, 1997), 85–97, and McCormick, *Technology*, 249–58.

140. Leo Strauss, "Notes on Carl Schmitt, *The Concept of the Political*," trans. J. Harvey Lomax, in *The Concept of the Political*, by Carl Schmitt, ed. George Schwab, exp. ed. (Chicago: University of Chicago Press, 2007), 97–122 (at 106–7).

141. Peter C. Caldwell, *Popular Sovereignty and the Crisis of German Constitutional Law: The Theory and Practice of Weimar Constitutionalism* (Durham, NC: Duke University Press, 1997), 112–14.

142. Schmitt, *Political Theology*, 12.

feeds into the "decisionistic and personalistic element in the concept of sovereignty."[143] Such a state of affairs offers as much predictability as the sovereign's whim. If liberalism's fault inheres in the normative and utopian nature of its structures, Schmitt's fault lies with the apologetic overtones of his proposals. Against liberalism's rigidity, Schmitt puts forward an all too flexible alternative. Whatever the sovereign decides is legitimate. There is no substantive content against which legitimacy of such actions can be measured—not even Hobbes's minimalist principle of self-preservation.

Despite Schmitt's attacks against the content-neutrality of liberalism and positivism, his theory, in the last account, is nihilistic.[144] In its purest form, a decision emerges out of nothing; that is, it does not presuppose any given set of norms, and it does not owe its validity or its legitimacy to any preexisting normative structure. No such structure, therefore, can attempt to limit the decision's scope in any meaningful way.[145] As William Scheuerman pointedly notes: "A rigorous decisionist legal theory reduces law to an altogether arbitrary, and potentially inconsistent, series of power decisions, and thus proves unable to secure even a modicum of legal determinacy. It represents a theoretical recipe for a legal system characterized by a kind of permanent revolutionary dictatorship.... Decisionism, at best, simply reproduces the ills of liberal legalism, and, at worst, makes a virtue out of liberalism's most telling jurisprudential vice."[146]

The German Constitutional State of Adolf Hitler

No one represented more fully Schmitt's "decisionistic and personalistic element in the concept of sovereignty" than Adolf Hitler. Hitler's rise to power allowed Schmitt to see his ideas put into action. His general musings about political and legal theory now turned into concrete actions in support of the National Socialist cause by formulating the case for the Führer state and for purifying the ranks of the legal profession of "alien" elements—first and foremost Jews—and

---

143. Ibid., 48.
144. Carty, "Interwar," 1270–71. Carty argues that Schmitt, like Kelsen, demonstrates "a flight from the complexity of political compromise into a nihilistic one-dimensionality which leaves completely open who is deciding what for whom."
145. McCormick, *Technology*, 153. McCormick notes that "if the constitution's primary purpose is to establish an institution, such as a presidency, to exclusively embody the preconstitutional sovereign will in a time of crisis, then the constitution is inviting its own disposability."
146. William E. Scheuerman, "After Legal Indeterminacy: Carl Schmitt and the National Socialist Legal Order, 1933–1936," *Cardozo Law Review* 19 (1998): 1743–69 (at 1755–56).

ensuring its ethnic, racial, cultural, spiritual, and ideological homogeneity.[147] It is here that Schmitt's legal and political model became unmistakably colored in shades of black and red.

The Third Reich epitomized the departure from liberalism and its substitution by *Gleichschaltung*, that is, achieving coordination and uniformity through policies and measures of repressing individual rights and freedoms. It also epitomized the departure from what Schmitt derisively called the *bürgerlicher Rechtsstaat* [state based on the liberal rule of law] to the Führer state. Under the Reich, "the state and the law acquire an identical meaning for the Volk."[148] Thus, not only was the rule *of* law replaced by rule *by* law,[149] but to the extent that all law was to be understood in the light of German spirit and value, it was also replaced by the "rule of ethos."[150] The Führer personified the purest form of decisionism replacing all useless forms of constitutional and legal discussion. Inasmuch as "discussion is liberalism,"[151] ridding Germany of the former, meant the destruction of the latter. On the whole, the "führer state," declared Schmitt, was an "exemplary constitutional state."[152] In that "constitutional state of Adolf Hitler,"[153] he proclaimed, "we do not determine what National Socialism is according to a preexisting concept of the constitutional state, but rather the reverse; the constitutional state [is determined] according to National Socialism."[154] "German blood and German honor have become the basic principles of German law, while the state has become an expression of racial strength and unity."[155]

Schmitt harnessed his talents and immense prestige in the service of National Socialism. His strong antisemitic views certainly did not prove an obstacle in that regard. Thus, for example, on May 10, 1933, when Nazi students burned books by Jewish authors, Schmitt published an article in which he celebrated the burning out of the "un-German spirit" and "anti-German filth," mocked anyone who appreciated Jewish authors as "unmanly," and criticized the students for targeting too few authors' works for the pyre. According to

---

147. Ibid., 1756–64.
148. Müller, *Hitler's Justice*, 70–71.
149. On this distinction, see David Dyzenhaus, *The Constitution of Law: Legality in a Time of Emergency* (Cambridge: Cambridge University Press, 2006), 17–19.
150. Kaufmann, "Jurisprudence," 1637.
151. Ibid., 1646 (quoting Schmitt).
152. Ibid., 1639.
153. Carl Schmitt, "Was bedeutet der Streit um den 'Rechtsstaat'?," *Zeitschrift für die gesamte Staatswissenschaft* 95 (1935): 189–201 (at 199).
154. Müller, *Hitler's Justice*, 71 (translating another source by Schmitt).
155. Sherratt, *Philosophers*, 101.

Schmitt, writings by non-Jewish authors who had been influenced by Jewish ideas should have also been destroyed.[156]

In 1934, following the Night of the Long Knives, Schmitt publicly proclaimed that the bloody purge had been the "highest form of administrative law"[157] and as such legitimate and legal. Even more odious was his support and legitimation of the Nuremberg Race Laws of September 15, 1935, that were to become the foundational basis for the racial policies of the Nazi regime. Two weeks after the adoption of the laws, Schmitt published an article under the title "Verfassung der Freiheit" [Constitution of Freedom] in the leading *Deutsche Juristen-Zeitung*, of which he himself was the editor.[158] In the article, Schmitt referred to the racial laws as the first German constitution of freedom for centuries. He emphasized that the laws were not merely to be numbered among other equally important pieces of legislation. Rather, they would "determine what we may call morality and public order, decency and good practice. They are the constitution of freedom, the core of our German law today. Everything that we German lawyers do gains its meaning and honor from them."[159]

For his fervent support of the Nazi Party, Schmitt was rewarded with numerous honors, official appointments, and offers of positions in the most prestigious German universities such as Munich, Cologne and Berlin (where he eventually joined the faculty).[160] Hermann Göring conferred on Schmitt the title of Prussian councilor of state. In June 1933, Schmitt was appointed a member of the newly created Akademie für deutsches Recht [Academy for German Law], which had "its full share" in drafting the vast part of the Nazi legislation, including the aforementioned Nuremberg Race Laws.[161]

Another group in which Schmitt played a major part was the Reichsgruppe Hochschullehrer des Nationalsozialistischen Rechtswahrerbundes [University Instructors Group of the National Socialist Lawyers League]. This organization, presided over by Schmitt, held a conference on "Jewry in Jurisprudence" on October 3–4, 1936.[162] In his introductory comments before an audience of

---

156. Ibid., 98–99.
157. Ibid., 100; Stolleis, *Swastika*, 97.
158. Carl Schmitt, "Die Verfassung der Freiheit," *Deutsche Juristen-Zeitung* 40 (1935): 1133–35.
159. Carl Schmitt, "The Constitution of Freedom (1935)," in Jacobson and Schlink, *Weimar*, 323–25 (at 325). For the original, see Schmitt, "Verfassung," 1135.
160. Sherratt, *Philosophers*, 99.
161. Weinreich, *Professors*, 38.
162. Morris, "Discrimination," 121. Morris notes: "With new forms of legal discrimination against Jewish lawyers lagging behind economic discrimination and anti-Semitic rhetoric, Nazi academics inflamed the matter with a new forum for propaganda."

over one hundred jurists, Schmitt declared, "We must free the German spirit from all Jewish falsifications,"[163] reminding the audience that "year after year, semester after semester, for almost one hundred years thousands of young Germans, future judges and lawyers, have been schooled by Jewish legal teachers, that standard texts and commentaries in the most important legal disciplines are by Jews, that influential legal journals were dominated by them."[164] "The Jew's relationship to our intellectual work," he declared, "is parasitical, tactical and commercial."[165] Hence, he highlighted the "genuine battle of principles" between Jews' "cruelty and impudence" and Germans' "ethnic honor."[166]

Like many other German scholars,[167] legal and otherwise, Schmitt expressed strong support for the war.[168] For him, it was the means to establish Germany's place as the largest empire in Europe. The German Reich, "through species and origin, blood and soil," was destined to constitute not only a new internal, domestic order but also a new political reality and a new order of international law.[169] That new reality, centered on *Großräume*, would replace the "universalistic-humanitarian," that is, "Jewish"[170] existing world law. Under this new world order, the Reich's *völkisch* order would be finally freed from "the interference of spatially alien and un*völkisch* powers."[171]

---

163. Weinreich, *Professors*, 40.
164. Morris, "Discrimination," 121.
165. Sherratt, *Philosophers*, 101.
166. Ibid.
167. Weinreich notes the "complete unanimity of German scholarship as to the war" (*Professors*, 124).
168. Remy, *Heidelberg*, 96. Remy discusses the Aktion Ritterbusch, a project spearheaded by Paul Ritterbusch, a legal scholar who was the Rector of Kiel University, assembling "publications and lectures on war-related issues solicited from four to five hundred university professors representing twelve disciplines. Collectively, the endeavor produced 67 books and brochures, including 24 edited collections containing 299 different contributions." "Ritterbusch," writes Michael Stolleis, "conducted himself like a fervent National Socialist" (*History*, 293). See further the chapters in this volume by Suzanne L. Marchand and Thomas Schneider.
169. Carl Schmitt, "The *Großraum* Order of International Law with a Ban on Intervention for Spatially Foreign Powers: A Contribution to the Concept of Reich in International Law," in *Writings on War*, trans. Timothy Nunan (Cambridge: Polity Press, 2011), 75–124 (at 111).
170. Schmitt, "*Großraum*," 121–22 ("The relation of a nation to a soil arranged through its own work of colonization and culture and to the concrete forms of power that arise from this arrangement is incomprehensible to the spirit of the Jew ... Jewish authors ... were here an important fermenting agent in the dissolution of concrete, spatially determined orders").
171. Ibid., 111.

V. THE DESCENT TO HELL

The story of the moral decline of German universities and professors in general, and of German law professors in particular, is one in which professional myopia, personal opportunism, moral weakness, and antisemitism were inexorably intermingled. For a significant group of legal intellectuals, Weimar's perceived failures stood in stark contrast to Germany's grandeur under Bismarck, and the culture and politics of endless debate and discussion to the image of the man of action and decision. This was especially the case for the generation of young scholars who ascended the ranks of academia as World War I came to an end, due not to the war but to the coincidental passing of older scholars. This new, younger generation of jurists was shaped by the war and by its disastrous outcomes.[172]

Furthermore, Weimar, with its leveling consequences of democratization,[173] did not sit well with the academic intellectual and social elitism that characterized German academia. Coming, as most of them did, from the nationalistically minded middle and upper classes of German society, academics "found it psychologically difficult to accept the reality created by the 'November revolution' and 'Versailles.'"[174] Political instability with constantly changing governments and petty party politicking, personal and financial insecurity with high inflation, coup attempts and a mounting crime rate, and even the perceived role of Weimar in promoting "sexual degeneracy"[175] resulted in the republic having very few supporters and many more vocal opponents among legal academics.[176] Many of the latter rejected the popular sovereignty at the

---

172. Stolleis, *History*, 24.
173. Grüttner, "Universities," 78.
174. Stolleis, *History*, 23. See also Hubert Rottleuthner, "Legal Positivism and National Socialism: A Contribution to a Theory of Legal Development," *German Law Journal* 12 (2011): 100–14. As Rottleuthner points out: "Various items can be compiled on which the assumption might be based that the majority of jurists during the Weimar Republic shared a conservative, authoritarian, nationalistic, anti-republican attitude" ("Positivism," 105).
175. See Eric D. Weitz, *Weimar Germany: Promise and Tragedy* (Princeton, NJ: Princeton University Press, 2007), 330, and generally at 297–330.
176. Stolleis, *History*, 65. Stolleis puts matters thus: "In the eyes of the revolutionaries the [Weimar] constitution sealed the failure of the revolution and the betrayal by the majority socialists. For the monarchists it was the symbol of the hated 'Republic' imposed by the Allies. The extreme right generally rejected the parliamentary model. Federalists criticized the Unitarian tendencies, which they believed had come to be too strong. The Unitarians in turn lamented the powerful return of particularism and the unresolved problems of the reform of the Reich. The bourgeoisie found itself in a disastrous forced marriage with the majority socialists."

foundation of the Weimar Republic and either pined to replace it entirely with a sort of monarchical sovereignty like the one that existed before the war or sought to inject the Weimar constitution with attributes and features derived from that competing sovereignty.

Even those who begrudgingly accepted the republic argued for a strong role for its president. Most notably, the president was granted dictatorial powers to deal with emergencies under article 48 of the Weimar Constitution.[177] In crises it would be he, rather than parliament, who would steer the ship of the state and guide it to safety. The Weimar constitution was thus regarded as a "felicitous synthesis because it promised to reconcile the democratic and the monarchic elements"[178] with the president playing the role of its powerful guardian. Warnings that the president's dictatorial powers could be abused and misused had gone largely unheeded. Rather, "the stress of the times had forced men to whom arbitrary government had been lifelong anathema, to put into their model charter a device of emergency government that was a relic of the past and a possible platform for despotism. It was their hope and somewhat over-confident expectation that only good democrats devoted to the cause of the Republic would ever be in a position to resort to this unusual fund of power."[179]

Article 48 integrated into the constitutional system of the republic radical powers that could be traced back to the German empire's institution of the "state of war" and sought to add them to the menu of protective mechanisms available to the republic.[180] Under article 48, the president could use the armed forces to compel a state to fulfill its constitutional obligations. He was authorized, when in his opinion public safety and order were seriously disturbed or endangered, to take measures necessary for the restoration of public safety and order and could use the armed forces for that purpose.[181] Moreover, the

---

177. Gross and Ní Aoláin, *Emergency Powers*, 84–85.
178. Stolleis, *History*, 93.
179. Clinton L. Rossiter, *Constitutional Dictatorship: Crisis Government in the Modern Democracies* (Princeton, NJ: Princeton University Press, 1948), 35. Stolleis quotes Richard Schmidt, the speaker of the German Social Democratic Party (SPD), who, during the first reading of the draft of the constitution, cautioned: "We must reckon with the fact that one day another man from another party, perhaps from a reactionary party eager for a coup, will stand in this position. We must take precautions against such cases" (Stolleis, *History*, 49).
180. Rossiter, *Constitutional Dictatorship*, 33–37; John E. Finn, *Constitutions in Crisis: Political Violence and the Rule of Law* (Oxford: Oxford University Press, 1991), 146.
181. As a matter of constitutional law, the president alone was authorized to judge whether such serious disturbance or danger to the public safety and order had in fact existed. See Finn, *Constitutions in Crisis*, 148.

president could temporarily suspend several of the fundamental rights guaranteed by the constitution. The use of article 48 was subject, theoretically, to certain limitations that were either explicitly prescribed in the constitution or implicit in the nature of the constitutional order.[182] However, in practice none of these limitations proved a meaningful obstacle to the exercise of unfettered dictatorial powers.

Between 1919 and 1932, article 48 was invoked more than 250 times.[183] It became a constitutional source for the promulgation of an extensive array of executive decrees, most frequently in the context of economic disturbances.[184] The extensive use of article 48 during the Weimar years led to a broad construction of the range of circumstances in which article 48 powers could be employed so as to encompass crises that did not fall within the traditional understanding of threats "endangering the public safety and order." For example, the German Reichsgericht announced that article 48 allowed the president to "take any measure necessary to the restoration of the public safety and order.... Absolutely everything that the circumstances demand is to be allowed him in warding off the dangers that imperil the Reich."[185] In fact, toward the end of the life of the Weimar Republic, especially within the context of the worldwide economic depression that dominated the late 1920s and early 1930s, article 48 was used as practically the exclusive legal source for governmental action, with the ordinary legislative and administrative processes virtually suspended.[186] In addition, the Reichstag—assigned the crucial role of a check on the powers of the president—proved to be no more than a rubber stamp to presidential emergency measures. With the collapse of parliamentary restraint on the presidency, combined with the president's use of the power to dissolve the Reichstag and

---

182. Rossiter, *Constitutional Dictatorship*, 65–68; Finn, *Constitutions in Crisis*, 149–51. Thus, for example, presidential actions under article 48 required ministerial countersignature. They were to be notified to the Reichstag and to be revoked upon the demand of the legislature. The constitution also made available various mechanisms for presidential accountability, such as impeachment or removal of the president from office and even making him the subject of criminal prosecution. Other limitations on the presidential powers under article 48 were implicit in the nature of the constitutional order; for example, they could only be employed for the purpose of restoring normal conditions, and thus were supposed to be of brief temporal duration to be revoked as soon as the goal of restoring public safety and order had been achieved. The presidential oath to observe and defend the constitutional provisions was similarly considered to impose limitations on the president's powers in this regard.
183. Finn, *Constitutions in Crisis*, 151–70; Rossiter, Constitutional Dictatorship, 37–60.
184. Rossiter, *Constitutional Dictatorship*, 51–53.
185. 55 RGStr. 115, quoted in Rossiter, *Constitutional Dictatorship*, 64.
186. Finn, *Constitutions in Crisis*, 165–68; Rossiter, *Constitutional Dictatorship*, 51–60.

employ article 48 emergency powers,[187] even that mechanism of control and supervision became a dead letter.

For their part, the German courts were not at any time a real factor in circumscribing presidential authoritarian powers. As Rossiter notes, the courts would, from time to time, "put the stamp of judicial approval upon the latitudinarian conception of the scope of these emergency powers."[188] Finally, and perhaps most importantly, the German people lacked any real sense of constitutionalism and deep appreciation of democracy, being accustomed to and supportive of an authoritarian regime.[189] And so it came to be, as Justice Robert Jackson was to observe years later, that when Hitler became chancellor in 1933, article 48 was ready to be used by the Nazis in order to finish off the republic.[190]

The chaotic conditions of the late 1920s and early 1930s, together with their own disposition to strong decisionistic leadership and what Oscar Hammen termed their "*Führer* consciousness,"[191] led many in legal academia to embrace an expansive interpretation of the dictatorial powers enshrined in article 48 and the circumstances for their use. However, prior to 1933, most law professors did not advocate (at least not openly) for the destruction of the republic. Even when the clouds of the storm were raging overhead, they clung to the traditionalist view of the academic's work as separate and removed from politics. Their authoritarian-flavored writings, opinions, and teachings had been, or so they pronounced to themselves and to others, apolitical. Of course, even at that early stage there had been voices in legal academia that supported the NSDAP and its agenda. But even professors such as Otto Koellreutter, who was among the very first to jump on the Nazi bandwagon, still wrote about the coming of the "national *Rechtsstaat*," apparently believing that Nazism and the rule of law could, somehow, be reconciled. In all, German universities, not merely the faculties of law, were primed for the advent of National Socialism. As Eric Weitz notes, "The major institutions like the churches, the army, schools and universities, and industrial organizations were largely hostile or recklessly indifferent

---

187. Rossiter, *Constitutional Dictatorship*, 55–57; Finn, *Constitutions in Crisis*, 162–63.
188. Rossiter, *Constitutional Dictatorship*, 70–71; Finn, *Constitutions in Crisis*, 151.
189. Rossiter, *Constitutional Dictatorship*, 71.
190. *Youngstown Sheet & Tube Co. v. Sawyer*, 343 U.S. 579 (1952). For Justice Robert Jackson's concurring opinion, on the Weimar Republic and Hitler, see pp. 634–55 (at 650–51).
191. Oscar J. Hammen, "German Historians and the Advent of the National Socialist State," *Journal of Modern History* 13, no. 2 (1941): 161–88 (at 174). Hammen notes: "A significant principle in German history as expressed by most historians was the decisive role of a Führer in the destiny of a nation" (at 173).

to the republic, and those institutions were at the upper levels populated by the well-connected and the powerful."[192]

The academics' professional myopia was soon bolstered by rank personal opportunism. As noted previously, the Nazis' seizure of power in 1933 brought with it opportunities for advancement in academia. With almost a third of those teaching at law faculties removed from their positions, mostly on racial grounds, the vacant positions were filled, in short order, by untenured faculty demonstrating nationalistic orientation. By 1939, 60 percent of professors teaching in German law faculties had been appointed in or since 1933 with a majority of those belonging to the NSDAP. The swift purge of the legal profession—students, lawyers, judges, and professors—left practically no dissenting voices within the profession. Furthermore, as academic promotion was inexorably tied to support for the National Socialist cause, the newly promoted professors were at great pains to demonstrate their allegiance.

For all of the moral depravity of the many who willingly flocked to the Nazis' camp and cause, many legal scholars, judges, lawyers and law students simply remained silent in a self-imposed state of "voluntary coordination" with the Nazi machine.[193] Indeed, it was "striking how few legal philosophers emigrated or withdrew into the so-called 'inner emigration.'"[194] As Michael Stolleis notes, "We look in vain ... for the members of the Association of Constitutional Lawyers in the circles of active resistance. Officers, clergy, students, and workers were represented, but as far as we know not a single professor of constitutional and administrative law."[195] This was all the more odious where university professors were involved since German professors had been revered by their compatriots. Their position in that respect was unparalleled anywhere outside of Germany.[196] That position conferred on them a unique opportunity to resist the new regime. They "commanded a great deal of respect and easily could have assumed leadership positions had they so desired."[197]

Last, but certainly not least, the seizure of power by the Nazis also made it acceptable, indeed desirable, to express one's antisemitic sentiments. If in the Weimar years such sentiments had been overtly expressed by the Communists

---

192. Weitz, *Weimar*, 366.
193. For the medical establishment, see similarly Michael H. Kater, *Doctors under Hitler* (Chapel Hill, NC: University of North Carolina Press, 1989), 19.
194. Kaufmann, "Jurisprudence," 1633; Morris, "Discrimination," 124.
195. Stolleis, *Swastika*, 99.
196. Grüttner, "Universities," 77 (quoting Carl Heinrich Becker describing the power of full Professors as "nearly absolute").
197. Sims, "Historians," 247.

on the left, Nazism allowed for such expressions to come from the right wing of the political spectrum, where most professors already belonged. "Jewish" content could and was poured into legal vessels that appeared not to be antisemitic to start with. Thus, the "international" and "other" that had been posited in contradistinction to the "national" and "German" became associated first and foremost with Jews and that which was Jewish.

VI. THE MYTH OF DEFENSELESS LAWYERS AND THE PANACEA OF NATURAL LAW

In a famous article published in 1945, Gustav Radbruch, a former minister for justice in the Weimar Republic and a Professor of Law in Heidelberg dismissed from that position as part of the purges of 1933, wrote that legal positivism, with its central theory that "law is law," had "rendered jurists and the people alike defenceless [sic] against arbitrary, cruel, or criminal laws, however extreme they might be."[198] Radbruch, a former leading legal positivist, now called for the return to a natural law legal thinking, having concluded that legal positivism was responsible for the conduct of jurists during the Nazi era.

Legal positivists adhered to the distinction and separation of law from morality, "is" from "ought to be."[199] For positivists, "a law, which actually exists, is a law, though we happen to dislike it, or though it vary from the text, by which we regulate our approbation and disapprobation."[200] According to Hans Kelsen, "the validity of a positive legal order does not depend on its conformity with some moral system."[201] As soon as the war had ended, the charge was made that the majority of the German legal profession were positivists and that their unwillingness to inquire into the morality of law "led to an easy capture of the legal system by the Nazis and facilitated its modification to meet evil Nazi goals."[202]

---

198. Gustav Radbruch, "Five Minutes of Legal Philosophy (1945)," trans. Bonnie Litschewski Paulson and Stanley L. Paulson, *Oxford Journal of Legal Studies* 26 (2006): 13–15 (at 13). See also Frank Haldemann, "Gustav Radbruch vs. Hans Kelsen: A Debate on Nazi Law," *Ratio Juris* 18 (2005): 162–78.

199. See Brian Bix, *Jurisprudence: Theory and Context*, 8th ed. (London: Sweet and Maxwell, 2019), 33–34.

200. John Austin, *The Province of Jurisprudence Determined*, ed. Wilfrid E. Rumble, rev. ed., Cambridge Texts in the History of Political Thought (Cambridge: Cambridge University Press, 1995), 157.

201. Hans Kelsen, *Pure Theory of Law*, trans. Max Knight (Berkeley: University of California Press, 1967), 67.

202. James E. Herget, *Contemporary German Legal Philosophy* (Philadelphia: University of Pennsylvania Press, 1996), 2.

Positivism, the argument went, had not provided a basis on which to reject evil laws and immoral legal systems. For the positivist, an evil legal system, such as that put forward by the Nazis, was still a legal system. A law which was morally evil but that was properly (i.e., procedurally appropriately) promulgated was still a valid law that needed to be obeyed and complied with. The remedy, as per Radbruch and others, was the return to natural law and to the recognition of law that lay beyond positive statutes. Others have strenuously argued that legal positivism had little, if anything, to do with the way in which jurists conducted themselves in the face of Nazism.[203]

Alas, it seems that much of the debate about positivism's role in the shift from Weimar to the Third Reich and during the twelve years of the Nazi regime, as well as the arguments regarding natural law as a panacea for the ills of positivism in this regard, lack nuance and provide cover, rather than clarity. First, it is not clear at all that positivism was, in fact, the dominant theory in Germany prior to the Nazi seizure of power. As Rottleuthner comments, "One could group together those authors who called themselves at that time 'positivists.' Besides Hans Kelsen, however, there would not be many. When one says 'positivist'—one means most often the Others."[204] Second, if one were to adopt the claim that positivism was the dominant theory, the further claim that positivists could not and would not challenge state authority would be clearly at odds with the willingness of law professors, judges and lawyers to challenge the authority of the Weimar Republic.[205] As Dubber notes: "The same judges who applied eugenic laws after 1933 had not felt compelled by their sense of loyalty to the Weimar government to apply the laws of the republic."[206] In fact, during the Weimar years it had been legal positivism, rather than antipositivism, that tried but ultimately failed to defend the republic and democracy.[207]

---

203. See, for example, Richard A. Posner, "Courting Evil," *New Republic* 204, no. 24 (June 17, 1991): 36–41, and famously H. L. A. Hart, "Positivism and the Separation of Law and Morals," *Harvard Law Review* 71 (1958): 593–629.

204. Rottleuthner, "Positivism," 102. Rottleuthner also argues that "positivism as a philosophy or theory of law ... was by no means the dominant perspective during the Weimar period, and also not in the public law theory" (106).

205. Shklar, *Legalism*, 72.

206. Markus Dirk Dubber, "Judicial Positivism and Hitler's Injustice," *Columbia Law Review* 93 (1993): 1807–31 (at 1824).

207. Peter C. Caldwell, "Legal Positivism and Weimar Democracy," *American Journal of Jurisprudence* 39 (1994): 273–301. As Caldwell argues, "as long as the Weimar Constitution remained in force, legal positivism served, not as a handmaiden of fascism, but as a bulwark against it in theoretical discussions, and a guarantee that social forces had access to the process of state will-formation" (at 278).

There is a third and more significant problem with blaming legal positivism for the failure of German law professors, judges, and lawyers to oppose the Nazi regime. It was the Nazis themselves who called for the unification of law and morality, a stance in direct opposition to the positivist worldview.[208] Practically each and every one of the Nazi legal theorists discussed in sections 1 and 2 of this chapter had made the claim that law must conform to the values of National Socialism, calling for the elimination of the distinction between law and (Nazi) morality. Positivism was castigated as responsible for the "ethical disorientation" of Germany under the Weimar Republic[209] and as a theory reflecting "intellectual foreign (i.e., Jewish) infiltration,"[210] separating law from its connectedness to "national (i.e., German) mores."[211] Carl Schmitt celebrated the end of the era of legal positivism while Karl Larenz argued that "law [was] an order closely connected with the moral and religious life of the community." Morality was not left as a matter for individuals as such but rather was a matter for the whole community, and it was with the mores of the volk that positive legal norms must align and comport.[212] It was precisely under National Socialism that the distinction between moral duty and legal duty collapsed. Thus, Rottleuthner argues correctly: "After 1933 ... [i]nstead of [positivism's] value-blindness we find the most abundant adjuration of law and justice by the legal philosophers, an ecstasy of values in face of the German legal state of Adolf Hitler. Instead of defenselessness we find efforts to ingratiate themselves in the form of declarations of loyalty.... Instead of defenselessness, one should rather speak of lack of contradiction—on the ground of inclination, agreement or 'to prevent something worse.'"[213] Indeed, "the fusion of law and morality serv[ed] the NS-jurists as a welcome means to extend the authority and power of the Nazi regime."[214] It was not inattention to values that marred the postwar reputation of the German legal profession but rather devotion to a base and odious set of values.

---

208. Ibid., 276–77. Caldwell writes that "far from excluding natural law from judicial practice, the Nazis developed a kind of secular, biological 'natural law' of race and nation."
209. Forsthoff, *Totale Staat*, 13.
210. Karl Larenz, *Deutsche Rechtserneuerung und Rechtsphilosophie*, Recht und Staat 109 (Tübingen, Germany: J. C. B. Mohr, 1934), 11.
211. Ibid., 12.
212. Ibid., 9.
213. Rottleuthner, "Positivism," 108.
214. Herlinde Pauer-Studer, "Kelsen's Legal Positivism and the Challenge of Nazi Law," in *European Philosophy of Science: Philosophy of Science in Europe and the Viennese Heritage*, ed. Maria Carla Galavotti, Elisabeth Nemeth, and Friedrich Stadler, Vienna Circle Institute Yearbook 17 (Cham, Switzerland: Springer, 2014), 223–40 (at 236).

Thus, National Socialism benefited from a perfect storm of legal theory. While legal positivists were, by and large, supportive of the Weimar Republic and democracy, they had been "unable to respond"[215] effectively when the constitutional order crumbled and the Nazis seized power. Moreover, positivism then "permitted lawyers to rationalize to themselves and others their interpretation and application of laws they might, upon reflection, have considered to be grotesquely unjust or immoral."[216] Antipositivists who hailed the unity of law and morality undermined the foundations of the Weimar constitution by "grant[ing] legitimacy to the judiciary and president as they usurped power from the Reichstag."[217] Furthermore, once the Nazis seized power the same jurists were quick to tie the law to the mast of Nazi morality. As Rottleuthner argues: "It would be naïve to appeal to natural law against the Nazis, realizing that the Nazis had their own natural law. . . . It would be naïve to speak of the *Rechtsstaat* as a guarantee against injustice without taking into consideration what the Nazis meant by the '*Rechtsstaat Adolf Hitlers*'. . . . We can learn from the Nazi era that everything can be justified."[218]

VII. THE HEIDELBERG MYTH

The end of the Second World War saw the evolution in postwar Germany of a myth erected on the foundations of a collective "culture of forgetting."[219] Steven Remy defines what he calls the "Heidelberg myth" as a network of elaborate narratives that served to absolve of connection to National Socialism all but a few professors and served as a shield against (mostly) American denazification policies after the war.[220] The myth consisted of the claims that the number of "genuine Nazis" on faculties was very small and that they had been imposed on the universities by the Nazi regime against the opposition of the professoriate.[221] The Heidelberg myth, which was in no way limited to that one university, facilitated a "stunning continuity"[222] post-1945 in that "[German] law professors teach, students study, lawyers cite, and judges rely on the views of many of the scholars that [had been] enthusiastic supporters of the Nazi

---

215. Caldwell, "Positivism," 278.
216. Dubber, "Hitler's Injustice," 1826.
217. Caldwell, "Positivism," 287.
218. Rottleuthner, "Positivism," 113.
219. Remy, *Heidelberg*, 218–33.
220. Ibid., 240–41.
221. Ibid., 241.
222. For analysis of the reasons for such continuity, see Reimann, "Continuity," 1655–59.

regime."[223] Indeed, "continuity of academic careers was the rule rather than the exception."[224] By and large, former Nazi supporters were able to return to or maintain their academic positions relatively easily, while those fired for racial or ideological reasons, or the very few who resigned for similar reasons, "were much less welcome."[225] Thus, "after 1945, the law faculties consisted almost exclusively of professors who had served in the previous period. This meant, virtually by definition, that they were either favorably inclined to National Socialism, or indifferent, or at least not strongly opposed."[226]

When the war ended, Carl Schmitt, who staunchly refused to undergo denazification, was barred from holding academic jobs. He returned to his hometown of Plettenberg, where he lived to the ripe age of ninety-six. While no longer a university professor, many continued to seek his company and his ideas continued to influence generations of Germans.[227] However, to the extent that the unrepentant Schmitt had been made to answer for his Nazi past, his was the exception to the general rule. As Michael Stolleis comments, after 1945, it was "enough to single out a few 'black sheep,'" one of whom was Carl Schmitt, who was unable to resume his university position, to show that cleansing had occurred. However, "beyond that, the attitude was that anybody who had not been 'excessively' National Socialist, who had merely commented on the prevailing law, could soon return, perhaps clutching a democratic textbook on constitutional theory under his arm."[228]

Otto Koellreutter refused to undergo the formal denazification process. He was tried and sentenced to five years in prison, leading to his imprisonment in June 1947. However, he was released just over a year later, after an appeals court held that he had been merely a "fellow traveler." This also resulted in overturning his dismissal from the university and the resumption of his academic

---

223. Reimann, "Continuity," 1652. As Reimann trenchantly comments there: "Many of the Nazis' staunchest intellectual supporters rose to academic and political power and fame in reconstructed West Germany. The number is enough to fill a book."

224. Ibid., 1654.

225. Ibid., 1656–57. Only 17 percent of those who had lost their academic positions after 1933 were able to return to the law faculties.

226. Ibid., 1656. Remy also notes the "continuities in both personnel and research agendas before and after National Socialism" (*Heidelberg*, 3, 5).

227. As Remy notes: "By the late 1940s, former students like Forsthoff and younger admirers of Schmitt had formed an organization, Academia Moralis, and several informal circles that served not only to keep Schmitt's ideas alive but also to provide a kind of support network for former Nazis" (*Heidelberg*, 223).

228. Stolleis, *Swastika*, 88.

position until retirement in 1952.[229] Karl Larenz, who had initially been banned from teaching after the war, resumed his position in Kiel in 1949. In 1960, he was appointed to a chair at the University of Munich, where he remained until his retirement. Ernst Forsthoff had initially been removed from the Heidelberg faculty in 1946 at the insistence of the Americans (and despite support by the university senate for his retention)[230] after being charged by the Heidelberg Spruchkammer in November of that year.[231] However, he resumed his teaching career four years later and soon thereafter was reappointed to his former full Professorship.[232] Forsthoff then became "the leading transmitter of Carl Schmitt's ideas to West German academic culture."[233]

Theodor Maunz's teaching career at the University of Freiburg remained uninterrupted until 1952, when he moved to the Ludwig Maximilian University in Munich, teaching there until his retirement. The high esteem in which he had been held was evident when he was elected, in 1948, to be a member of the constitutional convention that drafted the new constitution for West Germany. This, together with the publication of his authoritative commentary on the constitution (published in 1958), established Maunz, as noted earlier, as a leading expert on the West German constitution and earned him the moniker of "der Kronjurist des Grundgesetzes."[234] Maunz's postwar career was not entirely free of reminders of his enthusiasm for Nazi ideas in the past, however. Though he served as the minister of education in Bavaria from 1957 to 1964, he was forced to resign that position after his pro-Nazi publications were brought to light.[235] Nonetheless, Maunz held on to his position at the university.[236] It was only three decades later, in 1993, that his image was tarnished posthumously. This occurred not due to his pro-Nazi writings before 1945 but to the discovery that Maunz had written hundreds of anonymous articles for a right-radical postwar newspaper. He had also prepared scores of legal opinions for the party—the German People's Union

---

229. Jörg Schmidt, *Otto Koellreutter, 1883–1972: Sein Leben, sein Werk, seine Zeit*, Rechtshistorische Reihe 129 (Frankfurt, Germany: Peter Lang, 1995), 135–37.
230. Remy, *Heidelberg*, 158.
231. Ibid., 191.
232. Ibid., 193–94.
233. Ibid., 222.
234. Mauz, "Wütend."
235. Konrad Redeker, "Bewältigung der Vergangenheit als Aufgabe der Justiz," *Neue Juristische Wochenschrift* 17, no. 24 (1964): 1097–1100 (at 1098).
236. "Bavarian Minister of Education Resigns; Justified Nazi Laws on Jews," *Jewish Telegraphic Agency*, July 14, 1964.

(DVU)—with which that paper was associated and whose leader described Maunz as "a quarter-century . . . wonderful [and] loyal companion and authoritative adviser."[237]

VIII. THE ACCOUNTABILITY OF THE SCHOLAR: WHAT A TOPIC THAT WOULD MAKE!

For ten out of twelve people in my paternal grandfather's immediate family in Poland (four of them young children), the Final Solution exercised by the murderous Nazi machine was no political exercise or theoretical debate. It was their "existential negation." Unlike Carl Schmitt, they neither lived to be ninety-six years old nor fulfilled their individual potential, because they had been decreed to be the public enemy and, for so many of Schmitt's ilk, also a very private enemy. Saul Lande, my maternal grandfather, was luckier. He merely lost his career, not his life, on the altar of racial homogeneity of the legal profession—necessary, according to Schmitt, in order to achieve determinacy and predictability in the legal order.

While legal scholars did not, by and large, participate directly in the crimes perpetrated by the Nazis, they facilitated those by conferring a veneer of legality and legitimacy to the actions of the regime. As Stolleis notes, "The responsibility of a constitutional lawyer as teacher, scholar, expert witness, and counsel, against the backdrop of what we have learned from cases like that of Maunz—what a topic that would make!"[238] The support of legal scholars made it possible for the Nazi leadership to proclaim, and for ordinary Germans to accept the claim, that theirs was, when all was said and done, a Rechtsstaat. The role of the professors' failure to protect and defend the very basic values of democracy, liberty, and civilization and, indeed, their active role in dismantling those and substituting them for National Socialist values was captured poignantly by Victor Klemperer:

> If one day the situation were reversed and the fate of the vanquished lay in my hands, then I would let all the ordinary folk go and even some of the leaders.... But I would have all the intellectuals strung up, and the professors three feet higher than the rest; they would be left hanging from the lampposts for as long as was compatible with hygiene.[239]

---

237. Mauz, "Wütend"; Stolleis, *Swastika*, 185–92.
238. Stolleis, *Swastika*, 189.
239. Victor Klemperer, *I Will Bear Witness: A Diary of the Nazi Years, 1933–1941*, trans. Martin Chalmers (New York: Modern Library, 1999), 184.

BIBLIOGRAPHY

Aderet, Ofer. "A Jew from Palestine Was Awarded Law Degree from Nazi Germany, Exhibition Reveals." *Ha'Aretz*, April 18, 2012. Accessed January 23, 2018. https://www.haaretz.com/jewish/1.5214906.

Austin, John. *The Province of Jurisprudence Determined*. Edited by Wilfrid E. Rumble. Rev. ed. Cambridge Texts in the History of Political Thought. Cambridge: Cambridge University Press, 1995.

"Bavarian Minister of Education Resigns; Justified Nazi Laws on Jews." *Jewish Telegraphic Agency*, July 14, 1964. https://www.jta.org/1964/07/14/archive/bavarian-minister-of-education-resigns-justified-nazi-laws-on-jews.

Bix, Brian. *Jurisprudence: Theory and Context*. 8th ed. London: Sweet and Maxwell, 2019.

Caldwell, Peter C. "Ernst Forsthoff and the Legacy of Radical Conservative State Theory in the Federal Republic of Germany." *History of Political Thought* 15, no. 4 (1994): 615–41.

———. "Ernst Forsthoff in Frankfurt: Political Mobilization and the Abandonment of Scholarly Responsibility." In *"Politisierung der Wissenschaft": Jüdische Wissenschaftler und ihre Gegner an der Universität Frankfurt am Main vor und nach 1933*, edited by Moritz Epple, Johannes Fried, Raphael Gross, and Janus Gudian, 249–84. Schriftenreihe des Frankfurter Universitätsarchivs 5. Göttingen, Germany: Wallstein, 2016.

———. "Legal Positivism and Weimar Democracy." *American Journal of Jurisprudence* 39 (1994): 273–301.

———. *Popular Sovereignty and the Crisis of German Constitutional Law: The Theory and Practice of Weimar Constitutionalism*. Durham, NC: Duke University Press, 1997.

Carty, Anthony. "Interwar German Theories of International Law: The Psychoanalytical and Phenomenological Perspectives of Hans Kelsen and Carl Schmitt." *Cardozo Law Review* 16 (1995): 1235–92.

Cristi, Renato. *Carl Schmitt and Authoritarian Liberalism: Strong State, Free Economy*. Cardiff, UK: University of Wales Press, 1998.

Dubber, Markus Dirk. "Judicial Positivism and Hitler's Injustice." *Columbia Law Review* 93 (1993): 1807–31.

Dyzenhaus, David. *The Constitution of Law: Legality in a Time of Emergency*. Cambridge: Cambridge University Press, 2006.

———. *Legality and Legitimacy: Carl Schmitt, Hans Kelsen, and Hermann Heller in Weimar*. Oxford: Oxford University Press, 1997.

———. "'Now the Machine Runs Itself': Carl Schmitt on Hobbes and Kelsen." *Cardozo Law Review* 16 (1994): 1–19.

Finn, John E. *Constitutions in Crisis: Political Violence and the Rule of Law*. Oxford: Oxford University Press, 1991.

Forsthoff, Ernst. *Der Totale Staat*. Hamburg, Germany: Hanseatische Verlagsanstalt, 1933.

Galli, Carlo. "Carl Schmitt's Antiliberalism: Its Theoretical and Historical Sources and Its Philosophical and Political Meaning." *Cardozo Law Review* 21 (2000): 1597–617.

Gross, Oren, and Fionnuala Ní Aoláin. *Law in Times of Crisis: Emergency Powers in Theory and Practice*. Cambridge: Cambridge University Press, 2006.

Gross, Rina. Interview by author, April 18, 2012. Tel Aviv.

Grüttner, Michael. "German Universities under the Swastika." In *Universities under Dictatorship*, edited by John Connelly and Michael Grüttner, 75–111. University Park: Pennsylvania State University Press, 2005.

Haldemann, Frank. "Gustav Radbruch vs. Hans Kelsen: A Debate on Nazi Law." *Ratio Juris* 18 (2005): 162–78.

Hammen, Oscar J. "German Historians and the Advent of the National Socialist State." *Journal of Modern History* 13, no. 2 (1941): 161–88.

Hart, H. L. A. "Positivism and the Separation of Law and Morals." *Harvard Law Review* 71 (1958): 593–629.

Hartshorne, Edward Yarnall, Jr. *The German Universities and National Socialism*. Cambridge, MA: Harvard University Press, 1937.

Herf, Jeffrey. *Reactionary Modernism: Technology, Culture, and Politics in Weimar and the Third Reich*. Cambridge: Cambridge University Press, 1984.

Herget, James E. *Contemporary German Legal Philosophy*. Philadelphia: University of Pennsylvania Press, 1996.

Jacobson, Arthur J., and Bernhard Schlink, eds. *Weimar: A Jurisprudence of Crisis*. Translated by Belinda Cooper. Philosophy, Social Theory, and the Rule of Law 8. Berkeley: University of California Press, 2000.

Kater, Michael H. *Doctors under Hitler*. Chapel Hill: University of North Carolina Press, 1989.

Kaufmann, Arthur. "National Socialism and German Jurisprudence from 1933 to 1945." *Cardozo Law Review* 9 (1988): 1629–49.

Kelsen, Hans. *Pure Theory of Law*. Translated by Max Knight. Berkeley: University of California Press, 1967.

Kierkegaard, Søren. *"Repetition" and "Philosophical Crumbs."* Translated by M. G. Piety. Oxford World's Classics. Oxford: Oxford University Press, 2009.

Klemperer, Victor. *I Will Bear Witness: A Diary of the Nazi Years, 1933–1941*. Translated by Martin Chalmers. New York: Modern Library, 1999.

Koellreutter, Otto. *Parteien und Verfassung im heutigen Deutschland*. Leipzig, Germany: Hirschfeld, 1932.

———. *Vom Sinn und Wesen der Nationalen Revolution*. Recht und Staat in Geschichte und Gegenwart 101. Tübingen, Germany: J. C. B. Mohr, 1933.

Koonz, Claudia. *The Nazi Conscience*. Cambridge, MA: Belknap Press of Harvard University Press, 2003.

Lang, Hubert. *Zwischen allen Stühlen: Juristen jüdischer Herkunft in Leipzig (1848–1953)*. Leipzig, Germany: Biographiezentrum, 2014.
Larenz, Karl. *Deutsche Rechtserneuerung und Rechtsphilosophie*. Recht und Staat 109. Tübingen, Germany: J. C. B. Mohr, 1934.
Maunz, Theodor. *Neue Grundlagen des Verwaltungsrechts*. Der Deutsche Staat der Gegenwart 9. Hamburg, Germany: Hanseatische Verlagsanstalt, 1934.
———. *Verwaltung*. Hamburg, Germany: Hanseatische Verlagsanstalt, 1937.
Mauz, Gerhard. "Ich bin nicht nur wütend." *Der Spiegel*, October 18, 1993. http://www.spiegel.de/spiegel/print/d-13680349.html.
McCormick, John P. *Carl Schmitt's Critique of Liberalism: Against Politics as Technology*. Cambridge: Cambridge University Press, 1997.
Meinel, Florian. "Ernst Forsthoff and the Intellectual History of German Administrative Law." *German Law Journal* 8 (2007): 785–99.
Morris, Douglas G. "Discrimination, Degradation, Defiance: Jewish Lawyers under Nazism." In *The Law in Nazi Germany: Ideology, Opportunism, and the Perversion of Justice*, edited by Alan E. Steinweis and Robert D. Rachlin, 105–35. New York: Berghahn, 2013.
Müller, Ingo. *Hitler's Justice: The Courts of the Third Reich*. Translated by Deborah Lucas Schneider. Cambridge, MA: Harvard University Press, 1991.
Neumann, Franz L. *Behemoth: The Structure and Practice of National Socialism, 1933–1944*. 2nd ed. Oxford: Oxford University Press, 1944. Reprinted with an introduction by Peter Hayes. Chicago: Ivan R. Dee, 2009.
Neumann, Volker. "Carl Schmitt: Introduction." In Jacobson and Schlink, *Weimar*, 280–89.
Pauer-Studer, Herlinde. "Kelsen's Legal Positivism and the Challenge of Nazi Law." In *European Philosophy of Science: Philosophy of Science in Europe and the Viennese Heritage*, edited by Maria Carla Galavotti, Elisabeth Nemeth, and Friedrich Stadler, 223–40. Vienna Circle Institute Yearbook 17. Cham, Switzerland: Springer, 2014.
Posner, Richard A. "Courting Evil." *New Republic* 204, no. 24 (June 17, 1991): 36–41.
Radbruch, Gustav. "Five Minutes of Legal Philosophy (1945)." Translated by Bonnie Litschewski Paulson and Stanley L. Paulson. *Oxford Journal of Legal Studies* 26 (2006): 13–15.
Redeker, Konrad. "Bewältigung der Vergangenheit als Aufgabe der Justiz." *Neue Juristische Wochenschrift* 17, no. 24 (1964): 1097–1100.
Reimann, Mathias. "National Socialist Jurisprudence and Academic Continuity: A Comment on Professor Kaufmann's Article." *Cardozo Law Review* 9 (1988): 1651–62.
Rein, Gustav Adolf. *Die Idee der politischen Universität*. Hamburg, Germany: Hanseatische Verlagsanstalt, 1933.

Remy, Steven P. *The Heidelberg Myth: The Nazification and Denazification of a German University*. Cambridge, MA: Harvard University Press, 2002.

Ringer, Fritz K. *The Decline of the German Mandarins: The German Academic Community, 1890–1933*. Hanover, NH: University Press of New England, 1969.

Rossiter, Clinton L. *Constitutional Dictatorship: Crisis Government in the Modern Democracies*. Princeton, NJ: Princeton University Press, 1948.

Rottleuthner, Hubert. "Legal Positivism and National Socialism: A Contribution to a Theory of Legal Development." *German Law Journal* 12 (2011): 100–14.

Scheuerman, William E. "After Legal Indeterminacy: Carl Schmitt and the National Socialist Legal Order, 1933–1936." *Cardozo Law Review* 19 (1998): 1743–69.

———. *Between the Norm and the Exception: The Frankfurt School and the Rule of Law*. Cambridge, MA: MIT Press, 1994.

Schmidt, Jörg. *Otto Koellreutter, 1883–1972: Sein Leben, sein Werk, seine Zeit*. Rechtshistorische Reihe 129. Frankfurt, Germany: Peter Lang, 1995.

Schmitt, Carl. *The Concept of the Political*. Translated by George Schwab. New Brunswick, NJ: Rutgers University Press, 1976. Reprinted and expanded, Chicago: University of Chicago Press, 2007.

———. "Die Verfassung der Freiheit." *Deutsche Juristen-Zeitung* 40 (1935): 1133–35. Translated by Belinda Cooper as "The Constitution of Freedom (1935)." In Jacobson and Schlink, *Weimar*, 323–25.

———. "The *Großraum* Order of International Law with a Ban on Intervention for Spatially Foreign Powers: A Contribution to the Concept of *Reich* in International Law." In *Writings on War*, 75–124. Translated by Timothy Nunan. Cambridge: Polity Press, 2011.

———. *The Leviathan in the State Theory of Thomas Hobbes: Meaning and Failure of a Political Symbol*. Translated by George Schwab and Erna Hilfstein. Westport, CT: Greenwood, 1996. Reprinted with a foreword by Tracy B. Strong, Chicago: University of Chicago Press, 2008.

———. *Political Romanticism*. Translated by Guy Oakes. Cambridge, MA: MIT Press, 1986.

———. *Political Theology: Four Chapters on the Concept of Sovereignty*. Translated by George Schwab. Cambridge, MA: MIT Press, 1985.

———. "Was bedeutet der Streit um den 'Rechtsstaat'?" *Zeitschrift für die gesamte Staatswissenschaft* 95 (1935): 189–201.

Schwab, George. *The Challenge of the Exception: An Introduction to the Political Ideas of Carl Schmitt between 1921 and 1936*. 2nd ed. New York: Greenwood Press, 1989.

Sherratt, Yvonne. *Hitler's Philosophers*. New Haven, CT: Yale University Press, 2013.

Shklar, Judith N. *Legalism: Law, Morals, and Political Trials*. Cambridge, MA: Harvard University Press, 1964.

Sims, Amy R. "Intellectuals in Crisis: Historians under Hitler." *Virginia Quarterly Review* 54, no. 2 (1978): 246–62.
Stolleis, Michael. *A History of Public Law in Germany, 1914–1945*. Translated by Thomas Dunlap. Oxford: Oxford University Press, 2004.
———. "Law and Lawyers Preparing the Holocaust." *Annual Review of Law and Social Science* 3 (2007): 213–31.
———. *The Law under the Swastika: Studies on Legal History in Nazi Germany*. Translated by Thomas Dunlap. Chicago: University of Chicago Press, 1998.
Strauss, Leo. "Notes on Carl Schmitt, *The Concept of the Political*." Translated by J. Harvey Lomax. In Schmitt, *Concept of the Political*, 97–122 (expanded edition).
Trials of War Criminals before the Nuernberg Military Tribunals under Control Council Law No. 10: Nuernberg, October 1946–April 1949. Vol. 3, "The Justice Case" (*The United States of America v. Altstoetter et al.*). Washington, DC: United States Government Printing Office, 1951.
Weber, R. G. S. *The German Student Corps in the Third Reich*. Basingstoke, UK: Palgrave Macmillan, 1986.
Weinreich, Max. *Hitler's Professors: The Part of Scholarship in Germany's Crimes against the Jewish People*. New York: Yiddish Scientific Institute (YIVO), 1946. Reprinted with a foreword by Martin Gilbert. New Haven, CT: Yale University Press, 1999.
Weitz, Eric D. *Weimar Germany: Promise and Tragedy*. Princeton, NJ: Princeton University Press, 2007.
Youngstown Sheet & Tube Co. v. Sawyer. 343 U.S. 579 (1952).

OREN GROSS is the Irving Younger Professor of Law at the University of Minnesota Law School. He holds an LLB degree magna cum laude from Tel Aviv University and LLM and SJD degrees from Harvard Law School. He has taught and held visiting positions in prominent institutions, such as Harvard Law School and Princeton University. His work has been published extensively in leading academic journals, such as the *Yale Law Journal* and *Yale Journal of International Law*. His book *Law in Times of Crisis: Emergency Powers in Theory and Practice* (Cambridge, 2006) was awarded the prestigious Certificate of Merit for Preeminent Contribution to Creative Scholarship by the American Society of International Law in 2007. His most recent book, *Guantanamo and Beyond: Exceptional Courts and Military Commissions in Comparative Perspective* (edited with Fionnuala Ni Aoláin), was published by Cambridge in 2013. In 2017, he received the Stanley V. Kinyon Tenured Faculty of the Year Award, University of Minnesota Law School.

TEN

THE MUSIC OF ARNOLD SCHOENBERG: CATASTROPHE AND CREATION

MICHAEL CHERLIN

I. THE EXCISION OF PROGRESSIVE COMPOSERS FROM UNIVERSITY MUSIC CURRICULA DURING THE THIRD REICH

Music, especially art music, is dependent on the three-linked chain of composer, performers, and audience.[1] Musical practice, like all else, changes over time. As music changes, composers lead the way. New compositional practices entail new modes of musical imagination. These give rise to new demands on performers and new pedagogical practices that address new technical demands, including the development of muscle-memory, something requiring time and effort. Finally, the third link requires that audiences build new musical intuitions, not necessarily through structured training but rather through enough familiarity with the new music so that it "makes sense." At the very least, since the nineteenth century, universities and music conservatories have been essential in forging the first two links of the chain: the training of composers and the training of performing musicians. Less centrally, but important nonetheless, universities educate prospective audiences in the general historical and cultural contexts within which music exists, the context in which music makes sense. The new comes out of the old—whether out of resistance to what was, or out of the development of implications suggested, but not fully realized, in what came

---

1. In 2011, Harold Bloom wrote: "Reading Ezekiel, the trope of splintering always afflicts me: text, prophet, Jerusalem, God. *Everything breaks apart*" (*The Shadow of a Great Rock: A Literary Appreciation of the King James Bible* [New Haven, CT: Yale University Press, 2011], 137 [emphasis added]). Although he did not write about music, Harold Bloom has long influenced my musical scholarship in too many ways to count. This essay is respectfully dedicated to his memory.

before. Music, more so than music's sibling arts, is dependent on a continuity of practice, composition, and performance.

Changing our metaphor from mechanical to organic, we can say that with the rise of the Third Reich, the most progressive elements of music, denounced as *Entarte Kunst* (decadent art), were excised from the body of musical works studied in universities and music schools, as well as from the work performed in concert. The excision, lasting some thirteen years from the installation of Adolf Hitler until the end of World War II, left a deep scar, a wound that has never fully healed. After the war, a new generation of composers and performers worked toward understanding and further developing the compositional advances that had been suppressed, but continuity within musical practice had been severed. And while in postwar Europe, state-supported orchestras were mandated to perform new music as part of their work, the new music emerging out of the work banned by the Third Reich has remained culturally marginalized, though not eradicated. Instead of being widely understood in continuity with its musical antecedents, the "new music" gave rise to specialists, a community of composers, performers, and audiences separate and apart from the main body of "classical music." For most audiences, "classical music" ends somewhere in the early twentieth century; we do not even have a widely accepted name for the music spawned by the generation excised by the Third Reich.

As with other disciplines in the arts, humanities, and sciences, music studies and music performance in North America was profoundly impacted by immigrants lucky enough to escape Hitler's Germany. Musicologists, composers, and performers entered into American universities profoundly changing the teaching of music in America. Arnold Schoenberg, who had settled in the Brentwood neighborhood of Los Angeles, held teaching positions at first the University of California, Los Angeles, and then the University of Southern California.[2] Paul Hindemith, another significant composer, held a prestigious position at Yale. Refugees from Europe trained a new generation of musicians. Yet the most progressive music, so rooted in European practice, never entered mainstream American culture.

The posthumous career of Schoenberg in America took a surprising turn with the emergence of speculative music theory as a university-taught discipline. Emerging in the 1970s, with antecedents beginning in the 1950s, the new discipline had Schoenberg's music at its very center. Princeton University, especially with the work of Milton Babbitt, and later Yale University, with the

---

2. Schoenberg's years in America are chronicled in Sabine Feisst, *Schoenberg's New World: The American Years* (New York: Oxford University Press, 2011).

work of Allen Forte and then David Lewin, became the centers of this new discipline, whose roots reached back to Greek antiquity.[3] Nonetheless, the gap in performance practice separating that which came before World War II from that which came afterward remains.

In what follows, I trace the outlines of the career of one composer, Arnold Schoenberg. Each human story is individual. Yet as I hope these introductory remarks make clear, the trajectory of Schoenberg's story is part of a much larger one affecting humanity at large, to include the universities on both sides of the Atlantic.

II. SCHOENBERG: CATASTROPHE AND CREATION

In August 1925, Arnold Schoenberg was offered the position of director of the Master Class in Composition at the Preußische Akademie der Künste [Prussian Academy of Arts] in Berlin.[4] The position was a particularly prestigious one; Schoenberg would fill the seat left empty the previous year by the death of Ferruccio Busoni. Schoenberg began teaching the following October despite an intense campaign against his appointment, a campaign deeply colored by antisemitic rhetoric. In an article published in *Zeitschrift für Musik* in October 1925, Alfred Heuss, editor in chief of the journal, argued vehemently against Schoenberg's appointment. In the course of the article, Heuss makes a distinction between "rooted and rootless Jews," describing Schoenberg as the kind of "Jew who relies only on himself, is no longer rooted in any soil, and consciously defies tradition."[5]

The darkening situation for German and Austrian Jews intensified over the following years, coming to a boil with Hitler's rise to chancellor in 1933. On March 20 of that year, Schoenberg, facing imminent dismissal, voluntarily resigned from the Prussian Academy.[6] That July, Schoenberg and his family

---

3. Milton Babbitt, *The Collected Essays of Milton Babbitt*, ed. Stephen Peles et al. (Princeton, NJ: Princeton University Press, 2003); Allen Forte, *The Structure of Atonal Music* (New Haven, CT: Yale University Press, 1973); David Lewin, *Generalized Musical Intervals and Transformations* (New Haven, CT: Yale University Press, 1987); David Lewin, *Studies in Music with Text* (Oxford: Oxford University Press, 2006).

4. Hans Heinz Stuckenschmidt, *Schoenberg: His Life, World, and Work*, trans. Humphrey Searle (New York: Schirmer Books, 1978), 366–68.

5. As previously noted by Alexander Ringer, *Arnold Schoenberg: The Composer as Jew* (Oxford: Oxford University Press, 1990), 56, 225. The entirety of Heuss's article is translated and included by Ringer as appendix A, 224–26. The original is Alfred Heuss, "Arnold Schönberg: Preussischer Kompositionslehrer," *Zeitschrift für Musik* 92, no. 10 (October 1925): 583–85.

6. Stuckenschmidt, *Schoenberg*, 366.

emigrated from Berlin to Paris, and Schoenberg reconverted to Judaism, the religion of his ancestors that he had abandoned as a young man. By the fall of the same year, Schoenberg had emigrated to the United States, eventually settling in Los Angeles, where he lived out the remainder of his life.[7]

The linking of creation and catastrophe in the title of this chapter, "Schoenberg, Creation, and Catastrophe," can be read in two interrelated ways: (1) that creativity can be a response to looming or realized catastrophe and, (2) more strongly, that creation itself involves catastrophe, a traumatic breaking that is a necessary condition of making. The aphorism that "you have to break an egg to make an omelet" hides a darker truth behind its homey metaphor. Creation as a response to catastrophe has been a recurrent theme in Jewish history: from the destruction of the first temple and the Babylonian exile to the Holocaust, the calamities of Jewish history have given rise to art and literature that have been central in defining Jews as a people. *Creation-as-catastrophe* has also been a recurrent theme in Jewish history, perhaps most famously in the Kabbalah of Isaac Luria but closer to our own time exemplified in the work of Sigmund Freud, Franz Kafka, and, as I will argue here, Arnold Schoenberg.[8]

My own approach toward understanding creation-as-catastrophe is deeply indebted to the writings of Harold Bloom.[9] Bloom's 1975 book *Kabbalah and Criticism*, developing ideas out of Gershom Scholem's scholarship, advances a model for literary criticism based on Lurianic Kabbalah. Creation-as-catastrophe begins with a shattering of the divine, Luria's "breaking of the vessels," which then gives rise to a process of cosmic redemption and restitution, which Luria terms תיקון עולם [*tikkun olam*, generally translated "repair of the world," but carrying a theological and cosmic significance]. Bloom imagines the process as entailing a three-staged dialectic of breaking and healing, as redemptive restitution moves us from absence to presence, from emptiness to fullness, and from outsideness to innerness.[10]

---

7. Ibid., 368.
8. For an introduction to the thought of Isaac Luria (1534–1572), see Gershom G. Scholem, *Major Trends in Jewish Mysticism*, with a new foreword by Robert Alter (New York: Schocken Books, 1995), 244–86. I discuss parallels among Freud, Kafka, and Schoenberg in Michael Cherlin, *Schoenberg's Musical Imagination*, Music in the Twentieth Century 24 (Cambridge: Cambridge University Press, 2007), 10–19.
9. Among other places, Harold Bloom addresses creation-as-catastrophe in his *A Map of Misreading* (Oxford: Oxford University Press, 2003), 9–11; Harold Bloom, *Kaballah and Criticism* (New York: Continuum, 1984), 41, 77–78; and Harold Bloom, *The Breaking of the Vessels* (Chicago: University of Chicago Press, 1982), 57–58.
10. Bloom, *Kaballah and Criticism*, 77–78.

More recently, Bloom has cautioned scholars about adapting his model: "Like all exegetical instruments, it is subject to abuse, and I have ceased to recommend it to my students or to anyone else. I regard it now as a purely personal dialectical dance, part of the Kabbalah of Harold Bloom."[11] I am appreciative of Bloom's warning, but I will read it as a cautionary tale rather than a prohibition—all ideas are subject to abuse: the more splendid the idea, the more abuse that it will reap.

For most musical applications, the paired terms *absence/presence*, *emptiness/fullness*, and *outsideness/innerness* are almost interchangeable. Music with text aside, the oppositions of absence/presence and emptiness/fullness are particularly difficult to distinguish in musical contexts. For example, if a richly orchestrated musical texture is later stripped down to a softly played single line, we will tend to hear the latter passage as a veiled recollection of the first. In such cases we can hear the process either as an emptying out or as suggesting absence where presence was formerly found. Moreover, since memory involves the internalization of a past event, in most musical contexts the first two oppositions are indistinguishable from the third, outward/inward.[12]

And yet for my purposes in this chapter, the terms in their specific order are particularly apt. And so, I will adopt them whole cloth. I find Bloom's fiction to be useful toward shaping my own story about Schoenberg and toward choreographing my own dialectical dance with Schoenberg's life, times, and works. Adapting Bloom's model, I posit three "moments" of creation-as-catastrophe in understanding Schoenberg's place in music history and general history, each "moment" standing for conceptual breakthroughs that give rise to an extended period of new creativity. Needless to say, the three moments take on meaning within the whirlwind of events that fold musical thought into the greater fabric of human history. It is the third moment of creation-as-catastrophe that is most immediately connected with the overall focus of this volume, *The Betrayal of*

---

11. Harold Bloom, *The Anatomy of Influence: Literature as a Way of Life* (New Haven, CT: Yale University Press, 2011), 195.

12. This technique for expressing musical memory is already found in passages by Mozart (musical recollections in *Don Giovanni* for example) and Beethoven (most famously in the final movement of the Ninth Symphony). Specifically associated with loss, presence/absence, and/or fullness/emptiness, it is central to many of Schubert's songs. Variants of the technique are commonplace, for example, in the music of Richard Wagner and Gustav Mahler as well as that of Arnold Schoenberg. Schoenberg's orchestral songs *Gurrelieder* (1900–1901, 1910–11) and his tone poem *Pelleas und Melisande* (1902–3) both make extensive use of this means toward musical expression. Passages of musical recollection are also an essential part of Schoenberg's opera *Moses und Aron*, discussed later in this essay.

the Humanities: The University during the Third Reich. Schoenberg's leaving the Prussian Academy and his subsequent immigration to the United States will serve as a convenient marker for beginning a longer span that extends until Schoenberg's death in 1951 and the continuing reception and impact of his music and thought beyond his death.

III. THE ABANDONMENT OF TONALITY

The first great breaking apart in Schoenberg's musical evolution occurs in 1908 with his momentous abandoning of tonality. Although the antecedents of tonal music reach much further back in the modal practices of earlier periods, full-fledged tonality emerged during the eighteenth century. Two complementary aspects help define classical "tonality": first, music as a hierarchical system and, second, music as emerging out of and returning to a single conceptual and acoustic source. The latter aspect imagines the tonic as the acoustic and conceptual source that engenders the work as a whole, the inevitable return to which brings the work to "perfection" at its conclusion. By this way of thinking, the tonic is akin to a combination of Aristotle's first cause and final cause. The final state of rest entails what is still called "a perfect cadence," the final resolution into the tonic triad that brings a tonal work to its conclusion. Parallels with theological thought are readily at hand.

The hierarchical aspect of tonality entails a single note (the tonic) and its associated major or minor triad (the tonic triad, having the tonic as its "root"), which function as a kind of center of gravity for an entire work. The result is a complex hierarchical system, where notes other than the tonic, along with their associated harmonies, function as subordinate to the tonic, each also capable of creating embedded hierarchies, each with its local centers of gravity. Along these lines, Schoenberg, in his *Harmonielehre*, develops a metaphor where the tonic is analogous to the sun in a solar system, subordinate key areas (each with its local tonic) are analogous to the planets, and yet other musical events are analogous to moons, each circling around its planet. The idea of internal conflict and centripetal and centrifugal forces counterbalancing one another in the solar system metaphor, becomes magnified in another of Schoenberg's metaphors for the tonal system where he imagines tonality in terms of a conflict among competing tonics (analogous to warring armies): although challenged for preeminence by other potential tonics, only one single tonic emerges as predominant.

If we extend and expand the solar system metaphor, Schoenberg's post-tonal music (often called "atonal," a term that he did not like) might be likened to a galaxy containing local suns, each with its local systems, but where perceived centers shift as we move through time/space. If we transform the war metaphor into a psychology of musical conflict, then Schoenberg's post-tonal music can be conceptualized as expressing unresolved and unresolvable conflicts, somewhat akin to the competing unresolvable drives in Freudian psychology. Perhaps most important of all, Schoenberg's post-tonal music does not and cannot imagine a final state of perfection, an idea to which we will return shortly.

IV. THE SIGNIFICANCE OF THE PERSONAL

The motivations for creation-as-catastrophe are always complex, and they often combine elements that are very personal with those that loom large on history's stage. In 1908, while Schoenberg was composing his Second String Quartet, his wife, Mathilde, had an ill-fated affair with the painter Richard Gerstl.[13] The Gerstl-Schoenberg affair was devastating for the Schoenbergs, and it led directly to Gerstl's suicide.[14] How important this personal tragedy was in stimulating Schoenberg's momentous step in music history must remain a subject for conjecture. Here it will suffice to say that the personal crisis in Schoenberg's life is coincident with his music taking a new course, a reconceptualization that continues to ramify in art music even today.

The last two movements of Schoenberg's four-movement Second String Quartet add the human voice, setting two poems by Stephan George. In his 1937 article, "How One Becomes Lonely," Schoenberg recalled his George settings, not mentioning the personal aspects behind the work. The passage is worth quoting at length:

> But after having composed almost two movements, that is, about half of the whole work, I was inspired by poems of Stefan George, the German poet, to compose music to some of his poems and, surprisingly, without any expectation on my part, these songs showed a style quite different from everything I had written before. And this was only the first step on a new

---

13. The Second String Quartet, Op. 10, was composed between March 1907 and August 1908. It was premiered on December 21, 1908, in the Bösendorfer-Saal in Vienna by the Rosé String Quartet and Marie Gutheil-Schoder, soprano. A study score along with extensive historical background is found in Severine Neff, *Arnold Schoenberg: The Second String Quartet in F-sharp Minor, Opus 10* (New York: W. W. Norton, 2006). The Gerstl affair is documented and interpreted on pages 108–11 of Neff's critical edition of the score. Extensive background on all of Arnold Schoenberg's music and writings can be found at the website for the Arnold Schönberg Center in Vienna, http://www.schoenberg.at/ (accessed July 12, 2012).

14. Neff, *Schoenberg*, 108–11.

path, but one beset with thorns. It was the first step towards a style which has since been called the style of 'atonality'. Among progressive musicians it aroused great enthusiasm. New sounds were produced, a new kind of melody appeared, a new approach to expression of moods and characters was discovered.... I always insisted that the new music was merely a logical development of musical resources. But of what use can theoretical explanations be, in comparison with the effect the subject has on the listener? What good can it do to *tell* a listener, 'This music is beautiful', if he does not *feel* it? How could I win friends with this kind of music?[15]

The third movement of the quartet, recollecting melodic fragments from the first two movements, sets George's *Litanei*. The poem speaks of suffering and asks for release. Its final stanza sums up the sentiment of the whole: "Töte das sehnen, schliesse die wunde! Nimm mir die liebe, gib mir dein glück!" [Kill my longing, close the wound, take from me love, give me thy peace!].[16] The final movement sets George's *Entrückung* [Transport], a poem whose closing lines express a mystical union with the Godhead.

In einem meer kristallinen glanzes schwimme—	I am afloat upon a sea of crystal splendor,
Ich bin ein funke vom heiligen feuer	I am only a spark of the holy fire,
Ich bin ein dröhnen nur der heiligen stimme.	I am only a roar of the holy voice.[17]

Although tonality is quite attenuated throughout the quartet, it is effectively abandoned (or repressed) in the work's final movement. Schoenberg opens the movement with an extraordinary instrumental passage of ascending and then floating musical lines, suspending tonality and expressing an altered sense of time and space.[18] When the voice enters with the first line of George's text, "Ich fühle Luft von anderen Planeten" [I feel air of other planets], its rising line coincident with the lowest part of an ethereal chorale in the string quartet, we are fully in the new world of post-tonal music.

---

15. Arnold Schoenberg, "How One Becomes Lonely," in *Style and Idea: Selected Writings*, ed. Leonard Stein, trans. Leo Black, 2nd ed. (Berkeley: University of California Press, 2010), 30–53 (at 49–50).

16. The full text along with Schoenberg's preferred translation (Carl Engel, as used here) is given in Neff, *Schoenberg*, 160–61.

17. Neff, *Schoenberg*, 170.

18. For an interpretive analysis of this passage see Cherlin, *Schoenberg's Musical Imagination*, 182–85.

Prior to Schoenberg's abandoning of tonality, changes in the ways we think about evolution and biology, philosophy, psychology, and physics had challenged the notion of a final state of resolution, a state denoted in theology, grammar, and music theory by the term *perfection*. The history of musical tonality, the idea that a piece of music has a single, stable tonic that engenders the whole and gives perfection to the whole at its conclusion, has antecedents that reach at least as far back as Pythagoras with the idea that universal dissonance and consonance eventually and inevitably lead to a final state of concord.[19] This is the final perfection of things. In Western music theory, with direct precursors in medieval thought, this was the conceptual source behind the idea of the perfect cadence that ended all tonal works. Schoenberg's move to atonality told a different story—music no longer had a stable center to its universe, and it no longer inevitably wended its way to a final perfection. On the contrary, in Schoenberg's new musical universe, a final perfection could no longer be imagined. The loss of temporal and tonal stability was a calamity of sorts, a shattering of musical time that was no longer anchored in directionally stable musical progressions, and a shattering of musical space that had lost its privileged centering on a musical tonic. The compositions of the period express a sense of crisis, spiritual, psychological, and historical. Ironically, the Jewish people, who in the language of the antisemites had been maligned as a people without roots in the native soil, had given birth to a composer who destroyed the rootedness of tonality. The myth of a German identity forged through art and literature has antecedents long before the rise of National Socialism. It is a bitter irony that Schoenberg, who understood himself wholly and without equivocation as a product of German *Bildung* [self-formation], had created a new musical language that radically undermined one of its chief metaphors.[20]

V. THE DIALECTIC OF SCHOENBERG'S ATONALITY: "EVERYTHING BREAKS APART"

In Schoenbergian atonality there is a dialectic between the atonal surface and the repressed tonality expressive of a world that is not there. Freud's concept of negation, *Verneinung*, is particularly apposite for understanding the role

---

19. William Keith Chambers Guthrie, *A History of Greek Philosophy*, vol. 1, *The Earlier Presocratics and the Pythagoreans* (Cambridge: Cambridge University Press, 1962), 220. See also Cherlin, *Schoenberg's Musical Imagination*, 46–47.

20. For background on the history of the term *Bildung*, see David Sorkin, "Wilhelm von Humboldt: The Theory and Practice of Self-Formation (*Bildung*), 1791–1810," *Journal of the History of Ideas* 44, no. 1 (January–March 1983): 55–73.

of tonality as it is repressed in Schoenberg's post-tonal music, and it applies equally well for all three periods of catastrophe-as-creation. Harold Bloom's brilliant essay "Jewish Culture and Jewish Identity" includes an illuminated description of Freudian Verneinung: "Freudian *Verneinung* is anything but an Hegelian dialectical negation. Rather, it is properly dualistic, as befits a High Freudian concept, and mingles simultaneously and so ambivalently a cognitive return of the repressed and an affective continuation of repression, or flight away from the prohibited and yet desired images, memories, desires. Call Hegelian negation the most profound of gentile idealizations, and then say of the Freudian and Kafkan mode of negation that always it was fated to re-enact endless repetitions of the Second Commandment."[21] The passage is difficult and needs some unpacking for most readers. Hegelian negation is part of a dialectical process whereby an idea or event engenders its opposite, the opposition leading to an *Aufhebung* [sublation], essentially a higher-level synthesis that maintains the opposition within it. The key aspect of Hegelian dialectics is its progressive, future-oriented movement.[22] In contrast, Freudian dualism involves a different kind of dynamic conflict, neither progressive nor synthetic. In his earlier writings, Freud posits a dualistic opposition between ego instincts and sexual instincts. In his late thought, this is redefined as the conflict between life instincts and the death drive.[23] Later in this essay, I will suggest that Schoenberg's 1946 String Trio can be understood precisely in those terms. We will return to the final thought of the passage cited from Bloom, "say of the Freudian and Kafkan mode of negation that always it was fated to re-enact endless repetitions of the Second Commandment," in our discussion of Schoenberg's *Moses und Aron*.

For purposes of understanding the most general aspects of Schoenbergian negation, the most cogent passage in Bloom's commentary is that Freudian negation "mingles simultaneously and so ambivalently a cognitive return of the repressed and an affective continuation of repression, or flight away from

---

21. Harold Bloom, "Jewish Culture and Jewish Identity," in *Poetics of Influence: New and Selected Criticism*, ed. John Hollander (New Haven, CT: Henry R. Schwab, 1988), 347–68 (at 366–67).

22. A proper understanding of Hegelian dialectics is no easy matter and still hotly contested among Hegel scholars. J. N. Findlay's classic study remains a good introduction: John Niemeyer Findlay, *Hegel: A Re-Examination* (Oxford: Oxford University Press, 1976).

23. Freud discusses his ideas concerning dualism, contrasting them with the monism of Carl Jung, in *Beyond the Pleasure Principle*, trans. James Strachey (New York: W. W. Norton, 1989). The pertinent passage is cited and discussed in Harold Bloom, "Freud and the Poetic Sublime," in *Poetics of Influence*, 187–212 (at 203).

the prohibited and yet desired images, memories, desires." Just so, the gestures, harmonies, and musical associations of his tonal precursors are never fully evaded in Schoenberg's negations of tonality. A dialectical healing emerges as the absence of a tonic-centered universe anchored in the stability of metric time gives rise to a new presence of rhythmic, harmonic, and contrapuntal possibilities, creating a new music capable of expressing ideas that had heretofore been inexpressible. Schoenberg's breaking of tonality is the precondition for the post-tonal world of musical meaning and expression. But the healing is only partial: Schoenberg's new world is a shattered world.

Any number of works might be chosen as emblematic of the period that opens with the Second String Quartet, but no work expresses the potential for Schoenberg's new musical language more powerfully than *Erwartung* [Expectation]. Composed in 1909, *Erwartung* portrays a psychotic episode: what is real and what is hallucinated cannot be distinguished.[24] Has there been a murder, or is it imagined? Is the protagonist literally lost in a wood, or is all that metaphor? The work, famous for its incredibly concentrated style and quickly shifting musical textures, brings us to a psychological intensity never before achieved in music. There can be no doubt that despite the highly controversial nature of Schoenberg's post-tonal music, it was the achievements of this period that brought Schoenberg into international recognition. The first moment of creation-as-catastrophe provides the preconditions for Schoenberg's appointment to the Prussian Academy after World War I.

The second moment of creation-as-catastrophe emerges after the defeat of the Central Powers in World War I. The end of the war saw the dismantling of the Austro-Hungarian Empire, shortages of food and fuel, massive inflation, and a period of great social and political instability. To a significant extent, the old world, the source of Schoenberg's Bildung and his connection to the great German-Austrian musical tradition, no longer existed. The third moment, the rise of the Third Reich, would intensify this aspect of loss.

The interwar period was also a time of rising antisemitism, with rampant claims that Austria and Germany had been defeated because they had been "stabbed in the back" by Jews.[25] Schoenberg experienced the racial policies

---

24. Bryan R. Simms, "Whose Idea was *Erwartung*," in *Constructive Dissonance: Arnold Schoenberg and the Transformations of Twentieth-Century Culture*, ed. Juliane Brand and Christopher Hailey (Berkeley: University of California Press, 1997), 100–111. See also Cherlin, *Schoenberg's Musical Imagination*, 194–208.

25. A general history of the interwar period is Howard M. Sachar, *Dreamland: Europeans and Jews in the Aftermath of the Great War* (New York: Alfred A. Knopf, 2002). The Wikipedia

of antisemitism firsthand during the summer of 1921, when he and his family were required to leave the Austrian summer resort at Mattsee because of a new policy forbidding the area to Jews.[26] Schoenberg's poignant letter to Kandinsky, dated April 20, 1923, remembers the event with bitter irony: "For I have at last learnt the lesson that has been forced upon me during this year, and I shall never forget it. It is that I am not a German, not a European, indeed perhaps scarcely even a human being (at [the very] least, the Germans prefer the worst of their race to me), but I am a Jew."[27] A second letter to Kandinsky, written some two weeks later, is prescient of the horrors to come: "But what is anti-Semitism to lead to if not to acts of violence? Is it so difficult to imagine that? You are perhaps satisfied with depriving Jews of their civil rights. Then certainly Einstein, Mahler, I and many others, will have been got rid of. But one thing is certain: they will not be able to exterminate those much tougher elements thanks to whose endurance Jewry has maintained itself unaided against the whole of mankind for 20 centuries."[28]

Like so many others, Schoenberg rethought his positions on creativity and spirituality. As with the motives that gave rise to Schoenberg's abandonment of tonality in 1908, the emergence of the twelve-tone method of composition during the early 1920s cannot be explained by any single factor.[29] The method that Schoenberg developed is easy to mischaracterize and difficult to properly understand without a deeper technical study. Schoenberg, throughout his career, was interested in discovering ways that an underlying unity could give rise to diversity. The ramifications of the unifying seed idea for a work, his term was *Grundgestalt* [basic shape], would pervade every aspect of an expressive

---

article "Stab-in-the-back myth" includes an illustration derived from an Austrian postcard from 1919 depicting a Jew stabbing a German soldier in the back. See Wikipedia, s.v. "Stab-in-the-Back Myth," last modified August 4, 2021, http://en.wikipedia.org/wiki/Stab-in-the-back_myth.

26. Ringer, *Arnold Schoenberg: The Composer as Jew*, 3.

27. Schoenberg to Wassily Kandinsky, Mödling, April 20, 1923, in *Arnold Schoenberg Letters*, ed. Erwin Stein, trans. Eithne Wilkins and Ernst Kaiser (Berkeley: University of California Press, 1987), 88–89 (at 88). The words added in brackets are my emendation to the translation.

28. Schoenberg to Wassily Kandinsky, Mödling, May 4, 1923, in *Arnold Schoenberg Letters*, 89–93 (at 92–93).

29. The formal aspects of the emergence of the twelve-tone method are extensively described in Ethan Haimo, *Schoenberg's Serial Odyssey: The Evolution of His Twelve-Tone Method, 1914–1928* (Oxford: Oxford University Press, 1990).

musical idea, comprising the musical composition.[30] Incorporating another aspect of Schoenbergian duality, the Grundgestalt contained two contradictory impulses. Combining "centrifugal" and "centripetal" tendencies, it moved outward, as it were, propelling extension and development, and at the same time it embodied a kind of inward force, the source for compositional coherence. In the twelve-tone method, a specific ordering of the twelve chromatic notes would function as a source idea for all of the pitch material in a work—harmony, melody, and counterpoint would be generated by the basic shape of the tone row. The internal conflicts within the row, its mutually incompatible subdivisions, would generate the bases of rhythmic development.

In Schoenberg's twelve-tone music, the dialectic of post-tonal surface and tonal repression continues, but another layer of dialectic is added. In the ways that the row divides into smaller segments to form the harmonic, melodic, and rhythmic surfaces of the music, the twelve-tone row itself becomes the locus of dialectical conflict among its naturally induced but mutually exclusive subdivisions. The affiliations of subsegments of the row are inherently unstable, and while tonal centers are expressed, these too are evanescent and inherently unstable. The single unifying Grundgestalt, the basic underlying shape of twelve-tone music, subsumes irresolvable tonal conflict. This was not music suitable for myths of homogenous national unity![31] The old world of musical forms and musical grammar is emptied of meaning and then filled with new content, a plenum achieved through the workings of twelve-tone syntax, a new fullness that Schoenberg hoped would bind the shattered elements together. But once again, the healing is only partial: a world of loss informs Schoenberg's twelve-tone music. This is particularly vivid during the interwar period but hardly attenuated during the American years.

The twelve-tone compositions engage the genres and forms of the tonal tradition in ways that are more obvious than in the works after 1908 but before the war. Perhaps in Schoenberg's mind, his sense of loss would be compensated by more self-consciously engaging the tradition from which he sprang. Ironically, the twelve-tone music remembers the past through broken fragments in a complex dialectic of loss and gain. Twelve-tone composition allowed Schoenberg to

---

30. On Schoenberg's concept of *Grundgestalt*, see Severine Neff, "Schoenberg and Goethe: Organicism and Analysis," in *Music Theory and the Exploration of the Past*, ed. Christopher Hatch and David W. Bernstein (Chicago: University of Chicago Press, 1993), 409–33. Also see Cherlin, *Schoenberg's Musical Imagination*, 58–63.

31. A technical discussion of dialectical oppositions embedded within the tone row for *Moses und Aron* is found in Cherlin, *Schoenberg's Musical Imagination*, 237–98.

fill the void left by the abandonment of tonal syntax with a new musical syntax generated by the twelve-tone row and its various transformations, but the music simultaneously evokes memories of what it is not and cannot be.[32]

No work develops the twelve-tone method more extensively than Schoenberg's opera *Moses und Aron*.[33] The product of over a decade of spiritual and musical reevaluation, *Moses und Aron* occupied Schoenberg in the years and months just prior to his stepping down from the university position in Berlin. Schoenberg had completed the second act late in the summer of 1932. Despite plans of a third act, and despite nearly twenty years of continued activity as a composer, Schoenberg was never able to complete the final act. I am one of many scholars who feel that the drama has reached an impasse at the end of act 2, and that there is no way to convincingly resolve the problem.[34]

The opera both begins and ends with an image of shattering. The opening sets the revelation before the burning bush (Exodus 3), as Moses gropes toward an understanding of the inconceivable: "Einziger, ewiger, allgegenwärtiger, unsichtbarer und unvorstellbarer Gott" [One, eternal, omnipresent, invisible, and inconceivable God].[35] The music splinters pulsing time into uneven shards, breaking the underlying tone row into fragments. If ever there was a musical depiction of the Lurianic "breaking of vessels" this is it. The world, as Moses had known it, is shattered by his new knowing. Near the end of the second act, Moses comes down from the mountain, tablets in hand, only to discover the Golden Calf and his betrayal by Aron[36] and the people (Exod 32:15–19). Moses's wrath is formidable. In vivid contrast to the biblical account, in Schoenberg's telling the Golden Calf simply vanishes at Moses's word.[37] The actors representing the nation of Israel then leave the stage as Moses castigates

---

32. A more extended discussion of Schoenberg's motives for developing the twelve-tone technique is found in Cherlin, *Schoenberg's Musical Imagination*, 215–17.

33. Schoenberg was triskaidekaphobic. After realizing that his original title, "Moses und Aaron," contains thirteen letters, he changed the spelling of Aaron to Aron.

34. The scholarship on this issue is discussed in Cherlin, *Schoenberg's Musical Imagination*, 233–35.

35. Arnold Schoenberg, *Moses und Aron: Oper in drei Akten* (Mainz, Germany: B. Schott's Söhne, 1977). Moses speaks the words describing the Divine attributes in Act I, scene 1, mm. 8–10. There is no parallel to this in the biblical account (Exod 3:1–23). For a more extensive discussion of this passage its relation to the biblical text, see Michael Cherlin, "Schoenberg's Representation of the Divine in *Moses und Aron*," *Journal of the Arnold Schoenberg Institute* 9, no. 2 (November 1986): 210–16.

36. Here, Schoenberg's own spelling is retained rather than the standard English "Aaron."

37. In the biblical account, Moses burns the gold calf, grinds it to a powder, strews it on the water, and makes the Israelites drink it (Exod 32:20).

his brother Aron. Aron responds by arguing that the allegedly holy tablets of the Decalogue are, after all, themselves only images. Aron's words express the very crux of the opera's insolvable dilemma: "Die auch nur ein Bild, ein Teil des Gedankens sind" [They too are only an image, a part of the Idea]. Moses, furious and wounded, responds by smashing the tablets. We had previously invoked Freudian negation as a way to understand the repressed and return of the repressed in Schoenberg's music. Here we can recall Harold Bloom's observation that "the Freudian and Kafkan mode of negation [was always] fated to re-enact endless repetitions of the Second Commandment."[38] Moses's final words before the curtain closes on act 2 are: "O Wort, du Wort, das mir fehlt" [O word, you word, that fails me]. Moses, defeated, falls to his knees, for he can find no way to convey his vision aside from images that are inherently inadequate to that vision.

VI. DEPARTURE FROM BERLIN: "EVERYTHING BREAKS APART"

As I have already indicated, the third moment of creation-as-catastrophe is initiated by Schoenberg's leaving Berlin, reconverting to Judaism, and immigrating to the United States. Schoenberg expressed his situation with deep irony: he had been "driven into paradise."[39] The emigration from Europe seals off the Old World, and then the Holocaust effectively destroys it. The third "moment" differs from the first two in that there is no dramatic change in Schoenberg's musical language. The twelve-tone approach would be modified over time, but unlike the earlier transformations, there is no sea change. And while Schoenberg's formal reentry into Judaism coincides with his leaving Germany, this move was the result of a process that had long been put into place. Works of the American years, such as *The Survivor from Warsaw* and his setting of *Kol Nidre*, solidified his musical identification with the Jewish people.[40] Yet his

---

38. Bloom, "Jewish Culture," 366–67.
39. Schoenberg's comment "I was driven into paradise!" is the closing sentence of a speech that he gave in Hollywood, October 9, 1934. The speech is included in Schoenberg, *Style and Idea*, 501–2. The phrase "driven into paradise" was later adopted as the title of a book of essays dealing with the immigration of musician into the United States during the Nazi period. See Reinhold Brinkmann and Christoph Wolff, eds., *Driven into Paradise: The Musical Migration from Nazi Germany to the United States* (Berkeley: University of California Press, 1999).
40. Schoenberg's setting of *Kol Nidre*, Op. 39, was composed between August and September 1938. Its premiere performance was on October 4, 1938, in Los Angeles. First published by G. Schirmer in 1938, it is currently published by Belmont Music Publishers (Los

impact on European art music would have to wait until after the war when the generation of Pierre Boulez, Karlheinz Stockhausen, Luigi Nono, and Luciano Berio began to transform the legacy of Schoenberg and his students. In the United States, Schoenberg's legacy would be explored over the remainder of the twentieth-century on into our own time by Milton Babbitt, Elliott Carter, and many others.[41]

Like so many immigrants, Schoenberg carried his heritage with him, and although he tried to find ways to adapt to his new homeland, his music remained the product of Austro-German Bildung. As much as Schoenberg admired American jazz and the music of Gershwin and others, Bach, Mozart, Beethoven, Schubert, Brahms, Wagner, and Mahler had forged his musical world.[42] As early as the late eighteenth century, German intellectuals debated the meaning of Bildung: Was it to fill the needs of the state as the politically right insisted, or were its goals to cultivate human beings [Menschen bilden] and to develop a sense of inwardness, [Innerlichkeit], as liberals proposed?[43] By Schoenberg's generation, art and literature had become the center of internal and external life for many Austrian and German Jews. Its outward manifestations were libraries, theaters, museums, and concert halls; as a source of inner life, it had to a significant degree supplanted the previous role of religion.

For Schoenberg's Bildung to survive the move to North America, it had to become more radically internalized. The move from outsideness to innerness completes a trajectory that begins with the loss of the Old World after World War I. This final healing also opens a new wound. Earlier on, I had noted the irony of the Jew, accused of being without roots, effectively destroying the rootedness of music. The metaphor of rootedness takes on another meaning in Schoenberg's context as a transplant to the United States. Despite the presence

---

Angeles: Belmont Music Publishers, n.d.), Bel-1027. *A Survivor from Warsaw* was composed between July and August 1947. It was premiered in Albuquerque, New Mexico, on November 4, 1948. Originally published in 1949 by Bomart Music Publications, the corrected edition is *A Survivor from Warsaw*, rev. ed. (Hillsdale, MI: Bomart Music Publishers, 1974).

41. The rejection of Schoenbergian aesthetics is as important for many of the postwar composers as was his continuing impact. For interested readers not familiar with developments in classical music through the twentieth century, I would recommend Arnold Whittall, *Musical Composition in the Twentieth Century* (Oxford: Oxford University Press, 1999).

42. For Schoenberg's time in America and his attitudes toward American culture, see Feisst, *Schoenberg's New World*.

43. Jeffrey A. Grossman, *The Discourse on Yiddish in Germany: From the Enlightenment to the Second Empire* (Rochester, NY: Camden House, 2000), 53.

then and now of philharmonic societies, chamber music societies, and the like, the world of European music has never taken deep root in the United States. Yes, Schoenberg had been "driven into paradise," but his music remained an enigma for all but a very small segment of society. Would things have been different in a Europe not torn by two devastating world wars, or was his music inherently too forbidding to enter a popular canon? I do not think we can say for sure. We must remember that late works of Beethoven, too, were enigmas for his time; the continuation of his tradition in Europe corrected things. Music may seem like small potatoes in light of the larger problems of mankind, but the double catastrophe of the world wars arguably caused a wound in the continuity of music as thought, a rupture that has never been fully repaired.

For me, the American work that best exemplifies Schoenbergian creation-as-catastrophe is the String Trio, a magnificent work from 1946.[44] Like the majority of Schoenberg's compositions, the trio has an underlying personal narrative. Shortly after beginning work on the piece, Schoenberg experienced a near fatal heart attack.[45] The trio opens with a shattering that depicts the anguish and disorientation of the event. The anguished opening builds to a climax that is abruptly cut off by a "grand pause," silence in all of the voices.[46] After the silence, the music resumes but now with ethereal tremolos and chords sul ponticello all played very softly. The silence effectively expresses blacking out—the pain of the opening having reached its highest intensity, the suffering subject can no longer maintain consciousness. As the trio continues, the use of expressive silence becomes a key aspect of its fractured rhetoric. How much of the trio portrays waking consciousness and how much portrays dream consciousness must remain a matter of interpretation. In Schoenberg's astounding portrayal of sickness near unto death, the flow of musical thought, from time to time, drifts into silence, nodding off into a quiet sleep.

As the work progresses, fragments of a Viennese waltz gradually emerge, strands that rise to the surface and then break off again and again, constantly transformed but always recognizable as evocations of old Vienna. I have written elsewhere about the ways that the waltz strands within the trio transform

---

44. The *String Trio*, Op. 45, was composed between June and September 1946. It was premiered at Harvard University on May 1, 1947, performed by members of the Walden String Quartet. Originally published by Bomart Music Publishers in 1950, it is now available through Belmont Music Publishers (Los Angeles: Belmont Music Publishers, 1978).

45. Walter B. Bailey, *Programmatic Elements in the Works of Schoenberg* (Ann Arbor: UMI Research Press, 1984).

46. Schoenberg notated this as a fermata at the bar line at the end of m. 44.

a musical trope that had already had a long history, from the most benign of movements, to the macabre dances of Liszt, Mahler, and earlier Schoenberg. In the trio, the near-death experience moves from anguish to inner peace.[47]

The moment of healing at the end of the composition paradoxically lacks a sense of finality. Over the very last bars, the music gradually slows down, becoming more and more quiet. The piece ends peacefully, mid-phrase in yet another evocation of the waltz, in a final nodding off. Although it could easily be argued otherwise, the ending, to my mind, does not signify death. After all, Schoenberg recovered and went on to compose the piece. As I noted earlier, in a vivid sense, the trio is a musical expression of the Freudian conflict between the instincts for life and death. While we are alive, the conflict is unresolved. This, for me, is expressed by the lack of resolution in Schoenberg's trio. *Tikkun*, the redemptive restitution at the end of the work, projects toward some unknown future. Schoenbergian imperfection realizes that so long as we live in body or in memory, there is no closure.

Our humanity, broadly conceived, straddles two overlapping spheres: things public (including all things political, all having to do with the rule of law, the meaning of language, a sense of history and identity within a larger cultural, religious, and economic group) and things private (personal interrelationships and all that combines to form a sense of individuated self, as opposed to the self as citizen, coreligionist, or consumer functioning within a larger social/economic framework). The disciplines of the humanities straddle both of these spheres: a betrayal of the humanities is a violation of trust that causes harm both public and private. That the arts and the humanities are inextricably bound together, should, I hope, take no convincing. To betray one is to betray the other. And like the humanities, art straddles both spheres, public and private. Art (fiction, poetry, theater, music, dance, cinema, painting, sculpture, etc.) always involves a larger ongoing practice, whether confirmed or confronted by the individual, as well as a social context where that practice either thrives or goes into decline: the audience in the theater or music hall, the visitors to the gallery, readers en masse. Art also depends on the imagination and values of the singular individual, the artist, in interaction with the singular individual who reads the book, hears the music, sees the painting, and so forth. The betrayal of the arts during the Third Reich involved both living individuals as well as ongoing practices where the individual is part of a larger social enterprise that continues and transforms a living tradition. In music, that tradition included the compositions of Haydn, Mozart, Beethoven, Schubert,

---

47. Cherlin, *Schoenberg's Musical Imagination*, 299–338.

and Brahms; it also included those of Schoenberg. Because the individual artist speaks to our common humanity, deep subjectivity gives rise to an augmented commonality. The betrayal of the humanities breaks the circuit that connects the individual to the whole.

BIBLIOGRAPHY

Recommended Recordings of the Schoenberg Compositions Discussed in the Chapter

Erwartung

Phyllis Bryn-Julson, soprano; Sir Simon Rattle, conductor. Birmingham Symphony Orchestra. EMI Classics 5 55212 2, 1995.

Jessye Norman, soprano; James Levine, conductor. Metropolitan Opera Orchestra. Philips 426 261–2, 1993.

Moses und Aron

Philip Langridge (Moses); John Tomlinson (Aron); James Levine, conductor. Metropolitan Opera Orchestra and Chorus. Metropolitan Opera 10044556, 1999.

David Pittman-Jennings (Moses), Chris Merritt (Aron), Pierre Boulez. Royal Concertgebouw Orchestra. Deutsche Grammophon GmBH 449 174–2, 1996.

Günter Reich (Moses); Richard Cassilly (Aron); Pierre Boulez, conductor. BBC Symphony Orchestra. Sony Classical SM2K 48 456, 1993.

Second String Quartet

Quatuor Diotima; Sandrine Piau, soprano. Naïve V 5240, 2010.
Schoenberg Quartet; Susan Narucki, soprano. Chandos 9939(5), 2001.

String Trio

Juilliard String Quartet. Sony Classical SK 47 690, 1992
Schoenberg Quartet. Chandos 9939(5), 2001.

Secondary Sources

Babbitt, Milton. *The Collected Essays of Milton Babbitt*. Edited by Stephen Peles et al. Princeton, NJ: Princeton University Press, 2003.

Bailey, Walter B. *Programmatic Elements in the Works of Schoenberg*. Ann Arbor: UMI Research Press, 1984.

Bloom, Harold. *The Anatomy of Influence: Literature as a Way of Life*. New Haven, CT: Yale University Press, 2011.

———. *The Breaking of the Vessels*. Chicago: University of Chicago Press, 1982.
———. "Freud and the Poetic Sublime." In *Poetics of Influence*, 187–212.
———. "Jewish Culture and Jewish Identity." In *Poetics of Influence*, 347–68.
———. *Kaballah and Criticism*. New York: Continuum, 1984.
———. *A Map of Misreading*. Oxford: Oxford University Press, 2003.
———. *Poetics of Influence: New and Selected Criticism*. Edited by John Hollander. New Haven, CT: Henry R. Schwab, 1988.
———. *The Shadow of a Great Rock: A Literary Appreciation of the King James Bible*. New Haven, CT: Yale University Press, 2011.
Brinkmann, Reinhold, and Christoph Wolff, eds. *Driven into Paradise: The Musical Migration from Nazi Germany to the United States*. Berkeley: University of California Press, 1999.
Cherlin, Michael. *Schoenberg's Musical Imagination*. Music in the Twentieth Century 24. Cambridge: Cambridge University Press, 2007.
———. "Schoenberg's Representation of the Divine in *Moses und Aron*." *Journal of the Arnold Schoenberg Institute* 9, no. 2 (November 1986): 210–16.
Feisst, Sabine. *Schoenberg's New World: The American Years*. Oxford: Oxford University Press, 2011.
Findlay, John Niemeyer. *Hegel: A Re-Examination*. Oxford: Oxford University Press, 1976.
Forte, Allen. *The Structure of Atonal Music*. New Haven, CT: Yale University Press, 1973.
Freud, Sigmund. *Beyond the Pleasure Principle*. Translated by James Strachey. New York: W. W. Norton, 1989.
Grossman, Jeffrey A. *The Discourse on Yiddish in Germany: From the Enlightenment to the Second Empire*. Rochester, NY: Camden House, 2000.
Guthrie, William Keith Chambers. *A History of Greek Philosophy*. Vol. 1, *The Earlier Presocratics and the Pythagoreans*. Cambridge: Cambridge University Press, 1962.
Haimo, Ethan. *Schoenberg's Serial Odyssey: The Evolution of His Twelve-Tone Method, 1914–1928*. Oxford: Oxford University Press, 1990.
Heuss, Alfred. "Arnold Schönberg: Preussischer Kompositionslehrer." *Zeitschrift für Musik* 92, no. 10 (October 1925): 583–85.
Lewin, David. *Generalized Musical Intervals and Transformations*. New Haven, CT: Yale University Press, 1987.
———. "Schoenberg and Goethe: Organicism and Analysis." In *Music Theory and the Exploration of the Past*, edited by Christopher Hatch and David W. Bernstein, 409–33. Chicago: University of Chicago Press, 1993.
———. *Studies in Music with Text*. Oxford: Oxford University Press, 2006.
Neff, Severine. *Arnold Schoenberg: The Second String Quartet in F-Sharp Minor, Opus 10*. Norton Critical Scores. New York: W. W. Norton, 2006.
Ringer, Alexander. *Arnold Schoenberg: The Composer as Jew*. Oxford: Oxford University Press, 1990.

Sachar, Howard M. *Dreamland: Europeans and Jews in the Aftermath of the Great War*. New York: Alfred A. Knopf, 2002.
Schoenberg, Arnold. *Arnold Schoenberg Letters*. Edited by Erwin Stein. Translated by Eithne Wilkins and Ernst Kaiser. Berkeley: University of California Press, 1987.
———. "How One Becomes Lonely." In *Style and Idea: Selected Writings*, edited by Leonard Stein, translated by Leo Black, 30–53. 2nd ed. Berkeley: University of California Press, 2010.
———. *Kol Nidre*, Op. 39 [1938]. Los Angeles: Belmont Music Publishers, n.d.
———. *Moses und Aron: Oper in drei Akten*. Mainz, Germany: B. Schott's Söhne, 1977.
———. *String Trio*, Op. 45. Los Angeles: Belmont Music Publishers, 1978.
———. *A Survivor from Warsaw*. Revised ed. Hillsdale, MI: Bomart Music Publishers, 1974.
Scholem, Gershom G. *Major Trends in Jewish Mysticism*. With a new foreword by Robert Alter. New York: Schocken Books, 1995.
Simms, Bryan R. "Whose Idea Was *Erwartung*." In *Constructive Dissonance: Arnold Schoenberg and the Transformations of Twentieth-Century Culture*, edited by Juliane Brand and Christopher Hailey, 100–111. Berkeley: University of California Press, 1997.
Sorkin, David. "Wilhelm von Humboldt: The Theory and Practice of Self-Formation (*Bildung*), 1791–1810." *Journal of the History of Ideas* 44, no. 1 (January–March 1983): 55–73.
Stuckenschmidt, Hans Heinz. *Schoenberg: His Life, World, and Work*. Translated by Humphrey Searle. New York: Schirmer Books, 1978.
Whittall, Arnold. *Musical Composition in the Twentieth Century*. Oxford: Oxford University Press, 1999.

MICHAEL CHERLIN is author of *Schoenberg's Musical Imagination* (Cambridge, 2007) and *Varieties of Musical Irony: From Mozart to Mahler* (Cambridge, 2017). His essay "Ritual and Eros in James Dillon's *Come Live with Me*," a study of a contemporary setting of verses from "Song of Songs," appears in *Transformations of Musical Modernism* (Cambridge, 2015). In 2019, he was awarded a lifetime membership in the Society for Music Theory. He is Professor Emeritus, University of Minnesota.

ELEVEN

POLITICAL PHILOSOPHY

Hannah Arendt and Aurel Kolnai as Interpreters of the Nazi Totalitarian State

EMMANUEL FAYE

TRADITIONAL HISTORIOGRAPHY OF NATIONAL SOCIALISM has long favored the study of political and social facts at the cost of underestimating the massive penetration of the Nazi worldview (*Weltanschauung*) into academic and cultural fields along with this penetration's success in impacting people's minds with Nazi ideology. In the last decades, things have changed and many new studies have appeared. It is due to this recent work that we more fully recognize the widespread enthusiasm of German scholars for the Nazi state, something that might today be considered a betrayal of humanistic values. Yet this new recognition has been slow to penetrate the widespread, traditional understanding of the Nazi phenomenon. That is due, at least in part, to an influential understanding of totalitarianism fostered since 1951 by Hannah Arendt. Arendt's understanding of totalitarianism tends to exonerate the figures that dominated academic life under the Third Reich, such as Martin Heidegger and Carl Schmitt. This is in striking contrast with the approach that Aurel Kolnai had proposed as early as 1938 in *The War against the West* and, even earlier, in several critical articles on Heidegger, Schmitt, and others published in Vienna from 1933 to 1934.[1] The following study will explore the contrast between Arendt's and Kolnai's interpretations of National Socialism.

I. HANNAH ARENDT AND HEIDEGGER'S NAZISM

Two major aspects of Arendt's work seem to contradict each other: on the one hand, her critical analysis of twentieth-century totalitarianism; on the other

---

1. See Francis Dunlop, *The Life and Thought of Aurel Kolnai* (Aldershot, UK: Ashgate, 2002), 136–41.

hand, her unequivocal defense of Heidegger in spite of his praise of the "inner truth and greatness" of the Nazi movement, published in 1953.[2] In reality, such contradiction is only superficial, as Arendt's interpretation of Nazi totalitarianism and the ways in which she exonerated Heidegger of all responsibility are intimately connected.

Consider how Arendt evokes Heidegger's relation to Nazism on the occasion of the philosopher's eightieth birthday. Arendt's speech was recorded in New York on September 25, 1969, and broadcast the next day by the *Bayerischer Rundfunk* before being published the same year in the journal *Merkur*, augmented by footnotes.[3] The author of *The Origins of Totalitarianism* recalls that she saw in Heidegger during the 1920s the "hidden king [who] reigned in the realm of thinking."[4] She elevates him to the level of a new Plato, and concludes by asserting that "the storm [*der Sturm*] that blows through Heidegger's thinking—like that which still sweeps toward us after thousands of years from the work of Plato—does not spring from the century he happens to live in. It comes from the primeval."[5] The choice of the word *Sturm* (which can be translated as "assault" as well as "storm") to end her tribute and the association of this word with the name of Plato appear to be one of those calculated provocations typical of Arendt. Members of her German audience acquainted with recent history might have noticed the allusion to Heidegger's address as rector of Freiburg given on May 27, 1933, in which he concluded with his German translation of a line from Plato: *Alles Große steht im Sturm* [All that is great stands in the storm].[6] In 1933, this line echoed the calling up of the Nazi movement's Storm Troopers: the SA, or Sturmabteilungen, who paraded, all flags waving, around the stage on which the new rector was delivering his speech.

---

2. Martin Heidegger, *Einführung in die Metaphysik* (Tübingen, Germany: Max Niemeyer, 1953), 152; translated into English as *Introduction to Metaphysics*, trans. Gregory Fried and Richard Polt (New Haven, CT: Yale University Press, 2000), 213.

3. Hannah Arendt, "Martin Heidegger ist achtzig Jahre alt," *Merkur* 23, no. 10 (1969): 893–902.

4. Hannah Arendt, "Martin Heidegger at Eighty," trans. Albert Hofstadter, *New York Review of Books* 17, no. 6 (October 21, 1971): 50–54 (at 51).

5. Ibid., 54.

6. Martin Heidegger, "Die Selbstbehauptung der deutschen Universität," in *Reden und andere Zeugnisse eines Lebensweges (1910–1976)*, ed. Hermann Heidegger, Martin Heidegger Gesamtausgabe 16 (Frankfurt, Germany: Klostermann, 2000), 107–17 (at 117). A more accurate translation of Plato's text (*Republic* 6.497d) can be found in the Loeb Classical Library volume, which translates the text as "all great enterprises are prone to fail." See Chris Emlyn-Jones and William Preddy, *Plato: Republic, Books 6–10*, Loeb Classical Library 276 (Cambridge, MA: Harvard University Press, 2013), 53.

By decontextualizing the Heideggerian "storm," by brushing aside the historic reality of the twentieth century and by associating this storm with the so-called originary, Arendt exonerates Heidegger of his responsibility in the recognition, apology, and spiritual dissemination of the Nazi movement to which he so actively contributed. At the same time, Arendt's remark carries a great ambivalence, as it makes Heidegger himself the force that raises the "storm." Further, her evocation of the "storm" concludes her own tribute, after a development in which she attempts to exonerate Heidegger from what she calls *diese Eskapade* [this escapade], a term incorrectly translated in the American version as only "this episode."

Moreover, Arendt whitewashes Heidegger's speech as rector, with its celebration of the *Führung* [guidance] and *Gefolgschaft* [Hitlerian allegiance].[7] On March 26, 1967, in an unpublished letter to her friend J. Glenn Gray, the first American translator of Heidegger, Arendt asserted that this speech "is not Nazi" and "is obviously inspired by the *Republic*."[8] In short, Heidegger's main drawback is to have remained too Platonic! Thus, she opens the path to a whole lineage of exegetes who, in the manner of Jacques Taminiaux, would take over this whitewashed reading.[9]

In Arendt's own tribute, exactly as in the apologies of Jean Beaufret in France, Heidegger's National Socialism is reduced to "ten short months of fever."[10] Moreover, Heidegger's Nazism is doubly determined by Plato. Arendt compares his Nazi "escapade" both to Plato's voyage to the court of Dionysius at Syracuse (368 BC) and to the episode in *Theaetetus* in which a Thracian servant-girl laughs as Thales, too preoccupied with star-gazing, falls into a well.[11] But Heidegger's Nazism does not lend itself to laughter, and this double stylization is a red herring, since it is clearly not by excess of contemplation

---

7. Heidegger, "Die Selbstbehauptung," 112, 116 ("Alle Führung muß der Gefolgschaft die Eigenkraft zugestehen").

8. Arendt only criticizes the rector's address for being "a very unpleasant product of Nationalism." See Hannah Arendt to J. Glenn Gray, March 25, 1967, Hannah Arendt Papers, General Correspondence (1938–1976), J. Glenn Gray and family (1962–1967), Manuscript Division, Library of Congress, http://memory.loc.gov/cgi-bin/ampage?collId=mharendt_pub &fileName=02/020490/020490page.db (image 78 of 99).

9. See Jacques Taminiaux, *The Thracian Maid and the Professional Thinker: Arendt and Heidegger*, trans. and ed. Michael Gendre (Albany, NY: SUNY Press, 1997).

10. On the version spread by Beaufret, see his interview with Roger-Pol Droit, in Roger-Pol Droit, *La compagnie des contemporains: Rencontres avec des penseurs d'aujourd'hui* (Paris: Odile Jacob, 2002), 278.

11. For Plato's visit to Dionysius the Younger at Syracuse, see Plato, *Epistle* 7; for the story of Thales, see *Theaetetus* 174a.

that Heidegger espoused the exterminatory dynamic of the Nazi movement. In a footnote, Arendt makes Heidegger's self-apology her own: she paints in a favorable light his praise of the "inner truth and greatness" of the Nazi movement (pronounced in 1935 and published in 1953), which elicited the courageous and concerned reaction of the young Habermas in the newspaper *Frankfurter Allgemeine Zeitung*.[12] Indeed, Arendt gives credit to Heidegger for having seen in Nazism "the encounter between global technology and modern man."[13] Could she genuinely have been unaware that Heidegger himself added that explanatory parenthesis in 1953? Former students of Heidegger, such as Rainer Martin, knew this, and later said so.[14] Furthermore, we now know what the relationship between the National Socialist movement and technology meant to Heidegger. In May/June 1940, when the tank divisions of the Third Reich were attacking Holland, Belgium, and the French Ardennes, in his course titled *Nietzsche: Der europäische Nihilismus*, he celebrated the "total 'motorization' of the Wehrmacht," which represented to him "a metaphysical act."[15] In a letter to his wife, Elfride, that same year, moreover, he also praised the unconditional technologizing of war.[16]

In short, in contrast with Karl Löwith or Emmanuel Levinas, Hannah Arendt publicly criticized Heidegger's Nazism very little. When she did so, it was only at the end of the 1940s, and in a very restrained and questionable way. She thus reproached him in her 1946 essay on the philosophy of existence for being "the last Romantic" and, the same year, in her disapproving review of Max Weinreich's remarkable book *Hitlers's Professors*, for being no more than

---

12. Jürgen Habermas, "Mit Heidegger gegen Heidegger denken: Zur Veröffentlichung von Vorlesungen aus dem Jahre 1935," *Frankfurter Allgemeine Zeitung*, July 25, 1953; translated by William S. Lewis as "Martin Heidegger: On the Publication of the Lectures of 1935," in *The Heidegger Controversy: A Critical Reader*, ed. Richard Wolin (Cambridge, MA: MIT Press, 1992), 190–97.

13. Heidegger, *Introduction to Metaphysics*, 213.

14. Rainer Marten, "Ein rassistisches Konzept von Humanität," *Badische Zeitung*, December 19–20, 1987, 14.

15. Martin Heidegger, *Nietzsche: Der europäische Nihilismus*, ed. Petra Jaeger, Martin Heidegger Gesamtausgabe 48 (Frankfurt, Germany: Klostermann, 1986), 333.

16. Martin Heidegger, *"Mein Liebes Seelchen!" Briefe Martin Heideggers an seine Frau Elfride, 1915–1970*, ed. Gertrud Heidegger (Munich: Deutsche Verlags-Anstalt, 2005), 210. For an English translation, see Martin Heidegger, *Letters to His Wife, 1915–1970*, trans. Rupert Glasgow (Malden, MA: Polity, 2008), 167. Heidegger's praise of the relationship between Nazism and modern technology concerns more than the motorization of the German army: on that topic, see Emmanuel Faye, "Being, History, Technology, and Extermination in the Work of Heidegger," *Journal of the History of Philosophy* 50, no. 1 (2012): 111–30, esp. 126–28.

an "old-fashioned nationalist."[17] Beginning in the 1950s, on the contrary, she did everything she could to cover up her previous disparaging remarks and defend his reputation. She also contributed more than anyone else to the global proliferation of his thought by organizing and revising the first English translations of his writings by her friend Gray at Harper and Row.[18] It is true that in the late forties, in her private letters to Karl Jaspers, she was sharply critical of Heidegger's personality before resuming her relationship with him on February 8, 1950. She accused him of lying and saw him as a "potential murderer."[19] Such criticisms make the public praises that she would later make sound all the more disturbing. In 1953, she ironically wrote in her diary about the traps of the "fox."[20] But her personal criticisms do not bear directly on his involvement in Nazism.

Once Jaspers died in February 1969, once the last restraint that still held her back was removed, she delivered and published her 1969 celebration in which she expressed toward Heidegger a boundless idolatry. In the long footnote in which she clears Heidegger entirely from his relationship with Nazism, she

---

17. Max Weinreich, *Hitler's Professors: The Part of Scholarship in Germany's Crimes against the Jewish People* (New York: Yiddish Scientific Institute [YIVO], 1946). For Arendt's review, see Hannah Arendt, *Essays in Understanding, 1930–1945: Formation, Exile, and Totalitarianism*, ed. Jerome Kohn (New York: Harcourt, Brace, 1994), 187 and 202. Given the importance of Weinreich's work and Arendt's review of it, Alan E. Steinweis is right to introduce his volume by referencing that review. See Alan E. Steinweis, *Studying the Jew: Scholarly Antisemitism in Nazi Germany* (Cambridge, MA: Harvard University Press, 2008), 2. But Steinweis presents Arendt as corroborating Weinreich's book, while in fact she challenges its thesis. Indeed, she maintains that "Dr. Weinreich's main thesis . . . that 'German scholarship provided the ideas and techniques which led to and justified unparalleled slaughter' . . . is a highly controversial statement. . . . Dr. Weinreich's book pays too great a compliment to these professors by taking them too seriously" (*Essays in Understanding*, 201, 203). In that ultimately disapproving review of the book's orientation, we see Arendt's general strategy, which is to exculpate Nazism's intellectual elite by making light of them.

18. "Hannah Arendt had nominated him for the general editor's position." See Martin Woessner, *Heidegger in America* (New York: Cambridge University Press, 2011), 151. Woessner dedicates a whole chapter to "An Officer and a Philosopher: J. Glenn Gray and the Postwar Introduction of Heidegger into American Thought" (132–58). He also shows that Gray was disturbed by the way Arendt downplayed Heidegger's political past (153).

19. Hannah Arendt, letter to Karl Jaspers, July 9, 1946, in Hannah Arendt and Karl Jaspers, *Briefwechsel 1926–1969* (Munich: Piper, 1993), 84. See also the very harsh criticism of Heidegger's *Charakterlosigkeit* [lack of character] in her letter to Jaspers on September 29, 1949 (Arendt and Jaspers, *Briefwechsel*, 178).

20. See Arendt, "Heidegger the Fox," in *Essays in Understanding*, 361–62; Hannah Arendt, *Denktagebuch: 1950 bis 1973*, ed. Ursula Ludz and Ingeborg Nordmann (Munich: Piper, 2002), 404.

claims that he never read *Mein Kampf*.²¹ This is almost certainly a misrepresentation when confronted with former students' testimonies and a comparison between Hitler's and Heidegger's writings.²² She also claims that to speak of Heidegger in relation to Nazism instead of speaking only of "Hitler, Auschwitz, genocide, and 'extermination' as a policy of permanent depopulation," amounts "to dress[ing] up the horrible gutter-born phenomenon with the language of the humanities and the history of ideas."²³ Yet we know today that Heidegger in his seminars was telling his students to prepare, over the long haul, for the *völligen Vernichtung* [total extermination] of the internal enemy grafted onto the "root of the people," that is, the Jew assimilated to the German people.²⁴ He also used his seminars to heap the greatest praise on Hitler's speeches, whose

---

21. This assertion does not appear in the version of her speech titled "Martin Heidegger ist achtzig Jahre alt" (see note 3 in this chapter), which Arendt sent to Heidegger. See Hannah Arendt, letter to Martin Heidegger, September 26, 1969, in Hannah Arendt and Martin Heidegger, *Briefe 1925 bis 1975 und andere Zeugnisse*, ed. Ursula Ludz, 3rd ed. (Frankfurt, Germany: Klostermann, 2002), 332.

22. Hermann Mörchen recounts how, in 1930, Elfride Heidegger put *Mein Kampf* down on the table of the Todtnauberg cabin and exclaimed: "Das müssen Sie lesen!" [You must read that book!]. It is hard to imagine how Elfride could have made such a demand from the student if Heidegger himself had not read Hitler. Mörchen's account can be found in Thomas Rentsch, *Martin Heidegger: Das Sein und der Tod; Eine kritische Einführung* (Munich: Piper, 1989), 163. For parallels between several statements of Heidegger and Hitler, see Emmanuel Faye, "Heidegger, der Nationalsozialismus, und die Zerstörung der Philosophie," in *Politische Unschuld? In Sachen Martin Heidegger*, ed. Bernhard H. F. Taureck (Munich: Wilhem Fink, 2008), 45–80 (at 61–62, 65–66). At page 65n27, the translator refers by mistake to *Mein Kampf*, while mentioning a quote from Heidegger, *Sein und Wahrheit*, ed. Hartmut Tietjen, Martin Heidegger Gesamtausgabe 36/37 (Frankfurt, Germany: Klostermann, 2001), 225.

23. Arendt, "Heidegger at Eighty." It is interesting to note that in the American version of her praise of Heidegger previously cited (see note 4 in this chapter), Arendt added to her comment on the issue of the Nazi commitment a parallel between the literature focusing on Hitler's era and that focusing on Stalin's in the following terms: "One can indeed say that escape from reality has in the meantime blossomed into a profession, and this in the literature of both the Hitler and the Stalin period. In the latter we still find the notion that Stalin's crimes were necessary for the industrialization of Russia—even though this 'industrialization' quite obviously was a gigantic failure—and in the former we still read grotesquely highfalutin and sophisticated theories with whose spirituality the gutter never had anything to do" (54).

24. In early 1934, Heidegger taught his students

> The enemy is one who poses an essential threat to the existence of the people and its members. The enemy is not necessarily the outside enemy, and the outside enemy is not necessarily the most dangerous. It may even appear that there is no enemy at all. The root requirement is then to find the enemy, bring him to light or even to create him, so

eloquence he compared to that of Thucydides.²⁵ Even if Arendt did not know these texts, she had enough elements to be warned, had she only wanted to. I will later highlight the contrast between her and the philosopher Aurel Kolnai, who, as early as 1934, was lucid on that question.

II. ARENDT'S INTERPRETATION OF NAZISM

In 2009, the historian Bernard Wasserstein from the University of Chicago called into question the way in which Arendt approached and described National Socialism, in a noted essay published in the *Times Literary Supplement*.²⁶ Nor is he the only one, for as he himself reminds us, a number of major historians of Nazism (of whom Ian Kershaw was a pioneer) deem Arendt's concept of

---

> that there may be that standing up to the enemy, and so that existence does not become apathetic. The enemy may have grafted himself onto the innermost root of the existence of a people, and oppose the latter's ownmost essence, acting contrary to it. All the keener and harsher and more difficult is then the struggle, for only a very small part of the struggle consists in mutual blows; it is often much harder and more exhausting to seek out the enemy as such, and to lead him to reveal himself, to avoid nurturing illusions about him, to remain ready to attack, to cultivate and increase constant preparedness and to initiate the attack on a long-term basis, with the goal of total extermination.

See Martin Heidegger, *Sein und Wahrheit*, 90–91; translated in Emmanuel Faye, *Heidegger: The Introduction of Nazism into Philosophy in Light of the Unpublished Seminars of 1933–1935*, trans. Michael B. Smith (New Haven, CT: Yale University Press, 2009), 168.

25. See Martin Heidegger, "'Über Wesen und Begriff von Natur, Geschichte, und Staat': Übung aus dem Wintersemester 1933/34," in *Heidegger und der Nationalsozialismus I: Dokumente*, ed. Alfred Denker and Holger Zaborowski, Heidegger-Jahrbuch 4 (Freiburg, Germany: Alber, 2009), 53–88 (at 86).

> Als politisches Machtmittel galt die Rede bei den Griechen in ausgezeichneter Weise, ihr politischer Instinkt erkannte die Überzeugungskraft der Rede in vorbildlicher Art, und in unvergeßlicher Form wissen wir durch Thukydides davon. Es ist eine unbewußte Erkenntnis der Macht der Rede, wenn in unseren Tagen die Reden des Führers einen Eindruck machten, der in dem Wort vom 'Trommler' zum Ausdruck kam.
>
> [For the Greeks, speech was a preeminent means to political power. Their political instinct recognized the persuasive force of speech in an exemplary manner; we know this unforgettably from Thucydides. It is an unconscious recognition of the power of speech that in our own day, the speeches of the Führer made an impression that came to be expressed by the term, "the drummer."]'

(Translated in Martin Heidegger, *Nature, History, State: 1933–1934*, trans. and ed. Gregory Fried and Richard Polt [London: Bloomsbury, 2013], 62.)

26. Bernard Wasserstein, "Blame the Victim—Hannah Arendt among the Nazis: The Historian and Her Sources," *Times Literary Supplement*, October 9, 2009, 13–15. An expanded and footnoted version of the article appeared in Dutch together with three ripostes. See

totalitarianism irrelevant to understanding Nazism.[27] The most original point of Wasserstein's study is his insistence on the fact that *The Origins of Totalitarianism* not only uses as sources but also invokes favorably Nazi authors, such as the historian Walter Frank, the editor of the sinister journal *Forschungen zur Judenfrage* (1936–1944) [Research on the Jewish Question].[28] Arendt's praise extended to other Nazi "thinkers," such as the legal scholar Carl Schmitt, whom she deemed a man of "great achievement." She praised his "very ingenious theories about the end of democracy and legal government," which "still make arresting reading."[29] Indeed, she quoted one of Schmitt's worst books, *Staat, Bewegung, Volk*, three times as a reliable source to reflect on the modern state. Yet it is in this very book that Schmitt suggests that the party and the SA be exonerated of all civil responsibility, which meant the end of habeas corpus and the denial of the victims' right to legal recognition.[30]

More generally, Arendt clears the great National Socialist thinkers of all responsibility. As a matter of fact, in *The Origins of Totalitarianism*, she asserts that "in all fairness to those among the elite, on the other hand, who at one time or another have let themselves be seduced by totalitarian movements, and who

---

Bernard Wasserstein et al., *Hannah Arendt en de geschiedschrijving: Een controverse*, ed. Joos van Vugt (Nijmegen, Netherlands: Damon, 2010).

27. "Hannah Arendt's *Origins of Totalitarianism* ... offers no clear theory or satisfactory concept of totalitarian systems. And its basic argument explaining the growth of totalitarianism—the replacement of classes by masses and the emergence of a 'mass society'—is clearly flawed." See Ian Kershaw, *The Nazi Dictatorship: Problems and Perspectives of Interpretation*, 2nd ed. (London: Edward Arnold, 1989), 22.

28. For a critical overview of Frank's journal, see Reinhard Markner, "*Forschungen Zur Judenfrage*: A Notorious Journal and Some of Its Contributors," *European Journal of Jewish Studies* 1, no. 2 (2007): 395–415.

29. Hannah Arendt, *The Origins of Totalitarianism*, 3rd ed. with new prefaces (New York: Harcourt, Brace, and World, 1966), 339. Arendt's praise of Carl Schmitt is even more extended and explicit in the German edition of her book, in which Schmitt is presented as belonging to the "kleinen Zahl wirklicher Künstler und Gelehrter" [the small number of real artists and scholars] and as being "zweifellos der bedeutendste Mann in Deutschland auf dem Gebiet des Verfassungs- und Völkerrechts" [undoubtedly the most important figure in Germany in the field of constitutional and international law]. See Hannah Arendt, *Elemente und Ursprünge totaler Herrschaft: Antisemitismus, Imperialismus, totale Herrschaft* (Munich: Piper, 1986), 724.

30. "Daher können auch die Gesichtspunkte der Haftung, insbesondere die der Körperschaftshaftung für Amtsmißbrauch (Art. 131 der Weimarer Verfassung, § 839 BGB) nicht auf die Partei oder die SA übertragen werden." See Carl Schmitt, *Staat, Bewegung, Volk: Die Dreigliederung der politischen Einheit* (Hamburg, Germany: Hanseatische Verlagsanstalt, 1933), 22.

sometimes, because of their intellectual abilities, are even accused of having inspired totalitarianism, it must be stated that what these desperate men of the twentieth century did or did not do had no influence on totalitarianism whatsoever."[31]

This thesis, set forth shortly before the laudatory remarks on Carl Schmitt and Walter Frank, is deeply mistaken. Arendt conceives of totalitarianism in general and Nazism in particular as being an essentially plebian movement, composed of déclassé individuals manipulated by a mafia-like pseudo-elite. She deals exclusively with essentialized social groups—the lowest of the low, the mob, the elite, the déclassés, and the underworld—but she does not take up the writings of the Nazi thinkers as an object of critical study. This represents a considerable flaw that distorts our understanding of the Nazi movement. Worse, her description of the totalitarian movement as a nihilistic dynamic of grabbing power without any real political goal is broadly borrowed from Hermann Rauschning's highly problematic book. Rauschning was a former Nazi and president of the Danzig Senate who broke with Hitler and published *The Revolution of Nihilism* in exile in 1938. In that work, the Nazi movement is described as a mafia-like group with no other goal than the quest for power through violence. Thus, Arendt misses a fundamental truth about Nazism. It was not just by its SA hordes, turned loose in the city streets, that National Socialism was able to win over so many minds in Germany and elsewhere. It was by a carefully planned and methodical penetration of all areas of cultural, intellectual, social, and spiritual life: not only medicine, law, history, and philosophy, but also religion, poetry, art, and so on. The Nazi literature that proliferated before and after 1933 is extensive, and among that veritable army of authors, the "great names" possessing a certain cachet—Martin Heidegger for philosophy, Carl Schmitt for law, Friedrich Gogarten for theology, and Eugen Fischer for biology—bear considerable responsibility in the systematic conquest of hearts and minds.[32]

---

31. Arendt, *Origins of Totalitarianism*, 339.

32. Friedrich Gogarten (1887–1967), a Lutheran theologian, is, with Karl Barth and Rudolf Bultmann, one of the main representatives of dialectic theology. In August 1933, he officially joined the German Christians who rallied around Hitler. Gogarten is the most frequently cited theologian by Kolnai in Aurel Kolnai, *The War against the West* (London: Victor Gollancz; New York: Viking, 1938). Eugen Fischer (1874–1967), a Nazi medical doctor and advocate of racial hygiene and eugenics under the Third Reich, became the rector of the University of Berlin in 1933. He participated with Heidegger in the "Profession of Faith in Adolf Hitler" at the time of the referendum of November 12, 1933. When Fischer was

What is deeply problematic in Arendt's evocation of Nazism can first be seen in its numerous oversights: a lack of inquiry into the rise and growth of the Nazi movement in Germany, into its links to Italian Fascism, and, above all, a lack of any critical and in-depth study of the writings of Nazi theorists, academics, and thinkers. But there are two especially problematic points in what she says.

The first is dilettantism in the use of historical terms. To say that Fascism is not totalitarian when Mussolini practically created the word by asserting his "ferocious totalitarian will" in a 1925 speech delivered to justify the assassination of Giacomo Matteotti shows a lack of sensitivity to the language actually used in politics and history.[33] To maintain that Nazism does not become totalitarian until 1938 or even 1939 is equally problematic.[34] In reality, it is at the moment of the seizing of power in the years 1933–35 that Nazism may be accurately called a totalitarian movement, with the advent of the concept of the *totaler Staat* ["total state"]. This terminology was coined by Carl Schmitt in 1931 and developed in an explicitly racist sense by his disciples Ernst Forsthoff and Ernst Rudolf Huber.[35] The term was also used by Hitler himself to refer to the abolition of any distinction between law and morality.[36] This implies the disappearance, beginning in 1933, of all protection of private life in the total

---

director of the Kaiser Wilhelm Institute, his assistant was Josef Mengele, a doctor of medical experiments at Auschwitz. Fischer and Heidegger maintained friendly relations long after 1945.

33. "The nontotalitarian nature of the Fascist dictatorship" (Arendt, *Origins of Totalitarianism*, 308n11). For a sophisticated rebuttal of Arendt's disjunction between Italian fascism and totalitarianism, see Meir Michaelis's study, "Anmerkungen zum italienischen Totalitarismusbegriff: Zur Kritik der Thesen Hannah Arendts und Renzo de Felices," *Quellen und Forschungen aus italienischen Archiven und Bibliotheken* 62 (1982): 270–302.

34. Hannah Arendt, *Eichmann in Jerusalem: A Report on the Banality of Evil*, with an introduction by Amos Elon (New York: Penguin, 2006), 68.

35. See Carl Schmitt, "Die Wendung zum totalen Staat," *Europäische Revue* 7, no. 4 (1931): 241–50; Ernst Forsthoff, *Der Totale Staat* (Hamburg, Germany: Hanseatische Verlagsanstalt, 1933); and Ernst Rudolf Huber, "Die totalität des völkischen Staates," *Die Tat* 26, no. 1 (1934): 30–42. On the openly racist and antisemitic intention of Forsthoff's book, see Emmanuel Faye, *Heidegger: Introduction of Nazism into Philosophy*, 161.

36. Adolf Hitler's statement addressing the 1933 *Juristentag* ("Der *totale Staat* wird keine Unterschied dulden zwischen Recht und Moral" ["The totalitarian state will not tolerate any difference between law and morality"]) was reported in *Völkischer Beobachter*, October 5, 1933. The German text and English translation quoted here come from Max Domarus, ed., *Hitler: Reden und Proklamationen, 1932–1945*, vol. 1 (Neustadt an der Aisch, Germany: Schmidt, 1962), 305; translated by Mary Fran Gilbert as *Hitler: Speeches and Proclamations, 1932–1945: The Chronicle of a Dictatorship*, vol. 1 (Wauconda, IL: Bolchazy-Carducci, 1990), 364. Arendt herself quotes Hitler's statement in *Origins of Totalitarianism*, 394, to illustrate

state—which, as we have seen, Carl Schmitt commits himself to legitimizing.[37] At the end of the 1930s, and throughout the war, the National Socialist movement stands out in its true light, that of a movement that is not only totalitarian but also radically exterminatory, which Heidegger had clearly proclaimed and encouraged in his courses since the winter of 1933–34. Furthermore, to say that Nazism does not become totalitarian until 1938 exculpates the intellectuals who lent their strongest public support to the movement before that date, as is the case not only of Schmitt and Heidegger but also, to a lesser degree, of Eric Voegelin, as Aurel Kolnai has demonstrated.[38] Voegelin was, it is true, opposed to the National Socialists by the end of 1938, when he was writing the foreword to the second edition of *Political Religions* during his US exile, but he was not during his writings from the years 1933 to 1936. His articles published in Germany in 1934 are especially explicit and overwhelming. In *The Origins of Totalitarianism*, Arendt praises his 1933 book, *Rasse und Staat* [*Race and State*], even though its introduction contains a positive mention of Alfred Rosenberg, and despite the fact that Voegelin embraces the positions of Ludwig F. Clauss, one of the main theoreticians of Nazism's racial doctrine.[39]

The second problematic point is her laying of blame on concentration camp victims. Indeed, it is not without reason that Wasserstein titled his essay on Arendt "Blame the Victim." Consider the "lesson" that Voegelin drew from his

---

"The So-Called Totalitarian State" (the title of the first section of chapter 12, "Totalitarianism in Power"). She in turn found that statement in Hans Frank, *Nationalsozialistische Leitsätze für ein neues deutsches Strafrecht* (Berlin: Ludwig Fischer, 1936), 8. Arendt does not seem to notice the contradiction between using a signal declaration made by Hitler in 1933 to define the total state and her own thesis that Nazi Germany does not become totalitarian until 1938 or even 1939, when the Third Reich went to war.

37. See the reference to Carl Schmitt, *Staat, Bewegung, Volk* in note 30 of this chapter.

38. On the critique of Voegelin, see Kolnai, *War against the West*, 187–88, 191: "He [Voegelin] quotes with approval the passage from Werner Haverbeck's article in *Nationalsozialistische Monatshefte* (1933) which states that it is a new experience of the 'harmony of *Leib-Seele-Geist*' [body, soul, spirit] which 'has found its symbol in the consciousness of the Blood.'" See further critical passages on pp. 315–16, 447–49, 458–59, 478, 487–88, and 507.

39. See Eric Voegelin, *Race and State*, ed. Klaus Vondung, trans. Ruth Hein, Collected Works of Eric Voegelin 2 (Baton Rouge: Louisiana State University Press, 1997), 14–15, originally published in German as *Rasse und Staat* (Tübingen, Germany: Mohr, 1933). For Arendt's praise of *Rasse und Staat*, see *Origins of Totalitarianism*, 158n3. Ludwig Clauss began publishing on the "soul of the race" with the National Socialist press Lehmann as early as 1929. See Ludwig Ferdinand Clauss, *Von Seele und Antlitz der Rassen und Völker: Eine Einführung in die vergleichende Ausdrucksforschung* (Munich: J. F. Lehmann, 1929).

reading of *The Origins* and made his own: "She [Arendt] is even uneasily aware that not all the misery of National Socialist concentration camps was caused by the oppressors, but that a part of it was caused by the spiritual lostness that so many of the victims brought with them."[40] In her response to Voegelin's review, Arendt says nothing to contest this argument that he attributes to her. Yet after all that we know about the Nazi genocidal system, to transfer part of the responsibility to the victims is to further the physical, moral, and spiritual dehumanization of the political and racial victims of Nazism—namely, the Résistants and the Jews—a dehumanization inherent in the Nazi mentality.

III. ARENDT'S CONCEPTION OF NAZI TOTALITARIANISM

Hannah Arendt proposes the idea of *structural* totalitarianism, a worldview or ideology which would have merely an instrumental function in the service of total domination. This allows her to diminish the importance of the theoretical content of Nazism, to never seriously and rigorously study it for what it is, and finally to exonerate its thinkers, from Carl Schmitt to Martin Heidegger, who, according to her, had nothing to do with the "essence" of the phenomenon. According to this interpretation, Nazi totalitarianism would be only one possible twentieth-century "crystallization" of certain elements, such as the decline of the nation-state and the emergence of a mass society. Arendt, strongly inspired by the Heideggerian concept of historical destiny, proceeds to depersonalize and essentialize historical situations. That concept proves irrelevant for understanding and criticizing the formation of the Nazi movement. To try to determine the "essence" of totalitarianism is meaningless if, at the same time, one blinds oneself to the overwhelming responsibility of the men who planned, accompanied, and legitimized, through their writings and speeches, the carrying out of the Nazi movement and its genocidal intents. It is not enough to repeat, as Arendt keeps doing, that "this *should* never have happened."[41] It was likely that writings as radical and destructive as those of a Heidegger or a Schmitt would eventually transition into a genocidal politics. One cannot, in the context of the year 1934, call for the total extermination of the enemy within—given all the authority of a Rector-Führer over his students, of a famous thinker over his German audience—without expecting one's words to be carried out.

---

40. Eric Voegelin, "The Origins of Totalitarianism," *Review of Politics* 15, no. 1 (1953): 68–85 (at 73).

41. "Dies hätte nie geschehen *dürfen*." See Arendt, *Denktagebuch*, 7.

Jaspers was keen in perceiving some of the oversights of *The Origins of Totalitarianism*, but, perhaps out of friendship to his former student, he excused her in part. In a letter to Heinrich Blücher dated July 20, 1952, he wrote the following about Arendt: "Her respect for the mind kept her from making the great thinkers partially responsible for the horrors that occurred in the reality that her book analyzes."[42] Unfortunately, Arendt's attitude amounts to magnifying a decisive dimension of Nazi evil and in whitewashing some of its primary agents. How can one respect a "mind" that is congruent with the mind of Nazism, or a "greatness" that feeds on the power given by the destruction and the extermination of the human being at all levels? This power was not ordinary or "banal" in the form it took in Nazism.

The preceding analyses have carried us merely to the threshold of our critical examination of Arendt's phenomenology of totalitarianism. Further analysis should be pursued by contrasting the English and German versions of *The Origins of Totalitarianism*, often subtly different, and by studying the long-term effects of her work. After having long served Heidegger's cause, Arendt's work is used today in a series of books and studies that rehabilitate Carl Schmitt as a respectable political scientist. It would also be important to determine what she retained from authors such as Hans Freyer or Ernst Forsthoff, who both appear in the bibliography of the English version of her book, but not in the German edition.[43] Yet I have already established one central flaw of Arendt's work on totalitarianism: whenever she uses Nazi thinkers—historians, philosophers, legal scholars—it is always as sources rather than as objects of critical study. Such a problematic orientation is even more visible when one compares Arendt's work on totalitarianism to the seven-hundred-page summa on Nazi thought published by Aurel Kolnai in 1938.

---

42. Karl Jaspers, letter to Heinrich Blücher, in Hannah Arendt and Karl Jaspers, *Correspondence, 1926–1969*, trans. Robert Kimber and Rita Kimber (New York: Harcourt, Brace, Jovanovich, 1992), 186. For the original German text, see Arendt and Jaspers, *Briefwechsel*, 223.

43. It is interesting to note that Ernst Forsthoff, in his correspondence with Carl Schmitt, speaks in favorable terms about Arendt's book: "Eben lese ich Hannah Arendt, Elemente und Ursprünge totaler Herrschaft, ein ungewöhnlich gescheites, aufregend interessantes Buch. Ich möchte es ihnen gern schicken, weiß aber nicht, ob Sie es nicht bereit haben und kennen. . . . Es wäre mir eine besondere Freude, Ihnen dieses Buch zu übermitteln, in dem übrigens Ihre Politische Romantik außerordentlich verständnisvoll gewürdigt wird." See Ernst Forsthoff, letter to Carl Schmitt, Heidelberg, December 30, 1955, in Ernst Forsthoff and Carl Schmitt, *Briefwechsel Ernst Forsthoff Carl Schmitt (1926–1974)*, ed. Dorothee Mußgnug, Reinhard Mußgnug, and Angela Reinthal (Berlin: Akademie, 2007), 116.

IV. AN INTRODUCTION TO AUREL KOLNAI

Without claiming to summarize Kolnai's intellectual biography—he himself has done so in his *Political Memoirs*—it would be beneficial nonetheless to briefly survey the career of this long-forgotten author.[44] Aurel Kolnai was a Hungarian philosopher of Jewish origin who was trained at the University of Vienna. He participated in the formation of the psychoanalytic movement—before distancing himself from it—and became acquainted with Husserlian phenomenology and, to a certain degree, with Max Scheler's thought. He also identified with the biting spirit of G. K. Chesterton, the reading of whom contributed to his conversion to Catholicism in 1926. His inquiries into the function of feelings in ethics led him to publish, in the 1920s, three deeply original essays on disgust, shame, and hatred.[45] The essay on disgust influenced Jean-Paul Sartre's *Nausea*, although Sartre never acknowledged his debt toward him.[46] Georges Bataille also read the essay on disgust closely, as witnessed by his own handwritten notes.[47]

The present study will focus on Kolnai's critique of Nazi thought in the 1930s. Due to his progressive and democratic ethos, Kolnai was able to assess early on the threat represented by the National Socialists' rise to power, especially for the future of Austria, but also for the future of all Western democracies. He envisioned his project as a way to trigger awareness of a growing threat for democracies. It was also a way for him to prepare his exile. He left Vienna for London and Paris in 1937, and the following year he published his critical work *The War against the West* in English—in London and New York.[48]

Several years before the composition of his book, Kolnai had already written against the thought of both Schmitt and Heidegger. As early as 1933, he wrote a long critical study of Carl Schmitt's concept of the political, titled "The Content

---

44. Aurel Kolnai, *Political Memoirs*, ed. Francesca Murphy (Lanham, MD: Lexington Books, 1999).

45. These three essays have been republished as Aurel Kolnai, *Ekel, Hochmut, Haß: Zur Phänomenologie feindlicher Gefühle*, ed. Axel Honneth (Frankfurt, Germany: Suhrkamp, 2007).

46. See Aurel Kolnai, *On Disgust*, ed. with an introduction by Barry Smith and Carolyn Korsmeyer (Chicago: Open Court, 2004), 17.

47. See Georges Bataille, *Écrits posthumes, 1922–1940*, vol. 2 of *Œuvres complètes*, ed. Denis Hollier (Paris: Gallimard, 1970), 438–39. Bataille's reading of Kolnai is commented on at length by Claire Margat in her preface to the French edition of Aurel Kolnai, *Le dégoût*, trans. Olivier Cossé (Paris: Agalma, 1997), 6, 15–20. See also Aurel Kolnai, *On Disgust*, 17.

48. For full publication details of *War against the West*, see note 32 in this chapter.

[*Inhalt*] of Politics."⁴⁹ In June 1934, he published a bold criticism of the rector of Freiburg, "Heidegger and National Socialism," for which he cautiously assumed the pen name Dr. A. van Helsing, since the Nazis were already active in Austria.⁵⁰

Kolnai, as opposed to Arendt, understood from the very beginning that Nazism was not simply a mass movement animated by a vague ideology that seduced the people. He understood that he was confronted with a well-defined worldview that one had to know in-depth in order to describe, criticize, fight, and neutralize it by showing in particular the commonalities between its menial ideologues, such as Hans Frank or Ernst Krieck, and its most famous thinkers, such as Heidegger, Gogarten, or Schmitt. These latter thinkers, precisely because of their alleged greatness, were intellectually and morally the most responsible and most formidable of all in the long run. Indeed, in the case of Heidegger and Schmitt, their influence survived the military defeat of the Third Reich.

We must also inquire into why Kolnai has been entirely forgotten since 1945, beyond the small circle of his former students and colleagues at Bedford College, London, such as Bernard Williams. The contrast with Voegelin, who was clever enough to hide his support for Nazism in the years 1933–36 and secure for himself a prestigious career that propelled him from Munich to Stanford, is stunning. During the very years when Kolnai was planning his forced exile, Voegelin kept approaching and seducing the most radical Nazi philosophers, such as Alfred Baeumler and Ernst Krieck, in order to get published and invited to Germany. While that strategy ended up succeeding, his hope of securing a position in Frankfurt or Berlin failed.⁵¹ On the other hand, Kolnai went through much rougher ordeals, of which the French government should be ashamed. Unable to obtain a visa in time from the British government at

---

49. Aurel Kolnai, "Der Inhalt der Politik," *Zeitschrift für die gesamte Staatswissenschaft* 94 (1933): 1–38.

50. Dr. A. van Helsing [Aurel Kolnai], "Heidegger und der Nationalsozialismus," *Der christliche Ständestaat: Österreichische Wochenhefte* 1, no. 28 (17 June 1934): 5–7. Aurel Kolnai cunningly adopted "the pseudonym of Abraham van Helsing, who, in Bram Stoker's *Dracula*, fights the spiritual power of demonic evil." See Dunlop, *Life and Thought of Aurel Kolnai*, 137. In the reuse of that pseudonym, the new target became self-evident. The title "Heidegger's Nihilism" [Heideggers Nihilismus] given to this essay in the bibliography of the 2008 reprint of Kolnai's *Ethics, Value, and Reality*, with Opening Essays by Bernard Williams, David Wiggins, and Graham McAleer, 2nd ed., Library of Conservative Thought (Piscataway, NJ: Transaction Publishers, 2008), 234, is a mistake, corrected by Francis Dunlop in *Life and Thought of Aurel Kolnai*, 334.

51. See Emmanuel Faye, "Eric Voegelins Haltung zum Nationalsozialismus: Überlegungen zum Briefwechsel Krieck-Voegelin (1933–1934)," in *"Politisierung der*

the end of the 1930s, he was detained as a German national, although he had renounced Austrian citizenship after the *Anschluss* and was freed just in time: "about two hours before the Germans [the Wehrmacht] reached the camp."[52]

Perhaps this trauma, linked to his dismay at the blind pacifism of the Munich agreement, led Kolnai to distance himself from his democratic ethos and to adopt, as of 1943, a conservatism that was disconcerting, though always open to critical discussion, as witnessed by the mutual esteem between Kolnai and Karl Popper that endured until the end.[53] In any case, as already mentioned, the Kolnai of the present study is the lucid, courageous, and visionary thinker of the 1930s. The conservative Kolnai of the years 1943–73, the period during which he went from Laval to London, from neo-Thomism to an ethical thought open to analytic philosophy, belongs to a different chapter of intellectual history. One should not, however, dissimulate the contradictions of that later period. To be sure, Kolnai calls himself an anti-Fascist until the very end, but he nevertheless expresses a disturbing sympathy for Franco's Spain, and he contributes, one year before his death, to the work of a mentor of the new right, Gerd-Klaus Kaltenbrunner's *Rekonstruktion des Konservatismus* [Reconstruction of Conservatism].[54] A critical study of the contradictions and dark sides in the later Kolnai remains to be written; in order to do so, researchers must take an interest in Kolnai, the progressive of the 1930s, and not just the post-1943 conservative, as is by and large the case at present.

V. AUREL KOLNAI AND THE TOTAL STATE

To return to the Kolnai of the 1930s, the value of *The War against the West* consists in the remarkably broad sample of Nazi authors that Kolnai investigates. His bibliography is impressive, with over 120 references to fascist and Nazi writers. The book's value also rests on the way it reconstitutes the main points

---

Wissenschaft": *Jüdische Wissenschaftler und ihre Gegner an der Universität Frankfurt am Main vor und nach 1933*, ed. Moritz Epple et al., Schriftenreihe des Frankfurter Universitätsarchivs 5 (Göttingen, Germany: Wallstein, 2016), 111–46.

52. See Dunlop, *Life and Thought of Aurel Kolnai*, 175.

53. In Karl Popper's *The Open Society and Its Enemies*, the conclusions of the chapter dedicated to "Hegel and the New Tribalism" are explicitly based on Kolnai's book. See Karl Popper, *The Open Society and Its Enemies* (London: Routledge, 2002), 324, 325, 331, 624, 777. On Kolnai's conservative turn in 1943, the year of what he called his "second conversion," see his own account in his *Political Memoirs*, 211.

54. See Aurel Kolnai, "Konservatives und revolutionäres Ethos," *Rekonstruktion des Konservatismus*, ed. Gerd-Klaus Kaltenbrunner (Freiburg, Germany: Rombach, 1972), 95–136.

of the Nazi worldview and its importance in the writings of legal scholars, historians, theologians, and philosophers. Kolnai's book helps us assess the enormous Nazi literature that still lies dormant in libraries and continues to pop up when one postmodern author or another takes inspiration from Klages or Schmitt, at the risk of reactivating that worldview.

In addition to the breadth of Nazi theoreticians that Kolnai examines, the range of topics he explores is equally impressive. The list of chapter titles alone easily conveys that breadth: (introduction) The Challenge to Europe; (1) The Central Meaning of National Socialist Attitude; (2) Community; (3) State; (4) Human Nature and Civilization; (5) Faith and Thought; (6) Morals, Law, and Culture; (7) Society and Economics; (8) Nation and Race; (9) The German Claim; (conclusion) Nazi Germany and the Western World.

Two points are important to emphasize in this conclusion. First, whereas Hannah Arendt completely whitewashed Nazi authors, Kolnai demonstrates his full awareness of the responsibility of Nazi authors whose work he explores. For Kolnai, it was neither opportunism nor servility toward power that characterized the thought of Alfred Baeumler, Friedrich Gogarten, Martin Heidegger, Kurt Hildebrandt, Carl Schmitt, or Wilhelm Stapel but rather the force of conviction and "Nazi substance" of their worldview. As Kolnai writes: "Contrary to cheap criticism, the essential thing about Nazi Professors is not their servility toward the Fascist State, not their truckling to the owners of power, remarkable though it may be, but their genuine Nazi substance which could not actually be simulated at all."[55] It is the convergence in the same "Nazi substance" of authors such as Gogarten, Schmitt, Heidegger, and Stapel, as well as Baeumler, Krieck, and Rosenberg, that Kolnai attempted to portray in his book. Through well-chosen quotations, he showed that "great thinkers" and "ideologues" defend the same theses, albeit in different idioms. The statement concerning the "Nazi substance" of Nazi professors, moreover, appeared in a critical discussion of Heidegger's address as rector and his conception of the university as a "battle community of teachers and pupils." Kolnai even went so far as to present Heidegger as the one who somehow gave shape to Hitlerism: "It is of the greatest consequence to understand that Nazism is not a calamitous accident but a secular heresy, not a mischievous adventure but a metaphysical reality. If Heidegger cajoles Hitler, it is because figuratively speaking he has made Hitler."[56]

---

55. Kolnai, *War against the West*, 316.
56. Ibid.

Second, instead of understanding the "totalitarian state" as an essentialized category, as Arendt would do later, Kolnai uses it in a historically and philologically rigorous sense, to translate into English the German *totale Staat*.[57] He explores the writings of Ernst Forsthoff, Carl Schmitt, Ernst Rudolf Huber, and Othmar Spann, as well as Hitler, in order to lay bare the foundation that will allow for a precise definition of that "phrase," not to say of that "concept." Kolnai begins by making clear that the totalitarian state cannot be defined by the control of the state apparatus over the social or even private life of citizens: this would correspond more to "communism" or "collectivism." What is at stake is something much more radical and intimate: that is, the total domination of the heart and mind of each individual. He writes: "A succinct vocabulary of the Totalitarian State may be found in Forsthoff's book bearing that proud title. The individual is made to be 'totally duty-bound' (*totale Inpflichtanahme*) towards the nation. Each individual, in every detail of his life, is 'totally responsible' for the fate of his nation. The privacy of individual existence is abolished."[58] Kolnai highlights that for Hitler himself, what matters is not the party but the *Weltanschauung* deemed infallible.[59] According to Baeumler, moreover, the Nazi "feels himself as the soldier of a concretely materialized idea, a historical mission."[60] Finally, it is in Carl Schmitt's "doctrine of a threefold partition of political unity" where "*State, Movement, and People* [Staat, Bewegung, Volk] form the new trinitarian totality of the Nation" that Kolnai rightly saw one of the most advanced conceptions of the totalitarian state.[61]

In short, Kolnai's work can help us maintain a rigorous critical use of the terminology of the Nazi worldview. This, in my view, is more useful to the historian and the philosopher than the dubious attempts at drawing essentialized categories meant to characterize such a political regime, as Arendt has done. It is an indubitable fact that between 1932 and 1935 such notions as *totale Staat* (Schmitt, Forsthoff), *totale völkische* [racialist] *Staat* (Huber), or *Führerstaat* (Hitler, Heidegger, etc.) were instrumental to the *Selbstbehauptung* [self-affirmation] of National Socialism's political and existential domination. As Ernst Forsthoff himself admitted in a letter to Jean-Pierre Faye, while the phrase *totale Staat* was able to take shape through "conceptual means that go back to Hegel," the notion of *völkische Staat* pertains to a totally different tradition or at least interpretation

---

57. Ibid., 159–68.
58. Ibid., 163.
59. Ibid., 165.
60. Ibid., 166 (quoting Baeumler).
61. Ibid (italics original). For additional study of Schmitt's political theology, see Oren Gross's contribution to this volume, "Hitler's Willing Law Professors."

of *Volksgeist* [people's spirit]—one that is no longer Hegelian.[62] It is thus inaccurate to maintain without any nuances, as did Arendt, that the Nazis did not have a philosophy of the state and were aiming at the destruction of the national state. Among other texts, the two seminars delivered by Heidegger in the years 1933–35, recently unearthed, show exactly the opposite.[63] What is true is that after 1935, the emphasis that Nazi rhetoric put on the philosophy of the state would morph into a philosophy of expansion and imperial domination in which the concepts of *Raum* [space], *Macht* [power], and *Vernichtung* would take over. This corresponds to the time when Heidegger's interest shifts from Hegel to Nietzsche.[64] Soon enough, Nazi totalitarianism would no longer be that of the total state but of total war. As early as 1936, when he wrote the first draft of his book, Kolnai had foreseen that evolution. As Raphael Gross has rightly indicated, Kolnai's phenomenological analysis of hatred, the drive that targets the *Vernichtung* of its object, had provided him with a solid conceptual ground to anticipate critically the enacting of the Nazi Weltanschauung.[65] In short, works such as those of Aurel Kolnai or Max Weinreich are more enlightening than *The Origins of Totalitarianism* for understanding the fascination that National Socialism was able to exert on so many minds, and more helpful in supplying the critical means necessary to resist any return of that fascination.[66]

---

62. Ernst Forsthoff, letter to Jean-Pierre Faye, August 31, 1963, quoted in Jean-Pierre Faye, *Théorie du récit: Introduction aux Langages Totalitaires* (Paris: Hermann, 1972), 49.

63. See Emmanuel Faye, *Heidegger: Introduction of Nazism into Philosophy*, chapters 5 and 8.

64. In his seminar on Hegel and the state during the winter of 1934–35, Heidegger presents Hegel as the one who leads Western philosophy to its conclusion and Nietzsche not as a philosopher but as a "man without category" (see Faye, *Heidegger: Introduction of Nazism into Philosophy*, 213). In his courses on Friedrich Nietzsche that begin in 1936, however, he presents Nietzsche in turn as the one who concludes metaphysics.

65. Raphael Gross, "Hass auf den Westen: Warum wir Aurel Kolnai wieder lesen sollten," *Frankfurter Allgemeine Zeitung*, February 20, 2009, 35. Furthermore, an anthology of the writings of Kolnai that engages our purposes has recently appeared as *Politics, Values, and National-Socialism*, ed. Graham McAleer, trans. Francis Dunlop (Piscataway, NJ: Transaction Publishers, 2013).

66. This essay revises the introduction to Emmanuel Faye, *Arendt et Heidegger: Extermination nazie et destruction de la pensée* (Paris: Albin Michel, 2016). An earlier version had been published as "Nationalsozialismus und Totalitarismus bei Hannah Arendt und Aurel Kolnai," in *"Doppelte Vergangenheitsbewältigung" und die Singularität des Holocaust*, ed. Lucia Scherzberg, theologie.geschichte Beihefte 5 (Saarbrücken, Germany: Universaar, 2012), 61–82. I have deliberately refrained from dealing here with secondary literature on Arendt, in order to leave room for a direct confrontation between her approach to Nazism and Kolnai's much more critical approach one. My warmest thanks go to Bruno Chaouat, Michael B. Smith, Justin Buol, and Bernard Levinson for their generous assistance in translating and editing this chapter.

BIBLIOGRAPHY

Archival Sources

Hannah Arendt Papers, General Correspondence (1938–1976), J. Glenn Gray and family (1962–1967). Manuscript Division, Library of Congress, Washington, DC. http://memory.loc.gov/ammem/arendthtml/arendthome.html.

Secondary Sources

Arendt, Hannah. *Denktagebuch: 1950 bis 1973*. Edited by Ursula Ludz and Ingeborg Nordmann. Munich: Piper, 2002.

———. *Eichmann in Jerusalem: A Report on the Banality of Evil*. With an introduction by Amos Elon. New York: Penguin, 2006.

———. *Elemente und Ursprünge totaler Herrschaft: Antisemitismus, Imperialismus, totale Herrschaft*. Munich: Piper, 1986.

———. *Essays in Understanding, 1930–1945: Formation, Exile, and Totalitarianism*. Edited by Jerome Kohn. New York: Harcourt, Brace, 1994.

———. "Martin Heidegger ist achtzig Jahre alt." *Merkur* 23, no. 10 (1969): 893–902. Translated by Albert Hofstadter as "Martin Heidegger at Eighty." *New York Review of Books* 17, no. 6 (October 21, 1971): 50–54.

———. *The Origins of Totalitarianism*. 3rd ed., with new prefaces. New York: Harcourt, Brace, and World, 1966.

Arendt, Hannah, and Martin Heidegger. *Briefe 1925 bis 1975 und andere Zeugnisse*. Edited by Ursula Ludz. 3rd ed. Frankfurt, Germany: Klostermann, 2002.

Arendt, Hannah, and Karl Jaspers. *Briefwechsel 1926–1969*. Edited by Lotte Köhler and Hans Saner. Munich: Piper, 1985. Hannah Arendt and Karl Jaspers, *Correspondence, 1926–1969*, translated into English by Robert Kimber and Rita Kimber, New York: Harcourt, Brace, Jovanovich, 1992.

Bataille, Georges. *Écrits posthumes, 1922–1940*. Vol. 2 of *Œuvres complètes*. Edited by Denis Hollier. Paris: Gallimard, 1970.

Bialas, Wolfgang. *Aurel Kolnais "Krieg gegen den Westen": Eine Debatte*. Berichte und Studien 74. Göttingen, Germany: Vandenhoeck & Ruprecht, 2018.

Clauss, Ludwig Ferdinand. *Von Seele und Antlitz der Rassen und Völker: Eine Einführung in die vergleichende Ausdrucksforschung*. Munich: J. F. Lehmann, 1929.

Domarus, Max, ed. *Hitler: Reden und Proklamationen, 1932–1945*. Vol. 1. Neustadt an der Aisch, Germany: Schmidt, 1962. Translated by Mary Fran Gilbert as *Hitler: Speeches and Proclamations, 1932–1945: The Chronicle of a Dictatorship*. Vol. 1. Wauconda, IL: Bolchazy-Carducci, 1990.

Droit, Roger-Pol. *La compagnie des contemporains: Recontres avec des penseurs d'aujourd'hui*. Paris: Odile Jacob, 2002.

Dunlop, Francis. *The Life and Thought of Aurel Kolnai*. Aldershot, UK: Ashgate, 2002.

Faye, Emmanuel. *Arendt et Heidegger : Extermination nazie et destruction de la pensée.* Paris: Albin Michel, 2016.

———. "Being, History, Technology, and Extermination in the Work of Heidegger." *Journal of the History of Philosophy* 50, no. 1 (2012): 111–30.

———. "Eric Voegelins Haltung zum Nationalsozialismus: Überlegungen zum Briefwechsel Krieck-Voegelin (1933–1934)." In *"Politisierung der Wissenschaft": Jüdische Wissenschaftler und ihre Gegner an der Universität Frankfurt am Main vor und nach 1933*, edited by Moritz Epple, Johannes Fried, Raphael Gross, and Janus Gudian, 111–46. Schriftenreihe des Frankfurter Universitätsarchivs 5. Göttingen, Germany: Wallstein, 2016.

———. "Heidegger, der Nationalsozialismus, und die Zerstörung der Philosophie." In *Politische Unschuld? In Sachen Martin Heidegger*, edited by Bernhard H. F. Taureck, 45–80. Munich: Wilhem Fink, 2008.

———. *Heidegger: The Introduction of Nazism into Philosophy in Light of the Unpublished Seminars of 1933–1935.* Translated by Michael B. Smith. New Haven, CT: Yale University Press, 2009.

———. "Nationalsozialismus und Totalitarismus bei Hannah Arendt und Aurel Kolnai." In *"Doppelte Vergangenheitsbewältigung" und die Singularität des Holocaust*, edited by Lucia Scherzberg, 61–82. Theologie.geschichte Beihefte 5. Saarbrücken, Germany: Universaar, 2012.

Faye, Jean-Pierre. *Théorie du récit: Introduction aux Langages Totalitaires.* Paris: Hermann, 1972.

Forsthoff, Ernst. *Der Totale Staat.* Hamburg, Germany: Hanseatische Verlagsanstalt, 1933.

Forsthoff, Ernst, and Carl Schmitt. *Briefwechsel Ernst Forsthoff Carl Schmitt (1926–1974).* Edited by Dorothee Mußgnug, Reinhard Mußgnug, and Angela Reinthal. Berlin: Akademie, 2007.

Frank, Hans. *Nationalsozialistische Leitsätze für ein neues deutsches Strafrecht.* Berlin: Ludwig Fischer, 1936.

Gross, Raphael. "Hass auf den Westen: Warum wir Aurel Kolnai wieder lesen sollten." *Frankfurter Allgemeine Zeitung*, February 20, 2009, 35.

Habermas, Jürgen. "Mit Heidegger gegen Heidegger denken: Zur Veröffentlichung von Vorlesungen aus dem Jahre 1935." *Frankfurter Allgemeine Zeitung*, July 25, 1953. Translated by William S. Lewis as "Martin Heidegger: On the Publication of the Lectures of 1935." In *The Heidegger Controversy: A Critical Reader*, edited by Richard Wolin, 190–97. Cambridge, MA: MIT Press, 1992.

Heidegger, Martin. "Die Selbstbehauptung der deutschen Universität." In *Reden und andere Zeugnisse eines Lebensweges (1910–1976)*, edited by Hermann Heidegger, 107–17. Martin Heidegger Gesamtausgabe 16. Frankfurt, Germany: Klostermann, 2000.

———. *Einführung in die Metaphysik.* Tübingen, Germany: Max Niemeyer, 1953.

———. *Introduction to Metaphysics*. Translated by Gregory Fried and Richard Polt. New Haven, CT: Yale University Press, 2000.

———. *"Mein Liebes Seelchen!" Briefe Martin Heideggers an seine Frau Elfride, 1915–1970*. Edited by Gertrud Heidegger. Munich: Deutsche Verlags-Anstalt, 2005. Translated by Rupert Glasgow as *Letters to His Wife, 1915–1970*. Malden, MA: Polity, 2008.

———. *Nietzsche: Der europäische Nihilismus*. Edited by Petra Jaeger. Martin Heidegger Gesamtausgabe 48. Frankfurt, Germany: Klostermann, 1986.

———. *Sein und Wahrheit*. Edited by Hartmut Tietjen. Martin Heidegger Gesamtausgabe 36/37. Frankfurt, Germany: Klostermann, 2001.

———. "'Über Wesen und Begriff von Natur, Geschichte, und Staat': Übung aus dem Wintersemester 1933/34." In *Heidegger und der Nationalsozialismus I: Dokumente*, edited by Alfred Denker and Holger Zaborowski, 53–88. Heidegger-Jahrbuch 4. Freiburg: Alber, 2009. Translated as *Nature, History, State: 1933–1934*. Translated and edited by Gregory Fried and Richard Polt. London: Bloomsbury, 2013.

Huber, Ernst Rudolf. "Die totalität des völkischen Staates." *Die Tat* 26, no. 1 (1934): 30–42.

Kershaw, Ian. *The Nazi Dictatorship: Problems and Perspectives of Interpretation*. 2nd ed. London: Edward Arnold, 1989.

Kolnai, Aurel. "Der Inhalt der Politik." *Zeitschrift für die gesamte Staatswissenschaft* 94 (1933): 1–38.

———. *Ekel, Hochmut, Haß: Zur Phänomenologie feindlicher Gefühle*. Edited by Axel Honneth. Frankfurt, Germany: Suhrkamp, 2007.

———. *Ethics, Value, and Reality*. With Opening Essays by Bernard Williams, David Wiggins, and Graham McAleer. 2nd ed. Library of Conservative Thought. Piscataway, NJ: Transaction Publishers, 2008. Reprinted, New York: Routledge, 2017.

———. "Konservatives und revolutionäres Ethos." In *Rekonstruktion des Konservatismus*, edited by Gerd-Klaus Kaltenbrunner, 95–136. Freiburg, Germany: Rombach, 1972.

———. *On Disgust*. Edited with an introduction by Barry Smith and Carolyn Korsmeyer. Chicago: Open Court, 2004. Translated as *Le dégoût*. Translated by Olivier Cossé, with a preface by Claire Margat. Paris: Agalma, 1997.

———. *Politics, Values, and National-Socialism*. Edited by Graham McAleer. Translated by Francis Dunlop. Piscataway, NJ: Transaction Publishers, 2013.

———. *Political Memoirs*. Edited by Francesca Murphy. Lanham, MD: Lexington Books, 1999.

———. *The War against the West*. London: Victor Gollancz; New York: Viking, 1938. Translated into German as *Der Krieg gegen den Westen*. Edited by Wolfgang Bialas. Göttingen, Germany: Vandenhoeck & Ruprecht, 2015.

———. [Dr. A. van Helsing, pseud.] "Heidegger und der Nationalsozialismus." *Der christliche Ständestaat: Österreichische Wochenhefte* 1, no. 28 (June 17, 1934): 5–7.
Marten, Rainer. "Ein rassistisches Konzept von Humanität." *Badische Zeitung*, December 19–20, 1987, 14.
Michaelis, Meir. "Anmerkungen zum italienischen Totalitarismusbegriff: Zur Kritik der Thesen Hannah Arendts und Renzo de Felices." *Quellen und Forschungen aus italienischen Archiven und Bibliotheken* 62 (1982): 270–302.
Plato, *Republic, Books 6–10*, translated into English and edited by Chris Emlyn-Jones and William Preddy, Loeb Classical Library 276, Cambridge, MA: Harvard University Press, 2013.
Popper, Karl. *The Open Society and Its Enemies*. London: Routledge, 2002.
Rentsch, Thomas. *Martin Heidegger: Das Sein und der Tod; Eine kritische Einführung*. Munich: Piper, 1989.
Schmitt, Carl. "Die Wendung zum totalen Staat." *Europäische Revue* 7, no. 4 (1931): 241–50.
———. *Staat, Bewegung, Volk: Die Dreigliederung der politischen Einheit*. Hamburg, Germany: Hanseatische Verlagsanstalt, 1933.
Steinweis, Alan E. *Studying the Jew: Scholarly Antisemitism in Nazi Germany*. Cambridge, MA: Harvard University Press, 2008.
Taminiaux, Jacques. *The Thracian Maid and the Professional Thinker: Arendt and Heidegger*. Translated and edited by Michael Gendre. Albany, NY: SUNY Press, 1997.
Voegelin, Eric. "The Origins of Totalitarianism." *Review of Politics* 15, no. 1 (1953): 68–85.
———. *Race and State*. Edited by Klaus Vondung. Translated by Ruth Hein. The Collected Works of Eric Voegelin 2. Baton Rouge: Louisiana State University Press, 1997. Originally published in German as *Rasse und Staat*. Tübingen, Germany: Mohr, 1933.
Wasserstein, Bernard. "Blame the Victim—Hannah Arendt among the Nazis: The Historian and Her Sources." *Times Literary Supplement*, October 9, 2009, 13–15.
Wasserstein, Bernard, Dirk De Schutter, Remi Peeters, and Irving Louis Horowitz. *Hannah Arendt en de geschiedschrijving: Een controverse*. Edited by Joos van Vugt. Nijmegen, Netherlands: Damon, 2010.
Weinreich, Max. *Hitler's Professors: The Part of Scholarship in Germany's Crimes against the Jewish People*. New York: Yiddish Scientific Institute (YIVO), 1946. Reprinted with a foreword by Martin Gilbert. New Haven, CT: Yale University Press, 1999.
Woessner, Martin. *Heidegger in America*. New York: Cambridge University Press, 2011.

EMMANUEL FAYE is Professor of Modern and Contemporary Philosophy at the University of Rouen and has written or edited ten books, including *Heidegger, l'introduction du nazisme dans la philosophie: autour des séminaires inédits de 1933–1935* (Albin Michel, 2005), which has been translated into seven languages and published in English as *Heidegger: The Introduction of Nazism into Philosophy in Light of the Unpublished Seminars of 1933–1935* (Yale, 2009). He has recently published *Arendt et Heidegger: Extermination nazie et destruction de la pensée* (Albin Michel, 2016). He serves on the editorial board of the German open-access journal *theologie.geschichte*.

PART III

NAZI GERMANY AND BEYOND

TWELVE

THE NAZIFICATION AND DENAZIFICATION OF THE UNIVERSITY OF GÖTTINGEN

ROBERT P. ERICKSEN

WHEN ADOLF HITLER ROSE TO power, receiving his appointment as chancellor of Germany on January 30, 1933, professors at German universities had good reason to be concerned. Hitler himself had only the equivalent of an eighth-grade education but quite a high opinion of the insights he claimed to have achieved without benefit of university training. His very appointment thus seemed to violate the level of respect traditionally paid to education within German politics and German culture. Furthermore, Nazi ideology disparaged "ivory tower intellectuals," and it favored action over thought. Professors also had every right to be worried about the radical rightwing politics evidenced by their students. Already in 1931, Nazi students won majorities and took over the student government organization, Allgemeiner Studenten-Auschuss (AStA), at more than half of German universities. This allowed them to take over the national German Student Union, Deutsche Studentenschaft (DSt), by July 1931, eighteen months before Hitler took control of the nation. These students then proved themselves very disruptive of academic norms, boycotting lectures and insisting on their right to protect the "purity" of the university against left-wing and Jewish professors.[1]

I will argue that professors at German universities, despite having good reasons to be worried by the rise of Hitler and the Nazi state, simply did not

---

This chapter builds on my book *Complicity in the Holocaust: Churches and Universities in Nazi Germany* (Cambridge: Cambridge University Press, 2012). All translations from the German are mine, unless otherwise noted.

1. Geoffrey Giles, *Students and National Socialism in Germany* (Princeton, NJ: Princeton University Press, 1985), 68–72, and see below.

see as unacceptable the brutal politics and practices and the attack on academic freedom and other humanistic values that we so widely condemn today. German professors had inherited a strong tradition of freedom of research, freedom of ideas, and a collegial form of governance, all of which were anathema to the ideological nature and authoritarian claims of the Nazi state. Yet as a group, these professors quickly showed their approval, rather than disapproval, of Hitler's rise to power. Nazi leaders wanted *Gleichschaltung*, a coordination that would bring all German institutions into line with the Nazi worldview. Within universities, it seems most accurate to describe the subsequent process as one of *Selbstgleichschaltung* [self-coordination]. Despite the worries of pro-Nazi students and the Nazi regime that ivory tower professors would stand in opposition to the Nazi transformation of Germany, they did not. Not wanting to seem out of step with the new mood of confidence, unity, and excitement in Hitler's Germany, professors proved eager to coordinate themselves with Nazi ideology. If we accept that academic freedom, freedom of ideas, and freedom of research are significant humanistic values, nazification of German universities represents a betrayal of these values.

I begin this chapter with the period before 1933, when certain indicators already suggested that Hitler's politics would find approval within the academy. I then note the first months of the Nazi era, when professors quickly accepted the politicization of German universities, including a purge of professors with a Jewish background or leftist political views, and an ongoing, dramatic disruption in terms of hiring policies and curriculum. This is when a willingness to betray humanistic values comes clearly into view. Very few professors showed any sign of resistance to Nazi ideas; rather, the majority accepted and advocated a deep-seated and widespread nazification of their work. Once German universities had been transformed in this manner, little stood in the way of full cooperation with the regime by professors, whether in the late 1930s or throughout the period of World War II and the Holocaust.

I next move to the early postwar period, using the mirror of denazification to reflect on academic issues and academic behavior during the Nazi period. "Denazification" was a postwar attempt to cleanse Germany of Nazi ideas and practices, insisted on by the victorious Allies and focusing on all professions and occupations considered important in German society. Any job with public significance—from police work or politics to leadership within industry—required individuals to pass through an investigation. University professors, as teachers of the next generation, could not escape this scrutiny. First, all universities were closed, and professors considered the most committed to Nazism were dismissed immediately. Then, all professors had to fill out a *Fragebogen* [questionnaire], testifying to their membership in Nazi organizations, their record of employment, and even their pay level in the period between 1933 and 1945. If this questionnaire showed Nazi connections, individuals had to go through a legal process to try to prove they were not a significant proponent of the Nazi cause. Failing that, they lost—or could not reclaim—their job. Denazification records provide a body of evidence by which we can identify and assess what happened in German universities, including the widespread betrayal of humanistic values within the academy. They also give us insight into the complicated path of Germany's eventually successful transition into the postwar world, with humanistic values once again intact.

All of these claims refer to German universities as a whole in their relationship to the Nazi state. However, Göttingen University will be used as a main source of evidence to substantiate those claims. I use Göttingen in the conviction that it gives us an appropriate window on the behavior of German universities as a group. Göttingen was and is one of the best German universities, widely admired in the United States and in Great Britain as well as in Germany, and marked, for example, by nearly fifty Nobel Prizes accumulated over the years. Important figures such as Arthur Schopenhauer, Max Planck, and Max Weber all studied there, as did Otto von Bismarck. Carl Friedrich Gauss made Göttingen famous for math and physics in the nineteenth century, a tradition continued at the turn of the century by David Hilbert and Felix Klein. In the 1920s, Göttingen was arguably the best place in the world to study physics and math, with present or future Nobel laureates such as James Franck and Max Born on the faculty. The university was strong in many other fields as well.

In addition to its impressive academic credentials, Göttingen University has a special place in the history of humanistic education. It was founded in 1737 by the local head of the Hanoverian state at the time, King George II of England.[2] Acting in response to the Enlightenment, he wanted scholars at Göttingen to exercise academic freedom, push the boundaries of knowledge, and foster humanistic values. One century later, the political atmosphere changed, and seven professors at Göttingen, the famous "Göttingen Seven," rose up in protest. This part of the story begins with King William IV of England. Acting in the nineteenth-century spirit of reform and on the heels of the Reform Act of 1832 in England, he introduced a liberal constitution for his Kingdom of

---

2. When George I was crowned king of England in 1714, it was because he was the closest heir to Queen Anne not of the Catholic faith. He and his heirs in the House of Hanover united their duchy (later kingdom) in Germany with their Kingdom of England and Ireland for more than a century.

Hanover. Upon his death in 1837, Hanoverian law did not allow a woman, specifically the newly crowned Queen Victoria, to serve as monarch. Therefore, William IV's brother, Ernest Augustus, became King of Hanover.[3] Holding a more authoritarian view than William, he chose to abolish the constitution, rescinding its rights for citizens and its limitations upon the power of the king. Friedrich Christoph Dahlmann, a Göttingen historian, responded to this act by composing a protest petition. The brothers Grimm and four other professors at the university added their signatures, and all seven were quickly dismissed. Dahlmann and two others of the seven were also sent into exile. Students at Göttingen reacted by printing numerous copies of this petition and spreading it throughout Germany. The Göttingen Seven thus earned widespread fame and admiration. They continue to represent one of the most famous examples of civil courage in the face of political repression in European history, at least within the academy. This chapter, by contrast, describes circumstances a century later, in which academics at Göttingen and elsewhere in Germany failed to follow their example.

I. PRE-1933 INDICATORS

Achim Gercke, a chemistry student at Göttingen University, gives us an early example of pro-Nazi student activism. He established already in 1925 an "Archive for Racial Statistics by Profession." Supported by the local Nazi *Gauleiter*,[4] as well as by an Honorary Professor of History and open antisemite, Hugo Willrich,[5] Gercke and his fellow students gained free access to a treasure trove of documents collected in the basement of the Göttingen University

---

3. In 1837, Victoria, daughter of the fourth son of George III, succeeded her uncle, William IV, third son to George III, and ascended the throne of England. However, Salic Law applicable in Hanover did not allow a female ruler. Therefore, George III's fifth son, Ernest Augustus, became king of Hanover, and the long-standing legal connection between Great Britain and Hanover disappeared.

4. *Gauleiter* was an organizational term developed by the Nazi Party in an attempt to suggest its deep roots in the German past. Each Gauleiter was the Nazi Party leader of a *Gau*, a traditional, medieval term for individual regions.

5. Hugo Willrich, a *Privatdozent* at Göttingen since 1896 and Honorary Professor in ancient history since 1917, clearly indicates his hostile attitude toward Jews and portrays his "scholarly" method by this comment in his first publication: "With Jewish literature, one must never forget that almost always the main objective . . . is to create a positive view of Jewishness." And then he adds, "It is an old fact that the most stupid person can stay with the truth, but a successful lie requires a certain cleverness in order not to get caught in contradiction. Fortunately, almost none of the Hellenistic Jews had this cleverness;

Library. Examining Abitur records for those entering university and curriculum vitae for all those completing a doctorate, they created a card file system to track individual connections to Jews or Judaism. Their goal was to identify all professors who were Jewish, who were married to Jews, or who were connected to Jews in order to protect Germany from the alleged Jewish menace of the antisemitic imagination. Gercke's archival group eventually published eight small books, focusing on the Universities of Göttingen, Berlin, Königsberg, and Breslau.[6] Gercke later took his records, methods, expertise, and anti-Jewish animus to Nazi headquarters—the "Brown House" in Munich—where he served as head of racial statistics from 1931 to 1933. There he checked on and disproved the rumor that Reinhard Heydrich, head of the Sicherheitsdienst [Security Service (SD)] of the Schutzstaffel (SS), had been born to a Jewish father. He also confirmed the charge of Jewish "taint" that then destroyed the career of Heinrich Düsterberg, a leading figure in the right-wing and antisemitic veterans' organization, the *Stahlhelm*. From 1933 to 1935, he served as a racial expert in the Ministry of the Interior in Berlin.[7]

---

they betray themselves very quickly." See Hugo Willrich, *Juden und Griechen vor der makkabäischen Erhebung* (Göttingen, Germany: Vandenhoeck & Ruprecht, 1895), ii, vii–viii. After World War I, Willrich became founder and leader of the "Deutschvölkischen Schutz- und Trutzbund" [German Nationalist Protection and Defiance Federation] in Göttingen, a predecessor to the Nationalsozialistische Deutsche Arbeiterpartei [National Socialist German Workers' Party, or NSDAP]. See Robert P. Ericksen, "Kontinuitäten konservativer Geschichtsschreibung am Seminar für Mittlere und Neuere Geschichte: Von der Weimarer Zeit über die nationalsozialistische Ära bis in die Bundesrepublik," in *Die Universität Göttingen unter dem Nationalsozialismus: Das verdrängte Kapitel ihrer 250jährigen Geschichte*, ed. Heinrich Becker, Hans-Joachim Dahms, and Cornelia Wegeler, 2nd ed. (Munich: K G. Saur, 1998), 427–53 (at 431–34).

6. See, for example, [Achim Gercke,] *Der jüdische Einfluss auf den Deutschen Hohen Schulen: Ein Familienkundlicher Nachweis über die jüdischen und verjudeten Universitäts- und Hochschulprofessoren*, Heft 1, Universität Göttingen (Göttingen, Germany: Kreis der Freunde und Förderer der Deutschen Auskunftei, 1928). The "Archiv für berrufsständische Rassenstatistik," created by Achim Gercke, produced these books. However, no author is listed on the title page. That might be because in the mid-1920s Nazi students such as Gercke worried about keeping their activities secret from the "Novembersystem" (their derogatory name for the Weimar Republic, emphasizing its revolutionary origins in November 1918). See Hans-Joachim Dahms, "Einleitung," in Becker, Dahms, and Wegeler, *Universität Göttingen*, 31.

7. See Ericksen, *Complicity in the Holocaust*, 75–76. See also Dahms, "Einleitung," 31–32 and 39. I am further indebted to Dahms for the opportunity to view his unpublished manuscript, "The Professionalization of National Socialist Jewish Statistics: Preparation for the Holocaust."

Gercke began with the goal of identifying Jewish professors. The next step for him and other Nazi students was to try to get rid of unwelcome professors by boycotting their classes or loudly demonstrating outside their lecture rooms. One early story involves Emil Gumbel at the University of Heidelberg. In 1925, he made a seemingly disparaging comment regarding German soldiers in the Great War: "I do not actually mean to say that they fell on the field of dishonor; yet they lost their lives in a dreadful way."[8] Despite his half-hearted attempt to avoid the word *dishonor*, right-wing students and faculty saw only treasonous disrespect in Gumbel's stance. As a result, he suffered a temporary ban on his teaching. He then remained a lightning rod for controversy for the next six years, since he was not only a socialist and pacifist but also Jewish. Nationalistic and antisemitic critics maintained their attack until Gumbel suffered permanent removal from the faculty in 1932, a year before Hitler's rise to power.[9]

The Göttingen historian Paul Darmstädter experienced a somewhat similar fate, also before 1933, though the circumstances were more subtle. In 1921, Darmstädter got into a public quarrel with Hugo Willrich, the Honorary Professor who later supported the antisemitic activities of Achim Gercke. Willrich did not like Darmstädter, finding both his Jewish background and his prodemocratic, left-wing politics reprehensible. He also must have resented Darmstädter having a chair in history, since Willrich held only an honorary position and had to maintain a day job teaching at a gymnasium. He saw his chance for an attack when an anonymous letter appeared in the *Frankfurter Zeitung*.[10] This letter complained about two antidemocratic, German nationalist professors recently appointed to the Göttingen Faculty of History. The letter writer argued that this replicated practices under the authoritarian kaiser, despite the newly democratic auspices of the Weimar Republic. Willrich wrote to the local newspaper in Göttingen, attacking that anonymous letter and strongly implying that Darmstädter must have written it. He then described this "fervently democratic" individual, the probable author, as having tried to evade military service during World War I. Worse yet, that unwilling soldier further

---

8. Quoted in Fritz K. Ringer, *The Decline of the German Mandarins: The German Academic Community, 1890–1933* (Cambridge, MA: Harvard University Press, 1969), 219.

9. See Steven P. Remy, *The Heidelberg Myth: The Nazification and Denazification of a German University* (Cambridge, MA: Harvard University Press, 2002), 10–11, 235–36.

10. "Bemerkungen," *Frankfurter Zeitung und Handelsblatt*, 65, 276 (April 15, 1921), 1. A clipping of this letter (published on the first page of the paper) can also be found in the Göttingen University Archive (hereafter cited as GUA) Phil.Fak.II Ph Nr. 49, "Angelegenheit Darmstädter-Willrich."

dishonored himself by declaring his support for the postwar republic before being released from his service oath to the kaiser.[11]

Darmstädter, recognizing himself as the obvious target of Willrich's letter, angrily approached his dean, demanding support. He denied having had anything to do with the original letter to the *Frankfurter Zeitung*. He also denied having tried to evade military service, having requested only to finish his semester of teaching; and he explained that his support for the democratic republic came nine days after the kaiser had fled the country, which Darmstädter considered an "adequate release" from his oath of loyalty. He thought Willrich should be forced to retract his letter and that his faculty colleagues should publish a letter in his defense. None of this happened. Willrich refused to withdraw, and Darmstädter's dean and colleagues advised him just to let the affair die down.[12]

This unsatisfactory outcome of his quarrel with Willrich must have confirmed for Darmstädter his sense of being an outsider within his department, both as a Jew and as someone on the political left. Willrich had specifically attacked Darmstädter, even if anonymously, for being "fervently democratic"; for being a coward, allegedly trying to evade military service; and for being disloyal, violating his oath to the kaiser. Willrich never attributed Jewishness to the unnamed subject of his attack. However, Willrich's accusations perfectly matched the right-wing, stab-in-the-back legend that rose up in the 1920s, blaming internal enemies—especially Jews and leftists—for weakening Germany during the war and thus being the cause of Germany's defeat. Willrich's antisemitism was well known in Göttingen, and even if coded, his message—that the coward who had tried to evade military service and turned his back on the kaiser must also have been a Jew—would likely have been apparent to many.[13]

Further evidence for Darmstädter's outsider status came in 1928, when he was listed in the book on Jewish professors at Göttingen published by Achim

---

11. Hugo Willrich, "Ein demokratischer Willkommensgruss für unsere neu berufenen Historiker," *Göttinger Tageblatt*, April 20, 1921, 3. A clipping of this letter can also be found in Phil.Fak.II Ph Nr. 49, GUA.

12. See letters between Darmstädter and Dean Sethe, April 21 and 22 and May 3 and 4, 1921, in Phil.Fak.II Ph Nr. 49, GUA. See Robert P. Ericksen, "Kontinuitäten konservativer Geschichtsschreibung," 224–25.

13. The stab-in-the-back legend has been thoroughly discredited. It had a wonderful attraction for patriotic Germans who did not want to think that real Germans would have been so weak as to lose the war. However, all evidence points to exhaustion and collapse in Germany's military effort by October 1918. As for leftists and Jews, the SPD [Social Democratic Party of Germany] voted war credits in support of the war, and Jews volunteered for service at numbers above their percentage of the population.

Gercke's "Archive for Racial Statistics by Profession."[14] Gercke intended that book to highlight what he considered the problem of Jews in the German academy, and Darmstädter certainly would have seen this as a barely veiled threat. University records do not tell us more about his sense of identity or the extent to which he saw either his Jewishness or his left-wing politics as a source of vulnerability. They do show, however, that his career came to an odd end. In early October 1931, Darmstädter wrote to the Faculty of Philosophy from Switzerland, complaining of ill health and requesting an early retirement on medical grounds.[15] The outcome of this request gives us a last hint at Darmstädter's outsider status as a professor of Jewish background with prodemocratic political views in pre-Nazi Germany. When asked for evidence, he provided a medical diagnosis of arteriosclerosis as well as a doctor's recommendation that he stay in the salubrious climate of Switzerland.[16] Despite that, the Prussian Ministry of Education would only agree to accept his resignation, not his medical retirement. He would have to give up any claim to further remuneration, benefits, or a pension: the sort of retirement arrangements anyone in his position would have expected. After twenty-four years at Göttingen, eleven as a tenured professor, Darmstäder must have considered this an almost unimaginable slight, but he signed the papers. Nothing further in Darmstädter's personnel file clarifies these odd circumstances or helps overcome the suspicion that a harsh atmosphere of antisemitism played a role. If the Ministry of Education thought Darmstädter was exaggerating his ill health, he at least proved that wrong. He died in June 1934, just over two years after signing away his rights as a civil servant.[17]

Günther Dehn provides another and less subtle example of discrimination against left-wing academics before Hitler's rise to power. He received two formal offers of a professorship in practical theology, the first from Ruprecht Karls University of Heidelberg in 1930 and the second from the University of Halle in 1931. German academic appointment procedures allow the recipient of a formal offer an extended time to negotiate. While Dehn pondered his choice, right-wing critics turned his offer of appointment into a very public controversy. Dehn had no Jewish background and thus did not suffer from

---

14. [Gercke], *Jüdische Einfluss auf den deutschen Hohen Schulen*, 8.

15. Darmstädter to Phil. Fak., October 2, 1931, in Personalakten Darmstädter, GUA.

16. Ärztliches Attest von Dr. L. Mechaud, March 15, 1932, in Personalakten Darmstädter, GUA.

17. Minister für Wissenschaft to Darmstädter, September 8, 1932, in Personalakten Darmstädter, GUA.

antisemitic prejudice, as did both Gumbel and Darmstädter, but he was clearly on the political left, supporting the democratic Weimar Republic and questioning the traditional, authoritarian conservatism and widespread hypernationalism to be found in both church and university. One talk Dehn gave in 1928 in Magdeburg questioned whether dead soldiers should be celebrated in churches as if they were Christian martyrs. This proved his undoing. An angry woman yelled at Dehn afterward, "If the fallen cannot be honored with plaques in churches, then they might be seen as merely murderers."[18] These were not Dehn's words, but he was soon castigated by right-wing students and the right-wing press as if they were. As the Heidelberg Faculty of Theology contemplated its offer to Dehn, Nazi students attacked him for having tarnished the reputation of German soldiers, and Gottfried Traub, editor of the right-wing *Eisernen Blätter*, spread among his readership of students and others the "murderers" charge. Dehn, with the luxury of an offer from Halle, told the Heidelberg Faculty of his preference to join them. However, he asked for a vote of confidence from Heidelberg, given the right-wing campaign against him, before he rejected his second offer. Six of seven theology professors at Heidelberg, alarmed by the threat of student unrest, refused his request, so Dehn opted for Halle.[19]

By the time of Dehn's first lecture at Halle in November 1931, he had received the full support of his rector and the faculty senate, despite student unrest. However, Nazi students were undeterred:

> We will categorically reject with the most complete, elemental, and forceful outrage of which German youth is capable any teacher or leader ... who does not clearly and unconditionally advocate a national strengthening and renewal.... How can German students relate to a man who, according to his words and his fundamental stance, has rendered homage to pacifist and Marxist ideas, even if he is not happy today admitting that? ... [U]nder cover of academic freedom one may not deprecate things to which millions of people are devoted with their entire hearts.[20]

---

18. This comment is recorded by Günther Dehn in his memoir, *Die alte Zeit, die vorigen Jahre: Lebenserrinerungen* (Munich: Chr. Kaiser, 1962), 256.

19. See my treatment in *Complicity*, 76–84. See also Dehn, *Die alte Zeit*, 250–61. Dehn's extensive documentation of the Halle conflict is found in his *Kirche und Völkerversöhnung: Dokumente zum Halleschen Universitätskonflikt* (Berlin: Furche, 1931), and the story of Dehn is recounted in Ernst Bizer, "Der Fall Dehn," in *Festschrift für Günther Dehn*, ed. Wilhelm Schneemelcher (Neukirchen: Neukirchener Verlag, 1957), 239–61.

20. Quoted in Bizer, "Der Fall Dehn," 250.

Angry students filled the room at Dehn's first lecture and made so much noise he could not be heard. Additional students made a commotion outside the lecture hall, singing the Deutschlandlied [the German national anthem] and chanting slogans. They finally burst through the barred door, and Dehn had to be escorted home by police. The next day, Dehn rescheduled his lecture for the evening, thinking fewer students would choose to attend; but once again loud crowds caused chaos and police arrived with rubber truncheons. Two weeks later, students from Halle were joined by others from Leipzig and Jena, so that a group of two thousand students staged an anti-Dehn rally. Though Dehn persevered through that academic year, by the summer of 1932, he was forced by his superiors to take a one-year research leave. They apparently hoped that opposition would quiet down, but instead, Hitler came to power. Dehn never returned to a classroom until after the Third Reich had met its end.[21]

All of this right-wing activity on campuses prior to 1933, especially by students, suggested that Hitler and the Nazi movement would not be a friend to academia and its basic values. Nazi students flexed their muscles already in 1931, denying the principles of academic freedom and hoping to enforce a campus atmosphere of antisemitism, right-wing politics, and hypernationalism. Students may have set the early tone of agitation and brutality, but professors and university administrators also played a role. When Gumbel suffered removal from the faculty at Heidelberg in 1932, he had failed to receive the support of his faculty colleagues, and university administrators processed his removal. When Darmstädter came under attack from his antisemitic and hypernationalistic colleague Willrich, his dean and other colleagues at Göttingen refused his request for support. Later, the Ministry of Education rejected his seemingly legitimate request for an honorable medical retirement and forced him to give up all his accumulated rights and resign instead. He too was gone by 1932. When Günther Dehn came under right-wing attack in 1931, the Faculty of Theology at Heidelberg refused to accept his request for a vote of confidence. At Halle, university administrators and the local police tried to protect Dehn during 1931–32, his first academic year. By the end of that year, however, radical Nazi students had won the day, silencing a voice they did not want to hear. Dehn was forced into a leave of absence in 1932, followed by a formal dismissal the following year.

Even before the Nazi rise to power, therefore, academic freedom and humane values came under attack at German universities. Despite their longstanding tradition of academic freedom, their defense of intellectual inquiry,

---

21. Ericksen, *Complicity*, 81–84.

and their support of humanistic values, German universities learned to tolerate significant political interference in their work. Student agitation, faculty removals, and university acquiescence, even before 1933, hint at the horror, or at least the disappointment, underlying the title of this book, *Betrayal of the Humanities*. In 1933, with Hitler's surging popularity and a widespread spirit of national renewal, politicization of universities and betrayal of the humanities became the norm.

II. EARLY NAZI VIOLATIONS OF THE ACADEMY

Two episodes in the first four months of Hitler's rule help illustrate the Nazi violation of academic values. They also prefigure forms of betrayal within the academy yet to come. The first of these episodes involved a new law passed in April 1933: the Law for the Restoration of the Professional Civil Service. This law, whereby the Nazis thought they were "cleansing" the Civil Service, resulted in the wholesale purging of Jews and leftists from the university. Günther Dehn was fired.[22] The more famous Paul Tillich was fired, leading to the American phase of his career at Union Theological Seminary, Harvard, and the University of Chicago.[23] Dehn and Tillich were dismissed because of their politics. Jews, by contrast, were dismissed for being Jewish. In fact, Jews were dismissed for having Jewish forebears, no matter what their sense of identity might have been. This represented the Nazi version of antisemitism, in which Jewishness was considered racial, not religious or cultural, which therefore also made it immutable. The "Jewish Paragraph" in the law of 1933 did allow some exceptions in terms of dismissal. Jews who had served in World War I or those whose civil service appointment had preceded the Weimar Republic would not lose their jobs at this point, though that exception disappeared by 1935.[24]

The case of James Franck, a Nobel Prize–winning physicist at Göttingen, illustrates an early disappointment for any who might have hoped that German professors would stand up against Nazi violation of academic values and practices. Franck had served Germany in World War I. This meant that, despite

---

22. Bizer, "Der Fall Dehn," 261.
23. See, for example, Wilhelm Pauck and Marian Pauck, *Paul Tillich: His Life and Thought*, vol. 1: *Life* (New York: Harper and Row, 1976).
24. The reference to appointments before the Weimar Republic represented the right-wing belief that the "cleansing" of the civil service especially involved removing individuals appointed under Weimar. It was thought that Weimar had corrupted the process, with people appointed only for their politics rather than their credentials. In fact, virtually no examples of that sort of corruption could be found for the Weimar period. Ironically, however, politicized appointments occurred quite often in the Nazi period, as indicated later in this

his Jewish forebears, he would not have been removed from his professorship in 1933. However, he resigned his position at Göttingen, hoping to use his stature and example to generate a collective protest against the academic purge of Jews and leftists precipitated by the new Civil Service Law. Franck sent a letter to the local newspaper, announcing his resignation and thinking he could inspire colleagues to rise up with him. Instead, however, he prompted a reaction of a very different sort. In the immediate aftermath of his Friday letter, in the course of only one weekend, forty-two of his colleagues signed a letter labeling him a traitor to Germany. These forty-two signatures represented approximately 20 percent of the teaching faculty at Göttingen. Their letter not only condemned Franck's behavior but also called for an "accelerated cleansing" of the university.[25] The failed protest by someone as prominent as James Franck gives this Göttingen example an unusually high profile. However, the end result at Göttingen proved the norm throughout Germany. Faculty at German universities simply did not protest the purging of 15–25 percent of their colleagues—a purge based entirely on Nazi views of race and politics—despite this attack on tenure and on academic freedom.[26]

A second alarming event occurred on May 10, 1933, when great mounds of books went up in flames at universities across Germany. Twenty thousand books were burned that day on the square of the Deutsche Staatsoper [German State Opera] in Berlin, directly across Unter den Linden from the Humboldt University of Berlin. An additional two thousand to three thousand books were burned on or near each of the other university campuses in Germany.[27] Students participated enthusiastically across the nation. "Black Lists" were

---

chapter. It should be added that these two qualifications—for war veterans and for older civil servants—came about at the instigation of President von Hindenburg. He died in August 1934, and in 1935, the exceptions he had requested disappeared. All Jews and leftists could then be summarily removed.

25. See Ulf Rosenow, "Die Göttinger Physik unter dem Nationalsozialismus," in Becker, Dahms, and Wegeler, *Universität Göttingen*, especially 555–58. See also Dahms, "Einleitung," in the same volume, 41–45. For a description of the April 1933 purging of three world-renowned Jewish mathematicians, Richard Courant, Emmy Noether, and Felix Bernstein, plus the Nobel Prize–winning physicist, Max Born, see Norbert Schappacher, "Das Mathematische Institut der Universität Göttingen," in Becker, Dahms and Wegeler, *Universität Göttingen*, 523–32, and my treatment of these matters in *Complicity*, 85–87.

26. See, for example, Anikó Szabó, *Vertreibung, Rückkehr, Wiedergutmachung: Göttinger Hochschullehrer im Schatten des Nationalsozialismus* (Göttingen, Germany: Wallstein, 2000), especially section 2, "Die nationalsozialistischen Verfolgungen an der Hochschulen," 31–84.

27. These figures are found in Saul Friedländer, *Nazi Germany and the Jews*, vol. 1, *The Years of Persecution, 1933–1939* (New York: HarperCollins, 1997), 57.

circulated to guide them, condemning anything written by a Jew or by those writers out of favor with the regime. Marx, Freud, and Einstein's books were burned. Erich Maria Remarque's *All Quiet on the Western Front* was burned, due to its negative portrayal of German martial valor. Works of the brothers Heinrich Mann and Thomas Mann were burned. Books came from public libraries, lending libraries, private collections, and university libraries. Student leaders organized the bonfires and gave speeches. German professors did not protest this outrage against free ideas and the printed word. Rather, they cheered, they gave patriotic speeches, and they contributed books themselves.[28]

The purging of professors and the burning of books were all part of the Gleichschaltung of German universities mentioned previously, coordination in line with the Nazi worldview. Since *Gleichschaltung* is a term that was employed by the Nazi government, this could easily give the impression that the regime forced these changes on universities. However, much evidence suggests otherwise. Not only did professors fail to protest violations of academic values—the purging of tenured faculty members and burning of tens of thousands of books—but many also openly supported these measures. Famous scholars across Germany, from Martin Heidegger in Freiburg to Eugen Fischer in Berlin, greeted the changes of 1933 and advocated the creation of a "political university," including the active development of politically enthusiastic scholarship.[29] They and their colleagues eagerly worked to align the university with the goals of the Nazi regime. This is why the process of Gleichschaltung is best understood as Selbstgleichschaltung. Coordination in line with the Nazi worldview was not so much forced on German professors and students as willingly taken up in support of the national cause.

Space in this chapter does not allow a full rehearsal of academic cooperation with the Nazi regime throughout its twelve years of brutality and destruction. However, the almost complete lack of opposition and the widespread enthusiasm shown for the rise of Hitler in 1933 proved neither unique nor shortlived. Instead, it was symptomatic. Scholarly study of German universities and

---

28. See Matthew Fishburn, *Burning Books* (New York: Palgrave Macmillan, 2008), and Gerhard Sauder, ed., *Die Bücherverbrennung 10. Mai 1933* (Berlin: Ullstein, 1985).

29. For a recent critical treatment of Martin Heidegger, see Emanuel Faye, *Heidegger: The Introduction of Nazism into Philosophy in Light of the Unpublished Seminars of 1933–1935* (New Haven, CT: Yale University Press, 2009). See also Faye's contribution to this volume, "Political Philosophy: Hannah Arendt and Aurel Kolnai as Interpreters of the Nazi Totalitarian State." For an example of Eugen Fischer's remarkably antisemitic methodology, see Robert P. Ericksen, *Theologians under Hitler: Gerhard Kittel, Paul Althaus, and Emanuel Hirsch* (New Haven, CT: Yale University Press, 1985), 64–66.

academic disciplines has grown significantly within the past three decades and the trajectory seems clear. The more we know, the more we recognize that enthusiasm for Nazi ideas and collaboration in Nazi policies crossed all academic disciplines. We also know that the most active perpetrators of Nazi horrors, including the Holocaust, were among the best educated.[30] Professors proved far more willing to praise than to criticize the new directions undertaken by the Nazi state and far more willing to betray than to stand up for humanistic values.

III. NARROWING OUR GAZE: THE MIRROR OF DENAZIFICATION AT GÖTTINGEN UNIVERSITY

I will now turn to the denazification records of the early postwar period at Göttingen University as a way to reflect back on the politicized university in Nazi Germany. The entire Allied insistence on denazification (as described previously) has long suffered from a very negative reputation. Many or most Germans at the time considered the process far too harsh, with too many people losing their jobs, at least in the short term. Many on the Allied side thought it far too lenient, with enthusiastic Nazis slipping too easily through the net. A book by Lutz Niethammer from 1982 describes denazification as a *Mitläuferfabrik*, a factory in which you fed Nazis in at one end and turned out harmless *Mitläufer* at the other, individuals who went along with Nazi rule but should bear no responsibility for Nazi crimes.[31]

I use denazification and other archival records of a number of German professors to try to establish three things: First of all, these records indicate that universities were heavily politicized in the Nazi period. Contrary to the claims of many postwar Germans, widespread nazification really did take place in Germany, including within academia. Secondly, the denazification process produced a high level of dishonesty and denial among Germans. This almost certainly contributed to the conscious and subconscious repression of memory

---

30. See, for example, Michael Wildt, *An Uncompromising Generation: The Nazi Leadership of the Reich Security Main Office* (Madison: University of Wisconsin Press, 2010).

31. Lutz Niethammer, *Die Mitläuferfabrik: Die Entnazifizierung am Beispiel Bayern* (Berlin: Dietz, 1982). See also, James F. Tent, *Mission on the Rhine: "Reeducation" and Denazification in American-Occupied Germany* (Chicago: University of Chicago Press, 1984), and Remy, *Heidelberg Myth*. For a look at the Soviet sector, see Norman Naimark, *The Russians in Germany: A History of the Soviet Zone of Occupation, 1945–1949* (Cambridge, MA: Harvard University Press, 1995), and for a view of the economic issues, see Rebecca Boehling, *A Question of Priorities: Democratic Reform and Economic Recovery in Postwar Germany* (New York: Berghahn Books, 1996).

and misrepresentation of the past that marked German attitudes toward Nazism and the Holocaust—both public and scholarly—until at least the 1980s. The common German attitude might best be described with the cynical phrase, "I am not the one, Hitler did it."[32] Finally, I argue that the process of denazification did contribute to the remarkable success story that is present-day Germany. Denazification had as its primary goals the cleansing of Nazi ideas from German society and the creation of a democratic state. Those two goals clearly have been achieved. I claim that denazification, despite all criticisms, made a contribution to that happy result.

After the purging of university faculties in April and book burnings in May 1933, there followed an energetic politicization of the hiring process. Prior to the Nazi era, German universities had established a rigorous path for anyone wanting to become a university professor. First one would earn a doctorate. Then one had to research and write a second dissertation on a different topic. Completion of this *Habilitation* allowed one to become a *Privatdozent*. Privatdozenten could teach at a university, but they had neither job security nor decent pay. These individuals tried to build their reputation as scholars and teachers, hoping for appointment as an *Ordinarius*—that is, a full tenured professor with high pay, lifetime security, and considerable prestige. Privatdozenten would apply for open professorships, submitting their academic credentials, the names of referees, and evidence of their scholarly accomplishments. If shortlisted by a faculty committee, a Privatdozent would give a test lecture, hoping for a recommendation by the faculty committee and eventual appointment by the state Ministry of Education. The entire process involved rigorous standards and significant local control.

During the Nazi period, this process changed dramatically, as can be seen with several examples from Göttingen University. After 1933, a man like Walter Birnbaum followed a very different path to his position as ordinarius in the Faculty of Theology at Göttingen. Birnbaum had no habilitation. He had no doctorate. He had no reputation as a scholar. On the one occasion when he pursued a graduate degree, the licentiate (roughly equivalent to a master's degree), he failed the final exam. However, Birnbaum established his *political* credentials by working for the Deutsche Christen [German Christians], an

---

32. "Ich bin's nicht, Hitler hat es getan" is the title of a satirical play written, directed and performed in Berlin by Hermann van Harten in his own small theater, the Freie Theateranstalten. Since the first performance in May 1984, he performed this play in fourteen different versions six nights a week for nearly thirty years. See his website, www.freietheateranstalten-berlin.de.

enthusiastically pro-Nazi faction within the German Protestant Church.[33] This Nazi credential was enough to earn him first a temporary appointment in 1935 and then a permanent appointment the following year. He thus became a full Professor without the normal requirements for such a position and without having to go through the normal search process. Nonetheless, he received all the pay and privileges attached to his professorship.

Eugen Mattiat followed a similarly unconventional path onto the faculty at Göttingen. He was a simple pastor who chose to side with the pro-Nazi Deutsche Christen in 1932. His politics soon brought him an appointment in the bishop's office in Hannover and then a job as the expert on humanities within the Ministry of Education in Berlin. He spent three years overseeing the appointment of professors of humanities at universities across Germany, taking special care, for example, that members of the Deutsche Christen would be appointed to theological faculties—including Walter Birnbaum's appointment at Göttingen.[34] Then he received an appointment himself as a fully tenured professor at Göttingen. This came without benefit of doctorate, habilitation, or scholarly publications and without any sort of search process. The Ministry of Education simply appointed Mattiat professor of German *Volkskunde* [folklore] in the Faculty of Philosophy.[35] This was a discipline that proved popular in Nazi Germany. Since Nazis wanted to worship the German *Volk*, they also wanted an educational process that would highlight the glories of being German.[36]

---

33. For information on the politicized and controversial nature of Birnbaum's appointment from the point of view of the Hanoverian regional church, see files S 1 H II 133 and 133a in the *Landeskirchlichesarchiv* (hereafter cited as LKA) in Hannover. Birnbaum's memoir is also useful. Though argumentative and defensive in places, he describes his career prior to his professorship and his lack of academic credentials quite openly. For example, he notes that when he first learned of his surprising appointment to a provisional professorship in Practical Theology at Göttingen, he had to go to a library and consult a dictionary to learn what the field of practical theology actually involved. See Walter Birnbaum, *Zeuge meiner Zeit: Aussagen zu 1912 bis 1972* (Göttingen, Germany: Musterschmidt, 1973), 210.

34. The denazification judgment against Mattiat in June 1949 indicated that he secured professorial appointments for twenty-three theologians associated with the pro-Nazi Deutsche Christen during his tenure at the Ministry of Education. By 1936, therefore, forty-one of sixty-six professors of theology in Germany sided with the DC. See "Entnazifizierungs-Entscheidung," June 13, 1949, in the file on August-Eugen Mattiat, Nds. 171 Hild., 20039, in the *Niedersächsisches Hauptstaatsarchiv* in Hannover (hereafter cited as NSA). As for Mattiat's role in Birnbaum's appointment at Göttingen, see letters from Emanuel Hirsch, dean of the Göttingen Faculty of Theology, to Eugen Mattiat in the Ministry of Education, May 13, 1935, November 22, 1935, and November 26, 1935, in file 140, Faculty of Theology, in the GUA.

35. See Rolf Wilhelm Brednich, "Volkskunde—Die völkische Wissenschaft von Blut und Boden," in Becker, Dahms, and Wegeler, *Universität Göttingen*, 491–98 (at 492–93).

36. Ibid.

Apparently, Mattiat's love of Germany and love of Hitler implied that he would be prepared to teach German *Volkskunde*. Here is one piece of testimony by a colleague found in Mattiat's denazification file: "It is like this, he placed himself 100% in favor of NS [National Socialism] and was opposed to any concession. He was radically against Jews. According to his view, there were no decent ones among them."[37] This is the sort of thing that made Mattiat politically acceptable. However, his manifest lack of qualification for a professorship meant that he had first to be granted one year of research leave in order to prepare himself. Teaching and scholarship never became meaningful parts of his role at Göttingen. But as someone with the right political convictions, he quickly established himself as one of the most significant professors on campus, becoming within his first year the head of the local National Socialist German Professor's League.[38]

Shortly after the appointment of Mattiat, a position had to be filled in the Faculty of History. The first stages of this hiring process seemed almost normal. A faculty committee vetted possible candidates and shortlisted a group of three. These did not suit Otto Sommer, however, a professor of agriculture who had been recently appointed rector. Sommer wanted candidates with more evidence of passion for the Nazi cause. Under the new Nazi policy of *Führerprinzip* [Führer Principle], in which the rector received a political appointment and no longer served as merely an elected first among equals, Sommer's views prevailed. The faculty committee then selected a new group of three, trying to balance scholarly credibility with evidence of the necessary political enthusiasm.[39] The seemingly strongest candidate in terms of scholarship immediately got struck off the list for inadequate political credentials. However, Walter Hinz, Dean of the Faculty of Philosophy, rejected the other two as well. Though both were members of the Nazi Party, and one was both a Storm Trooper and in the Wehrmacht [the German Army], Hinz apparently thought neither could provide the level of political enthusiasm needed.[40]

---

37. Testimony by Amtsrat Draeger, April 25, 1949, "Anlage," in the Mattiat denazification file, NSA.

38. For these details, see "Das Spruchgericht XII. Spruchkammer. Urteil im Namen des Rechts!" from a hearing on March 16, 1948, in the Mattiat denazification file, NSA.

39. Internal correspondence at Göttingen over vacant positions in history can be found in file R 3205 b, GUA. See also the extensive documentation of these circumstances in the *Personalakten Botzenhart*, GUA.

40. These and other details about the peculiarities of Botzenhart's appointment are taken from a letter by Siegfired Kaehler to the Dean of the Faculty of Philosophy, May 28, 1945, in the *Personalakten Botzenhart*, GUA.

Suddenly a new name appeared on the list, giving a strong indication that political considerations would now take precedence. Erich Botzenhart arrived at Göttingen and gave a lecture on Heinrich Friedrich Karl *Freiherr* vom Stein, a German national hero from the early nineteenth century who had helped drive Napoleon off German soil. As one Göttingen historian, Siegfried Kaehler, commented, "Even for non-historians it was clear that the topic was a very slick attempt to show this [the events of 1806–13] as a prelude to the Revolution of 1933, based upon a complete violation of the historical facts."[41] Prior histories of vom Stein had noted his left-wing side, encouraging political change in Germany that pointed toward a democratic future. In fact, vom Stein hoped that Germany could borrow from the best elements of the French Revolution, but that aspect of the story disappeared entirely in Botzenhart's talk, since the French Revolution was anathema to right-wing Germans. Others noted Botzenhart's lack of a habilitation, even suggesting that it would be hard to get students to complete such a hard piece of work if it were shown to be completely unnecessary. As for Botzenhart's narrow emphasis on vom Stein (*Stein* being the German word for "stone"), one wag suggested Botzenhart should be considered more geologist than historian. These critics could not prevail, however, and Botzenhart received his appointment.[42]

Botzenhart came to Göttingen from the pro-Nazi think tank, the Reich Institute for the History of the New Germany, founded and directed by Walter Frank.[43] Frank was one of the most ambitious of those young historians in Germany who rejected the "sterile" objectivity practiced by historians and nurtured by an older generation, individuals such as Friedrich Meinecke, a Professor of History at the Humboldt University of Berlin and editor of a major journal, *Historische Zeitschrift*, for nearly forty years.[44] Frank was aware of something important in Hitler's new Germany. The study of history was vital both to Hitler and to the Nazi worldview, an essential tool for establishing the German claim to greatness and the Aryan claim of superiority. But historians could only be trusted by Nazis if they would avoid the trap of objectivity

---

41. Ibid.

42. Ibid.

43. See Helmut Heiber, *Walter Frank und sein Reichsinstitut für Geschichte des neuen Deutschlands* (Stuttgart, Germany: Deutsche Verlag-Anstalt, 1966).

44. Meinecke was too reserved toward the Nazi regime for young enthusiasts like Walter Frank. However, he still represented both nationalism and antisemitism, as was common in his pre-Nazi generation. This can be seen even in his postwar assessment, *The German Catastrophe: Contemplations and Reflections* (Cambridge, MA: Harvard University Press, 1946).

and endorse the Nazi passion for the German Volk. Botzenhart did so while working with Walter Frank in his Reich Institute for the History of the New Germany, and now Frank hoped to boost Botzenhart's career with a position as a tenured professor.

When the final meeting took place at Göttingen, the day after Botzenhart's lecture, various faculty members expressed their hesitation. However, Eugen Mattiat, newly arrived at Göttingen, announced that Botzenhart was the first choice of the Nationalsozialistischer Deutscher Dozentenbund [National Socialist German University Instructors' League (NSDDozB)]. He said that the lecture had made the "spark of history" visible to the audience, and he added that there existed "decisive, relevant reasons and fundamental considerations" behind this choice. When challenged to explain these reasons and considerations, Mattiat responded, "That won't do, for that would bring to an end this opportunity for us to work successfully together here."[45] It may seem odd that Mattiat, a new professor in his mid-thirties who carried no reputation as a scholar, could control the outcome of this meeting and selection process. However, he was already on the political inside and was local head of the NSDDozB. Walther Hinz, the dean, backed him up, and Botzenhart received the appointment. In all of these appointments to full Professor—Birnbaum, Mattiat, and Botzenhart—old academic ideals disappeared and politicized Nazi influence prevailed.

A similar thing happened with scholarship and the curriculum at universities all across Germany. Philosophers, economists, law professors, and others began to remove Jewish books from their syllabi and so-called Jewish ideas from their teaching. For example, Jewish philosophers like Baruch Spinoza, long considered important to the German tradition, had to be repositioned as never really important; instead, Spinoza and others were now described as inferior to their lesser-known Aryan counterparts.[46] Professors of music,

---

45. This quote and other details about the hiring of Botzenhart are found in Kaehler's letter of May 28, 1945, as noted previously (note 41). It has the problem of being postwar testimony, when, in my view, the temptation to misrepresent and prevaricate about the past blossomed. However, Kaehler's version of the hiring of Botzenhart seems consistent with other evidence, as found in Botzenhart's personnel file in the GUA. That file includes description of a long postwar process in which the faculty successfully continued to reject the return of Botzenhart to its ranks. See my treatment of this material in "Kontinuitäten konservativer Geschichtsschreibung," in Becker, Dahms, and Wegeler, *Universität Göttingen*, 427–53 (at 441–48).

46. See Max Wundt, "Das Judentum in der Philosophie," in "Sitzungsberichte der Zweiten Arbeitstagung der Forschungsabteilung des Reichsinstituts für Geschichte des neuen

literature, political science, and theology found ways to incorporate the Nazi worldview into their work.[47] In physics, the extraordinary accomplishments of Albert Einstein had to be dismissed, with his relativity theory denigrated as "Jewish physics" and replaced by "German physics."[48]

For many decades after 1945, the thoroughgoing nazification of research and of the teaching curriculum under Hitler went largely unmentioned, with only a few exceptions.[49] The postwar history of history provides a good example. For several decades historians inside Germany probed many aspects of the Nazi past but not the role of historians during that period. Finally, in 1998 at the annual meeting of the profession, the Deutscher Historikertag [the major annual meeting of the German Association of Historians], the dam burst. Suddenly two of the most important postwar historians in the federal republic, Werner Conze and Theodor Schieder, were shown to have had a Nazi past, working on the Generalplan Ost [General Plan (for the) East], with its endorsement of aggressive war and "ethnic cleansing."[50] Then, in the first decade of the twenty-first century, at least four major conferences took place in Germany or

---

Deutschlands vom 12. bis 14. Mai 1937," *Forschungen zur Judenfrage* 2 (1937), 75–87 (at 79–81). Many similar examples can be found in the eight volumes of this journal, a publication of Walter Frank's Reich Institute for the History of the New Germany, in which the former place of importance of Jewish scholars in various fields of scholarship is dismissed as mistaken.

47. Gerhard Kittel, an important theologian teaching at Tübingen University, wrote a book on the Jewish Question (*Die Judenfrage* [Stuttgart, Germany: Kohlhammer, 1933, 3rd ed. 1934]). He also became the single most prolific contributor to *Forschungen zur Judenfrage*, with six articles and one entire volume of the journal contributed by him. The latter, authored with Eugen Fischer, appeared as "Das antike Weltjudentum: Tatsachen, Texte, Bilder," *Forschungen zur Judenfrage* 7 (1943). Among the articles published by Kittel were "Die ältesten Judenkarikaturen: Die 'Trierer Terrakotten,'" *Forschungen zur Judenfrage* 4 (1940): 250–59; and "Die Behandlung des Nichtjuden nach dem Talmud," *Archiv für Judenfragen* (Berlin) 1, Group A1 (1943): 7–17. For further discussion of Gerhard Kittel's antisemitic project, see Ericksen, *Theologians under Hitler*, 28–78, and the analysis by Anders Gerdmar in "Jewish Studies in the Service of Nazi Ideology: Tübingen's Faculty of Theology as a Center for Antisemitic Research" in the present volume.

48. See Alan Beyerchen, *Scientists under Hitler: Politics and the Physics Community in the Third Reich* (New Haven, CT: Yale University Press, 1976).

49. Exceptions include the remarkable postwar study by Max Weinreich, *Hitler's Professors: The Part of Scholarship in Germany's Crimes against the Jewish People* (New York: Yiddish Scientific Institute [YIVO], 1946; repr., foreword by Martin Gilbert, New Haven, CT: Yale University Press, 1999). Alan Beyerchen then published his *Scientists under Hitler* in 1976, and I published my *Theologians under Hitler* in 1985.

50. See Götz Aly, "Theodor Schieder, Werner Conze oder: Die Vorstufen der physischen Vernichtung," in *Deutsche Historiker im Nationalsozialismus*, ed. Winfried Schulze and Otto Gerhard Oexle, 2nd ed. (Frankfurt, Germany: Fischer, 1999), 163–82.

the United States, with subsequent large volumes appearing that examined scholarship on the humanities in Nazi Germany. In all cases, these volumes have revealed widespread and enthusiastic support for Nazi ideas and the Nazi state, providing a wealth of evidence for what we can label the betrayal of the humanities.[51]

I now describe two famous historians from Göttingen, Karl Brandi[52] and Percy Schramm,[53] to illustrate how easily Nazi-friendly ideas infiltrated the university. Theirs seems to me a subtle story, for they did not hold a significant position within a Nazi organization or participate directly in Nazi crimes.[54] Nor did Brandi or Schramm support the Nazis prior to 1933; rather, both were active in the more moderate, right-of-center German People's Party (DVP). However, each of them took a stance that meshed comfortably with major elements of the Nazi worldview. This included their German nationalism, and especially their eagerness to advocate Germany's right to reclaim former provinces lost to Poland after World War I. Both Brandi and Schramm made this a special cause, and that fit quite well within Hitler's concept of *Lebensraum* for the "Aryan super race," a "drive to the East," and the broader Nazi plans for an *Ostpolitik*. As a result, these two important and respected figures found themselves more comfortable praising the Nazi state than voicing criticism.

Brandi began focusing on the Ostmark [Eastern march] in the 1920s, gathering materials and giving speeches to encourage Germans to retain their connection to regions in Poland that had been taken from Germany after World

---

51. See Frank-Rutger Hausmann, ed., *Die Rolle der Geisteswissenschaften im Dritten Reich 1933–1945: Schriften des Historischen Kollegs*, Kolloquien 53 (Munich: Oldenbourg, 2002); Hartmut Lehmann and Otto Oexle, eds., *Nationalsozialismus in den Kulturwissenschaften. Band 1: Fächer, Milieus, Karrieren*, and *Band 2: Leitbegriffe, Deutungsmuster, Paradigmenkämpfe* (Göttingen, Germany: Vandenhoek & Ruprecht, 2004); Wolfgang Bialas and Anson Rabinbach, eds., *Nazi Germany and the Humanities: How German Academics Embraced Nazism* (2006; Oxford: Oneworld, 2014); and Jürgen Elvert and Jürgen Nielsen-Sikora, eds., *Kulturwissenschaften und Nationalsozialismus* (Stuttgart, Germany: Franz Steiner, 2008).

52. Karl Brandi is best known for his magisterial book, *The Emperor Charles V* (New York: Alfred A. Knopf, 1940), first published in German in 1939.

53. Percy Ernst Schramm combined political history, art history, and the use of ritual and regalia, creating a new way of understanding European politics in the Middle Ages. This approach appeared first in *Kaiser, Rom, und Renovatio* (Leipzig, Germany: B. G. Teubner, 1929). He wrote about the British monarchy as well, for example, in *A History of the English Coronation* (Oxford: Clarendon Press, 1937). He also wrote military history, based on his wartime experience as official historian for the German High Command during World War II, including *Hitler: The Man and the Military Leader* (Chicago: Chicago Review Press, 1999).

54. The one exception is that Percy Schramm did serve in the Wehrmacht during World War II, as noted below.

War I.[55] In 1931, Percy Schramm led a group of students on a bus tour to this area, arguing that every German student should travel "once to the East."[56] In April 1932, Brandi and Schramm traveled together to Gleiwitz, now in Poland, getting positive press in local German language newspapers.[57] Then in the summer of 1932, Brandi and Schramm hosted the annual Historikertag at Göttingen. A scholar who studied the history of Historikertag meetings draws a dramatic picture: "The one-sided thematic arrangement of the Göttingen program of lectures signaled unmistakably the almost brutal politicization of this gathering. No Historikertag before this one had shown itself so ready for 'service to the entire Volk,' for service to the Ostmark."[58]

Brandi reached the mandatory retirement age of sixty-five in 1935, though he continued to do some teaching. Schramm continued to play an active role, living and working comfortably within Nazi expectations. In 1936 he wrote, "Since the year 1933, which brought the concepts of Volk and *Volksgemeinschaft* close to the students, one can note the strong resonance of these topics, as lecture and seminar classes in social history have shown."[59] In 1938, he wrote, "The extraordinary pace of historical developments in recent years throws up one problem after another with which the historian must deal: war politics, Eastern history, colonial history, social history—these categories may indicate how the tasks of the history seminar have grown since 1933."[60] Naturally, letters such as these were signed with "Heil Hitler!"

---

55. The box containing these materials is labeled #75, in the *Brandi Nachlass* in the *Handschriftskammer* of the Göttingen University Library. For more than a century, Poland had not existed as an autonomous nation. It was created in 1919 from territories recently belonging to Russia and Austria as well as Germany. This loss created an especially sensitive issue for German nationalists.

56. "Bericht über die Ostpreussenfahrt Göttinger Studenten, vom. 1.–14. August 1931," in *Personalakten Schramm*, File 1, 82, GUA.

57. "Oberschlesienreise vom Geh.-Rat Dr. Brandi und Dr. Schramm, Göttingen," *Ostdeutsche Morgenpost*, 104 (April 15, 1932). This article, with no author listed, can be found in the *Brandi Nachlass*, File 74, 71.

58. Peter Schumann, "Die deutschen Historikertage von 1893 bis 1937: Die Geschichte einer fach-historischen Institution im Spiegel der Presse" (PhD diss., Philipps University of Marburg, 1974).

59. Schramm to Kurator [chief administrative officer] Bojunga, October 22, 1936, in K, XVI, IV, C.k.2, Bd II, GUA. This translation is mine and has appeared also in *Complicity in the Holocaust*, 154.

60. Schramm to Kurator Bojunga, November 28, 1938, in K, XVI, IV, C.k.2, Bd II, GUA. The seminar referred to is the "Seminar für mittlere und neuere Geschichte," for which Schramm held the corresponding chair.

Though Schramm's comments might not have been as passionate as thoroughgoing Nazis would have liked, they suggest his full acceptance of the changed atmosphere since 1933. In 1938, he jubilantly greeted the successful outcome of the Munich crisis[61] and the German acquisition of the Sudetenland with the words, "Our grandchildren will envy us, because we live in the age of Adolf Hitler!"[62] This sentiment in response to a land grab is entirely consistent with his passion for Germany's right to the Ostmark before 1933. In fact, there is nothing in Schramm's role that indicates anything but satisfaction during the Nazi years. He belonged to the Reiter-SA (Sturmabteilung), the mounted branch of the Storm Troopers, from 1934 to 1938, and he joined the Nazi Party in 1939.[63] When World War II broke out, he served in the military, despite being in his mid-forties. In 1943, Schramm was appointed to the High Command of the Armed Forces (OKW) in order to write the *Kriegstagebuch* [war diary], a position that gave him access to top generals as well as to Hitler.[64]

Brandi and Schramm each occupied a place near the high end of international fame among historians in Germany and scholars in the humanities in their era. Brandi served as a vice president of the International Society of Historians, and Schramm, due to his work on royal rituals in England, received invitations to attend the coronations of King George VI in 1937 and Queen Elizabeth II in 1953. Though this prominence may have been above the norm, in one thing they were quite representative of their colleagues. Nearly everywhere scholars have probed into German academia, we find a similar willingness to go along. We see much enthusiasm. We see almost no one willing to criticize the nazification of the university. We see little evidence even of foot dragging, much less of actual opposition to Nazi ideas.

---

61. The "Munich Crisis" involved a summit meeting between the leaders of Germany, Italy, Great Britain, and France in September 1938. Hitler's many threatening comments about the Sudetenland, a part of Czechoslovakia, threatened the outbreak of war. The resolution agreed on by these four nations allowed Hitler to take the Sudetenland, without asking Czechoslovakia, in hopes of appeasing German anger over the Versailles postwar settlement. Instead of avoiding war, it merely postponed war by one year.

62. See David Thimme, *Percy Ernst Schramm und das Mittelalter: Wandlungen eines Geschichtsbildes* (Göttingen, Germany: Vandenhoek and Ruprecht, 2006), 368.

63. See Schramm's *Fragebogen*, signed April 8, 1947, in his denazification file, Nds. 171 Hild., 7494, NSA, 1–6. His Nazi Party membership number was 7,048,995.

64. See Percy Ernst Schramm, *Kriegstagebuch des Oberkommandos der Wehrmacht*, 8 vols. (Frankfurt, Germany: Bernhard und Graefe Verlag für Wehrwesen, 1961). See also his denazification file, as mentioned in note 63.

IV. LYING AND PREVARICATION DURING AND AFTER THE DENAZIFICATION PROCESS

When we assess German universities between 1933 and 1945, we see Nazis. That image then changed dramatically after German defeat. Suddenly no one had been a Nazi. Everyone—even those who had been members of the Nazi Party, officers in Nazi organizations, or members of the SS—explained that they had simply been working from the inside, trying to protect academic values against the Nazi onslaught. Before considering this seemingly dishonest state of affairs (a dishonesty to be found throughout the nation, not just in universities), we can briefly consider one element in the crucible of postwar Germany: the circumstances of denazification.

All four occupying powers in postwar Germany—the United States, Britain, France, and the Soviet Union—agreed that Germany must be cleansed of the Nazi ideology. They focused especially on those categories of individuals expected to play a significant role in Germany after 1945, whether as schoolteachers, police, journalists, politicians, business leaders, or in any other important occupation. University professors occupied a place of special importance in Allied thoughts, since they would produce the next generation of German leaders. In the first weeks of occupation, German universities were simply shut down. The Allies then assigned intelligence and security officers with the task of removing those professors considered the most egregious Nazis on the faculty in preparation for reopening the universities in the fall of 1945 or the spring of 1946.

After these first removals, there developed a more organized process of denazification, with authority for implementation gradually being handed to Germans. Those involved included German prosecutors and defense attorneys, plus German civilian panels to hear and judge the evidence. Despite this German participation, however, the process remained under Allied oversight and control for about three years before continuing for another three years under full German authority. Individual denazification always started with completion of a questionnaire, or *Fragebogen*, followed by a hearing to assess the extent and significance of one's prior support of Nazism. The Allied Control Council in Berlin established five categories for anyone processed through denazification. With Categories I and II reserved for actual criminals, those described as "major offenders" or "offenders," denazification panels for university professors typically would place individuals in Category III for "promoters" of Nazism, Category IV for "supporters," or Category V for those entirely exonerated. The results could be serious, since individuals in Category III were ejected from their career path, restricted to manual labor in terms of employment, and denied the right to vote or run for office. Individuals in Category IV also suffered restrictions in their professional and political lives.[65] Perhaps it is no surprise that Germans began to lie rather than give up their careers and their livelihood.

We see opposition from the beginning, both to the very idea of German guilt and to the Allied view that Germany needed cleansing. For example, on May 2, 1945, Cardinal Faulhaber of Munich compared the Allied bombing of German cities to Nazi crimes in concentration camps.[66] In June, he then complained to the clergy in his archdiocese: "For weeks one [i.e., the Allies] brought representatives of American newspapers and American soldiers to Dachau, and then they showed slides and movies of the most horrible sights from there, in order to place the disgrace and shame of the German people before the entire world, right down to the last village in Africa [Negerdorf]."[67] This statement perhaps indicates merely a reflexive support of the German people in the immediate aftermath of a bitter war. However, it is also typical of a very widespread tendency among church leaders to downplay, deny, or ignore the seriousness of "the disgrace and shame" to which Faulhaber refers. In addition, this eagerness to downplay the seriousness of German crimes went along with a nearly complete unwillingness of church figures to accept any responsibility for the harshness of German behavior. Even the *best* Protestant response to be found in 1945, the Stuttgart Declaration of Guilt from October, describes Christian guilt in very vague terms. The Stuttgart Declaration apologizes for Christians not "acting more courageously" in the fight against National Socialism. Such a formulation completely fails to acknowledge the opposite problem, the many enthusiastic Christian statements in favor of National Socialism. The Declaration also fails even to mention Jews or other specific victims.[68]

The Protestant Bishops Meiser of Bavaria and Wurm of Württemberg, in their first reactions to denazification, immediately protested blanket sanctions against members of the Nazi Party and of the SS. Bishop Wurm warned in July 1945 that removing such individuals from the German bureaucracy

---

65. For a description of the denazification process, see Ericksen, *Complicity*, ch. 6–7. See also Niethammer, *Die Mitläuferfabrik*; Tent, *Mission on the Rhine*; and Remy, *Heidelberg Myth*.
66. Quoted in Ernst Klee, *Persilscheine und falsche Pässe: Wie die Kirchen den Nazis halfen* (Frankfurt, Germany: Fischer, 1991), 13.
67. Quoted in ibid.
68. See Matthew Hockenos's treatment of these issues in, *A Church Divided: German Protestants Confront the Nazi Past* (Bloomington: Indiana University Press, 2004), 75–100 (at 76).

would result in others "unsuited in terms of character" taking their place. Quite clearly, Wurm meant socialists and Jews in his assessment of those who would be unsuited to lead postwar Germany. As he defended the other group, Christians who became Nazis, he referred to the "elemental reaction of the German people to the horrible Versailles *Diktat*," and he added, "For all these reasons, many of our best within and without the civil service then followed Hitler's call."[69] We now know that Wurm was including among "our best" Germans his own son, Hans Wurm, who was imprisoned postwar for falsifying his Fragebogen, denying his early entry into the Nazi Party.[70]

The same Bishop Wurm who protested blanket sanctions against party members and members of the SS was quite willing to write letters in support of significant criminals. For example, he provided a letter in support of SS Hauptsturmführer Karl Sommer, praising him for reading the New Testament while in prison at Nuremberg. Wurm added, "If he really committed crimes worthy of death, he must have done so under the pressure of especially unfortunate circumstances, so that ... [he] as a believing Christian is worthy of a show of mercy."[71] Wurm and other representatives of the churches, from bishops to priests and pastors, recognized that the Allies, especially the British and Americans, showed themselves ready to respect people of religious faith. Thus, clergy members produced an outpouring of letters, letters that soon became known by the derisive term, *Persilscheine*. Persil was a standard brand of German soap, so that a Persilschein was the equivalent of a "soap certificate," intended for a whitewash. Persilscheine saturated the process of denazification with overwhelmingly positive claims and widespread clergy testimony. According to the Persilscheine, no German was ever a real Nazi.

Consider a letter from Otto Fricke, a pastor who had been active in the Confessing Church. He wrote a Persilschein for Otmar Freiherr von Verschuer, the mentor who inspired Joseph Mengele's twins research and received regular reports from Mengele on his work. While he was director of the Kaiser Wilhelm Institute for Anthropology, Human Heredity, and Eugenics in Berlin, von Verschuer also received body parts from Mengele's ample supply. Yet according to Fricke:

> He and his family belong to my confessional congregation and he supported me most energetically during the difficult years of struggle over the Confessing Church and the freedom of the church and its message....

---

69. See Clemens Vollnhals, *Evangelische Kirche und Entnazifizierung, 1945–1949: Die Last der nationalsozialistischen Vergangenheit* (Munich: Oldenbourg, 1989), 52–57.
70. Ibid.
71. Quoted in Klee, *Persilscheine*, 101.

People of his type and his character are suited to guide the redirection of the German academic world onto a Christian foundation and promote the rebuilding of German life.[72]

Kommandoführer Waldemar Klingelhöfer of Einsatzgruppe B, sentenced to death for the mass murder of Jews in Estonia, received a Persilschein from his pastor, who described him as "a person of upright, honest character, an enemy to all lies and every injustice ... the sort of person we need today, outside, among our Volk, for a return to health and a rebuilding where so much corruption now prevails."[73] Pleas such as this helped Klingelhöfer win a pardon in 1951.[74] These examples suggest a rigidly defensive posture in support of German perpetrators, along with what now seems like a remarkable willingness to excuse the crimes of individuals in their service to the Nazi state. It would seem that pastors, bishops, and others in Germany ignored the significance of German crimes, including perhaps especially crimes against Jews, either by refusing to allude to Jewish victimization at all or by responding to someone like Waldemar Klingelhöfer, who murdered Estonian Jews, only to describe his "upright character" and label him "the sort of person we need today."

I will now describe several examples from the denazification experience of professors at Göttingen University in which a similar failure to recognize the size, scope, or implications of Nazi crimes seems to linger. The dishonesty of Persilscheine, as described, certainly made an appearance in these cases. However, another form of dishonesty also can be found in the claims and stories fabricated by individuals as they tried to get out from under a negative judgment. For example, Eugen Mattiat had joined the Sicherheitsdienst [Security Service (SD)] of the SS in 1937. This fact loomed large in his denazification proceedings, since the SS had been declared a criminal organization by the Allies. Membership in the SS meant almost automatically that a person would be placed in Category III, a promoter of Nazism, or at least Category IV, a supporter. The former was certain to result in removal from one's job and the latter likely to do so. Mattiat's service in the SD branch of the SS exacerbated the problem, since SD members, especially in the university, were regularly engaged to spy on their colleagues and send secret reports to Berlin.

Mattiat responded to his SS problem with the surprising claim that he had joined the organization merely for the chance to wear a uniform. He felt

---

72. Quoted in Klee, *Persilscheine*, 128.
73. Quoted in Klee, *Persilscheine*, 99–100.
74. Klee, *Persilscheine*, 99.

embarrassed, he said, attending formal events in a business suit, when most others had some sort of uniform to wear. When questioned by his postwar prosecutor, Mattiat claimed to have known nothing about the reputation of the SS, its crimes against Jews, or the reality that a sister organization, the Gestapo, arrested people without charge and imprisoned them without trial. Mattiat's panel relegated him to Category III, adding this wry comment:

> When the accused claims that he never had the consciousness of being a member of the SS, ... the fact that he received the rank ... of an SS Hauptsturmführer [captain] and wore a black SS officer's uniform with SS insignia and SS rank ... makes it impossible to understand to what organization other than the SS [he] felt he belonged.... The objection that he did not have the consciousness of belonging to the SS is a claim invented for his defense in this trial and is based on nothing else.[75]

In a final blast, the panel added that "the accused was extremely sparing of the truth, a reproach that he as a professor and theologian would better have avoided."[76] It is worth noting that Mattiat's legitimacy as a university professor had always been in doubt (see the earlier account of his approval process), making him an easier target for scorn. However, this judgment conforms to the way someone today almost certainly would read the evidence, with little willingness to give credence to Mattiat's farfetched denials and a strong sense that he was "extremely sparing of the truth." Mattiat's 1948 placement in Category III meant he could not return to his position at Göttingen, nor could he return to his former job as a pastor or any job of public significance. Three years later, however, he had been granted a Category V, full exoneration.[77] This was a very typical trajectory.

Walter Birnbaum's case followed a similar path, but with a twist. He secured his professorship in the Faculty of Theology due to his support of Nazi politics and despite his lack of habilitation, doctorate, or even graduate degree (see earlier discussion). The British recognized this and removed him upon their arrival in 1945. He then went through the normal denazification process. At first this mirrored the British decision, placing him in Category III, indicating he had been a "substantial promoter" of the Nazi regime, and confirming the

---

75. "Das Spruchgericht XII. Spruchkammer. Urteil im Namen des Rechts!" from a hearing on March 16, 1948, in the Mattiat denazification file, NSA.

76. Ibid.

77. Given Mattiat's lack of a doctorate or other academic credentials, no one considered bringing him back into the university. Instead, he returned to the church and finished his career as pastor in Osterode, a village just outside Göttingen.

loss of his professorship. Birnbaum appealed, however, and experienced the fairly common end result. By 1951, his five separate appeals managed to bring him to Category V, full exoneration. Despite that success, however, the Faculty of Theology at Göttingen never accepted him back into its ranks, almost certainly because of his egregiously politicized appointment and lack of academic credentials. However, he received an anomalous appointment as "professor of the university." This involved no specific duties. After failing to attract any students to lectures he offered, he kept an official address in Göttingen but lived in Munich, drawing his full Professor's salary until his retirement in 1961. He then received a full Professor's pension until his death at the age of ninety-three, a far cry from the fate of Paul Darmstädter in the 1930s.[78]

The cases of Mattiat and Birnbaum illustrate the norm. During the first years of denazification, Allied oversight combined with a willingness of German prosecutors and German panel members to deliver relatively harsh judgments. This resulted in many individuals being placed in Category III. By 1948 the English gave up their oversight. Also by 1948 and thereafter, public acceptance of denazification among Germans weakened considerably. German prosecutors and panel members, who had been selected originally for their distance from Nazism, began to feel public stigma attached to their role. The same was true for many of those asked to give testimony in individual cases. Seemingly honest testimony early in the process turned into prevarication thereafter. As a result of these changes, denazification gradually weakened until by 1951 it had collapsed. Almost everyone received a Category V in the end. Despite all the evidence against them, this would seem to confirm that none of those individuals originally placed in Category III or Category IV had ever really been Nazis. That was the claim they made in court, as we can observe in additional cases of denazification at Göttingen in the period after 1948.[79]

Several Göttingen professors had been widely considered the most committed Nazis on the faculty. This included, for example, Professors Siegfried Wendt and Klaus-Wilhelm Rath in economics and Karl Siegert in law. Each suffered immediate removal from the faculty by British occupation authorities. At their first denazification hearings, Rath and Siegert received placement in Category III and Wendt in Category IV.[80] When each of them appealed that first decision,

---

78. See file S1 H2 133a in the LKA in Hannover. See also my treatment of Birnbaum in *Theologians under Hitler*, 168–76 and 195–97.
79. For examples of these patterns within denazification, see Ericksen, *Complicity*, ch. 7.
80. Geoffrey Bird, the British officer in charge at Göttingen, protested the Category IV for Wendt, though to no avail. He argued that other professors would protest, either at

their attorneys protested, among other things, that their clients had been unfairly accused of being part of a so-called terror group. The attorneys argued that this was an imprecise term, representing no concrete reality but merely a subjective claim by persons of ill will.[81]

The first postwar rector at Göttingen, Rudolf Smend (1882–1975), a professor in the Faculty of Law, was one who had used the term *terror group* in his comments about colleagues. For example, he gave testimony in 1947 against Wendt, describing him as "belonging to the group of Schürmann-Rath, which exercised a regime of real terror here." He added that Wendt "was fully involved in support of the terror activities of that group, for example, in faculty meetings, and for that reason I would not wish ever again to sit with him in a faculty gathering."[82] In February 1949, Smend gave testimony describing Rath as also belonging to the "terror group."[83] Five months later, however, Smend significantly modified that claim. In July he noted that a friend of Rath "has sent out a number of long, written pieces... that direct a polemic against me," a polemic about Smend's allegedly careless use of the "terror group" charge. Smend then told the court that the minutes of his earlier testimony did not reflect the nuance of what he had said. In particular, "[I] expressly refused to claim that I could place responsibility on any single member" of the terror group.[84]

Rath's first hearing occurred in February 1949, and he received a Category III. His appeal hearing took place in August 1949. Despite Smend's watered-down testimony, Rath's Category III was still upheld. Among other things, the panel's judgment mentioned that he had written on the Jewish Question in a way that conformed with Nazi ideology.[85] This charge would seem hard to deny, since Rath had written a number of books and articles that included

---

being placed in the same category as someone with as much Nazi baggage as Wendt or at not being shown the same lenience as he was shown. See Bird, Univ. Edn. Control Officer, University of Göttingen, to Special Branch, HQ Hild., December 9, 1947, in Siegfried Wendt's denazification file, Nds. 171 Hild., 18531, NSA.

81. See, for example, attorneys Gonell and von Waldow to the *Entnazifizierungsausschuss*, May 23, 1949, in Klaus-Wilhelm Rath's denazification file, Nds. 171 Hild. 9223, NSA, 96–102, especially section 9.

82. Rudolf Smend to Vorsitzender des Unterausschusses für die politische Überprüfung des Lehrkörpers der Universitäts Göttingen, July 7, 1947, in Wendt's denazification file, NSA.

83. Smend's testimony in "Öffentliche Sitzung der Entnazifizierungs-Hauptausschuss, Göttingen," February 1, 1949, in Rath's denazification file, NSA, 59–64.

84. Smend to Vorsitzenden der Entnazifizierungs-Hauptausschuss, July 18, 1949, in Rath's denazification file, NSA, 119–20.

85. "Entnazifizierungs-Entscheidung," August 2, 1949, in Rath's denazification file, NSA, 135–36.

"the removal of Jewish influence" in either their title or their table of contents. Rath defended himself, protesting that his research "always dealt solely with the Jewish ideology, i.e., a certain type of thought, and therefore had nothing to do with a racial struggle" and nothing to do with National Socialism.[86]

Rath's lawyer solicited testimony on this question of antisemitism for Rath's final appeal, although from only one individual who had read only one short article among Rath's many works on "the removal of Jewish influence." This "expert" felt able to testify, echoing Rath's own argument, that the article dealt appropriately with the "Jewish Question," a "problem that plays a great role in our [economic] scholarship." He found no "hatefulness" or anything likely to create a "contemptuous view of Jewry."[87] It is possible that this witness was defending Rath as a friend. It is also likely that he simply could not recognize the stereotypes and exaggerations about Jewish nature and about the role of Jews in the world that are the raw material of antisemitic prejudice.

Any observer not corrupted by the anti-Jewish atmosphere of Nazi Germany could hardly fail to note antisemitic intentions in Rath's work. For example, his book from 1944, *Um Volk und Wirtschaft*, includes a section entitled, "Zum Kampf gegen das Judentum" [The struggle against Jewry], Rath begins with these words: "The Jewish Question is not an economic question, it goes far beyond that. However, Jewry uses economic power as a means to establish and to maintain its dominance."[88] He then argues that Jews amass money merely as a way to attack "the otherwise unreachable domains of European culture and politics." Furthermore:

> It remains a fact, that Jewry uses its economic position as the most effective way to achieve its actual goal of world domination. That applies even where, in most recent times, the path appears to be completely different—the path of bolshevization, which seems merely to destroy the economy. But in destroying the wealth of others, Jewry enriches itself and also turns the angry, impoverished masses against the remainder of the middle classes still in place.[89]

---

86. Rath, "Zur Frage der Behandlung des Judentums in der Nationalökonomie," a statement with no date, in Rath's denazification file, NSA, 209–10.

87. This witness, designated by the name Schaeder, testified during Rath's final appeal: "After the first proceedings against Herr Rath, I studied everything [in one of Rath's anti-Jewish articles] to get clarity for myself." See the trial record of June 23, 1950 in Rath's denazification file, NSA, 220–30 (at 222).

88. Klaus Wilhelm Rath, *Um Volk und Wirtschaft* (Leipzig, Germany: August Lutzeyer, 1944), 339.

89. Ibid., 340.

It is hard to separate these sentiments from normal antisemitic propaganda, exaggerating the power and place of Jews in the world, echoing the *Protocols of the Elders of Zion*, and even adopting the seemingly absurd argument that Jews can be capitalists or communists, but still be working in league with each other.

We find another example of Rath's ideas about Jews in a letter written in 1943. In this case Rath was defending a book he had written on the German insurance industry:

> My book did have a certain direction, a "tendency"... Perhaps you are surprised to hear that I not only advocate this "tendency," but I am happy to claim this publicly.... We scholars in the Germany of Adolf Hitler can finally and openly advocate the "tendency" only to serve the German *Volk*, and in the sense of this "tendency" we can research and speak the truth.

Rath then clarifies what "truth" meant to him:

> Ever since the Jew Manes served for decades as the pope of an allegedly German insurance scholarship, enjoying copious support from the German private insurance industry,... perhaps a scholarly presentation... will have surprised you. But you will need to put up with that. The times of Jews like Manes, Berliner, Goldschmidt, and their glorifiers as well as their parrots are in the past, also for scholarship.[90]

The prosecutor in Rath's denazification case did not ignore his antisemitism. In fact, he wanted to extend the trial in Rath's second appeal in order to inquire more carefully into the anti-Jewish nature of Rath's writings. However, Rath had connections in the government of Lower Saxony pressuring the process in his favor. He also filled the hearing room with friends, who booed decisions that went against him; and he claimed that none of his "scholarship" about Jews ever represented antisemitism or pushed the Nazi ideology. The final denazification decision in August 1950 accepted Rath's claims. It left him in Category IV, not the Category V that he wanted, but it raised him from Category III at least partly because he "never showed an agitating tendency against Jews, either in his review of Jewish literature or his writings." The panel added that he was "not at all an antisemite."[91]

---

90. Rath to Generaldirektor Dr. K. Schmitt, Vorsitzer des Vorstandes der Münchner Rückversicherungs-Gesellschaft, March 12, 1943, in Rath's denazification file, NSA, 271.

91. "Entnazifizierungs-Entscheidung," signed August 30, 1950, in Rath's denazification file, NSA, 253–54. For more on Rath's denazification process as well as his antisemitism, see Ericksen, *Complicity*, 202–18.

The conclusion that Rath was "not at all an antisemite" seems outrageous in light of the evidence. We find other outrageous claims if we go back to that group of Göttingen professors accused of Nazi terror. Each of these allegedly most enthusiastic Nazis on the faculty claimed that they had never really been Nazis. They all pointed to one person, Artur Schürmann, and claimed that he was the real Nazi at Göttingen. Any membership in a Nazi organization or any positive thing these others had ever said about Adolf Hitler or the Nazi Party had simply been camouflage. They worked within the system, only pretending to accept Nazi ideas, in an effort to protect academic values and practices against true Nazis like Schürmann.

Friedrich Neumann was one of many who pointed to Schürmann as the one genuine Nazi on campus. Neumann served as rector of Göttingen University from 1933 to 1938, appointed for his political views, according to the new Führer Principle, rather than being elected by his peers. He presided over the removal of Jewish faculty members and the nazification of the university while praising Nazi ideology in all of his writings. However, during denazification, Neumann claimed to have used his party membership "only to protect the life of the university against attack."[92] His final appeal moved him from Category III to Category IV, with his hearing panel giving this explanation: "Through his misunderstanding of the true essence of National Socialism, whose exponent at Göttingen was Schürmann, and through his belief that the 'childhood illnesses' [of the Nazi Party] could be overcome, *he can in a certain sense be considered a victim of National Socialism*" [emphasis added].[93]

The attempt by Neumann and others to claim innocence, or even victimhood, almost always involved shifting blame onto Artur Schürmann. That made me very interested to read Schürmann's file. This professor of agriculture, who measured the milk production of cows in the Ruhr, had been without question a leading Nazi at Göttingen. He served as head of the NSDDozB for all of Lower Saxony. One witness gave testimony at Schürmann's hearing, based on stenographic notes he had taken at an NSDDozB meeting. He reported these words from Schürmann at that meeting: "We will work until everyone is either with us or has been pushed out.... The former years [of Weimar] have one advantage—we know exactly who is who. When one of them tries to raise

---

92. Friedrich Neumann to Entnazifizierungs-Hauptausschuss, Göttingen, March 14, 1948, in Neumann's denazification file, Nds. 171 Hild., 18915, NSA, 23.
93. "Entnazifizierungs-Entscheidung," February 8, 1949. The quotation comes from the public prosecutor in Göttingen to the Entnazifizierungs-Hauptausschuss, January 4, 1949, in Neumann's denazification file, NSA, 35.

his head, I will smash it. I will destroy them, those liberal dogs. Whoever sets himself against me, I will annihilate."[94] Despite these words reported at his denazification trial, and despite the claims of all other Nazi professors that they were merely working undercover to protect academic values against Schürmann, he made exactly the same claim, but in reverse. He had accepted Nazi office only to protect academic values against the true Nazis, like those various men who had been accusing him.[95]

Just as with the Persilscheine, the denazification testimony of each professor at Göttingen stretches credulity. Taken at face value, this testimony would show that not a single one had ever actually been a Nazi. Each had secretly opposed Hitler. Each had taken on the *appearance* of being a Nazi but only in order to fight the regime more effectively from within. It seems impossible to accept this, impossible not to conclude that prevarication, dissimulation, and repression marked the denazification process. A very similar pattern of denial and prevarication can be seen within Germany for approximately the next forty years. For a generation or two, Germany was a nation filled with secrets, with denial, and with taboo topics not to be mentioned in public.

I witnessed some of this in person in the 1980s. When I published *Theologians under Hitler* in 1985, highlighting the Nazi enthusiasm of three important Protestant theologians, a reviewer in the *Frankfurter Allgemeine Zeitung* liked the book but expressed his regret that even forty years after the collapse of the Nazi state, it had taken an American to tell this story.[96] About the same time, I was asked to contribute to a book describing Göttingen University during the Third Reich. I agreed to write a chapter on the theological faculty, led by Emanuel Hirsch, one of the enthusiastic Nazi theologians I had described earlier. Then Hans-Joachim Dahms, a leader of this Göttingen project, asked if I would also write a chapter on professors of history. Several young historians at Göttingen had been approached to write this chapter. They were then each warned against the project, for fear that exposing Nazi-era secrets would be bad for their careers. A colleague at Tübingen told me a similar story. She and

---

94. Testimony of Professor Mortensen in the trial of February 1, 1949, in Artur Schürmann's denazification file, Nds 171 Hild., 20265, NSA, 59.

95. See Schürmann's statement at his hearing on February 22, 1949 in Schürmann's denazification file, NSA, 86–92. Schürmann received placement in Category III. His subsequent appeals failed to achieve a Category IV. Although this negative outcome lost its full significance after 1951, when Germans gained final control over the legal impact of denazification, he was one of those at Göttingen who never returned to his professorship.

96. See Klaus Goebel, "Theologen, die Hitler unterstützten: Über Gerhard Kittel, Paul Althaus, Emanuel Hirsch," *Frankfurter Allgemeine Zeitung*, June 5, 1986, 11.

I had both written about the important Tübingen theologian, Gerhard Kittel. She had described his abhorrent book, *Die Judenfrage,* written in 1933, but she claimed that he soon saw the truth about the Nazi regime and turned against it. I had written, by contrast, that his pro-Nazi, anti-Jewish stance grew more and more vitriolic, at least until 1944.[97] When I asked why she treated him so gently, she told me that she would have no hope for a career if she told the full story. This was a hero of the theological faculty at Tübingen, so she could not allow herself an entirely truthful presentation.

These stories of mine are clearly anecdotal. However, we also can note that by the 1980s Germans were just beginning to work on *Vergangenheitsbewältigung,* their willingness to take responsibility for the past and deal with it honestly. Prior to that time, German universities and German professors in the humanities had hardly been investigated. Since the 1980s, one university after another and one academic discipline after another has been scrutinized. The general outcome corresponds to the one I have described here.[98] Until 1945, Nazi professors played a large role in German academic life. After German defeat, denial, prevarication, and repression of the story set in. I would argue that this denial, prevarication, and repression that continued for several decades grew out of the pattern of dishonesty set during denazification.

V. THE IRONIC BENEFIT OF GERMAN LIES

Despite many problems in the denazification process, I believe it still played a useful role. We can begin by noting that postwar Germany represents a remarkable success story. In contrast to Germany after World War I, there was no significant attempt to return to the past, no bitter attempt to take back Germany's place in the world through nationalistic and militaristic extremism. For seven postwar decades, the threat of a neo-Nazi resurgence in Germany has remained tiny and inconsequential, and Western Europe as a whole became an almost unbelievable story of economic success and cultural accomplishment. Yet by 2015, some of this luster diminished in the face of significant challenges. A flood of refugees from conflicts in North Africa and the Middle East reached Europe that year, creating a border crisis that threatened European stability. In Germany, Chancellor Angela Merkel offered the most generous response by far, welcoming more than a million asylum seekers. As a result of the changing

---

97. On Kittel, see note 47.
98. See, for example, Becker, Dahms, and Wegeler, *Universität Göttingen*; Remy, *Heidelberg Myth*; and the sources listed in notes 49, 50, and 51.

demographics, for the first time since 1945, a far-right party, Alternative für Deutschland [Alternative for Germany], gained significant numbers, reaching 12 percent in the federal election of 2017. A resurgence in nationalism and a diminishing tolerance for democratic principles also occurred elsewhere, especially in several Eastern European nations within the European Union. A variation on this trend toward nationalism reached the United Kingdom in 2016, when voters surprisingly gave a small majority to "Brexit," the dramatic British withdrawal from the European Union. Despite these setbacks for European integration, democratic norms remain strong in Germany. Postwar Germany has provided a model for democratic elections and honest courts, along with free speech and freedom of the press. More importantly, the prospect of something like a German-French war or a German-British war, so prominent at the turn of the nineteenth century, still seems beyond our imagination.

These decades of German postwar success surely arise from many sources. The *Wirtschaftswunder* [economic miracle] played a role, teaching Germans to value material comfort while giving up on the allure of war and conquest. The Cold War encouraged Britain and the United States to treat Germans gently, in order to secure West Germany's place in the anti-Soviet NATO coalition. Another impediment to postwar glorification of Hitler's ideas involved their disastrous outcome. The brutal and costly defeat that left Germany in ruins certainly could be traced to Hitler and his misguided goals. Furthermore, the national shame placed on Germans for the extraordinary crimes of the Holocaust also cost Hitler any sort of posthumous admiration from all but his most radical admirers on the right.

All of these are factors that separated post–World War II Germany from post–World War I Germany. They helped West Germany—and since 1990 a unified Germany—jettison its Nazi past and become a thoroughly democratic nation. However, I think that denazification made a useful contribution in two ways. First of all, denazification made the claim that nazification had been widespread in Germany, despite the many Germans who claimed: "I am not the one, Hitler did it." Scholarship in the last generation has, in my view, shown us that the Allies got it right. Nazification really had been very widespread; that is important to acknowledge. Second, the denazification process produced an entire nation of Germans claiming they had never really been Nazis. They had always secretly opposed the terrible Nazi ideas. Many or most of them must have been lying when they said this, but I think those lies produced an ironic form of inoculation against any resurgence of Nazism.

University professors reclaimed their jobs by saying they had never been Nazis. After that they might have retained some right-wing ideas or certain hidden prejudices. However, they could hardly begin leading their students toward a return to the Nazi ideology. Their denial and repression of memory contributed, I believe, to a suppression of the actual Nazi past, with its complications, but it also rendered difficult or impossible any attempt to argue on behalf of Nazi ideals. The betrayal of the humanities that lay at the heart of the Nazi worldview, with its prejudice against open inquiry and academic freedom, had to be condemned after 1945. At that moment, those who claimed never to have been Nazis had to speak, almost by necessity, in support of humanistic values. Whether they meant it or not, it worked.

BIBLIOGRAPHY

Archival Sources

GUA   Universitätsarchiv in Göttingen
LKA   Landeskirchlichesarchiv in Hannover
NSA   Niedersächsisches Hauptstaatsarchiv in Hannover

Secondary Sources

Aly, Götz. "Theodor Schieder, Werner Conze oder: Die Vorstufen der physischen Vernichtung." In *Deutsche Historiker im Nationalsozialismus*, edited by Winfried Schulze and Otto Gerhard Oexle, 163–82. 2nd ed. Frankfurt, Germany: Fischer, 1999.

Aly, Götz, and Susanne Heim. *Architects of Annihilation: Auschwitz and the Logic of Destruction*. Princeton, NJ: Princeton University Press, 2003.

Becker, Heinrich, Hans-Joachim Dahms, and Cornelia Wegeler, eds. *Die Universität Göttingen unter dem Nationalsozialismus*. Second, expanded edition. Munich: K. G. Saur, 1998.

Berg, Nicolas. *Der Holocaust und die westdeutschen Historiker: Erforschung und Erinnerung*. Berlin: Wallstein, 2003.

Berghahn, Volker. *Der Stahlhelm: Bund der Frontsoldaten 1918–1935*. Düsseldorf: Droste, 1966.

Besier, Gerhard. *"Selbstreinigung" unter britischer Besatzungsherrschaft: Die Evangelisch-Lutherische Landeskirche Hannovers und ihr Landesbischof Marahrens 1945–1947*. Studien zur Kirchengeschichte Niedersachsens 27. Göttingen, Germany: Vandenhoek & Ruprecht, 1986.

Beushausen, Ulrich, Hans-Joachim Dahms, Thomas Koch, Almuth Massing, and Konrad Obermann. "Die Medizinische Fakultät im Dritten Reich." In Becker, Dahms, and Wegeler, *Universität Göttingen*, 183–286.

Beyerchen, Alan D. *Scientists under Hitler: Politics and the Physics Community in the Third Reich*. New Haven, CT: Yale University Press, 1977.

Bialas, Wolfgang, and Anson Rabinbach, eds. *Nazi Germany and the Humanities: How German Academics Embraced Nazism*. Oxford: Oneworld, 2014. Originally published 2006.

Biddescomb, Perry. *The Denazification of Germany 1945–1950*. Stroud, UK: Tempus, 2006.

Birnbaum, Walter. *Zeuge meiner Zeit: Aussagen zu 1912 bis 1972*. Göttingen, Germany: Vandenhoek and Ruprecht, 1973.

Bizer, Ernst. "Der Fall Dehn." In Wilhelm Schneemelcher, ed. *Festschrift für Günther Dehn*. Neukirchen, Germany: Neukirchener Verlag, 1957, 239–61. .

Boehling, Rebecca. *A Question of Priorities: Democratic Reform and Economic Recovery in Postwar Germany*. New York: Berghahn, 1996.

Botzenhart, Erich. *Die deutsche Revolution 1806/1813*. Hamburg, Germany: Hanseatischer, 1940.

Brandi, Karl. *The Emperor Charles V*. New York: Alfred A. Knopf, 1940.

———. *Versailles, 28. Juni 1919*. Göttingen, Germany: Göttinger Studentenschaft, 1929.

Brednich, Rolf Wilhelm. "Volkskunde—Die völkische Wissenschaft von Blut und Boden." In Becker, Dahms, and Wegeler, *Universität Göttingen*, 491–98.

Burleigh, Michael. *Germany Turns Eastwards: A Study of Ostforschung in the Third Reich*. Cambridge: Cambridge University Press, 1988.

Cantor, Norman. *Inventing the Middle Ages*. New York: William Morrow, 1991.

Dahms, Hans-Joachim. "Einleitung." In Becker, Dahms, and Wegeler, *Universität Göttingen*, 29–74.

———. "The Professionalization of National Socialist Jewish Statistics: Preparation for the Holocaust." Unpublished manuscript, n.d., in the possession of the author.

Dehn, Günther. *Die alte Zeit, die vorigen Jahre: Lebenserinnerungen*. Munich: Chr. Kaiser, 1962.

———. *Kirche und Völkerversöhnung: Dokumente zum Halleschen Universitätskonflikt*. Berlin: Furche, 1931.

Elvert, Jürgen, and Jürgen Nielsen-Sikora, eds. *Kulturwissenschaften und Nationalsozialismus*. Stuttgart, Germany: Franz Steiner, 2008.

Ericksen, Robert P. *Complicity in the Holocaust: Churches and Universities in Nazi Germany*. New York: Cambridge University Press, 2012.

———. "Die Göttinger Theologische Fakultät im Dritten Reich." In Becker, Dahms, and Wegeler, *Universität Göttingen*, 75–101.

———. "Kontinuitäten konservativer Geschichtsschreibung am Seminar für Mittlere und Neuere Geschichte: Von der Weimarer Zeit über die nationalsozialistische Ära bis in die Bundesrepublik." In Becker, Dahms, and Wegeler, *Universität Göttingen*, 427–53.

———. *Theologians under Hitler: Gerhard Kittel, Paul Althaus, and Emanuel Hirsch*. New Haven, CT: Yale University Press, 1985.

Faye, Emanuel. *Heidegger: The Introduction of Nazism into Philosophy in Light of the Unpublished Seminars of 1933–1935*. New Haven, CT: Yale University Press, 2009.
Fishburn, Matthew. *Burning Books*. New York: Palgrave Macmillan, 2008.
Frei, Norbert. *Vergangenheitspolitik: Die Anfänge der Bundesrepublik und die NS-Vergangenheit*. Munich: Beck, 1996.
Friedländer, Saul. *Nazi Germany and the Jews*. Vol. 1, *The Years of Persecution, 1933–1939*. New York: Harper Collins, 1997.
———. *Nazi Germany and the Jews*. Vol. 2, *The Years of Extermination, 1939–1945*. New York: Harper Collins, 2007.
"Georgia Augusta—Universität im Dritten Reich." *Politikon: Göttinger Studentenzeitschrift für Niedersachsen* 9 (January 1965): 3–4.
[Gercke, Achim.] *Der jüdische Einfluss auf den Deutschen Hohen Schulen: Ein Familienkundlicher Nachweis über die jüdischen und verjudeten Universitäts- und Hochschulprofessoren*. Heft 1, *Universität Göttingen*. Göttingen, Germany: Kreis der Freunde und Förderer der Deutschen Auskunftei, 1928.
Giles, Geoffrey. *Students and National Socialism in Germany*. Princeton, NJ: Princeton University Press, 1985.
Goebel, Klaus. "Theologen die Hitler unterstützten: Über Gerhard Kittel, Paul Althaus, Emanuel Hirsch." *Frankfurter Allgemeine Zeitung*, June 5, 1986, 11.
Gross, Matthias. "Die nationalsozialistische 'Umwandlung' der ökonomische Institute." In Becker, Dahms, and Wegeler, *Universität Göttingen*, 156–82.
Halfmann, Frank. "Eine 'Pflanzstätte bester nationalsozialistischer Rechtsgelehrter': Die juristische Abteilung der Rechts- und Staatswissenschaftlichen Fakultät." In Becker, Dahms, and Wegeler, *Universität Göttingen*, 102–55.
Hausmann, Frank-Rutger, ed. *Die Rolle der Geisteswissenschaften im Dritten Reich 1933–1945: Schriften des Historischen Kollegs* Kolloquien 53, Munich: Oldenbourg, 2002.
Heiber, Helmut. *Universität unterm Hakenkreuz*. Teil 1, *Der Professor im Dritten Reich: Bilder aus der akademischen Provinz*. Munich: K. G. Saur, 1991.
———. *Walter Frank und sein Reichsinstitut für Geschichte des neuen Deutschlands*. Stuttgart, Germany: Deutsche Verlag-Anstalt, 1966.
Hirsch, Emanuel. *Das Alte Testament und die Predigt des Evangeliums*. Tübingen, Germany: Katzmann, 1936.
Hockenos, Matthew D. *A Church Divided: German Protestants Confront the Nazi Past*. Bloomington: Indiana University Press, 2004.
Jarausch, Konrad H. *After Hitler: Recivilizing Germans, 1945–1995*. Oxford: Oxford University Press, 2006.
———. *The Unfree Professions: German Lawyers, Teachers, and Engineers, 1900–1950*. New York: Oxford University Press, 1990.
Kaehler, Siegfried A. "Wehrverfassung und Volk in Deutschland von den Freiheitskriegen bis zum Weltkriege. Rede zur Reichsfeier am 30. Januar 1937,

gehalten in der Aula der Georgia Augusta." *Mitteilungen des Universitätsbundes Göttingen* 18, no. 2 (1937): 1–27.

Kater, Michael H. *Studentenschaft und Rechtsradikalismus in Deutschland 1918–1933: Eine sozialgeschichtliche Studie zur Bildungskrise in der Weimarer Republik.* Berlin: Hoffmann und Campe, 1975.

Kittel, Gerhard. "Die ältesten Judenkarikaturen: Die 'Trierer Terrakotten.'" *Forschungen zur Judenfrage* 4 (1940): 250–59.

———. "Die Behandlung des Nichtjuden nach dem Talmud." *Archiv für Judenfragen* (Berlin) 1, Group A1 (1943): 7–17.

———. *Die Judenfrage.* Stuttgart, Germany: Kohlhammer, 1933, 3rd ed. 1934.

Kittel, Gerhard, and Eugen Fischer. "Das antike Weltjudentum: Tatsachen, Texte, Bilder." *Forschungen zur Judenfrage* 7 (1943).

Klee, Ernst. *Persilscheine und falsche Pässe: Wie die Kirchen den Nazis halfen.* Frankfurt, Germany: Fischer, 1991.

Lehmann, Hartmut, and Otto Gerhard Oexle, eds. *Nationalsozialismus in den Kulturwissenschaften, Band 1: Fächer—Milieus—Karriere; Band 2: Leitbegriffe—Deutungs- Muster-Paradigmenkämpfe. Erfahrungen und Transformationen im Exil.* Göttingen, Germany: Vandenhoek and Ruprecht, 2004.

Marshall, Barbara. "Der Einfluss der Universität auf die politische Entwicklung der Stadt Göttingen." *Niedersächsisches Jahrbuch für Landesgeschichte* 49 (1977): 265–301.

Marten, H.-G. *Der niedersächsische Ministersturz: Protest und Widerstand der Georg-August-Universität Göttingen gegen den Kultusminister Schlüter im Jahre 1955.* Göttingen, Germany: Vandenhoek and Ruprecht, 1987.

Meinecke, Friedrich. *The German Catastrophe: Contemplations and Reflections.* Cambridge, MA: Harvard University Press, 1946.

Naimark, Norman M. *The Russians in Germany: A History of the Soviet Zone of Occupation, 1945–1949.* Cambridge, MA: Belknap Press of Harvard University Press, 1995.

Niethammer, Lutz. *Die Mitläuferfabrik: Die Entnazifizierung am Beispiel Bayern.* Berlin: Dietz, 1982.

Ostdeutsche Morgenpost. "Oberschlesienreise vom Geh.-Rat Dr. Brandi und Dr. Schramm, Göttingen." No. 104, April 15, 1932.

Pauck, Wilhelm, and Marian Pauck. *Paul Tillich: His Life and Thought.* Vol. 1, *Life.* New York: Harper and Row, 1976.

Rath, Klaus-Wilhelm. *Konkurrenzsystem, Organisationsform und Wirtschaftlichkeit im Versicherungswesen.* Leipzig, Germany: Meiner, 1942.

Remy, Steven P. *The Heidelberg Myth: The Nazification and Denazification of a German University.* Cambridge, MA: Harvard University Press, 2002.

Ringer, Fritz K. *The Decline of the German Mandarins: The German Academic Community, 1890–1933.* Cambridge, MA: Harvard University Press, 1969.

Rosenow, Ulf. "Die Göttinger Physik unter dem Nationalsozialismus." In Becker, Dahms, and Wegeler, *Universität Göttingen*, 552–88.
Rüegg, Walter, ed. *A History of the University in Europe*. Vol. 3, *Universities in the Nineteenth and Early Twentieth Centuries (1800–1945)*. Cambridge: Cambridge University Press, 2004.
Saller, Hans. *Die Rassenlehre des Nationalsozialismus in Wissenschaft und Propaganda*. Darmstadt: Progress, 1961.
Sauder, Gerhard, ed. *Die Bücherverbrennung 10. Mai 1933*. Berlin: Ullstein, 1985.
Schappacher, Norbert. "Das Mathematische Institut der Universität Göttingen 1920-1950," in Becker, Dahms, and Wegeler, *Universität Göttingen*, 523–551.
Schramm, Percy Ernst. *A History of the English Coronation*. Oxford: Clarendon Press, 1937.
———. *Hitler: The Man and the Military Leader*. Chicago: Chicago Review Press, 1999.
———. *Kaiser, Rom, und Renovatio*. Leipzig, Germany: B. G. Teubner, 1929.
———. *Kriegstagebuch des Oberkommandos der Wehrmacht*. 8 vols. Frankfurt, Germany: Bernhard und Graefe Verlag für Wehrwesen, 1961.
Schumann, Peter. "Die deutschen Historikertage von 1893 bis 1937: Die Geschichte einer fach-historischen Institution im Spiegel der Presse." PhD diss., Philipps University of Marburg, 1974. Self-published by the author in 1975.
Steinweis, Alan. *Studying the Jew: Scholarly Antisemitism in Nazi Germany*. Cambridge, MA: Harvard University Press, 2008.
Szabó, Anikó. *Vertreibung, Rückkehr, Wiedergutmachung: Göttinger Hochschullehrer im Schatten des Nationalsozialismus*. Göttingen, Germany: Wallstein, 2000.
Tent, James F. *Mission on the Rhine: "Reeducation" and Denazification in American-Occupied Germany*. Chicago: University of Chicago Press, 1984.
Thimme, David. *Percy Ernst Schramm und das Mittelalter: Wandlungen eines Geschichtsbildes*. Göttingen, Germany: Vandenhoek and Ruprecht, 2006.
Vollnhals, Clemens. *Evangelische Kirche und Entnazifizierung, 1945–1949: Die Last der nationalsozialistischen Vergangenheit*. Studien zur Zeitgeschichte 36. Munich: Oldenbourg, 1989.
Weinreich, Max. *Hitler's Professors: The Part of Scholarship in Germany's Crimes against the Jewish People*. New York: Yiddish Scientific Institute (YIVO), 1946. Reprinted with a foreword by Martin Gilbert. New Haven, CT: Yale University Press, 1999.
Wildt, Michael. *An Uncompromising Generation: The Nazi Leadership of the Reich Security Main Office*. Translated by Tom Lampert. Madison: University of Wisconsin Press, 2009.
Willrich, Hugo. "Ein demokratischer Willkomensgruss für unsere neu berufenen Historiker." *Göttinger Tageblatt*, April 20, 1921, 3.
———. *Juden und Griechen vor der makkabäischen Erhebung*. Göttingen, Germany: Vandenhoek and Ruprecht, 1895.

Wundt, Max. "Das Judentum in der Philosophie." In "Sitzungsberichte der Zweiten Arbeitstagung der Forschungsabteilung der Reichsinstituts für Geschichte des neuen Deutschlands vom 12. bis 14. Mai 1937." *Forschungen zur Judenfrage* 2 (1937): 75–87.

ROBERT P. ERICKSEN is the Kurt Mayer Chair of Holocaust Studies Emeritus at Pacific Lutheran University in Tacoma, Washington. He has written or edited six books, including *Theologians under Hitler* (Yale, 1985), *Complicity in the Holocaust: Churches and Universities in Nazi Germany* (Cambridge, 2012), and *Betrayal: German Churches and the Holocaust* (edited with Susannah Heschel, Fortress, 1999). He is Fellow of the Alexander von Humboldt Foundation; serves as Chair of the Committee on Ethics, Religion, and the Holocaust at the United States Holocaust Memorial Museum; and sits on the board of editors of *Kirchliche Zeitgeschichte* and an online journal, the *Contemporary Church History Quarterly*.

THIRTEEN

THE UNIVERSITY OF GÖTTINGEN AND ITS POSTWAR RESPONSE TO PERSECUTED COLLEAGUES

A Broken Relationship

ANIKÓ SZABÓ

I. REBUILDING THE UNIVERSITY AFTER THE WAR

As Robert Ericksen described in the previous chapter, the University of Göttingen experienced a pronounced nazification beginning in 1933 and a denazification beginning in 1945. That first wrenching change involved a removal of all Jewish and leftist faculty members, beginning with the April 1933 Law for the Restoration of the Professional Civil Service, intended to "cleanse" the German Civil Service in line with Nazi ideology. This change was perpetrated by the regime as an effort toward *Gleichschaltung* [the coordination of all German institutions with Nazi ideology]. This process involved a betrayal of the humanities not only by the Nazi regime but also by many of the remaining faculty who endorsed Hitler's leadership and, embracing his goals, strived toward *Selbstgleichschaltung* [self-coordination]. The subsequent process, the denazification of universities, began with Germany's defeat in 1945 and the division of Germany into four zones of occupation under British, American, French, and Soviet control. The two bookends of this dramatic interruption of university life—the nazification beginning in 1933 and the denazification beginning in 1945—each involved external as well as internal actors.

The external force in 1945 at the university was the British Military Government, exercising its prerogatives within the British Zone of Occupation. After the distortions of the National Socialist years, the British hoped to rebuild universities physically but also intellectually.[1] In order to democratize the universities, the British Military Government held that structural and personnel changes were necessary, but it hoped to avoid an aggressive confrontation by relying on a policy of indirect control.[2] This meant that Germans themselves were expected to reform and democratize all institutions, but especially universities, whose legal conventions for university autonomy were largely accepted by the British. Universities played only a subordinate role in the larger framework of British occupation plans, yet as a component of reeducation and given their role as educational institutions for German youth, it was hoped universities would make an important contribution toward the long-term democratization of Germany.

Very early on the British occupation plan considered the continuation of education to be sensible and controlled research to be tenable.[3] By September 17, 1945, course instruction began at the University of Göttingen. Fifteen months later, on January 1, 1947, responsibility for educational matters was once again completely turned over to the Germans.[4] The British retained for themselves *only* the right of veto. The designated agency in the state of Lower Saxony, led by a member of the Social Democratic Party, Adolf Grimme, also allowed the university to act broadly and independently. Initially, this meant the Department of Culture and/or the Department of Science, Art, and Education, established on November 1, 1946, in the High Office [*Oberpräsidium*] in Hannover. Later, universities fell under the Culture Ministry of the State of Lower Saxony.

The first postwar rector at the University of Göttingen, the jurist Rudolf Smend,[5] later described the situation with these words: "it was a heartening situation after the end of the horrors of war and after the fall of a disgraceful

---

1. This chapter draws on Anikó Szabó, *Vertreibung, Rückkehr, Wiedergutmachung: Göttinger Hochschullehrer im Schatten des Nationalsozialismus* (Göttingen, Germany: Wallstein, 2000). Gerald Fetz prepared a preliminary translation of this chapter from the original German, which was then shaped for this volume by Robert P. Ericksen. Tina M. Sherman contributed editing expertise. The Center for Holocaust and Genocide Studies at the University of Minnesota generously extended a subvention in support of translation costs.

2. Siegfried Müller, "Einleitung," in *Nordwestdeutsche Hochschulkonferenzen 1945–1948*, ed. Manfred Heinemann, 2 vols. (Hildesheim, Germany: Lax, 1990), 1:1–30 (at 3).

3. Ulrich Schneider, "Zur Entnazifizierung der Hochschullehrer in Niedersachsen 1945–1949," *Niedersächsisches Jahrbuch für Landesgeschichte* 61 (1989): 325–46 (at 326–28).

4. Müller, "Einleitung," 3.

5. Rudolf Smend (1882–1975), a professor of state, church, and administrative law, was forced to transfer in 1935 from his full Professorship at the University of Berlin to the same rank at Göttingen. He then served as the acting rector at the University of Göttingen from

tyranny, [to enter] into the red dawn of a difficult, yet certainly better and liberated future. Following the evil and filth of Nazi rule, it appeared to the academic sensibility... to be doubly heartening to be able to rebuild the German university within the boundaries of the possible, on a path toward academic autonomy, without a board of control and within what was allowed by the English."[6] By pointing to university autonomy, the professorial faculty succeeded in turning back not only a structural university reform, which could have limited its influence at the university, but also ensured that the professoriate could make largely autonomous decisions about hiring and filling positions.[7] Being able to assess the qualifications and reputations of applicants allowed them to help former colleagues gain a position and also became a method for keeping out unwanted faculty colleagues. After 1945, positions and conditions at the university were open to arrangement. Holdover professors at Göttingen, having secured their overall control, realized that their actions had to be newly defined, negotiated, protected, and made public.[8]

II. THE INITIAL STAGES OF REHABILITATING FACULTY MEMBERS WHO WERE DISMISSED BETWEEN 1933 AND 1945

After the peaceful surrender of the city of Göttingen on April 8, 1945, followed by the arrest of the university rector on April 10, faculty attempted to shape the new start of the university themselves. On April 12, all deans stepped down and their successors were elected from among members of the senate who had

---

April 12, 1945, until July 27, 1945, and continued as the elected rector from July 28, 1945, to March 31, 1946. See Wilhelm Ebel, ed., *Catalogus Professorum Gottingensium 1734–1962* (Göttingen, Germany: Vandenhoeck & Ruprecht, 1962), 28, 54.

 6. Rudolf Smend, ["Adolf Grimme,"] in *Wirkendes, sorgendes Dasein: Begegnungen mit Adolf Grimme. Gruß der Freunde und Weggefährten zum 70. Geburtstag*, ed. Walther G. Olischewski (Berlin: Arani, 1959), 105–8 (at 105). In contrast to the British, Smend showed himself to be extremely antireform. See Waldemar Krönig and Klaus-Dieter Müller, *Nachkriegssemester: Studium in Kriegs- und Nachkriegszeit* (Stuttgart, Germany: Franz Steiner, 1990), 92.

 7. Falk Pingel, "Wissenschaft, Bildung, und Demokratie: Der gescheiterte Versuch einer Universitätsreform," in *Grenzgänger: Aufsätze von Falk Pingel*, ed. Georg-Eckert-Institute, Studien des Georg-Eckert-Instituts zur internationalen Bildungsmedienforschung 125 (Göttingen, Germany: Vandenhoeck & Ruprecht, 2009), 233–63.

 8. Mitchell G. Ash, "Verordnete Umbrüche—Konstruierte Kontinuitäten: Zur Entnazifizierung von Wissenschaftlern und Wissenschaften nach 1945," *Zeitschrift für Geschichtswissenschaft* 43, no. 10 (1995): 903–23.

not belonged to the Nazi Party. Following that, the new senate, the highest decision-making body in the university, named the sixty-three-year-old Professor of Constitutional Law, Rudolf Smend, to be the acting rector. Due to this "self-cleansing," a caesura was formally drawn and the responsibility to act appeared to be secured. The military government confirmed Smend as rector but retained for itself further personnel decisions.[9]

On May 2 and 5, 1945, just days before Germany's surrender to the victorious Allies, professors in the Göttingen senate proposed the rehabilitation of university faculty members who had been dismissed during the Nazi period. They were aware that an explanation would be expected and decided to create one while it was still possible to do so, calmly, and also within certain limits. Due to unclear legal conditions at the university, a distinction was made "between personal and abstract rehabilitation and specific re-introduction into the realm of planning and institute leadership."[10] Four days after this meeting of the senate, a message to the professors who had been dismissed during the Nazi period was drawn up:

> The university welcomes as a fortunate result the cancellation of a part of the previous legislation that caused premature dismissals of a number of highly regarded members of its teaching staff, resulting in loss of their positions. Drawing legal conclusions from this change for individual cases must be left to the future. With the agreement of the Senate and the Curator (the chief administrative officer), however, I ask you to regard yourselves already as fully entitled members of Georgia Augusta.[11]

Not one word of apology, remorse, or regret for past actions was included in this message, yet the university (there referenced by its formal Latin name) followed

---

9. Wiebke Fesefeldt, *Der Wiederbeginn des kommunalen Lebens in Göttingen: Die Stadt in den Jahren 1945 bis 1948* (Göttingen: Vandenhoeck & Ruprecht, 1962), 140. In the following period all persons were automatically fired who had, before April 1, been members of the NSDAP, had belonged as officers in the SA, SS, or the Gestapo or had assumed tasks for the Security Service of the SS. Their possessions were confiscated, and they were prohibited from stepping foot into the workplace (Wolfgang Krüger, *Entnazifiziert: Zur Praxis der politischen Säuberung in Nordrhein-Westfalen* [Wuppertal, Germany: Peter Hammer, 1982], 22). In the process of denazification, sixteen tenured professors and thirty-eight lecturers were fired between May 1945 and July 1947, but in total, the University of Göttingen received through new hiring twenty-eight tenured professors and ninety-six lecturers as well as assistants, a noticeable increase in personnel numbers. See Schneider, "Zur Entnazifizierung," 341.

10. Göttingen University Archive (hereafter indicated as GUA), Senatsprotokolle, Bd. 1. Sitzung vom May 5, 1945.

11. GUA, K, IX, 83, Bl. 214, Schreiben vom May 9, 1945.

the new order of the day. The handful of professors who were easily reachable were quickly declared to be members of the university administration and faculty. Recipients of this message were seventy-year-old Julius von Gierke, full Professor for civil law; sixty-five-year-old Herman Nohl, full Professor for philosophy and pedagogy; sixty-five-year-old Hans von Wartenberg, full Professor for inorganic chemistry; and sixty-year-old Rudolf von Ehrenberg, a nontenured associate Professor for physiology, who had also previously been a senior assistant.

On June 9, 1945, the senate again took up the issue of colleagues yet to be rehabilitated, discussing broader lists of university employees who had been dismissed during the Nazi period. The agenda remained focused on future actions with the addition of one important stipulation: "We are in agreement that those who were dismissed are not necessarily and merely due to rehabilitation to be appointed to Göttingen positions, but only in the course of the appointment process's goal of appointing only the best."[12] This appointment policy as formulated in the minutes, including the subjective phrase, "only the best," proved to be programmatic for the future. Rectifying past injustice did not have priority but rather the academic reputation of the appointee and, with that, the reputation of the university. Also, in accord with a further decision of the senate on July 5, 1945, a position could only be filled if it were vacant.[13] This latter issue quickly became rancorous in the rehabilitation of Rudolf von Ehrenberg. His position as a salaried assistant and as a nontenured associate professor had been taken by Hans Joachim Deuticke, by this time a full Professor[14] and heir to the place that should have been awarded to Ehrenberg.[15] It was resolved that Ehrenberg should be offered only a "Diäten-Professorship,"

---

12. GUA, Senatsprotokolle, Bd. 1, Sitzung vom June 9, 1945.

13. GUA, Senatsprotokolle, Bd. 1, Sitzung vom July 5, 1945. This included protection for administrators and professors, even if they were still prisoners of war or awaiting the result of their denazification process.

14. Hans Joachim Deuticke (1898–1976) moved from his 1930 position as a *Privatdozent* at the University of Frankfurt to a nontenured associate professorship in 1934 at Bonn, adjusted to a tenured associate professorship in 1938, followed by a tenured associate professorship in physiological chemistry at Göttingen in 1939. He was promoted to full Professor in 1946 and was granted emeritus status in 1966. From the summer semester of 1952 to the winter semester of 1953–54, he served as rector of the University of Göttingen. See Ebel, *Catalogus Professorum*, 29, 79, 84. See also the Lower Saxony Archive (hereafter indicated as NSA), Nds. 171. Hild., Nr. 71577, Personalbogen 1945; NSA, Nds. 171 Hild., Nr. 63814, Personalbogen 1947; and Katharina Trittel, *Hermann Rein und die Flugmedizin: Erkenntnisstreben und Entgrenzung* (Paderborn, Germany: Schöningh, 2018), 143–44.

15. GUA, Senatsprotokolle, Bd. 1. Sitzung vom June 6, 1945.

an academic status created by the Nazi regime with even lower status as well as an even lower financial benefit than the meager income available to a *Privatdozent*.[16]

In the course of the next months, fifty-four-year-old philologist Kurt Latte, sixty-four-year-old business economist Richard Passow, and sixty-one-year-old international law specialist Herbert Kraus were rehabilitated as full Professors. However, Kurt Latte could only assume his chair temporarily as a stand in. His official installation took place in November 1946 after the chair holder, Hans Drexler,[17] who had been rector until April 1945, became one of the few professors removed permanently from his professorship due to his role as an important Nazi functionary as well as his membership in the Security Service of the Schutzstaffel (SS).[18] With those appointments, all of the dismissed professors who lived in Germany were rehabilitated. It became more difficult regarding the rehabilitation of the nontenured associate professors and Privatdozenten. For those in these categories, reinstating their previous academic titles and their places on the path toward an academic career did not mean placement in an actual position. Only if they had been appointed as a tenured associate professor did they have a right to that position. In the immediate postwar period, associate professor positions were not unimportant financially. When former Privatdozenten who had been dismissed registered with the university, they regained to be sure their *Venia Legendi*,[19] their right to teach. The faculty members already in place, however, were reluctant to offer them an actual

---

16. The right to teach at a German university was based on the habilitation, a second thesis on a different topic required after the completion of a doctoral dissertation. The acceptance of this thesis by a university offered the individual a *Venia Legendi*, the authorization to lecture at that university as a Privatdozent, normally without pay. Various paid assistant positions might become available to that Privatdozent or a contract to teach a specific course. The German system also included a rank roughly corresponding to nontenured associate professor [*ausserordentlicher* (extraordinary) *Professor*]. Scholars holding that rank were paid for teaching assignments but did not have security from term to term. They could be offered tenure and hold a secure position with financial stability, but only an ordinary or full Professor [*ordentlicher Professor*] enjoyed the substantial income and security available to the German professoriate.

17. Hans Drexler (1895–1984), full Professor of classical philology, moved in 1940 from the University of Breslau to the University of Göttingen, where he served as rector from January 10, 1943, to November 4, 1945. See GUA, K., IX. 1. Bd. II, Bll. 172–73, Kurator der Univ. Göttingen, Feb. 6, 1951; and NSA Nds. 171 Hild., Nr. 17389, Personalbogen 1947.

18. See NSA, Nds. 401, Acc. 92/85, Nr. 266 Bl. 30, Kurator der Univ. Göttingen to the Minister für Volksbildung, Kunst, und Wissenschaft in Hannover, December 17, 1946.

19. See note 16 in this chapter regarding the Venia Legendi.

position.[20] One striking exception was the rehabilitation of the Privatdozent Heinrich Düker. Although Düker had not been employed by the Psychology Institute but rather had been funded by a grant, he was fully rehabilitated in the summer of 1945. Düker received his teaching rights again, was appointed to a position as associate professor, and received enhanced pay as well.[21] Göttingen professors could not and did not want to deny their esteem for a man who had participated in the resistance against National Socialism, was arrested, and suffered in prison and in a concentration camp.[22]

On the other hand, the university showed itself to be reluctant regarding the rehabilitation of Karl Saller. Saller had last been a Privatdozent and a salaried assistant in the Anatomical Institute. Initially he had fully welcomed Hitler's rise to power, but he then quarreled with leading scientists about race theory. These scientists represented and soon advanced Hitler's notions about race, which Saller disputed as unscientific. Saller's study of human genetics traced only hard characteristics, such as hair color, in human reproduction. The geneticists attractive to Hitler, however, claimed that "soft" characteristics—for example, the sort of behavioral stereotypes long attributed to Jews by antisemites—could also be measured through genetics. More importantly, those advocating this broader, more careless view of genetics were attracted to and supportive of eugenics, the purging of unwanted characteristics in unwelcome populations. Saller already by the summer of 1933 had called these ideas, the ideas also

---

20. In September 1945 there were twenty-five *Diäten-professoren* positions (the appointments with limited budgets explained earlier) that were open for hiring. Therefore, there could have been restitutions through a re-hiring of all Privatdozenten. See NSA, Nds. 92/85, Nr. 135, Kurator der Univ. Göttingen, Bojunga, to the Oberpräsidium Hannover, September 9, 1945, and Szabó, *Vertreibung*, 90. The rehabilitation of the Privatdozent for pediatrics, Hugo Fasold, and the Privatdozent for gynecology, Robert Brühl, both of whom had been forced to leave Göttingen as political opponents, was made possible through the renewed awarding of the Venia Legendi to them (Szabó, *Vertreibung*, on Fasold, 162–66, and on Brühl, 167–71).

21. GUA, Senatsprotokolle, Bd. I, Aug. 29, 1945, as well as NSA, Nds. 401, Acc. 92/85, Nr. 135, Rein als Vertreter des Rektors to the Kurator [Rein as representative of the rector to the curator], August 30, 1945.

22. Heinrich Düker (1898–1986) had his leg amputated as the result of an injury in the First World War. As a member of the International Socialist Combat Group, he had actively provided opposition to the Nazi regime and had distributed leaflets. After being freed from the concentration camp Sachsenhausen in early May 1945, he had to spend several months in a military hospital before he could return to Göttingen. Still in 1945, however, he was elected mayor of Göttingen. On October 1, 1946, he became full Professor and director of an institute at the University of Marburg. For more information, see Szabó, *Vertreibung*, 205–9.

advocated by Hitler, "nonsense."[23] As a result of his stance, Saller was denied the teaching assignment for human genetics, his Venia Legendi was revoked, and a plan to name him to an associate professorship was rescinded. When he wanted to settle in south Germany as a doctor, he was denied a license, so he had to earn his money as a homeopath.[24] In September 1945, Saller approached the Faculty of Medicine in Göttingen, and as a result, his Venia Legendi was restored; however, as the files document, the faculty was not interested in any actual assignment or further rehabilitation for him. When Saller requalified in Munich and was promoted to full Professor status a year later, the Göttingen faculty was relieved.

The Faculty of Medicine in the meantime had hired Fritz Lenz, one of the leading race theorists in the Nazi period and a prominent advocate of both soft genetics and the practice of eugenics.[25] Saller was well-informed about the event. Already in December 1945, when Saller's move to Munich was in no way anticipated, the faculty wanted to submit a request in order to establish a chair in Saller's field, human genetics. The dean expressed how pleased he would be to appoint the "best representative in this discipline in Germany."[26] It is now clear that "only the best" in human genetics by 1945 could favor someone like Fritz Lenz, who had coauthored the most prominent book on human genetics in Germany in 1921 and prospered throughout the Nazi period. He was given initially a teaching position at Göttingen and in October 1946 an Extraordinary Professorship for Human Genetics. It was precisely Fritz Lenz with whom Saller, during the Nazi era, had engaged in the public dispute about race theory that ended his career as an academic and medical doctor. The hiring of Lenz, whom Saller later described as a "pioneer of National Socialist sterilization

---

23. For more on these issues, see Robert P. Ericksen, *Complicity in the Holocaust: Churches and Universities in Nazi Germany* (Cambridge: Cambridge University Press, 2012), 154–58.

24. For details, see Szabó, *Vertreibung*, 172–97; as well as Ulrich Beushausen et al., "Die Medizinische Fakultät im Dritten Reich," in *Die Universität Göttingen unter dem Nationalsozialismus*, ed. Heinrich Becker, Hans-Joachim Dahms, and Cornelia Wegeler, 2nd ed. (Munich: K. G. Saur, 1998), 183–286 (at 198–205, 243, 246–48).

25. Fritz Lenz (1887–1976) was a full Professor of eugenics at the University of Berlin and also a head of department at the Institute for Racial Hygiene and Heredity Research of the Kaiser Wilhelm Institute (KWI) for Anthropology. He fled to Westfalen shortly before the end of the war, where his denazification process declared him a *Mitläufer* [Nazi sympathizer]. After his appointment as a tenured associate professor in 1946, he was promoted to full Professor in 1952 and reached emeritus in 1955 (GUA, K, PA Lenz). See also *Deutsche Biographische Enzyklopädie* (1997), s.v. "Lenz, Fritz."

26. GUA, Rektorat, PA Lenz, Rudolf Schoen as Dean of the Med. Fakulty to the Oberpräsidium, Hannover, December 28, 1945.

orgies," did not only anger Saller.[27] In the spring of 1947, the hiring of Lenz caused a noticeable storm. Yet the waves calmed quickly, and Lenz's career was not damaged for long.[28] The Göttingen faculty in its appointment of Lenz had undoubtedly appointed someone with a prominent career. However, that left it showing respect for a career rooted in the Nazi world of 1933 to 1945 as well as a polluted scientific tradition now able to influence a new generation of colleagues. Only a few faculty members saw that as a significant problem, however, since Lenz was regarded by them as an outstanding scientist, one of "the best." Saller objected to the behavior of his colleagues not only in personal letters but also in publications as a public critic of his profession.[29]

Problems of another kind arose in the attempted rehabilitation of the mathematician, Kurt Hohenemser. Hohenemser's Venia Legendi had been rescinded due to his Jewish background, and he had been fired from his position as an assistant. On June 25, 1945, he applied to return to the university as a Privatdozent and assistant. In his letter, Hohenemser mentioned political implications during the change in leadership of the Institute for Mechanics in 1933. Although that was meant to clarify his removal, it also tended to incriminate the leader of the Institute at that time, who remained on the faculty.[30] Immediately, other faculty members responded with anger and with complete solidarity. The professors in the faculty regarded "any fruitful, collegial work or cooperation with Dr. Hohenemser to be impossible."[31] Hohenemser further damaged his hopes when he proposed, in an additional letter, that there be a full investigation of personnel changes during the NS period.[32] Despite this fracas, Hohenemser's claim for rehabilitation was indisputable. At the end of March 1946, he had to be granted renewal of his Venia Legendi.[33] The faculty, however, never forgot

---

27. GUA, Med. 91, Saller to Hermann Rein, April 20, 1948, Rückseite von Seite II.
28. GUA, Rektorat, PA Lenz, Aktennotiz von Hermann Rein als Rektor der Universität Göttingen, March 6, 1947.
29. Karl Saller, *Die Rassenlehre des Nationalsozialismus in Wissenschaft und Propaganda* (Darmstadt, Germany: Progress, 1961); Karl Saller, "Der Rassenmord und Heldenwahn des Nationalsozialismus," in *Unmenschliche Medizin*, vol. 1, ed. the Internationales Auschwitz Komitee (Warsaw: Internationales Auschwitz Komitee, 1969), 74–193.
30. NSA, Nds. 401. Acc. 92/85, Nr. 135, Hohenemser an Kurator, June 25, 1945.
31. GUA, K, PA Hohenemser, Bl. 19, Dekan der Math.-Nat. Fak., Arnold Eucken, an den Rektor der Univ. Göttingen, July 7, 1945.
32. GUA, K, PA Hohenemser, Bl. 23, Hohenemser an den Rektor der Univ. Göttingen, July 30, 1945.
33. NSA, Nds. 401, Acc. 92/85, Nr. 135. Oberpräsidium, Abt. IV/2 an Hohenemser, March 25, 1946.

and energetically opposed any further form of rehabilitation of his position, drawing out the process for so long that Hohenemser finally capitulated. In the summer of 1947 he took a position in St. Louis in the United States. Hohenemser had the law on his side; however, professors already at Göttingen had the power. Seldom were the motives for a rejection so obvious as in this case.[34] Hohenemser had miscalculated the situation completely, thinking there would be some kind of interest on the part of the faculty or the university in addressing harsh practices that had taken place during the Nazi period.

III. THE UNWANTED TASK OF REHIRING ÉMIGRÉS

The quarrels regarding rehiring had just gathered steam when on September 26 and 27, 1945, the first regional university conference took place in Göttingen, a convenient location in a city that had almost completely avoided war damage. Representatives from universities and university administrations met with members of the British Military Government. Under the agenda item "New Hiring and Rehabilitation," the establishment of a "Central Certification Office" for unemployed university teachers was discussed. First on the list were "professors from the eastern German territories that had been lost and from the zone occupied by the Russians." Second on the list were "professors from Austria, Czechoslovakia, and Alsace," that is, from regions recently part of greater Germany. Third on the list were "professors abroad who had earlier held professorships at German universities." Finally, "there was a large number of domestic professors from Germany who had been more or less ruthlessly pushed out by the National Socialist regime, and these should be reactivated." After this recounting, representatives of the military government intervened to urge universities to give specific priority in the hiring of university faculty to those "who had been expelled or had emigrated due to National Socialist laws," and they ordered conference participants to make a formal commitment along those lines.

Rudolf Smend, who chaired the conference, then took the podium and responded immediately to the British proposals. He noted that "not every professor who came into question for being appointed again would be appointed," citing age and illness as possible reasons as well as a lack of academic activity

---

34. Szabó, *Vertreibung*, 214–32; see also Gerhard Rammer, "Die Nazifizierung und Entnazifizierung der Physik an der Universität Göttingen" (PhD diss., Universität Göttingen, Germany, 2009), 519–32, doi: http://hdl.handle.net/11858/00-1735-0000-0006-B49F-4.

in recent years. "A rehabilitation of such professors would only be possible after a new examination of conditions for appointment, and complete and total usefulness must be evident."[35] In formulating the official decision, Smend's objections were ultimately included. Professors who were dismissed or had emigrated should be assigned "in all suitable cases" to their earlier positions, but only if they had "academic usefulness," and if they could help reestablish the "character of German university faculty." If their earlier position "were occupied," an equivalent position should be offered. In the case of "decreased academic usefulness," however, appropriate treatment, particularly retirement, should be guaranteed. If the occasion allows, former positions of those affected should be held open for them. The acceptance of this carefully limited decision was regarded by those at this university conference as "an honorable duty and sign of solidarity from all German university administrations, universities and faculties."[36]

Despite these words about "an honorable duty and sign of solidarity," any hope for a positive result for most faculty dismissed for political and racial reasons between 1933 and 1945 proved futile. Göttingen University inquired of several full Professors whether everyone eligible for reappointment had signed in, but that could not be determined.[37] Individual professors named émigrés who had participated in the new appointment process, but these candidates for reappointment were hardly given serious consideration. Rehabilitation was never in the forefront of faculty minds but rather the "goal of appointing only the best."[38] Existing professors of the university claimed to be the ones possessing the power to define abilities and renown, and the Culture Ministry of Lower Saxony did not offer any corrective. It followed, rather, the suggestions of Göttingen professors. A further obstacle to rehabilitation soon appeared as well. The Lower Saxony State Chancellery required German citizenship as a qualification for any university position. Faculty members forced to emigrate, however, had usually lost citizenship under National Socialist law and, as a result, had taken the citizenship in their countries of exile. It must be regarded as a scandal that, after 1945, laws reflecting Nazi ideology were still having this sort of impact.[39] Only later were new regulations adopted, though these were only intended for individual cases.

---

35. Heinemann, *Nordwestdeutsche Hochschulkonferenzen* 1, 68–69.
36. Ibid. 1, 70.
37. Szabó, *Vertreibung*, 253–64.
38. GUA, Senatsprotokolle, Sitzung vom June 9, 1945.
39. Szabó, *Vertreibung*, 247–51.

Alongside organizational obstacles standing in the way of rehiring faculty persecuted in Nazi times, there also existed a large group of academic candidates available who represented competition for émigrés. That actually included university faculty removed during the denazification process after 1945. The Central Certification Office established at the first university conference counted as early as in August 1946 close to one thousand names of potential candidates for academic appointments.[40] Participants in the next conference occupied themselves with offering assistance for those seeking to resume academic careers but with hardly any extra assistance for victims of forced emigration.[41]

IV. THE ÉMIGRÉS AND THEIR FORMER UNIVERSITY

Corresponding to the ideas of the British University Officer, the rehabilitation of émigrés as well as the exchanging of professors and visiting professors were central measures intended for democratizing the universities.[42] However, the hope of British university officers that university professors who had been persecuted and/or those who had emigrated would receive appointments often met with resistance from the professors in place.[43] The military representative could push for rehiring emigrated professors, but that decision remained solely with the university. Visiting professorships and visiting lectures represented an intermediate step, a nonbinding opportunity for émigrés to test the situation in postwar Germany, and many made use of this opportunity early on. But very few took up their former chairs. One exception was Georg Misch, a sixty-seven-year-old philosopher who returned at the beginning of July 1946 directly from exile in England. He had fled to England in 1939 without his wife,

---

40. Müller, "Einleitung," 15. From March 1946, the universities from the French and American Occupation Zones sent lists of the names of university faculty members without positions.

41. See also Anikó Szabó, "Verordnete Rückberufungen: Die Hochschulkonferenzen und die Diskussion um die emigrierten Hochschullehrer," in *Nationalsozialismus und Region: Festschrift für Herbert Obenaus*, ed. Marlis Buchholz and Hans-Dieter Schmied (Bielefeld, Germany: Verlag für Regionalgeschichte, 1996), 339–52.

42. Heinemann, *Nordwestdeutsche Hochschulkonferenzen* 1, 69n51.

43. Walter Dorn, personal advisor to the American General Lucius L. Clay, also reported, on May 22, 1946, on the behavior of the Munich professors' refusal to fill the faculty positions in order to save them for the professors who were yet to be denazified. See Walter L. Dorn, *Inspektionsreisen in der US-Zone: Notizen, Denkschriften, und Erinnerungen aus dem Nachlaß*, ed. and trans. Lutz Niethammer, Schriftenreihe der Vierteljahrshefte für Zeitgeschichte 26 (Stuttgart, Germany: Deutsche Verlagsanstalt, 1973), 87.

who had stayed in Göttingen, but he had not found a secure position there. In Germany, he could count on his connections to be of help.[44]

A few other dismissed professors were able to return to the University of Göttingen, especially if they could match their prominence as scholars with their desire for professional and financial security. The mathematician Carl Siegel, as well as the jurist Gerhard Leibholz, had this in mind when they returned to Germany at the beginning of the 1950s. Siegel had taken a professorship in Göttingen in early 1938. Then, due to the political situation after the outbreak of war and the suspect nature in Nazi Germany of his own conscientious objection during World War I, he did not return from abroad after beginning a lecture tour in February 1940. By way of Denmark and Norway he emigrated to the United States, where he then worked at the Institute for Advanced Study at Princeton. As early as 1946 Siegel visited Göttingen and gave visiting lectures. At that point, he found the situation in postwar Germany too problematical and insecure. Only in 1951 did he, at the age of fifty-four, take over the chair for mathematics at Göttingen.[45]

Like Siegel, Gerhard Leibholz was in no hurry to risk the incalculable situation in postwar Germany. He had been forced to emigrate to England via Switzerland due to his Jewish ancestry. After initial squabbles about the regulations for returning, members of the faculty and the university, but also relevant people in the offices of the State of Lower Saxony, recognized the benefits to be gained through Leibholz's contacts with British politicians and academics.[46] He was first given the advantage of a permanent Visiting Professorship, whereby he would receive his emeritus pay during his stays in Germany. When he finally moved from England to Germany at the age of fifty in 1951 to take up the prestigious position of a judge on the Federal Constitutional Court, he remained connected to the university as a lecturer. Upon ending his judicial role in 1959, he became a full Professor at Göttingen University and filled the newly created chair for political science and government, a position that corresponded to his personal interests.[47]

Other émigrés with Jewish ancestry, like the prominent mathematician Richard Courant and the expert on criminal law Richard Martin Honig, came

---

44. On Georg Misch (1878–1965), see Szabó, *Vertreibung*, 341–44.
45. On Carl Ludwig Siegel (1896–1981), see Szabó, *Vertreibung*, 432–37.
46. Gerhard Leibholz was married to a sister of Dietrich Bonhoeffer. During the Nazi period, the Bonhoeffer family played a prominent role in both academic circles and the resistance. Their prominence did not win them widespread approval in early postwar Germany but would have been seen in England as a positive.
47. On Gerhard Leibholz (1901–1982), see Szabó, *Vertreibung*, 378–91.

to Göttingen regularly for visits. Courant, despite a close connection to Germany, and especially to Göttingen, never seriously thought about returning. Honig visited, but he left his land of exile, America, only in 1974 at the age of eighty-four and after the death of his wife. Then he finally lived once again in Göttingen. Honig had not been able to make that decision in 1946 partly for family reasons but mostly for political considerations. This avoidance remained true for nearly three decades, even though he had not been able to establish himself professionally in America and lived there in poverty.[48]

The prominent physicist Max Born was seventy-two years old when he decided in 1953 to return to Germany. Albert Einstein disapproved of his friend's decision to go back to the "Land of Mass Murderers."[49] After his small number of years working in Scotland, however, Born would have had to live on an income that was "less than that of an unskilled worker."[50] In Germany, by contrast, a regular stipend as an emeritus professor awaited him.[51] Even better, the transfer of his emeritus stipend to a foreign country was arranged in 1954.[52] Born did not return to Göttingen, but his residence in Bad Pyrmont was not very far from that university city. Shortly after his return, Born received the Nobel Prize for Basic Research in Quantum Mechanics, work that he had previously developed in 1926 and a strong reminder of what Germany had given up when it chose to force out Jews.[53] Another Jewish physicist, Nobel Prize recipient James Franck, suffered under Nazi rule even as early as 1925. Post-1945, he could not forget that suffering inflicted on himself and on all Jews by Nazi Germany, nor could he pull himself completely away from the power of attraction that the university city of Göttingen radiated, together with his own positive memories from there. Franck first visited postwar Göttingen in 1953, when he, Max Born, Richard Courant, and Herman Nohl were awarded honorary citizenship of the city. Franck's letter to a Göttingen newspaper on that occasion shows something of his frame of mind, noting that he and Born wanted to "interpret the award in such a way that the magistrate through us

---

48. On Richard Martin Honig (1890–1981), see Szabó, *Vertreibung*, 372–78.
49. Albert Einstein to Max Born, October 12, 1953, in Albert Einstein, Hedwig Born, and Max Born, *Briefwechsel 1916–1955*, commentary by Max Born, preface by Bertrand Russell, foreword by Werner Heisenberg (Munich: Nymphenburger, 1969), 259.
50. Einstein, Born, and Born, *Briefwechsel*, 261.
51. Max Born to Albert Einstein, September 29, 1953, in Einstein, Born, and Born, *Briefwechsel*, 258.
52. Szabó, *Vertreibung*, 332–33.
53. On Max Born (1882–1970), see Szabó, *Vertreibung*, 414–18.

wants to honor the memory of the innumerable dead who fell victim to the racist insanity of National Socialism."[54]

V. THE GÖTTINGEN ACADEMY OF SCIENCES IN 1947: REAPPOINTING FRANCK AND BORN

Six years before Max Born and James Franck were made honorary citizens of Göttingen, they got caught up in a drama over the prestigious Academy of Sciences in Göttingen. This drama was rooted in the drastically different experience of victims of the Nazi regime and those who "got along" with the Nazi state. It also shows the difficulty of finding a way to communicate over this chasm of differing experience. Repeated misunderstandings and perhaps unintended insults made the strained nature of the relationship clear. Possible reconciliations, which started with letters and then visits to Germany, were often accompanied by remarkably painful experiences, such as when Rudolf Smend wrote to James Franck and Max Born at the end of 1946. As president of the Göttingen Academy of Sciences, Smend implored both of them to regard themselves again as members of the Academy. Born and Franck received this letter: "On August 21, 1945, we wrote the following letter to you and several other members of our Academy: 'Since the unfortunate circumstances that led earlier to your dismissals no longer exist, we ask you to allow us to consider you again as members.' Apparently, most of these letters got lost. We are therefore asking you again, in that spirit, to regard yourselves as members. It is our great pleasure that Mr. Misch and Mr. Latte some time ago joined our circle again and are once more working with us."[55]

In a similar tone in May 1945, Smend had declared four easily reachable professors to be members of the university again. He matter-of-factly had termed

---

54. Franck's letter was also sent to the *Göttinger Presse* (March 5, 1953). See James Franck, "Rede des Ehrenbürgers Prof. Dr. James Franck," *Göttinger Jahrbuch* 3 (1954): 101. On James Franck (1882–1964), see Szabó, *Vertreibung*, 424–32.

55. Staatsbibliothek Berlin, Preußischer Kulturbesitz, NL Born 1850, Bl. 1, President of the Akademie der Wissenschaften, Smend, to Max Born, December 28, 1946. This exchange of letters is also published in Jost Lemmerich, *Science and Conscience: The Life of James Franck*, trans. Ann M. Hentschel (Stanford, CA: Stanford University Press, 2011), 265–67. Regarding the Göttingen Academy of Science in the Nazi period, see Désirée Schauz, "Wissenschaft und Politik: Zum Selbstverständnis der Göttinger Akademiemitglieder im Nationalsozialismus," in *Akademien und andere Forschungseinrichtungen im Nationalsozialismus und nach 1945*, ed. Dirk Schumann and Désirée Schauz (Göttingen: Wallstein, 2020), 191–226.

their renewed affiliation as a "happy result of the removal of a part of what had been up to now the law."[56] In neither case did Smend's messages to six colleagues, who had been treated very unjustly, include personal words that mentioned the injustice or formulated an apology. Instead, memberships were formally renewed and the fact that these former colleagues had been expelled in the years of National Socialism was dismissed as "unfortunate circumstances."

Franck was outraged at that minimizing word choice. He wrote to Born on March 8, 1947:

> I can completely imagine that a group of humanists are meeting, who perhaps still regard it as a sacrifice when they ask people like you and me to regard ourselves as fellow members and that it should be an honor for us. I feel that I cannot let such an attitude stand. The letter I wrote was more positive than what I believe to have sent to you. But I emphasized that I would like my letter to be read aloud in a meeting and that I will only join again if the gentlemen in attendance can agree with my point of view.[57]

In his letter of response (March 25, 1947), Rudolf Smend treated Franck's objection as unjustified and sought to clear up the "misunderstanding":

> You take issue with the wording of our earlier letter to you, in which we described how we on the executive committee had finally given in to the pressure on the Academy from the Ministry back then, after long opposition, and called it "unfortunate circumstances." In contrast to the unspeakable that otherwise had happened, we did not want to emphasize this matter excessively. But also, deep loathing arises in us against all big words after the horrible inflation of words in the Third Reich. And added to that is the aversion for strong words about the Third Reich, which are cheap these days and in which the fellow travelers of the Third Reich scream at each other as fellow travelers of the present, where it has become safe and advantageous to stomp on the dead monster belatedly.[58]

In justifying himself, Smend could not find respectful words for the émigrés and their fate. He shielded himself against further criticism by contrasting the

---

56. GUA, K, IX, 83, Bl. 214, Smend as the managing Rector, "Explanation regarding the Gentlemen Gierke, Nohl, von Wartenberg, and Ehrenberg," May 9, 1945.

57. Staatsbibliothek Berlin, Preußischer Kulturbesitz, NL Born 229, Bl. 18, Franck to Born, March 8, 1947.

58. Bibliothek und Archiv zur Geschichte der Max Planck Gesellschaft, Berlin, NL Hahn, N 12, Mappe 303–1, Smend as President of the Academy of Sciences to James Franck, on March 25, 1947.

"unspeakable" (the National Socialist brutal crimes) with expulsion from the Academy. Smend failed to see that the expulsion was a National Socialist action that had been preceded by numerous others. Franck had implicitly tied them together with many other actions that finally led to genocide. Smend chose to ignore that Franck—as a Jew—had been personally threatened by exactly that fate. In diminishing the professional persecution of Franck by mentioning the greater horrors of the Holocaust, Smend displayed the temptation of postwar Germans toward protective self-justification along with a narrow understanding of the impact of Nazi criminality on the victims.

Despite Smend's claimed aversion to "big words" in his letter to Franck, in the same letter he chose to describe Hitler and the Nazi regime as "monstrous." This blanket description was typical for the time, an easy dismissal intended to separate one from the regime now viewed throughout most of the world as brutally criminal. The majority of postwar professors in Germany felt themselves to be, or at least pretended to be, among those victims who had lived under constant threat. None, however, were willing to count themselves among the perpetrators, or even the fellow travelers who cheered Hitler, approved the changes, and supported National Socialism as long as it had seemed successful. In order to stress his victimization and to deter further discussion, Smend reported that he had been watched by the Gestapo (a somewhat common postwar claim), though he had "at least avoided the gallows."[59]

In truth, the National Socialist authorities and Nazi fellow professors had not seen Smend as their ally. When he arrived in Göttingen, it was because a more enthusiastic Nazi had been pushed into his position in Berlin.[60] After the failed coup against Hitler on July 20, 1944, Smend was interviewed by the Gestapo. This was part of a very broad search for coconspirators, but it might have added to his impression that he was being watched and pursued by the most active Nazis. Furthermore, he had supported the appointment of Ambassador Ulrich von Hassel to the Chair for Civil Law at Göttingen, the same von Hassel who later was sentenced to death for his participation in the resistance and hanged on September 8, 1944.[61] Smend mentioned these things to Franck,

---

59. Ibid.
60. Regarding Smend, see Frank Halfmann, "Eine 'Pflanzstätte bester nationalsozialistischer Rechtsgelehrter': Die juristische Abteilung der Rechts- und Staatswissenschaftlichen Fakultät," in Becker, Dahms, and Wegeler, *Universität Göttingen*, 102–55 (at 121), and Helmut Fangmann, "Die Restauration der herrschenden Staatsrechtswissenschaft nach 1945," in *Das Recht des Unrechtsstaates: Arbeitsrecht und Staatsrechtswissenschaften im Faschismus*, ed. Udo Reifner (Frankfurt, Germany: Campus, 1981), 211–24 (at 221–23).
61. Halfmann, "Pflanzstätte," 127.

in hopes of winning Franck's understanding of his own difficulties with the Nazi regime.

Smend also sought to up the ante. He told Franck that he had cosigned the important Stuttgart Declaration of Guilt, presented by the Council of the German Protestant Church on October 19, 1945, whereby the church formally confessed guilt for its inadequate opposition to the Nazi regime. This declaration caused outrage and demonstrations among the German population, being understood as an admission of collective guilt, a position that most Germans categorically rejected.[62] According to Eric Colledge, head of the British University administration in its Education Branch,[63] Smend considered himself criticized by his students, some of whom thought him a traitor because of his signature. In the report by Colledge, one can sense that Smend was hurt by hostility on this issue.[64] Smend then added this to Franck about the response of the Academy to the Stuttgart Declaration of Guilt: "I do not have the impression that any member of the Academy disapproves of this position [signing the Declaration], and when I asked in our regular meeting if I should present my position as typical, I found lively agreement. That is our position—only that we would not like to make ourselves appear important by being particularly loud about it."[65]

Following receipt of this letter, Franck felt the need for a sort of justification, since Smend's formulation of the problem "seemed to suggest that only the Nazi regime's handling of the Academy" was at issue. Not wanting anyone to think he and Born cared only about the impact of Nazi ideas on the Academy and its membership, Franck wrote: "[Do not think] that we regarded our expulsion from the Academy back then as something that played in any way a role, when compared to the horrible disaster that the Nazis otherwise caused. I also do not belong among those people who want to check every little thing, and I have, I believe, made that amply clear through my behavior toward many

---

62. Jochen Vollmer, "Die Schuld der Stuttgarter Schulderklärung," *Junge Kirche* 56, no. 10 (1995): 546–57. Regarding collective guilt, see Norbert Frei, "Von deutscher Erfindungskraft, oder: Die Kollektivschuldthese in der Nachkriegszeit," in *1945 und Wir: Das Dritte Reich im Bewußtsein der Deutschen* (Munich: Beck, 2005), 145–55.

63. Müller, "Einleitung," 10.

64. PRO/FO 1050/372, Colledge, Visit to Göttingen, Nov. 10–11, 1945, November 13, 1945.

65. As further evidence of this attitude among Academy members, Smend pointed to a memorial service they held for Ernst Julius Cohn (1869–1944), an Academy member and professor of chemistry at the University of Utrecht who was murdered at Auschwitz. See Smend, as President of the Academy of Sciences, to James Franck, March 25, 1947, Bibliothek und Archiv zur Geschichte der Max Planck Gesellschaft, Berlin, NL Hahn, N 12, Mappe 303–1.

people in Germany." He hoped for understanding of his reaction to Smend's letter, because "**our** interpretation gives your words meaning that had to appear to us as being provocative."[66]

Smend's response to Franck's complaint seems proof of the widespread refusal to reflect on individual responsibility or to wrestle with the situation of someone who was persecuted. That supports the likelihood that an individual guilt was actually felt but rejected. The widespread explanation, instead, was that one was himself a victim of an enforced system. With this justification, one distorted the National Socialist past and disguised one's own role in that time. The victim myth and manipulation of the Nazi reality attached to it is a part of the founding consensus of the Federal Republic of Germany that for many years determined the political and intellectual atmosphere.

VI. THE GÖTTINGEN ACADEMY OF SCIENCES IN 1957: ÉMIGRÉS AGAINST FORGETTING

In 1947, an attempt had been made to reenlist the famous physicists Max Born and James Franck among the members of the Göttingen Academy of Sciences. As already noted, this step was meant to counteract their unwarranted expulsion under Nazi rule, but matters became complicated. In 1957, another attempt was made to deal with the past. In this case it involved the 1945 decision to expel the anthropologist Hans Plischke from the Academy of Sciences because of his pro-Nazi behavior during the Third Reich. The reconsideration of that decision went awry.

Hans Plischke had been at the University of Göttingen since 1928. Initially he taught anthropology as a Privatdozent with a contract, the following year as an associate professor, and in 1934 as a full Professor with a chair. Plischke had belonged to the Nationalsozialistische Deutsche Arbeiterpartei [National Socialist German Workers' Party (NSDAP)] since May 1933, and in addition, he was a supporting member of the SS and worked as an evaluator for the official party Examining Commission for Anthropological Publications.[67] As rector from the middle of 1941 to the end of September 1943, Plischke held the

---

66. James Franck to Prof. Smend, Akademie der Wissenschaften Göttingen, May 12, 1947, Bibliothek und Archiv zur Geschichte der Max Planck Gesellschaft, Berlin, NL Hahn, N. 12, Mappe 303-1 [emphasis on "our" in the original text].

67. For Hans Plischke (1890–1972), Professor of Volkskunde, see NSA, Nds. 401, Acc. 92/85, Nr. 17, Bl. 55; Ebel, *Catalogus Professorum*, 118, 166, 170, 176; *Kürschners Deutscher Gelehrten-Kalender*, 9th ed. (1961), s.v. "Plischke, Hans"; and Helmut Heiber, *Universität*

most visible position of authority at Göttingen University, and he represented with full conviction the National Socialist system. Previously he had served as dean of the Faculty of Philosophy from November 1934 to October 1935 and, together with the Rector Friedrich Neumann,[68] was responsible for the "reorganization" (i.e., nazification) of the university.[69] He pushed out professors with "Jewish ancestry" who were still working in the Faculty of Philosophy—the philologist, Kurt Latte and the Anglicist Hans Hecht—convincing them "voluntarily" to allow themselves to be removed from their responsibilities because he (Plischke) wanted to appoint replacements who were politically reliable for the party. It also must be assumed that Plischke had worked on the philosopher Georg Misch in similar fashion, leading him to apply for emeritus status at the end of March 1935.[70] All three of these men—Latte; Hecht, a former frontline fighter [*Frontkämpfer* in World War I]; and Misch, a seasoned civil servant [*Altbeamter*]—fell under the Exception Rules of the Law for the Restoration of the Professional Civil Service, which should have protected their positions. However, they became victims of the overzealousness of Dean Plischke and Rector Neumann, even before the Nuremberg Race Laws of November 1935 would have impacted them and forced them into retirement.

In April 1946, Plischke was removed from the faculty for having been an active National Socialist. However, despite his engagement as a Nazi functionary, he was not regarded as having been an "extremist." It helped that he had removed himself from his exposed position as rector at just the right time, when he foresaw the defeat of National Socialism. He even found himself placed on

---

unterm Hakenkreuz, part 2, *Die Kapitulation der Hohen Schulen: Das Jahr 1933 und seine Themen*, 2 vols. (Munich: K. G. Saur, 1992–1994), 2:506–12.

68. Friedrich Neumann (1889–1978), professor of German philology and literature, had taught previously in Leipzig. In 1927, he was appointed to a position at the University of Göttingen. From May 6, 1933, to August 31, 1938, Neumann was the rector at the University of Göttingen, and from 1935 to 1945 he was a councilor of the city. At the end of the war, he was removed both from his professorship and his place on the city council. In 1954, according to Article 131 GG [*Grundgesetz*, the Basic Law of Germany], he was given emeritus status. See NSA, Nds. 171. Hild., Nr. 18915, Fragebogen 1945, and Ebel, *Catalogus Professorum*, 28, 117, 150.

69. Cornelia Wegeler, "*. . . wir sagen ab der internationalen Gelehrtenrepublik*": *Altertumswissenschaft und Nationalsozialismus. Das Göttinger Institut für Altertumskunde 1921–1962* (Vienna: Böhlau, 1996), 173–74. Hans Heyse was appointed against the explicit wish of the Faculty of Philosophy. See Hans-Joachim Dahms, "Einleitung," in Becker, Dahms, and Wegeler, *Universität Göttingen*, 29–74 (at 54).

70. See Hans-Joachim Dahms, "Aufstieg und Ende der Lebensphilosophie: Das Philosophische Seminar der Universität zwischen 1917 und 1959," in Becker, Dahms, and Wegeler, *Universität Göttingen*, 287–317 (at 295).

a postwar list of university members who "stood distant from National Socialism," which favorably affected the outcome of his denazification process.[71] Moreover, during that process he was supported by many colleagues. Not only the postwar rector, Rudolf Smend, and the postwar dean of the Faculty of Philosophy, Herbert Schöffler,[72] but also the formerly persecuted professors Richard Passow, Georg Misch, Kurt Latte, and Hans Hecht submitted favorable character references for him.[73] This secured Plischke's right to teach again in 1949 and his rights as a full Professor in 1950.[74]

Plischke's full reinstatement seemed ensured when the historian Percy E. Schramm nominated him for readmission to the prestigious Göttingen Academy of Sciences in 1957.[75] Plischke had already been a member from 1936 until 1945, when he was removed by the British Military Government from his faculty position and membership in the Academy. Schramm's renomination thus reflected the softer view that had emerged by the 1950s regarding complicity in the Nazi regime. However, several members vigorously opposed implementing

---

71. Wegeler, "... wir sagen ab," 254.

72. Herbert Schöffler (1888–1946), professor of English philology, was transferred involuntarily from Cologne to Göttingen in 1942. See Ebel, *Catalogus Professorum*, 118, 131, and Lars U. Scholl, "Zum Besten der besonders in Göttingen gepflegten Anglistik: Das Seminar für Englische Philologie," in Becker, Dahms, and Wegeler, *Universität Göttingen*, 391–426 (at 415–18).

73. Heiber, *Universität unterm Hakenkreuz*, 2:508; see as well Renate Kulick-Aldag, *Die Göttinger Völkerkunde und der Nationalsozialismus zwischen 1925 und 1950* (Hamburg, Germany: LIT, 2000), 75–77.

74. Kulick-Aldag, *Göttinger Völkerkunde*, 50–51, 73–77, and Katja Geisenhainer, "'Aus innerer Zustimmung zu den Programmpunkten der NSDAP': Der Völkerkundler Hans Plischke (1880–1972) und sein Wirken in Göttingen," in Schumann and Schauz, *Akademien und andere Forschungseinrichtungen*, 263–96 (at 292–93).

75. Percy E. Schramm (1894–1970). For further details, see David Thimme, *Percy Ernst Schramm und das Mittelalter: Wandlungen eines Geschichtsbildes* (Göttingen, Germany: Vandenhoeck & Ruprecht, 2006). Of the group of members released due to their political incrimination, only Schramm was immediately reelected to membership in the Academy, which occurred on November 12, 1948, as soon as he was reinstalled in his professorship. Later, all politically incriminated professors received the right by law to be reinsituted into their rights as faculty members. Kurt Latte, who had been persecuted in Nazi times, was president of the Academy at the time. On March 31, 1953, he urged the Cultural Ministry of Lower Saxony not automatically to make membership retroactive for those who had been removed from the Academy post-1945. Otherwise, he warned, the international reputation of the Academy would be endangered. See Norbert Schappacher, "Ideologie, Wissenschaftspolitik, und die Ehre, Mitglied der Akademie zu sein: Ein Fall aus dem zwanzigsten Jahrhundert," *Nachrichten der Akademie der Wissenschaften zu Göttingen: Neue Folge* 2 (2015): 1–30 (at 9), doi: http://hdl.handle.net/11858/00-001S-0000-0023-9A17-2.

such an approach toward Plischke. This group of critics included the mathematicians Carl Ludwig Siegel and Richard Courant, the latter of whom was visiting at that moment in Göttingen. As a result of their questions, Schramm's suggestion quickly to readmit Plischke as a member was rejected. But that was not the end of the matter. One of the questions raised by Siegel involved the rumor that Plischke had only gained his position as full Professor in 1934 for political reasons, and for that same reason was admitted to the Academy. Therefore, critics suggested it should be determined whether Plischke had published sufficient academic scholarship by that time that actually justified his membership. If that were the case, his behavior during the National Socialist period should not be underestimated but could also be evaluated in a broader light.[76] Siegel had also been informed that Plischke had spoken up for the retention of Jewish members in the Academy, though in a losing battle, and that as rector "in the later years of the war had acted properly." Yet Siegel also remembered a statement from the mathematician Franz Relich, by then deceased, that Plischke might have been one of the signatories to a very controversial public statement against James Franck. This changed the picture.

In 1933, James Franck, already a Nobel Prize–winning physicist, resigned voluntarily from his position, hoping that such a gesture would resonate against the Law for the Restoration of the Professional Civil Service, the first Nazi effort to purge Jews from all government jobs. As a Frontkämpfer in the First World War, Franck would not have been subject to dismissal himself at that time. However, Franck chose to use his prominence as a famous scientist and a German recipient of the Nobel Prize to protest against the policies of the new dictator, and he published his resignation letter in the press for maximum effect. However, his hopes would soon be crushed. The following week a document appeared in the *Göttinger Tageblatt* that attacked Franck's resignation letter, describing it as an "act of sabotage" against the "work of the national government." This document was signed by forty-two of Franck's Göttingen colleagues, about 20 percent of the teaching faculty, who had responded on very short notice to attack his protest against the regime.[77]

Siegel was not aware personally of what had happened in 1933, since he arrived in Göttingen only in 1938 and completed an emigration to the

---

76. Staatsbibliothek Berlin, Preußischer Kulturbesitz, NL Born, Nr. 728, Bl. 1, Siegel to Born, July 9, 1957. On the question of whether to readmit into the Academy, see also Schappacher, "Ideologie," 10–13.

77. See Robert P. Ericksen, "The Nazification and Denazification of the University of Göttingen," in this volume, and Szabó, *Vertreibung*, 47–48.

United States by 1940. As this issue developed in 1957, he wrote to Max Born, who had spent many years in Göttingen, informing him about Schramm's application:

> They wanted to reappoint someone who was in good standing with the [Nazi] government and yet had not behaved like a terrorist. It is very difficult to be sure about these things, since many of the men who were already in the Academy in 1936 have themselves some dirt on their hands. For that reason, it would be very important if you could possibly comment on the behavior of Plischke around 1933, and, if it comes to that, explain whether it would be embarrassing and painful for you to think that a man could be voted into the Academy who had signed that blasphemous pamphlet against Franck.[78]

Born declared himself prepared to intervene against the readmission of Plischke if he had signed the document against James Franck. Siegel then located the issue of the *Göttinger Tageblatt* from April 19, 1933, in which the declaration of the forty-two faculty members against Franck was printed. He found that Plischke was indeed among those who had signed.[79] That ended the discussion, confirming that Plischke did not deserve membership in the Academy. In order to avoid an embarrassing situation, this decision was not even allowed to come up for a vote; Schramm simply withdrew his nomination. Siegel then reported to Born: "By the way, Courant was of the opinion that one should let grass grow over the entire sad affair. This seemed to me, however, to go too far in the interest of the Academy, because the declaration against Franck will remain a stain on all those who signed."[80]

One year later, the possible reappointment of Plischke again appeared as a topic in the correspondence between Siegel and Born. Although Siegel was of the opinion that Plischke absolutely deserved scientific recognition for his scholarship, he still did not believe Plischke should be readmitted, as he told Born: "But even if he had achievements like Hilbert and Einstein to show, I would still be of the opinion that he **does not** belong in the Academy, because he had signed the shameful document against our member Franck back then. I discussed the issue again with several others, informed President Bartels of

---

78. Staatsbibliothek Berlin, Preußischer Kulturbesitz, NL Born, Nr. 728, p. 1, Siegel to Born, July 29, 1957.
79. See Szabó, *Vertreibung*, 48n76.
80. Staatsbibliothek Berlin, Preußischer Kulturbesitz, NL Born, Nr. 728, p. 2, Siegel to Born, July 29, 1957.

our misgivings, and explained that I would resign, if Plischke were admitted. After that, nothing else happened."[81]

VII. ERASING THE NAZI PAST IN GERMAN UNIVERSITIES

The post-1945 path to reconciliation between the persecuted, the émigrés, and the professors who had cooperated with and prospered under National Socialism was long and arduous. To speak of the "normalizing" of relationships would certainly be an overstatement, since these groups would remain "exceptional" forever, at least for actual participants and to some extent for later generations. How could it be otherwise? The experience of German universities during this period, universities which had developed to a very high level upon a strong foundation of the humanities and of humanistic values, gives us pause. The Nazi world of politics and of ideas brutally violated these values. However, German universities learned how to prosper within that new world, even to celebrate it.

Professors in 1933 at Göttingen and elsewhere in Germany had experienced a generation of remarkably dramatic and challenging events: the outbreak of World War I, the loss of that very costly war, the widespread rejection of the Versailles Treaty, and frustrations under Weimar democracy, including the huge impact of the Great Depression. Within months of Hitler's rise to power, he moved to reshape German universities, both by purging Jewish and left-wing professors and by urging support for the Nazi point of view. As noted previously, when the Nazi regime urged the institutional *Gleichschaltung*, professors at Göttingen and other German universities largely accepted and worked toward that goal with their own personal *Selbstgleichschaltung*, despite the very large cost for victims, outsiders, and the humanistic principles of a university.

During the first two years of postwar occupation, the British Military Government tried to encourage a return to the best values of a university, but without much success in terms of justice for those Jewish and leftist members of the professoriate who had been purged. Professors at Göttingen and elsewhere watched the firings and expulsions of these victims before 1945, perhaps with enthusiasm, or at least without choosing to take any action. Some may have remained silent out of cowardice and fear, others out of opportunism or their approval of Germany's new path. By not taking the side of their persecuted colleagues, they went along with National Socialism in a *Grundkompromiß* [basic

---

81. Staatsbibliothek Berlin, Preußischer Kulturbesitz, NL Born, Nr. 728, p. 3, Siegel to Born, May 4, 1958. The emphasis on "does not" appears in the original text.

compromise] that contained both a tolerance of Nazi politics and, in many cases, an offer of collaboration.

The firings in 1933 were the first step toward a National Socialist *Umbau* [rebuilding] of the universities, including their academic institutes, facilities, and organizations. Professors who accepted this new reality followed Nazi trends in new research. They sought out research grant opportunities and projects to secure funding and position themselves in the new evaluation and paradigm shift for the individual academic disciplines.[82] They made use of the possibilities and creative spaces that the new regime offered. Professors published their research results in line with the goals and frequently with the rhetoric of National Socialism. Despite what we might expect from the strong academic and humanistic tradition within German universities, this generation either devoted their skills and effort toward the academic goals, structures, and plans of the Nazi state or, at minimum, avoided giving offense.[83]

After the collapse of this Nazi state and a political review by the British occupation authorities, the existing professoriate managed to control future hiring policies under the watchword "only the best." Most professors then kept their position at the university, even if their past was clearly stamped by cooperation with Nazi ideas. Under these new circumstances, it became necessary to try to erase that cooperation from their record, from their conversation, and, if possible, from their memory. Academic projects that had served the goals of the Nazi regime needed to be buried or disguised. Lists of publications were shortened and elided to remove the most objectionable. If the faculty members had the slightest knowledge of, contact with, or participation in Nazi crimes, they did not want it known; they became assiduous and creative in denying it. Soon professors created the argument that they had only pursued "pure"

---

82. Herbert Mehrtens, "Kollaborationsverhältnisse: Natur- und Technikwissenschaften im NS-Staat und ihre Historie," in *Medizin, Naturwissenschaft, Technik und Nationalsozialismus: Kontinuitäten und Diskontinuitäten*, ed. Christoph Meinel and Peter Voswinckel (Stuttgart, Germany: Verlag für Geschichte der Naturwissenschaft und der Technik, 1994), 13–32 (at 26).

83. Extensive studies in recent years have traced the reciprocal relationships between academia and politics, based on the example of actors, disciplines, universities, institutes, facilities, and organizations. See, for example, the series Geschichte der Kaiser-Wilhelm-Gesellschaft im Nationalsozialismus, Beiträge zur Geschichte der Deutschen Forschungsgemeinschaft, and Studien zur Geschichte der Forschungsgemeinschaft. For studies about the University of Göttingen, see also Dirk Schumann, Petra Terhoeven, and Kerstin Thieler, "Die Georg-August-Universität im Nationalsozialismus," Georg-August-Universität Göttingen, accessed August 28, 2020, http://www.ns-zeit.uni-goettingen.de/.

scholarship in "politically free" space. Just as the excuse among the German population developed as a claim that Hitler had misused the German people for his deeds, academics used this same rhetorical construct to exonerate themselves from any responsibility or any shared guilt regarding Nazi crimes. Only an "abnormal" or a "crooked" scholar would have allowed himself to be used by the Nazi system to perpetuate such crimes, they claimed.[84] Any and all individual responsibility was repressed and denied.

Professors who had successfully worked within the Nazi paradigm did not want to confront their own failure with regard to the victims of the Nazi expulsion program: neither the removals in 1933 nor the barriers to returning in 1945. Empathy toward the fate of the persecuted or those forced to emigrate was lacking. Instead, professors occupied themselves with their own needs and cares. In addition, the professors, like many other people in Germany, nurtured the image in their minds that things had gone well for the émigrés, perhaps in sunny California or elsewhere, with a good salary and a pleasant life. From this point of view, there was no need to invite them back. Additionally, Nazi propaganda had taught that the émigré was an enemy and opponent of Germany and the German people. These prejudices were still in effect in postwar German society and gained new force as resentment toward émigrés exceeded any sort of empathy.

The impact of such thoughts helps explain a broader phenomenon, the one-sided *Vergangenheitspolitik* [politics of the past][85] among professors in Germany as well as the public at large. Instead of acknowledging the problems of those exiled by the Nazi state, they worried about those postwar Germans who had experienced denazification as well as those colleagues who had been part of the Nazi era but who were then deported or forced to flee. They felt responsible for these colleagues and were joined with them in a *Schicksalsgemeinschaft* [community of fate]. Supposed or real injustices during denazification stiffened the defensiveness toward émigrés and strengthened the solidarity with the university faculty who were without positions due to denazification. The solidarity soon went so far that nobody asked about individual guilt. Concern about financial as well as professional problems, along with the need to

---

84. See Herbert Mehrtens, "'Missbrauch': Die rhetorische Konstruktion der Technik in Deutschland nach 1945," in *Technische Hochschulen und Studentenschaft in der Nachkriegszeit*, ed. Walter Kertz (Braunschweig, Germany: Universitätsbibliothek der Technischen Universität, 1994), 33–50 (at 34).

85. Norbert Frei, *Vergangenheitspolitik: Die Anfänge der Bundesrepublik und die NS-Vergangenheit* (Munich: Beck, 1996).

rehabilitate colleagues thought to have been harshly treated post-1945, moved to the fore.

This reaction was also to be found even among those who had stayed completely distant from National Socialism. All research about postwar circumstances at the University of Göttingen, as well as at other universities, shows that almost all colleagues from 1933 to 1945 whose National Socialist collaboration and political incrimination led to their denazification were soon offered generous assistance and welcomed back. The university denied reintegration only to a very few of those formerly enthusiastic Nazis, those who had celebrated the new "political university."[86] As a rule, those who did integrate then proved themselves capable of adapting and changing. Yet German universities for a generation or more were hesitant to turn a critical eye on their own past or their own place in the human tragedy that was Nazi Germany.

The discrepancy in experience between professors who had cooperated with National Socialism and the university faculty members who had been forced to emigrate was immense. Members of the first group were not prepared to reflect on their own responsibility and their failure of conscience. Instead, they justified themselves by pointing to their difficulties under the dictatorship during the war, and then with the postwar conditions. Professors in Germany complained—sometimes secretly, sometimes openly—that the émigrés had not experienced the constraints and pressures of the dictatorship, had not known the deprivations and losses due to the war, and had not undergone the hunger and misery of the postwar period. The mix of all these judgments, impressions, and feelings grew to the point that émigrés were not regarded as the real victims! Rather, it was the Germans who had stayed behind who felt themselves the actual victims of dictatorship and war. On that basis they bestowed on themselves the term *the resistance* while deftly resisting any confrontation with or careful look into the recent past. The notion of having been victims themselves covered any consciousness of having cooperated with National Socialism. It also kept them from thinking that they had failed those who were persecuted. It is not easy in individual cases to know how and to what degree this mindset had negative effects on the university, academic research, or the development of German democracy. Many students in the 1960s generation, however, grew critical of that mindset and began to demand change. Since the 1980s, scholarship has followed suit.

---

86. See Einar Brynjolfsson, "Die Entnazifizierung der Universität Göttingen am Beispiel der Philosophischen Fakultät" (Master's thesis, Göttingen University, Germany, 1996); Szabó, *Vertreibung*, 308–9; and Ericksen, "Nazification and Denazification," in this volume.

BIBLIOGRAPHY

Archival Sources

Bibliothek und Archiv zur Geschichte der Max Planck Gesellschaft, Berlin
GUA   Universitätsarchiv in Göttingen
NSA   Niedersächsisches Hauptstaatsarchiv in Hannover
PRO/FO   Public Record Office, Foreign Office, London-Kew
Staatsbibliothek Berlin, Preußischer Kulturbesitz

Secondary Sources

Ash, Mitchell G. "Verordnete Umbrüche—Konstruierte Kontinuitäten: Zur Entnazifizierung von Wissenschaftlern und Wissenschaften nach 1945." *Zeitschrift für Geschichtswissenschaft* 43, no. 10 (1995): 903–23.

Becker, Heinrich, Hans-Joachim Dahms, and Cornelia Wegeler, eds. *Die Universität Göttingen unter dem Nationalsozialismus.* 2nd ed. Munich: K. G. Saur, 1998.

Beushausen, Ulrich, Hans-Joachim Dahms, Thomas Koch, Almuth Massing, and Konrad Obermann. "Die Medizinische Fakultät im Dritten Reich." In Becker, Dahms, and Wegeler, *Universität Göttingen*, 183–286.

Brynjolfsson, Einar. "Die Entnazifizierung der Universität Göttingen am Beispiel der Philosophischen Fakultät." Master's thesis, Göttingen University, Germany, 1996.

Dahms, Hans-Joachim. "Aufstieg und Ende der Lebensphilosophie: Das Philosophische Seminar der Universität zwischen 1917 und 1959." In Becker, Dahms, and Wegeler, *Universität Göttingen*, 287–317.

Dorn, Walter L. *Inspektionsreisen in der US-Zone: Notizen, Denkschriften, und Erinnerungen.* Edited and translated by Lutz Niethammer. Stuttgart, Germany: Deutsche Verlagsanstalt, 1973.

Ebel, Wilhelm, ed. *Catalogus Professorum Gottingensium 1734–1962.* Göttingen, Germany: Vandenhoeck & Ruprecht, 1962.

Einstein, Albert, Hedwig Born, and Max Born. *Briefwechsel 1916–1955.* Commentary by Max Born. Preface by Bertrand Russell. Foreword by Werner Heisenberg. Munich: Nymphenburger, 1969.

Ericksen, Robert P. *Complicity in the Holocaust: Churches and Universities in Nazi Germany.* Cambridge: Cambridge University Press, 2012.

———. "Die Göttinger Theologische Fakultät im Dritten Reich." In Becker, Dahms, and Wegeler, *Universität Göttingen*, 75–101.

———. "Kontinuitäten konservativer Geschichtsschreibung am Seminar für Mittlere und Neuere Geschichte: Von der Weimarer Zeit über die nationalsozialistische Ära bis in die Bundesrepublik." In Becker, Dahms, and Wegeler, *Universität Göttingen*, 427–53.

Fangmann, Helmut. "Die Restauration der herrschenden Staatsrechtswissenschaft nach 1945." In *Das Recht des Unrechtsstaates: Arbeitsrecht und Staatsrechtswissenschaften im Faschismus*, edited by Udo Reifner, 211–24. Frankfurt, Germany: Campus, 1981.

Fesefeldt, Wiebke. *Der Wiederbeginn des kommunalen Lebens in Göttingen: Die Stadt in den Jahren 1945 bis 1948.* Göttingen, Germany: Vandenhoeck & Ruprecht, 1962.

Franck, James. "Rede des Ehrenbürgers Prof. Dr. James Franck." *Göttinger Jahrbuch* 3 (1954): 101.

Frei, Norbert. *Vergangenheitspolitik: Die Anfänge der Bundesrepublik und die NS-Vergangenheit.* Munich: Beck, 1996.

———. "Von deutscher Erfindungskraft, Oder: Die Kollektivschuldthese in der Nachkriegszeit." In *1945 und Wir: Das Dritte Reich im Bewußtsein der Deutschen*, 145–55. Munich: Beck, 2005.

Geisenhainer, Katja. "'Aus innerer Zustimmung zu den Programmpunkten der NSDAP': Der Völkerkundler Hans Plischke (1980–1972) und sein Wirken in Göttingen." In Schumann and Schauz, *Akademien und andere Forschungseinrichtungen*, 263–96.

Halfmann, Frank. "Eine 'Pflanzstätte bester nationalsozialistischer Rechtsgelehrter': Die juristische Abteilung der Rechts- und Staatswissenschaftlichen Fakultät." In Becker, Dahms, and Wegeler, *Universität Göttingen*, 102–55.

Heiber, Helmut. *Universität unterm Hakenkreuz.* Part 2, *Die Kapitulation der Hohen Schulen: Das Jahr 1933 und seine Themen.* 2 vols. Munich: K. G. Saur, 1992–94.

Heinemann, Manfred, ed. *Nordwestdeutsche Hochschulkonferenzen 1945–1948.* 2 vols. Hildesheim, Germany: Lax, 1990.

Krönig, Waldemar, and Klaus-Dieter Müller. *Nachkriegssemester: Studium in Kriegs- und Nachkriegszeit.* Stuttgart, Germany: Franz Steiner, 1990.

Krüger, Wolfgang. *Entnazifiziert: Zur Praxis der politischen Säuberung in Nordrhein-Westfalen.* Wuppertal, Germany: Peter Hammer, 1982.

Kulick-Aldag, Renate. *Die Göttinger Völkerkunde und der Nationalsozialismus zwischen 1925 und 1950.* Hamburg, Germany: LIT, 2000.

Lemmerich, Jost. *Science and Conscience: The Life of James Franck.* Translated by Ann M. Hentschel. Stanford, CA: Stanford University Press, 2011.

Mehrtens, Herbert. "Kollaborationsverhältnisse: Natur- und Technikwissenschaften im NS-Staat und ihre Historie." In *Medizin, Naturwissenschaft, Technik und Nationalsozialismus: Kontinuitäten und Diskontinuitäten*, edited by Christoph Meinel and Peter Voswinckel, 13–32. Stuttgart, Germany: Verlag für Geschichte der Naturwissenschaft und der Technik, 1994.

———. "'Missbrauch': Die rhetorische Konstruktion der Technik in Deutschland nach 1945." In *Technische Hochschulen und Studentenschaft in der Nachkriegszeit*, edited by Walter Kertz, 33–50. Braunschweig, Germany: Universitätsbibliothek der Technischen Universität, 1994.

Müller, Siegfried. "Einleitung." In Heinemann, *Nordwestdeutsche Hochschulkonferenzen*, 1:1–30.

Pingel, Falk. "Wissenschaft, Bildung, und Demokratie: Der gescheiterte Versuch einer Universitätsreform." In *Grenzgänger: Aufsätze von Falk Pingel*, edited by Georg-Eckert-Institute, 233–63. Studien des Georg-Eckert-Instituts zur internationalen Bildungsmedienforschung 125. Göttingen, Germany: Vandenhoek & Ruprecht, 2009.

Rammer, Gerhard. "Die Nazifizierung und Entnazifizierung der Physik an der Universität Göttingen." PhD diss., Universität Göttingen, Germany, 2009. http://hdl.handle.net/11858/00-1735-0000-0006-B49F-4.

Saller, Karl. "Der Rassenmord und Heldenwahn des Nationalsozialismus." In *Unmenschliche Medizin*, vol. 1, edited by the Internationales Auschwitz Komitee, 74–193. Warsaw: Internationales Auschwitz Komitee, 1969.

———. *Die Rassenlehre des Nationalsozialismus in Wissenschaft und Propaganda*. Darmstadt, Germany: Progress, 1961.

Schappacher, Norbert. "Ideologie, Wissenschaftspolitik, und die Ehre, Mitglied der Akademie zu sein: Ein Fall aus dem zwanzigsten Jahrhundert." *Nachrichten der Akademie der Wissenschaften zu Göttingen: Neue Folge* 2 (2015): 1–30. http://hdl.handle.net/11858/00-001S-0000-0023-9A17-2.

Schauz, Désirée. "Wissenschaft und Politik: Zum Selbstverständnis der Göttinger Akademiemitglieder im Nationalsozialismus." In Schumann and Schauz, *Akademien und andere Forschungseinrichtungen*, 191–226.

Schneider, Ulrich. "Zur Entnazifizierung der Hochschullehrer in Niedersachsen 1945–1949." *Niedersächsisches Jahrbuch für Landesgeschichte* 61 (1989): 325–46.

Scholl, Lars U. "Zum Besten der besonders in Göttingen gepflegten Anglistik: Das Seminar für Englische Philologie." In Becker, Dahms, and Wegeler, *Universität Göttingen*, 391–426.

Schumann, Dirk, and Désirée Schauz, eds. *Akademien und andere Forschungseinrichtungen im Nationalsozialismus und nach 1945*. Göttingen, Germany: Wallstein, 2020.

Schumann, Dirk, Désirée Schauz, Petra Terhoeven, and Kerstin Thieler. "Die Georg-August-Universität im Nationalsozialismus" Georg-August-Universität Göttingen. Accessed August 28, 2020. http://www.ns-zeit.uni-goettingen.de/.

Smend, Rudolf. ["Adolf Grimme."] In *Wirkendes, sorgendes Dasein: Begegnungen mit Adolf Grimme. Gruß der Freunde und Weggefährten zum 70. Geburtstag*, edited by Walther G. Olischewski, 105–8. Berlin: Arani, 1959.

Szabó, Anikó. "Verordnete Rückberufungen: Die Hochschulkonferenzen und die Diskussion um die emigrierten Hochschullehrer." In *Nationalsozialismus und Region: Festschrift für Herbert Obenaus*, edited by Marlis Buchholz and Hans-Dieter Schmied, 339–52. Bielefeld, Germany: Verlag für Regionalgeschichte, 1996.

———. *Vertreibung, Rückkehr, Wiedergutmachung: Göttinger Hochschullehrer im Schatten des Nationalsozialismus*. Göttingen, Germany: Wallstein, 2000.

Thimme, David. *Percy Ernst Schramm und das Mittelalter: Wandlungen eines Geschichtsbildes*. Göttingen, Germany: Vandenhoek & Ruprecht, 2006.

Trittel, Katharina. *Hermann Rein und die Flugmedizin: Erkenntnisstreben und Entgrenzung*. Paderborn, Germany: Schöningh, 2018.

Vollmer, Jochen. "Die Schuld der Stuttgarter Schulderklärung." *Junge Kirche* 56, no. 10 (1995): 546–57.

Wegeler, Cornelia. "*. . . wir sagen ab der internationalen Gelehrtenrepublik*": *Altertumswissenschaft und Nationalsozialismus. Das Göttinger Institut für Altertumskunde 1921–1962*. Vienna: Böhlau, 1996.

ANIKÓ SZABÓ is a German historian and archivist who directs the Archive of the University of Paderborn, Germany. She has previously published a major study of the impact of National Socialist racist and political persecution on the German university system: *Vertreibung, Rückkehr, Wiedergutmachung: Göttinger Hochschullehrer im Schatten des Nationalsozialismus* (Wallstein, 2000). Her work, appearing here for the first time in English, examines the postwar experience of professors who had been persecuted and expelled from their academic positions during the Nazi period.

GERALD FETZ is Dean Emeritus of Humanities and Sciences and Professor Emeritus of German Studies at the University of Montana. He received his PhD at the University of Oregon. He has received major fellowships (DAAD, NEH, American Philosophical Society) and was appointed Fulbright Visiting Professor at the University of Heidelberg. He served as Secretary-Treasurer of the German Studies Association for twenty years. He was also the refounding director and chief editor of the University of Montana Press and is on the editorial board for Ariadne Press. His publications include a book on Martin Walser (Metzler, 1997) as well as articles and essays on Thomas Bernhard, Franz Kafka, Friedrich Wolf, Franz Innerhofer, Lilian Faschinger, Walser, W. Georg Sebald, and German Theater at the Wende. He is editor of a new book on Christa Wolf (Spektrum, 2021). He is currently writing a book on Vienna novels since 1945.

FOURTEEN

ITALIAN FASCISM

Decentering Standard Assumptions about Antisemitism and Totalitarianism

FRANKLIN HUGH ADLER

IT MIGHT SEEM OBVIOUS TO begin a discussion of the betrayal of the humanities by invoking the case of Nazi Germany. For many, it represents pure evil and negates all the values associated not only with the Western humanistic tradition but also with humanity itself. Yet to confine the discussion to Nazi Germany would be misleading; its singularity hardly exhausts the universe of discourse and its practices neither typify nor serve as an adequate yardstick against which other suspect cases might be measured. If we confine our attention to interwar Europe, for example, Nazi Germany is often taken as the pure Platonic form of Fascism and the manifold antisemitic policies associated with the Holocaust seen as little more than German racial policy writ large. Without trivializing or ethically relativizing the Nazi case, one might nevertheless suggest that it occupies too much conceptual space and ends up occluding an understanding of other cases where betrayals of the humanities took place. Elsewhere, antisemitic measures were instituted for reasons that had little or nothing to do with Nazi Germany. For a comparative understanding, decentering Germany might be a useful first step.

For illustrative purposes, our attention will be focused on Italy, where Fascism first emerged during the early twenties and lasted roughly twice as long as the German case.[1] Moreover, I consider the world of culture more broadly,

---

1. In English, the most recent and comprehensive study is Michele Sarfatti, *The Jews in Mussolini's Italy: From Equality to Persecution*, trans. John and Anne C. Tedescschi, George L. Mosse Series in Modern European Cultural and Intellectual History (Madison: University of Wisconsin Press, 2007). For a fuller elucidation of the position taken here, see Franklin Hugh

not confining the "betrayal of the humanities" to what specifically happened in universities. Unlike Nazism, racism and antisemitism were not part of Italian Fascism's formative program and ideology. Jews had figured among Fascist leadership and the rank-and-file, and Nazis had been viewed with suspicion as late as the mid-thirties, particularly on account of their crude, biological racism. Mussolini himself, during a meeting with young Fascist intellectuals from Florence at the Palazzo Venezia in 1934, dismissed such racism as *roba da biondi* [that nonsense blonds come up with].[2]

However, during the late thirties, the Fascist regime would abruptly turn toward antisemitism and enact discriminatory laws against the Jews. After the war, Italy was hardly alone in blaming such policies exclusively on the Germans, whether by diplomatic alliance or through annexation or occupation, though in fact, many local and autonomously generated antisemitic measures were enacted that had little to do with any German master plan. I should note that, to date, no one has discovered a shred of evidence in German or Italian archives that Germany in any way put pressure on the Italian government to encourage either the 1938 campaign against the Jews or the antisemitic legislation that almost immediately went into effect.[3] A focus on Italy would suggest that, unlike Germany, neither an antisemitic past nor a long-term ideological commitment to racism was necessary for this and other betrayals of humanistic values.

George Mosse and many others have argued that the antisemitism that surfaced in Europe during the thirties was largely a redeployment of movements and ideologies that had emerged earlier, during the final decades of the nineteenth century and early decades of the twentieth. This position, too, needs qualification, because postunification Italy experienced nothing comparable to what took place in such major cases as France, Germany, Austria, and Russia. Of course, no Christian nation was totally free of antisemitism. Nonetheless, in Italy, unlike France, there were no antisemitic leagues, Dreyfus affairs, or a literary establishment that was largely antisemitic; unlike Austria, there were

---

Adler, "Jew as Bourgeois, Jew as Enemy, Jew as Victim of Fascism," *Modern Judaism* 28 (2008): 306–26.

2. The pejorative comment was reported by the journalist Indro Montanelli, *Corriere della Sera*, April 13, 1997, 35. This translation is courtesy of Professor Susan Noakes. Compare to Franklin H. Adler, preface to *The Jews in Fascist Italy: A History*, by Renzo De Felice, trans. Robert L. Miller, 3rd ed. (New York: Enigma, 2015), vii.

3. The 1938 campaign against the Jews is explored in more detail under "Mussolini's Campaign against the Jews." See also Franklin Hugh Adler, "Why Mussolini Turned on the Jews," *Patterns of Prejudice* 39 (2005): 285–300.

no self-professed, antisemitic mayors of major cities, such as Vienna; unlike Germany, there were no long, protracted debates concerning Jewish emancipation; unlike Russia, there were no pogroms.

These were all absent in Italy, whose small Jewish population was so assimilated that it had the highest intermarriage rate of any Jewish community in Europe (roughly 30 percent), hardly an indicator of deep-seated prejudice.[4] Add to that the fact that, by the outbreak of World War I, Italy—alone in Europe—had already had three prime ministers of Jewish origin, and it would be difficult to argue that prior antisemitic history was an explanatory variable to account for Fascist Italy's campaign against the Jews in 1938.[5] In fact, what makes the Italian case so fascinating, in a comparative sense, is the relative absence of this and other factors typically identified with 1930s antisemitism in Central and Western Europe, such as separate linguistic and cultural Jewish identities, big Jewish banks, and, especially, significant immigration of *Ostjuden*. (The great westward migration of East European Jews to Vienna, Berlin, Paris, London, and New York almost totally bypassed Italy).

I suggest that the abrupt turn toward antisemitism in Fascist Italy was due largely to a legitimation crisis that befell the regime during the mid-thirties, necessitating ideological revision to redress internal contradictions that threatened its continued stability. These contradictions were linked not only to an increasingly adventurous foreign policy (such as invading Ethiopia and intervening in the Spanish Civil War) but also to the internal dynamics of Fascism itself. I specify and illustrate these in short order. First, however, I propose a related comparative hypothesis, which is nonetheless beyond the substantive scope of this essay and cannot be fully explored here. Unlike the German case, recourse to state-sponsored antisemitism (or similar ascriptive persecutory policies) in illiberal autocracies may be due more to legitimation crises than to the regime's founding ideology, deeply rooted historical precedents, or long-term cultural practices, all factors that may or may not be significant or even determinative. What we confront here is a change in line, or a midterm correction, driven more by immediate political contingencies than by longer-term structural causes. We know that "betrayals of the humanities" are not infrequent in illiberal autocracies, and occasionally

---

4. In fact, such a high intermarriage rate is attested even in the years immediately preceding the 1938 campaign against the Jews. See Renzo De Felice, *The Jews in Fascist Italy* (New York: Enigma, 2001), 11.

5. Italy's three prime ministers of Jewish origin were Alessandro Fortis (1905–6), Sidney Sonnino (1906, 1909–10), and Luigi Luzzatti (1910–11).

even in liberal regimes, though the latter have constitutional principles and practices that serve as safeguards rarely found in the former. By decentering the German case, which in my view is singular, if not exceptional, we may work toward a better understanding of the general phenomenon.

Before turning to the internal contradictions of Italian Fascism, and to the legitimation crisis that led directly to the antisemitic campaign of 1938, I briefly underscore an important difference with the German case regarding antisemitism. Not only did the turn toward antisemitism occur relatively late in the regime's history (during the sixteenth year of its twenty-year duration), but also those directly responsible for its implementation were hardly convinced antisemites or ones of long standing. Nazi leaders often prided themselves for never having even shaken the hand of a Jew, whereas such a biological-hygienic fixation had never existed in Italy, even with respect to intimate relations. Mussolini had any number of Jewish mistresses, most notably Margherita Sarfatti, who during the twenties undoubtedly was the dominant cultural figure in Italy as well as the author of Il Duce's official biography. His daughter Eda had been engaged to a Jew, but Mussolini forced an end to this relationship after the Lateran Accords with the Vatican in 1929. She then married Count Galeazzo Ciano, a notorious philanderer who, like Mussolini, had multiple Jewish mistresses. Giuseppe Bottai, who as minister of public education would expel Jewish students and professors from schools and universities in 1938, just five years earlier had joined the philosopher Giovanni Gentile in helping establish on Italian-soil private schools for German Jewish children [*Landschulheime*] whose educational opportunities in Germany had become uncertain.[6] Though in 1938 Bottai stated that schools, so central to the transmission of Fascist values and Italian identity, had to be defended and protected from any Jewish presence, he himself had cultivated friendships with Jews as a teenager at Rome's celebrated *liceo classico Tasso*, none of whom apparently had infected him with the distinctively alien, nomadic, and degenerate influences he later attributed to the Jewish spirit. Jewish friendships also marked, without apparent injury, Bottai's days as a Futurist and, then, a Fascist. In fact, the cofounder of Bottai's influential journal *Critica Fascista*, Gino Modigliani, was a Jew, as were some of his best friends and collaborators, such as Enrico Rocca and Gino Arias. Similarly, Alessandro Pavolini, who became the influential minister of popular culture as the racial laws were being rigorously instituted in 1939, had been

---

6. Klaus Voigt, "Le scuole dei profughi in Italia," *Storia contemporanea* 19, no. 6 (1988): 1153–88.

partially raised by a Jewish couple, Giorgo and Elisa Uzielli, when his father, a famous professor of Sanskrit, ran off with a Finnish woman half his age. As a teenager in Florence, Pavolini was friendly with Carlo and Nello Rosselli, Jewish brothers who would become major anti-Fascist intellectuals and were murdered in exile in France in June 1937. Pavolini's brother, Corrado, himself a Fascist writer of some note, married a Jew.[7]

Italy—particularly Rome—became a haven for prominent German Jews during the first years of Nazi rule. When George Mosse's family arrived in Rome, a bouquet of flowers for his mother greeted them at their hotel, sent by no less than Mussolini, who knew that Rudolf Mosse had been a powerful publishing magnate in Berlin. In 1934, Mussolini brought to Rome Rudolf Arnheim, a German Jewish authority on cinema, to teach at a new center for experimental film housed in his personal residence, Villa Torlonia. There Arnheim taught a young generation of filmmakers, later to become famous after the war, and collaborated in the prestigious film journal *Cinema*, edited by Mussolini's son Vittorio. Arnheim was not alone. Soon he would be joined by such other German Jewish notables as Walter Benjamin, Max Reinhardt, Max Neufeld, and Max Ophüls, whose film *La Signora di tutti* was nominated as Italy's official entry for the best film of 1934 (the Mussolini Cup) at the Venice Film Festival. Also nominated, among seven finalists for the Mussolini Cup in 1934, were films by two other Jews: *Little Women*, by George Cukor (a US entry), and *The Private Lives of Don Juan*, by Alexander Korda (the British entry). Max Reinhardt produced *A Midsummer's Night Dream* in Florence in 1933 and *The Merchant of Venice* in Venice in 1934. Max Neufeld, a Jewish actor in Austria and later a celebrated film director in Germany, left Berlin for Rome due to Nazi racial legislation. Because he was able to secure documentation that his mother was a gentile, Neufeld was able to continue making films in Italy after 1938, until the time of his death in 1957. Ironically, his first major Italian film, *Mille Lire Al Mese*, was released in 1939, after the racial laws had already gone into effect. To date, no Italian film historian specializing in the Fascist period has noted the irony of a full-page ad for *Mille Lire Al Mese* appearing immediately next to an unprecedented and pernicious editorial denouncing Jewish influence in the November 1938 issue of *Cinema*.

In order to grasp how Fascist Italy changed so significantly in its policy toward the Jews, from criticizing Nazi antisemitism and hosting German Jews in 1934 to the adoption of racial legislation in 1938, we must examine the internal

---

7. The only serious biography of Pavolini is Arrigo Petacco, *Il Superfascista: Vita e morte di Alessandro Pavolini* (Milan: Mondatori, 1998).

contradictions of the regime. I will demonstrate that the attack on the Jews responded to a legitimation deficit, which arose from the growing gap between Fascism's inflated revolutionary aspirations, on the one hand, and its ultimate failure to enact any substantive social and economic policies that threatened the traditional order, on the other.

I. THE CULTURAL CONTRADICTIONS OF 1930S FASCISM

During the 1920s, the Fascist regime was almost exclusively focused on eliminating sources of opposition and erecting an authoritarian institutional order that would take the place of the previous liberal one. Totalitarian aspirations had been kept in check by virtue of the compromises Mussolini chose to make with the traditional elites, particularly the industrialists, in order to secure their support. These liberal elites, hoping to preserve as much of the liberal *status quo ante* as they could, were under constant attack by intransigent Fascists, intent on immediately establishing a new order. By the early 1930s, a dictatorship had been established, but without any apparent legitimating project that had been carried over from the previous decade. Now the traditional elites had been weakened, and their autonomy eroded further due to the coming of the Great Depression, which made them ever more dependent on state assistance. Capitalism, if not industrial society itself, was in crisis; perhaps, it was thought, a terminal one. As Mussolini put it, the crisis in the system had become a crisis of the system. In this situation, the old compromises with the liberal elite were no longer legitimate, and through the exigencies of autarky, Italy became more and more a command economy.

By the early 1930s, the violent suppression of dissent had given way to an emergent consensus. Anti-Fascist historiography has always resisted the term *consensus*, insisting that Fascism became an ever more repressive dictatorship. Yet the fact remains that Mussolini's new and extensive social programs were popular, such as calls for social justice, articulation of corporatism as a new *terza via* [third way] between communism and capitalism, and generous subsidies for culture. Oddly enough, this concession can easily be found in the writings of contemporary Communist leaders such as Antonio Gramsci and Palmiro Togliatti, who both remarked that only someone with a Socialist background—like Mussolini—could have taken this path. An amnesty in 1932, celebrating the tenth anniversary of the Fascist March on Rome, freed more than half of those detained for oppositional activity. No less than the communist Giorgio Amendola would later note that former prisoners, like himself, were left alone so long as they refrained from politics, and that Italian Fascism, in this sense, was altogether different from German Nazism.[8]

By 1931, six years after the Matteotti assassination and Croce's famous anti-Fascist manifesto (signed by more than four hundred intellectuals), Mussolini imposed an oath of fidelity to the Fascist regime that was refused by only twelve university professors in the entire country. Practically all the university professors who earlier had signed Croce's manifesto not only took the loyalty oath but also ended up collaborating, to one degree or another, with the regime. Intellectuals later noted for their anti-Fascism, such as Norberto Bobbio and Antonio Banfi, not only signed the oath but later attested, following the 1938 racial legislation, that they had no Jewish blood.[9] In fact, the only intellectual of note who refused to do so was Croce himself. Of course, not taking the required oath and not attesting to one's "Aryan" status would have jeopardized or ended university careers, but that stick was more than offset, in the calculation of most Italian intellectuals, by the conspicuous carrots of collaboration.

There was no era in contemporary Italian history when culture was as richly subsidized as during the thirties. As Marla Stone demonstrates in *The Patron State*, Mussolini, before 1938, simply wanted intellectuals on board without imposing any particular aesthetic, as was the case in Stalin's Russia and Hitler's Germany.[10] In fact, the analytic category Stone deploys to describe this practice

---

8. Giorgio Amendola, *Intervista sull'antifascismo*, ed. Piero Melograni (Bari, Italy: Laterza, 2008), 94, 152–54.

9. In the June 21, 1992, issue of *Panorama*, the journalist Giorgio Fabre revealed a servile letter that Bobbio had written to Mussolini in 1935, assuring the dictator of his Fascist family background, his membership in the GUF (Gruppi universitari fascisti [Fascist University Youth]), and his Fascist faith. Bobbio feared his academic career was jeopardized by an arrest for having been at the periphery of the Justice and Liberty group. Fabre's revelation immediately led to polemics regarding Bobbio's conduct, especially for having kept his Fascist past hidden. Bobbio handled the affair with exemplary honesty in his 1997 autobiography and in several interviews, especially one published in *Il Foglio* on November 12, 1999. As for why he never mentioned his Fascist past, Bobbio repeatedly used the term *vergonia* [shame], for emphasis actually spelled "ver-gogn-ia." At roughly the same time, the Fascist past of Eugenio Scalfari, editor of the independent left newspaper *La Reppublica*, another noted left-wing intellectual, was revealed. Scalfari played a major role in the Rome GUF journal *Roma Fascista*, which published some of the worst antisemitic pieces during the campaign against the Jews (although none were written by him). Scalfari, too, would use the word *vergonia* repeatedly in interviews, reflecting on this period and his role in it. On Banfi and other intellectuals in Fascist Italy, see Mirella Serri, *I Redenti: Gli intellettuali che vissero due volte, 1938–1948* (Milan: Corbaccio, 2005).

10. Marla Stone, *The Patron State: Culture and Politics in Fascist Italy* (Princeton, NJ: Princeton University Press, 1998).

is "hegemonic pluralism," where intense debate often took place between antithetical movements (e.g., traditionalists vs. modernists), and ample room was afforded even for dissident and nonconforming tendencies. In any event, as it developed after the 1920s, Italian Fascism became less coercive and more consensual, and intellectuals became both subjects and objects of this process.

By the mid-1930s, it had become clear that joining the Gruppi universitari fascisti [Fascist University Youth (GUF)] and participating in annual competitions [the *Littoriali*] conferred elite status, ensured upward mobility, and gained entry for ambitious aspirants into networks of power and influence in the universities, cultural institutions, state administration, and Fascist Party. Those who joined the GUF automatically became party members, whether or not they were Fascists by deep conviction. For this reason, literally all those who became prominent after the war in academia, culture, journalism, and public administration had, like Norberto Bobbio, passed through the GUF. Enrollment in the GUF jumped from 8,854 in 1927 to 75,436 in 1935, to 105,883 in 1939, and reached 164,667 by the time the regime collapsed in 1943.[11] The ascent in membership was constant and linear; neither the presumably "unpopular" racial laws, the alliance with Germany, nor the entrance into the Second World War precipitated any reversal. For this reason, one should not be surprised that GUF membership included most notables, including those not at all associated with Fascism after the war. For example, economists such as Paolo Sylos Labini and Guido Carli (future governor of the Bank of Italy and president of Confindustria), writers such as Pier Paolo Pasolini and Elio Vittorini, philosophers such as Enzo Paci and Antonio Banfi, historians such as Carlo Morandi and Luigi Salvatorelli, filmmakers such as Roberto Rossellini and Michaelangelo Antonioni, and journalists such as Enzo Biagi and Indro Montanelli. A recent anthology of interviews (*I giovani di Mussolini*) reveals that GUF activities, especially the Littoriali competitions, were the highlight of their university years for members of this generation, across the political spectrum.[12]

The brightest individuals within the GUF, including many who would become leading Communists after the war, were recruited by Giuseppe Bottai, the so-called Fascist Gramsci, intent on cultivating a new *classe dirigente* and creating a new fascist cultural hegemony. At the time, this group was actually called *la covata Bottai* [Bottai's kids]. As we shall see, Bottai, as minister of

---

11. Tracey H. Koon, *Believe, Obey, Fight: Political Socialization of Youth in Fascist Italy: 1922–1943* (Chapel Hill: University of North Carolina Press, 1985), 190.

12. Aldo Grandi, *I giovani di Mussolini: Fascisti convinti, fascisti pentiti, antifascisti*, Storie della storia d'Italia 59 (Milan: Baldini & Castoldi, 2001).

education, personally distributed posts vacated by Jews in 1938 to these young clients while offering stipends and favors to nonconformist journals and even to an ascendant "anti-Fascist" (or rather unorthodox) publishing house of undeniable quality, Einaudi.

During the thirties, organized anti-Fascism within Italy was isolated and thoroughly marginal. A number of previously anti-Fascist Socialists, including the former mayor of Milan, Emilio Caldara, sought reconciliation with the regime, believing in its anticapitalist rhetoric and the consequent transformation of Fascism into a new form of Socialism. Socialist trade union leaders such as Rigola and Baldesi already had joined the regime, while the Partito Comunista Italiano [Italian Communist Party (PCI)] in 1936 issued an "appeal to our brothers in black shirts," calling for Communists and Fascists to join forces to realize the 1919 Fascist Program, which they called "democratic and progressive."[13] The PCI also adopted a policy of *entrismo* whereby members were encouraged to penetrate Fascist mass organizations, highlight unfulfilled promises, and push them further to the left.

It is therefore hardly astonishing, under these circumstances, that the so-called second generation, the *generazione di Mussolini*, which grew up under Fascism and came of age during the thirties, identified strongly with the regime. This held true for young Jews as well, many of whom, such as the aspiring writers Fausto Coen and Giorgio Bassani, competed in the Littoriali, and some even occupied leadership positions in the GUF. Recalling those years, some of the participants from the South or rural zones noted this was the first time they came into contact with and befriended Jewish intellectuals of their generation. As late as the 1938 Littoriali held in Palermo, numerous Jews participated, and one panel was actually presided over by Enrico Rocca, a noted Jewish author and German specialist.[14] The text in question was a book by Rudolf Arnheim, the German Jewish authority on the cinema mentioned earlier. Harsh protests erupted at the 1938 Palermo Littoriali, when some participants, for the first time in this forum, uttered antisemitic comments. In fact, it was participation in the GUF, and especially in the Littoriali (which

---

13. The original Italian text can be found in Bruno Grieco, *Un partito non stalinista: PCI 1936, "Appello ai fratelli in camicia nera,"* Gli specchi della memoria (Venice: Marsilio, 2004). For an English translation of this remarkable document, see Ruggiero Grieco, "Appeal to Our Brothers in Black Shirts," *Telos* 133 (2005): 131–49. See also Franklin Hugh Adler and Danilo Breschi, "Introduction," *Telos* 133 (2005): 3–14 (at 11–12). This entire special issue of *Telos*, coedited by Franklin Hugh Adler and Danilo Breschi, is devoted to new scholarship on Italian Fascism.

14. Grandi, *Giovani di Mussolini*, 82–87.

took place with unusual freedom of expression) where future anti-Fascists from throughout Italy first became acquainted and began crucial conversations that led in some cases eventually to opposition.

Beyond the diffuse leftism (anticapitalism, corporatism, a rhetoric of social justice, and mass incorporation) that appealed particularly to university students and trade union leaders, the other ideological strain of Fascism that would become important in the mid-thirties was radical nationalism. In fact, radical nationalism largely preceded Fascism, developing in the 1912–22 decade (spanning Italy's war in Libya, the First World War, the postwar crisis, and the Fascist March on Rome). Imperial expansion was its central concern, articulated most truculently by Enrico Corradini, who famously argued that Italy was a "proletarian nation," in struggle against the plutocratic ones.[15] What Italy lacked in financial resources was offset by its demographic potential, which was more important, they argued, in sustaining wars and conquering territory in the long run.

During the 1920s, while Mussolini was preoccupied with domestic politics and establishing a dictatorship, radical nationalism remained dormant. With the exception of the Corfu incident in September 1923, Mussolini had been fully aware of the constraints within which he had to operate and made no expansionist or imperial claims until the mid-thirties. In fact, he had been so eminently responsible during the negotiations relating to the Locarno Pact, the Briand Plan, and the Austro-German Customs Union that he was broadly praised for his diplomatic skill. With the invasion and conquest of Ethiopia in 1935, and subsequent claims regarding *mare nostrum* [Mediterranean dominance], the proletarian nation theme became dominant, so much so that when Mussolini entered the Second World War in June 1940, his declaration was uttered in the explicit name of *Italia proletaria e fascista*, a war on the part of poor people against those who monopolized the wealth of the world, a war of young and fecund people against sterile powers in decline.

As persuasively argued by Emilio Gentile, radical nationalism provided the very transcendent project that had been absent during the 1920s, when Mussolini had created a dictatorship but failed to coherently articulate the reason for which this had been done.[16] Radical nationalism was not identical to the diffuse

---

15. Enrico Corradini, *Il nazionalismo italiano* (Milan: Treves, 1914), 53–70.
16. See especially Emilio Gentile, *Il mito dello Stato nuovo: Dal radicalismo nazionale al fascismo*, 2nd ed., Biblioteca universale Laterza 510 (Rome: Laterza, 1999), and Emilio Gentile, *La Grande Italia: The Myth of the Nation in the 20th Century*, trans. Suzanne Dingee and Jennifer Pudney, George L. Mosse Series in Modern European Cultural and Intellectual History (Madison: Univerity of Wisconsin Press, 2008).

leftism mentioned earlier, but it would not be difficult to fuse the two themes into a grandiose synthesis whereby the Fascist state would totally transform the wretched and corrupt Italy Mussolini had inherited from liberalism into a magnificent imperial nation of workers and soldiers. Emilio Gentile appropriately called this a projected "anthropological revolution," as the stated intent was no less than creating, as the expression put it, the "New Fascist Man."[17] Renzo De Felice similarly referred to this as Mussolini's "cultural revolution." What they have in common is the notion of a totalitarian state that makes a new society or, in this case, a Fascist totalitarian state that fabricates a future Fascist society, a state that creates not only new institutions but also new historical subjects, new men, and a new race.

Unlike the diffuse leftism of the early thirties, radical nationalism from the very beginning had attacked Zionism and particularly international Jewish finance, though in tracts on the latter, a distinction usually had been made between "international Jewry," on the one hand, and Italian Jews, on the other. This distinction would collapse in the 1930s when it was argued that Italian Jews refused to distance themselves from attacks made by Jews elsewhere against Nazi antisemitism, especially when relations between Italy and Germany were growing closer. Mussolini was convinced that international Jewish organizations played a leading role in sanctions levied against Italy by the League of Nations following the invasion of Ethiopia, and increasingly identified these same anonymous international Jewish organizations as the primary source of global anti-Fascism. Mussolini, until this time, had made both philosemitic and antisemitic statements, depending on the situation and consequence. For example, he was pro-Zionist in 1934–35, when he imagined Zionists could be alienated from the British and emerge as a pawn in Italy's Mediterranean strategy, but anti-Zionist thereafter, when, together with the Germans, he opted for an anti-British, pro-Arab position.[18] But right up to 1938, in countless public statements, Mussolini said that there was no "Jewish Problem" in Italy and that no antisemitic policies were being contemplated.[19] Privately, however, one can detect an antisemitic drift in privileged conversations and in permitting, if not

---

17. See Emilio Gentile, *The Struggle for Modernity: Nationalism, Futurism, and Fascism*, Italian and Italian American Studies (Westport, CT: Praeger, 2003), 84–86.

18. In my view, the best overall assessment of Mussolini's conflicted and conflicting views on the Jews remains the first chapter of Giuseppe Mayda, *Ebrei sotto Salò: La persecuzione antisemita 1943–1945* (Milan: Feltrinelli, 1978), 9–24.

19. See Sarfatti, *Jews in Mussolini's Italy*, 43, and Emil Ludwig, *Talks with Mussolini*, trans. Eden and Cedar Paul (Boston: Little, Brown, 1933), 70.

encouraging, progressively more aggressive antisemitic polemics in the Italian press. It should be noted, however, that an antisemitic tone did not yet appear in journals published by the pillars of the Fascist left—the GUF and the trade unions—which were focused on themes of social justice, corporatism, and the need to affect real anticapitalist reforms.

II. MUSSOLINI'S CAMPAIGN AGAINST THE JEWS

We come now to a long-neglected question in studies of Italian Fascism, especially from the perspective of unredeemed transformative promises. What happens when a political revolution is not accompanied by a social one? Italian Fascism certainly was a political revolution that fundamentally altered institutions, imposed new political principles, created a new political culture, and recruited a new political class. Moreover, unlike the liberal state that never seriously attempted to integrate the masses into political life, the Fascist state was Italy's first attempt to incorporate the masses into public life, albeit hierarchically, through new youth organizations, leisure activities, labor syndicates, and social welfare programs. These efforts were typically superficial, stopping well short of violating the prerogatives of private property, class privilege, and altering the social order itself. For this reason, Mussolini was always reinventing himself and the regime, and when domestic options ran out by the mid-thirties, he then turned toward an aggressive foreign policy to compensate for a growing deficit in domestic legitimacy. This accounts for his turn toward racism, which was also related to imperialism, especially after Ethiopia had been conquered and Italy ruled over a large black African population. It further accounts for Mussolini's campaign against the Jews in 1938. Although the conventional explanation for this new antisemitic policy is based almost exclusively on Italy's growing diplomatic relationship with Nazi Germany, and the consequent need to harmonize domestic policy, it can be argued that there were internally generated causes for the campaign against "the Jews" as well.

By 1937, the regime was coming under attacks from all quarters for failed economic and social reforms: the corporatist restructuring of productive life; the growing economic hardship caused not only by the Great Depression but also by an economy that had lost any dynamism; deficits attributed directly to Italy's protracted and unpopular intervention in the Spanish Civil War; and massive colonial expenses. Despite an ideology that called for imperial expansion and greater sacrifices, in reality Italy's trade with its colonies was only 2 percent of its total trade in 1939. According to Denis Mack Smith, Italy was spending on its colonies ten times their value to it, ironically at a time when the Italian population of New York City alone was ten times that of the entire Italian colonial empire.[20] The consensus of the early thirties was coming apart at the seams, especially among the "second generation" for whom Fascism's unredeemed leftism stimulated a revolutionary appetite it was unable to satisfy. To them, as well as the more radical syndical leaders, the undeniable social transformations of the communist Soviet Union appeared all the more attractive.

Beginning in 1937, intelligence reports submitted to the Ministry of Internal Affairs indicated growing mass dissatisfaction and disaffection from Fascism.[21] Worse still was the growing demoralization within the Fascist Party itself, including those at the summit. The diaries of both Bottai and Galeazzo Ciano, Mussolini's son-in-law and foreign minister, reflect this sense of drift. When in 1937 the Communist Giorgio Amendola was released from prison and returned to Rome, Bottai and Ciano wished to meet with him. Amendola had been a childhood friend of both, but as a "Communist functionary," he refused to meet with them. He later regretted that decision, because the disaffection that motivated their requests might have provided useful information for the PCI regarding contradictions within the top Fascist leadership group.[22]

Confronted with this legitimation crisis, Mussolini launched the so-called *antiborghese* campaign, promising to deliver "three belly punches to the bourgeoisie." The first two were relatively innocuous: adopting the so-called *passo romano*, an Italian version of the goose step that Mussolini insisted was of Roman origin, and the *anti-lei* campaign against the Italian pronoun that Mussolini said was not only archaic but antipopular. The third was a frontal attack against the Jews, principal bearers, in Mussolini's words, of "the bourgeois spirit."[23]

The clearest articulation of this *antiborghese* stance is contained in the speech Mussolini delivered to the national council of the Fascist Party in October 1938, as the official racial campaign had just begun. Mussolini argued that "the enemy of our regime has a name: '*borghesia.*'" The borghesia, he claimed, was not so much an economic category as a politico-moral one: pessimistic, self-interested, and parasitic. The bourgeois spirit was an obstacle

---

20. Denis Mack Smith, *Modern Italy: A Political History* (New Haven, CT: Yale University Press, 1997), 388.

21. On public opinion, see Simona Colarizi, *L'opinione degli italiani sotto il regime 1929–1943*, Biblioteca universale Laterza 518 (Bari, Italy: Laterza, 2000).

22. This disaffection ultimately led to Mussolini's dismissal at the famous July 25, 1943, meeting of the Fascist Grand Council. See Amendola, *Intervista sull'antifascismo*, 106–7.

23. The text of Mussolini's speech is reproduced in Luigi Preti, *Impero fascista: Africani ed ebrei* (Milan: Mursia, 1968), 285–96.

to further development; "it must be isolated and destroyed." This was hardly an exceptional outburst, as throughout the diaries of Bottai and Ciano there are numerous entries that record Mussolini's many extemporaneous fulminations against the bourgeoisie. Both diaries recall Mussolini saying that, had he a true understanding of what the bourgeoisie really signified when he was still a socialist, he would have led such a merciless revolution that, by comparison, the one led by "Comrade Lenin" would seem like an innocent joke.[24]

Once the "bourgeois spirit" became identified with the "Jewish spirit," Jews became conflated with the bourgeoisie, and attacks against the latter became transformed rhetorically into attacks against the former. What followed was a discursive game in which hostility toward capitalism and frustration over stalled corporatist reforms became displaced onto Jews and their sympathizers, the so-called pietists (denigrated in the Fascist press as *filogiudei* and "moral mongrels"). For members of the Fascist left, and particularly labor leaders, this was the only sanctioned way to extend the *antiborghese* campaign beyond the small number of Jews to the bourgeois class itself. This was readily apparent in an article the labor leader Luigi Fontanelli wrote in *Il lavoro fascista* on September 4, 1938. "Justly it has been written that no less dangerous than the Jews are the friends of the Jews." In a thinly veiled attack against the broader bourgeoisie, not merely the Jews, Fontanelli sought, as he put it, to "fill in the gray areas":

> The race problem, and particularly the resulting, indispensable anti-Semitic attitude of Fascism, is an excellent reactive agent to isolate not only the Jews but all those gray areas where—under the cover of the most "petit bourgeois spirit"—those representatives of the old ruling classes were hiding, whose motto could be: "I have changed my badge because it was convenient, nothing else." It is very well, therefore, that through the problem of race, revolutionary Fascism doubles its uncompromising vigilance over those elements that nurture the most deleterious and corrosive individualistic spirit, which is anti-Fascist.... The circles that show little sensitivity toward the race problem will identify closely with those who are insensitive to the collective spirit imposed by a superior civilization, who do not believe in corporatism, reducing it to a system thought up to avoid or delay the solution of the biggest social problems of our time.... The revolution gives no pause to these elements and gray areas representing the vestiges of that extremely ingrained mentality of the old conceited, empty, intellectualistic, and

---

24. Giuseppe Bottai, *Diario 1935–1944*, ed. Bruno Guerri (Milan: BUR, 2001), 237; Galeazzo Ciano, *Diario 1937–1943* (Milan: BUR, 2000), 486.

underhanded Italy that was useful to everyone and didn't scare anyone.... Now they will find out that it wasn't just a flash of lightning: it is raining and it will continue to rain.[25]

There never was one unitary conception of Fascist racism; it was a complex and contradictory mélange of biological, spiritual, and political components, used by different actors in different contexts and at different moments.[26] The image of the Jew, however, as the class enemy has particular salience for two important reasons: first, this was the form of antisemitism deliberately used by Mussolini to launch the campaign against the Jews, and second, this basis for attacking Jews was the form most prevalently deployed by labor leaders and intellectuals, particularly those of the second generation. As Emilio Gentile has argued, the distinctive project of the final and most radical phase was launching an anthropological revolution that would create nothing less than a new historical subject. Jews, who had achieved emancipation and relative prosperity under the preceding liberal state, were now portrayed as obstacles to this cultural transformation because they were historically bound to the old, decadent order, as well as the corrupting bourgeois spirit that informed it.

The attack on Jews served two complementary ends: diplomatically, it helped overcome Italy's isolation and solidify the strategic alliance with Germany; domestically, by identifying an enemy "other," it served the purpose of helping fabricate the myth of the New Fascist Man. Here, the imaginary Jew represented both an obstacle to and negation of the new Italy and the new Italians. The imaginary Jew was fatally linked to liberal Italy and to the bourgeoisie, both of which Mussolini viscerally detested. In fact, in the imaginary Jew these somewhat abstract phenomena became targeted, focused, and concretized. For Mussolini, it was seldom the "real Jew" that was at issue. This ideological projection (the "imaginary Jew"), however, in the hands of his subordinates and in the context of a totalitarian regime, took on a life of its own, ironically removed not only from ordinary Italian Jews, but from Italian public opinion as well. At no time, even in the vile state-sponsored journal *Difesa della Razza*, were specific Italian Jews ever targeted as living incarnations of the "bourgeois spirit," as opposed to the menacing imaginary Jew. As Mussolini cynically observed,

---

25. Quoted in De Felice, *Jews in Fascist Italy*, 381–82, and Renzo De Felice, *Lo Stato totalitario (1936–1940)*, vol. 2 of *Mussolini il duce* (Turin, Italy: Einaudi, 1996), 260–61.

26. On the diverse and often conflicting interpretations of Fascist racial theory, see Aaron Gillette, *Racial Theories in Fascist Italy*, Routledge Studies in Modern European History 5 (London: Routledge, 2003).

"Now anti-Semitism has been inoculated into the blood of the Italian people. It will continue to circulate and develop by itself."²⁷ Rumors circulated that Jews had either simply set up gentile front men to conserve their control of banned enterprises, or they had turned the family business into a *società anonima* (or corporation), masking its Jewish identity. The imaginary Jew here was identified with anonymous capital and linked to international Jewish finance, long-standing themes in the standard repertoire of European antisemitism.

Italy's racial laws were enacted during the same time that Kristallnacht gave graphic evidence regarding the drift of racial policy in Italy's new ally. Yet in Italy there were no pogroms, no obligatory Jewish stars on garments, no mass mobilization of Italians against their Jewish compatriots. The watchword was "discrimination not persecution." In some cities, such as Trieste, where Jewish property had been vandalized, party and state officials quickly intervened and took appropriate action against those involved. Intelligence reports submitted to the Ministry of Internal Affairs indicate that public opinion, not prepared for this abrupt change in policy, and not believing that the small Jewish population was a credible threat, was generally repulsed by the antisemitic campaign and the related preemptive attack on Jewish sympathizers [*pietisti*]. Yet at the same time, the new discrimination against the Jews elicited only a reaction of silence and growing indifference.²⁸ Indifference, in this case, was certainly preferable to virulent antisemitism, but far from compatible with the postwar myth of the good Italian, unless "good" in this case is simply the absence of being actively "bad." As with most people in circumstances where difficult ethical choices need to be faced, Italians in 1938 responded to the racial legislation in a cynical, self-interested manner, not rallying to state invoked invectives against the Jews, but not supporting their Jewish compatriots either or passing up opportunities that derived from discrimination against them. Few followed Croce's example of refusing to sign forms attesting to the fact that they had no Jewish blood or, for that matter, hesitated for a minute before accepting a post vacated by a Jew whose service had been terminated because of the racial legislation.

Many noted Jewish intellectuals left the country, such as the classics scholar Arnaldo Momigliano. Enrico Fermi won the Nobel Prize for physics in 1938 but went to the United States after accepting the award in Norway rather than return to Italy, where his Jewish wife would face humiliation. Among the many remarkable Italian Jews who came to the United States were four future Nobel Prize winners whose promising careers were terminated abruptly with the 1938

---

27. Quoted in De Felice, *Jews in Fascist Italy*, 290.
28. Colarizi, *L'opinione degli italiani*, 242–61.

racial laws—Franco Modigliani, economics; Emilio Segrè, physics; Rita Levi-Montalcini, medicine; and Salvatore Luria, medicine. Considering that Italy, to this day, has won but thirteen Nobel Prizes in the sciences, four of which went to Jews of this generation who were forced to leave, it is obvious that the impact of the antisemitic campaign on Italian science itself was devastating.[29] Internationally renowned faculties, such as the department of mathematics at the University of Rome, were devastated, as even bright "Aryan" students were now lost with the departure of Jewish *capi scuola* such as Vito Volterra, Tullio Levi-Civita, Guido Castelnuovo, and Federigo Enriques, all supplanted with relatively mediocre replacements.

III. INTELLECTUALS AND FASCIST ANTISEMITISM

If, as Antonio Gramsci once remarked, politics is always a combination of *dominio* [coercion] and *direzione* [consensus], the balance during the early thirties tipped toward consensus.[30] Intellectuals were generously rewarded for their part in legitimating Fascism, both established intellectuals and especially the younger ones of the second generation. Until 1938, Jewish intellectuals were no different, so far as being attracted to the benefits derived from activity in the GUF and especially participation in the Littoriali. They too were part of a cultural consensus generated by the regime and most likely would have continued, like all the others, to respond opportunistically to the positive and negative inducements orchestrated by the government. Continued collaboration after 1938, of course, took on a different and far more sinister significance, as the regime now made Jews objects of vituperation, and aspiring, ambitious intellectuals were expected to participate in, if not promote, official antisemitism.[31]

---

29. This is amply demonstrated by Giorgio Israel and Pietro Nastasi in their book on science and race in Fascist Italy (*Scienza e razza nell'Italia fascista* [Bologna, Italy: Il Mulino, 1998]).

30. See Antonio Gramsci, *Selections from the Prison Notebooks of Antonio Gramsci*, trans. Quintin Hoare and Geoffrey Nowell Smith (New York: International Publishers, 1971), 313–449.

31. There were even some cases where, for reasons of pure opportunism, some young intellectuals would write especially vile, antisemitic pieces once the racial campaign began, despite particularly close friendships they had enjoyed with Jews before 1938. The worst was probably Guido Piovene, later to become one of Italy's most important writers. He engaged in the crudest characterizations of the Jews and of Jewish culture, though he had close ties with Jews at least since his university days in Milan. His best friend in fact had been Eugenio Colorni, a Jewish socialist imprisoned in 1938 for oppositional activity, later to perish in the Resistance (in May 1944). Piovene, writing in *Corriere della Sera* of November 1, 1938,

Thanks to Giovanni Sedita's *Gli intelletuali di Mussolini*, we now know the full degree to which intellectuals, journalists, artists, and musicians were actually subsidized, openly and covertly, by the regime to promote its efforts and what happened in those few cases where opposition was publically expressed to the campaign against the Jews. For example, the monthly stipend of 1,500 lire that routinely went to the poet Giuseppe Ungaretti was abruptly suspended in February 1939, when he publicly dissented from the racial policy in an article published in the Italian cultural magazine *Omnibus*. Not only poets but also such leading composers as Mascagni, Cilea, and Giordano were given secret funds. In fact, well beyond university-based intellectuals, the entire cultural world was enlisted with subsidies that became significantly more generous after 1939.[32] In December 1938, the famous Austrian conductor Erich Kleiber refused to honor a contract to conduct Beethoven's *Fidelio* at La Scala, learning that Italy's most famous opera house had canceled Jewish subscriptions and fired the celebrated Jewish chorus master Vittorio Veneziani.[33] Kleiber and Arturo Toscanini were solitary dissidents; the world of music quickly accommodated itself to the new racial policy. Mascagni raised no objection that a central character in his opera *L'Amico Fritz* was changed from Rabbi David to Dr. David. American cinema, a model previously emulated for the developing Italian film industry, was now denounced as a cultural instrument in the hands of influential Jews. The Marx brothers' *A Night at the Opera*, initially greeted with critical acclaim, even in the Fascist press, was now roundly denounced as a vehicle for "three dirty Jews" to ridicule Italian culture.

After the war, skeletons and Blackshirts were consigned to the closet, so far as prominent and aspiring politicians, journalists, artists, and academics were concerned, intent on creating a new world and artfully forgetting the past. Yet

---

showered praise on Telesio Interlandi's collection of viciously antisemitic essays *Contra judeos*, agreeing with the author that Jews are always enemies of whatever host country they enter and then exploit for their own selfish benefit. Piovene actually wrote this less than a week after his Jewish friend Colorni had been arrested. After the war, Piovene was one of those young Fascist intellectuals "redeemed" and situated himself close to the PCI, thanks to the *perdonismo* of Togliatti. In the immediate postwar period, he unsurprisingly became a rank apologist for Stalinism. On the Piovene-Colorni relationship, see Sando Gerbi, *Tempi di malfede: Una storia italiana tra fascismo e dopoguerra* (Turin, Italy: Einaudi, 1999).

32. Giovanni Sedita, *Gli intellettuali di Mussolini: La cultura finanziata dal fascismo* (Florence: Le Lettere, 2010), 36, 49–51.

33. See the remarkable essay by Annalisa Capristo, "La Scala, gli ebrei, ed Erich Kleiber: Una vicenda antisemita del dicembre 1938," *Quaderni di Storia* 67 (2008): 205–20. I should add that Vittorio Veneziani initially had been brought to La Scala by none other Toscanini, and was quickly, if unceremoniously, reengaged after the war.

the situation was far more complex, given the pitiful demise of Fascism and the somewhat contrived birth of the new republic, symbolically if not substantively anti-Fascist. Beneath the level of official rhetoric and high culture, ample space was found for an alternative, popular public sphere of the center-right, where Fascism became an object not so much of rehabilitation, as apologia and nostalgia. This is hardly surprising, given the fact that principled anti-Fascism represented a small minority, and most Italians had supported Fascism, with varying degrees of enthusiasm, until the very end. What had happened to Italy's Jews during the final four years of Fascism was rarely mentioned, despite the genesis of the myth of the "good Italian," who protected and saved their Jewish compatriots from the "bad Germans" after Mussolini had fallen and Germany occupied the north. In the world of politics and high culture, no attention was given to the Jews either, other than the fact that they too, stripped of all particularity, were part of a long list of "victims of Fascism"—as if they had been targeted because they were anti-fascists, rather than Jews.

As Mirella Serri illustrated in her 2005 bestseller *I Redenti*, intellectuals who had collaborated with Fascism buried their pasts in an all-too-accommodating postwar political atmosphere, in part because many joined the Italian Communist Party and were "redeemed" by its leader, Palmiro Togliatti, intent on using them to forge a new anti-Fascist hegemony. Dealing openly with the Jewish Question risked uncovering the worst period of their collaboration, 1938–43, the most extreme and degenerate phase of Fascism. Togliatti, who served as minister of justice in the first postwar government, orchestrated an *epurazione* so ineffectual that the jails were emptied. Even Fascists who had collaborated with the Gestapo and committed acts of bestial violence against *partigiani* were released and returned to normal life well before Italian Jews—minimally assisted by the government—began to retrieve lost occupational posts and pilfered property.

The reintegration of Jews into public life was an incredibly long and difficult process (the last remaining racial law was abrogated only in 1987), especially regaining pilfered property and jobs. When Jews sought to reclaim their university posts, they were generally treated with little generosity and understanding. As one of the leading authorities on the subject put it, they went from "victims of Fascism" to "usurpers" trying to take away the jobs of real Italians.[34] There were some especially grotesque instances where famous

---

34. Roberto Finzi, *L'università italiana e le leggi antiebraiche*, 2nd ed. (Rome: Riuniti, 2003), 131–32. For the most comprehensive study of the subject, see Annalisa Capristo, *L'espulsione degli ebrei dalle accademie italiane* (Turin, Italy: Silvio Zamorani editore, 2002).

Jewish professors expelled in 1938 regained their posts after the war, only to be expelled once more for having been fascists. Indeed, this happened to the noted biologist Tullio Terni and to the philosopher of law Giorgio Del Vecchio. And this despite the fact that almost none of the non-Jewish university professors who also had been Fascists—*virtually the entire professoriate*—were subjected to comparable treatment. For the most part, they became nominal anti-Fascists, without ever having renounced Fascism, and continued in their posts as if nothing had happened.

With the exception of some noteworthy articles in *Il Ponte*, little of substance was written on what had happened to the Jews until Renzo De Felice's book in 1965 and nothing specifically on the difficult postwar reintegration of Italian Jews until the 1980s. Jews who had lived through the war were too traumatized to raise the issue, which is why the Jewish community actually solicited De Felice to write their history, giving him full access to their own archival materials. That no doctoral dissertations were written on the subject is not at all surprising. University professors who had received their posts under Fascism were hardly enthusiastic about supervising research on such an embarrassing subject, since even those who were not themselves antisemitic, or directly implicated in the expulsion of their Jewish colleagues, nevertheless benefited indirectly from the absence of traditionally high-qualified Jewish competitors for the limited number of available university positions. It is highly significant that dissertations on the subject, as well as several fine scholarly monographs, began to emerge only after a newer generation of university professors replaced the old. Indeed, the copious literature now available on Italian Jews under Fascism dates back only to 1988, the fiftieth anniversary of the racial laws.[35]

At first glance, this phenomenon of professors being reluctant to turn a critical eye toward their own discipline's involvement in and benefit from antisemitic propaganda has a familiar ring. First, the development of critical scholarship about the major disciplines of the humanities during the Nazi era in Germany took a similar course.[36] Second, as in Germany, Mussolini's campaign against Italian Jews in 1938 resulted in many scholars fleeing the country. Notwithstanding these similarities, to insist on fitting the Italian case into a rubric designed for the German situation would lead to a misunderstanding

---

35. For an overview of this literature, see Franklin Hugh Adler, review of *Storia della Shoah in Italia: Vicende, memorie, rappresentazioni*, ed. Marcello Flores et al., *Quest: Issues in Contemporary Jewish History* 3 (July 2015), https://www.quest-cdecjournal.it/franklin-h-adler/.

36. See the essay by Alan Steinweis in this volume, "The History of the Humanities in the Third Reich."

of what actually caused Italian Jews to be singled out as an enemy and have to flee from their homeland to save their lives. As we have seen, Italian Jews had long been successfully integrated into Italian culture at large, and they played very important roles in Italy right up to Mussolini's 1938 antiborghese campaign. In that year, Mussolini attacked Jews as "bearers of the bourgeois spirit" and thereafter introduced antisemitic legislation. If we allow the Italian case to stand on its own, the truth emerges that Mussolini's sudden turn against the Jews came about when his regime faced a legitimation crisis over its failed economic and social reforms and stood in need of a convenient scapegoat: an all-too-familiar story.

This volume explores in detail how many professors in a variety of humanistic disciplines promoted Nazi propaganda and research. Scholars took active roles in betraying the values that upheld their fields of study. But a betrayal just as significant can be observed in those who silently accepted the discrimination against their former friends and colleagues. They reaped the benefits of newly available jobs and decreased competition for academic positions and promotions. Research in twentieth-century antisemitism and its legacy within the academy certainly builds on the vital work that has uncovered the complicity of so many within Nazi Germany. Such betrayals of the humanities also took place for reasons having nothing to do with Nazi policies, as this essay has shown. Moving forward, therefore, it becomes essential to decenter Germany. Doing so will facilitate comparative understandings of other betrayals, allowing a fuller perspective on twentieth-century antisemitism to emerge.

BIBLIOGRAPHY

Adler, Franklin Hugh. "Jew as Bourgeois, Jew as Enemy, Jew as Victim of Fascism." *Modern Judaism* 28 (2008): 306–26.

———. Preface to *The Jews in Fascist Italy: A History*, by Renzo De Felice, i–ix. Translated by Robert L. Miller. 3rd ed. New York: Enigma, 2015.

———. Review of *Storia della Shoah in Italia: Vicende, memorie, rappresentazioni*, ed. Marcello Flores et al. *Quest: Issues in Contemporary Jewish History* 3 (July 2015). https://www.quest-cdecjournal.it/franklin-h-adler/.

———."Why Mussolini Turned on the Jews." *Patterns of Prejudice* 39 (2005): 285–300.

Adler, Franklin Hugh, and Danilo Breschi. "Introduction." *Telos* 133 (2005): 3–14.

Amendola, Giorgio. *Intervista sull'antifascismo*. Edited by Piero Melograni. Bari, Italy: Laterza, 2008.

Bottai, Giuseppe. *Diario 1935–1944*. Edited by Bruno Guerri. Milan: BUR, 2001.

Capristo, Annalisa. "La Scala, gli ebrei ed Erich Kleiber: Una vicenda antisemita del dicembre 1938." *Quaderni di Storia* 67 (2008): 205–20.

———. *L'espulsione degli ebrei dalle accademie italiane*. Turin, Italy: Silvio Zamorani editore, 2002.

Ciano, Galeazzo. *Diario 1937–1943*. Milan: BUR, 2000.

Colarizi, Simona. *L'opinione degli italiani sotto il regime 1929–1943*. Biblioteca universale Laterza 518. Bari, Italy: Laterza, 2000.

Corradini, Enrico. *Il nazionalismo italiano*. Milan: Treves, 1914.

De Felice, Renzo. *The Jews in Fascist Italy: A History*. Translated by Robert L. Miller. 3rd ed. New York: Enigma, 2015.

———. *Lo Stato totalitario (1936–1940)*. Vol. 2, *Mussolini il duce*. Turin, Italy: Einaudi, 1996.

Finzi, Roberto. *L'università italiana e le leggi antiebraiche*. 2nd ed. Rome: Riuniti, 2003.

Gentile, Emilio. *Il mito dello Stato nuovo: Dal radicalismo nazionale al fascismo*. 2nd ed. Biblioteca universale Laterza 510. Rome: Laterza, 1999.

———. *La Grande Italia: The Myth of the Nation in the 20th Century*. Translated by Suzanne Dingee and Jennifer Pudney. George L. Mosse Series in Modern European Cultural and Intellectual History. Madison: University of Wisconsin Press, 2008.

———. *The Struggle for Modernity: Nationalism, Futurism, and Fascism*. Italian and Italian American Studies. Westport, CT: Praeger, 2003.

Gerbi, Sando. *Tempi di malfede: Una storia italiana tra fascismo e dopoguerra*. Turin, Italy: Einaudi, 1999.

Gillette, Aaron. *Racial Theories in Fascist Italy*. Routledge Studies in Modern European History 5. London: Routledge, 2003.

Gramsci, Antonio. *Selections from the Prison Notebooks of Antonio Gramsci*. Translated by Quintin Hoare and Geoffrey Nowell Smith. New York: International Publishers, 1971.

Grandi, Aldo. *I giovani di Mussolini: Fascisti convinti, fascisti pentiti, antifascisti*. Storie della storia d'Italia 59. Milan: Baldini & Castoldi, 2001.

Grieco, Bruno. *Un partito non stalinista: PCI 1936, "Appello ai fratelli in camicia nera."* Gli specchi della memoria. Venice: Marsilio, 2004.

Grieco, Ruggiero. "Appeal to Our Brothers in Black Shirts." *Telos* 133 (2005): 131–49.

Israel, Giorgio, and Pietro Nastasi. *Scienza e razza nell'Italia fascista*. Bologna, Italy: Il Mulino, 1998.

Koon, Tracey H. *Believe, Obey, Fight: Political Socialization of Youth in Fascist Italy: 1922–1943*. Chapel Hill: University of North Carolina Press, 1985.

Ludwig, Emil. *Talks with Mussolini*. Translated by Eden and Cedar Paul. Boston: Little, Brown, 1933.

Mayda, Giuseppe. *Ebrei sotto Salò: La persecuzione antisemita, 1943–1945.* Milan: Feltrinelli, 1978.
Montanelli, Indro. *Corriere della Sera,* April 13, 1997, 35.
Petacco, Arrigo. *Il Superfascista: Vita e morte di Alessandro Pavolini.* Milan: Mondadori, 1998.
Preti, Luigi. *Impero fascista: Africani ed ebrei.* Milan: Mursia, 1968.
Sarfatti, Michelle. *The Jews in Mussolini's Italy: From Equality to Persecution.* Translated by John and Anne C. Tedeschi. George L. Mosse Series in Modern European Cultural and Intellectual History. Madison: University of Wisconsin Press, 2007.
Sedita, Giovanni. *Gli intellettuali di Mussolini: La cultura finanziata dal fascismo.* Florence: Le Lettere, 2010.
Serri, Mirella. *I Redenti: Gli intellettuali che vissero due volte, 1938–1948.* Milan: Corbaccio, 2005.
Smith, Denis Mack. *Modern Italy: A Political History.* New Haven, CT: Yale University Press, 1997.
Stone, Marla. *The Patron State: Culture and Politics in Fascist Italy.* Princeton, NJ: Princeton University Press, 1998.
Voigt, Klaus. "Le scuole dei profughi in Italia." *Storia contemporanea* 19, no. 6 (1988): 1153–88.

FRANKLIN HUGH ADLER is the G. Theodore Mitau Professor of Political Science Emeritus at Macalester College, Saint Paul. He specializes in political theory, comparative politics, movements of the Far Right, and Holocaust studies. He is the author of *Italian Industrialists from Liberalism to Fascism: The Political Development of the Industrial Bourgeoisie, 1906–1934* (Cambridge, 1995) and has published articles in numerous academic journals. He has also contributed to the anthologies *Antonio Gramsci: Critical Assessments of Leading Political Philosophers* (Routledge, 2001) and *Dizionario del Fascismo* (Einaudi, 2002) and serves as an editor of the journal *Telos.*

FIFTEEN

IS THERE AN ANTI-JEWISH BIAS IN TODAY'S UNIVERSITY?

ALVIN H. ROSENFELD

DO THE HUMANITIES HUMANIZE? GEORGE STEINER raises this question in *Language and Silence* (1967) with the crimes of the Third Reich prominently in mind: "It is not only the case that the established media of civilization—the universities, the arts, the book-world—failed to offer adequate resistance to political bestiality; they often rose to welcome it and give it ceremony and apologia. Why? . . . When barbarism came to twentieth-century Europe, the arts faculties in more than one university offered very little moral resistance. . . . In a disturbing number of cases [they] gave servile or ecstatic welcome to political bestiality."[1] Steiner is eloquent in formulating the critical questions about possible links between the humanities and the "temptations of the inhuman," but his answers are sometimes more suggestive than definitive.[2] That is not the case with Max Weinreich, whose still-valuable pioneering study of 1946, *Hitler's Professors*, offers an abundance of empirical evidence to demonstrate "the part of scholarship in Germany's crimes against the Jewish people" (to quote his book's subtitle).

Weinreich sets out to prove that "German scholars from the beginning to the end of the Hitler era worked hand in glove with the murderers of the Jewish people."[3] He cites many of these scholars by name, institutional affiliation,

---

1. George Steiner, *Language and Silence: Essays on Language, Literature, and the Inhuman* (New York: Atheneum, 1967), ix, 61.
2. Ibid., ix.
3. Max Weinreich, *Hitler's Professors: The Part of Scholarship in Germany's Crimes against the Jewish People* (New York: Yiddish Scientific Institute [YIVO], 1946; repr., foreword by Martin Gilbert, New Haven, CT: Yale University Press, 1999), 9. Page references to the 1999 edition.

and academic discipline, quotes liberally from their speeches and writings, and shows how, in their zeal to propagate the tenets of racial science and the "German spirit," they succeeded in aligning Germany's institutions of higher learning with the ideological and political goals of the national government. While only partly successful, the regime's efforts to co-opt German academicians were widespread and involved anthropologists, biologists, chemists, economists, engineers, geographers, historians, legal scholars, linguists, political scientists, philosophers, theologians, and others. Working chiefly within the established universities but also within newly fashioned research institutes devoted to addressing the Jewish Question, these scholars actively pursued teaching and research agendas that would advance such spurious notions as political biology, racial hygiene, racial linguistics, Aryan mathematics, German physics, and other pseudoscientific fields.[4] In the words of the prominent legal and political theorist Carl Schmitt, their work was integral to winning a fateful "ideological contest with Jewry," a contest whose ultimate aim was to "free the German spirit from all Jewish falsifications."[5]

These "falsifications" included such major achievements as Albert Einstein's work in physics and a broad range of other significant contributions to science and the humanities by eminent Jewish scholars. The new racial state made it impossible for these scholars to continue their university careers, and in short order they, together with Jewish students, were expelled en masse. As Weinreich notes, by 1936, some 1,500 professors had been dismissed from their posts, most of them for racial or political reasons. According to Jeremy Noakes: "Between 1933–8, and mainly during 1933–4, 3,120 German academics left Germany, of whom 756 were full Professors.... Among those who left were many of the ablest scholars in Germany, including 24 existing and future Nobel Prize winners."[6]

---

4. See Alan Steinweis, *Studying the Jew: Scholarly Antisemitism in Nazi Germany* (Cambridge, MA: Harvard University Press, 1966).

5. Weinreich, *Hitler's Professors*, 40, citing and translating Carl Schmitt's speech in *Das Judentum in der Rechtswissenschaft: Ansprachen, Dorträge und Ergebnisse der Tagung der Reichsgruppe Hochschullehrer des NSRB. am 3. und 4. Oktober 1936, Die deutsche Rechtswissenschaft im Kampf gegen jüdischen Geist* 1 (Berlin: Deutscher Rechtsverlag, 1936), 14–17 (at 14 and 15). For a recent examination of Schmitt, see Raphael Gross, *Carl Schmitt und die Juden: Eine deutsche Rechtslehre* (Frankfurt am Main, Germany: Suhrkamp, 2000); for the English translation, see Raphael Gross, *Carl Schmitt and the Jews: The "Jewish Question," the Holocaust, and German Legal Theory*, trans. Joel Golb (Madison: University of Wisconsin Press, 2007).

6. Jeremy Noakes, "The Ivory Tower under Siege: German Universities in the Third Reich," *Journal of European Studies* 23 no. 4 (1993): 371–407 (at 379). See also Saul Friedlander, "The Demise of the German Mandarins: The German University and the Jews, 1933–1939," in

Many of these scholars were Jews, and their purge was as thorough as it was devastating for German universities. As for the non-Jews who stayed on, many kept their heads down, sought to continue their work, and rarely offered any significant moral or political resistance to the dismissal of their Jewish colleagues and students. With only few exceptions, many others—true believers, fellow travelers, or professional opportunists—actively contributed to making academic scholarship subservient to the political requirements of the Nazi state. In Weinreich's summary assessment of their work, these German scholars provided many of the "ideas and techniques which led to and justified" the persecution and slaughter of the Jews.[7]

Subsequent scholars of this subject largely support the main lines of Weinreich's findings. Nevertheless, in the postwar period, it was common for German academics to whitewash this history by constructing a convenient past for themselves that would absolve all but a few of their colleagues from complicity with National Socialism. But as Steven P. Remy demonstrates in *The Heidelberg Myth*, his revealing study of the nazification and denazification of the Ruprecht Karls University in Heidelberg, this whitewashed history, which was widely adopted, obscured the fact that sizable numbers of German academics "put their talents in the service of the regime."[8] Following one maneuver or another, most were exonerated in the postwar period; nevertheless, Jeremy Noakes's assessment is accurate: "The most striking feature of the history of universities in the Third Reich is the relative ease with which they adapted themselves to the new order. Indeed, many German academics—for a time at least—actually welcomed and eagerly co-operated with a movement and a regime which was blatantly at odds with the traditional values of their profession."[9] Noting the extent to which these German academics sympathized with Nazi ideas and goals and were involved "in some of the worst crimes of the Third Reich," Noakes does not hesitate to call their behavior "treason in the Ivory Tower."[10]

Other authors contributing to this book have taken it upon themselves to study the forms such complicity took during the Third Reich. My task is different. While keeping in mind the historical dimensions of our subject, I have

---

Von der Aufgabe der Freiheit: Politische Verantwortung und bürgerliche Gesellschaft im 19. und 20. Jahrhundert. Festschrift für Hans Mommsen zum 5. November 1995, ed. Christian Jansen, Lutz Niethammer, and Bernd Weisbrod (Berlin: Akademie, 1995), 69–82.

7. Weinreich, *Hitler's Professors*, 6.

8. Steven P. Remy, *The Heidelberg Myth: The Nazification and Denazification of a German University* (Cambridge, MA: Harvard University Press, 2002), 245.

9. Noakes, "Ivory Tower under Siege," 371.

10. Ibid., 399, 371.

been asked to take a hard look at today's universities and identify any analogous developments. Might such scrutiny uncover signs of a contemporary betrayal of the humanities? This is an unnerving but necessary question, and I will do my best to address it in as sober and clarifying a manner as I can.

On the positive side, nothing akin to the kind of academic collusion with a dictatorial state that occurred during the Hitler period is observable within North American and West European institutions of higher learning today. No attempts at *Gleichschaltung*, or the systematic coordination of scholarship with governmental dictates, are taking place.[11] No efforts are apparent to reproduce or inculcate nationalist or ideological tendencies like the "German spirit," or to "cleanse" Jewish books and authors from university libraries, or to remove Jewish professors or Jewish students from institutions of higher learning on racial or religious grounds. Nor are our universities encouraging the development of ideologically fabricated subjects like racial biology or American or Canadian physics or German or French mathematics. In all of these respects, Western universities are by and large free of the kinds of professional deformations that the nazification of scholarship introduced into German universities.

But there is another hand. However, here I feel the need to pause and remind myself, as well as my readers, that when dealing with a historical experience as extreme as that of Nazi Germany, one should introduce parallel experiences cautiously, if at all. Whatever our problems today, and we are not free of them, we are not witnessing anything within the educational cultures of the Western world that resembles the onset of the political bestiality, to use George Steiner's term, that led to and legitimized the persecution and mass murder of the Jews. Some of the material presented in the following pages is cause for concern, but not on the scale of concerns that should have accompanied the corruption of academic standards within German universities during the Third Reich. Then,

---

11. Some recent developments in central and eastern Europe, by contrast, are cause for concern. The present government in Hungary, for instance, has put the Central European University in Budapest under extreme pressure and evidently threatened it with closure; see Ben Chapman, "George Soros' Central European University Faces Closure after Hungary Law Targets Foreign Institutions," *Independent*, April 5, 2017, http://www.independent.co.uk/news/business/news/george-soros-central-european-university-hungary-law-protests-foreign-institutions-parliament-a7667451.html. There are also efforts underway in Poland to introduce revisionist histories of World War II and the Holocaust and to curb the work of such scholars of the subject as Jan Gross; see Alex Duval Smith, "Polish Move to Strip Holocaust Expert of Award Sparks Protests," *Guardian*, February 13, 2016, https://www.theguardian.com/world/2016/feb/14/academics-defend-historian-over-polish-jew-killings-claims.

matters had reached the point where the German political philosopher Bruno Amann could propose that "there should be no German university that would not have at least one chair in the Jewish Question, which would make accessible the Jew-problem to each student."[12] In many of today's American universities, programs of Jewish studies flourish. They have not been established, however, because of any perceived "Jew-problem" but out of the recognition that knowledge of Judaism and the Jews can add significantly to the understanding of major facets of both Western and Eastern cultures.

Nevertheless—and here I will introduce my now-qualified "other hand" reflections—our universities, like the broader surrounding cultures in which they exist, are not altogether free of a version of the so-called Jewish Question.[13] It is not a version that anyone in his right mind believes requires a "final solution," but it is troubling all the same. And some of the troubles relate to changing attitudes toward how the victims and perpetrators of the Nazi Final Solution of the Jewish Question should be remembered, including how they should be presented in university-level teaching and research. Another source of concern, as described later in this chapter, are certain campus attitudes toward Israel, especially as some of these go well beyond normative political criticism and expose connections between anti-Zionism and antisemitism.[14]

---

12. Weinreich, *Hitler's Professors*, 83.

13. For scholarly studies of some of the issues discussed in this chapter, see Manfred Gerstenfeld, ed., *Academics against Israel and the Jews* (Jerusalem: Jerusalem Center for Public Affairs, 2007); Kenneth L. Marcus, *Jewish Identity and Civil Rights in America* (New York: Cambridge University Press, 2010); Eunice G. Pollack, ed., *Antisemitism on the Campus: Past & Present* (Boston: Academic Studies Press, 2011); Gary A. Tobin, Aryeh K. Weinberg, and Jenna Ferer, eds., *The Uncivil University: Intolerance on College Campuses*, rev. ed. (Lanham, MD: Lexington Books, 2009); Tammi Rossman-Benjamin, "Identity Politics, the Pursuit of Social Justice, and the Rise of Campus Antisemitism: A Case Study," in *Resurgent Antisemitism: Global Perspectives*, ed. Alvin H. Rosenfeld (Bloomington: Indiana University Press, 2013), 482–520; Cary Nelson and Gabriel Noah Brahm, eds., *The Case against Academic Boycotts of Israel* (Chicago: MLA Members for Scholars' Rights, distributed by Wayne State University Press, 2015); Cary Nelson, *Israel Denial: Anti-Zionism, Anti-Semitism, & The Faculty Campaign against the Jewish State* (Bloomington: Indiana University Press, 2019); and Andrew Pessin and Doron Ben-Atar, eds., *Anti-Zionism on Campus: The University, Free Speech, and BDS* (Bloomington: Indiana University Press, 2018).

14. See Alvin H, Rosenfeld, ed., *Anti-Zionism and Antisemitism: The Dynamics of Delegitimization* (Bloomington: Indiana University Press, 2019); Elhanan Yakira, *Post-Zionism, Post-Holocaust: Three Essays on Denial, Forgetting, and the Delegitimization of Israel* (Cambridge: Cambridge University Press, 2010); and Bernard Harrison, "Anti-Zionism, Antisemitism, and the Rhetorical Manipulation of Reality," and Elhanan Yakira, "Antisemitism and Anti-Zionism as a Moral Question," in Rosenfeld, *Resurgent Antisemitism*, 8–41 and 42–64.

Questions about Holocaust memory are as complex as they are consequential. That has been the case from the start. So, too, has been the struggle between recollection and repression, which dates back to the time of the mass killings themselves. From the standpoint of the perpetrators, the genocide of the Jews was to be an unrecorded, or silent, crime—"an unwritten and never-to-be-written page of glory," as Heinrich Himmler put it in a famous speech he delivered to SS officers in Poznan, on October 4, 1943.[15] From the standpoint of the intended victims, the brutal persecutions and mass killings, far from being a source of glory, were a cause of deep anxiety. Jews in Nazi-dominated Europe feared not only that they would be murdered in large numbers but also that there would be no lasting record of their violent end. One hears the torments they suffered in the final words of Chaim A. Kaplan's Warsaw Ghetto diary, which convey the anguish of the remembrancer worried that his words would be lost: "If my life ends—what will become of my diary?"[16] Kaplan's concern was widely shared. Looking back decades later, the Auschwitz survivor and Nobel laureate Imre Kertész recalls, "From the very first moment, when it was far from being revealed to the world, when it was as yet unnamed, ... from the very first moment, there was a terrible anxiety, a fear of forgetfulness attached to the Holocaust."[17]

To counter forgetting, historians have labored for decades to document, describe, and explain the history of the Third Reich and the Nazi campaign of oppression and elimination of subject peoples, the Jews foremost among them. Their work has been invaluable. And yet historical memory broadly conceived depends less on the record of events drawn up by scholars than on the projection of these events by writers, filmmakers, artists, architects, museum

---

15. Himmler's speech can be read in English translation in Lucy S. Dawidowicz, ed., *A Holocaust Reader* (New York: Behrman House, 1976), 130–40, and the specific quote can be located at 133. It can be accessed in the original German through the Bundesarchiv Berlin, NS 19/4010; printed as Nuremberg Doc. PS1919 in International Military Tribunal, *Trial of the Major War Criminals before the International Military Tribunal: Nuremberg 14 November 1945–1 October 1946*, vol. 29, *Documents and Other Material in Evidence, Numbers 1850-PS to 2233-PS*, ed. S. Paul A. Joosten (Nuremberg, Germany: International Military Tribunal, 1948), 145–46, https://www.loc.gov/rr/frd/Military_Law/NT_major-war-criminals.html.

16. See Chaim A. Kaplan, *Scroll of Agony: The Warsaw Diary of Chaim A. Kaplan*, trans. and ed. by Abraham I. Katsh (New York: Macmillan, 1965), 400.

17. Imre Kertész, "The Holocaust as Culture," *Szombat*, July 1, 1998, 6–9, http://www.szombat.org/archivum/imre-kertesz-the-holocaust-as-a-culture-1352774022. The translation given here is by Tuende Vajda and appears on page 6. The same essay, translated by Thomas Cooper, appears in Imre Kertész, *The Holocaust as Culture* (Chicago: University of Chicago Press, 2012), 57–78.

designers, television producers and directors, and others. Because most of us acquire a sense of the past through the cultural artifacts given us by these people, one has to look carefully at their productions to understand how the collective memory of the Holocaust is being created, transmitted, and received.

A review of these productions shows that Holocaust memory has become a volatile area of contending images, interpretations, and historical claims and counterclaims.[18] Far from being fixed, it is continually in flux. That is increasingly so within our universities. Some proponents of genocide studies, for instance, decry ongoing attention to the Holocaust as being too narrow, or too parochial, and argue that it is time to insert study of the Nazi crimes against the Jews into the broader comparative framework of their discipline.[19] For instance, Marianne Hirsch and Irene Kacandes, the editors of *Teaching the Representation of the Holocaust*, argue that because scholars who teach the Holocaust in the United States do so as part of "a people with its own troubled history of suffering, persecution, and genocide," an "acknowledgment of the relation of Holocaust representation and memorialization to the representation of slavery and Native American genocide is fundamental to any Holocaust course taught in the United States."[20]

The premises of this view need to be closely questioned. American scholars who offer courses on American slavery and the fate of Native Americans, after all, may feel no obligation to focus their curricula along comparative lines but instead may treat their subjects as fully sufficient unto themselves. But if they are right to do so, why is a focus on the Holocaust deemed to be insufficient? And why is there a supposed need to encompass study of the Nazi crimes against the Jews within an American context that will expose students to what Hirsch and Kacandes call "the workings of racism and prejudice that we can find within our own culture"?[21] Racism and prejudice are well-established facts of American national life, but to date they have not culminated in anything remotely like Auschwitz or Treblinka. To situate study of the Nazi crimes against the Jews within a specifically American framework, therefore, risks distorting

---

18. See Alvin H. Rosenfeld, *The End of the Holocaust* (Bloomington: Indiana University Press, 2011).

19. For a detailed study of some of the issues involved in the debates between scholars of Holocaust studies and genocide studies, see Gavriel D. Rosenfeld, "From History to Memory and Back Again: Debating the Holocaust's Uniqueness," in *Hi, Hitler! How the Nazi Past Is Being Normalized in Contemporary Culture* (Cambridge: Cambridge University Press, 2015), 78–121.

20. Marianne Hirsch and Irene Kacandes, eds., *Teaching the Representation of the Holocaust* (New York: Modern Language Association, 2004), 10.

21. Ibid., 10.

the histories of both the Nazi Holocaust and the American experience, including that of racism. The imperative to reorient Holocaust studies in this way is but one illustration among many of a growing impatience with the place of the Holocaust in American life, which mirrors similar, even more strongly expressed, feelings of dissatisfaction with Holocaust history and memory in parts of Europe and throughout the Muslim world.

Other professors—they include David Stannard, Ward Churchill, Peter Novick, Norman Finkelstein, and numerous others[22]—argue that Holocaust studies, by awarding supreme victim status to the Jews, deny it to other victim groups and thereby assign a "permanent privilege" to the Jews alone. Inclined to engage Holocaust history and memory polemically, they claim that Jewish suffering during the Nazi era has become the subject of exclusive concentration as part of a "Zionist" scheme to make Israel the beneficiary of universal sympathy. Thus, in his preface to Ward Churchill's *A Little Matter of Genocide: Holocaust and Denial in the Americas, 1492 to the Present*, David Stannard writes that "it is official Israeli policy to undermine the efforts of others to have their own historical victimhood acknowledged" and that "the most prominent proponents" of what he calls "Jewish exclusivism" are "Jewish American writers."[23] In his own introduction to the book, Churchill asserts that "a substantial component of Zionism . . . contends not only that the American holocaust never happened, but that *no* 'true' genocide has ever occurred, other than the Holocaust suffered by the Jews at the hands of the Nazis."[24]

Moreover, Jews today are said to use their own past history of suffering as a pretext to inflict suffering on others. In the name of Auschwitz, it is alleged, Jews are actively carrying out genocide against the Palestinians, who are commonly referred to within these rhetorical codes as the "new Jews," the Israelis being figured as perpetrators on a par with the Nazis.[25] To put an end to such alleged Jewish chauvinism, it is time, in the words of Marc Ellis, to "end

---

22. For more on the works of the scholars mentioned here by name, including page numbers for the arguments to which I refer, see Rosenfeld, *End of the Holocaust*, 251–52, 257–59, and 262–64.

23. David Stannard, preface to *A Little Matter of Genocide: Holocaust and Denial in the Americas 1492 to the Present*, by Ward Churchill (San Francisco: City Lights Books, 1997), xvi.

24. Ward Churchill, *Little Matter of Genocide*, 7.

25. Omar Barghouti, one of the founders of the BDS movement, for instance, claims that some of Israel's "racist" and "sadistic" actions against the Palestinians "are reminiscent of common Nazi practices against the Jews." See Institute for NGO Research, "Omar Barghouti," NGO Monitor, February 9, 2011, http://www.ngomonitor.org/reports/omar_barghouti/; and Omar Barghouti, "'The Pianist' of Palestine," *Countercurrents.org*, November 30, 2004, https://www.countercurrents.org/pa-barghouti301104.htm.

Auschwitz";[26] or, as the influential French philosopher Alain Badiou puts it more bluntly, the time has come "to forget the Holocaust."[27]

And that precisely is what growing numbers of people seem intent on doing. A 2019 public opinion poll conducted by the Anti-Defamation League shows that antisemitic attitudes remain pervasive in Europe and that over 40 percent of people in Germany and Austria and some other European countries think that "Jews talk too much about the Holocaust." In Poland the figure was 74 percent.[28] In another poll, 42 percent of people in eight European countries believe that "Jews exploit the past to extort money."[29]

The implications of these findings are clear: a sizable part of the European population has heard all they want to hear about the tribulations of the Jews. They've grown tired and resentful of having to confront yet again stories of Jewish victimization and suffering and want to move on. As Lord Baker of Dorking, who served for three years as British education secretary under Margaret Thatcher, put it in 2011, it is time to stop teaching British youngsters about the Holocaust: "I would ban the study of Nazism from the history curriculum totally."[30] In certain French schools, such courses are no longer taught, seemingly because Muslim pupils object to them or act aggressively in the classroom when the subject is presented. In 2010, some officials in the French education ministry suggested that the very words "Shoah" and "Holocaust" might be removed from school curricula and textbooks, for their connotations were judged to be too specific to the Jewish experience. Instead, a more generalized French word for "annihilation"—"anéantissement"—was recommended.[31] None of these

---

26. Marc H. Ellis, *Ending Auschwitz: The Future of Jewish and Christian Life* (Louisville, KY: Westminster/John Knox, 1994), 43.

27. Alain Badiou, *Polemics*, trans. Steve Corcoran (London: Verso, 2006), 214. For commentary on Badiou and his views on Israel and the Jews, see Mark Lilla, "A New Political Saint Paul?" *New York Review of Books* 55, no. 16 (October 23, 2008): 69–73.

28. Anti-Defamation League, "ADL Global Survey of 18 Countries Finds Hardcore Anti-Semitic Attitudes Remain Pervasive," ADL, accessed August 26, 2020, https://www.adl.org/news/press-releases/adl-global-survey-of-18-countries-finds-hardcore-anti-semitic-attitudes-remain. For further discussion on these public opinion polls, see Rosenfeld, *End of the Holocaust*, 243.

29. Nir Hasson, "More Global Anti-Semitic Incidents Reported in 2009 Than Any Year since WWII," *Haaretz*, January 24, 2010, www.haaretz.com/1.5049341.

30. Tom Rowley, "Stop Teaching about the Holocaust So Children See Germany in a Better Light, Says Lord Baker," *Telegraph*, December 24, 2011, http://www.telegraph.co.uk/education/educationnews/8976283/Stop-teaching-about-the-holocaust-so-that-children-see-Germany-in-a-better-light-says-Lord-Baker.html.

31. Guido Meotti, "France Bans the 'Shoah,'" *Israel National News*, January 9, 2011, http://www.israelnationalnews.com/Articles/Article.aspx/10566.

ideas was implemented, but similar examples of a desire to distance students in the classroom from the Holocaust have appeared elsewhere.[32]

In the United States, many colleges and universities continue to offer courses on the Nazi persecution and destruction of European Jewry, but at some of these institutions, faculty members are encouraged to broaden the focus of what they teach and include other historical examples of mass violence as well. The idea is to avoid a "Jewish monopolization of suffering" in order to broaden awareness of "man's inhumanity to man" in general. The same goals may account for the conversion of institutes originally conceived as centers for the study of the Holocaust to centers of Holocaust and genocide studies; or Holocaust, genocide, and human rights studies; or holocaust, genocide, and peace studies, and so on. As part of this trend, there is a tendency to see the Holocaust more as a universal symbol of human rights violations wherever these may occur and less as a crime that specifically targeted the Jews. To be sure, the latter is acknowledged, but chiefly for its emblematic value as a referent that can be extended to others and less so as a historical event with its own distinctive features. Thus, the Holocaust as a genocidal crime against the Jews becomes recontextualized into a series of moral lessons about problems of injustice that periodically beset humanity as such and is used didactically for teaching the lessons of human rights, tolerance, justice, and other socially progressive ideals.

What might be concluded from these developments? While considerable attention continues to be given to stories of Jewish fate under the Nazis, Holocaust fatigue and Holocaust resentment seem to be increasing. Many people, it appears, have had enough of the Jews and their sorrows and want relief from all of that.[33] Complaints about "the hegemony of Jewish Holocaust memory" and of a self-serving "Holocaust industry" are symptomatic of this changed mood. In sum, a number of signs—cultural, ideological, political, and psychological—indicate a growing dissatisfaction with the spread of Holocaust consciousness and point to a range of moves against it. How much influence such negative reactions are likely to have is impossible to predict, but if these trends continue unchecked, Holocaust memory may be less compelling, and also less sustainable, in the years ahead than it has been in the recent past.

---

32. See Etgar Lefkovits, "Berlin Official: German Kids Tired of Holocaust," *Jerusalem Post*, March 10, 2008, http://www.jpost.com/International/Berlin-official-German-kids-tired-of-Holocaust. See also Madeline Chambers, "Over 40 Percent of Germans Want Closure on Nazi Past," *Haaretz*, April 15, 2015, http://www.haaretz.com/jewish/news/1.651971.

33. See Catherine Chatterley, "Leaving the Post-Holocaust Period: The Effects of Anti-Israel Attitudes on Perceptions of the Holocaust," in Rosenfeld, *Anti-Zionism and Antisemitism*, 158–74.

In fact, one already sees a troubling decline in what Americans know about the Holocaust. In February 2018, the Conference on Material Claims against Germany released the results of a new survey of Holocaust awareness in the United States. Major findings of the survey, include:

- Thirty-one percent of all Americans and 41 percent of all millennials believe that the number of Jews killed during the Holocaust was two million or fewer.
- Forty-five percent of American adults and 49 percent of millennials "cannot name one of the over 40,000 concentration camps and ghettos in Europe during the Holocaust."
- Forty-one percent of respondents "did not know what Auschwitz was." Among millennials, that number rises to 66 percent.
- Seventy percent of Americans say "fewer people seem to care about the Holocaust than they used to."[34]

If knowledge of the history and memory of the Holocaust is now diminished and contested on several fronts, including the university, the same holds true, but even more so, regarding knowledge of the State of Israel. Complaints about the two are often cojoined, with calls for "the end of Auschwitz" often emanating from the same people who publicly question the legitimacy and future of the State of Israel. Alain Badiou, already mentioned as an advocate of "forgetting" the Holocaust, also calls for the dissolution of Israel as a Jewish state. He is joined by numerous others who object to Jewish particularity as such.[35] They see it as an offense against a worldview that stresses what they take to be universalist principles and cosmopolitan, emancipatory ideals. To such people, Jews as individuals may pose no serious problems, but the idea of corporate or collective Jewish existence, especially when established in the form of an independent state, is out of sync with the way they think social and political life should be organized. Add to this source of unease with the Jews the fact that, in an age when many intellectuals endorse notions of postnationalism, postmilitarism, and an emphatic preference for secularism, the Jewish state

---

34. Conference on Jewish Material Claims against Germany, Inc., "New Survey by Claims Conference Finds Significant Lack of Holocaust Knowledge in the United States," Claims Conference, accessed August 26, 2020, http://www.claimscon.org/study/.

35. See Eric Marty, *Radical French Thought and the Return of the "Jewish Question"* (Bloomington: Indiana University Press, 2015); Vivian Liska, *German-Jewish Thought and Its Afterlife: A Tenuous Relationship* (Bloomington: Indiana University Press, 2017), 82–84, 154–55, 167; and Bruno Chaouat, *Is Theory Good for the Jews? French Thought and the Challenge of the New Antisemitism* (Liverpool, UK: Liverpool University Press, 2016).

has a strong national and religious character and a powerful army, and the gap between a prominent strain of contemporary thinking and the Jews as an ethnic-religious-national entity widens.

The tensions that accompany this divide frequently appear in the writings of today's anti-Zionists. Prominent among them, the late Tony Judt no doubt spoke for many when he pronounced Israel to be "anachronistic" and "bad for the Jews" and called for its replacement by a binational state.[36] Judt's hostility to Israel is widely shared on college and university campuses, where, as Stanley Fish describes it, "anti-Israel sentiment flourishes and is regarded more or less as a default position."[37] If we are witnessing the emergence of new versions of the Jewish Question—and an abundance of evidence indicates that we are—one of its most prominent strains is found right here: in the "Israel question."

With the possible exception of the United States, no other country draws as much negative attention today as the State of Israel. On some university campuses, Israel, in fact, plays something of the same role that it does at the United Nations. As Walter Laqueur reminds us, some "25 million people were killed in internal conflicts since World War II, of them, 8,000 in the Israeli-Palestinian conflict, which ranks forty-sixth in the list of victims. But Israel has been more often condemned by the United Nations and other international organizations than all other nations taken together."[38] Israel is not blameless—no country is—but the criticisms heaped on it at the United Nations are clearly out of proportion to the country's faults and reveal hostile passions at work. A similar hostility is displayed on campuses in an array of Israel-oriented programs that often carry well beyond critical discussion of specific Israeli policies to impassioned denunciations of the country as such and calls for its elimination.

These negative trends date back over a number of years. When one encounters campus-based lectures and conferences with titles like "Israel: The Fourth Reich,"[39] "Israel: The Politics of Genocide,"[40] "Zionism: America's Disease,"[41]

---

36. Tony Judt, "Israel: The Alternative," *New York Review of Books* 50, no. 16 (October 23, 2003): 8–10.

37. Stanley Fish, "Is It Good for the Jews?" *New York Times*, March 4, 2007, https://opinionator.blogs.nytimes.com/2007/03/04/is-it-good-for-the-jews/.

38. Walter Laqueur, *The Changing Face of Anti-Semitism* (New York: Oxford University Press, 2006), 8.

39. Amir Abdel Malik Ali, "Israel: The Fourth Reich" (lecture, University of California, Irvine, May 18, 2006).

40. "Israel: The Politics of Genocide" (lecture series, University of California, Irvine, May 5–21, 2009).

41. Amir Abdel Malik Ali, "Zionism: America's Disease" (lecture, University of California, Irvine, June 10, 2004).

"From Auschwitz to Gaza,"[42] and so on, it is clear that a blatantly anti-Israel political agenda is operating. It aims to brand Zionism as a form of racism; to make Israel into an apartheid state on the model of South Africa; to accuse the country of committing the most brutal crimes against humanity, including ethnic cleansing and genocide; and to denounce its behavior as so evil as to be comparable to that of Nazi Germany. Add to all of this ideological animosity practical efforts to bar Israeli speakers from campuses or otherwise keep them from being heard by heckling them or shouting them down; guerrilla theater productions or other campus "happenings" that feature the building of Israeli "Apartheid Walls" and staged "die-ins" of students dressed up like Arabs supposedly massacred by other students dressed up like Israeli soldiers; leaflets and posters that routinely mingle the Star of David with the swastika and other versions of anti-Israeli and antisemitic graffiti; verbal abuse and sometimes physical assaults against Jewish students; the vandalism of Jewish property; and such well-organized annual events as "Israel Apartheid Week," now a decade old and held on dozens of campuses around the world, and "Boycott, Divestment, and Sanctions" (BDS) campaigns, and it is clear that universities have become popular venues for determined efforts to delegitimize and criminalize the State of Israel.[43] It is also little wonder that, as shown in a recent study, more than 50 percent of Jewish students at American colleges and universities confirm the presence of antisemitism on their campuses.[44] On some campuses, the environment for Jewish students has become so strained as to bring about the filing of complaints with the United States Department of Education's Office for Civil Rights under Title VI of the 1964 Civil Rights Act, whose recent extension now includes the protection of the rights of Jewish students.[45]

---

42. Mohammad al-Asi, "From Auschwitz to Gaza: The Politics of Genocide" (lecture, University of California, Irvine, February 7, 2008). For a summary of this and other public lectures by al-Asi, see Anti-Defamation League, "Mohammad al-Asi," ADL, accessed September 8, 2020, https://www.adl.org/resources/profiles/mohammad-al-asi.
43. These activities are copiously documented and carefully analyzed in Nelson and Brahm, *Case against Academic Boycotts of Israel*, and Pessin and Ben-Atar, *Anti-Zionism on Campus*.
44. See Barry A. Kosmin and Ariela Keysar, "National Demographic Survey of American Jewish College Students 2014: Anti-Semitism Report (February 2015)," Trinity College and Louis D. Brandeis Center for Human Rights under Law, accessed October 18, 2021. https://www.jewishvirtuallibrary.org/jsource/anti-semitism/trinityantisemreport.pdf.
45. For example, in 2019 at least five Title VI complaints were filed on behalf of Jewish students, including at Duke University/University of North Carolina; New York University; University of California, Los Angeles; Columbia University; and the Georgia Institute of Technology. See Tammi Rossman-Benjamin, "A Survey of Antisemitic Activity and Trends on U.S. Campuses in 2019 and Efforts to Address It (March 2020)," AMCHA Initiative,

The growing unease of some of these American students is paralleled by the experience of Jewish students at Canadian and British universities, some of whose campuses have long been hospitable to anti-Israel activists. In Great Britain, the leadership of the 120,000-member University and College Union (UCU) issues annual calls for the institution of discriminatory measures against Israeli universities and academic scholars. This situation reached such a troubled point some years ago as to bring Lady Deech, former head of Oxford University's St. Anne's College and also one-time adjudicator for higher education, to issue a statement that included these words: "'Zionist' has become a word of opprobrium—all Jews are so labelled... Once the equation is made between Zionism and Jews, anti-semites then feel free to attack all Jewish students without distinction. Protests start as attacks on Israel and conclude with threats to all Jews."[46] In his comprehensive analysis of British antisemitism, Anthony Julius illustrates this latter point graphically: "At a meeting of the School of Oriental and African Studies [in London] a Hizb al-Tahrir activist stated: 'Let's be open about this—the Koran does not mention Zionists—it mentions Jews. They are our enemy and, inshaallah [God willing], we shall kill them.'"[47]

This equation of Zionists and Jews has long been commonplace in the countries of the Middle East and now finds a home in some of the anti-Zionist discourse and anti-Jewish harassment on British and North American college campuses. It lends credence to Stanley Fish's contention that "when hostility to Israel comes, anti-Semitism is not far behind."[48]

To what degree such biases inform faculty sentiment and behavior is difficult to determine, but sufficient evidence already exists to confirm the reality of some highly questionable professional conduct. Consider the case of Michael Sinnott, a British Professor at the University of Manchester who, claiming to speak for many, denounces Israel as "the mirror image of Nazism";[49] or the case of Mona Baker, his Manchester colleague, who dismisses two Israeli scholars from the editorial boards of two academic journals she manages solely

---

accessed August 26, 2020, https://amchainitiative.org/wp-content/uploads/2020/07/Kantor-Center-Campus-Antisemitism-US-March2020.pdf.

46. Donald MacLeod, "Universities Urged to Combat Campus Anti-Semitism," *Guardian*, June 13, 2007, https://www.theguardian.com/education/2007/jun/13/highereducation.uk.

47. Anthony Julius, *Trials of the Diaspora: A History of Anti-Semitism in England* (New York: Oxford University Press, 2011), 576.

48. Fish, "Is It Good for the Jews?"

49. Peter Hetherington, "Anti-Israel Row Recurs at College," *Guardian*, September 30, 2002, http://www.guardian.co.uk/uk/2002/sep/30/highereducation.internationaleducationnews.

on the basis of their nationality ("I can no longer live with the idea of Israelis as such," she said, "unless it is explicitly in the context of campaigning for human rights in Palestine");[50] or Andrew Wilkie, a prominent scientist at Oxford University, who refuses to accept an Israeli graduate student into his laboratory because the student's résumé shows he has done his obligatory national military service;[51] or Julio Pino, a historian at Kent State University, who shouts "Death to Israel" at a campus speech by a former Israeli diplomat;[52] or David Klein, a mathematician at California State University, Northridge, who uses his university-sponsored webpage to disseminate anti-Israel propaganda among his students, denouncing Israel as "the most racist state in the world at this time" and promoting articles that speak of Israeli "death camps" and plans for "genocide."[53]

A fuller compilation of incidents of this kind could easily be made. While such behavior is not typical of how most professors conduct themselves, it is no longer rare and points to the emergence of an intensely negative, aggressively hostile mood toward Israel and its supporters. Troubled by manifestations of this mood on his own campus, former Harvard president Lawrence H. Summers criticized some of his colleagues and students for activities that were "antisemitic in their effect, if not in their intent."[54] The criticism did not go over well and may have contributed to his dismissal from the Harvard presidency. All the same, Summers was more accurate than not in describing campus attitudes toward Israel in the terms he used. The March 2012 Harvard-based

---

50. David Tell, "Boycotting the Juden," *Weekly Standard*, July 10, 2002, http://www.weeklystandard.com/boycotting-the-juden/article/2731.

51. Diana J. Schemo, "Oxford Investigates Scientist Who Denied Israeli Application," *New York Times*, July 2, 2003, http://www.nytimes.com/2003/07/02/world/oxford-investigates-scientist-who-denied-israeli-application.html.

52. Scott Jaschik, "When a Prof Shouts 'Death to Israel,'" *Inside Higher Ed*, October 31, 2011, https://www.insidehighered.com/news/2011/10/31/debate-over-professor-who-shouted-anti-israel-statement.

53. See David Klein's homepage ("Welcome to Prof. David Klein's Home Page," accessed August 28, 2020, http://www.csun.edu/~vcmthoom/). Klein provides a link to the Boycott Israel Resource Page, which contains the quoted material ("Boycott Israel Resource Page," accessed August 28, 2020, http://www.csun.edu/~vcmthoom/boycott.html). For more on the British professors, see Alvin H. Rosenfeld, *Anti-Zionism in Great Britain and Beyond: A 'Respectable' Antisemitism?* (New York: American Jewish Committee, 2004); for more on Professor Pino, see Karen Farkas, "Kent State Professor Comes under Fire for Shouting 'Death to Israel' during Diplomat's Speech," *Cleveland Plain Dealer*, October 28, 2011.

54. David H. Gellis, "Summers Says Anti-Semitism Lurks Locally," *Harvard Crimson*, September 19, 2002, http://www.thecrimson.com/article/2002/9/19/summers-says-anti-semitism-lurks-locally-university/.

conference on the "one-state solution" to the Israeli-Palestinian conflict, which basically promoted the idea of the dissolution of the Jewish state, is a case in point. As stated in the now widely adopted International Holocaust Remembrance Alliance (IHRA) "Working Definition of Antisemitism," which the US State Department adopted in 2008 as this country's own source for defining antisemitism, "denying the Jewish people their right to self-determination," a right they have enjoyed since 1948, is a manifestation of antisemitism.[55] So, too, is "drawing comparisons of contemporary Israeli policy to that of the Nazis," regarding Israel as a "racist" state, accusing Israel and the Jews of inventing or exaggerating the Holocaust, and numerous other instances of anti-Jewish and anti-Israeli vilification, denunciation, and demonization that appear on university campuses.[56]

To the degree that they become normalized, these defamatory views corrode the academic and moral integrity of university life, including what goes on in the classroom, lecture halls, and research and publication. They represent a clear betrayal of the humanities by encouraging forms of groupthink rather than independent reflection and analysis based on reason and supported by demonstrable evidence. At bottom, groupthink is invested in advocacy or indoctrination rather than the rigors of critical analysis and interpretation. As such, it is antithetical to one of the oldest and most important aims of the university, which is to foster a climate of free inquiry that will enable us to draw distinctions between truth and falsehood, what is real and what distorts and undermines our sense of reality.

Some notable malformations of truth are visible today within certain well-known writings on Zionism and Israel by prominent academic scholars, as can be illustrated by looking briefly at such tendentious works as Jacqueline Rose's *The Question of Zion* and John Mearsheimer and Stephen Walt's *The Israel Lobby and U.S. Foreign Policy*. The first of these books, written by a professor of English

---

55. See International Holocaust Remembrance Alliance (IHRA), "Working Definition of Antisemitism (May 26, 2016)," IHRA, accessed August 27, 2020, https://www.holocaustremembrance.com/resources/working-definitions-charters/working-definition-antisemitism.

56. U.S. Department of State, Office of the Special Envoy to Monitor and Combat Anti-Semitism, *Contemporary Global Anti-Semitism: A Report Provided to the United States Congress*, Washington, DC, 2008, https://2009-2017.state.gov/documents/organization/102301.pdf. These understandings have been adopted by the thirty-one member states of the International Holocaust Remembrance Alliance and the United States State Department; see International Holocaust Remembrance Alliance, "Working Definition of Holocaust Denial and Distortion (October 10, 2013)," IHRA, accessed August 27, 2020, https://www.holocaustremembrance.com/resources/working-definitions-charters/working-definition-holocaust-denial-and-distortion.

at London's Queen Mary University and fashioned as a companion piece to Edward Said's *The Question of Palestine*, and dedicated to Said, is not only replete with egregious factual errors but contains statements like this one: "We take Zionism to be a form of collective insanity."[57] In order to portray Zionism as not only mad but morally corrupt, Rose manufactures blatantly false parallels between the Jewish national movement and Nazism, at one point linking Herzl and Hitler in an altogether bogus way: "It was the same Paris performance of Wagner," she writes, "when—without knowledge or foreknowledge of each other—they [Theodor Herzl and Adolf Hitler] were both present on the same evening, that inspired Herzl to write *Der Judenstaat* and Hitler *Mein Kampf*."[58] Since Herzl died in 1904 and Hitler never set foot in Paris until his triumphal entry into the city in 1940, this story is entirely apocryphal, as are other claims in this book. None of that, however, kept Princeton University Press from publishing the book, a dubious undertaking for one of this country's premier academic presses and probably explainable only because the press sensed that a damning book on Zionism, even if written by someone who had no credentials whatsoever as a scholar of the subject, would fit the current anti-Israel mood and sell well.

Similar reasons must have led Farrar, Straus and Giroux to reportedly give John Mearsheimer and Stephen Walt an advance of $750,000 to write *The Israel Lobby and U.S. Foreign Policy*.[59] While both authors are distinguished scholars in their own fields, neither Mearsheimer, of the University of Chicago, nor Walt, of Harvard, had ever before written anything of note about Zionism or Israel. Unsurprisingly, their book has been rejected by most scholars who have reviewed it as poorly conceived, ill-informed, simplistic in its analysis, and slipshod in its handling of evidence.[60] In sum, there is virtual unanimity that this book is not serious scholarship.

---

57. Jacqueline Rose, *The Question of Zion* (Princeton, NJ: Princeton University Press, 2005), 17. For the companion piece, see Edward Said, *The Question of Palestine* (New York: Vintage Books, 1992).
58. Rose, *Question of Zion*, 64–65.
59. See the review essay by Christopher L. Ball et al., Review of *The Israel Lobby and U.S. Foreign Policy*, by John J. Mearsheimer and Stephen M. Walt," *H-Diplo Roundtables* 8, no. 18 (2007): 1–33 (at 16), https://issforum.org/roundtables/PDF/IsraelLobby-Roundtable.pdf.
60. Among the many highly critical reviews of *The Israel Lobby*, see the following: Jeffrey Goldberg, "The Usual Suspect," *New Republic*, October 8, 2007; Samuel G. Freedman, "Conspiracy Theory: Who Really Drives America's Policy toward the Middle East?" *Washington Post*, October 7, 2007; Leslie H. Gelb, "Dual Loyalties," *New York Times*, September 23, 2007; Jeff Jacoby, "The Big Lie about the 'Great Silencer,'" *Boston Globe*,

What then drives it? Since the authors' argument implies that those who make up "the Israel lobby" work determinedly and almost conspiratorially for a foreign power rather than in the American national interest, and thereby might be guilty of dual loyalty, the question has been frequently asked: Does the book express an anti-Jewish bias? Walter Russell Mead, reviewing the work in *Foreign Affairs*, believes the authors are not antisemites but then notes: "This may be a book that anti-Semites will love, but it is not necessarily an anti-Semitic book."[61] Expanding on this notion, Mead adds the following:

> The authors do what anti-Semites have always done: they overstate the power of Jews. Although Mearsheimer and Walt make an effort to distinguish their work from anti-Semitic tracts, the picture they paint calls up some of the ugliest stereotypes in anti-Semitic discourse. The Zionist octopus they conjure—stirring up the Iraq war, manipulating both U.S. political parties, shaping the media, punishing the courageous minority of professors and politicians who dare to tell the truth—is depressingly familiar. . . . It is no crime to be wrong, and being wrong about Jews does not necessarily make someone an anti-Semite. But rhetorical clumsiness and the occasional unfortunate phrase makes their case harder to defend.[62]

For these and other reasons, Mead finds *The Israel Lobby* to be insensitive and often incoherent and concludes that, "written in haste, the book will be repented at leisure."[63]

September 23, 2007; Jeff Robbins, "Anti-Semitism and the Anti-Israel Lobby," *Wall Street Journal*, September 9, 2007; Michael Gerson, "Seeds of Anti-Semitism," *Washington Post*, September 21, 2007; Richard Cohen, "Rationalizing Israel Out of Existence," *Washington Post*, September 11, 2007; William Grimes, "A Prosecutorial Brief Against Israel and Its Supporters," *New York Times*, September 6, 2007; David Remnick, "The Lobby," *New Yorker*, September 3, 2007; Steve Huntley, "Unfair Charge vs. Israel Lobby," *Chicago Sun-Times*, September 7, 2007; Tim Rutten, "Israel's Lobby as Scapegoat," *Los Angeles Times*, September 12, 2007; Mark LeVine, "No, It's the Dog That Wags the Tail," *Asia Times*, September 8, 2007.

61. Walter Russell Mead, "Jerusalem Syndrome: Decoding the Israel Lobby," *Foreign Affairs* 86, no. 6 (November/December 2007): 160–68 (at 162). As Mead describes what Walt and Mearsheimer have wrought, the authors "do not seem to know who, exactly, belongs to this amoebic, engulfing blob they call the lobby and who does not" (162). "[They] have come up with a definition of 'the Israel lobby' that covers the waterfront, including everyone from Jimmy Carter and George Soros to Paul Wolfowitz and Tom Delay" (163). "If everyone from AIPAC to Americans for Peace Now is part of the lobby, what exactly is the political agenda the lobby supports?" (162).

62. Ibid., 167.

63. Ibid., 160.

On this latter point, Mead has not been proven right. Far from expressing any regret over their work, Walt and Mearsheimer have reaped the rewards that come with open displays of anti-Israel animus. And the more forceful the assault, the larger the rewards. *The Israel Lobby* has already been translated into more than twenty foreign languages and sold hundreds of thousands of copies. In addition, it has brought Walt and Mearsheimer more lecture invitations in the few years that have passed since its publication than most professors can ever hope to receive in a lifetime. In short, precisely because *The Israel Lobby* is a book "that anti-Semites will love," Walt and Mearsheimer have won both fame and fortune. The only other author I can think of who rivals them in this regard is Norman Finkelstein, who likewise enjoys fame of a sort by producing pseudoscholarship about the Jews, some of it published by major academic presses. Although his deeply flawed book *The Holocaust Industry* is not taken seriously by scholars of the Holocaust, it has had a wide readership, no doubt because it, too, is a work "that anti-Semites will love." It now exists in numerous foreign language translations, has also sold hundreds of thousands of copies, and has made its author a frequent speaker on the anti-Zionist campus lecture circuit.

Both of these books tap into a popular strain of anti-Jewish feeling, which is running high these days in certain circles and expresses itself in a conspiratorial sense of Jewish power. Walt and Mearsheimer locate this alleged power in the ability of Israel's supporters to redirect and essentially undermine America's national interests on behalf of the Jewish state. Finkelstein locates it in the ability of Jews to supposedly exploit the Holocaust for political and venal communal ends and "sell" it to a gullible public. In fact, as conceptual categories, both "the Israel lobby" and "the Holocaust industry" are little more than polemically driven intellectual constructs, assembled from a broad range of disparate phenomena, some of them half-true, others not true at all, and ultimately far more the products of their author's imaginations than they are cohesive entities that operate in the real world. To readers who have made both books best-sellers, though, these facts are irrelevant. What matters to them is that these authors have seemingly exposed well-organized, manipulative forms of Jewish power at work in important areas of political life, the media, and financial circles. Add Jacqueline Rose's assault, which portrays Zionism as inherently mad, violent, and unjust, and the result is an accumulating image of the Jews as a crafty and domineering people, who use their allegedly excessive influence and control to the detriment of others and should be exposed as what they are: a malign and destructive social force.

This is not an image of the Jews or of Israel that prevails in the American public at large. Nor is it likely to ring true among most students and faculty members on American campuses. As every recent poll of European public opinion demonstrates, however, such negative attitudes toward Israel are now common in Europe, where they go hand in hand with feelings of impatience with Holocaust memory and resentment toward the Jews for keeping such memory alive. To the degree that such hostility is now finding a voice on American campuses—and it is—it points to the emergence of a new version of the Jewish Question (redefined as the Israel question) within sectors of our universities. It is not a wholesome development and should not be encouraged.

We are not right now looking at a reprise of the 1930s, but if these developments continue and become more widely embraced, we will be witnessing—to some degree, we are already witnessing—a serious challenge to the core missions of the university, which are to encourage free inquiry, discourage attachments to every kind of intellectual or ideological bias or dogma, and search out truths that reasonable people can agree are demonstrable and worthy of serious attention. When we remain faithful to such goals, the humanities do humanize, but they can never do so if they are employed to dehumanize the Jews or anyone else.

BIBLIOGRAPHY

Al-Asi, Mohammad. "From Auschwitz to Gaza: The Politics of Genocide." Lecture, University of California, Irvine, February 7, 2008.

Anti-Defamation League. "ADL Global Survey of 18 Countries Finds Hardcore Anti-Semitic Attitudes Remain Pervasive." ADL. Accessed August 26, 2020. https://www.adl.org/news/press-releases/adl-global-survey-of-18-countries-finds-hardcore-anti-semitic-attitudes-remain.

———. "Mohammad al-Asi." ADL. Accessed September 8, 2020. https://www.adl.org/resources/profiles/mohammad-al-asi.

Badiou, Alain. *Polemics*. Translated by Steve Corcoran. London: Verso, 2006.

Ball, Christopher L., Andrew Preston, David Schoenbaum, and Tony Smith. Review of *The Israel Lobby and U.S. Foreign Policy*, by John J. Mearsheimer and Stephen M. Walt." *H-Diplo Roundtables* 8, no. 18 (2007): 1–33. https://issforum.org/roundtables/PDF/IsraelLobby-Roundtable.pdf.

Barghouti, Omar. "'The Pianist' of Palestine." *Countercurrents.org*, November 30, 2004. https://www.countercurrents.org/pa-barghouti301104.htm.

Chambers, Madeline. "Over 40 Percent of Germans Want Closure on Nazi Past." *Haaretz*, April 15, 2015. http://www.haaretz.com/jewish/news/1.651971.

Chaouat, Bruno. *Is Theory Good for the Jews? French Thought and the Challenge of the New Antisemitism*. Liverpool, UK: Liverpool University Press, 2016.

Chapman, Ben. "George Soros' Central European University Faces Closure after Hungary Law Targets Foreign Institutions." *Independent*, April 5, 2017. http://

www.independent.co.uk/news/business/news/george-soros-central-european
-university-hungary-law-protests-foreign-institutions-parliament-a7667451.html.
Chatterley, Catherine. "Leaving the Post-Holocaust Period: The Effects of Anti-
Israel Attitudes on Perceptions of the Holocaust." In Rosenfeld, *Anti-Zionism
and Antisemitism*, 158–74.
Churchill, Ward. *A Little Matter of Genocide: Holocaust and Denial in the Americas
1492 to the Present*. Preface by David Stannard. San Francisco: City Lights Books,
1997.
Cohen, Richard. "Rationalizing Israel out of Existence." *Washington Post*,
September 11, 2007.
Conference on Jewish Material Claims against Germany, Inc. "New Survey by
Claims Conference Finds Significant Lack of Holocaust Knowledge in the
United States." Claims Conference. Accessed August 26, 2020. http://www
.claimscon.org/study/.
Dawidowicz, Lucy S., ed. *A Holocaust Reader*. New York: Behrman House, 1976.
Ellis, Marc H. *Ending Auschwitz: The Future of Jewish and Christian Life*. Louisville,
KY: Westminster/John Knox, 1994.
Farkas, Karen. "Kent State Professor Comes under Fire for Shouting 'Death to
Israel' during Diplomat's Speech." *Cleveland Plain Dealer*, October 28, 2011.
First International Resources, LLC. *Attitudes toward Jews in Seven European
Countries*. Anti-Defamation League, February 2009. https://www.adl.org/sites
/default/files/documents/assets/pdf/israel-international/Public-ADL-Anti
-Semitism-Presentation-February-2009-_3_.pdf.
Fish, Stanley. "Is It Good for the Jews?" *New York Times*, March 4, 2007. https://
opinionator.blogs.nytimes.com/2007/03/04/is-it-good-for-the-jews/.
Freedman, Samuel G. "Conspiracy Theory: Who Really Drives America's Policy
toward the Middle East?" *Washington Post*, October 7, 2007.
Friedlander, Saul. "The Demise of the German Mandarins: The German
University and the Jews, 1933–1939." In *Von der Aufgabe der Freiheit: Politische
Antwortung und bürgerliche Gesellschaft im 19. und 20. Jahrhundert. Festschrift
für Hans Mommsen zum 5. November 1995*, edited by Christian Jansen, Lutz
Niethammer, and Bernd Weisbrod, 69–82. Berlin: Akademie, 1995.
Gelb, Leslie H. "Dual Loyalties." *New York Times*, September 23, 2007.
Gellis, David H. "Summers Says Anti-Semitism Lurks Locally." *Harvard Crimson*,
September 19, 2002. http://www.thecrimson.com/article/2002/9/19/summers
-says-anti-semitism-lurks-locally-university/.
Gerson, Michael. "Seeds of Anti-Semitism." *Washington Post*, September 21, 2007.
Gerstenfeld, Manfred, ed. *Academics against Israel and the Jews*. Jerusalem:
Jerusalem Center for Public Affairs, 2007.
Goldberg, Jeffrey. "The Usual Suspect." *New Republic*, October 8, 2007.
Grimes, William. "A Prosecutorial Brief against Israel and Its Supporters."
New York Times, September 6, 2007.

Gross, Raphael. *Carl Schmitt and the Jews: The "Jewish Question," the Holocaust, and German Legal Theory*. Translated by Joel Golb. Madison: University of Wisconsin Press, 2007.

———. *Carl Schmitt und die Juden: Eine deutsche Rechtslehre*. Frankfurt am Main, Germany: Suhrkamp, 2000.

Harrison, Bernard. "Anti-Zionism, Antisemitism, and the Rhetorical Manipulation of Reality." In Rosenfeld, *Resurgent Antisemitism*, 8–41.

Hasson, Nir. "More Global Anti-Semitic Incidents Reported in 2009 Than Any Year since WWII." *Haaretz*, January 24, 2010. www.haaretz.com/1.5049341.

Hetherington, Peter. "Anti-Israel Row Recurs at College." *Guardian*, September 30, 2002. http://www.guardian.co.uk/uk/2002/sep/30/highereducation.internationaleducationnews.

Hirsch, Marianne, and Irene Kacandes, eds. *Teaching the Representation of the Holocaust*. New York: Modern Language Association, 2004.

Huntley, Steve. "Unfair Charge vs. Israel Lobby." *Chicago Sun-Times*, September 7, 2007.

Institute for NGO Research. "Omar Barghouti." NGO Monitor, February 9, 2011. http://www.ngo-monitor.org/reports/omar_barghouti/.

International Holocaust Remembrance Alliance (IHRA). "Working Definition of Antisemitism (May 26, 2016)." IHRA. Accessed August 27, 2020. https://www.holocaustremembrance.com/resources/working-definitions-charters/working-definition-antisemitism.

———. "Working Definition of Holocaust Denial and Distortion (October 10, 2013)." IHRA. Accessed August 27, 2020. https://www.holocaustremembrance.com/resources/working-definitions-charters/working-definition-holocaust-denial-and-distortion.

International Military Tribunal. *Trial of the Major War Criminals before the International Military Tribunal: Nuremberg 14 November 1945–1 October 1946*. Vol. 29, *Documents and Other Material in Evidence, Numbers 1850-PS to 2233-PS*. Edited by S. Paul A. Joosten. Nuremberg, Germany: International Military Tribunal, 1948. https://www.loc.gov/rr/frd/Military_Law/NT_major-war-criminals.html.

"Israel: The Politics of Genocide." Lecture series, University of California, Irvine, May 5–21, 2009.

Jacoby, Jeff. "The Big Lie about the 'Great Silencer.'" *Boston Globe*, September 23, 2007.

Jaschik, Scott. "When a Prof Shouts 'Death to Israel.'" *Inside Higher Ed*, October 31, 2011. https://www.insidehighered.com/news/2011/10/31/debate-over-professor-who-shouted-anti-israel-statement.

Judt, Tony. "Israel: The Alternative." *New York Review of Books* 50, no. 16 (October 23, 2003): 8–10.

Julius, Anthony. *Trials of the Diaspora: A History of Anti-Semitism in England.* New York: Oxford University Press, 2011.

Kaplan, Chaim A. *Scroll of Agony: The Warsaw Diary of Chaim A. Kaplan.* Translated and edited by Abraham I. Katsh. New York: MacMillan, 1965.

Kertész, Imre. "The Holocaust as Culture." Translated by Tuende Vaida. *Szombat,* July 1, 1998. http://www.szombat.org/archivum/imre-kertesz-the-holocaust-as-a-culture-1352774022. Revised and expanded as "The Holocaust as Culture," in *The Holocaust as Culture,* translated by Thomas Cooper. Chicago: University of Chicago Press, 2012, 57–78.

Klein, David. "Boycott Israel Resource Page." Accessed August 28, 2020. http://www.csun.edu/~vcmthoom/boycott.html.

———. "Welcome to Prof. David Klein's Home Page." Accessed August 28, 2020. http://www.csun.edu/~vcmthoom/.

Kosmin, Barry A., and Ariela Keysar. "National Demographic Survey of American Jewish College Students 2014: Anti-Semitism Report (February 2015)." Trinity College and Louis D. Brandeis Center for Human Rights under Law. Accessed October 18, 2021. https://www.jewishvirtuallibrary.org/jsource/anti-semitism/trinityantisemreport.pdf.

Laqueur, Walter. *The Changing Face of Anti-Semitism.* New York: Oxford University Press, 2006.

Lefkovits, Etgar. "Berlin Official: German Kids Tired of Holocaust." *Jerusalem Post,* March 10, 2008. http://www.jpost.com/International/Berlin-official-German-kids-tired-of-Holocaust.

LeVine, Mark. "No, It's the Dog That Wags the Tail." *Asia Times,* September 8, 2007.

Lilla, Mark. "A New Political Saint Paul?" *New York Review of Books* 55, no. 16 (October 23, 2008): 69–73.

Liska, Vivian. *German-Jewish Thought and Its Afterlife: A Tenuous Relationship.* Bloomington: Indiana University Press, 2017.

MacLeod, Donald. "Universities Urged to Combat Campus Anti-Semitism." *Guardian,* June 13, 2007. https://www.theguardian.com/education/2007/jun/13/highereducation.uk.

Malik Ali, Amir Abdel. "Israel: The Fourth Reich." Lecture, University of California, Irvine, May 18, 2006.

———. "Zionism: America's Disease." Lecture, University of California, Irvine, June 10, 2004.

Marcus, Kenneth L. *Jewish Identity and Civil Rights in America.* New York: Cambridge University Press, 2010.

———. "Tackling Anti-Semitism on College Campuses." *Algemeiner,* February 2, 2012. http://www.algemeiner.com/2012/02/02/tackling-anti-semitism-on-college-campuses/.

Marty, Eric. *Radical French Thought and the Return of the "Jewish Question."* Bloomington: Indiana University Press, 2015.

Mead, Walter Russell. "Jerusalem Syndrome: Decoding the Israel Lobby." *Foreign Affairs* 86, no. 6 (November/December 2007): 160–68.

Meotti, Guido. "France Bans the 'Shoah.'" *Israel National News*, January 9, 2011. http://www.israelnationalnews.com/Articles/Article.aspx/10566.

Nelson, Cary. *Israel Denial: Anti-Zionism, Anti-Semitism, & The Faculty Campaign against the Jewish State.* Bloomington: Indiana University Press, 2019.

Nelson, Cary, and Gabriel Noah Brahm, eds. *The Case against Academic Boycotts of Israel.* Chicago: MLA Members for Scholars' Rights, 2015.

Noakes, Jeremy. "The Ivory Tower under Siege: German Universities in the Third Reich." *Journal of European Studies* 23:4 (1993): 371–407.

Pessin, Andrew, and Doron S. Ben-Atar, eds. *Anti-Zionism on Campus: The University, Free Speech, and BDS.* Bloomington: Indiana University Press, 2018.

Pollack, Eunice G., ed. *Antisemitism on the Campus: Past & Present.* Boston: Academic Studies, 2011.

Remnick, David. "The Lobby." *New Yorker*, September 3, 2007.

Remy, Steven P. *The Heidelberg Myth: The Nazification and Denazification of a German University.* Cambridge, MA: Harvard University Press, 2002.

Robbins, Jeff. "Anti-Semitism and the Anti-Israel Lobby." *Wall Street Journal*, September 9, 2007.

Rose, Jacqueline. *The Question of Zion.* Princeton, NJ: Princeton University Press, 2005.

Rosenfeld, Alvin H., ed. *Anti-Zionism and Antisemitism: The Dynamics of Delegitimization.* Bloomington: Indiana University Press, 2019.

———. *Anti-Zionism in Great Britain and Beyond: A 'Respectable' Antisemitism?* New York: American Jewish Committee, 2004.

———. *The End of the Holocaust.* Bloomington: Indiana University Press, 2011.

———, ed. *Resurgent Antisemitism: Global Perspectives.* Bloomington: Indiana University Press, 2013.

Rosenfeld, Gavriel D. "From History to Memory and Back Again: Debating the Holocaust's Uniqueness," in his *Hi, Hitler! How the Nazi Past Is Being Normalized in Contemporary Culture.* Cambridge: Cambridge University Press, 2015.

Rossman-Benjamin, Tammi. "Identity Politics, the Pursuit of Social Justice, and the Rise of Campus Antisemitism: A Case Study." In Alvin Rosenfeld, *Resurgent Antisemitism*, 482–520.

———. "A Survey of Antisemitic Activity and Trends on U.S. Campuses in 2019 and Efforts to Address It (March 2020)." AMCHA Initiative. Accessed August 26, 2020. https://amchainitiative.org/wp-content/uploads/2020/07/Kantor-Center-Campus-Antisemitism-US-March2020.pdf.

Rowley, Tom. "Stop Teaching about the Holocaust So Children See Germany in a Better Light, Says Lord Baker." *Telegraph*, December 24, 2011. http://www.telegraph.co.uk/education/educationnews/8976283/Stop-teaching-about-the-holocaust-so-that-children-see-Germany-in-a-better-light-says-Lord-Baker.html.

Rutten, Tim. "Israel's Lobby as Scapegoat." *Los Angeles Times*, September 12, 2007.

Said, Edward. *The Question of Palestine*. New York: Vintage Books, 1992.

Schemo, Diana Jean. "Oxford Investigates Scientist Who Denied Israeli Application." *New York Times*, July 2, 2003. http://www.nytimes.com/2003/07/02/world/oxford-investigates-scientist-who-denied-israeli-application.html.

Schmitt, Carl. *Das Judentum in der Rechtswissenschaft: Ansprachen, Dorträge und Ergebnisse der Tagung der Reichsgruppe Hochschullehrer des NSRB. am 3. und 4. Oktober 1936. Die deutsche Rechtswissenschaft im Kampf gegen jüdischen Geist 1*. Berlin: Deutscher Rechtsverlag, 1936.

Smith, Alex Duval. "Polish Move to Strip Holocaust Expert of Award Sparks Protests." *Guardian*, February 13, 2016. https://www.theguardian.com/world/2016/feb/14/academics-defend-historian-over-polish-jew-killings-claims.

Stannard, David. Preface to *A Little Matter of Genocide: Holocaust Denial in the Americas 1492 to the Present*, by Ward Churchill, xiii–xix. San Francisco: City Lights Books, 1997.

Steiner, George. *Language and Silence: Essays on Language, Literature, and the Inhuman*. New York: Atheneum, 1967.

Steinweis, Alan. *Studying the Jew: Scholarly Antisemitism in Nazi Germany*. Cambridge, MA: Harvard University Press, 1966.

Tell, David. "Boycotting the Juden." *Weekly Standard*, July 10, 2002. http://www.weeklystandard.com/boycotting-the-juden/article/2731.

Tobin, Gary A., Aryeh K. Weinberg, and Jenna Ferer, eds. *The Uncivil University: Intolerance on College Campuses*. Revised edition. Lanham, MD: Lexington Books, 2009.

US Department of State, Office of the Special Envoy to Monitor and Combat Anti-Semitism. *Contemporary Global Anti-Semitism: A Report Provided to the United States Congress*. Washington, DC, 2008. https://2009-2017.state.gov/documents/organization/102301.pdf.

Weinreich, Max. *Hitler's Professors: The Part of Scholarship in Germany's Crimes against the Jewish People*. New York: Yiddish Scientific Institute (YIVO), 1946. Reprinted with a foreword by Martin Gilbert. New Haven, CT: Yale University Press, 1999.

Yakira, Elhanan. "Antisemitism and Anti-Zionism as a Moral Question." In Rosenfeld, *Resurgent Antisemitism*, 42–64.

———. *Post-Zionism, Post-Holocaust: Three Essays on Denial, Forgetting, and the Delegitimization of Israel*. Cambridge: Cambridge University Press, 2010.

ALVIN H. ROSENFELD holds the Irving M. Glazer Chair in Jewish Studies at Indiana University, where he has taught since 1968, and is Director of the university's Institute for the Study of Contemporary Antisemitism. He is the author of numerous books and articles on Holocaust literature and contemporary antisemitism and has lectured widely on these subjects in the United States, Europe, and Israel. He held a five-year presidential appointment on the United States Holocaust Memorial Council and also served on the US Holocaust Memorial Museum's Executive Committee. For ten years, he was Chair of the Academic Committee of the Museum's Center for Advanced Holocaust Studies. He has been honored with Indiana University's Distinguished Service Award, the Provost's Medal, and, most recently, the President's Medal in recognition of "sustained excellence in service, scholarly achievement, and leadership."

INDEX OF SCHOLARS AND RELATED ACADEMIC FIGURES EXAMINED

Albright, William F., 78, 104–7, 316, 319
Althaus, Paul, 25, 126, 129, 147, 206, 208n7, 211, 215, 228–33, 239, 241, 246–51, 254
Andrae, Walter, 85–86, 86n47
Andreas, Willy, 76
Anthes, Rudolf, 96–97
Arendt, Hannah, 31, 44, 76n19, 423–41
Astel, Karl, 168–69

Babinger, Franz, 81–82, 85, 326
Baumstark, Anton, 75
Becker, Carl, 73, 74, 91, 326, 389n196
Berve, Helmut, 84–85, 95–96, 104–6
Bieberbach, Ludwig, 287, 289
Birnbaum, Walter, 463–64, 464n33, 467, 476–77
Bissing, Friedrich Freiherr von, 75n18
Bonhoeffer, Dietrich, 114–15, 166n36, 503n46
Born, Max, 460n25, 504, 505n55, 506n57, 512n76, 513, 514n81
Bornkamm, Günther, 174, 226n111
Bornkamm, Heinrich, 126, 131
Botzenhart, Erich, 466–67
Brandi, Karl, 469–70, 471
Breasted, James Henry, 75n18, 105, 107
Brockelmann, Carl, 65n3, 74, 101–2, 321n42
Buchwald, Georg, 24, 114, 117n11, 118, 122, 133–47
Büsching, J. G. G., 336

Capart, Jean, 283–84, 288, 289, 292
Christian, Viktor, 307, 321–22, 323–24, 325
Cohn, Ernst Julius, 508n65
Conze, Werner, 50, 468
Courant, Richard, 503–4, 512, 513
Croce, Benedetto, 528, 537

Darmstädter, Paul, 454–58, 477
Dehn, Günther, 456–59
Delitzsch, Friedrich, 73
Deuticke, Hans Joachim, 495
Drexler, Hans, 496
Düker, Heinrich, 497

Ebeling, Erich, 311, 325n55
Ehelolf, Hans, 311, 325n55
Ehrenberg, Rudolf von, 495
Eisenhuth, Heinz, 173–74, 176, 177, 180, 193–94
Erman, Adolf, 74, 95, 96, 267, 283–85, 296

Fermi, Enrico, 537
Fischer, Eugen, 219, 258, 277–79, 280, 431n32, 461, 468n47, 488
Forsthoff, Ernst, 368–72, 392n209, 394n227, 395, 398, 432, 435, 435n43, 440, 441n62, 443
Franck, James, 451, 459–60, 504–9, 512–13, 519
Frank, Carl, 307, 311, 321
Frank, Walter, 45, 79, 91, 213n33, 218n61, 256, 312, 430, 431, 466–67

INDEX OF SCHOLARS AND RELATED FIGURES

Franke, Otto, 72, 89–90, 93, 109
Frauwallner, Erich, 83, 98, 103
Friedrich, Johannes, 311, 324, 327

Gercke, Achim, 452–54, 456
Graetz, Heinrich, 134
Grapow, Hermann, 26, 98, 103, 263–98,
Grau, Wilhelm, 46, 121, 127, 128, 128n44, 131
Grimme, Adolf, 492
Grundmann, Walter, 25, 174–77, 180, 193–94, 195n146, 206–7, 208n7, 211, 227, 233–37, 239, 241, 243–53
Gumbel, Emil, 454, 457, 458

Hartmann, Richard, 101n92, 102, 276, 279–80, 296, 314
Hauer, J. W., 314
Hecht, Hans, 510, 511
Hecker, Rudolf, 276
Heidegger, Martin, 5, 23, 30–31, 56–59, 76n19, 79, 121, 122n23, 429–37, 439–41, 461
Heisenberg, Werner, 309, 504n49
Hermelink, Heinrich, 132
Herzfeld, Ernst, 310, 311, 327
Heuss, Alfred, 404
Heussi, Karl, 174, 180
Hintze, Fritz, 276
Hinz, Walter, 81, 82, 85, 307, 313n18, 321, 322–23, 326, 465, 467
Hirsch, Emanuel, 115, 130, 131, 213n38, 241, 242n199, 464n34, 482
Hohenemser, Kurt, 499–500
Holsten, Walter, 117n11, 118, 122, 126–33, 147
Honig, Richard Martin, 503–4

Jankuhn, Herbert, 29, 333, 334n4, 337, 341, 347–54

Kahle, Paul, 82–83, 320, 321n42, 326
Kees, Hermann, 84, 266n5, 270, 273, 274, 277, 295, 296, 327
Kittel, Gerhard, 9–10, 16, 25, 79, 121, 123, 146n106, 171–72, 174, 205–11, 216–27, 230, 235–45, 248–51, 253, 468n47, 483
Koellreutter, Otto, 371, 372–73, 388, 394
Kolnai, Aurel, 31, 76n19, 423, 429, 431n32, 433, 435, 436–41, 461n29
Koschaker, Paul, 313n18, 322–23, 361

Kossinna, Gustaf, 335–36, 338, 342, 344, 347, 350, 351
Kraus, Fritz Rudolf (F. R.), 77n25, 310, 319, 327
Krebs, Norbert, 279
Kuhn, Karl Georg, 25, 56, 206, 208, 211, 216, 219–27, 235, 237, 238, 241, 242–43, 246, 249–51, 254
Kühnel, Ernst, 89, 90, 92
Kümmel, Otto, 89–90, 92–93, 94

Lande, Saul, 361–62, 396
Landsberger, Benno, 27–29, 77n25, 307, 309, 310–12, 316, 317n31, 318–19, 322, 323, 324, 325n55, 326, 327
Larenz, Karl, 368, 371–72, 392, 395
Latte, Kurt, 496, 505, 510
Leffler, Siegfried, 117n10, 169–70, 170n54, 171, 234
Leibholz, Gerhard, 503
Lenz, Fritz, 498–99
Levy, Kurt, 83
Lewy, Julius and Hildegard Lewy, 310, 325n55, 327
Littmann, Enno, 74, 220, 242, 326
Lüddeckens, Erich, 276
Lüders, Heinrich, 74, 89, 93, 94, 100

Macholz, Waldemar, 170, 174, 180
Mattiat, Eugen, 464–65, 467, 475–76, 477
Maunz, Theodor, 368–70, 371, 372, 395–96
Meinecke, Friedrich, 466, 466n44
Mentzel, Rudolf, 288n91, 293
Meyer, Eduard, 73, 74, 77
Meyer(-Erlach), Wolf, 119, 169, 170–71, 234
Misch, Georg, 502–3, 505, 510, 511
Mittwoch, Eugen, 77, 81
Mommsen, Theodor, 135
Moortgat, Anton, 316, 320n41
Müller, Karl Alexander von, 45

Neugebauer, Otto, 310, 327
Neumann, Friedrich, 481, 510
Nohl, Herman, 495, 504
Norden, Eduard, 284, 289

Pauls, Theodor, 140–42
Plischke, Hans, 509–14

INDEX OF SCHOLARS AND RELATED FIGURES 573

Rad, Gerhard von, 24–25, 154–95, 226n11, 236n170
Radbruch, Gustav, 390, 391
Rath, Klaus-Wilhelm, 477–81
Reinerth, Hans, 29, 333, 334n4, 337, 338n20, 339n24, 340, 342–54
Richthofen, Bolko von, 345, 347, 350, 352
Riek, Gustav, 337, 345
Ritterbusch, Paul, 50, 98, 99–100, 274, 276, 384n168
Rosenberg, Alfred, 46, 76n21, 127–28, 141n90, 164n28, 209, 249, 288n91, 293, 312, 313, 323, 325, 326, 338, 340, 342, 344, 433, 439
Rössler, Otto, 280
Rothfels, Hans, 3, 43n6, 53
Rückert, Hanns, 122–25

Saller, Karl, 497–99
Schaeder, Hans Heinrich, 81–82, 85, 86, 86n48, 89, 91–92, 95, 98–99, 100–101, 276n42, 277n46, 326, 327
Scheel, Helmuth, 101n92, 102n96, 276, 279, 280, 284, 287n88, 292, 293n112
Schieder, Theodor, 50, 468
Schlatter, Adolf, 25, 206–7, 208, 210–16, 219, 227, 228, 230, 233, 235–53
Schlichting, Günter, 221
Schmidt, R. R., 337, 343, 344
Schmitt, Carl, 23, 30, 31, 56–57, 58, 59, 121, 215n47, 366, 368, 370, 371n75, 372, 373–84, 392, 394, 395, 396, 423, 430–37, 439–40, 546
Schneider, Carl, 174
Schoenberg, Arnold, 30, 402–20
Schöffler, Herbert, 511
Schramm, Percy E., 469–71, 511–12, 513
Schürmann, Artur, 478, 481–82
Siegel, Carl Ludwig, 503, 512–14

Siegert, Karl, 477
Smend, Rudolf, 72n10, 157n7, 159n15, 160–61nn17–18, 167n43, 169n51, 174n71, 178nn85–86, 179n90, 183n107, 188n129, 194n144, 478, 492, 493n6, 494, 500–501, 505–9, 511
Soden, Wolfram von, 27–29, 307, 311, 315–21, 324–25, 327–28
Sommer, Otto, 465
Steindorff, Georg, 65n2, 95n74, 263, 264n2, 264n4, 266–69, 282–83, 285, 286, 288–90, 292–93, 295–96
Stille, Hans, 287, 479–80

Tillich, Paul, 459
Treitschke, Heinrich von, 84, 105, 106, 134–35

Unger, Eckhard, 307, 311, 319, 321
Ungnad, Arthur, 83, 307, 316, 320–21, 324–25

Vahlen, Theodor, 283, 286
Verschuer, Otmar Freiherr von, 474
Voegelin, Eric, 433–34, 437
Vogelsang, Erich, 115, 129, 131

Waerden, Bartel Leendert van der, 309
Weber, Wilhelm, 89–91
Wendt, Siegfried, 477–78
Werner, Friedrich, 127
Westermann, Diedrich, 277, 278n51, 279–80, 296
Wiegand, Theodor, 88–90
Willrich, Hugo, 452, 453n5, 454–55, 458
Wolf, Walter, 95, 96n75, 277
Wundt, Max, 222, 467n46
Wüst, Walther, 86–88, 94, 98, 103, 107, 277, 281

Zotz, Lothar, 339

INDEX OF PARAMILITARY AND MILITARY ROLES HELD[1]

OFFICER RANKS

Scholar, University	Officer Rank	Translation/ Equivalent	Discussion
Karl Astel Rector University of Jena	SS Standartenführer	SS Colonel	168–69
Herbert Jankuhn University of Kiel University of Rostock Directed archaeological research unit in *Ahnenerbe* [Ancestral Heritage Research Institute]	SS Untersturmführer	SS Second Lieutenant	348 (347, 349–54)
	SS Sturmbannführer	SS Assault Unit Major Head of "Sonderkommando Jankuhn"	

(*Continued*)

---

1. The SA and SS were technically paramilitary units. Page references signify places where a scholar's paramilitary or military roles are mentioned; parenthetical references then follow for a more detailed discussion of the individual. If only parenthetical references are provided, the individual's paramilitary or military role has not been the focus. For a complete list of references to each scholar, see the Index of Scholars and Related Academic Figures Examined. More broadly, please note that the translations of the German military or paramilitary ranks here represent approximate equivalents. Even for German speakers, the equivalences between ranks of the SS and the armed forces (*Wehrmacht*) are not easily recognized. The distinctive designations arose from the widespread Nazi attempt to use native German words rather than more conventional terms for rank that had a French military background.

INDEX OF PARAMILITARY AND MILITARY ROLES HELD

Scholar, University	Officer Rank	Translation/ Equivalent	Discussion
Erich Lüddeckens Professor of Egyptology University of Würzburg	SS Totenkopf Standarte "Ostmark" Rottenführer	SS Death's Head Regiment "Ostmark" Section Leader	276
	Waffen SS Unterscharführer	Waffen SS Junior Squad Commander	
Eugen Mattiat Professor of German Folklore University of Göttingen	SS Hauptsturmführer	SS Captain	475–76 (464–67)
	Sicherheitsdienst (SD) of the SS	Security Service of the SS	
Rudolf Mentzel President, Deutsche Forschungsgesellschaft	SS Brigadeführer Member of the SA	SS Major General (conducted research on chemical weapons and on Nazi atomic bomb project)	288n91, 293
Percy Schramm Chair of History University of Göttingen	Member of Reiter-SA	Mounted Branch, SA	471 (469–70, 511–13)
	Oberkommando der Wehrmacht	Captain, High Command of the Armed Forces (military historian)	
Theodor Vahlen President of the Prussian Academy of Sciences Professor of Mathematics University of Berlin	SS Brigadeführer	SS Major General	283, 286
Walther Wüst Professor of Indology, Dean, and Rector University of Munich; President of the *Ahnenerbe* [Ancestral Heritage Research Institute]	SS Oberführer	SS Senior Colonel	281 (86–88, 98, 103, 277)

NON-OFFICER ROLES

Scholar, University	Membership	Discussion
Ludwig Bieberbach Professor of Mathematics University of Berlin	Member of the SA	287 (289)
Viktor Christian Professor of Ancient Semitic Philology Prorector University of Vienna	As a leading member of the SS *Ahnenerbe*, also included in the *Persönlicher Stab* (Personal Staff of) *Reichsführer-SS Heinrich Himmler*	321–22 (323–25)
Hans Drexler Professor of Classical Philology University of Breslau Rector University of Göttingen	Member of the Sicherheitsdienst (SD) of the SS	496
Heinz Eisenhuth Professor of Systematic Theology University of Jena Active Member, Institute for the Investigation and Eradication of Jewish Influence on German Church Life, Eisenach (Acting Director in 1943)	Enlisted in the Wehrmacht, 1943[2]	(173–77, 193–94)
Ernst Forsthoff Professor of Law University of Frankfurt, University of Hamburg, University of Königsberg, University of Vienna, University of Heidelberg	Member of the SA	370–71 (394–95, 432)
Richard Hartmann Professor of Islamic Studies University of Göttingen, University of Berlin	Consultant to the SS	279 (280, 296)
Rudolf Hecker Research Assistant Dictionary of the Egyptian Language	Soldier in the Wehrmacht (died in combat October 24, 1943)	276

(Continued)

---

2. Oliver Arnhold, *Das "Institut zur Erforschung und Beseitigung des Jüdischen Einflusses auf das deutsche kirchliche Leben" 1939–1945*, vol. 2 of *"Entjudung" – Kirche im Abgrund*, Studien zu Kirche und Israel 25 (Berlin: Institut Kirche und Judentum, 2010), 795.

Scholar, University	Membership	Discussion
Walther Hinz Professor of Iranian Studies, Dean of the Faculty of Philosophy University of Göttingen	Member of the SS	322–23 (81–82, 326, 465, 467)
Karl Georg Kuhn Lecturer University of Tübingen Institute for Research into the Jewish Question	Member of the SA	220 (206, 219–27, 241–43)
Gerhard von Rad Professor of Theology University of Jena	Member of the SA, 1933–1937	172–73 (154–95)
	Drafted into the Air Defense militia, 1944	178, 194 (154–95)
Wolfram von Soden Chair of Assyriology University of Berlin	Joined the SA 1934 Arabic translator in the Wehrmacht and military intelligence; after 1942, served as a reserve lieutenant on the Eastern Front[3]	311 (28–29, 307, 315–19, 321, 324–25, 327–28)

INDIRECT AFFILIATIONS AND SUPPORTING ROLES

Scholar/University	Affiliation	Translation	Discussion
Hermann Grapow Chair of Egyptology University of Berlin	Förderndes Mitglied, SS	SS Sustaining Member (membership involved regular formalized financial contributions but no active military duty; lapel pin provided)	271, 285–86 (26, 98, 103, 263–97)
	Blockwart/Blockleiter, NSDAP	NSDAP Block Warden	

(Continued)

---

3. See chapter 7 of this volume and Jakob Flygare, "Assyriology in Nazi Germany: The Case of Wolfram von Soden," in *Perspectives on the History of Ancient Near Eastern Studies*, ed. Agnès Garcia-Ventura and Lorenzo Verderame (University Park, PA: Penn State University Press, 2021), 44–60.

Scholar/University	Affiliation	Translation	Discussion
Walter Grundmann Chair of New Testament Faculty of Theology University of Jena Director, Institute for the Investigation and Eradication of Jewish Influence on German Church Life Eisenach	Förderndes Mitglied, SS (from 1934)	SS Sponsoring Member	(174, 176–77, 193–94, 206, 233–37, 243–52)
	In the post-war period, active and paid as a secret informer for the Stasi against fellow theologians in East and West Germany (1956–69)[4]		
Fritz Hintze Professor of Egyptology Humboldt University	Scharführer, Hitler Youth	Hitler Youth Squad Leader	276
Emanuel Hirsch Professor of Theology University of Göttingen	Förderndes Mitglied, SS	SS Sponsoring Member	130 (115, 213n38, 241–42, 464n34)
Hans Plischke Professor of Anthropology Dean of Faculty of Philosophy; Rector University of Göttingen	Förderndes Mitglied, SS	SS Sponsoring Member	509 (510–14)
Hans Reinerth[5] Privatdozent, Pre- and Early History; and Director of the Institute for Prehistory and Germanic Early History University of Berlin	Reichsamtsleiter der Abteilung für Ur- und Frühgeschichte im Amt Rosenberg	Director of the Department of Pre- and Early History in the Rosenberg Office	343–44 (333–34, 337, 340, 341–47, 349–54)
	Reichsamtsleiter im Reichsamt für Vorgeschichte der NSDAP	Director of the NSDAP Reich Office for Prehistory	
	Leiter des Sonderstabes Vorgeschichte im Einsatzstab Reichsleiter Rosenberg	Director of the Special Staff for Prehistory in the Reichsleiter Rosenberg Task Force	

---

4. Lukas Bormann, "Walter Grundmann und das Ministerium für Staatssicherheit: Chronik einer Zusammenarbeit aus Überzeugung (1956–1969)," *Kirchliche Zeitgeschichte* 22, no. 2 (2009): 595–632.

5. Reinerth's career is discussed in chapter 8 of this volume. Additional details regarding his paramilitary supporting roles may be found in Gunter Schöbel, "Hans Reinerth: From Archaeologist to Reichsamtsleiter," in *L'archéologie nazie en Europe de l'Ouest*, ed. Jean-Pierre Legendre, Laurent Olivier, and Bernadette Schnitzler (Gollion: Infolio, 2007), 45.

INDEX OF UNIVERSITIES AND ACADEMIC INSTITUTIONS EXAMINED

Academy for German Law [Akademie für deutsches Recht], Munich, 383
Ahnenerbe [Ancestral Heritage Research Institute], Berlin, 29, 46–47, 88, 97, 103, 277, 280, 281, 312, 314, 320, 322, 323, 325, 326, 333, 334, 337, 340–41, 345, 348, 353
Amt Rosenberg. *See* Rosenberg Office

Berlin-Brandenburg Academy of Sciences and Humanities. See Prussian Academy of Sciences
Berlin, Friedrich Wilhelm University of [renamed after 1949: Humboldt University], 21, 26, 70, 72, 76, 81, 89, 97, 134–35, 212–13, 263–64, 270–72, 274, 276n40, 284–85, 289–97, 307, 310–311, 317, 321, 322–23, 326, 344, 383, 415, 431n32, 437, 453, 460–61, 466, 492n5, 498n25, 507. *See also* Seminar for Oriental Languages, Berlin (1887)
Berlin, Technische Universität, 86n47
Breslau Rabbinical Seminary, 219, 226–27
Breslau, Silesian Friedrich Wilhelm University of [until 1911, Royal University of Breslau – Universitas litterarum Vratislaviensis], 307, 320, 336, 453, 496n17

Cologne, University of, 383

Department for Research into the Jewish Question [Forschungsabteilung Judenfrage], Frankfurt, 121n21, 127, 208n7, 218–19, 221–22, 225–26, 243, 244
Dresden, University of, 312

Freiburg, Albert Ludwig University of, 5, 58, 121, 368, 395, 424, 437, 461

German Academic Institute, Budapest, 282n69
German Archaeological Institute, Isfahan, 79, 315n26
Göttingen Academy of Sciences [Akademie der Wissenschaften zu Göttingen], 505–14
Göttingen, Georg August University of, 21, 22, 28, 31–33, 82, 115, 126, 186, 194, 226, 228, 273, 296, 307, 313n17, 317, 319, 322, 349, 449–90, 491–521

Halle, Martin Luther University of, 96, 372, 456–58
Hamburg, University of, 344
Heidelberg, Ruprecht Karl University of, 56, 76, 194, 226, 344, 365, 368, 370, 390, 393, 395, 454, 456–58, 547
Heidelberg Academy of Sciences [Heidelberger Akademie der Wissenschaften], 226, 242

Hohe Schule [Advanced School of the NSDAP], Frankfurt, 312, 323, 325, 326

Institute for the Investigation and Eradication of Jewish Influence on German Church Life [Institut zur Erforschung und Beseitigung des jüdischen Einflusses auf das deutsche kirchliche Leben], Eisenach, 141, 177, 208n7, 233–35, 244–45

Institute for Near Eastern Research [Institut für Orientforschung], East Berlin, GDR, 280, 296

Institutum Judaicum, Berlin, 210

Institutum Judaicum, Leipzig, 210, 211, 216, 238, 323

Jena, Friedrich Schiller University of [until 1920, Grand-Ducal and Ducal Pan-Saxon University; 1920–1934, Thuringian State University], 24, 95, 119, 160, 162, 167, 168–82, 193–95, 206, 208, 234, 236n170, 237, 239, 344, 372, 458

Kaiser Wilhelm Institute for Anthropology, Human Heredity, and Eugenics [Kaiser-Wilhelm-Institut für Anthropologie, menschliche Erblehre, und Eugenik], Berlin, 277, 431–32n32, 474, 498n25

Kiel, Christian-Albrecht University of, 50, 98, 274, 349, 371–72, 384n168, 395

Königsberg, University of, 53, 115, 314, 370, 453

Kriegseinsatz der Geisteswissenschaften. *See* Project Ritterbusch [*Aktion Ritterbusch*]

Leipzig, University of, 24, 28, 76, 81, 84, 95–96, 118, 132–33, 135, 142, 144, 171, 236, 237, 263, 267, 308–12, 322, 324, 326, 361–62, 458, 510n68

Marburg, Philips University of, 14, 132, 242, 293n112, 310–11, 317n30, 321, 497n22

Munich, Ludwig Maximilian University of, 81, 82, 86, 88, 208, 277, 295, 326, 336, 368, 372, 383, 395, 437, 498, 502n43

Oriental Institute of the University of Vienna, 322

Prague, University of, 344

Project Ritterbusch [*Aktion Ritterbusch*], or formally (*Arbeitsgemeinschaft für den*) *Kriegseinsatz der Geisteswissenschaften* [(Working Group for the) War Deployment of the Humanities], Berlin, 50–51, 98–100, 264, 270, 273–77, 297, 384n168

Prussian Academy of Arts [Preußische Akademie der Künste], Berlin, 30, 267, 284, 286–88, 293n112, 294–97, 404, 407, 412

Prussian Academy of Sciences [Königlich-Preußische Akademie der Wissenschaften], Berlin, 26, 264–65, 272, 273, 275–76, 277, 279–81, 288, 290, 292, 294, 297

Reich Institute for German Volkskunde, 49

Reich Institute for the History of the New Germany [Reichsinstitut für Geschichte des neuen Deutschlands], Berlin, 45–46, 121, 127, 208n7, 218–19, 466–68

Rosenberg Office [Amt Rosenberg], *or formally* Einsatzstab Reichsleiter Rosenberg, Berlin, 29, 46–47, 76n21, 312–14, 333–34, 337, 339, 340, 342, 343–44, 346, 353

Seminar for Oriental Languages, Berlin (1887), 72, 77, 81

Teaching and Research Institute for North African Cultural Studies [Lehr- und Forschungsstätte für nordwestafrikanische Kulturwissenschaft], unit of SS-Ahnenerbe, 280

Tübingen, Eberhard Karl University of, 9, 21, 25, 53, 76, 118, 121, 122–25, 171, 205–62, 314, 343–45, 468n47, 482–83

Vienna, University of, 10n18, 28, 42, 54–55, 69, 103, 319, 322, 324–25, 327, 370, 423, 436

INDEX OF AUTHORS

Abt, Jeffrey, 105n103
Ackermann, Zeno, 328
Adam, Klaus-Peter, 245n220, 245n222
Adam, Uwe Dietrich, 206n2, 209n13
Aderet, Ofer, 362nn5–6
Adler, Franklin Hugh, 522n1, 523nn2–3, 530n13, 541n35
Allinson, Mark, 175n72
Almgren, Birgitta, 328
Alt, Albrecht, 182n106, 183n108
Altekamp, Stefan, 312n14
Aly, Götz, 48, 468n50
Amendola, Giorgio, 527, 528n8, 534
Anderson, Benedict, 335n6
Andrássy, Petra, 291n103
Anoonshahr, Ali, 82nn36–37
Applebaum, Anne, 332, 332n2
Applegate, Celia, 123n32
Arnold, Bettina, 29, 334n5, 335n8, 336n13, 338n22, 349n58
Arnold, Bill T., 73n12
Arthur, Thomas C., 189n131
Arvidsson, Stefan, 71n9
Ash, Mitchell G., 54, 493n8
Asi, Mohammad, al-, 557n42
Austin, John, 390n200
Autengruber, Peter, 302

Babbitt, Milton, 403, 404n3, 417
Badiou, Alain, 553, 555

Bailey, Walter B., 418n45
Bainton, Roland H., 115n5
Ball, Christopher L., 561n59
Bambach, Charles, 79n29
Baranowski, Shelley, 163n24, 164n27, 165n32, 166
Barghouti, Omar, 552n25
Barner, Wilfried, 78n25
Barnes, Kenneth C., 115n3
Barnett, Victoria, 114n2, 115n3, 163n23, 163n25, 166n34, 179n91, 188n130, 240n190
Barth, Karl, 157n9, 165, 179, 189n132, 240n190, 247, 431n32
Bataille, Georges, 436
Baumeister, Ralf, 343n34
Bautz, Friedrich-Wilhelm, 132n57, 133n58
Becker, Heinrich, 453nn5–6, 460n25, 464n35, 467n45, 483n98, 498n24, 507n60, 510nn69–70, 511n72
Beckman, Gary, 27n42, 34
Beek, M. A., 220n73
Begrich, Joachim, 182n106, 183n108
Ben-Atar, Doron, 549n13, 557n43
Bendersky, Joseph W., 57n36
Berg, Nicolas, 52
Berg, Wieland, 286n86
Bergen, Doris L., 122n22, 164n28,
Berghahn, Volker, 485
Bergmann, Werner, 212n30
Bertram, Marion, 335n7, 338n21, 339n23

583

Besier, Gerhard, 193n141
Bethge, Eberhard, 115n3
Beushausen, Ulrich, 498n24
Beyerchen, Alan D., 15, 468nn48–49
Bialas, Wolfgang, 4n6, 41n1, 53, 76n20, 80n31, 81n32, 85n45, 95n72, 155n3, 194n145, 274n36, 296, 297n133, 469n51
Bickel, Susanne, 266n5, 267n9, 273n34
Biddescomb, Perry, 486
Biermann, Frank, 286n83
Binding, Karl, 1n1
Bix, Brian, 390n199
Bizer, Ernst, 457nn19–20, 459n22
Blasius, Dirk, 59
Bloom, Harold, 30, 402n1, 405–6, 411, 416
Blumenthal, Elke, 266n7
Boehling, Rebecca, 462n31
Boehm, Laetitia, 287n89
Böhm, Susanne, 160n17, 175n74, 180n97, 181nn99–103, 194n144
Bollenbeck, Georg, 80, 81n32, 93
Bollmus, Reinhard, 46–47, 76n21, 80n31, 340n27, 345n47
Borcherdt, H. H., 127n42, 128n43, 130n52
Bormann, Lukas, 194n142
Born, Hedwig, 504nn49–51
Bott, Marie-Louise, 271n29, 272n32
Bottai, Giuseppe, 525, 529–30, 534, 535
Böttner, Heike, 168n46, 169n49
Botzenhart, Erich, 465nn29–40, 466–67, 467n45
Bousset, Wilhelm, 216, 238
Bracher, Karl Dietrich, 43n6
Brahm, Gabriel Noah, 549n13
Bräuer, Siegfried, 123nn28–29
Braune, Walther, 102
Brednich, Rolf Wilhelm, 464n35
Breschi, Danilo, 530n13
Brettler, Marc Z., 185n118
Breuer, Stefan, 59n45
Brinkmann, Reinhold, 416n39
Brinks, Jan Herman, 135n63
Browning, Christopher R., 12, 18
Bruch, Rüdiger vom, 278n52
Brueggemann, Walter, 161–62, 161n19
Bruhn, Mike, 168n46, 169n49
Brumlik, Micha, 183n110

Brynjolfsson, Einar, 517n86
Buber, Martin, 183, 191
Buchheim, Hans, 164n28
Burchardt, Axel, 181n104
Burleigh, Michael, 48, 76n21, 118n13, 120n16, 142n97
Buss, Martin, 161–62, 161n20

Caldwell, Peter C., 370nn71–73, 371n75, 372n88, 380n141, 391n207, 392n208, 393n215, 393n217
Callmer, Johan, 350n62, 351
Cantor, Norman F., 6
Cappel, Alexandra, 264n4, 282n70, 283n73
Capristo, Annalisa, 539n33, 540n34
Carruthers, William E., 26n41, 266
Carty, Anthony, 379n133, 381n144
Casey, Maurice, 172n63, 227n116
Chamberlain, Houston Steward, 71, 87, 212n26, 213n38, 338
Chambers, Madeline, 554n32
Chaouat, Bruno, 4, 441n66, 555n35
Chapman, Ben, 548n11
Chatterley, Catherine, 554n33
Cherlin, Michael, 30, 405n8, 409n18, 410n19, 412n24, 414nn30–31, 415n32, 415nn34–35, 419n47
Churchill, Ward, 552
Ciano, Galeazzo, 524, 534, 535
Clauss, Ludwig Ferdinand, 433
Cohen, Richard, 562n60
Colarizi, Simona, 534n21, 537n28
Conard, Nicholas, 345n44
Confino, Alon, 123n32
Cooper, Jerrold S., 316n29
Corradini, Enrico, 531
Crenshaw, James L., 161, 161n18
Cristi, Renato, 377n122
Czerniakow, Adam, 221n79

Dahms, Hans-Joachim, 313n16, 453nn5–7, 460n25, 464n35, 467n45, 482, 483n98, 498n24, 507n60, 510nn69–70, 511n72
Davies, Alan T., 214n38
Dawidowicz, Lucy S., 550n15
De Felice, Renzo, 432n33, 523n2, 524n4, 536n25, 537n27, 541

INDEX OF AUTHORS

Deines, Roland, 177n80, 213n34, 235n161, 236n166, 238n176
Delitzsch, Franz, 210, 227, 238, 239n182
Deutscher Orient-Verein, 90n57
Dietz, Burkhard, 76n21
Diner, Hasia R., 13n26, 16
Domarus, Max, 432n36
Dorn, Walter L., 502n43
Dow, James R., 49nn17–18
Droit, Roger-Pol, 425n10
Dubber, Markus Dirk, 391, 393n216
Dunlop, Francis, 423n1, 437n50, 438n52, 441n65
Dyzenhaus, David, 374n106, 380n139, 382n149

Ebbinghaus, Angelika, 43n4
Ebel, Wilhelm, 493n5, 495n14, 509n67, 510n68, 511n72
Eckel, Jan, 52, 53
Eckert, Astrid M., 52n25
Edwards, Mark U., 137n75
Eickhoff, Martijn, 351n66, 352n69, 353n76
Einstein, Albert, 313, 345, 413, 461, 468, 504, 513, 546
Elert, Werner, 230n137, 232
Ellinger, Ekkehard, 278n51, 281n63, 315n25
Ellis, Marc H., 552, 553n26
Elsmann, Thomas, 285n81
Elvert, Jürgen, 4n6, 53, 65n2, 307n1, 308nn2–3, 309n7, 312n14, 313n16, 313n20, 315n26, 469n51
Endesfelder, Erika, 270n24, 290–91, 296n125
Ericksen, Robert P., 1, 3nn4–5, 10nn17–18, 13n25, 16n32, 31–32, 38, 79n29, 114n2, 115nn3–4, 120n18, 122n23, 130n51, 146n106, 155n3, 156n5, 163n24, 164n26, 164n28, 165n30, 172n62, 177n82, 180n93, 183n110, 193nn40–41, 218n62, 222n83, 229n130, 231n138, 231n143, 242n199, 361, 453nn5–7, 455n12, 458n21, 461n29, 468n47, 473n65, 477n79, 480n91, 491, 492n1, 498n23, 512n77, 517n86
Evans, Richard J., 118n13, 119n14

Fahlbusch, Michael, 52, 54
Fangmann, Helmut, 507n60

Farías, Victor, 58
Farkas, Karen, 559n53
Faye, Emmanuel, 31, 58, 76n19, 426n16, 428n22, 429n24, 432n35, 437n51, 441nn63–64, 441n66, 461n29
Faye, Jean-Pierre, 440, 441n62
Feisst, Sabine, 403n2, 417n42
Ferer, Jenna, 549n13
Fesefeldt, Wiebke, 494n9
Fichtner, Paula Sutter, 69n7
Findlay, John Niemeyer, 411n22
Finn, John E., 386nn180–81, 387nn182–83, 387n186, 388nn187–88
Finzi, Roberto, 540n34
First International Resources, LLC, 565
Fischer, Wolfram, 270n25, 272n31, 275n39
Fischer-Elfert, Hans-Werner, 298
Fish, Stanley, 556, 558
Fishburn, Matthew, 461n28
Fleming, Michael, 11n20
Flygare, Jakob, 27n42, 318nn31–32,
Forstman, Jack, 240n190
Forte, Allen, 404
Frahm, Eckart, 315n27
Frank, Hans, 433n36, 437
Franz, Leonhard, 338nn18–19
Franzmeier, Henning, 273n34, 288n92, 293n114, 296n128
Freedman, Samuel G., 561n60
Frei, Norbert, 508n62, 516n85
Freud, Sigmund, 405, 408, 410–11, 416, 419, 435, 461n43
Friedländer, Saul, 125n38, 460n27, 546n6
Friedrich, Gerhard, 172n63, 218n60
Fritzsche, Peter, 18

Galli, Carlo, 377n126, 378n130
Geisenhainer, Katja, 511n74
Gelb, Leslie H., 561n60
Gellis, David H., 559n54
Gentile, Emilio, 531–32, 536
Gerbi, Sando, 539n31
Gerdmar, Anders, 16n32, 25, 56n34, 79n29, 123n29, 191n135, 206n2, 208n6, 210n16, 210n18, 212n24, 213n34, 213n37, 214n39, 214n42, 215nn46–47, 215n49, 216n51, 217n56, 219n62, 225n106, 226n112, 226n115,

227n116, 227n118, 227n120, 228n125, 232n144, 234n159, 235nn161–62, 237n174, 238n177, 239n181, 239n185, 239n187, 240n190, 244n216, 245n219, 247n227, 250n242, 262, 468n47
Geringer, Sandra, 335n10, 337nn16–17, 348n56, 351n66
Gerlach, Wolfgang, 114n2, 116n6, 166n34, 240n190
Gerson, Michael, 562n60
Gerstenfeld, Manfred, 549n13
Gertz, Jan Christian, 158n14
Gertzen, Thomas L., 75n18, 95n74, 263, 264nn2–4, 267nn7–8, 267n11, 268–70, 271nn26–28, 271n30, 277n48, 282, 283nn73–74, 283n76, 284, 285, 286, 287nn88–89, 288n92, 289n93, 291, 292, 293nn111–13, 294n115, 296nn129–32
Gilbert, Martin, 14n27, 15, 44n8, 65n2, 121n19, 172n62, 366n39, 468n49, 545n3
Giles, Geoffrey, 449n1
Gillette, Aaron, 536n26
Gimmel, Jürgen, 217nn56–57
Girard, Ilse, 42n3
Goebel, Klaus, 482n96
Goldberg, Jeffrey, 561n60
Goldhagen, Daniel Jonah, 349n61
Gorsemann, Sabine, 285n81
Gottwald, Herbert, 168–69nn45–47
Götz, Norbert, 249n240
Graf, Friedrich Wilhelm, 240n189
Grafton, Anthony, 5n7
Gramsci, Antonio, 527, 529, 538
Grandi, Aldo, 529n12, 530n14
Gressmann, Hugo, 216, 238
Grieco, Bruno, 530n13
Grieco, Ruggiero, 530n13
Grimes, William, 562n60
Grimm, Gerhard, 82n36
Grimm, Harold J., 132n54
Grimsted, Patricia Kennedy, 128n43
Gritsch, Eric W., 149
Grobman, Alex, 11n19
Gross, Matthias, 487
Gross, Oren, 30, 56n35, 191n134, 374n105, 386n177
Gross, Raphael, 57, 441, 441n65, 546n5

Gross, Rina, 362n5
Grossman, Jeffrey A., 417n43
Grüttner, Michael, 119n14, 277n47, 364n18, 364nn22–23, 385n173, 389n196
Guthrie, William Keith Chambers, 410n19

Haar, Ingo, 52, 54
Habermas, Jürgen, 426
Hagen, Anders, 349
Hagen, Gottfried, 74n15
Haimo, Ethan, 413n29
Haldemann, Frank, 390n198
Halfmann, Frank, 507nn60–61
Halle, Uta, 337n17, 341n30, 347n54
Hammen, Oscar J., 388
Hammerstein, Katrin, 42n2
Hanisch, Ludmila, 65n2, 66, 75n18, 77n23, 77n25, 78, 80n31, 81, 82n38, 83n39, 86n48, 99, 271n25, 284n78, 308n2, 309n6, 310n11, 312n14, 314n22, 315n25, 321n42, 326n58, 326n60
Härke, Heinrich, 337nn14–15
Harrison, Bernard, 549n14
Hart, H. L. A., 391n203
Hartshorne, Edward Yarnell, Jr., 120, 364n17, 364nn19–21,
Hartung, Wolfdietrich, 289n97
Hass, Aaron, 13n26
Hassmann, Henning, 337n15, 338n18, 339n24, 339n26, 343nn35–36, 346n50, 349n58
Hasson, Nir, 553n29
Hauger, Martin, 179n88
Hausmann, Frank-Rutger, 4n6, 50–51, 54, 66, 98, 99n88, 272, 273, 274nn35–37, 275n38, 276n43, 277n45, 282n69, 469n51
Heiber, Helmut, 45–46, 80n30, 211n23, 218n61, 221n78, 466n43, 509n67, 511n73,
Heim, Gerd, 3n5,
Heim, Susanne, 48
Heimes, Claus, 59n45
Heinemann, Manfred, 492n2, 501n35, 502n42
Heinsius, Wilhelm, 127n42
Helmreich, Ernst Christian, 165n29, 167n40, 167n43
Herf, Jeffrey, 67n5, 80n31, 103, 374n100
Herget, James E., 390n202

INDEX OF AUTHORS

Hermelink, Heinrich, 132
Herpolsheimer, Ralf, 286n83
Heschel, Susannah, 55, 95n72, 101n93, 114n2, 115nn3–4, 117n10, 119n15, 130n51, 141n92, 160n17, 162, 163n24, 164n28, 167n43, 169nn50–51, 170nn53–54, 170n56, 171nn58–59, 171n62, 174nn68–71, 176nn75–76, 176n78, 177nn82–83, 180nn94–95, 181n99, 181nn102–3, 183n110, 191n134, 193n141, 194n143, 194n145, 214n38, 234n156, 234n158, 235n161, 236n165, 239n184, 245n219
Hetherington, Peter, 558n49
Hetzer, Tanja, 230n137, 231n143, 232n146
Heuss, Alfred, 404
Hilberg, Raul, 11–12, 221n79
Hillgruber, Andreas, 43n6
Hirsch, Marianne, 551
Hitschler, Daniel, 59n45
Hoche, Alfred, 1n1
Hockenos, Matthew D., 167n42, 190n132, 473n68
Hoffmann, Andrea, 206n4
Hoffmann, Dieter, 286n85
Hoffmann, Petra, 278n51, 281n62
Hoffmann, Stanley, 332–33, 333n3, 352
Hofmann, Andreas, 55n33
Hohlfeld, Rainer, 270n25, 272n31, 275n39, 278n51, 280n57, 286nn85–86, 287nn88–89, 290n101
Hohls, Rüdiger, 43n5, 52n23
Horowitz, Irving Louis, 445
Hoßfeld, Uwe, 160n17, 162n21, 168n45, 170n55, 181n104, 237n172
Huber, Ernst Rudolf, 432, 440
Hundt, Hans-Jürgen, 345n45
Huntley, Steve, 562n60
Hutter, Manfred, 329
Hutton, Christopher M., 142n97
Hyatt, J. Philip, 158n14

Institute for NGO Research, 552n25
International Holocaust Remembrance Alliance, 560
International Military Tribunal, 550n15
Irmscher, Johannes, 287n88
Israel, Giorgio, 538n29

Jacoby, Jeff, 561n60
Jaeger, Ludwig, 274n37
Jagemann, Norbert, 281
Jagust, Frederick, 350n62, 351n64, 351n66, 352n68, 354n77
Jahr, Christoph, 278n52
Jansen, Christian, 547n6
Jantzen, Detlef, 338n18, 343n35
Jarausch, Konrad H., 43n4, 52n23
Jaschik, Scott, 559n52
Jaspers, Karl, 427, 435
Jauernig, Reinhold, 131–32nn53–54, 132n57, 133nn58–59
Jeremias, Gert, 219n67, 242
Jerke, Birgit, 245n219
John, Jürgen, 170n55
Judt, Tony, 556
Julius, Anthony, 558
Junginger, Horst, 55, 56n34, 122, 206n2, 206n4, 209n9, 209n11, 209n14, 211n23, 218n61, 219n63, 220–22nn69–82, 222n84, 242n205, 243nn208–10, 280n59, 309n7, 312n14, 313n21, 314n24, 321n42, 325n57
Junker, Hermann, 268, 270, 277

Kacandes, Irene, 551
Kaehler, Siegfried A., 465n30, 466, 467n45
Kampe, Norbert, 135nn64–65
Kampp-Seyfried, Friederike, 298
Kant, Immanuel, 5, 7–8
Kaplan, Chaim A., 550
Kasher, Aryeh, 224n96
Kater, Michael H., 46–47, 98, 312n14, 335n9, 340n27, 341n29, 389n193
Kaufmann, Arthur, 336n33, 336nn37–38, 367n40, 367n47, 368, 369n63, 370n69, 371n74, 371n78, 371n80, 372nn84–85, 382nn150–52, 389n194
Kaufmann, Thomas, 135n67, 145n104
Keefer, Erwin, 343n37, 344n39, 345n43, 346
Kelsen, Hans, 374n106, 379n133, 381n144, 390, 391
Kerig, Tim, 343n38
Kern, Martin, 77n22
Kershaw, Ian, 429, 430n27
Kertész, Imre, 550
Keysar, Ariela, 557n44

Kierkegaard, Søren, 377n127
Kinzig, Wolfram, 212n26
Klee, Ernst, 271n25, 473n66, 474–75nn71–74
Klein, David, 559
Klemperer, Victor, 396
Kloft, Hans, 285n81
Koch, Thomas, 485, 518
Koenen, Klaus, 161n17
Köhler, Ludwig, 184–85
König, Christoph, 78n25
Koon, Tracey H., 529n11
Koonz, Claudia, 122n23, 367n42
Kosmin, Barry A., 557n44
Krall, Katharina, 353n75
Krause, Reinhold, 123, 164–65
Krieg, Robert A., 155n2
Krieger, Karsten, 134–35nn62–64
Krönig, Waldemar, 493n6
Krüger, Wolfgang, 494n9
Kulick-Aldag, Renate, 511nn73–74
Kupisch, Karl, 115n5
Kurlander, Eric, 88n55
Kusber, Jan, 308n3
Kvidahl, Cliff, 213n35

Lamparter, Eduard, 129, 130n50
Landesverein für Innere Mission, 133n60
Lang, Hubert, 361, 362n2
Langmuir, Gavin I., 117n12
Laqueur, Walter, 11n20, 556
Lefkovits, Etgar, 554n32
Legendre, Jean-Pierre, 342n32
Lehmann, Hartmut, 4n6, 469n51
Lemberg, Joseph, 291n107
Lemmerich, Jost, 505n55
Lemuth, Oliver, 170n55
Leppin, Volker, 160n17, 172n65, 177n80, 194nn144–45, 235n161, 236n166
Lerchenmüller, Joachim, 279n56
Lessing, Eckhart, 228n122
Leube, Achim, 339n24, 350n62, 351n67
Levenson, Alan, 227
Levenson, Jon D., 191n135
LeVine, Mark, 562n60
Levinson, Bernard M., 1, 4, 8n14, 24, 38, 95n72, 119n15, 123n31, 157n8, 179n89, 185n119, 192n139, 203, 215n45, 226n111,
227n116, 232n145, 234n155, 236n170, 263, 286n85, 361, 441n66
Lewin, David, 404
Liebenberg, Roland, 229n128, 233n152, 249n237
Lifton, Robert J., 3n4
Lilla, Mark, 553n27
Lipstadt, Deborah, 11n12, 361
Liska, Vivian, 555n35
Lixfeld, Hannjost, 49
Lohfink, Norbert, 192n139
Longerich, Peter, 88n54
Lönnendonker, Siegward, 271n25
Loprieno, Antonio, 298
Lösch, Niels C., 277n49, 277n51, 279n53, 280
Losemann, Volker, 47–48, 85n45, 91n60
Luther, Martin, 8, 19n38, 20, 23–24, 67, 116–17, 128n43, 129, 130, 132, 137, 138, 139, 141–43, 145

Maas, Utz, 274n36
MacLeod, Donald, 558n46
Mählert, Ulrich, 61
Mahsarski, Dirk, 335n10, 337n16, 344, 348n56
Maier-Metz, Harald, 310n10
Malik Ali, Amir Abdel, 556n39, 556n41
Marchand, Suzanne L., 23, 41, 47–48, 70n8, 71–72nn9–10, 73nn12–13, 74–75nn15–17, 77n23, 78n27, 79n29, 80n31, 87n52, 90n56, 92n64, 103n97, 113, 315n25, 384n168
Marcus, Kenneth L., 549n13
Marsch, Ulrich, 278n52
Marshall, Barbara, 488
Marten, H.-G., 488
Marten, Rainer, 426n14
Marty, Eric, 555n35
Massing, Almuth, 485, 518
Maunz, Theodor, 368–72, 395–96
Mauz, Gerhard, 368n56, 395n234, 396n237
Mayda, Giuseppe, 532n18
McCormick, John P., 74n16, 377n122, 380n139, 381n145
Mead, Walter Russell, 562–63
Mehring, Reinhard, 59n45
Mehrtens, Herbert, 515n82, 516n84
Meinel, Florian, 370n67, 515n82
Meiser, Martin, 242nn199–200

INDEX OF AUTHORS

Meissner, Bruno, 307, 310, 311, 320, 324–25
Meister-Karanikas, Ralf, 171n59
Mekhitarian, Arpag, 283n75
Meotti, Guido, 553n31
Merz, Georg, 127–28nn42–43, 130n52
Meyer, Michael A., 134n63
Meyer-Drawe, Käte, 53
Michaelis, Meir, 432n33
Mischek, Udo, 278n51
Mode, Markus, 75n18, 84n43
Mohn, Josef, 345n48
Mommsen, Wolfgang J., 290
Morris, Douglas G., 363n9, 363nn11–16, 367n48, 383n162, 384n164, 389n194
Motadel, David, 67n5, 279n56
Müller, Ingo, 3n4, 362, 363n10, 363n14, 364n20, 364n22, 364n24, 366n33, 366nn35–36, 382n148, 382n154
Müller, Klaus-Dieter, 493n6
Müller, Sandra, 266n7
Müller, Siegfried, 492n2, 492n4, 502n40, 508n63
Murphy, David Thomas, 279n55

Nagel, Anne C., 282n68
Naimark, Norman M., 462n31
Nastasi, Pietro, 538n29
Neff, Severine, 408nn13–14, 409nn16–17, 414n30
Nelson, Cary, 549n13, 557n43
Nemec, Birgit, 302
Neuer, Werner, 208n6, 212n24, 212nn26–29, 213n32, 235, 237n173, 241n191, 241n195, 251n43
Neukirch, Johannes, 135n67
Neumann, Franz L., 11, 365n27–28, 373n95, 374n98
Neumann, Georg, 322n49
Neumann, Volker, 59n45, 375n106
Ní Aoláin, Fionnuala, 374n105, 386n177, 401
Nicolaisen, Carsten, 120n17, 180n93, 205n1
Niebuhr, Karl-Wilhelm, 177n80, 235n161, 236n166
Nielsen-Sikora, Jürgen, 4n6, 53, 307–8nn1–3, 309n7, 312n14, 313n16, 313n20, 315n26, 469n51
Niess, Wolfram, 54

Niethammer, Lutz, 462, 473n65, 502n43, 547n6
Niewyk, Donald L., 130n50
Noakes, Jeremy, 88n54, 546, 547
Norden, Günther van, 166n35, 167n39
Norwood, Stephen H., 20n39
Nötzoldt, Peter, 270n25, 272n31, 275n39, 278n51, 280n57, 286nn85–86, 287nn88–89, 290n101, 294nn118–19

Oberkrome, Willi, 50
Oberman, Heiko A., 139n82
Obermann, Konrad, 485, 518
Oexle, Otto Gerhard, 3n5, 4n6, 468–69nn50–51
Olender, Maurice, 352n71
Osten-Sacken, Peter von der, 141n89, 141n92, 235n161, 236n166
Ott, Hugo, 58
Ott, Thomas, 3n5
Otto, Eckart, 157n8

Pältz, Eberhard H., 160n17, 171n59
Pape, Wolfgang, 348n57
Papen, Patricia von, 121n21, 128n43
Pasch, Helma, 277n50
Pauck, Marian, 459n23
Pauck, Wilhelm, 459n23
Pauer-Studer, Herlinde, 392n214
Paul, Ludwig, 82n37
Pauls, Theodor, 140–42
Peeters, Remi, 445
Perles, Felix, 238n179
Pessin, Andrew, 549n13, 557n43
Petacco, Arrigo, 526n7
Petersen, Hans-Christian, 42n3, 308n3
Petersmann, Werner, 141
Phillips, Jonathan, 125n38
Pieper, Max, 77n24
Pils, Ramon, 54
Pingel, Falk, 493n7
Platt, Kristin, 53
Poewe, Karla, 278n51
Pollack, Eunice G., 549n13
Pollock, Sheldon, 66, 78, 87
Popper, Karl, 438
Posner, Richard A., 391n203

Potter, Pamela M., 51
Preston, Andrew, 564
Preti, Luigi, 534n23
Price, David H., 139n82
Pringle, Heather, 88n54, 103n98, 349n60
Probst, Christopher J., 19n38, 23, 115n3, 115n5, 116n9, 117n12, 119n15, 120n17, 131n53, 132n56, 140n85, 145n105, 153, 163n24, 164n28, 169n52, 170n57, 171n59, 177n81
Puschner, Uwe, 249n240

Rabenau, Konrad von, 172n64, 174n71, 180n94, 180n98
Rabinbach, Anson, 4n6, 41n1, 53, 76n20, 80–81nn31–32, 85n45, 155n3, 194n145, 274n36, 296, 297n133, 469n51
Rabinowitz, Dorothy, 13n26
Rammer, Gerhard, 500n34
Raschzok, Klaus, 170n53
Rathkolb, Oliver, 54n31, 279n55, 280n58
Raue, Dietrich, 264n2, 264n4, 266n5, 266n7, 267n9
Raulwing, Peter, 75n18, 80n31, 95n74, 263
Rebenich, Stefan, 283n76, 287n87
Reddy, William M., 252
Redeker, Konrad, 395n235
Reimann, Mathias, 368, 369n58, 371, 393–94nn222–23
Rein, Gustav Adolf, 364n25
Reineke, Walter F., 303
Remnick, David, 562n60
Remy, Steven P., 76n20, 120n18, 168n44, 365, 366n39, 367n41, 367n44, 367n46, 368n50, 371n76, 374n102, 384n168, 393, 394nn226–27, 395nn230–33, 454n9, 462n31, 473n65, 483n98, 547
Renger, Johannes, 27–29, 65n2, 78n25, 80n31, 81n34, 82n37, 83nn40–41, 308n4, 309n8, 311–12nn13–15, 313n17, 313n19, 315nn25–26, 317n30, 318n33, 319n35, 319n37, 320n40, 321nn42–44, 322n48, 322n50, 323n53, 325n56, 326n59, 331
Rentsch, Thomas, 428n22
Richarz, Monika, 116n7
Richter, Tonio Sebastian, 298
Riis, Ole, 252n252
Ringer, Alexander, 404n5, 413n26

Ringer, Fritz K., 367, 454n8
Rinnen, Anja, 169n50
Ritterbusch, Eugen, 275n38
Robbins, Jeff, 562n61
Röhm, Eberhard, 116n7
Rohrbacher, Peter, 277n51, 280n58
Rose, Jacqueline, 561nn57–58
Rosenfeld, Alvin H., 33, 549nn13–14, 551n18, 552n22, 553n28, 554n33, 559n53, 570
Rosenfeld, Gavriel D., 551n19
Rosenow, Ulf, 460n25
Rossiter, Clinton L., 386nn179–80, 387–88nn182–89, 388
Rossman-Benjamin, Tammi, 549n13, 557n45
Rost, Leonhard, 184n113
Roth, Karl Heinz, 43n4
Roth, Philip, 13n26
Rottleuthner, Hubert, 385n174, 391, 392, 393
Rowley, Tom, 553n30
Rubin, Barry, 279n56
Rüegg, Walter, 489
Rupnow, Dirk, 55
Rüthers, Bernd, 57n36
Rutten, Tim, 562n60

Sabrow, Martin, 42n2
Sachar, Howard M., 412n25
Safranski, Rüdiger, 58
Said, Edward, 64n1, 561
Saller, Hans, 489
Sarfatti, Michelle, 522n1, 532n19
Sauder, Gerhard, 461n28
Sauer, Wolfgang, 43n6
Schaarschmidt, Rebecca, 278n52
Schäfer, Gerhard, 214n44
Schäfer, Hans Dieter, 289n97
Schaller, Helmut W., 313n20
Schappacher, Norbert, 460n25, 511–12nn75–76
Schauz, Désirée, 505n55, 511n74
Scheler, Werner, 289n97
Schemo, Diana Jean, 559n51
Schenk, Wolfgang, 236n166
Schermaul, Ulrich, 280n59
Scheuerman, William E., 375n109, 381
Schmidt, Jan, 310n11
Schmidt, Jörg, 395n229

INDEX OF AUTHORS 591

Schmidt, Kurt Dietrich, 205n1, 233n154
Schmidt, Wolfgang, 330
Schmuhl, Hans-Walter, 1n1, 277–78n51
Schneider, Thomas, 26, 65n2, 80n31, 98n81, 174, 266n5, 267n10, 270n24, 271n27, 271n30, 273n34, 275n39, 276n40, 280n59, 283n73, 287n87, 289n96, 290n100, 295n121, 296nn126–27, 305, 309n5, 312n14, 314n23, 315n25, 318n34
Schneider, Ulrich, 492n3, 494n9
Schöbel, Gunter, 335n10, 339n25, 342, 344, 346n51, 351n67, 353
Schoenbaum, David, 564
Scholem, Gershom G., 405
Scholl, Lars U., 511n72
Schönwälder, Karen, 49–50
Schreiber, Maximilian, 277n44
Schröder, Wilt Aden, 284nn78–79
Schüfer, Tobias, 160n17, 170n54, 171nn59–61, 175n73
Schulz, Gerhard, 43n6
Schulze, Winfried, 3n5, 468n50
Schumann, Dirk, 505n55, 511n74, 515n83
Schumann, Peter, 470n58
Schutter, Dirk de, 445
Schwab, George, 376n115
Schwanitz, Wolfgang G., 279n56
Scott, James C., 332
Scriba, Christoph J., 286n86
Sedita, Giovanni, 539
Seidel, Thomas A., 161n17, 171n59
Seidler, Eduard, 286n86
Sénécheau, Miriam, 339n26
Serri, Mirella, 528n9, 540
Sherratt, Yvonne, 373n95, 373n97, 382n155, 383n160, 384nn165–66
Shklar, Judith N., 375n110, 391n205
Siegele-Wenschkewitz, Leonore, 120n17, 121n21, 180n93, 205n1, 217n57, 245n219
Simms, Bryan R., 412n24
Simon, Gerd, 280n59, 312n14, 322n46
Sims, Amy R., 364n18, 365n26, 389n197
Ska, Jean-Louis, 157n9, 161, 162
Smith, Alex Duval, 548n11
Smith, Denis Mack, 533, 534n20
Smith, Tony, 564
Solberg, Mary M., 164n28

Sommer, Ulrike, 336, 337, 342n31, 344n40
Sonne, Hans-Joachim, 171n59
Sorensen, Lee, 108
Sorkin, David, 410n20
Spicer, Kevin P., 155n2
Spinoza, Baruch, 8, 57, 467
Stackert, Jeffrey, 185n119
Stadnikow, Sergei, 96n76
Stannard, David, 552
Stegmann, Erich, 203
Steigmann-Gall, Richard, 155n1, 162n22, 166n38, 167nn40–41, 173n67, 189n130, 190n133
Steinbach, Matthias, 168–69nn45–47,
Steinel, Monika E., 350–51
Steiner, George, 545, 548
Steiner, John M., 271n27
Steinweis, Alan E., 3n4, 22–23, 55n32, 63, 80n31, 121, 146, 206n4, 207, 363n9, 427n17, 541n36, 546n4
Stern, Selma, 137n73
Steuer, Heiko, 347n53, 348n57, 349n59
Stoecker, Adolf, 212–13, 215, 216n50, 218n61, 237, 239, 249
Stoecker, Holger, 278n51
Stolleis, Michael, 365n31, 366, 368n49, 369, 370n66, 370n69, 371n79, 372nn82–83, 372nn86–87, 372nn89–92, 373n96, 383n157, 384n168, 385n172, 385n174, 385n176, 386nn178–79, 389, 394, 396
Stone, Marla, 528
Strack, Hermann L., 210, 227, 227n119, 237n174, 239
Strauss, Claudia, 240
Strauss, Leo, 58, 380n140
Streck, Michael P., 310n9
Stuckenschmidt, Hans Heinz, 404n4, 404n6
Stutz, Rüdiger, 169n47, 169n52, 171n59, 172n65, 173
Sýkorová, Jitka, 28n43
Szabó, Anikó, 32, 460n26, 492n1, 497n20, 497n22, 498n24, 500n34, 501n37, 501n39, 502n41, 503nn44–45, 503–4nn47–48, 504–5nn52–54, 512n77, 513n79, 517n86, 521

Taminiaux, Jacques, 425
Tell, David, 559n50

Tenorth, Heinz-Elmar, 277n47
Tent, James F., 462n31, 473n65
Terhoeven, Petra, 515n83
Theissen, Gerd, 206n4, 219n66, 220n68, 220n71, 222n83, 225–26nn105–12, 226, 227n116, 242nn201–4, 242n206, 243, 251n250
Thieler, Kerstin, 515n83
Thierfelder, Jörg, 116n7, 123n28, 180n93
Thimme, David, 471n62, 511n75
Tobin, Gary A., 549n13
Tolischus, Otto D., 11n19
Trappe, Julie, 61
Trittel, Katharina, 495n14
Trümpler, Charlotte, 74n15

Urban, Otto, 355
U.S. Department of State, Office of the Special Envoy to Monitor and Combat Anti-Semitism, 560n56

Vacín, Luděk, 28n43
Valla, Lorenzo, 7
Veijola, Timo, 192n139
Voigt, Klaus, 525n6
Vollmer, Jochen, 508n62
Vollnhals, Clemens, 474n69
Von der Haar, Frauke, 355
Vos, J. S., 227n116
Voss, Susanne, 264n2, 264n4, 266n5, 266n7, 267–68, 269, 280n61

Walravens, Hartmut, 112
Walter, Karin, 355
Walther, Peter, 270n25, 271n27, 275n39, 294nn116–19, 295n123
Walther, Wilhelm, 139, 140n84
Wasserman, Nathan, 310n9
Wasserstein, Bernard, 429–30, 433
Weber, Anke, 273n34, 288n92, 293n114
Weber, R. G. S., 365n29

Weber, Wilhelm, 89–91
Wegeler, Cornelia, 453nn5–6, 460n25, 464n35, 467n45, 483n98, 498n24, 507n60, 510–11nn69–72
Weger, Tobias, 347n52
Weinberg, Aryeh K., 549n13
Weinfeld, Moshe, 187n124, 192n139
Weinreich, Max, 14–15, 16n32, 18n36, 44–45, 55, 65n2, 80n31, 95n72, 121n19, 172n62, 174n69, 177n79, 366–67nn39–40, 383n161, 384n163, 384n167, 426, 427n17, 441, 468n49, 545, 546–47, 549n12
Weisberg, David B., 73n12
Weitz, Eric D., 361, 385n175, 388, 389n192
Wendelin, Adolf, 138, 139n81
Wenninger, Florian, 302
Werner, Karl Ferdinand, 45n9
Weyde, Karl William, 203
Whittall, Arnold, 417n41
Wiese, Christian, 212n26, 237n174
Wiesehöfer, Joseph, 315n26
Wildt, Michael, 2, 462n30
Wilhelm, Gernot, 323n53
Wimmer, Walter, 228
Winau, Rolf, 286n86, 287n90, 295n122
Wippermann, Wolfgang, 118n13, 142n97
Wischnath, Michael, 123n30
Witte, John E., Jr., 189n131
Woessner, Martin, 427n18
Wojak, Irmtrud, 55n33
Wokoeck, Ursula, 28n44, 81n33, 276n41
Wolff, Christoph, 416n39
Wolfrum, Edgar, 61
Wolgast, Eike, 120n17
Wolin, Richard, 58, 426n12
Woodhead, Linda, 252n252
Wrogemann, Henning, 126n40

Yakira, Elhanan, 549n14

Ziegeldorf, Vera, 52n25

SUBJECT INDEX

Note: This subject index does not provide page ranges for entire chapters. Thus, for entries that employ words, concepts, or ideas clearly reflected in one or more chapter titles, please see the volume's table of contents for the relevant page numbers.

Ahasveros, the "Wandering Jew," 223–24, 239
Akkadian, 319, 320, 328
Allied Military Government, 120n18, 219, 353, 472–73, 491–92, 494, 500, 502, 511, 514
anti-Judaism, 15–16, 24, 33, 115, 117, 117n12, 118, 120, 126, 129, 131, 142, 144, 145–47, 176, 218, 223, 226, 227, 227n116, 239, 253, 288, 453, 479–80, 479n87, 483, 545, 558, 560, 562, 563
antimodernism, 25, 238, 248–50, 253
anti-Zionism, 549. *See also* Zionism
anti-Zionist, 532, 556, 563. *See also* Zionist
apartheid, 34, 217, 557
appointing only the best [*Ergänzung der Besten*], 32, 495, 501. *See also* faculty appointment procedures
Aramaic, 68n6, 101–2, 221
"Archive for Racial Statistics by Profession," 452, 456
Archives
  Berlin, Bundesarchiv, 322n47, 328, 550n15
  Berlin (Dahlem), Geheimes Staatsarchiv, 83n39, 107, 348
  Berlin, Staatsbibliothek zu, 86n47, 107, 505n55, 506n57, 512n76, 513n78, 513n80, 514n81

Archives (*Cont.*)
  Biblioteca e Archivi di Egittologia, Milan, 292n110, 295n120, 296n124, 298, 298n135
  Bundesarchiv Koblenz, 233n153, 254, 345n46, 352, 353, 354
  Danish National Archives, 293n112, 298
  Hannah Arendt Papers, Library of Congress, 425n8, 442
  Landeskirchenarchiv Eisenach, 236n165, 236n170, 244n217, 245n221, 254
  Landeskirchlichesarchiv Hannover, 126n40, 464n33, 477n78, 485
  Landsberger Archives in Leipzig and Jerusalem, 310n9, 328
  Max-Planck-Gesellschaft, Archiv der, 506n58, 508n65, 509n66
  Niedersächsisches Hauptstaatsarchiv Hannover [Lower Saxony Archive], 464n34, 465nn37–38, 471n63, 476n75, 478nn80–85, 479nn86–87, 480nn90–91, 481nn92–93, 482nn94–95, 485, 495n14, 496nn17–18, 497nn20–21, 499n30, 499n33, 509n67, 510n68, 518
  Public Record Office, Kew, London, 508n64

Archives (*Cont.*)
  Thüringisches Hauptstaatsarchiv Weimar, 172n65, 195
  Universitätsarchiv der Friedrich-Schiller-Universität Jena, 171n58, 173n66, 174n68, 175n74, 176n78, 195
  Universitätsarchiv Göttingen, 454n10, 455nn11–12, 456nn15–17, 464n34, 465nn39–40, 467n45, 470n56, 470nn59–60, 485, 494nn10–11, 495nn12–13, 495n15, 496n17, 497n21, 498nn25–26, 499nn27–28, 499nn31–32, 501n38, 506n56, 518
  Universitätsarchiv Tübingen, 206n3, 217n58, 222n85, 223n86, 226n113, 235n161, 254
Aryanization, 229
Aryan Paragraph, 163–64, 166, 246
Aryan race, 70–71, 87–88, 94, 142, 168, 312, 313, 315–16, 318, 337–38
Assyriology, 22, 23, 27–29, 73, 77, 85, 306–31
Austria(n), 28, 69, 83, 321, 322n46, 362, 404, 412, 436, 437, 470n55, 539
  annexation of (Anschluss), 54, 310, 322, 438
  antisemitism in, 413, 523–24, 553
  cultural traditions of, 412, 417
  forced emigration from, 310, 526
  post-war, 42, 500
  universities, 54–55, 404, 500

Babylon(ian), 223, 310, 315, 318
  and Bible Affair (1901–2), 73.
  See also exile, Babylonian
Barmen Declaration, 165–67, 189n132, 231n143
Berlin Antisemitism Dispute [*Berliner Antisitismusstreit*], 134–35, 144, 216
Bethel Confession, the, 215n49, 247
Bible (dejudaized), 177, 234, 244–45
Bildung
  as liberal education, 74
  as self-formation, 410, 412, 417
Bolshevism, 126, 130–31, 147, 479
Bonnet, Hans, 291
book burning, 31, 382, 460–61, 463
boycott
  academic, against professors, 31, 449, 454
  economic, against German Jews, 11, 214, 220–21, 222
  recent, against Israel, 34, 557, 559n53

Brackmann, Albert, 291
British Zone of Occupation, 32, 474, 476–77, 491–93, 500–2, 514–15
Bultmann, Rudolf, 232n144, 240n190, 241–42, 431n32

catechism, 143, 159, 177, 234
Catholic, 19n38, 22, 25, 25n40, 67, 121n21, 127, 145, 155n2, 192, 322, 436, 451n2
Christian Social Party, 212
Church Struggle [*Kirchenkampf*], 115, 122n24, 159, 162–67, 167n42, 169, 178–80, 188–89n130, 193, 214, 244–45, 248
Civil Service Law (Law for the Restoration of the Professional Civil Service). *See under* laws, Nazi or fascist
Colonial League [*Kolonialbund*], 271, 285
Committee for the Study of White Africa [*Kommission für die Erforschung Weißafrikas*], 264, 270, 277–81, 290, 296, 297
Communist(s), 92, 220, 293n112, 308, 373, 389–90, 480, 527, 529, 530, 534
concentration camps, 33, 86n48, 292, 310, 371, 433–34, 473, 497, 555
  Buchenwald, 147, 168
  Dachau, 147, 473
  Sachsenhausen, 147, 497n22
Conference on Material Claims against Germany, 555
Confessing Church [*Bekennende Kirche*], 114–15, 122n24, 163n24, 165–67, 172n64, 174, 174n69, 178–80, 178n85, 181–82, 183n110, 185, 193, 214, 221n78, 240n190, 243n211, 244–45, 317n30, 474
conservatism
  political, 22, 41, 45, 47, 50, 53, 86, 115, 212, 229, 249, 367, 370n70, 373, 385n174, 438, 457
  theological, 25, 131, 179, 212–13, 228, 237n174, 238, 240–46, 248, 253

denazification [*Entnazifierung*], 22, 28, 32, 174n71, 193–95, 222, 226, 346, 349, 393, 394, 462–71, 491, 494n9, 495n13, 498n25, 502, 511, 516–17, 547
  categories of, 472–73, 475
  and its successful role in postwar Germany, 463, 483–85

and lying about the past, 13, 462–63, 472–83
process of, 32, 450–51, 472–73
reduced Allied role in, by 1948, 32, 477. See also *Persilschein*
Doktorvater, 27, 28, 206, 235–36
Ducki, Horst, 284

Egyptology, 22, 23, 26, 65n2, 77, 85, 95–96, 98, 263–98, 314, 315, 318, 326, 327
emigration, 27, 65, 78, 104, 116, 217, 276, 307, 327, 389, 403, 500–2, 514–17
Indians as Aryan emigrants, 93–94
émigrés, German professors as, 28–29, 30, 83, 267, 283, 288n91, 310, 318–21, 323, 327, 345, 405, 407, 416–17, 500–17
"emotional regime," 26, 238, 250–53
Enlightenment, the
critiques of, 129, 131, 237n174
as exemplar for cultural values, xviii, 7–10, 21, 69, 95, 125n39, 451
Entarte Kunst [decadent art], 403
Entnazifierung. See denazification
Erichsen, Wolja, 276n40, 292, 292n110, 293n112, 295, 295n120, 295–96n124, 298n135
"eternal Jew," 223
eugenics, 168, 231, 277, 431n32, 474, 497–98
ewige Jude, der [the "eternal Jew"]
antisemitic concept, 223
antisemitic film, 121n20
exile
Babylonian, 223–24, 405
from Hanover, 452
from Nazi Germany, 28, 66, 267, 269, 308, 310, 318–19, 327, 431, 433, 436–37, 501, 502, 504, 516, 526

Faculties (of German universities)
History, 45, 454–55, 465
Law, 361, 372, 389, 478
Law and Economics, 168
Medicine, 168, 498–99
Philosophy, 54, 70, 84, 223, 264, 272, 293, 456, 464, 465, 510, 511
Theology, 25, 25n40, 68, 70, 118, 120n17, 123, 125, 141, 160, 162, 169–178, 180–81, 193–94, 457, 458, 476, 477, 482–83

faculty appointment procedures
before Nazi era, 21–22, 463
during Nazi era, xvii, 119, 155–56, 160, 168–74, 180–81, 307–11, 313, 364–65, 389, 463–67
post-war, 32, 193–95, 319, 395, 493–517. *See also* appointing only the best
Fascism, 58
in Germany, xvii, 290, 391n207, 522
in Italy, xvii, 22, 33, 432
Fascist University Youth [Gruppi universitari fascisti; GUF], xv, 528n9, 529–31, 533, 538
Faulhaber, Michael von, Cardinal, 473
Final Solution, 34, 222, 396, 549
Fragebogen [denazification questionnaire], 450–51, 472, 474
Frankfurter Allgemeine Zeitung, 426, 482
Frick, Wilhelm, Interior Minister, 283, 288n91
Fricke, Otto, 474–75
Führer, 91, 100, 107, 119, 143–44, 146, 170, 173, 214–15, 229, 231, 250, 253, 271, 275, 284, 287, 289, 297, 369, 372, 373, 382, 388n191, 429. *See also* Hitler, Adolf
Führer consciousness, 388
Führer Principle, 286, 287n88, 465, 481
Führer state, 381–82
Führereid [oath of loyalty to Hitler], 310, 365n26

General Association of Student Representatives [Allgemeiner Studenten-Auschuss; AstA], xv, 449
Generalplan Ost, 468
genocide, 19–20, 48, 125, 335, 428, 507, 550–57, 559
George, Stefan, 408–9
German Christians (movement) [Deutsche Christen; DC], xv, 115, 121–22, 123, 130–31, 141, 154–55, 159–60, 162–67, 170–71, 173, 174, 176, 179, 182, 183, 183n110, 185, 189–90n132, 191–92, 214–15, 431n32, 463–64
and denazification, 193–95
German Christian Church Movement [Kirchenbewegung Deutsche Christen; KDC], xv, 117n10, 167, 169, 233–35

German Democratic Republic (GDR; East Germany), 26, 42, 48, 194, 236, 270, 290–91, 295–96
German Oriental Society [Deutsche Morgenländische Gesellschaft; DMG], xv, 82–84, 321, 323–24
German People's Party [Deutsche Volkspartei; DVP], xv, 469
German People's Union [Deutsche Volksunion; DVU], xv, 395–96
German Protestant Church [Deutsche Evangelishe Kirche], 23–24, 115, 121–22, 124, 126, 127, 130, 464, 508
German Student Union [Deutsche Studentenschaft; DSt], xv, 276n40, 449
Gerstl, Richard, 408
Gestapo [Geheime Staatspolizei, "Secret State Police"], 283–84, 341, 348, 369, 476, 494n9, 507, 540
Gleichschaltung [coordination], 154, 382, 450, 491, 548
   in the churches, 154–56, 165
   in universities, 155–56, 168–69, 286, 343
   Selbstgleichschaltung [self-coordination] in universities, 450, 461, 491, 514
Goebbels, Joseph, 219, 288n91, 339, 371
Göring, Hermann, 383
"Göttingen Seven" (famous signers of a petition for academic freedom in 1837), 9, 451–52
"Grüber Office," 116
Grundgestalt [basic shape], 413–14

Habilitation, 81, 126, 170, 174, 188, 221, 463, 464, 466, 476, 496n16
Hartung, Fritz, 291
Hebrew, 83, 140, 165, 177, 221
   study of, 67, 68, 68n6, 70, 77, 175–76, 180, 239
Heidelberg Myth, The, by Steven P. Remy, 393–94, 547
Heimat [native soil, homeland], 97, 123–24
Heydrich, Reinhard, 284, 313, 453
High Command of the Armed Forces (Oberkommando der Wehrmacht; OKW), xvi, 469n53, 471
Himmler, Heinrich, 87, 88, 88n54, 98, 284, 312, 313, 322, 325, 326, 341, 550

Historikertag, 3, 52, 468, 470
Hitler, Adolf, 5, 11, 13, 17, 31, 58, 79, 119, 175n72, 207, 284, 312, 333n3, 339, 373, 381–82, 393, 431, 432, 432–33n36, 439, 449, 461, 471n61, 484, 497–98, 507, 561
   and the Protestant Church, 115, 154–55, 162, 163, 167n41, 205n1, 474
   post-war opposition to, 463, 481, 482, 484, 507, 516
   in post-war scholarship, 3, 12, 23, 43, 428–29, 439, 440
   "reductio ad Hitlerum," 58
   support from academics, 5, 10, 15, 56, 75n18, 90, 121–22, 125n38, 205, 214, 225, 229, 267, 273, 286, 292n110, 392, 425, 428–29, 431n32, 450, 465, 470, 471, 480, 491.
   See also Führer
Hitler Youth, 18, 91n60, 101, 167, 276n40
Hitler's Professors: The Part of Scholarship in Germany's Crimes against the Jewish People, by Max Weinreich, 14–16, 44–45, 55, 65n2, 426–27, 441, 468n49, 545–47
Holocaust
   awareness, 10–17, 21, 555
   and genocide studies, 17–20, 554
   memory, 16–17, 34, 550–51, 552–555, 560, 563–64
   scholarship on, 11–16, 48, 52–53, 55, 332–33, 462–63, 548n11, 550–52, 554
Holocaust Museum, United States, 16
hymnal (dejudaized), 159, 165, 177, 234

Indology, 70–71, 73, 78, 86–89, 93–94, 98
Institutum Judaicum
   in Berlin, 210
   in Leipzig, 210, 211, 216, 238, 323
International Holocaust Remembrance Alliance (IHRA), "Working Definition of Antisemitism," 560
Israel
   biblical, 157, 158, 161n19, 179, 187, 189, 415
   in Christian antisemitism, 142, 175, 223–24, 230
   land of, 213, 223–24
   modern state of, 16–17, 34, 549, 552, 555–64
Italian Communist Party [Partito Comunista Italiano; PCI], xvi, 530, 534, 538–39n31

SUBJECT INDEX

Jesus, 101, 128, 133, 138, 159n16, 165, 175, 176, 177, 183, 189n132, 210, 213, 216–17, 230, 234, 239, 240, 244–45
Jewish Boycott. *See under* boycott
"Jewish Question, the," 34, 46, 55, 116, 127, 128, 136–38, 139, 140, 144–45, 176, 180, 352, 478–79, 540, 549, 556, 564
   research on [*Forschungen zur Judenfrage*], 55, 98, 121, 127, 218–19, 221, 224–25, 312, 430, 546, 549.
   See also *Judenforschung*
Jewish Question, The [*Die Judenfrage*], by Gerhard Kittel, 9–10, 209, 217–18, 223, 468n47, 483
Josel of Rosheim, 137, 139
Judenforschung [Jewish Research], 23, 45, 55–56, 80, 207, 211n23
Judenfrage, Die. See *Jewish Question, The*
Judenschriften [Martin Luther's writings about Jews and Judaism], 132, 133, 136, 141, 142, 143

Kafka, Franz, 405, 411, 416
Kant, Immanuel, 5, 7–8
Kaiserreich [Imperial Germany], 133, 146
Kirchenkampf. See Church Struggle
Klingelhöfer, Waldemar, Commander of Einsatzgruppe B, 475
Klotz, Leopold [publisher], 289, 292–93, 296
Kriegstagebuch [war diary], 471
Kristallnacht [Night of Broken Glass], 11, 83, 147, 225, 361, 537
Kyffhäuser-Verband, 217n57

Landeskirchen [Germany's state or regional churches], 120, 154–55, 162–63, 167, 175, 177, 193, 233, 464n33
Language and Silence, by George Steiner, 545
laws, Nazi or fascist
   Aryan Paragraph, 163, 166, 246
   Italian racial laws, 525, 526, 529, 537, 538, 541
   Law against the Overcrowding of German Schools and Universities, 118
   Law for the Restoration of the Professional Civil Service, 27, 83n39, 94, 118, 122, 155–56, 163–64, 173, 307–8, 311, 363–64, 459–60, 491, 510, 526, 537

Law on the Admission to the Bar, 362–63
Nuremberg Race Laws (the Reich Citizenship Law and the Law for the Protection of German Blood and Honor), 28, 83, 94, 147, 214, 225, 308, 346, 383, 510, 512
laws, other
   Article 48 (Weimar Constitution), 386–88
   Title VI of the 1964 Civil Rights Act, 557.
   See also natural law
Lebensraum, 279, 338, 469
Lepsius, Richard, 296
liberalism, 129–30, 367, 370, 371, 373, 374, 381, 382, 532
"life unworthy of life" [*Lebensunwertes Leben*], 1
Luria, Isaac, 405, 415
Luther Renaissance, 115–16, 130, 228–29

Marcion, 159, 192
Marx, Karl, 461
Marxism, 50, 377n122, 457
Meiser, Hans, Bishop, 473–74
Mengele, Joseph, 431–32n32, 474
Militant League for German Culture [*Kampfbund für deutsche Kultur*; KfdK], xv, 209, 217, 249, 344
military, 225, 252, 274–75, 281
   events, 267, 273, 278, 280, 280n57, 437, 455n13
   service, 28, 249, 307, 313n17, 317, 324, 348, 454–55, 469n53, 471, 497n22, 559
ministers. *See* pastors
Ministry of Church Affairs, 127n42, 167n41
Ministry of Culture, 492, 501
Ministry of the Interior, 119, 283, 288n91, 453
Mischlinge [person of mixed race], 82, 95, 294
Mitläufer [fellow travellers], 462, 498n25
Mitläuferfabrik, Die, by Lutz Niethammer, 462
Moeller, Georg, 280
Munich Crisis (1938), 333, 438, 471
Mutschmann, Martin, 312

national chauvinism, 25, 238, 248–50, 253, 552
National Socialist German Students' League [Nationalsozialistischer Deutscher

Studentenbund; NSDStB], xvi, 119, 155n3, 365
National Socialist German Teachers' League [Nationalsozialistischer Deutscher Lehrerbund], 271, 285
National Socialist German University Instructors' League [Nationalsozialistischer Deutscher Dozentenbund; NSDDozB], xvi, 75–76, 155n3, 271 285, 313, 322, 371, 467, 481
National Socialist German Workers' Party [Nationalsozialistische Deutsche Arbeiterpartei; NSDAP], xvi, 29, 154, 162, 163, 222, 344, 372, 452–53n5
  members, 171, 174, 208, 270–71, 285–86, 287, 289, 292, 317n30, 334, 337, 344, 364, 389, 494n9, 509
National Socialist People's Welfare Organization [Nationalsozialistische Volkswohlfahrt], 285
natural law, 369, 390–93
Night of the Long Knives, 56, 88, 383
Nobel Prize, 15, 286–87, 309, 451, 459, 460n25, 504, 512, 537–38, 546, 550
"Non-Aryan(s)," 82, 142, 163, 164, 166–67, 240n190, 294, 308, 316, 363, 364
Nordic (as racial or cultural concept), 90–91, 92, 269, 272, 278–79, 280, 322, 338, 340
Nuremberg Racial Laws of 1935. *See under* laws, Nazi or fascist
Nuremberg Trials, 11, 15, 340, 474

Old Testament, 24–25, 67, 80, 85, 86, 123n31, 139, 156n6, 161, 161n18, 171, 173, 175–76, 182–88, 225, 254
  possible removal from the Bible, 159, 162, 164–65, 166–67, 177–78, 190–92, 241, 244–45
On the Jews and Their Lies [*Von den Juden und ihren Lügen*], by Martin Luther, 19n38, 24, 116–17, 128–30, 133, 134n63, 136, 137–38, 140–41, 143–44
Ordnungen [orders], theology of, 215, 228, 231–33, 246–47
Orthodox Judaism, 238
Ostforschung [research on the East], 48, 76, 88
Ostmark [Eastern march], 469–70, 471

"Palestinian Judaism," 213, 216–17, 238
pastors, 3, 18, 69–70, 115, 116, 118, 126–31, 132, 140n85, 141, 144, 147, 159, 161n18, 164, 173n67, 175, 179, 233, 464
  and denazification, 193–94, 474–76
  Pastors' Emergency League, 165–66
  and *Persilscheine*, 474–75
patriotism, 249, 455n13, 461
Paul (the apostle), 123n31, 159, 165, 175, 213
Persilschein, 474–75, 482. *See also* denazification [*Entnazifierung*]
Pietism, 210, 211, 213, 236
Planck, Max, 286–87, 294, 451
"political university," the, 32, 118–19, 122, 170, 461, 517
Protestant church, 23–24, 115, 121–22, 124, 126–27, 154–55, 159, 163–67, 178, 188–89n130, 229, 464, 508
Protestantism, 114–18, 122n24, 124, 205, 240
Protocols of the Elders of Zion, 480

rabbinic literature, 81, 210, 217, 219–20, 238–39, 242, 243, 326
race, 46, 66, 84–85, 94, 96, 101–2, 103, 124, 129, 135, 138, 141n90, 164, 168–69, 175n72, 176, 209, 231–32, 246, 250, 269, 273, 278–79, 280, 312, 313–15, 318, 320–21, 334–35, 337–38, 370, 392n208, 413, 433n39, 439, 460, 469, 497–99, 532, 535
racial antisemitism, 225
"racial hygiene," 249, 431n32, 498n25, 546
racial mixing, 218–19, 225
"racial science," 55, 76, 97, 176, 180, 546
Rechtsstaat, 30, 368n49, 369–73, 382, 388, 393, 396. *See also* Total State
Reformation, 21, 23, 67, 115, 116, 124, 143, 144
Reformed Protestants, 188n130, 189, 211, 246
regional church. *See Landeskirchen*
Reich Air Defense League [Reichsluftschutzbund], 178, 271, 285
Reich Church [Reichskirche], 154–55, 163–64, 167, 188–89n130. *See also* German Christians
Reich Ministry for Church Affairs, 167n41
Reich Ministry of Education, 119, 155, 169, 280, 286, 288n91, 456, 458, 463, 464
Reich Ministry of Science, Art, and Education [Reichsministerium

für Wissenschaft, Kunst, und
Volksbildung; RMWKV], xvi, 83n39
Reich Ministry of Science, Education, and
Public Instruction [Reichsministerium
für Wissenschaft, Erziehung und
Volksbildung], 274, 312, 314, 322
Reich Security, Main Office for
[Reichssicherheitshauptamt; RSHA],
xvi, 2, 313
Reich's Association for Student Affairs
[Reichsstudentenwerk], 281
Richter, Liselotte, 293
rightwing students, 46, 75–76, 78, 119, 135,
145, 155n3, 156, 168, 217, 308, 320, 365,
382, 394n227, 428, 434, 449–50, 452–59,
460–61, 470, 508
Romans, 70
Rust, Bernhard, 50, 284, 287–88, 291, 293–94,
312

salvation history, 161, 229
Scharff, Alexander, 292n110, 295, 298n135
Selbstgleichschaltung. See under
Gleichschaltung
Semitic languages, 79, 81, 123, 219, 238, 315,
326
Sethe, Kurt, 267, 296
Sievers, Wolfram, 88
Social Democratic Party of Germany
[Sozialdemokratische Partei
Deutschlands; Sopade or SPD], xvi, 119,
308, 326, 386n179, 455n13, 492
soldier(s), 68, 124–25, 215n48, 233, 249, 275,
339, 412–13n25, 454–55, 457, 473, 532, 557
Sonderkommando Jankuhn, 348
Spinoza, Baruch, 8, 57, 467
Sports Palace Rally (1933), 123, 235
SS (Schutzstaffel), xvi, 2, 13, 18, 46, 48, 78, 87,
88, 93, 121n20, 264, 276n40, 279, 281–82,
290, 312–13, 322, 348, 453, 472, 473–76,
494n9, 496, 550
SS, sponsoring *or* supporting member of
[*Förderndes Mitglied*], 130, 271, 285, 509
SS Intelligence Service [Sicherheitsdienst,
"Security Service"; SD], xvi, 313, 322,
348, 453, 475
stab-in-the-back theory, 10, 412, 412–13n25,
455

Stasi (State Security Office of the GDR),
194, 236
state church. See *Landeskirchen*
Stein, Freiherr vom, 466
sterilization, 168–69, 498–99
Stormtroopers [Sturmabteilung; SA], xvi, 28,
119, 172–73, 215, 220, 229, 245, 247, 264,
287, 311, 317, 371, 424, 430, 431, 471, 494n9
Studienführer (SS publication), 264, 281, 282
Stuttgart Declaration of Guilt (1945), 473, 508

Talmud, 24, 56, 80, 117, 206, 219, 221–22, 225,
238
Theological Dictionary of the New Testament
[*Theologisches Wörterbuch zum Neuen
Testament*], 220, 227n116, 235
theology
of creation, 238, 243–44, 246–48
liberal, 212–13, 240n190, 242, 246
tikkun [repair or redemptive restitution],
405, 419
Total State, 215, 370, 380, 432–33, 441. See also
Rechtsstaat
total war, 97, 273–74, 441
Tübingen Network, 206–8, 211, 237–53
two kingdoms doctrine, 231, 246–47

University Instructors Group of the
National Socialist Lawyers League
[Reichsgruppe Hochschullehrer
des Nationalsozialistischen
Rechtswahrerbundes], 383–84

Vahlen, Theodor, 283, 286–87, 286n86
Vasmer, Max, 271, 272, 291
Venia Legendi, 496–99
Vergangenheitsbewältigung [coming to terms
with the past], 483
Verneinung [Freudian negation], 410–11
Versailles, Treaty of, 50, 353, 385, 471n61, 474,
514
Volk, völkisch, 50, 66, 90, 123–25, 126, 143, 147,
175n72, 230–32, 234, 245, 246, 249–50,
367, 440–41
völkische Wissenschaft [racial scholarship],
269
Volksgemeinschaft [racial community], 365,
374, 470

Volksgeschichte, 50
Volkskunde [folk studies], 49, 337, 464–65
Von den Juden und ihren Lügen. See *On the Jews and Their Lies*

Waffen-SS, 276n40, 348
war crimes, 103, 294
Wehrmacht, 124, 275–76, 426, 438, 465, 469n54
Weimar Republic, 9–10, 23, 43, 50, 74–75, 78, 104, 169, 232–33, 252, 364n18, 370, 373–74, 385–86, 391–93, 453n6, 459n24
 constitution, 122, 367, 373, 385–87, 391n207, 393
 economic crises, 385, 514
 moral decadence of (Protestant critique), 248–49, 385
White Africa (racist project). See Committee for the Study of White Africa
whitewashing the past, 76n19, 425, 435, 439, 474, 547
Wirzberger, Karl-Heinz, 291
Wölfel, Dominik Josef, 280

worldview [*Weltanschauung*], 10, 31, 87, 96, 313–14, 337, 423, 440, 441
World War I, 9, 10, 23, 28, 66, 73–74, 75n18, 81, 91–92, 122, 247, 248, 249, 252, 342, 350, 373, 385, 412, 454–55, 455n13, 469, 483–84, 497n22, 503, 510
 and Nazi racial laws, 28, 77, 94, 363, 459–60, 512
World War II, 2, 11, 12, 14, 43, 97–103, 124–25, 194, 273–77, 324, 325, 327, 332n2, 365, 384, 393, 426, 469nn53–54, 471, 483–84, 529, 531, 548n11
Wurm, Theophil, Bishop, 473–74

YMCA, 219, 236, 245

Zeitschrift der Deutschen Morgenländischen Gesellschaft (ZDMG), xvi, 83, 96, 276n41, 320
Zionism, 58, 549
 in the context of anti-Zionism, 532, 552, 556–58, 560–61, 563
Zionist, 91, 532, 552, 558, 562

BERNARD M. LEVINSON serves as Professor of Classical and Near Eastern Studies and of Law at the University of Minnesota, where he holds the Berman Family Chair in Jewish Studies and Hebrew Bible. He is the author of four books, including *Deuteronomy and the Hermeneutics of Legal Innovation*, and *Legal Revision and Religious Renewal in Ancient Israel*, and six edited volumes.

ROBERT P. ERICKSEN is the Kurt Mayer Chair of Holocaust Studies Emeritus at Pacific Lutheran University in Tacoma, Washington. He has written or edited six books, including *Theologians under Hitler*, *Complicity in the Holocaust: Churches and Universities in Nazi Germany*, and *Betrayal: German Churches and the Holocaust* (edited with Susannah Heschel).

www.ingramcontent.com/pod-product-compliance
Lightning Source LLC
Chambersburg PA
CBHW021713300426
44114CB00009B/120